STRATEGY FOR PERSONAL FINANCE

McGRAW-HILL SERIES IN FINANCE
Professor Charles A. D'Ambrosio
University of Washington
Consulting Editor

STRATEGY for PERSONAL FINANCE

LARRY R. LANG
THOMAS H. GILLESPIE
University of Wisconsin, Oshkosh

McGraw-Hill Book Company

New York   St. Louis   San Francisco   Auckland   Bogotá   Düsseldorf   Johannesburg
London   Madrid   Mexico   Montreal   New Delhi   Panama   Paris   São Paulo   Singapore
Sydney   Tokyo   Toronto

**To Pamela
and Sarah**

STRATEGY FOR PERSONAL FINANCE

1 2 3 4 5 6 7 8 9 0 D O D O 7 8 3 2 1 0 9 8 7 6

This book was set in Times Roman by Black Dot, Inc.
The editors were J. S. Dietrich and Edwin Hanson;
the cover design and cartoons were done by Phil Frank;
the production supervisor was Thomas J. LoPinto.
The drawings were done by ANCO/Boston.
R. R. Donnelley & Sons Company was printer and binder.

Library of Congress Cataloging in Publication Data

Lang, Larry R.
    Strategy for personal finance.

    (McGraw-Hill series in finance)
    Includes bibliographies and index.
    1. Finance, Personal. I. Gillespie, Thomas H., joint author. II. Title.
HG179.L26   332'.024   76-29349
ISBN 0-07-036247-5

Contents

Consumer Buyers' Clubs: What Are They? Other High-Pressure Sales Gimmicks. Outright Frauds. Avoiding High-Pressure Sales Tactics. Finding Information. Deceptive Advertising. Why Take Advertising to Task? Pricing. "Bait and Switch". Misleading Labels. Consumer Protection Legislation. *Consumer Protection Agencies. Recovering Your Losses: When, Where, How.*
Appendix: Consumer Complaint Agencies.

*Insurance. Summary of Policy Coverages. How Much
Insurance?* Compensation for Loss of Personal
Property. Homeowners Liability Insurance. Cost of
Homeowners Insurance. Automobile Insurance. *The Family
Auto Policy. Choosing Your Policy Limits. Who Is
Covered? Policy Cancelation. Shopping for Auto
Insurance. Getting the Most for Your Insurance
Dollar. Rates for Automobile Insurance. No-Fault
Insurance. Selecting an Agent and Buying Insurance.*

BUILDING FOR YOUR FUTURE

To the Student

Strategy for Personal Finance will help you with all phases of your personal money management, including your ability to increase the amount of money you earn, to obtain maximum satisfaction from each dollar you spend, to safeguard the money and resources you have, and to invest the money you plan to save for future goals. We feel that everyone will benefit in a very measurable dollars-and-cents way from the information contained in the next 21 chapters.

As an individual consumer, you must make a large number of financial decisions every year. And most of those decisions are becoming increasingly complex. The range of choices you must analyze and compare for each decision continues to expand and will likely do so over the foreseeable future.

We have all witnessed the sharp price increases on all types of raw materials, energy, and manufacturing costs. This rapid rise in prices has convinced the consumer that each personal financial decision must be carefully analyzed to determine whether the promised benefits really do justify the underlying costs. We feel you can obtain the greatest satisfaction from the money you have by becoming a competent money manager. This book assumes that none of us has to be rich to enjoy life and accomplish the things we want. Success means obtaining maximum satisfaction from what we have. It also means managing our personal finances so we will not worry over every financial decision. We believe this book will help you accomplish both objectives.

IT IS YOUR DECISION

Within each chapter we provide sufficient information so that you, as the key decision maker, will be able to make all the required financial decisions. Yet, at the same time, we have eliminated descriptive information that is of no value in the decision process. Each topical area has several examples to illustrate how you can analyze the potential benefits and costs associated with a particular financial decision. But we do not present a series of standards or set decisions everyone is supposed to follow. Instead, we show you the steps in the decision process. Because, in the final analysis, only you can decide what is best, given your particular financial goals and aspirations.

OVERVIEW OF THE BOOK

The first section of the book consists of a series of chapters to prepare and equip you for your financial decision-making role. Throughout, we stress the need to integrate all aspects of your personal finances into a total financial plan. The importance of establishing and clearly defining both your short- and long-term financial goals is emphasized. We discuss career planning as a means to achieving your desired income as well as your job satisfaction objectives.

Managing your income is the main topic of our second section. Selecting a bank to provide the essential services that are part of managing your personal finances is the leadoff topic. Next we discuss the unavoidable: taxes! This topic is covered early in the text because taxes have a profound impact on many financial decisions. Then we discuss the proper use, sources, and recent developments in consumer credit.

Major consumer expenditures—for automobiles, appliances, consumer durables, and housing alternatives—are the topic of section three. For each area we stress how you can obtain adequate service from these items at an affordable price. We do an in-depth analysis of the wide range of choices you have available within each area.

Section four examines the need and means of safeguarding what you own and what you earn. Rather than give a list of insurance coverages everyone should have (there probably is no single list), we provide the basic framework so you can decide what insurance coverage best meets your needs.

Building for your financial future is the emphasis of section five. Recognizing that for some people the "future" may be a short-term financial goal that is several years away, while for others it may be a long-term goal more than 20 years in the future, we discuss a wide variety of potential investment alternatives. We have strived to present investment alternatives that will be suitable and available to most people; yet we have refrained from placing undue emphasis on this section.

UNIQUE FEATURES OF THIS BOOK

We believe this book has some very important features that make it unique.

First, we concentrate on providing information which is directly beneficial to you as the chief financial decision maker. For example, we do not care how many millions of people have automobile loans. Rather, we are concerned about whether a loan is appropriate for you. If it is appropriate, where can you obtain it? At what cost? For what length of time?

Second, each chapter begins with a list of learning objectives. This permits you to see beforehand what will be covered and what we feel is essential.

Third, there is a list of important words and terms at the end of each chapter. If you can define and use these terms after reading the chapter, then you understand the new concepts introduced in the chapter.

Fourth, each chapter has a series of discussion questions and a case study, so you can practice and reinforce the subject matter of the chapter.

Fifth, a selective, annotated bibliography concludes each chapter, so you can pursue any of the subjects in more depth.

Strategy for Personal Finance will help you develop as a money manager who can handle all phases of your personal finances. We believe you will find it a useful guide and reference throughout your money management years.

Larry R. Lang / Thomas H. Gillespie

To the Instructor

We believe there are serious shortcomings in the introductory texts that are currently available for courses in personal or consumer finance. Despite the major dollar significance to the individual, topics such as automobile ownership, purchase of consumer durables, and analysis of the newer housing alternatives are given only the briefest coverage, if any, in some texts. To students who will soon be faced with major decisions in these areas, this is a gross oversight. Unfortunately, all too many texts include voluminous descriptive material and macro economic data that have limited interest and even less usefulness to students who want to become competent managers of their personal finances. Still other texts place such an emphasis on investments that they are really low-level investment books. Or, in contrast, some texts spend an inordinate amount of time on specialized investment alternatives or tax-sheltering opportunities, yet most students have neither interest nor immediate need for this information. And most are not likely to need this information for a considerable time. These shortcomings convinced us that there is a need for a personal finance text with this principal objective: to prepare and equip students for their lifelong role as key decision makers in the management of their personal finances. In that role, the individual must be able to skillfully analyze and compare the host of alternatives which are part of each financial decision.

This book is designed for a one-semester, trimester, or quarter personal finance course. The book is suitable for (1) the undergraduate personal or consumer finance courses offered by 4-year colleges, (2) consumer or personal finance courses offered by 2-year community colleges, and (3) personal finance courses that are part of a college's adult education program. We have produced a book which contains sufficient examples and illustrations so the student can understand and internalize the basics of personal finance. The stress has been on preparing a text that students will find highly readable, understandable, and interesting, and that can be applied to their present as well as their future financial situation. Our classroom experience with the preliminary drafts of this material has confirmed the text's ability to accomplish these goals.

PEDAGOGICAL FEATURES

Overall Organization   The 21 chapters are arranged in five major sections. The first section provides background and basic introductory materials to prepare and equip students for their role of key financial decision makers. The second section discusses the key points in managing their income. The third section analyzes the benefits and costs of major consumer expenditures: automobiles, consumer durables, and housing alternatives. Insurance coverage is the central thrust of the fourth section. The fifth section discusses the investment alternatives available to help individuals build for their financial future.

While the material has been laid out in what we consider an optimum order, the chapters can be rearranged to suit a particular instructor's preference. The topic coverage is sufficiently broad so that an instructor can emphasize those areas which he or she feels are most important. And with the broad coverage of topics, we feel an instructor can readily supplement the material should the course extend more than a single semester or quarter.

Chapter Layout   Within each chapter we have attempted to integrate the material as part of the individual's overall financial plan. Each time a new concept or term is introduced, we have included an example to illustrate the material. Likewise, we have included extensive numerical examples when a student should make a computation. At the same time, we illustrate each cost-benefit analysis with an example when it is part of the financial decision. Throughout the book, we have included numerous charts, graphs, and tables to illustrate the consequences of various financial decisions or alternatives. We are convinced that good visual displays, along with a plentiful supply of examples, are essential for the readability, teachability, and understandability of the material.

Learning Objectives and Chapter Summaries   Each chapter begins with a list of learning objectives directed toward the student. At the end of the chapter, there are succinct summary statements reemphasizing the essential points in the chapter. In addition, there is a list of key words and terms that students should understand from their reading of the material. These two features, combined with the learning objectives, should assist the student in identifying the important points of each chapter.

Discussion Questions and Case Study   There is a comprehensive set of questions and problems at the end of each chapter that test the students' understanding of the material. The case study provides them with an opportunity to apply the financial concepts they have learned.

We feel the strengths of *Strategy for Personal Finance* overcome the shortcomings of the currently available personal and consumer finance texts. We believe you will find this teaching package to be an asset in your teaching of personal or consumer finance.

Larry R. Lang / Thomas H. Gillespie

INTRODUCTION

Chapter 1

Personal and Financial Planning

After completing this chapter you should be able to:

recognize the importance of personal financial planning.

explain the interrelationship of long-term and short-term planning.

explain the importance of a regular savings program as a part of long-term planning.

develop long-term goals.

explain the importance of personal goals as a part of long-term financial planning.

recall the major spending decisions which are important in short-term financial planning.

Unless you plan to take the vow of poverty, you will regularly make decisions in personal financial areas such as budgeting, insurance, mortgages, savings, borrowing, and spending. Poor decisions can be financially penalizing for many years. By studying personal finance, you can make wise decisions and significantly improve your overall economic welfare.

The necessity for careful money management has never been greater. Daily, we are confronted with news stories of price increases, shortages, and other distressing economic news. These factors have produced a situation where most people find their income is insufficient for the things they would like to do. In many cases, insufficient income is only part of the problem. Poor spending decisions is the other part. Certainly, anybody offered a pay raise of $1,000 or $2,000 per year would not turn it down. Yet, many people waste this amount every year because of careless financial planning and poor buying and investing. You may not be able to get a raise of $1,000 this year, but you might be able to save as much by more careful planning. By doing so, you would be as well off as if you had received the raise.

This chapter will outline a framework for personal financial planning. Each of the topics mentioned here will be discussed in detail in later chapters. The purpose of this chapter is to provide an overview of the book and to make the essential point that finance decisions should be made to achieve certain goals. Without an overall plan, chances for achieving your goals are remote.

THE PLANNING PROCESS

Planning is the process of setting goals and identifying actions to achieve the goals. Total planning involves an understanding of the interrelationship between short- and long-term goals. As such, it concentrates on how to manage income and expenditures so that the specified goals will be met. The need for coordinating short-term decisions with long-term goals is crucial. For example, many people have as a long-term goal the accumulation of wealth. That can be realized only over an extended time period. However, the money to achieve the goal must be made available by careful short-term planning.

The planning process is depicted in Exhibit 1–1. Note the process includes a feedback system which enables planners to periodically review their progress and to take any necessary corrective action, thus ensuring that objectives are realized.

Saving Is a Part of Planning   The savings realized by careful day-to-day decisions can be used for other expenditures, or they may be used to accumulate wealth. Allocating some money to a long-term savings program is essential for truly successful personal financial management. And the best way to do it is to begin saving early in your life. For example, if you are twenty-five years old and save $1,000 per year, which you invest at 6 percent interest, you will have $154,762 at age sixty-five. If you postpone this annual savings program until age thirty-five, you will only have $79,058 at sixty-five. The delay of 10 years means that you have saved $10,000 less. Yet, by the time you reach

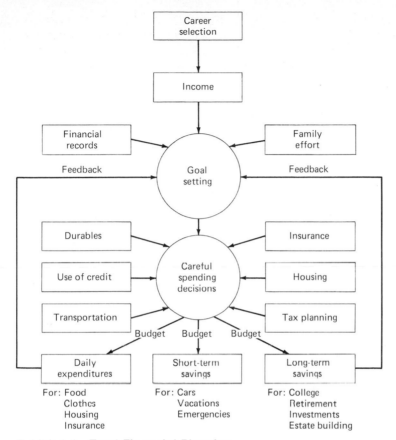

Exhibit 1-1   Total Financial Planning

age sixty-five, that $10,000 means lost interest of $65,704. That is a tremendous sacrifice to make for delaying a regular savings program for only 10 years.

Exhibit 1–2 summarizes the amount an investment of $1,000 per year will total, given different rates of interest and periods of investment.

Note how important it is to start saving early and to earn the highest possible interest. With only $1,000, the difference between 5 and 6 percent seems insignificant. Yet, over a 40-year period during which time you invest $1,000 per year, the difference between 5 and 6 percent interest amounts to $33,962: certainly a significant amount of money.

This is only one example of where the early identification of a goal, in this case saving money, makes achieving the goal much easier.

Setting Long-Term Personal Goals

Personal and financial goals are intertwined to an extent that separating them often becomes difficult. Yet, in achieving long-term success, identifying personal goals is at least as important as specifying financial objectives. It is very easy to state as a goal: I want to have $5,000 three years from now. It is far

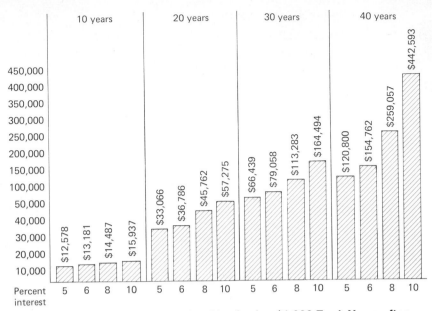

Exhibit 1-2   Total Amount Attained by Saving $1,000 Each Year, after 10, 20, 30, and 40 Years

more difficult to determine what you would like to achieve personally and to develop a strategy to reach the goals. The major personal goal to be covered in this text is the selection of a career.

Career Selection   Finding the right career determines, in large measure, the degree of economic and psychological satisfaction an individual derives from life. The decision should not be made in a haphazard fashion, nor should it be made by default, as is so often the case. Many people devote little thought or effort to making a real career choice. They drift into a job and end up with little ability to change their course. After you get married, have children, buy a house, and accumulate all the responsibilities of life, changing occupations is difficult. If you are now twenty-one years old, you will probably work for 44 years before you retire. That is over twice as long as you have lived so far. To spend that long in a job which you dread is a very sad thing, indeed. Positive steps can be taken to help you select a career that is best for you. Some of the more important factors you should consider in selecting a career are discussed in Chapter 2.

Setting Long-Term Financial Goals

Specifying goals and implementing actions is second only to career selection as the most important factor for achieving financial success. Most people have unfulfilled desires. They may want a house, a second home, a new car, a vacation of a lifetime, or college for their children. If the goals are just vague ideas in the back of your mind, most of them probably will not be realized. A good start in achieving your objectives is to formalize your thinking about

them. This involves specifying what you would like to accomplish financially over a 20- to 40-year time period. Many of the goals, such as buying a home, are typical of the ones many young people hold for themselves. In addition, everybody is ultimately faced with the prospect of retirement. Consequently, the accumulation of capital to supplement pensions and social security should be a high priority objective for most individuals.

Homeownership   This is probably most families' earliest and highest-priority long-term goal. Owning a home may have both financial and psychological advantages. Nevertheless, there are many situations where a family is ill-advised to purchase a house. And, even if ownership is in its best interests, it is one of the most difficult goals to achieve. Unless you are fortunate enough to inherit money for the down payment, you will need to have saved anywhere from 5 percent to 30 percent of the purchase price before you can buy the house. With today's average new home selling for $40,000 or more, even a 10 percent down payment is a substantial amount of money. You should make some estimate of how soon you would like to buy a home, figure how much money you will need, and then start to save that money right now.

College Education   The economic benefits of college are well known. Consequently, among the main goals for many people is a college education for their children. Like everything else, the cost of college has risen at an alarming rate. Unless you have a substantial income, college expenses are impossible to meet out of current income. Part-time jobs, savings, current income of parents, scholarships, and loans represent the major sources of funds for most students. The only one that can really be relied on is savings. Scholarships and loans are increasingly hard to obtain. Part-time jobs are difficult to find and they become even scarcer when the country is in a recession. A family's current income can help, but that is subject to other demands which may be even more important. Financing a college education is not going to get any easier. The sooner you begin to save, the easier it will be to finance college expenses.

Retirement   This is a difficult idea for a young person to think about. At a time when you are just starting a working career, the thought of retirement is the farthest thing from your mind. Yet, there are decisions which will confront you, very early in your career, which have a direct bearing on retirement planning. What type of pension plan does your employer have? Are you eligible? Does it have a death benefit? How much are you saving? How is it invested? Have you bought a house? Do you buy term or cash-value insurance? These are all long-term decisions and all have an impact on the amount of retirement income you will have.

When you look at the amounts in Exhibit 1–2, the need for early planning becomes very clear. Every year that you postpone a savings and investment program, which is the cornerstone of good retirement planning, the more difficult it becomes to accumulate the money necessary for a comfortable retirement.

Other Inputs to Planning

Setting goals is the first major step in financial planning. However, in the process of setting the goals, the impact of inflation, the family's role, and the use of financial records are necessary inputs as well.

Inflation and Financial Planning   Inflation is an increase in the cost of things you buy which is not accompanied by a change in the physical product. The shirt you paid $10 for last year, which now costs $11, is an example of inflation. For most of your parents' and grandparents' lifetimes, inflation was reducing the purchasing power of the dollar at about 2 percent a year. That is, the average prices increased each year 2 cents for every dollar spent.

The world seems to have undergone a sharp change. Beginning in the late 1960s, inflation rates increased between 5 and 12 percent a year. By incorporating inflation into your planning, its impact can be dampened. Is it worth buying now instead of postponing purchases? Which is better, homeownership or rental? What are the best places for savings when there is high inflation? Does it affect a decision on whether a car should be kept longer? In the past, inflation could be ignored when answering these questions. Now, it must be considered.

The Family's Role   Financial goal setting and financial planning should be a family venture—husband, wife, and even the children as they grow older, should be included in the discussions. Family finance has to involve everybody. If husband and wife do not jointly agree on major decisions, those decisions are probably doomed to failure. It is hard to go off a budget when all members of the family help set the budget and, individually, have kept their end of the bargain. Unilateral decisions are much easier to ignore.

Marriage counselors continually stress the point that money is often as important as sex to a sound marriage. Take the time to work out your family's finances with each member and it will pay tremendous dividends.

Using Records in Financial Planning Budgeting is the center of short run planning. Other statements, prepared on a periodic basis, provide the feedback for determining whether short-run and long-run plans are being adequately coordinated. These periodic statements, which summarize your income and expenditures for a year and your financial position at the end of the year, will help you to determine whether you are making progress toward achieving your financial objectives.

The planning process cannot be accomplished without the use of records. In starting to develop your own plans, keep in mind that some effort must be devoted to clerical paperwork. If you are unwilling to keep financial records, it is extremely unlikely that you will achieve the objectives you have set for yourself.

Short-Term Financial Planning

Short-term planning involves goals and actions which will be completed within a few years. The major parts of short-term planning are (1) goal setting, (2) investment decisions, (3) the analysis of spending decisions, and (4) coordination with long-term plans. The fourth aspect is necessary since the savings to achieve long-term goals must be provided for on a monthly or an annual basis.

Short-Term Goal Setting Short-term goals cannot be generalized about in the same manner as long-term ones: They are usually more personal or unique.

For example, you may have as an objective to purchase a $1,000 pool table 3 years hence. This is certainly not so common as saving for a house or retirement. However, like a long-term goal, it will not be realized unless you save for it. Ignoring the fact that your savings will earn interest, you must save $27.77 per month for 36 months to be able to buy the pool table 3 years from now.

The action to save the money to reach such a goal must be incorporated into your financial planning. This is done through the use of a family budget.

Savings and Investments   Once you have determined how much of your income you can regularly put aside, the next step is to decide how to invest it. Goals will never be realized unless careful attention is given to both the savings and the investment aspects of financial planning.

Selecting appropriate investments can be very helpful in reaching goals. For example, to accumulate $1,000 in 3 years without earning interest, $27.77 monthly must be saved. If the money is invested in a savings account at 5 percent, the same goal can be reached by saving $25.79 a month. At 8 percent it is necessary to save only $24.69 monthly. The details on these and similar calculations are covered in Chapter 17.

Spending Decisions   Careful attention to spending decisions can save a substantial amount of money. In addition to food and clothing, other major necessary family expenses are: (1) insurance, (2) transportation, and (3) housing. Careful evaluation of needs and costs in these areas can produce savings. Understanding taxes and making proper use of credit (borrowing money) can also produce significant benefits.

Insurance   Between life, health, auto, homeowners and disability income insurance, many people spend $300 to $2,000 or more each year. Savings can be substantial if attention is given to buying the correct types of insurance for specific needs and shopping for the lowest possible rates.

Questions which are crucial for developing a sound personal insurance program include: How much life insurance is necessary? Is there a difference between companies and policies? Does it pay to shop for insurance? How can different policies be compared? Is homeowners or tenant's insurance necessary for apartment renters? When should a personal insurance program be reviewed? The answers to these and many more questions concerned with insurance will be covered in Chapters 13 through 16.

Transportation   With the least expensive cars now costing in excess of $3,000, transportation represents one of a family's largest continuing expenditures. Questions which can assist in making the best decisions include: How much does it cost to own and operate various types of cars? What is the optimal length of time to own a car? Should a car be leased or purchased? Are there advantages to buying a used car instead of a new one?

Housing   Everybody must make a housing decision. Making the correct decision can be facilitated by answering some of the following questions: Is it better to rent or buy? How do condominiums compare with apartments? Are mobile homes a good alternative? When buying a house, what are the important factors to be aware of? How much can an individual afford to spend for a home? What alternatives are there for financing a home? Is it necessary to use a realtor? What is title insurance? Careful planning in each of these areas can be worth thousands of dollars. Failure to understand these points can be financially devastating.

Taxes   The thought of taxes makes most people shudder. With this subject, even the questions are difficult. Understanding things like deductions *for* and deductions *from* gross income, moving expenses, and contributions is an effort for even the best financial planners. The cost of failing to take every legitimate deduction can be substantial. Record keeping and awareness of some basic tax rules make the job much easier.

Credit   The use of credit enables a person to enjoy things like cars, appliances, and furniture sooner than if the money had to be saved before making the purchase. Credit carries with it certain costs and obligations. Being overextended, hounded by bill collectors, and unable to meet commitments is a frightening experience. Having a substantial income is no guarantee for avoiding credit problems. Every day, people earning $20,000 to $40,000 a year have to declare personal bankruptcy because they abused credit. Understanding the costs of credit, the amount of credit which can be handled at different income levels, and the remedies available in the event credit is overused can help significantly in deciding whether to be a cash or a credit buyer.

Coordinating Long-Term and Short-Term Plans   Budgeting is the mechanism for providing this necessary coordination. A budget permits you to specify the amount that you can spend for food, clothes, housing, and transportation, as well as how much you can save toward your long-term and short-term goals.

Identifying goals, the amount necessary to achieve them, and the time they are to be realized is essential if they are to be included in a budgeting system.

SUMMARY

1   Financial planning includes both short- and long-term considerations.
2   Planning involves both economic goals and personal goals.
3   Starting a regular savings program is essential for achieving financial success.
4   Inflation is becoming an increasingly important consideration in all aspects of personal financial planning.
5   Planning, to be successful, requires both careful thought and careful record keeping.
6   Planning should be a family process. Cooperation will enhance its chances for success.
7   Short-term planning involves decisions and actions which will be completed within a few years.

8 The essential aspects of short-term planning are: (*a*) goal setting, (*b*) investment decisions, (*c*) spending decisions, and (*d*) the coordination of long- and short-term plans.

REVIEW YOUR UNDERSTANDING OF

The planning process   Short-term planning
Long-term planning   Goals
   Personal goals   Savings and investments
   Financial goals   Budgets

DISCUSSION QUESTIONS

1 Why should a regular savings program be started as soon as possible?
2 Which is more important in accumulating a great deal of money, high interest rates or saving for a prolonged period? (*Hint:* look at Exhibit 1–2 very carefully.)
3 Set out an economic goal to be realized in 10 years. Ignoring interest, how much will you have to save to achieve the goal?
4 If retirement is so far in the future, why is it important to start thinking about it today?
5 Do you agree with the idea that goals and records are necessary for successful financial planning? Why?
6 Why should financial planning be a family decision-making process? What are the disadvantages of having one family member handle the process?
7 Inflation has become a significant factor in most financial decisions. Although we did not discuss the specific ways inflation may affect expenditures and savings, how do you think this factor should be incorporated in these decisions?
8 Why is short-term planning so important to achieving your long-term goals?

RECOMMENDED READINGS

Booklets

Reaching Your Financial Goals. Chicago: Household Finance Corporation, Money Management Institute, Chicago, 1971.
   A very readable and practical booklet which integrates budgeting, financial planning, and saving.

Magazines

Changing Times:
"How to Cope with This Inflation," November 1973, pp. 7–12.
   The article discusses ways for incorporating the effect of inflation into financial decisions.

Chapter 2

Career Selection: Choosing and Finding a Job

After completing this chapter you should be able to:

recall the major ways that occupations are classified.

classify occupations of interest to you into several major categories.

identify through research the educational requirements for most occupations.

recall the major sources of information which explain the characteristics of most occupations.

consider on the basis of objective factors whether a college education is necessary for your career goals.

recognize the important questions which should be answered in trying to select a career.

develop a list of your personal attributes which you feel will have an influence on your choice of a career.

recognize the most frequently used tests to assist people in career selection.

develop a personal résumé which can be used in applying for jobs.

Finding the right job is among the most important decisions a person ever makes. It influences daily life in numerous ways and largely determines an individual's economic and psychological satisfaction.

The decision's importance suggests that it be made only after exhaustive study of career alternatives. This would be easy if all the variables could be readily analyzed. Unfortunately, the problem is complex. The value judgments and perceptions of status and prestige associated with different occupations make it difficult to be objective in choosing a career. Consequently, the decision often gets made by default. After graduating from college, one accepts a job and launches firmly on a career path. Many of the preliminaries happened years before, such as the selection of a college and a major program of studies while at college, without an awareness of the decision's implications.

Given the complexity of finding the right career, is there really anything we can do to help the process? Obviously, we think there is. Rather than advocating a neat little checklist, this chapter will take a much broader and long-term approach to career selection. We hope the suggestions will raise more questions for you than they answer. Our purpose is to stimulate the general questions about a career choice: you must find your own specific answers.

While self-assessment is crucial to finding the right career, there are numerous external sources which can ease the process. The principal external source is published information such as standardized preference tests, booklets on selected careers, and job outlook studies. These references are of little use unless they are prefaced with a discussion, albeit brief, of available career choices. With over 40,000 specific job titles recognized by the U.S. Department of Labor, the discussion will necessarily be limited to a few categories, encompassing most people's career alternatives.

JOBS—HOW THEY ARE CLASSIFIED

Occupations are broadly classified according to either *function*, such as legal, technical, medical, educational, or *type of organization*, such as manufacturing, finance, or retailing. However, the specific occupations within each classification can vary considerably. Some occupations have the same title, but they actually might differ greatly, depending on the organization defining the job. For example, your school's plant engineer is really a kind of mechanic for the heating, plumbing, lighting, and general maintenance of the school buildings, whereas an engineer in an electronic company does work that is more closely associated with science in designing and developing electronic equipment. As another example, consider surgeons and psychiatrists, who are both broadly classified as doctors, yet, their daily routines are quite different. Moreover, their concept of job satisfaction is undoubtedly very different: the psychiatrist being closer to teachers, social workers, psychologists, or the clergy than to surgeons. The similarity between surgeons and psychiatrists probably ended with graduation from medical school.

Types of Employers

Employers are classified as profit or nonprofit organizations. Profit organizations include all business firms, ranging from the mom-and-pop grocery store to General Motors. Nonprofit organizations are the federal, state, and local governments, most medical facilities, and educational institutions.

Private Profit-making Organizations   Most business firms come under this heading. Within this group are a wide variety of organizations with a tremendous range of job and career possibilities. The major job classifications among the private profit-making organizations are: manufacturing, retailing, and finance.

Manufacturing   This subclassification includes all business firms engaged in production or manufacturing. Jobs within these organizations include accountants, engineers, personnel specialists, and production managers. Generally, a well-rounded business or liberal arts training is the route to the nontechnical jobs within these firms. If you are interested in working specifically for a chemical company or an electronics firm in a technical capacity, training in the appropriate engineering specialty is usually required.

Retailing   Job opportunities within the retailing sector do not require the specialized training which characterizes many of the technical jobs in the manufacturing firms. While retailers employ accountants, data processors, and personnel specialists, the unique jobs in this area involve merchandising. This includes purchasing, store design, sales promotion, and actual sales work. Entry into a retailing career is usually through a training program with a major department store. Every year, large stores hire thousands of college and junior college graduates for their on-the-job training programs. The activity in these programs ranges from buying the merchandise to selling it to the customer. After completing the training program (usually 6 months), the trainee may be assigned to a department as an assistant buyer. Job progression may lead to department management and higher levels.

No matter what your major course, retailers will consider hiring you for their training programs. If you have completed courses in marketing or retailing, they can be helpful, but they are not necessary. The real key to success in these jobs seems to be a flair for merchandising, something that may be hard to get from formal course work.

Finance   The last major subdivision in the private sector is finance, including banks, savings and loans, insurance companies, and accounting firms. The unique professional-level jobs in these organizations involve a great deal of personal contact. For example, commercial or retail lending officers of banks devote much of their time to working with clients arranging satisfactory loan agreements. Bank trust officers spend considerable time with individuals whose investments they are managing.

The specific training required for these jobs is oriented heavily toward finance and accounting. For administrative positions with a bank or insurance company, a college degree is usually necessary.

Entry to these jobs is normally through a training program or direct job assignment with one of the larger institutions. Job mobility within the industry depends on the individual's specialty. It appears that smaller banks are continually hiring trained individuals from larger ones.

The bank jobs have appeal for people wanting less personal contact than is required in pure selling jobs, but more variety and personal contact than there are in typical accounting administrative jobs.

Most corporations are required to have their accounting statements verified by firms specializing in accounting. These companies are known as public accountants, although they are, in fact, private organizations. Public accounting firms require an undergraduate degree in accounting. Jobs involve a great deal of variety, with the opportunity of meeting many different people. Job mobility tends to be high. Public accounting is viewed by many people as an excellent way to see a variety of businesses before finally selecting the one they would like to work for.

The major staffing requirement of the insurance industry is for new sales representatives. Attrition among first-year sales personnel is extremely high. Selling insurance can be difficult, and since most salespeople work on a straight commission basis, there is no weekly paycheck to support them until they become established. Potentially, the rewards in this line of work are above average. There are a number of life insurance agents who consistently earn in excess of $50,000 annually. Offsetting these success stories are the thousands of agents who tried and failed, or who are making a marginal living from their efforts.

Nonprofit Organizations   The nonprofit sector is distinguished by the fact that most jobs are classified as service occupations. That is, they deal directly with people and provide a service, not a product. Government agencies, ranging from the Internal Revenue Service to local municipal bodies, hire accountants, data processors, personnel specialists, and a variety of other skills which are also present in the private sector. However, the unique jobs in the nonprofit organizations are in education, social work, and medicine.

Education   Despite the fact that there is a tremendous oversupply of elementary and secondary school teachers, the number of teaching openings each year is among the largest for any profession. In the 1970s, the abundance of candidates for each opening has made finding a job highly competitive. The outlook is for a continued excess supply of qualified candidates.

The educational requirement for a teaching career is a college degree, including appropriate courses to qualify for state certification. There are exceptions for some specialized vocational teachers, where work experience or noncollege training meets the acceptance standards.

To enjoy teaching, you must enjoy working with young people. That is the main satisfaction to be derived from the job. Economically, teaching provides a reasonable standard of living, but places a very low maximum on potential earnings. The security of a teaching career is excellent relative to most occupations, and the fringe benefits in the form of pensions and insurance coverage are above average.

Other Services   The nonprofit sector has many additional service careers ranging from doctors, nurses, administrators, and psychologists to x-ray technicians, lab technicians, physical therapists, and medical assistants. Each of these occupations requires training, which may involve a year of specialized training for a technician to as much as 10 or 12 years for certain medical specialties. Income potentials in medicine are excellent, even for the technical specialties. Satisfaction levels among workers in these careers also seem to be high and security tends to be above average.

Social work is a career available in the public sector. Training includes a college degree with specialization in social work. The massive growth of federal and state welfare programs has made social work one of the growth industries of the 1960s and early 70s. The growth appears to have slowed, but there are still a great many openings each year. However, the situation will probably become more like the teaching profession, where competition is heightened by the large number of qualified personnel available for each of the openings.

Build Your Awareness of Jobs

Finding a career should be a sifting process. The more you know about different occupations, the better you will be able to choose your career. Gathering the information about various jobs should be a long-term effort. Much of it, of course, results from contact with family and friends. But making the search truly effective requires a basic curiosity and a willingness to seek information.

In addition to the informal sources of information, such as family and friends, there are a number of publications which can be useful in learning about different careers and occupations. Most of these publications are available in school placement offices or public libraries. The most useful publications (complete citations are given at the end of the chapter) are:

1   *Concise Handbook of Occupations.* This book provides a short description of 305 occupations. It discusses the type of work, educational requirements, and salaries.

2   *Career Monographs.* The Institute for Research has developed career research monographs for over 280 occupations. The monographs, which run 20 or more pages, discuss, in depth, all aspects of the career. They are an excellent source of information.

3 *College Placement Annual.* This is the official publication of college and university placement services. It contains articles advising students on finding a job and lists all employers with job openings who have registered with the College Placement Council. The book is usually distributed to college seniors at the start of their last year in school.

Do You Need a College Degree?

The college degree has been debased over the last 20 years. Competition for jobs which require a college education has increased to the point that the degree no longer guarantees a good job. Job security which once went along with college degrees has diminished as well. It appears that the economic advantage of a college degree is declining. Studies used to show that a college education would increase a person's lifetime earning power by 70 percent over that of a high school graduate. Recent figures indicate the differential is down to 30 percent and continuing to narrow.

The striking thing about these comparisons is the fact that they reflect the difference in lifetime income between college graduates and high school graduates. There are currently many occupations requiring some post–high school training which offer income potentials at least as attractive as a college degree promises.

Technological advances over the last 20 years have created many jobs which did not even exist at the end of World War II. Computer repair technicians, medical technicians, refrigeration repair personnel, and heavy equipment operators are examples of jobs where college training is unnecessary, but training beyond the high school level is required. The pay in these jobs often exceeds the pay in college-trained occupations by a substantial margin.

There are a number of issues which are important in deciding whether to follow the college or noncollege route to a career.

1   Do not choose a career simply because it promises higher income. If you would really rather teach school than repair air conditioners, choose the teaching career, but recognize there will be heavy competition which will limit salaries and mobility.

2   Equally important: Do not go to college without being sure that is the direction you want to follow. A college degree is of little value if some specialized training and career motivation do not accompany it. The undergraduate history major may find a job, but it probably will not be in a line of work which utilizes the individual's academic training.

3   College should be viewed as an enriching experience as well as a source of vocational training. The reason for majoring in history or philosophy is not vocational and the limitations of nonvocational major courses should be recognized before they are selected.

Education, whether college or specialized post–high school training, enhances a person's income potential. The figures in Exhibit 2–1, showing the relationship between income and education, illustrate conclusively that more highly educated people have larger incomes than individuals whose education stopped after a few years. One way to help ensure an adequate income is to obtain as much education as you can.

PERSONAL FACTORS

A career selection strategy should include some reasonably penetrating self-analysis. It is extremely important to find a career which is consistent with the

Exhibit 2-1   Income and Education for Heads of Households, 1974
(Percentage of total)

| | Years of school completed | | | | | |
| | Elementary school | | High school | | College | |
Income	Less than 8	8	1 to 3	4	1 to 3	4
Under $7,000	61.5	47.5	36.4	21.8	20.6	12.6
$ 7,000–$7,999	5.1	5.4	5.2	4.5	4.8	2.9
8,000– 8,999	5.2	5.2	4.6	4.6	4.5	3.0
9,000– 9,999	3.6	4.4	4.9	5.0	4.5	3.5
10,000–11,999	6.6	9.5	10.1	10.7	9.9	7.8
12,000–14,999	7.1	10.0	12.6	15.5	14.3	11.7
15,000–24,999	8.9	14.8	21.1	29.1	29.5	33.0
25,000–49,999	1.8	3.1	4.7	8.2	10.9	22.1
Over $50,000	.2	.1	.4	.6	1.0	3.4
Median income	$5,364	$7,447	$ 9,770	$12,664	$13,205	$18,300
Mean income	$7,307	$9,233	$11,087	$13,763	$14,716	$20,259

Source: Bureau of the Census, U.S. Department of Commerce, Series P-60, No. 100, August 1975.

things you consider to be important. It is equally important not to overrun your capabilities. Self-analysis should start to give you an idea of your values and your abilities. Remember, succeeding in a career with less demanding requirements is far better than attempting and failing at a career you are not capable of handling. Who would not like to be Jack Nicklaus or Chris Evert? Unfortunately, all but a few gifted people are precluded from pursuing, with any degree of success, the routes that Jack and Chris have chosen for themselves.

Individual Values

The critical factor in career selection is matching the career to your values. We all have thought about what is important to us as individuals. Logically, the same questions can be directed at a career choice. The values that are important to you permeate your life—and your career is an important aspect of daily existence.

Economics   Career selection has a large influence on your income level. Some jobs have limited salary potential while others can be extremely lucrative. Questions you might consider are:

1   Do you want to be wealthy or at least have an above-average income?
2   Would you be content with a low-paying job that offers great security?
3   Is income unimportant as long as you are doing something you consider to be important and worthwhile?

If money is your principal motivation, you had better be prepared to seek out and prepare yourself for those careers holding the highest possible returns. There is no point in training to be a teacher, member of the clergy, social worker, or law enforcement officer if a high income is your goal.

Occupations that have a potentially high income usually have a high probability of failure associated with them. The exceptions involve the professions, such as medicine and dentistry, where the supply-demand relationship is such that virtually all members of the profession are assured above-average incomes. Jobs such as insurance sales agent, stockbroker, or independent manufacturer's representative have the possibility of very high incomes. They carry with this opportunity, however, the strong likelihood of failure. For every life insurance sales agent making $100,000 a year, there are probably three or four hundred who tried to become salespeople and failed. Even the few who manage to stay with the job fall far below the income realized by the supersalesperson.

Satisfaction   Jobs have a host of intangible features which may be more important than economic considerations for many people. Again, ask yourself a few general questions about these intangibles. Your answers will help you to evaluate how important they are to your career.

1   Is a job where you feel you are improving the world important to you?

2 Is it important to have a job where you can be creative, can express yourself?

3 Do you need the feeling of independence that goes with working for yourself, or do you prefer taking directions from someone else?

4 Is a job with a great deal of security more important than one which has more income potential but far more risk?

5 Does the thought of constant traveling appeal to you, or would you prefer a job where you are home every night?

6 Does being moved to a new location periodically bother you, or are transfers something you can handle without any problems?

7 Do you want a job which puts you in direct contact with other people, or would you prefer a job where interpersonal contacts are limited?

Personal Assets

Values are only half the personal factors which should be inputs to career selection. The other half are the talents, abilities, or special skills you possess. Certain careers, for example, engineering, require a high level of mathematical ability. If you decide that you would like to be an engineer, you will have made a poor career choice unless you have the necessary ability.

Some of your skills and abilities are probably quite apparent. Others can be determined by the use of aptitude and intelligence tests. As a basic part of the career search, you should make an effort at identifying your personal assets to determine which careers are suitable for you and which careers you should reject.

The Role of Tests Organizations which provide vocational counseling often administer a battery of tests to assist in determining career aptitudes. The

tests measure basic intelligence, achievement, aptitude, interest, and personality.

The tests are not infallible predictors of the best career for an individual. They do provide additional information which can be useful in helping a person select a career. If you take these tests, do not expect "high" scores on all of them. The intelligence, or IQ tests will give you a score which is readily comparable with other individuals. But even if you come out comparatively low on the IQ portion, it is not a disaster. The score should be analyzed in conjunction with the results from the other examinations. Most occupations do not require superbright people. And it is often the average person, in the right job, who will turn out to be the happiest and most successful.

If you are interested in taking tests to help in identifying your assets, there are a number of likely sources. Many universities maintain full-time testing and counseling centers which will both administer and interpret the exams for you. Some universities and colleges may give the tests through the school's placement service. Finally, in larger cities, there are public vocational counseling centers which provide these testing services.

Exhibit 2–2 summarizes some of the more widely used tests in each area. Different organizations usually rely on one test in preference to others. It is usually a function of the experience of the counselor. All these exams are considered reliable, nothing strongly recommends one over the others.

Strategy: Most young people should take tests to help them in selecting a career. The sooner you have test results, the sooner you will be able to use the information in your own career selection process.

A diagram of the career selection process is shown in Exhibit 2–3. The exhibit summarizes the important factors which should enter the decision process and illustrates the idea that these factors are interrelated. Recognizing the interrelationship is crucial for making an objective analysis of individual career preferences. For example, status, money, and security are available in different amounts in careers; the individual needs for them are a function of personality. A measure of their importance for any individual can be obtained through the use of standardized guidance tests.

Look at Future Trends in Jobs

Finding out about different jobs is not enough: Awareness of future trends in those occupations is also important. Is demand for people in that occupation expected to remain high? Or is the supply of jobs dwindling while the numbers of applicants continue to rise? There may still be many jobs available in careers which have stopped expanding; but if there are more applicants than positions, competition is intensified for the available openings. A classic example of this has occurred in the teaching profession over the last decade. Education graduates in the post-Sputnik era from 1957 through the late 1960s had little difficulty finding jobs. This was the period when American education was trying

Exhibit 2-2   Tests Used in Vocational Counseling

Type of Test	Measures	Examples
1 Intelligence	Capacity for mastering problems (generally referred to as IQ or intelligence quotient)	Wonderlic Personnel Test Otis Self-administering Tests of Mental Ability Wechsler-Bellevue Scales of Mental Ability
2 Achievement	Extent of knowledge or skill in a particular subject	Iowa Placement Examinations Typing or shorthand examinations College midterm or final examinations
3 Aptitude	Facility and speed with which new information or skills may be learned	Army General Classification Test Purdue Pegboard Minnesota Clerical Test
4 Interest	Pattern of likes and dislikes in various activities	Kuder Preference Record Strong Vocational Interest Blank
5 Personality	Emotional stability and personal adjustment	Bernreuter Personality Inventory Minnesota Multiphasic Personality Inventory Thurstone Temperament Schedule

Source: Robert Calvert and John E. Steel, *Planning Your Career*. New York: McGraw-Hill, 1963, p. 14.

to close the technology gap between the United States and Russia; this gap had become apparent with the successful launch of Russia's satellite, Sputnik I. Potential teachers entering the job market in recent years have found a far different environment. Openings have continued at several hundred thousand annually, but the supply of graduates has exceeded this by 4 or 5 times.

A completely different situation has occurred for aspiring accountants. Increasingly, the government requires businesses to keep better financial records and to make them known to the public. This trend has forced industry to hire more accountants each year. However, business schools have not produced enough graduates to meet the demand. The outcome of these factors for students electing an accounting career has been higher starting salaries and numerous job possibilities.

None of this discussion is meant to suggest that you should become an accountant if you really want to be a teacher. It is intended to make you aware of trends and suggests that you consider them in making your career choice. The problems with careers which have a generous supply of workers relative to

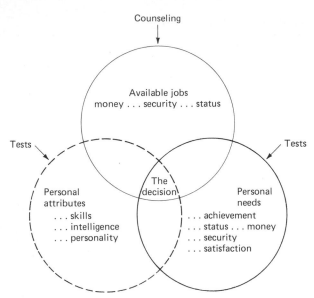

Exhibit 2-3   The Career Selection Process

available openings are numerous. The supply-demand relationship exerts a downward pressure on salaries. Job mobility is extremely limited and, with economic downturns, the security for individuals without seniority is poor.

Information on the outlook for specific occupations is available from the federal government. Periodically, the government surveys occupations and estimates the available openings each year and the potential supply of qualified applicants. These are reported by the Bureau of Labor Statistics of the U.S. Department of Labor.

Large or Small Firm?

For those people choosing a business career, one of the more important decisions is whether to work for a large or small firm. Underlying the decision should be many of the personal factors already discussed. Large firms, because of their more formal organizational structure, may tend to be stifling to some people. Other persons will thrive in that type of environment. Small firms offer the chance for broader exposure to all aspects of business: The advantage is experience in all areas; the disadvantage is no in-depth experience in any one area.

The larger firms may have greater promotional opportunities, more geographic locational possibilities, and greater job security (possibly). Small firms may be more fun to work for, and they may provide personal satisfaction which exceeds the monetary rewards of the giant corporations. The choice between the two is not an easy one and should be made with some care. Exhibit 2–4 summarizes the advantages of large and small employers. There are undoubtedly other factors which may be important. However, the exhibit does provide a reasonably comprehensive list of the most important variables.

Exhibit 2-4 Advantages of Large and of Small Employers

Large employer	Small employer
More job levels, therefore greater promotional opportunities.	Person of ability may stand out sooner and more prominently.
Greater potential earnings.	May offer eventual ownership possibilities.
Starting salary often higher.	Advancement often faster; competition may be less.
More extensive training programs.	Quicker assumption of responsibility and more immediate assignment to a specific job.
Greater security and fringe benefits.	More opportunity to benefit from growth of the organization.
Greater financial strength to weather depressions and technological changes.	Individual may be able to give more direction to work of organization and more readily see results of his own efforts.
Promotion from within policies enable graduate to make career with one employer on a lifetime basis.	More willing to hire older, experienced graduates.
More staff resources available to help solve problems as they arise.	Often greater opportunity for the independent person who works best alone.
Greater expenditures on research to ensure progress.	Work is often more varied and not as routine.
Diverse operations permit functional and geographic transfers.	Little need for geographical relocation, upsetting family life and friendships.
Often more scientific approach to management.	Policies and procedures more flexible; individual initiative may be more encouraged.
Less danger of being merged with large employer because of financial difficulties, competition of new products, or uneconomical size.	Often get better experience if you are interested in going into business for yourself.
More scientific promotion policies; little danger of relatives being favored as in a family-owned business.	Easier identification with goals of employer; more apt to be known by top management.

Source: Robert Calvert and John E. Steel, *Planning Your Career*. New York: McGraw-Hill, 1963, p. 29.

What Happens after You Pick a Career?

Getting your first entry-level job is only the beginning. If you are the typical young adult, you can look forward to 40 years or more before reaching retirement. A few things appear certain about your future, however. Once you pick a career, the odds are high that you will finish your working days in the same field. Job mobility from company to company may be easy, but job mobility across career lines is difficult unless you have a functional specialty, such as accounting or finance, where the type of business is immaterial to the job. People who start out as buyers in a retail store will almost invariably stay in retailing. Accounting trainees for the same retailer may become accountants for a manufacturer—they will remain accountants, however.

Progression within any chosen career depends in large measure on how well you do the job. Yet, with the exception of a few people who remain on the bottom and a few superstars who rapidly reach executive status, most people will find they conform to a fairly typical career pattern. The initial stage of 3 to 5 years involves training. After becoming familiar with the organization's operations, you may be moved into field sales or a lower-level supervisory job. This phase may last for 2 to 3 years. If you have shown satisfactory progress in your first 5 to 10 years with a company, you can reasonably expect to remain with the firm and receive future promotions. Most companies try to weed out marginal employees during the training and initial job-assignment phases. After that, the firm feels an obligation to continue your employment. The depth of this commitment is evidenced by the policy of the board chairman of a multibillion-dollar corporation who requires that all firings of employees with more than 8 years' service be approved by him. The manager recommending the termination of a long-service employee has to justify the decision on grounds other than incompetence. After all, incompetence should have been obvious long before 8 years had passed. This particular firm feels that short of theft or gross insubordination, an employee deserves a measure of job security after a reasonable probationary period.

Having survived the probationary period, the employee may expect future promotions that usually involve more direct supervision of other employees. Examples might include promotions from unit sales supervisor to district sales manager to regional sales manager. You will probably not make it to marketing vice-president. A company may have a sales organization of over 1,000 people,

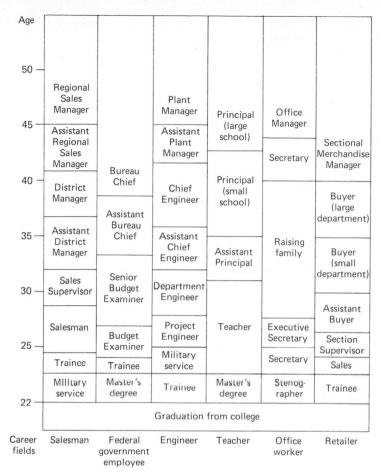

(*Source*: Robert Calvert and John E. Steel, *Planning Your Career*, McGraw-Hill, New York, 1963, p. 131.)

Exhibit 2-5 Career Patterns in Typical Fields

but there is only one V.P. for marketing. Accepting the fact that you might not reach the top is important for maintaining personal satisfaction with your career. It is not easy to do, and disappointment has adversely affected the life of many frustrated middle managers. Exhibit 2–5 shows typical career progression patterns.

Alternative Life-Styles

Thus far, we have briefly discussed some of the conventional careers and life-styles and suggested several ways to help you make a choice among them. However, there are also less conventional careers and life-styles, and they can be evaluated in the same way. Furthermore, if you are considering one of these alternatives, it is just as important, perhaps more so, to evaluate them carefully before you make a choice. We have raised some thoughts about personal values and the economic consequences of career choice, and they are equally important in deciding whether to rebel against the established roles of society and seek satisfaction in some less accepted role.

If you are considering making pottery or doing odd jobs to earn a living, you probably should examine yourself and think about your choice more intensely than if you are deciding to be an engineer or an accountant because of the economic sacrifices and, most likely, the adverse reaction from your family.

If you decide, after weighing the advantages and disadvantages, to live an unconventional life, much of the negative reaction you receive from older and more conservative people probably carries with it a tinge of envy. The fetters of accepted roles, the 9-to-5 job, the credit and mortgage problems, the effort of just coping with modern society look quite pale when contrasted with the thought of being a beachcomber.

Nevertheless, most people still lead a rather conventional life and are reasonably happy doing so. If you are disillusioned with the established system, however, you are not forced to abandon it entirely. Most people who try the alternatives end up even more disillusioned and slowly drift back to conventionality.

THE JOB SEARCH

The job search should start only after you have made a complete assessment of your strengths and weaknesses and your values. Assuming you have chosen a career and undertaken the appropriate training for it, the remaining thing is to find a job.

The Résumé

When you apply for a job, you should have an up-to-date résumé. Résumés should convey pertinent information to the reader, without undue length or detail. Younger people, those with little or no full-time work experience, should try to limit their résumés to one page. The résumé should include the following information:

1 Name, address, and phone number.
2 Personal data: birth date, marital status, health, and military status.
3 Professional objective: Specify the type of job you are seeking and indicate some long-term career goal.
4 Education: The most recent training should be listed first, earliest training listed last. It is unnecessary to list education prior to high school; the reference to high school can usually be eliminated if you have a college degree.
5 Degrees and awards: Following the names and location of the schools attended, list your degrees, major studies, and any honors or awards you have received.
6 Experience: In reverse chronological order (start with the most recent), list your work experience. Include the names and locations of the employers and the types of work you performed.
7 Miscellaneous: Included in this section are special skills, hobbies, and community services.

8 References: Include the names and addresses of at least three references. Make sure the individuals have been contacted and have agreed to act as a reference.

A sample résumé is shown in Exhibit 2–6.

Strategy: Even if you have very little work experience, you should try to write a résumé. Résumés take time to develop, and working on one over an extended period can improve its effectiveness.

Exhibit 2-6   Sample Résumé

ROBERT E. SMITH
115 Algoma Street
Oshkosh, Wisconsin 54901   Telephone 414–212–1234

PERSONAL	Married 5'8" 170 pounds 26 years old
PROFESSIONAL OBJECTIVE	Retail Sales Manager Ultimate goal—manager of major retail outlet for large national chain.
EDUCATION	B.B.A., 1975, University of Wisconsin-Oshkosh Major: Marketing Special emphasis on Retail Sales and Merchandising; considerable work in Accounting and Data Processing.
WORK EXPERIENCE 1975 to 1977	Glump's, Inc., Oshkosh, Wisconsin *Assistant Manager* in charge of all advertising and copy layout for this large department store. Worked closely with all buyers in planning sales campaigns.
1971 to 1975	Harold's, Inc., Oshkosh, Wisconsin *Retail Shoe Clerk.* Responsible for all display work, newspaper advertising, and sales promotion. The store had an annual volume of $250,000.
MILITARY SERVICE	United States Navy, 1967 to 1971. *Communications Specialist.* After graduation from high school, enlisted in the service. Spent most of the time in Europe working as a communications and personnel relations officer. Present draft status 1-C (Reserve).
BACKGROUND	Brought up in Oshkosh, Wisconsin. Active in community affairs such as Oshkosh Junior Chamber of Commerce; active alumnus of University of Wisconsin-Oshkosh. Member of social fraternity. Have traveled extensively throughout the western United States.
INTERESTS AND OTHER ACTIVITIES	Primarily interested in sports — outdoor activities — and reading. Member of Oshkosh area Consumer Council.
REFERENCES	Mr. John Glump, Owner, Glump's, Oshkosh, Wisconsin. Mr. Harold Glump, Owner, Harold's, Oshkosh, Wisconsin. Professor Ivy Twead, University of Wisconsin-Oshkosh, Oshkosh, Wisconsin.

Use Summers to Improve Job Chances   One of the important entries on your résumé is your work history. Employers often give preference to experienced candidates. As a student, you can use your summers to advantage by gaining experience which is directly related to your career choice. Doing so requires that you narrow your career possibilities as soon as possible. After taking that step, you should try to find summer employment related to your career choice. Such an effort can be invaluable in finding a good job after graduation. This same advice applies to part-time jobs and internships offered by many schools.

Help for Job Seekers

Finding a job is almost impossible without some form of assistance. Sources of help may range from the help-wanted advertisements in a local newspaper to executive search agencies, often referred to as headhunters. An understanding of those various sources and how they can help will significantly reduce the frustration in finding the right job.

College Placement Services   College students and alumni have the advantage of using the facilities and trained personnel of placement offices run by the schools. Placement offices arrange interviews with companies, assist students and alumni in preparing résumés, and provide career guidance when it is requested.

Placement advisors can also be a great help in teaching interview skills, which are necessary even for the most highly qualified applicants. An example of the suggestions for correctly handling the interview process is shown in Exhibit 2–7.

Exhibit 2-7

The Interview: Some Points to Remember

Analyze Strengths and Weaknesses. In preparing for interviews start by doing some solid, honest soul-searching. Analyze your strengths and weaknesses, your background, your academic performance, your vocational interests, and your personal aspirations and values. In other words, begin to formulate, in your own mind, not only what you would like to do but also what you feel you are best prepared to do.

Read Employer Literature. Next, study your prospective employers. It is imperative that you have some knowledge about their policies, philosophies, products, and services. Failure to do your homework before an interview can be the kiss of death. Nothing turns recruiters off faster.

Dress in Good Taste. Although most employers are becoming more liberal in their standard of dress and appearance, let basic good taste be your guide. If a beard or "Alice-in-Wonderland" look is going to jeopardize your chances for a job, that's your decision. With some employers appearance could be the deciding factor. The question you have to ask yourself is, "How important is it?"

Be Yourself. Your attitude is going to influence the interviewer's evaluation. Don't try to be something you aren't . . . just be yourself. Emphasize your strong points and remember that the recruiter is looking for inherent personal energy and enthusiasm. The interview is your opportunity to sell a product and that product is *you*!

Dwell on the Positive. Try always to dwell on the positive. While past failures and shortcomings need not be volunteered, don't try to cover them up or sidestep them. Should the recruiter ask about them, try to explain the circumstances rather than give excuses or blame others. Remember, he's human too . . . and probably has made a few mistakes. You'll create a better impression by being honest and candid.

Ask Questions—When Indicated. If appropriate, ask meaningful questions, particularly if you're not clear about the details of the job, the training program, or other job-related concerns. But, don't ask questions just because you think that's what is expected.

Follow Up. Finally, follow up on the interview. Provide whatever credentials, references, or transcripts are requested by the prospective employer as soon as possible. Be sure to write down the name, title, and address of the recruiter. You may want to consider a brief typed letter of appreciation for the interviewing opportunity.

Use Your Placement Office. These are, of course, only general suggestions and observations. For more detailed and personalized advice, take advantage of the services of your college's career planning and placement office.

Source: College Placement Council, *College Placement Annual,* 1976. Bethlehem, Pa., p. 13.

Private Employment Agencies   Assistance from private employment agencies ranges from excellent to terrible. Agencies may provide help in résumé preparation, or they may simply give you the names of companies having employment vacancies in your field.

The real difference between a good and a bad agency, as far as you are concerned, is whether or not it helps you find a job. Identifying good agencies on that basis depends on your success. A factor that can be measured, however, is whether the agency charges a fee or works on a fee-paid basis. Obviously, you would prefer to work through an agency that does not charge a fee. Some agencies will list both fee positions—you pay the agency a fee if you get the job—and fee-paid positions—the employer hiring you agrees to pay the agency fee. Quite often, employers will not absorb the agency's fee, but will reimburse the fee if you remain with the company for 6 months or a year. Be sure that the amount of the fee and the person who pays it are clearly specified, and these facts should be in writing before you sign a contract with an employment agency.

Working Wives?

Increasingly, more families have two sources of income. Among many couples, both partners have jobs. In the past, at the time the first child was born, the wife stopped working and seldom resumed full-time work, even after the children were grown and had left home. Now, many women return to work when the youngest child enters school, and in many cases even before that. The purpose of this section is to point out the economic and noneconomic factors which a wife should consider before deciding to return to work.

Is the Money All It Seems?   A woman considering a job which pays $500 a month will not realize anywhere near that amount. Taxes and social security will reduce the $500 gross by as much as $100. If extensive commuting via public transportation is necessary, another $50 to $100 could easily be spent. If commuting makes a second car necessary, the commuting costs could approach $200 monthly. Hiring a baby-sitter for young children could cost another $100 to $200. Put these costs together and it does not leave much from the $500 gross. What little is left will be spent on clothes (working women typically require a more varied wardrobe than men) and lunches. The result is that many wives decide it is just not worthwhile to return to work.

The Need for Satisfaction   Even if the financial considerations turn out to be marginal, many women want to return to work because they feel it is more satisfying than being a housewife. Cooking, doing laundry, tending to the children, and watching television soap operas have little appeal for many women. If this is your situation, then by all means consider a job. However, if you would rather tend to your house and the children and watch television, but you must return to work to help financially, then evaluate working on a dollar-and-cents basis only.

Minorities, Women, and Older Workers

Legally, employers cannot discriminate against minorities, women, and people over forty years old. Nevertheless, these groups have the most difficulty in finding jobs. Supposedly, they are protected by the Equal Opportunity legislation, the Equal Pay for Equal Work Act and the Age Discrimination in Employment Act. Unfortunately, there is much covert discrimination and it is difficult to detect. A woman may have her job application rejected for very legitimate reasons, or simply because she is a woman. Determining which reason caused the rejection can be almost impossible.

Despite these problems, recourse is available. The U.S. Department of Labor's Wage and Hour Division is charged with seeing that discrimination is eliminated. To date, the department has shown a willingness to work on behalf of people subject to discrimination.

Strategy: If you feel that you have been discriminated against because of age, sex, or race, contact the Labor Department's Wage and Hour Division. Complaints are not limited to situations where you are an applicant. If you are employed but feel that you are being discriminated against with respect to pay, recourse is also available.

SUMMARY

1   Understanding how jobs are classified is essential for starting the career selection process. A rough classification scheme is to define jobs based on the type of employer. Another classification is according to functional specialty.
2   Starting the career selection process early is necessary because of the educational requirements of many jobs. As soon as you know the career you would like to enter, you can select training which will help in finding employment.
3   A number of publications listed at the end of this chapter provide an excellent basis for expanding your knowledge of available careers.
4   A college degree is a requirement for many jobs. However, the economic advantages of college have been eroded. Many jobs not requiring college training now have as much income potential as the careers which require college training.
5   It is important to match your career choice with your personal values. Identifying the things you feel are important calls for objective self-analysis.
6   Choosing a career which is consistent with your skills and abilities is as important as matching the career to your values.
7   Standardized tests measuring skills, intelligence, aptitudes, interests, and personality can provide valuable assistance in selecting a career which matches your values and ability.
8   Understanding future trends in employment can help you select a career with the greatest growth potential. Choosing a career in which opportunities are not expanding limits salary potential and reduces job security and mobility.
9   Career progression for most people follows a fairly uniform pattern. Very few people make it to the top, but most people will progress at a steady rate, achieving a measure of job satisfaction and economic security.
10 The job search includes preparing a résumé listing your personal data, education, and work history. Placement offices, newspaper advertisements, personnel agencies, and friends can provide valuable help in finding a job.
11 A wife should consider both economic and noneconomic considerations in deciding to return to work.
12 Major federal legislation has been enacted in recent years to protect individuals subject to job discrimination because of sex, race, or age.

REVIEW YOUR UNDERSTANDING OF

Job classifications
Personal factors
    Values
    Skills
Tests
    Intelligence
    Achievement
    Aptitude

Interest
Personality
Job trends
The Occupational Outlook Handbook
Career progression
Job search
Résumé

Employment agencies   College placement services
   Fee paid   Antidiscrimination laws

DISCUSSION QUESTIONS

1 Why is it important to develop an understanding of the way jobs are classified?
2 Job security, satisfaction, and economic rewards are all important in selecting a job. Which of these factors is most important for you? Why?
3 Most large employers have formal recruiting and training procedures. Smaller firms are less structured in their recruiting practices. If you wanted to find work with a small firm, what strategy would you use for selecting the firm and for gaining access to an interview?
4 How much, do you feel, is luck a factor in finding the right job, and how much do you believe depends on the efforts of the individual?
5 What are the major sources of assistance in trying to find a job?
6 Some occupations will be more desirable in the future than others because of an expanding need for qualified individuals. What sources of information are available to help in choosing those careers with the greatest growth potential?
7 Why do jobs which have the greatest salary potential also have the highest failure rate?
8 How can tests assist you in finding the right career? What types of standardized tests are available and what do they measure?
9 What are the pros and cons a wife should consider in returning to work?

CASE PROBLEM

Harold Mudd was born in Oshkosh, Wisconsin, on January 3, 1959. He is currently enrolled at UW-Oshkosh as a first-year student with a declared major in history. Harold was a mediocre student in high school and is not setting academic records at college either. During the previous summer he sold pots and pans door to door and, despite a nasty run-in with an irate German shepherd, he managed to earn over $1,200. Most of that was promptly squandered on a used motorcycle and a four-week bender at a local campus bar.

    Harold has finally decided that he had better start thinking seriously about what he would like to do with his life. While in high school, he took a battery of tests which showed a high interest in people, average intelligence, little tolerance for structured tasks, and a personality suitable for sales or a career dealing with people. He is unsure of how to start a career search. He said he has heard about something called a résumé and would like your help in developing one.

    Also try to help out Harold by suggesting further tests that he could take to better understand himself. Finally, what sources of career information do you feel would be most appropriate for Harold to become more aware of the career opportunities that may be suitable for him, given his strengths and weaknesses?

RECOMMENDED READINGS

Books

There is an endless stream of books offering career advice. Most of the popular books are of little or no real value. If you would like useful text references, your public library would be a good place to start looking.

Booklets

Costello, Joan M., and Rita Parsont Wolfson, *Concise Handbook of Occupations.* Chicago: J. G. Ferguson Publishing Co., 1973.

The Institute for Research, *Career Monographs,* Chicago.

College Placement Council, Inc., *College Placement Annual.* Bethlehem, Pa. 18001. Latest edition.

Government Publications

U.S. Department of Labor, Bureau of Labor Statistics, *The Occupational Outlook Handbook.* Washington, D.C.: U.S. Government Printing Office 20402. Latest edition.

———, "Equal Pay," U.S. Government Printing Office, Washington, D.C. 20402.

———, "Sex Discrimination in Employment," U.S. Government Printing Office, Washington, D.C. 20402
The last two booklets describe the legal recourse available if there has been discrimination in pay or employment for women.

Magazines

Money:

Tarrant, Marguerite, "Careers from Here to 1985." September 1975, pp 60–61.
The outlook for specific occupations is discussed and areas of special importance are singled out.

Chapter 3

Financial and Personal Records: A Necessary Drudgery

After completing this chapter you should be able to:

identify the major types of records needed by an individual.

develop a good set of records for your particular needs.

use the records to start analyzing your financial condition.

recognize the types of records which should be kept in a safety deposit box.

From the day you are born, when a birth certificate officially attests to your existence, to the day you die, when a death certificate officially says you no longer exist, records are an important part of your life. There are checking accounts to balance, insurance policies to renew, mortgage or rent payments to record, as well as tax returns that must be prepared every year. It is at tax time when you wish you had kept a good set of financial records throughout the year. The person who has maintained clear records can complete the required tax returns in less time and suffer less frustration than someone with inadequate records. And with a good record-keeping system, you will miss fewer deductions.

Records are neither difficult nor time-consuming to maintain. Surprisingly, the organized record keeper spends less time on personal paperwork than the person who does everything on the backs of envelopes and matchbook covers.

The most difficult part of good record keeping is setting up the records. After that, the process is relatively mechanical. This chapter will help you develop a good personal record system by showing you a set of records designed to provide the information most people need.

Many of the records discussed in this chapter will be treated in greater detail in the following chapters.

SETTING UP YOUR RECORDS

The principal records most people should maintain are:

1 *Income statement.* This is a summary of income and expenses for a selected time period. It provides an important first step in planning and budgeting.

2 *Balance sheet.* This is a listing of assets and liabilities which shows a person's financial worth. It is important for summarizing a person's financial condition.

3 *Personal inventory.* This is a compilation of personal possessions, listing such factors as date of purchase and original cost. It can be very important for insurance purposes.

4 *Tax records.* Adequate records consist of income data and a list of deductions accumulated during the year. Also, copies of prior tax returns should be kept in the event the Internal Revenue Service questions your calculations.

5 *Homeownership records.* A record of the total investment in the property should be kept up to date.

6 *Insurance records.* Policies should be safeguarded, and a schedule of policy due dates should be set up to assist in periodically reviewing insurance coverages.

7 *Investment records.* A record of all sales and purchases of stocks, bonds, or other investments should be retained for tax purposes. Maintaining a record of the income from each investment can be helpful in periodically evaluating your investments.

8 *Working file.* Adequate record keeping includes the systematic handling of bills, the checking account, and worksheets for the family budget.

The Income Statement

An income and expense statement is important because it summarizes the revenues available to take care of a family's needs and desires. Often, by reviewing your past expenses, you can better plan future expenses, and if necessary, alter your life-style to fit your level of income.

The mechanics of completing a statement such as shown in Exhibit 3–1 are reasonably straightforward. Old check registers, bills, and your memory should enable you adequately to complete the income statement. Remember, this is for your benefit only: it is not an official document. Accuracy to the penny is not so important as the exercise of filling out the form.

Even if your records of expenses are incomplete, and some categories do not apply to you, it is still important to complete an income statement. Only by making yourself sit down and reconstruct *how you spent* your money will it be possible for you to decide *how you would like to spend it.* Probably the biggest surprise in completing the income statement will be the large amount of income that is unaccounted for. This fact alone should illustrate the need for a budgeting system. By specifying how you want to spend your money, you ultimately make far better use of your income than when expenses are totally unplanned.

Most of the items on the income statement are self-explanatory. The statement in the exhibit may not exactly fit your circumstances; however, minor modifications should make it work reasonably well. The first time you fill out an income statement you will probably find the catchall category "Other" (Exhibit 3–1, line 22) taking a disproportionate share of your total income. This will soon make you aware of "other" expenses. Specific things you should watch for are the following:

Lines 1 and 2 The amounts listed should be your after-tax income, after deductions for taxes and social security. Because these taxes are automatically deducted, there is little point in showing gross income on these lines. And besides, what you are really interested in is spendable income.

Line 4 "Other" income should represent true income, not sale of assets such as an old car. For example, a state income tax refund is considered income.

Line 6 Include in this category items such as kitchen supplies.

Line 10 List here only the cost of the clothes. Cleaning and repairs should be included under Personal, line 20.

Line 24 If this line shows a negative amount, you are in trouble. It means you are spending more than you make. If this line shows a positive amount, but one that is much larger than you think it should be, you have probably missed some expenses.

Balance Sheet

The next document you will need in determining your financial condition is a balance sheet. This lists all your *assets,* the things you own, and deducts your

Exhibit 3-1   Personal Income Statement for 19XX, Frank and Mary Swanson

Sources of Income		
1 Husband's job	$9,700	
2 Wife's job	3,800	
3 Dividends and interest	15	
4 Other, state tax refund	562	
5 Total income		$14,077
Expenses		
6 Food		
At home	$2,100	
Away from home	375	
7 Total Food		$ 2,475
8 Housing		
Rent or mortgage	$2,400	
Real estate taxes	—	
Heat and light	487	
Telephone	193	
Insurance	55	
Repairs	—	
9 Total housing		$ 3,135
10 Clothing		$ 875
11 Transportation		
Gas, oil, etc.	$ 417	
Insurance and license fees	218	
Loan payments	1,380	
Repairs and maintenance	225	
Other, public transportation	58	
12 Total transportation		$ 2,298
13 Recreation		
Vacations	$ 360	
Clubs, dues	—	
Sports equipment	50	
Other, entertainment	260	
14 Total recreation		$ 670
15 Life Insurance Premiums		$ 123
16 Medical		
Doctors	$ 55	
Dentists	125	
Medicine	36	
Health insurance	400	
17 Total medical		$ 616
18 Other fixed payments		
Loan repayment	$ 347	
School tuition	—	
Other	—	
19 Total fixed payments		$ 347
20 Personal		
Magazines	$ 36	
Cosmetics	47	
Barber	60	
Other	—	
21 Total personal		$ 143
22 Other, alimony		$ 3,600
23 Total expenditures (lines 7, 9, 10, 12, 14, 15, 17, 19, 21, 22)		$14,282
24 Amount left over (line 5 minus line 23)		($205)

liabilities, or the things you owe to other people. The difference between your assets and liabilities is referred to as *net worth.* Exhibit 3–2 is a sample balance sheet which you can use to calculate your net worth. A first effort at completing the balance sheet can be a frustrating experience. However, it is extremely important because it neatly summarizes your current financial value. Without understanding your current financial position, it is impossible to develop short-, intermediate-, or long-range financial plans. Making judgments about what you want to change over the next year becomes much easier with this information.

For example, after analyzing the balance sheet, you may decide that your cash position is far too low. Having more readily available cash could become one of your financial goals for the next year. Completing an annual balance sheet is a good way to keep a record of your financial progress. After you have done it for a few years, a review of previous statements will quickly tell you whether or not you are making progress.

In addition to thinking about short-term goals when developing a balance sheet, it is also a good time to think about your financial position 5, 10, or even 25 years hence. You might start by drawing up a condensed balance sheet showing your projected future financial position. If you do this, you can then ask yourself whether the projections are realistic. Do not try to fool yourself with dreams that cannot possibly be fulfilled. It may seem difficult, and even a little ridiculous, to project so far in the future, yet it is a good place to start if you really hope to make some significant long-term financial progress.

The spending and savings patterns shown in Exhibits 3–1 and 3–2 indicate a fairly conservative nature. The Swansons have few debts outstanding and an adequate savings account to handle any emergency situations which may arise.

Personal Inventory

Many people are unaware of the amount they have invested in furniture, china, jewelry, and clothes. In the "Other" category may be very valuable items like gun collections, cameras, or stereo equipment. If you came home some night and fire had destroyed your house or apartment or burglars had cleaned you out, could you itemize all your belongings for the insurance company? Most people would have difficulty doing so unless they had some systematic record of what they own. The more accurate your records, the more likely you will be to collect the fair value of your possessions in the event of fire or theft.

Your inventory of personal belongings should include a description of each item and its condition, the amount you paid for it, and the date you purchased it. If the item is of special value, such as an antique or a painting, it should be appraised to verify its value. The appraisal should become a part of your records.

The inventory can be maintained on loose-leaf pages, such as shown in Exhibit 3–3, or on index cards, so that additions and deletions can be made easily. Periodically—say, once a year—the inventory should be updated.

Exhibit 3-2   Balance Sheet for 19XX, Frank and Mary Swanson

Assets

1 Cash		
Checking account	$ 375	
Savings accounts	3,823	
On hand	15	
2 Total cash		$ 4,213
3 Life insurance cash value		$ 3,648
4 Investments		
Stocks (market value)	—	
Bonds	—	
Real estate (other than home)	—	
Other	—	
5 Total investments		—
6 Automobiles (current value)		$ 2,600
7 Personal belongings		
Furniture and appliances	$1,500	
China, silver	330	
Jewelry	500	
Clothes	1,200	
Other	—	
8 Total personal		$ 3,530
9 Home		—
10 Total assets (lines 2, 3, 5, 6, 8, 9)		$13,991

Liabilities

11 Bills outstanding		
Charge accounts	$ 135	
Oil company credit	56	
Doctors, dentists	25	
Other _____	—	
12 Total bills		$ 216
13 Installment loans		
Car	$1,200	
Furniture	175	
Other	—	
14 Total installment loans		$ 1,375
15 Home mortgage		—
16 Total liabilities (lines 12, 14, 15)		$ 1,591
Net worth (line 10 minus line 16)		$12,400

Tax Records

Income tax time is greatly simplified if you have kept systematic records. People who do not itemize deductions but, rather, take the standard deduction

Exhibit 3-3   Sample Personal Property Inventory

Room: Living room		Date of inventory: January 3, 19XX	
Description	*Condition*	*Price*	*Date purchased*
Sofa	Excellent	$475	Feb. 1972
Easy chair	Good	250	Mar. 1970
Table lamps (2)	Excellent	75	April 1970
Oriental rug (appraised by J. Smith, Aug. 1971)	Very good	500	Aug. 1971
Stereo	Excellent	500	Mar. 1976
End tables (2)	Good	200	Mar. 1973
Coffee table	Good	150	Mar. 1973

will need only a record of the income they have received. Ultimately, however, many people find it advantageous to itemize their deductions. (A complete discussion of this subject is covered in Chapter 6.) If you intend to itemize your deductions, you must set up your records for the following categories: (1) Income, (2) Taxes paid, (3) Interest payments, (4) Contributions, (5) Medical expenses, and (6) Miscellaneous deductions. About six pages in a loose-leaf notebook, to be updated as the need arises, will save you countless hours and dollars when you have to complete your tax returns. Exhibit 3–4 shows a sample of the type of tax record, for interest expenses, that you can easily maintain for yourself.

Exhibit 3-4   Sample Tax Records
Interest Expenses, 19XX

Date	Paid to/for	Amount	Cumulative total
1/5	Oshkosh NB/mortgage	$125.00	$ 125.00
2/5	Oshkosh NB/mortgage	124.50	249.50
2/7	Credit Union/car loan	23.00	272.50
.	.	.	.
.	.	.	.
.	.	.	.
12/5	Oshkosh NB/mortgage	119.00	1,703.00

	Summary		
Year	Oshkosh NB/mortgage		1,470.00
"	Credit Union/car loan		200.00
"	Master Charge/interest		23.00
"	Sears/interest		10.00
		Total	$1,703.00

A similar record for contributions is shown in Exhibit 3–5. It is important to have a separate record for each major category of deductible expense. For some expenses which occur frequently, it may be advisable to have individual sheets for each person or organization to which payments are made. If this is done, the summary process will be greatly facilitated.

Setting up adequate tax records is just the beginning. Knowing what should be included in the records is equally as important. This is covered in greater detail in Chapter 6.

After annual tax returns have been submitted, copies should be kept along with all supporting documentation. This would include the worksheets, such as Exhibit 3–5, and receipts to verify the worksheets. Tax returns, except in the event of fraud, should be kept for a minimum of 3 years from the date the return was due. On April 15, 1977, it is safe to dispose of your tax return for calendar 1973, since that return was due on April 15, 1974. The returns themselves can be kept in file folders or large manila envelopes. The latter are particularly useful if there are a lot of loose receipts and supporting documents.

Despite the 3-year time limit for reexamining returns by the government, however, we feel that returns should probably be kept for at least 10 years. It does not cost anything to keep the returns, and in the event they are needed, they will be readily available.

Homeownership Records

From the time a home is purchased until it is sold, records must be maintained. The deed must be safeguarded and additions to the property recorded for tax

Exhibit 3-5   Sample Tax Records
Contributions, 19XX

Date	To	Amount	Cumulative total
1/5	Heart Fund	$ 5.00	$ 5.00
2/11	Church	50.00	55.00
2/15	Girl Scouts	10.00	65.00
.	.	.	.
.	.	.	.
12/8	Church	50.00	485.00

	Summary		
Year	Heart Fund		$ 5.00
"	Church		400.00
"	Girl Scouts		50.00
"	United Way		30.00
		Total	$485.00

purposes. Every year, the total interest, tax, and casualty-loss expenses should be recorded for income tax deductions.

The Deed   A deed is the legal document which is proof of property ownership. It is extremely valuable since property cannot be transferred without it. In many localities a deed is difficult and often expensive to replace. Consequently, care should be taken to properly safeguard deeds to any real estate you own.

Other Ownership Records   Ownership documents which should be protected include the mortgage note, any surveys which define property boundaries, and title insurance policies when necessary. Title insurance protects your interest in a property from any financial claims that may arise because of improper recording of deeds or similar mistakes. Finally, if you have house blueprints, they should be saved: They can be quite useful if you plan to remodel the house at a future time.

Capital Addition Records   At the time a house is sold, a tax is levied on the difference between the cost of the property and its selling price, if higher. The tax may be avoided if money from the sale of the house is invested in another primary residence, of equal or higher value, within a specified period of time. The cost of additions to the property, such as a new room, central air conditioning, or a paved driveway, can be added to the basis, or cost, of the property for figuring the tax liability. Since a house may be owned for 10, 20, even 30 years or more, it will be necessary to keep accurate, well-documented records. A summary sheet should be maintained to record the property additions. An example of a recommended form is given in Exhibit 3–6. This form provides a summary of the total investment in the property. All the entries on the form should be substantiated with receipted bills, canceled checks, or some other acceptable proof of the expenditure. Proof that trees have been planted can also be demonstrated with pictures which show the property before

Exhibit 3-6   Record of Capital Additions to 210 Easy Street

Date	Item	Amount	Total cost of property
	Balance		$24,207
1/17/68	Driveway	$485	24,692
5/11/69	Trees	108	24,800
12/15/72	Paneled basement	480	25,280
.	.	.	.
.	.	.	.
.	.	.	.
5/18/73	Patio	400	27,211
6/26/75	New hot water heater	600	27,811

and after the addition. If there is some question as to whether an expenditure represents a capital expense, it is probably wise to record it as such. Examples of pure expense items which cannot be included are ordinary painting, papering, and general maintenance. Examples of questionable ones are a new furnace or roof. At times they are considered capital additions and at other times they are expenses. Generally, if they are done when a home is initially occupied, they represent capital additions. If they are done after the home has been occupied for a period of years, they represent an expense which cannot be used to offset taxes. The safe thing to do is record all questionable items so that at least the information is available at the time a decision must be made.

Yearly Expense Records   The interest on a home mortgage, real estate taxes, and unreimbursed casualty losses, such as damage from a fire, in excess of $100 are deductible for federal income tax purposes. The only difficult deduction to substantiate may be the casualty loss. If some damage occurs to your home, careful appraisals of the extent of the damage should be obtained from qualified individuals. When repairs are made, an accurate record of all costs should be compiled. If these two precautions are taken, there should be little problem in claiming this deduction.

Personal Records

Personal records, such as a birth certificate or military separation papers, are important for insurance, employment, and social security. Records which should be readily accessible include the following:

   1   *Birth certificate.* An official copy of the birth certificate for all family members should be kept in a safe place. Ready access to a birth certificate can uncomplicate the paperwork for school, jobs, the military, and social security.
   2   *Military separation papers.* Like birth certificates, these are often required by potential employers.
   3   *Marriage license.* This will not be needed often, but it is one of your important records.
   4   *Wills.* Most people, particularly if they are married, should have an executed will. In the absence of a will, a person's property, no matter how insignificant, will be distributed in accordance with state law, not according to the wishes of the individual. (This is discussed more fully in Chapter 21.) Consequently, make a will and keep it safeguarded with your other important records.
   5   *Letter of last instructions.* Accompanying the will should be a letter providing an inventory of financial records. Examples of things contained in the letter would be a statement of the location and number for (*a*) bank accounts, (*b*) life insurance policies, (*c*) certificates of automobile ownership, (*d*) deeds to real estate, (*e*) prior income tax returns, (*f*) canceled checks, (*g*) stock accounts, (*h*) mutual funds, and (*i*) other insurance policies. The information contained in the letter is very helpful to the person responsible for handling the decedent's affairs. Often it is difficult to be sure that all items are

accounted for unless the deceased has provided a comprehensive summary of all possessions.

Insurance Records

In subsequent chapters, a number of ways to save on insurance premiums will be discussed. Keep good records of your insurance and they can be an important initial step in reducing insurance costs. A checklist should be developed which lists the premium due date for each of your insurance policies. An example of a typical list is shown in Exhibit 3–7.

By referring to this insurance checklist periodically, you will be prepared for the premium notices. This knowledge will be a big help in setting a monthly budget. Equally important, it will give you enough advance warning to make changes in the coverage well before the due date. You may want to drop the collision insurance on your car after it reaches a certain age and its value has dropped below $1,000. Our experience has shown that many people will continue with coverages they may not want unless they make a specific point of periodically reviewing their insurance needs. An example may highlight the usefulness of an insurance checklist: Homeowners insurance is written for a specific value on the property, such as $25,000. As the property increases in value, the coverage should be raised to keep the property fully insured. Failure to arrange for full coverage will mean that only partial reimbursement will be made in the event of a loss. (The calculation is discussed in Chapter 16.) It is the

Exhibit 3-7   Insurance Policy Record

Policy number	Company	Amount	Due date	Premium
Life insurance				
283728	You Bet Your Life Co.	$10,000	June 20	$125
396278	Last Gamble Life	$15,000	July 8	$162
Auto insurance				
12876243	Fidelity Auto	$100/300/25	Aug. 20	$ 75
		$100 Ded*	Feb. 20	$ 75
		$ 5 Med		
Homeowners insurance				
4728316	Friendship Mutual HO-3†	$32,000	Jan. 15	$127
Other				
114732	Blue Cross–Blue Shield Health Insurance		Nov. 1	$635
143821	Mutual Casualty Boat Insurance	$ 2,000	Aug. 1	$103

*Refers to liability, collision, and medical limits (see Chapter 16 for a complete discussion).
†Refers to the type of homeowner's policy. (Also discussed in Chapter 16.)

policyholder's responsibility to make sure that insurance limits are adequate. Therefore, you must regularly evaluate needs, and accurate up-to-date records will make it easier.

Investment Records

If you ever invest in stocks or bonds, complete records are an absolute necessity. The information that you must keep includes (1) cost, (2) income, and (3) selling price. The income you receive will have to be included on your annual income tax returns in most cases. The difference between cost and selling price is a gain or loss, which must also be included on your tax returns. Therefore, for your investment records, make sure you keep all confirmation slips (records of purchases and sales) from your broker and maintain an up-to-date income record for each stock and bond you own.

Maintaining Your Records

The average person's financial and personal records are too complex to be kept in a shoe box. Be better organized than that. After all, organized record keeping is the start of successful financial planning. Get yourself a supply of manila folders and a small file cabinet (single, cardboard file drawers are commercially available), and you have the start to maintain your records.

A Safety Deposit Box

Some of the records and papers which you accumulate should be guarded more carefully than others. They may be very costly or even impossible to replace. You can obtain adequate protection by renting a safety deposit box at a

IT STARTED OUT TEN YEARS AGO AS A FOLDER FULL OF IMPORTANT PAPERS AND JUST GREW!

commercial bank, savings and loan association, or mutual savings bank. The cost depends on the size of the box. Five dollars probably represents a minimum annual charge.

> **Strategy: We feel the following documents should be kept in a safety deposit box: (1) a copy of the personal property inventory, (2) deeds to all real estate, (3) certified copies of birth certificates, (4) military separation papers, (5) wills, (6) marriage and/or divorce papers, (7) stock certificates, and (8) other investment certificates.**

SUMMARY

1 Each year, prepare a balance sheet and an income statement to summarize income, expenditures, and current financial condition. These can then be used for developing the next year's plans.
2 An inventory of personal property should be updated annually to assure that full insurance reimbursement can be collected in the event of fire or theft.
3 Tax records should be maintained for (*a*) income, (*b*) taxes paid, (*c*) interest payments, (*d*) contributions, (*e*) medical expenses, and (*f*) miscellaneous deductions.
4 Homeownership records involve safeguarding the deed, maintaining a record of capital additions, and maintaining a record of annual expenses deductible for income tax purposes.
5 Make sure that personal documents, such as family birth certificates, military discharge papers, and marriage licenses, are safeguarded.
6 Investment records should be kept up to date for all stocks, bonds, mutual funds, and other investments. Included in the records should be information of the property's cost and a historical record of income from the property.
7 Personal record keeping can be greatly facilitated by investing in a file cabinet and a good supply of manila folders.
8 Many records and documents should be protected from the possibility of loss. Renting a safety deposit box is the best way to ensure that such papers are adequately safeguarded.

REVIEW YOUR UNDERSTANDING OF

Income statement
Balance sheet
Personal property inventory
Tax records
Homeownership records
    Deed
    Capital additions
Safety deposit box

Personal records
    Birth certificate
    Military papers
    Wills
    Letter of instructions
Insurance records
Investments records
Working file

DISCUSSION QUESTIONS

1 What information can be found in an income statement which can assist you in developing sound financial plans?
2 Why is it important to complete a balance sheet as part of your financial records?

3   What information should be included in a personal inventory? Why is this information important?
4   What records are needed if you file a tax return using the standard deduction? What additional information should you accumulate if you plan to itemize deductions?
5   Why should the deed to property be kept in a safety deposit box?
6   What types of tax records should be kept if you own a home?
7   What types of personal records should be kept? Describe an instance where a personal document, such as a birth certificate or military separation papers, was required.
8   What are the two most important reasons for having an insurance policy checklist?
9   Give two reasons for keeping investment records. What information is required?
10 Why should certain papers be carefully safeguarded? What are the most common documents which should be kept in a safety deposit box?

CASE PROBLEM

Ed King has spent the last 4 years as the assistant manager of a local pizza parlor. He believes that he has developed the recipe for the best-tasting pizza in the area. He would like to open his own pizzeria, feeling it would succeed because of his secret recipe. A local banker is interested in lending the money for the venture, but he insists that Ed first draw up a personal balance sheet and income statement for the past year. The banker needs this information to determine whether Ed is financially responsible, how much money he can invest in the business, and whether he will be able to live during the first year before the business is established.

Ed does not know how to begin. He has asked for your help and he has brought you all the records for the past year. His tax return shows that he made $13,000 at the pizzeria. His taxes were: (1) social security, $760.50, (2) federal taxes $1,015, and (3) state taxes $200. He and his wife pay $200 a month for an apartment, including utilities. Ed figures that food has cost $175 a month, clothes about $55, and entertainment expenses $15. Telephone has run $12 monthly. Annual insurance premiums were (1) car, $220, (2) health insurance, $400, and (3) life insurance, $120. The loan repayment on his car has been $134 a month; he has spent $35 monthly on gas and oil; the registration fee is $25; and he just had a $250 repair bill to fix the power steering. Ed's pet poodle just had an infected rear leg and the veterinarian's fee was $400. The Kings also had a $1,200 medical bill which was not covered by their health insurance. Ed estimates they spent about $25 a month on personal items.

Financially, the Kings have a savings account of $1,100, savings bonds worth $600, and a checking account balance of $350. They own no stocks, bonds, or real estate. Their car is worth $2,300, but they still owe $1,500 on the loan. Ed figures their furniture and clothing are probably worth $1,800. They owe $250 on a sofa and $150 on their Master Charge.

a   Using Exhibit 3-1 as a guide, complete an income statement for Ed.
b   Using Exhibit 3-2 as a guide, complete a balance sheet for Ed.

RECOMMENDED READINGS

Books

Bailard, Thomas E., David L. Biehl, and Ronald W. Kaiser, *Personal Money Management*. Chicago: Science Research Associates, Inc., 1973.

Chapter 2 contains a discussion of record keeping and gives details for completing a personal income statement and a balance sheet.

Magazines

Changing Times:
"Which Family Records Should You Hang On To." December 1974, pp. 37–40.
The article discusses the most important records and papers a family should save.

DEVELOPING •AND• MANAGING YOUR INCOME

Chapter 4

Personal Budgeting

After completing this chapter you should be able to:

explain the major steps involved in the budgeting process.

recognize the importance of budgeting.

develop a complete budgeting system for yourself.

analyze your expenditures from a budget summary sheet.

recall the major problem areas which may make a budget unworkable.

explain why savings should be treated as a regular expense in the budgeting process.

A sound personal budget is an important aid in achieving your economic goals. Trying to get the most out of your income without budgeting is like trying to drive from one point to a far-distant point without a road map. It may turn out to be a successful trip, but then again, it may not. A budget is the road map that can guide you in making expenditures which will help you meet your goals. If you would like to save for a down payment on a house, a winter vacation, a new car, or any other major purchase, a budget can help you realize the goal.

A budget does not tell you how to spend your money. You are the one who makes that decision. How you spend your money is a very personal value judgment. Some ways may be more beneficial than others, but that is for you to decide. No matter what life-style you select, however, a budget can assist you in obtaining the maximum satisfaction from your income.

There are any number of good budgeting systems which have been developed. All good systems minimize clerical effort and maximize the information provided. The system developed in this chapter has only two repetitive clerical steps, both of which can be accomplished by spending a minute or two each day and about 1 hour at the end of each month. The output of the system reveals exactly how much was spent in each expense category and whether that figure is above or below the desired level.

The case of John and Sally Brown illustrates the need for careful money management. John worked for a large corporation, starting at $8,000 a year 6 years ago. He received regular raises and the increase to $16,000 last year made it appear that he had a promising future. When they were married, Sally worked as a grade school teacher and supplemented John's income by $6,400 a year. Life was great. The extra income was used for clothes, vacations, a new car, and rent on a luxury two-bedroom apartment complete with swimming pool. Three years ago, Amy Brown was born and a move to a three-bedroom, $35,000 home followed.

Living on John's income alone proved to be almost an impossible task. The house payments, taxes, utilities, and insurance claimed $450 per month. Car payments for a second car (John now had to commute to work) were $134, and gas, upkeep, and insurance were another $60. When they moved to suburbia, they bought furniture to fill the rooms in their new home. Installment payments for the purchases consumed another $150 per month. Every month they seemed to fall a little further behind. Second notices on bills came regularly, and harassing phone calls from bill collectors were so annoying that Sally needed tranquilizers to get through the day.

In desperation, Sally took all their bills and checkbooks to a counselor at a family service organization. The counselor found that the Browns owed $9,300 for cars, furniture, and general department store bills. John's take-home pay was $925 per month and their monthly expenses amounted to $1,150, of which over $800 were fixed obligations, not including food or clothing.

At work, promotions and raises stopped. Some of the bill collectors had contacted his boss, and while he did not fire John, he certainly was not going to entrust more responsibility to a person who could not handle his personal finances.

The Browns' home life also suffered. John and Sally fought constantly about money and the bickering caused Amy to become a problem child. Finally, Sally sued for divorce, and a long and bitter battle ensued.

What had started out as a seemingly perfect marriage ended in personal disaster in less than 6 years. Most of the troubles could be directly traced to poor money management. This little vignette may seem like overdramatization to you. It is not. There are thousands of John and Sally Browns who are going through this same process every day. To be sure, financial problems do not cause all marriages to end up in divorce proceedings like the Browns. Nevertheless, much of the trauma the Browns suffered will be present even in marriages which remain intact.

Studies have shown that financial problems resulting from poor planning and management are a primary source of marital difficulty and divorce. The man and woman who start their married life by working out their finances together can avoid many of the problems which ruined John and Sally's marriage. Budgeting is no guarantee of marital success, but if the statistics are correct, it can at least prevent one of the major causes of marital discord.

BUDGETING: THE PRELIMINARIES

A budget system will work smoothly if attention is paid to some planning details. The budgeting procedure consists of five distinct steps. They are:

1   Estimating available income
2   Defining major expense categories and setting budget levels
3   Developing worksheets to accumulate expenses
4   Using the budget summary sheet to monitor and control expenditures
5   Periodically reviewing the budgeting system to make sure that it is still appropriate for changing circumstances

The steps are shown in Exhibit 4–1. Note that the only ongoing clerical work occurs in steps 3 and 4, where expenses are recorded daily and transferred to the summary sheet at the end of each month. The benefits far outweigh the small clerical effort required to keep the records up to date once the system has been set up.

A successful budgeting program cannot be done without first completing some basic preparations. These preliminary steps are (1) estimating available income and (2) defining expense categories and setting budget levels. Figuring total income is relatively easy for most people. Step 2 is the most difficult part of the budgeting process. It may take a fairly substantial amount of time and effort to reconstruct your previous spending. After you have determined how you have spent your money in the past, you must evaluate that information to decide how you would like to spend it in the future. This may require a major

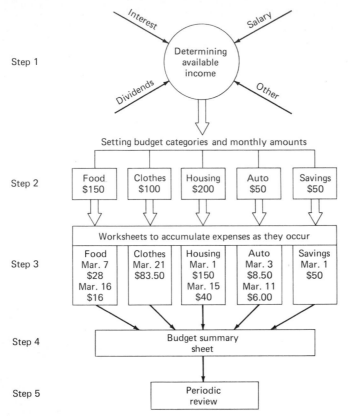

Exhibit 4-1   The Budgeting Process

realignment of your life-style, particularly if you have decided to begin budgeting because you find expenditures exceed income.

Estimating Available Income

For most people, the largest percentage of their income will be derived from their jobs. In estimating available income, look only at the amount that you will receive after all nonvoluntary deductions, such as federal, state, and city taxes, social security, and any required contributions to insurance programs or pension plans. If you belong to the "bond-a-month" plan or a voluntary savings plan through a credit union or stock-purchase plan, these amounts should not be deducted. They are voluntary and represent income which would be available if you should stop making contributions to them. These deductions represent savings or investments.

Other sources of income that you may have include: interest on savings accounts and bonds, dividends, bonuses, tax refunds, and rental income. Total monthly income for Sam and Samantha Jones is summarized in Exhibit 4–2.

Dividing your total expected income for the year by 12 will give you a good approximation of the amount that will be available each month to cover your expenses. If your income is received rather unevenly (throughout the year), you may want to list each month separately on the budget summary sheet (Exhibit 4–8). This would permit you to exercise even greater control by grouping major expenses in the months you have the highest income. However, to simplify the examples in this chapter, income is assumed to be received evenly throughout the year. Therefore, an equal amount is entered for each month on the summary sheet.

In planning your budget, you may want to pay some attention to income planning. For example, if you expect to receive a tax refund, instead of taking the refund at the end of the year, change your exemptions (number of dependents you claim) so that less money is withheld monthly. This will give you more spendable income during the year. And remember, while it may be nice to get a tax refund, the government does not pay interest during the year it holds your money. If you changed your withholding so that you had the money instead of the government, you would at least benefit by the interest it would earn in a savings account.

Defining the Major Budget Categories

How detailed do you want your budget to be? It can be a very simple statement with a few major categories, such as food or rent. Or it can be far more elaborate, containing detailed breakdowns of each of the major categories. A word of caution: A lot of detail will provide a great deal of information, but it will tend to make the budget overly time-consuming. Too little detail will make it difficult to analyze expenditures.

> **Strategy: Most people will find that a budget with 8 to 10 major budget categories will be sufficient. No more than 25 or 30 subcategories, or approximately 3 for each major category, should adequately summarize all normal expenditures.**

The income statement from Chapter 3 can assist you in setting a preliminary budget. From the income statement select the categories which best suit your expenditure patterns, and use them as the basis for a preliminary budget worksheet. You will probably need two or three tries to get the budget set up correctly, so do not get frustrated if things fail to work the way they should the first time.

Timing of Expenses   Identifying each of your major expense categories is the first step in budgeting. But, the next step is the critical one—knowing when

Exhibit 4-2   Sources of Income for Sam and Samantha Jones

Salary	$1,050.00
Interest	28.00
Dividends	22.00
Other (specify)	—
Total monthly income	$1,100.00

all your expenses must be paid and establishing a cash flow pattern between income and expenses so that cash becomes available as bills come due.

The greatest percentage of personal expenses occurs on a regular monthly basis. Examples would be rent, food, and utilities. Other expenses occur on an irregular basis. Auto insurance, life insurance, homeowners insurance, and real estate taxes may be paid once or twice a year. Bills for these expenses are an unpleasant surprise for many people who do not budget for them. They pay regular monthly expenses and do not set aside enough money to cover the expenses which occur on an infrequent basis. In your budgeting, be especially attentive to your irregular expenses. Your budget can help you to put aside enough money each month to meet these bills when they come due. By planning in this way, you are effectively converting irregular expenses to regular expenses.

In addition to known expenses, whether regular or irregular, every family can be faced with unforeseen bills which can ruin a budget, unless the budget provides for an "unforeseen" category of expenses. Examples of such costs include medical expenses and car repairs. By setting up an emergency fund as part of the budget, you will be prepared for sudden costs in these areas. These will be discussed in more detail in a later section.

Regular and Occasional Expenses   Many budgeting systems categorize expenses as either fixed or variable. However, this is somewhat unrealistic since very few expenses are fixed amounts. Even food expenses vary somewhat. Therefore the terms *regular* and *occasional expenses* more accurately describe the breakdown of normal expenditures. Regular expenses are the

costs of everyday living: food, housing, transportation, entertainment, regular savings, and monthly payments on installment debt. Occasional expenses are bills for insurance and major purchases which may occur only once or twice a year. Make sure that these occasional expenses are considered in your budget. An amount of money sufficient to cover the annual totals for these occasional expenses should be included as a major expense each month.

Exhibit 4–3 gives a detailed breakdown of major expense categories by month. If you complete this table showing your actual expenses during the past year, you will have a detailed analysis of how you spent your money in each area, every month. Using the information in the table, you should be able to make judgments about the way you want to spend money during the next year. By analyzing your regular monthly expenses, you should also be better able to plan for the occasional expenses.

Exhibit 4–3 has been completed for Sam and Samantha Jones to show how much variation there can be in typical monthly expenses. These variations occur to some extent with just about everybody and highlight the need for preparing for the big occasional expenses. The Jones's expenditures for last year ranged from a monthly low of $748 to a monthly high of $1,740. Sam's income after tax was $1,100 per month. Since there were 5 months during the year when his expenses exceeded income, it was important to set money aside during the low-expense months to prepare for the high-expense months. Without going through the exercise of listing monthly expenses for the past year, it would be extremely difficult to know how much to set aside for large expenses and when those expenses occur.

Note the absence of any savings in Sam's and Samantha's expenditures. Regular savings should also be a part of the budget. Yet, when most people review their past spending patterns, they find that savings has simply been the amount, if any, left over after expenses. Later, this chapter will show how to include savings as a regular monthly expense.

Deciding How to Spend Your Money   The next step in budgeting is setting amounts for each expense category. Everybody has a limited income and must decide how that income should be spent. How much for food? Clothes? Housing? Transportation? Recreation? and Savings? These are questions which have to be answered to develop a workable budget. How you divide your income will depend on what you feel is most important. Some people enjoy fine clothes and are willing to spend a large percentage of their income for them. Others consider expensive clothes a waste of money and would rather spend their money on cars or on a hobby such as photography. Remember, no matter what you would like to spend your money for, your expenses cannot exceed your income for a prolonged period. If you find, in setting up your budget, that you are spending too much, go back and reassess each of the expense categories. The greatest attribute of budgeting is that it enables you to check systematically on how you are spending your money and permits you to make adjustments before you get into trouble.

Exhibit 4-3 Record of Spending for 19XX,
for Sam and Samantha Jones

Expense	Jan	Feb	Mar	Apr	May	Jun	Jul	Aug	Sep	Oct	Nov	Dec	12-month total
Housing													
Rent or mortgage	$ 180	$ 180	$ 180	$ 180	$180	$180	$180	$180	$ 180	$ 180	$180	$ 180	$ 2,160
Real estate taxes	—	—	—	—	—	—	—	—	—	—	—	750	750
Water and sewer	—	—	25	—	—	25	—	—	25	—	—	25	100
Heat and light	60	55	40	35	30	20	20	15	25	30	40	50	420
Maintenance	—	—	30	—	—	85	—	—	15	—	—	—	130
Telephone	15	10	10	10	10	10	10	10	10	10	10	20	135
Total housing	$ 255	$ 245	$ 285	$ 225	$220	$320	$210	$205	$ 255	$ 220	$230	$1,025	$ 3,695
Food													
At home	$ 155	$ 160	$ 140	$ 160	$185	$140	$ 140	$175	$ 160	$ 150	$170	$ 190	$ 1,925
Away from home					(included in personal spending money)								
Total food	$ 155	$ 160	$ 140	$ 160	$185	$140	$ 140	$175	$ 160	$ 150	$170	$ 190	$ 1,925
Clothing													
Husband	$ 50	—	—	$ 125	—	—	$ 35	—	$ 110	—	$ 60	—	$ 380
Wife	—	$ 45	$ 45	—	$ 80	—	—	$ 17	25	$ 40	—	$ 60	312
Children	30	25	10	—	15	$ 5	25	10	18	23	10	14	185
Total clothing	$ 80	$ 70	$ 55	$ 125	$ 95	$ 5	$ 60	$ 27	$ 153	$ 63	$ 70	$ 74	$ 877
Insurance													
Life	—	—	—	$ 300	—	—	—	—	—	$ 300	—	—	$ 600
Car	$ 110	—	—	—	—	—	$110	—	—	—	—	—	220
Homeowners	—	—	$ 105	—	—	—	—	—	—	—	—	—	105
Other, *boat*	—	—	—	40	—	—	—	—	—	—	—	—	40
Total insurance	$ 110	—	$ 105	$ 340	—	—	$110	—	—	$ 300	—	—	$ 965
Medical													
Doctor	—	$ 30	$ 30	—	—	—	—	—	—	$ 45	$ 40	—	$ 145
Dentist	$ 25	—	—	—	$ 25	$ 25	—	—	—	25	—	—	100
Prescriptions	—	15	15	—	—	—	—	—	—	23	18	—	71
Total medical	$ 25	$ 45	$ 45	—	$ 25	$ 25	—	—	—	$ 93	$ 58	—	$ 316

Exhibit 4-3 Record of Spending for 19XX, (Continued)
for Sam and Samantha Jones

Expense	Jan	Feb	Mar	Apr	May	Jun	Jul	Aug	Sep	Oct	Nov	Dec	12-month total
Automobile													
Payments	$ 110	$ 110	$ 110	$ 110	$110	$110	—	—	—	—	—	—	$ 660
Gas, etc.	23	17	23	40	25	50	$ 25	$ 30	35	40	$ 25	$ 18	351
Repairs	—	—	105	—	—	—	—	—	80	—	—	—	185
Total auto	$ 133	$ 127	$ 238	$ 150	$135	$160	$ 25	$ 30	$ 115	$ 40	$ 25	$ 18	$ 1,196
Charity													
Church	$ 20	$ 20	$ 20	$ 20	$ 20	$ 20	$ 20	$ 20	$ 20	$ 20	$ 20	$ 20	$ 240
Other	—	5	—	5	—	—	—	—	20	—	—	15	45
Total charity	$ 20	$ 25	$ 20	$ 25	$ 20	$ 20	$ 20	$ 20	$ 40	$ 20	$ 20	$ 35	$ 285
Durables													
Furniture	—	$ 300	—	—	—	—	—	$250	—	—	—	—	$ 550
Appliances	—	—	—	$ 150	—	—	—	—	—	60	—	—	210
Total durables	—	$ 300	—	$ 150	—	—	—	$250	—	60	—	—	760
Personal													
Education	$ 150	—	—	—	—	—	—	—	$ 150	—	—	—	$ 300
Magazines	—	$ 30	—	—	—	—	$ 23	—	—	—	$ 18	—	71
Entertainment	20	—	15	10	25	$ 25	—	$ 15	30	40	25	18	223
Total personal	$ 170	$ 30	$ 15	$ 10	$ 25	$ 25	$ 23	$ 15	$ 180	$ 40	$ 43	$ 18	$ 594
Miscellaneous													
Husband	$ 100	$ 100	$ 100	$ 100	$100	$100	$100	$100	$ 100	$100	$100	$ 200	$ 1,300
Wife	50	50	50	50	50	50	50	50	50	50	50	150	700
Children	10	10	10	10	10	10	10	10	10	10	10	20	130
Total miscellaneous	$ 160	$ 160	$ 160	$ 160	$160	$160	$160	$160	$ 160	$160	$160	$ 370	$ 2,130
Grand total	$1,108	$1,162	$1,063	$1,345	$865	$855	$748	$882	$1,063	$1,146	$776	$1,720	$12,743

Sample Expense Totals   The percentage figures in Exhibit 4–4 are computed from budgets prepared by the U.S. Department of Labor, Bureau of Labor
Statistics, for an urban family of four at three income levels. The budgets are
not derived from actual data, but are the result of estimates of costs for
representative goods and services.

These figures can provide a good starting point for setting target expenditure totals in each of your major budget categories. If your past expenditures
varied only slightly from the percentages in the budget closest to your standard
of living, you probably have nothing to be concerned about. However, if your
expenditures are markedly different from these, the disparity indicates that you
should reevaluate your spending pattern. There may be a logical explanation
for the variance, but wide differences should at least cause you to examine
more carefully how you spend your income.

Do Not Make the Budget a Straitjacket   If the budget becomes too detailed and demanding, the burden of accounting for every penny can make
people lose interest in the process very rapidly. Included in the expenses
should be a miscellaneous category which does not have to be accounted for
each month. Each week, allocate a certain amount of spending money to each
family member and simply record the total as "Miscellaneous." The amount
does not have to be large. But not having to account for every candy bar and
magazine can reduce the bookkeeping by an appreciable amount. It will also

**Exhibit 4-4   Consumption Expenditures as a Percentage
of Income for Three Income Levels**

Budget category	Lower budget, $9,198	Intermediate budget, $14,333	Higher budget, $20,777	Typical $10,000 budget* Monthly	Annual
Food, at home	26.1	20.9	17.2	$217.50	$ 2,610
Food, away from home	3.9	3.8	4.2	32.50	390
Housing (includes furniture)	19.1	22.6	22.7	159.16	1,910
Transportation	7.0	8.2	7.3	58.33	900
Clothing	8.2	7.6	7.6	68.33	820
Personal care	2.5	2.2	2.1	20.83	250
Medical care	8.0	5.2	3.7	66.66	800
Other consumption†	4.6	5.5	6.2	38.33	460
Other‡	4.5	4.6	5.4	37.50	450
Taxes§	15.9	19.5	22.6	132.50	1,590
	100.00%	100.00%	100.00%	$833.33¶	$10,000

*Derived using the lowest budget percentages.
†Includes reading materials, recreation, tobacco, education, and miscellaneous.
‡Includes gifts, contributions, life insurance, and occupational expense.
§Social security and federal and state taxes.
¶Percentages and dollar amounts do not add to total because of rounding error.
Source: U.S. Department of Labor, Bureau of Labor Statistics, 1975.

increase everybody's enthusiasm for recording major expenditures. The amount that you should consider as miscellaneous expense will depend on your income and number of family members. A reasonable amount of free spending money will be well worth the sacrifice of not accounting for each penny in the budget.

Make Savings a Regular Expense

Most people regard payment of rent or mortgages and repayment of consumer loans as unavoidable expenses. Successful financial planners have the same attitude toward regular savings. They make savings one of the main budget categories and treat the item as an obligation which must be met. In doing so, they ensure that short-run fluctuations in income and expenses can be met out of an emergency fund, and that long-run goals can be realized from money set aside each month. The amount which you allocate to each of these categories will depend on your income level and your goals. Some recommended savings levels which may help you in deciding how much to save are discussed below.

Emergency Savings Everyone should have a savings account for an emergency reserve. Major expenses for car repairs, home repairs, or medical problems cannot always be met from current income. The amount that should be kept in an emergency reserve will depend to a large extent on the security of your job. The more secure your employment, the smaller the reserve you will need to keep.

> **Strategy: Your emergency reserve should be equal to at least 3 months' take-home pay. If your income after tax is $1,000, then your savings account should be at least $3,000. A more prudent reserve should represent about 6 months' take-home pay.**

PHIL FRANK

Amounts in excess of this should be allocated to long-term savings objectives.

The emergency fund should be kept in a passbook savings account so that you can have immediate access to the money if the need arises.

Long-Term Savings   The second portion of your savings program should be directed toward accumulating savings for long-term goals. Examples of the things you might wish to save for are a down payment on a home, a vacation home, or investments which can provide a second income. In Chapter 1 it was suggested that stating the goals in dollar terms and specifying how soon you would like to realize those goals are necessary if you are to determine how much you will have to save each month to achieve your objectives.

Sam and Samantha Jones have some goals which illustrate how these computations should be made. Sam would like to buy a new sailboat in 5 years. He estimates that it will cost about $3,000. A college education for their children is one of their primary goals. The children will be in college 10 and 12 years from now respectively, and Sam would like to have $20,000 in the bank at the time the oldest child starts college. The last goal they have is a European vacation when the children finish college. This will require $3,000 some 16 years from now. These goals with their respective timing are summarized in Exhibit 4–5.

Sam estimates that he can earn 5 percent on the money he saves. With this information he can calculate exactly how much he must save each month to reach these goals. This amount then becomes the long-term savings element of his budget.

Tables A17–1 and A17–2 in Chapter 17, Appendix A, are compound interest tables which can be used to compute exactly how much must be saved each year, at a given interest rate, to achieve a desired ending balance. For Sam to have $3,000 in 5 years to buy his sailboat, he will need to save $545 per year. This means Sam must save $45 every month for the next 5 years in order to be able to buy the sailboat. The calculation is $3,000 ÷ 5.5 = $545. The factor, 5.5, was obtained from Table A17–2. A detailed description of the tables' use is contained in Appendix A, Chapter 17.

Using Table A17–2, we have converted each of the Jones's goals to an amount that must be saved each month to reach the goals. This information is given in Exhibit 4–6.

Even for these modest goals, Sam must save almost $200 per month. The value in defining goals as Sam has done is that of determining whether they are realistic. If you had Sam's goals, could you save $187 a month? By having the information laid out before you, as in Exhibit 4–6, you can develop alternatives. Maybe the sailboat can be postponed, or the European vacation plans can be scaled down. Remember, without defining the goals and calculating the

Exhibit 4-5 Long-term Goals for Sam and Samantha Jones

Goal	Amount	When required
Sailboat	$ 3,000	5 years
College	20,000	10 years
Vacation	3,000	16 years

necessary monthly savings amount, it is impossible to see whether those goals are achievable.

The Budget Period Budgeting is usually done on a monthly basis for a one-year period. An annual budget seems to conform with the expenditure patterns of most families. It contains all the major expenses which are paid on an annual basis, such as insurance premiums, and includes a full year for tax purposes. Moreover, it really takes about a year to keep one-time expenses from making the budget look unrealistically low or high. For example, if an annual insurance premium is due during the first month of a budget, it will appear that insurance expenses are far greater than they should be because the premium will be 12 times the budgeted amount. Only after a full year's budgeting will the amounts be equal.

Once you have decided to prepare an annual budget, you should decide whether to break it down on a monthly or weekly basis. Most people find that the detail involved in maintaining a weekly budget is so cumbersome that they quickly lose interest in the process. For this reason, budgeting on a monthly basis is strongly recommended. Even if you are paid weekly, the monthly budget should be easier and just as useful. Recognize, however, that there are not four weekly paychecks in each calendar month—but that there are

$$\frac{52 \text{ weeks}}{12 \text{ months}} = 4^{1}/_{3} \text{ weeks per month over the year. It makes a}$$

difference.

Preliminary Worksheets Daily and weekly expenditures must be accumulated before they can be entered on the monthly budget. Loose-leaf sheets

Exhibit 4-6 Savings Goals for Sam and Samantha Jones

Goal	Amount	When required	Monthly savings needed to reach the goal
Sailboat	$ 3,000	5 years	$ 45
College	20,000	10 years	132
Vacation	3,000	16 years	10
		Total monthly savings	$187

should be set up for each of the budget categories. If these are kept in a three-ring binder in a convenient place, such as the kitchen, all members of the family can enter on the appropriate sheets each amount they spent shortly after they have spent it. Exhibit 4–7 gives a sample worksheet for food expenses. At the end of the month, the totals for each category can be entered on the budget.

A Trial Budget   As a preliminary step in budgeting, you may want to keep worksheets for each of the categories until you get a good idea of how you are spending your money. If you do this for a month or two, the job of maintaining a full-scale budgeting system will appear more manageable, since you will already have done a big part of the clerical portion of the job.

The Monthly Closing Process   At the end of each month, the totals on each of the monthly worksheets should be transferred to the budget summary sheet (Exhibit 4–8). The summary sheet serves as a check for overspending in each of the major categories. At the end of each month, you can see exactly how closely you are staying to each of the budget amounts you projected. Some of the items, such as food and rent, should conform very closely to the budget amount. Others, such as insurance and taxes, may show a very large positive or negative balance depending on whether the expense occurs near the beginning or end of the annual budgeting period. This difference may be disconcerting, but it should not be cause for concern, provided a monthly amount sufficient to cover these occasional expenses has been included in the budget.

The Periodic Review   If the budget is not used in making spending decisions, it represents nothing more than a clerical exercise. Consequently, it is strongly recommended that every 3 months an evening be set aside to review the previous quarter's budget. The budget summary sheet, Exhibit 4–8, has been set up to include quarterly totals. After these have been filled in for the last 3 months, the information can be used to evaluate how successfully you

Exhibit 4-7   Sample Worksheet for Recording Expenses to be Included in Family Budget

Food Expenses

Date	Items	Amount	Cumulative total for month
11/5	Groceries	$ 25.11	$ 25.11
11/12	Meat	18.00	43.11
11/23	Groceries	42.00	85.11
.	.	.	.
.	.	.	.
.	.	.	.
11/29	Groceries	40.37	183.18
		November total	$183.18
12/5	Groceries	$ 15.10	$ 15.10
12/8	Meat	18.43	33.53

Exhibit 4-8 Budget Summary Sheet for Sam and Samantha Jones

	Monthly Budget	Jan Actual	Jan Surplus (Deficit)	Feb Actual	Feb Surplus (Deficit)	Mar Actual	Mar Surplus (Deficit)	Quarterly summary Budgeted	Quarterly summary Actual	Quarterly summary Surplus (Deficit)
Total income (See Exhibit 4-2)	$1,100	$1,100		$1,100		$1,100		$3,300	$3,300	
Expenses:										
Food	175	185	(10)	160	15	200	(25)	525	545	(20)
Rent or mortgage	180	180	—	180	—	180	—	540	540	—
Taxes	65	—	65	—	65	—	65	195	0	195
Phone	10	15	(5)	15	(5)	15	(5)	30	45	(15)
Heat and light	60	75	(15)	70	(10)	65	(5)	180	210	(30)
Clothing	150	200	(50)	210	(60)	175	(25)	450	585	(135)
Insurance:										
Home	10	—	10	—	10	—	10	30	—	30
Car	20	120	(100)	—	20	—	20	60	120	(60)
Life	50	600	(550)	—	50	—	50	150	600	(450)
Car expense	50	40	10	35	15	100	(50)	150	175	(25)
Personal	50	150	(100)	—	50	—	50	150	150	—
Miscellaneous	160	150	10	160	—	160	—	480	470	10
Total Consumption	$ 980	$1,715	$(735)	$ 830	$(150)	$ 895	$(85)	$2,940	$3,440	$(500)
Savings										
Emergency	20	20	—	20	—	20	—	60	60	—
Long term	100	—	(100)	100	—	100	—	300	200	(100)
Total savings	$ 120	$ 20	$(100)	$ 120	—	$ 120	—	$ 360	$ 260	$(100)

Note: Deficits are shown in parentheses.

have lived within the budget you set out for yourself. Are there any expenditures which are well over the amounts budgeted? If so, is there a good reason for the overspending?

Exhibit 4–8 has been completed for Sam and Samantha Jones. Their income projections proved to be quite accurate. They were not so successful in making their expenditures stay within their budget. They overspent on clothing by $135, and their savings fell short by $100. The major problem area was insurance. Actual expenditures were $510 greater than budgeted. This is not so bad as it might be, however, since Sam's total life insurance premium for the year comes due in January and one-half the car insurance for the year is due at the same time. For the 3 months of the budget, Sam and Samantha actually overspent by $500 and undersaved by $100.

The budget summary sheet separates savings from consumption expenses so that it is very clear whether overconsumption or lack of savings was the reason the budget was not met.

Budgeting Problems

Any budgeting system will fail if you do not pay attention to details. In addition, there are other potential problems which can doom even the most carefully developed budget. There may be factors other than the ones discussed here which are unique to your situation. Recognizing them beforehand can help avoid the problems they create.

Past Mistakes   The chances for success are enhanced considerably if the budget starts without the burden of past mistakes. Such mistakes might include large department store bills or high fixed payments for nonessentials like boats or campers. An interim budget to rectify these errors can be a big aid in ensuring the success of the new budget. When the budget is finally started, it will be for a spending pattern which is more consistent with plans, not with the haphazard way income was spent in the past.

Car Payments   Sam and Samantha's spending record (Exhibit 4–3) shows they made car payments for the first 6 months of the year. After the payments were completed, there was no evidence that they made any provision to save an amount equal to the payments. If, after they had completed their car payments, they had continued to put aside the same amount each month in a savings account, they could buy their next car with cash. But apparently, instead of saving the amount of the monthly car payments, Sam and Samantha used the money to increase their spending in other areas. The problem with this is that when they eventually have to buy a new car, of course they must finance it with a loan, and they must reduce their increased spending in these other areas to come up with the monthly payments for the car. Once an increased spending pattern is established, it is very difficult to cut it back.

Two Incomes   Many young couples will both work before they decide to have children. The luxury of two incomes is nice. The danger of it is in getting used to living on two salaries. Some couples with two incomes may feel that money problems are insignificant and that budgeting seems totally unnecessary. Yet, failure to budget can create insurmountable problems when one of the incomes stops.

There is nothing wrong with spending one of the incomes for vacations, possibly some special furniture, or even eating out frequently. All these expenditures can be curtailed with little difficulty. The problems occur when normal living costs—food, housing, clothes, and insurance are paid for partially by the second income. Should the second income stop, those expenses must be reduced, but the cutback will be very difficult. For this reason, second incomes should be used for building savings and buying items which are not a regular living expense. To ensure that you do not become dependent on the second income, budget only your primary income for all routine living expenses. Experience has shown that if a conscientious effort is not made to live within the one income, ultimately both incomes will be consumed by normal expenditures.

Joint Effort   In Chapter 1 it was stressed that financial planning should be a family effort. This advice is equally important for budgeting. In younger families, both the husband and wife will be making purchase decisions. If the budget has not been jointly developed, there is little chance that it will succeed. In older families, the children should also be included in the budgeting process since they too will be spending part of the family's income.

A mutual commitment to the budget is as important as the budget itself. The budget is only the visible evidence that a family wants to control the way it spends money. The full cooperation of all family members is needed to make it work.

SUMMARY

1   Budgeting is important to help you live within your income.
2   Budgeting should assist you in directing your income to the expenditures which are most important to you.
3   Budgeting can be viewed as a four-step sequence where (*a*) you estimate cash income; (*b*) you estimate regular fixed expenditures, including savings; (*c*) you specify the amount desired for emergency savings; and (*d*) you estimate normal monthly living expenditures. The final part of budgeting is putting these steps together to see how well you are living within your income.
4   Budgeting is only part of successful money management. Carefully selecting goods and services and selecting the best way to pay for them can stretch income by a substantial percentage.
5   Savings should be treated as a regular part of the expense budget. You should

budget savings for two purposes; for an emergency fund, equal to 3 to 6 months' income; and for long-term goals.

6   To determine how much should be allocated to long-term savings, list all the major things you would like to save for, how much they will cost, and how long a time you will need to save for them. This information can be used to calculate the amount which must be saved each month.

7   Budgeting on a trial basis can improve chances for success when you put your budget into effect.

8   The periodic review of your budget is an important step in making it work for you.

9   Budgeting can be more successful if problem areas are avoided. The budget should not suffer from the past mistakes of poor planning. Special attention should be paid to budgeting when a family has two incomes.

10 Budgeting should be a family effort. Without the cooperation of all family members, the chances for success are limited.

REVIEW YOUR UNDERSTANDING OF

Expense categories
    Budget levels
Timing of expenses
    Regular expenses
    Occasional expenses
Savings
    Emergency Fund
    Long-term
Budget worksheets

Closing process
Summary sheet
Periodic review
Budget problems
    Past mistakes
    Car payments
    Two incomes
    Family cooperation

DISCUSSION QUESTIONS

1   How many budget categories should the average person have? Why?

2   In setting up a family budget, what is the most important decision that must be made?

3   Sam and Samantha Jones have decided that they would like to save $100 per month next year. From the information in Exhibit 4–3, giving the Jones's expenditures last year, make recommendations on the categories which could be reduced to allow them to reach their goal.

4   What is the best time interval for budgeting purposes? Does it make any difference if the budgeting period is monthly and your pay is received weekly?

5   Is it necessary to account for every expenditure in your budget?

6   For persons who have trouble living within their income, what budget categories do you feel are most critical to control for?

7   Using Table A17–2 in Chapter 17, calculate the amount that you must save each year at 5 percent to have $5,000 in 5 years. How much do you have to save each year at a 7 percent interest rate?

8   Complete a budget worksheet, similar to Exhibit 4–3, for yourself. How closely do

your expenditure patterns compare with those in Exhibit 4–4? Can you explain all the major divergences of your spending from the percentages in Exhibit 4–4?

CASE PROBLEM

Gloria Gonzalez recently graduated from college and started work as a management trainee for a large manufacturing firm. She is single, but plans to be married next June (a year hence) when her fiancé graduates from college, although he plans to continue in graduate school. Her salary is $950 per month and after deductions for social security, federal and state taxes, and health insurance, her take-home pay is $690. The major expenses facing her include car payments of $134 monthly, life insurance due in September of $287, and a bill at the local clothing store of $275. (She had to trade in her jeans for more suitable business clothes.)

Gloria would like to save at least $2,000 between now and next June so that she and Jamie can take a honeymoon trip that she estimates at $1,000—and still have money to buy some furniture for their apartment. She plans to share an apartment this year with a college friend. The monthly rent will be $90 each, including utilities. By eating most meals in the apartment, she feels that she can keep her food bill under $75 per month.

Using this information, complete a one-year budget, by months, which will enable Gloria to achieve her savings goal. Items that you should consider in making up the budget, in addition to the ones mentioned, include (1) additional clothing purchases; (2) entertainment; (3) personal care; (4) transportation expense; and (5) car insurance of $185 due in November. Notice how Gloria's fixed commitments give her very little leeway in each of the major budget categories.

RECOMMENDED READINGS

Booklets

Household Finance Corporation, Money Management Institute, *Reaching Your Financial Goals*. 1971.
   A very readable and practical booklet which integrates budgeting, financial planning, and saving.

Magazines

Money:

Main, Jeremy, "Bring Your Budget Back to Earth." May 1974, pp. 26–30.
   The article discusses four areas: housing, borrowing, savings, and food.
Mead, William B., "The Superinflation Squeeze." August 1974, pp. 26–30.
   The article discusses strategies for coping in the major budget areas.

APPENDIX A: Buying Food

Food prices in the United States have risen sharply during the past several years, and all indications are that they will continue to increase. Consumers who had become conditioned to seeing annual price rises of 4 percent during the late 1960s and early 1970s have reacted with shock and dismay to the 13 percent annual rise during the mid-1970s.[1] Unfortunately, there is little an individual can do to slow those price increases. But there are several things that can be done to reduce the effect of those increases. The central objective is to obtain maximum value for each dollar you spend for food.

More for Your Dollar

The suggestions outlined below are designed to help you become a more careful, demanding, and discriminating food shopper. Our recommendations do not require that your diet consist of some bland, unappetizing string of "bargain meals." Nor are we suggesting that you ignore the requirements of good nutrition solely to reduce your food outlay. We think you can serve appetizing and nutritionally sound food, yet still obtain maximum value for your food dollar. By doing your homework, we think food shopping can be a challenging and rewarding pursuit.

Unit Pricing   Many food stores have adopted some form of unit pricing (price per ounce) as well as the product's total price on the package or container. Thus, the price label on a 12-ounce box of cornflakes would show: cost 34 cents, 2.83 cents per oz. Typically, this detailed price label is placed on the shelf rather than on the product. By comparing the price per unit, you can decide which brand is cheapest. Likewise, the various sized containers of the same brand (family, giant, super, etc.) can be compared to decide which size is the best value. The largest size does not always have the lowest cost per unit. For example, a small-size package of 6 ounces may cost 62 cents while the large size of 16 ounces may cost $1.85. Yet, unit pricing shows that the small size costs 10.3 cents per ounce, and the large size costs 11.5 cents per ounce. Obviously, the small size is the better buy.

If the store where you shop has not adopted unit pricing, voice your displeasure to the manager. Until the practice is adopted, do your own pricing, using your pocket calculator or pencil and notepad.

> **Strategy: Always select the brand and the package size that minimizes the cost per unit, yet meets your needs. Obviously, that size should not be so large that you waste part of the product.**

House Brands   Many large supermarket chains package food products under their own private brand names. In most cases, their product's quality is comparable with that of the highly advertised national name-brand counterparts.[2] Rather than automatically

---

[1] Author's estimates based on price information in *Federal Reserve Bulletin*, "Consumer Prices," November 1975, p. A53.
[2] William B. Mead, "What's in a Name Brand?", *Money*, February 1974, pp. 40–44.

assume the national brand is superior, try some of the private brands before you decide. The potential savings vary widely, however. So compare prices to make certain the private brand is cheaper.

Convenience Foods   Convenience foods are designed either to ease the time and effort to prepare a particular meal or to present a food item in a more convenient form: packaged mixes, frozen dinners and entrées, food in aerosol cans or squeeze tubes. The consumer pays a dear price for the convenience. Except for several minor exceptions, all convenience foods cost more per serving than the same food item costs when you prepare it yourself, using the basic ingredients. Unfortunately, the consumer not only pays more, but many convenience foods deliver less nutrition than their made-from-scratch counterparts. Furthermore, many have only a faint resemblance in taste and texture to their real-life counterparts. If you want to receive maximum value and nutrition for your food dollar, do not use convenience foods heavily.

Try making an item from scratch rather than using a convenience food. You may be amazed at what real food tastes like; and the substantial savings provide a double bonus.

Using Store-Sponsored Specials   Nearly all food stores run a series of weekly specials at reduced prices. By planning your menus around these items, you can save two ways. First, by using the special items, you can save the amount of the price reduction. Second, some stores raise the price on other food items to recoup the profits lost on their special sale items. By concentrating your purchases on their specials, you will likely reduce your purchases of nonspecials that may have inflated prices. If the special is a staple food item that can be stored, consider buying ahead. Obviously, you should not carry this so far that you must discard part of the food because it is stale or unusable.

Always wait until a store has announced its weekly specials, even if you buy only a few of those items. Shopping several days early could mean forgoing some sizable savings. If the store includes coupons as part of its advertisement, use them. If the store is out of a special, demand a raincheck for the item so you can buy at the reduced price on a later date.

Plan! Plan! Plan!   We cannot overemphasize the need to carefully plan your food purchases. It is amazing how few people do any advance planning before they head for the food store, yet it is likely they are spending 25 percent of their total income on those shopping trips. Planning should begin with a menu for the next week. When estimating the perishable foods you need for that menu, try to match the quantities to your family's size so that you will not waste food.

Before you go to the store, have a detailed list of exactly what you need. Relying on your memory is an invitation to forget something. Even more important, a detailed list lessens the chance of your buying an item on impulse. Seriously underestimating your weekly food needs can be as wasteful as overestimating. Frequent trips to the store are costly. And if you supplement your week's shopping by purchasing at a small, late-hours convenience store, you will likely pay much higher prices.

When planning your menus, stress items that are currently in season; their cost should be low relative to the rest of the year and the quality will be high. Minimizing out-of-season items can substantially cut your food bill. Avoid doing your shopping immediately before closing time. The selection is likely to be more limited and heavily picked over.

When planning your weekly menu, consider substituting some lower-cost foods. Possibly a less luxurious cut of meat would be just as suitable. Or maybe you could try several meatless meals during the week. You will have to be your own judge on this particular point. Your individual preference will dictate how far you want to proceed on trying lower-cost substitutes.

Where to Shop   The best way to decide which store has the lowest prices is to do your own comparison test. Compare prices over a fairly broad range of items rather than just a few. As a result of your comparison, you may want to split your food purchases among several stores. For example, you might decide to buy fresh produce or meat at one store because it excels in those items. Then purchase your staple food items at a different store because its prices are lower than those at the first store. Given the recent rise in automobile operating costs, however, the strategy of shopping the specials at several different stores should be examined carefully.

Impulse Buying   A golden rule of successful food shopping is to avoid buying an item on impulse. There are several things you can do to protect yourself from impulse buying. Have a detailed shopping list with your needs clearly set out. Never shop when you are hungry. Avoid buying an item just because it has been heavily advertised. Despite the enticing odors in the bakery and delicatessen area, move through them quickly lest you be tempted to add something you do not need. Unless you can say no, leave your children at home. Unless you are certain the price is a good one, avoid the items that the store is featuring at the end of each aisle. Likewise, avoid those food items placed near the checkouts; frequently, they are convenience or junk foods that are very poor value.

Does It Pay to Buy in Bulk?

The question of whether you save money by buying in large quantities is difficult to answer. First, several other questions require answers. Is there a source in your area where you can buy food in quantity at a favorable price? Do you use a sizable amount of food each year? Can you preserve some of the food for later use? People who answer yes to these questions should carefully consider buying in large quantities.

Where to Buy   Many cities have a farmers' market where local growers bring their produce to be sold. Generally, the savings are greatest if you can buy in large quantities. If you need only a small amount, the saving probably is not worth the trip. The range of products you can buy at these markets varies depending on the area. Typically, your savings will be greatest on those products which are grown locally. If the seller is merely an agent who is selling products which have been shipped in, the savings are likely to be small or none at all.

The question of whether you should buy meat, such as a full side of beef, is much more difficult. First, be aware that the potential savings are not what some advertisements make them out to be. Second, buy only from a seller you know to be reputable.

Exhibit A4-1 Cost of Freezer Ownership

Description	Annual cost
Operating cost, 1905 kilowatt hours × 4¢*	$ 76.20
Lost interest on money used to purchase freezer:	
$350 × 5.25 percent	18.38
Annual decline in freezer's value:†	
$350 ÷ 15 years	23.33
Repair expense	5.00
Total	$122.91

*Operating cost for a medium efficiency freezer in the 15.5 to 18.5 cubic-foot range. Assumes energy cost of 4 cents per kilowatt hour (kwh).

†Assumes life of 15 years.

Third, make certain you really can use everything you are getting. A side of beef is not all steaks and filet. The references at this chapter's end can give you further guidance.

Storage Costs: A Freezer While many people are well aware of the potential savings from owning a freezer—buying fruits and vegetables in season, buying meats in large quantities, preparing foods in advance, storing convenience foods—few consider the total cost of freezer ownership. Exhibit A4–1 illustrates the principal operating costs for a freezer in the popular 15.5 to 18.5 cubic-foot capacity.

Several items in Exhibit A4-1 require further explanation. The lost interest is just that—it is interest lost on the amount of money taken from your savings account to purchase the freezer. The annual decline in the freezer's value stems from the fact that it will be essentially worthless after 15 years. Consequently, we assume that roughly one-fifteenth of the freezer's value is lost each year. The annual cost, $122.91, is much larger than most people expect. In essence, you must save at least $122.91 each year from using the freezer just to break even. If a family uses 1,000 pounds of various frozen foods annually, it would have to save 12.3 cents per pound ($122.91 ÷ 1,000 pounds) to justify owning a freezer.

Strategy: Unless you can identify some substantial savings from purchasing in large quantities, a freezer may cost more to own than it saves you in reduced food costs.

RECOMMENDED READINGS

Books

Margolius, Sidney, *The Great American Food Hoax.* New York: Walker, 1971.
    Excellent coverage of the pitfalls and inflated price of convenience foods. Suggestions on how to shop for convenience foods.
Travers, M. Evans, and David Greene, *The Meat Book.* New York: Scribner, 1973.
    Excellent discussion of the essentials of shopping for meat. Provides useful guides to selecting and preparing meat.

Booklets

Available from Consumer Information, Public Documents Distribution Center, Pueblo,
    Colorado 81009:
    "How to Buy Meat for Your Freezer"
    "What's in Your Food Bill?"
    "Your Money's Worth in Foods"
    "Food Is More than Just Something to Eat"
    "Nutrition: Food at Work for You"
    "Nutritional Labeling"

Chapter 5

Banking Services:
Using Them Effectively

After completing this chapter you should be able to:

explain the advantages of using a personal checking account.

describe the seven major types of checking accounts.

analyze the cost and features of competing checking accounts.

decide which checking account best meets your needs.

determine which endorsement would be most appropriate in a given situation.

formulate a plan for using a checking account effectively.

explain the purpose and use of a certified check.

illustrate the use of a stop-payment order.

describe a bank cashier's check and money order.

develop a plan for effectively using traveler's checks.

Increasingly, the American consumer is bombarded with advertisements by financial institutions, each one proclaiming to be a virtual one-stop personal finance center. At present, commercial banks are the closest thing to such a center. Their range of services includes several kinds of checking accounts, several savings alternatives, numerous lending options, financial counseling, and other services. However, in this chapter we will also cover mutual savings banks, hereafter called savings banks, and savings and loan associations, hereafter called S&Ls. Commercial banks have a significant advantage over both savings banks and S&Ls because they alone can offer the traditional checking account, although a few savings banks have accounts resembling checking accounts.

There are several reasons why an individual should understand what services are offered and how to use them effectively. First, today's business environment is so complex that you will have to use some of these services in managing your personal finances. Second, although the current range of services is large, it is likely to expand even more as a result of the increased competition among financial institutions. Third, the cost of these services varies so widely that it is worth the effort to thoroughly investigate what is available. For example, a heavily used checking account could easily cost $75 per year at one bank, while a competing bank might offer the same checking account absolutely free. Finally, the proper use of these services can be a tremendous convenience and assistance to your overall personal financial plan.

Why have financial institutions suddenly become interested in providing financial services to you as an individual consumer? Because they are discovering that providing their services to more than 200 million people can be very profitable. Even very large commercial banks, which have long relied on the deposits and loan activity of business firms, are rediscovering the profit potential in their consumer operations. Also, financial institutions have found that a customer, once attracted, remains a lifelong user of their services.

There is every indication that many of the present restrictive regulations imposed on some types of financial institutions will be lifted. Once they are, you can be sure that the variety of services will increase and that competition among the institutions will be even sharper.

CHECKING ACCOUNT

Most adults have a checking account which they use extensively in their daily financial transactions. A checking account offers a number of conveniences. You can pay your monthly expenses by mailing personal checks. Thus you do not have to travel around town with large amounts of cash and wait in line to pay bills. Another convenience is that your checkbook provides a record of deposits and payments. This record is especially helpful when you are itemizing deductible expenses for income tax purposes, or when you are formulating a new personal budget. One more convenience is that a canceled check provides a valid receipt that you have paid a particular item.

A check is merely your written order to your bank to pay a specified amount to a specified individual or organization.

Opening a Checking Account

Opening a checking account is a relatively simple procedure. Most banks require that you answer several questions on a signature card and, of course, provide your signature. Your signature on the card is essential because the bank uses it to verify that the signature on the checks drawn against your account are genuine and therefore should be honored.

When you open an account, you receive a supply of temporary checks until your personalized checks are printed. Many banks do not charge you for the checks if only your name is printed on them. If you want more than your name printed, you will be charged. The checks are available in a wide variety of designs from plain to exotic; checkbook covers are also available in many different colors and materials. You may select what you like, but be sure you know if there is any extra charge for exotic designs and covers, and consider if they are worth it.

In addition to your name, a number identifying your account is printed along the bottom of each check. This identification number, called your account number, is assigned when you open the account.

A reorder blank is usually attached to the last packet of checks for your convenience in ordering more checks before your present supply runs out.

Most personal checks come prenumbered. With this convenience you do not have to assign a number each time you write a check. However, the greatest convenience of prenumbering is that it helps to minimize or eliminate the errors made in recording checks in a checkbook.

Types of Accounts

Commercial banks currently offer several different types of personal checking accounts. They differ mainly with respect to their cost and the range of services provided. A feature common to all commercial banking accounts is that none pays interest on any checking account. A banking regulation, in force since 1933, prohibits commercial banks from doing so. While checking accounts are primarily the exclusive territory of commercial banks, several siates have authorized the savings banks within their borders to offer specialized personal checking accounts. Since savings banks are not covered by the 1933 banking regulation, they can pay interest on their checking accounts if they choose.

The major features of the seven widely available checking accounts are summarized in Exhibit 5-1.

Analysis   As the name suggests, the bank analyzes the activity in the account—deposits, checks cleared, and average account balance—each month to determine the monthly service charge. This is the traditional, older type of personal checking account, which is rapidly being phased out by most banks. In large part, the account is patterned after a commercial checking account. The higher the average balance the customer keeps in the account each month, the lower the monthly service charge.

The best way to illustrate how an analysis account works is through an example. Assume that our customer averages 25 checks per month, maintains an average monthly balance of $200, and makes approximately 3 deposits each month. The charges for the account are: 12 cents per check, 10 cents per deposit, and monthly maintenance of 50 cents; the credit is 20 cents for every $100 of account balance each month. The annual service charge will be $40.80, comprising checks (25 × 12 months × 12 cents = $36), plus deposits (3 × 12 months × 10 cents = $3.60), plus monthly maintenance (50 cents × 12 months = $6), less credit for average balance [($200 ÷ $100) × 12 months × 20 cents = −$4.80]. Because the credit feature encourages a large account balance, this account would fit an individual who has moderate to low account activity yet maintains a high average balance. In many parts of the country, this type of account is no longer available.

Special or Activity   The special or activity account still entails a service charge, but the computation is simpler than with an analysis account. Typically, when the customer purchases a supply of personalized checks, the bank's price includes the full service fee. Thus, if the check fee is 10 cents, a book of 50 checks will be $5. By charging in advance, the bank does not have to keep a record of how many checks a customer used during the month. Most of these

Exhibit 5-1   Major Types of Checking Accounts

Description	Minimum account balance	Service charges	Credit for balance in account	Extra services
1 Analysis	None	10¢–15¢ per check, 10¢–20¢ per deposit, and 50¢–$1.00 monthly maintenance fee	10¢–20¢ per month for each $100 balance maintained	None
2 Special or activity	None	10¢–15¢ per check and 50¢–$1.00 monthly maintenance fee	None	None
3 Minimum checking balance	$100–$1,000 in checking account	None	None	None
4 Minimum savings balance	$25–$500 in savings account	None	None	Regular interest on balance in savings account
5 Unrestricted free checking	None	None	None	None
6 Package account	None	$2–$5 per month	None	Typically includes safe-deposit box, traveler's checks, bank credit card, preferred loan rate, possibly more.
7 NOW	None	0–15¢ per check	None	Interest is paid on the account balance; similar to savings account.

accounts entail a monthly maintenance fee as well as the charge for checks, but there generally is no charge for deposits and the customer does not have to maintain a prescribed balance in the account. To keep their servicing costs low, some banks mail out an account statement only every other month.

Our example for this account uses the same check activity as our previous example (25 checks per month) and we assume a charge of 10 cents per check with a monthly maintenance fee of 75 cents. Based on this, the annual cost would be $39: checks (25 × 10 cents × 12 months = $30), plus maintenance fees (75 cents × 12 months = $9). Clearly, this checking account is designed for people who use their accounts infrequently.

Minimum Checking Balance   As the name suggests, a minimum checking balance account has a prescribed minimum balance that the customer must keep in the checking account to avoid all service fees. That minimum varies considerably, depending on the competitive situation within an area: minimums can range from $100 to $1,000. Some banks compute that minimum by averaging the daily balance during the period. Others use the lowest balance during the period. An example will quickly demonstrate why the latter technique is the most costly.

Suppose an account requires a $300 minimum balance. Under the first method, the balance could drop below $300 for several days as long as there were enough days above $300 to offset that shortfall. With the lowest balance technique, however, any time the balance dropped below $300, the account would be below the stipulated minimum that month, and therefore would be charged a service fee. When the account drops below the minimum, the bank generally assesses a flat monthly fee of $1 to $4.

Although these accounts are frequently touted as "free checking" if the minimum balance is maintained, they nevertheless do entail an implicit cost. That cost stems from the interest that could have been earned on the money that is tied up in the account where it is not earning interest. Thus, in our previous example, the individual could have deposited the $300 minimum balance in a savings account earning $5^{1}/_{4}$ percent annually. Had that been done, the annual interest would be $15.75 ($300 $\times$ $5^{1}/_{4}$ percent). In effect, the cost of this "free checking account" is the lost interest on the minimum balance. Of course, the lower the required minimum balance, the closer the account approaches truly free checking.

A minimum balance account is best suited to people who write a large number of checks each month, yet are able to maintain the necessary minimum balance.

Minimum Savings Balance   With a minimum savings balance account, the customer receives a free checking account provided a stipulated minimum balance is maintained in a regular savings account. The required minimum varies widely, depending on the competitive situation within an area: the minimum ranges from $25 upward. Should the customer's savings account balance drop below the minimum, the bank generally assesses a flat monthly fee of $1 to $4.

The principal advantage of this type of account is that the customer has a free checking account, yet still earns the regular interest on the minimum balance in the savings account. The only cost is the reduced flexibility caused by the requirement that you maintain the savings account; for most people, this would not be a serious restriction.

A checking account requiring a minimum savings balance would rank as the best among the ones discussed thus far. It is suitable for someone using many checks each month, as well as the infrequent user. With it, the customer can minimize the balance in the checking account, yet avoid all service charges on the account. This account is not available in all areas; however, its penetration is spreading.

Unconditional Free Checking   More and more banks have begun offering unconditional free checking to their customers. With this account there are no minimum balance requirements, no charge for checks, no charge for deposits, and no monthly maintenance fee. Unfortunately, the free checking account is not available in all areas. Even where it is available, it is often limited to a select group of bank customers: people over sixty-five, students, and certain professional people. To date, this type of account has generally been pioneered by small- to medium-sized banks in areas where the competition for banking customers is especially intense.

As long as there are no conditions attached, this checking account is the best of the ones discussed thus far. It is suitable for all kinds of users, has no requirements, and does not cost anything.

Package Plan   For a monthly fee of between $2 and $5, the package plan provides a number of banking services, including unlimited free checking, overdrafts of the checking account (the bank advances the money to cover a check if the account balance is insufficient), traveler's checks, money orders, bank credit card, safe-deposit box, and lower finance charges on certain loans (typically $1/2$ to 1 percent below the regular rate).

Whether or not a package account represents a good value depends upon how frequently the "extras" are used. The best way to evaluate a package account is to estimate the value of each service in the package. Based on that, we can decide whether the package is worth the fee. Consider an example: Assume the package costs $36 annually ($3 monthly) and provides free checking, traveler's checks, safe-deposit box, and a preferred lending rate $1/2$ percent below the regular loan rate. As a competing checking alternative, assume a $300 minimum balance account is available from another bank in the area. Recalling an earlier example, we know a $300 minimum account costs approximately $16 annually. The free safe-deposit box (more on this topic later) should be worth roughly $10. Let us assume we would normally have purchased $500 of traveler's checks each year; the service fee is $1 per $100 of checks, so the total cost for the traveler's checks would be $5. For these three services, the cost would be $16 + $10 + $5 = $31. The remaining service—the preferred lending rate—is the hardest one to place a price tag on. However, you would have to save at least $5 on this service to break even with the package accounts. To determine whether or not you can save on the preferred lending rate, consider two things. First, that service is worth nothing unless you borrow money during the year. Second, the annual finance charge on identical loans can vary widely, depending on the lender. (Since lenders and types of loans are discussed in detail in Chapters 7 and 8, our comments will be brief at this point.) You should become familiar with these loans and their finance charge to determine if the preferred lending rate of the package account is indeed a bargain. Therefore, to evaluate the preferred lending rate feature, answer these two questions: Is the preferred rate a bargain? Will you use the loan service? If both answers are yes, this feature may have some value.

The package account is probably best suited to people who not only use their checking account heavily, but also expect to use the extra services frequently. For people who rarely use the extra services, the package account is a poor value; these people should buy those services only when they need them.

   Negotiable Order of Withdrawal (NOW)   The NOW account is a newcomer among checking accounts. While commercial banks are prohibited from paying interest on checking accounts, savings banks are not governed by the same regulation. This has encouraged an account which not only pays interest, but on which the customer can also draw a negotiable order—effectively, a check. Just as NOW accounts were beginning to spread, Congress stepped in and banned them in all states but two; New Hampshire and Massachusetts. It is hoped that this is a temporary ban that will ultimately be lifted, allowing a further growth in this, or a similar type of account.

   Those NOW accounts which are available differ considerably in certain respects. Some assess a service charge of 10 to 15 cents per check, while others have no service charge. Some NOW accounts pay 5 to $5^{1}/_{4}$ percent interest rate on the account balance, the same as a traditional savings account. Still others set their interest rate substantially below the rate available on a savings account. This means, of course, that you should shop and compare features before deciding on a particular NOW account. While savings banks in New Hampshire and Massachusetts are requested to limit their advertising to residents and persons working in their respective states, they can and will accept accounts from outsiders. If you want more information on the NOW accounts of a particular savings bank, we suggest you look up its address and telephone number under the "bank-savings" listing in the commercial section of the appropriate telephone directory.

   In general, NOW accounts have a lot going for them, especially when they entail no service charge and when the interest rate is comparable with the rate for savings accounts. When a NOW account has both features, it offers the best of two worlds: free checking combined with interest on the account balance. If Congress can see its way to lifting the current interest restrictions, the NOW account would likely be the best among all the alternative accounts shown in Exhibit 5–1.

   Selecting Your Account   When selecting a checking account, ask for complete details on what the commercial banks currently offer. You should also include savings banks if you live in an area where NOW accounts are available. Of course, if you do not mind mailing to and from an out-of-state account, you should consider a NOW account regardless of where you live. Using your own data, you can construct a table similar to Exhibit 5–2 to decide which account best fits your needs.

   To construct a cost comparison similar to Exhibit 5–2, you will need complete details on the different checking accounts in your area: service charges, minimum balance, and services provided. Most institutions will readily provide this information over the phone, but you will have to ask because few volunteer the information. Some institutions, however, are reluctant to give details over the phone, so you may have to visit them. If the

Exhibit 5-2 Comparative Annual Costs of Different Checking Accounts

Type of account and charges	Checks per month					
	5	10	15	20	25	30
Analysis:* 10¢ per check, 10¢ per deposit, 50¢ monthly fee, and 10¢ credit per month per $100 balance	$13.20	$19.20	$25.20	$31.20	$37.20	$43.20
Analysis:* 15¢ per check, 20¢ per deposit, 75¢ monthly fee, and 20¢ credit per month per $100 balance	20.40	29.40	38.40	47.40	56.40	65.40
Special: 10¢ per check and 50¢ monthly fee	12.00	18.00	24.00	30.00	36.00	42.00
Special: 15¢ per check and $1.00 monthly fee	21.00	30.00	39.00	48.00	57.00	66.00
Minimum checking balance:† $100	5.25	5.25	5.25	5.25	5.25	5.25
Minimum checking balance:† $500	26.25	26.25	26.25	26.25	26.25	26.25
Minimum savings balance:‡ $200	0	0	0	0	0	0
Unrestricted free checking	0	0	0	0	0	0
Package account $2 per month	24.00	24.00	24.00	24.00	24.00	24.00
Package account $5 per month	60.00	60.00	60.00	60.00	60.00	60.00

*Assumes four deposits per month and $300 average balance.

†Lost interest on minimum balance assuming a 5¼ percent annual interest rate.

‡Assumes the $200 savings account paid interest at the regular savings rate and the account had no other costs.

institution is still unwilling to provide complete cost information, we recommend you drop it from your list. Once you have these cost data and an estimate of your account usage, it is an easy matter to make a comparison similar to Exhibit 5–2. As a general rule, if you anticipate writing less than five checks per month, it will probably be cheaper to use cashier's checks (more on these later) rather than a checking account unless you can obtain a truly free checking account.

Using Your Account

Using a checking account is reasonably easy and straightforward. However, there are several things that can make it work more smoothly and efficiently.

Writing Checks

Exhibit 5–3 illustrates a sample check and describes its key points. Most of the required information is self-explanatory. Contrary to what some people think, a check dated on Sunday [point (*a*) in Exhibit 5–3] is as valid as when dated on any other day. Most banks will not, however, accept a check that has been dated ahead of the current date (postdated). Thus, on June 10, they would not accept a check dated June 13.

Checks that have "Cash" as the payee [point (*b*) in Exhibit 5–3] become bearer instruments. That is, the check can be cashed by the person who holds the check. Obviously, care should be exercised when writing such checks because any finder could readily cash the check, should you lose it.

The amount of the check is written in two places: point (*c*), where it is written in numerals; and point (*d*), where it is spelled out.

The amount in numbers [point (*c*)] should begin close to the $ sign: for example, "$100.25," not "$ 100.25." Likewise, the written amount [point (*d*)] should begin at the far left, with the unused portion of the line filled with a wavy line: for example, write "One Hundred and $\frac{25}{100}$ ∼∼∼∼∼∼Dollars," and not "_____ One Hundred and $\frac{25}{100}$ Dollars." Both procedures ensure that the amount cannot be altered. Should there be a difference between the amounts in (*c*) and (*d*), the written amount (*d*) takes precedence.

The "memo" [point (*f*)] is a convenience feature which you should use to indicate the purpose of the check. A short description of its purpose can be extremely useful. So you should get in the habit of filling in the memo.

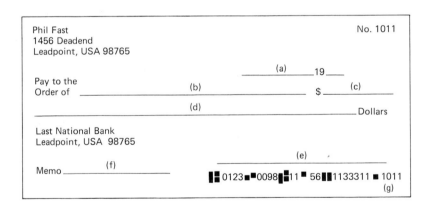

(a) Current date
(b) The person or business to whom the check is issued (the payee)
(c) Amount in numerals
(d) Amount in words
(e) Your signature (the drawer)
(f) Purpose of the check, for your information only
(g) Series of MICR characters showing: bank's identification number, account number, and check number. (The Magnetic Ink Character Recognition characters are machine readable so the entire clearing and recording process is mechanized to reduce error and increase speed.)

Exhibit 5-3   Writing a Check

Recording Checks and Deposits   Whenever you write a check or make a deposit, you should promptly enter the amount in the record portion of the checkbook. While this seems like an obvious thing to do, it is amazing how many people fail to keep their checkbooks current. As a consequence, they frequently receive a bank notice informing them their account is overdrawn: that is, they have written checks for more money than there is in the account. And each time the bank has to tell you that your account is overdrawn, you will be charged a penalty of $2 to $5. Another possible result of failing to promptly record the amount of the check is that you may forget the amount or remember it incorrectly when you record it later. The result is usually anguish at the end of the month when you attempt to reconcile the monthly balance shown on the bank statement with the balance in your checkbook record.

Making a Deposit   Nearly all checking accounts provide you with person-alized deposit slips for making deposits. Each slip has the bank's code number and the account identification number to ensure the deposit is credited to the correct account.

Whenever you receive a check, deposit it promptly. This minimizes the complications that can arise if a check has been outstanding a long time. Such complications might be: The bank is reluctant to cash an old check; the account the check is drawn on may have been closed; or the account may no longer have sufficient funds. Before a check can be cashed, it must be endorsed (signed on the reverse side) by the individual or business (the payee) the check is made payable to. If the check is lost before it is endorsed, it is relatively easy to have the drawer (the person who issued the check) stop payment on the check. Once payment is stopped, the drawer will issue a replacement check. The safest procedure is: Never endorse a check until the moment you are about to cash or deposit it.

While the traditional place for an endorsement is the extreme left end of the reverse side, the endorsement can go anywhere as long as it does not alter or obscure the check's essential information. The three basic endorsements are illustrated in Exhibit 5–4.

Blank Endorsement   A blank endorsement (top of Exhibit 5–4) converts the check to a bearer instrument. That means that the check can be cashed by any person who holds it. For that reason, a check should not be endorsed in blank until immediately before it is cashed. For a similar reason, a check should not be endorsed in blank if it is to be mailed to the bank.

Restrictive Endorsement   A restrictive endorsement limits the use of a check to a restricted purpose. For example, the money from the two checks shown in Exhibit 5–4 could only be deposited in the account of Fred Bear or Wilma Schultz, respectively. Because of this restriction, this type of endorse-ment is recommended whenever a check is included in a mail deposit.

Special Endorsement   A special endorsement is used when the payee wants to limit who can cash or transfer the check. For example, assume Sally Jones was the payee on a check and she wanted to endorse that check to Jack

Blank endorsements

Restrictive endorsements

Special endorsement

Exhibit 5-4   Types of Endorsements

Winter so that only he could cash the check. The endorsement illustrated at the bottom of Exhibit 5–4 would assure that. At this point, only Jack Winter could cash the check; he would have to endorse it below Sally's signature when he cashed it. But until he endorses it, the check remains unnegotiable. By endorsing a check to the order of your bank, credit union, or S&L, this endorsement could be used for a mail deposit.

Overdrawing the Account   The bank has two choices if you write checks for more than the money you have in the account. First, it can refuse to honor any check which would overdraw the account (such a check is called an overdraft): that check would then be returned to the person who deposited it with a note that your account does not have sufficient funds. (Your check has "bounced" back at you.) In all likelihood, the depositor would not waste any time before contacting you about the returned check. Second, the bank can honor the check even though the account is short the necessary funds. It would, however, request that you immediately deposit the necessary money in the account. Obviously, banks are not enthusiastic about this alternative because they are forced to make a temporary loan to the check writer. To show their displeasure, they charge the account holder a $2 to $5 penalty for the overdraft. While some overdrafts are intentional, many arise because the account holder made a numerical error in the checkbook record. Accurate and prompt record keeping should lessen the possibility of overdrawing your account.

Automatic Overdraft   Overdrafts are less frequent today because many banks have adopted an automatic overdraft system: that is, you can overdraw your account up to a prescribed limit. The bank will honor the checks and you will not be charged a penalty for the overdraft. When you use the overdraft, you pay a finance charge based on the amount and time period involved. Since automatic overdrafts are covered in Chapter 8, we defer further discussion until then.

> **Strategy: You should look for a checking account offering an automatic overdraft. Even if you do not plan to use it, it can cover those times when an error causes an overdraft.**

Effective Use of an Account   The balance in your checking account is one measure of whether the account is being used effectively. It should not be larger than your immediate cash needs. For example, assume John and Jane Yuven regularly make their $300 mortgage payment on the twenty-first of each month. Because they pay most of their other bills at the beginning of the month, they also deposit this $300 in their checking account on the first, even though they write the check 3 weeks later. Had that money been in a savings account for those 21 days, it would have earned 91 cents ($300 × 5¼ percent × 21 days/365 days). Over a 12-month period they have forgone $10.92 (91 cents × 12 months) in interest. True, the amount is not breathtaking, but if there were several payments like that, the amount would be considerable.

> **Strategy: Your checking account balance should not exceed your immediate cash needs to maximize the effective use of your money.**

Minimizing the Balance   One way to minimize your cash balance is have a checking and savings account that includes prepaid mail deposit services. In this way, you can readily transfer your checking account excess to savings. When the money is needed, you can make a two-part mail deposit: withdrawing the money from savings and depositing it to checking. To obtain maximum benefit, the savings account should (1) have prepaid mail deposits, (2) pay interest daily, and (3) have no service fee on deposits and withdrawals. In most localities, accounts with these facilities are easily available.

Special Features   Most checking accounts have several special features which you should know about because you may have the need to use them.

Certified Check   A certified check is a check drawn on a regular checking account, but the bank has "certified" that the account has sufficient funds to pay the check when it is presented for payment. This added assurance can be essential or necessary where the amount is sizable. To ensure there will be sufficient funds, the bank immediately reduces the account balance when the check is certified. This check is easily identified because the word "certified" is stamped across it and it is initialed by one of the bank's officers. Though most banks provide the service free, some charge a nominal fee. The cashed check is generally retained by the bank. Should the drawer need a copy, it can be obtained from the bank.

Stopping Payment   There are times when you may decide that you want to prevent payment on a particular check. As long as the check has not been presented for payment, this can be done by having a stop-payment order placed on the check. That order entails the completion of a form giving check number, date, payee, and amount. Once completed, it is circulated to the bank's tellers to alert them to the check. Most banks require one or two days before the order becomes effective. Once accepted, it remains in force for 6 months, but that can be extended by a renewal. As a temporary measure, most banks accept a verbal order over the telephone, but it remains in effect for only 14 days.

Generally, all banks charge a fee—$3 to $5—for placing a stop payment on a check. Nearly all stop-payment orders contain a clause exempting the bank from liability should the check be cashed by oversight or error. In effect, the bank does not guarantee performance; it merely promises to make its best effort to avoid paying the check.

A bank will not accept a stop-payment order on a certified check.

Reconciling Your Checking Account

Reconciling an account simply means comparing the balance in your checkbook records with the balance on the monthly bank statement to see if they agree. If they do, no problem. If not, the reconciliation process continues further until you have identified the items that caused the difference between the two balances.

There are three things you accomplish by reconciling your checking account. First, you test the accuracy of the bank's records as well as those in your checkbook. Second, you have the opportunity to update your records for any service fee or finance charge deducted during the period. And third, the reconciliation will show the adjusted account balance.

While reconciliation is done once each month, the closing date on the bank statement rarely coincides with the last day of the month. Because banks cannot possibly prepare and mail all their statements in one day, the last day of the month, they stagger the closing dates on their checking accounts, spreading them throughout the month. Typically, an account's closing date depends on the first letter of the customer's last name. For reconciliation purposes, the exact closing date is not critical because we reconcile all activity in the account since the closing date of the previous statement, thus covering a one-month period.

To complete a reconciliation, we must develop five items: balance per bank statement, balance per checkbook, bank service charges, outstanding check list, and deposits in transit. The best way to demonstrate how this information is compiled is through an example. In Exhibits 5–5 and 5–6, we have reproduced the essential records needed. Exhibit 5–5 includes the items that would normally be in the monthly bank statement: statement of the account, together with the canceled checks that have cleared the account. Exhibit 5–6 illustrates a selected page out of Fred Bear's checkbook. Our example spans the period April 10 through May 10. While many people's statements would have more checks than our example, the steps in all reconciliations are identical.

Balance per Bank Statement   The balance per bank statement is shown as the last entry on the bank statement. In addition, most statements summarize the month's activity (opening balance, total deposits, total checks, service charges, and ending balance) at the top or bottom of the statement. The balance per bank is $170.60 for the example in Exhibit 5–5. Again, we point out that we are not reconciling as of month-end, but rather as of the end of the statement period: May 10 for this example.

Balance per Checkbook   The balance per checkbook should be the balance the checkbook shows as of the closing date on the bank statement. For our example, the balance per checkbook was $78.00 on May 10 (Exhibit 5–6). Since there still are several steps, we would not yet expect this balance to equal the bank statement balance.

Bank Charges   The total bank service charge includes any service charge for the checking account, finance charge for using the automatic overdraft, cost of printing checks, fee for stop-payment order. In Exhibit 5–5, that charge is indicated as the final deduction; it is $2.40 (note the letters SC). This charge should be deducted from the checkbook to update that balance.

Outstanding Check List   Developing an outstanding check list requires some work. The initial step is to compare all returned checks with the checkbook record as to amount and payee. Not only does this test the accuracy of the checkbook, it also highlights any check which may have been cashed for

Fred Bear 1123 Ajax Place Anywhere, USA		Last National Bank 999-111-9876 Statement Period April 10th to May 10th

Opening Balance 80.00	Total Deposits For The Period 760.00	Total Charges For The Period 669.40	Ending Balance 170.60

Deductions			Credits	Date	Balance
				4-10	80.00
45.00				4-12	35.00
10.00	12.00			4-20	13.00
			425.00	4-21	438.00
65.00	265.00	45.00		4-23	63.00
20.00				4-24	43.00
			150.00	4-30	193.00
10.00	40.00			5-4	143.00
			185.00	5-9	328.00
35.00	120.00			5-10	173.00
2.40SC				5-10	170.60

SC Service Charge   RT Returned Item
DM Debt Memo   FC Finance Charge

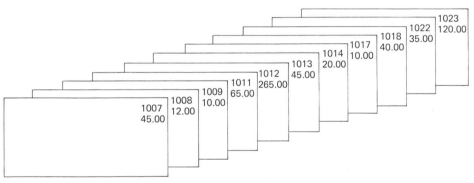

Exhibit 5-5 Monthly Bank Statement

an amount different from what the drawer intended. As you compare these, place a small mark (✓) next to any check that has been returned. Checks without a mark are still outstanding. That is, these are checks which you have deducted from your checking account balance but which have not yet cleared the bank and therefore are not deducted from the bank's balance. The list of outstanding checks for Exhibit 5–6 would include: #1010–$15.00, #1015–$15.00, #1016–$45.00, #1019–$35.00, #1020–$5.00, and #1021–$15.00. Total outstanding checks would be $130.00.

    Deposit in Transit   A deposit in transit is a deposit that you have recorded in the checkbook, but that has not yet been credited by the bank. To determine whether there are any such items, we compare the deposits per checkbook with those per bank statement. Comparing the deposits in Exhibit 5–6 with those in

Exhibit 5-6 Checkbook Details

Check number	Date	Check issued to	Check amount	Deposit amount	Balance
1007	4/9	Ace Plumbing Supply	$ 45.00√		$ 35.00
1008	4/11	Valley Telephone	12.00√		23.00
1009	4/15	Shopper's Market	10.00√		13.00
	4/20	Deposit		$425.00	438.00
1010	4/20	Ralph Smith	15.00		423.00
1011	4/20	Electric and Gas Co.	65.00√		358.00
1012	4/21	First Savings and Loan	265.00√		93.00
1013	4/21	Best Department Store	45.00√		48.00
1014	4/21	White Health Insurance	20.00√		28.00
1015	4/21	World Gift Specials	15.00		13.00
	4/28	Deposit		150.00	163.00
1016	4/29	John Waldo, M.D.	45.00		118.00
1017	4/31	Swift Drugs	10.00√		108.00
1018	5/2	Shopper's Market	40.00√		68.00
1019	5/4	Central TV Repair	35.00		33.00
1020	5/6	Action Cleaners	5.00		28.00
1021	5/8	Douglas Dog Hospital	15.00		13.00
	5/8	Deposit		185.00	198.00
1022	5/9	Cash	35.00√		163.00
1023	5/9	Dixon Insurance	120.00√		43.00
	5/10	Deposit		35.00	78.00
1024	5/11	Sully Oil Company	25.00		53.00
1025	5/15	Jones Nursery	6.00		47.00

Exhibit 5–5, we can see that the deposit of May 10 was not credited on the bank statement. Therefore, the deposit in transit would be $35.00

The Reconciliation At this point we have the information necessary to complete the reconciliation. The actual computations are illustrated in Exhibit 5–7.

Essentially, we are computing an adjusted balance that reflects the account's true cash balance. To do that, the deposit in transit must be added to the bank balance because that deposit will soon arrive at the bank. Likewise, the outstanding checks must be deducted because they represent future claims that will ultimately be honored by the bank. Adding the in-transit deposit and deducting the total amount of the outstanding checks from the balance on the bank statement gives the adjusted cash balance per the bank. Deducting the total bank charge from the balance in your checkbook gives the adjusted cash balance per your checkbook. If everything is in order, the two adjusted balances—line 5 and line 8 in Exhibit 5–7—should be equal. If the two are not equal, there is an error somewhere: in the reconciliation, your checkbook, or the bank statement. The checklist at the bottom of Exhibit 5–7 should help you locate the error. If the error is in your checkbook, you should make the necessary adjustments to correct it. Should the error be the bank's, contact the accounting department at the bank and request a correction.

Exhibit 5-7   Checking Account Reconciliation

Line	Description	Amount
	Per bank statement	
1	Balance per bank statement	$170.60
2	Add: Deposits in transit	35.00
3	Subtotal	$205.60
4	Less: Outstanding checks	130.00
5	Adjusted cash balance per bank	$ 75.60
	Per checkbook	
6	Balance per checkbook	$ 78.00
7	Less: Bank charge	2.40
8	Adjusted cash balance per checkbook	$ 75.60

Checklist

1 If line 5 equals line 8, you are done. If not, proceed to steps 2 through 6.
2 If line 5 is greater than line 8:
  a recheck your list of oustanding checks.
3 If line 8 is greater than line 5:
  a recheck your list of outstanding checks.
  b test your deposits in transit.
  c review bank statement for additional bank charges.
4 If line 8 and line 5 still do not agree:
  a test the addition and subtraction in your checkbook.
  b recompare the amounts on the returned checks to the amount originally recorded in the check-book.
5 If line 5 and 8 still do not agree:
  a take the checks returned with the bank statement and compare the amount per check with the amount deducted on the bank statement.
6 If the two lines still do not agree:
  a take a short break, you are probably overlooking an obvious error.

Selecting a Bank

While the cost of a checking account is important, there are several other things you should consider. First, what range of services do the different banks offer: personal loans, savings account, mortgage loan, bank credit card? You should also consider the convenience aspect: hours of operation, branch network, prepaid mail deposit service, telephone transfers between accounts. Every person must decide how important each service and convenience is to that individual and therefore how much weight it should receive in the final decision. We rank cost at the top and place convenience and range of services further down the list; but not everyone would agree with that ranking.

While it is hard to generalize, quite often small to medium-sized banks have the lowest cost. Most, however, offer a range of services that is adequate for most people. We put limited emphasis on whether a bank is among the 50 largest in the United States, whether it has branches overseas, or whether it provides extensive business banking services. Frankly, we doubt that many individuals really benefit from any of these features.

OTHER PAYMENT METHODS

In addition to the standard personal checking account, there are several other ways to make a payment.

Cashier's Check   The drawer on a cashier's check is an authorized officer of the financial institution itself. Because the check is backed by the promise of the financial institution, it is readily accepted in any transaction. Cashier's checks can be purchased in any amount from most financial institutions: commercial banks, S&Ls, and savings banks. Some institutions provide the checks free of charge if the person has an account with them. Others charge a nominal fee for the service. Since the check is made out to a specific payee, they are a convenient, safe way to make mail payments.

If a free checking account is not available, using cashier's checks is usually cheaper for anyone who uses fewer than five checks per month. The check is not returned to the purchaser once it has been cashed; instead, it is retained by the selling institution. The purchaser does, however, receive a duplicate copy of the check. And the selling institution can furnish a copy of the cashed check if necessary.

Money Order   Money orders are issued by a wide range of organizations, including financial institutions, the United States Post Office, specialized financial service firms, and others. Because they are backed by a well-known firm, they are readily accepted in most transactions. Since they are payable to a specific payee, they are also a safe, convenient way of making mail payments.

A money order is always made out to a specific dollar amount, but the payee section is frequently left blank for the purchaser to fill in. The fee varies depending on the amount of the money order as well as the issuer's fee schedule; a typical range would be 25 cents to $2.

As proof of purchase, the buyer retains a duplicate copy or a stub from the money order. The cashed money order itself is returned to the issuing organization. Should the buyer have a question about when and where a money order was cashed, the issuing organization can provide that information from their records.

Traveler's Check   Traveler's checks are a special payment vehicle, designed to meet the cash needs of people who are away from home. These checks are superior to personal checks because they are issued by large commercial banks (both United States and foreign-based) and specialized financial service companies. With this backing, they are readily accepted at hotels, motels, restaurants, airlines, major department stores, and others. This acceptability extends throughout the United States and abroad. To give the purchaser added safety assurance, the issuing organization promises to replace any checks that are lost or stolen. Traveler's checks eliminate the need to carry large amounts of cash and provide a widely accepted payment vehicle.

The checks are available from most financial institutions in denominations ranging from $10 to $1,000 per check. While the service fee typically runs $1 per $100 worth of checks, some financial institutions provide traveler's checks at no charge.

When you purchase the traveler's checks, you must sign each one in the space designated for your signature. Later, when you cash a traveler's check, you fill in the name of the payee and write your signature in the designated space. However, you must write your signature in the presence of the payee. This enables the payee to immediately compare the witnessed signature with the signature you wrote when you purchased the check. By requiring a double signature, the person accepting the check can decide whether the signer is the same person who originally signed the checks.

While the issuer promises to replace any lost or stolen checks, the buyer must furnish serial numbers of the missing checks. That makes it imperative that the buyer record those serial numbers and keep the record in a place separate from the checks.

Since these checks have no time limit, many people hold unused checks rather than cash them in. The issuing company is happy to see this because it has use of the purchaser's money as long as a check remains outstanding. But good financial practice suggests you hold the check no longer than 75 days. If you do not need the checks within that period, you could earn more by having the money in a savings account than it would cost to buy new checks (at $1 per $100) when you need them.

The widespread acceptance of travel and entertainment (T&E) credit cards—American Express, Diners Club, and Carte Blanche—has further reduced the need to carry money. But you will still probably need some traveler's checks because not all credit cards are accepted everywhere. Furthermore, unless you travel extensively, it may be less expensive to buy traveler's checks rather than pay the $15 to $25 annual fee for a T&E credit card; for that fee you could purchase $1,500 to $2,500 of traveler's checks annually.

> **Strategy: Check the financial institutions in your area to see whether any of them offers free traveler's checks. Cash all unused traveler's checks unless you expect to use them within 75 days.**

OTHER SERVICES OF FINANCIAL INSTITUTIONS

Financial institutions also provide other services in addition to the previously discussed payment alternatives.

Safe-Deposit Box   Most commercial banks rent safe-deposit boxes. These metal boxes vary in size and are located in the bank's vault. The rentals range from $5 upward, depending on the box size and the bank's rate schedule.

Opening a box requires two keys; one is held by the box renter and the other is retained by the bank. Since the bank does not have a master key to fit the customer's lock, the box cannot be opened unless the customer is present. Likewise, the customer cannot open the box without the bank's representative being present. Of course, the lack of a duplicate key means the lock on the box must be destroyed should the customer's key be lost.

When you want to open your box, you must sign your name on a card and the bank representative compares it with its copy of your signature. In general, the access to safe-deposit boxes is well controlled by the bank. Most banks carry insurance that covers the loss of contents in case of fire, flood, and other hazards. Few, however, insure against loss by theft. It is essential that you keep an up-to-date list of the box contents so you can estimate the dollar amount in case of loss. Chapter 3 discussed the records that should be stored in a safe-deposit box.

Electronic Terminals Increasingly, financial institutions are installing electronic terminals to provide deposit and withdrawal services for their customers. In addition, some terminals can grant a small cash advance when the customer has a preapproved line of credit.

These machines have a number of safeguards to prevent unauthorized withdrawal of funds or tampering with an account. Many require a plastic identification card and a user-supplied, multiple-digit "secret" identification number. The user has only a limited number of opportunities to give the correct "secret" number. Barring success in those trials, the machine retains the identification card and locks up the account. To recover that card and reactivate the account, the customer must visit the bank's main office.

Currently, the fate of electronic terminals remains heavily clouded by a dispute over whether they are "branch offices." Should they be declared branch offices, their spread will be slowed markedly because most financial institutions have restrictions on branch offices. Until this issue is resolved, the fate of terminals is unclear. What is clear, however, is that they can be a real benefit to customers.

Strategy: Other things being equal, select an institution that has a network of remote electronic terminals.

Investment Management Service   A number of larger commercial banks have established investment services to manage the portfolios of individuals. Since the smallest service currently requires a minimum $25,000 portfolio, these services are not yet directed toward most people. Even in the $25,000 to $35,000 range, the service fee substantially reduces the portfolio's net annual return. With most services, individual clients indicate which stocks they personally would like purchased from the bank's recommended list. The bank handles matters such as record keeping and physical storage of the securities. It remains to be seen whether additional banks decide the area is sufficiently lucrative for them to offer the service. At the same time, it is not clear whether the minimum investment will be reduced so the service will be available to more people.

Trust Services   Nearly all commercial banks provide a trust and estate management service. Traditionally, this service was restricted to sizable estates and trusts. But banks have become more willing to extend this service to small and medium-sized estates and trusts. The topic is covered in more detail in Chapter 20.

SUMMARY

1   Financial institutions have made a considerable effort to identify themselves as one-stop personal finance centers.
2   A checking account eliminates the need to carry large sums of cash, provides a ready and safe method of making mail payments, and results in canceled checks that provide valid payment receipts.
3   Most checks are personalized with the account holder's name, address, and account number.
4   Unrestricted free checking is the lowest-cost checking account currently offered by commercial banks.
5   NOW accounts—presently offered in two states—combine the best of both worlds: the interest of a savings account and the convenience of a checking account.
6   A check should not be endorsed in blank until immediately before it is to be cashed.
7   A restrictive or special endorsement is best when a check is deposited by mail.
8   Many checking accounts now provide an automatic overdraft that allows the customer to overdraw the account up to a prescribed ceiling.

9   The nonworking cash balance should be minimized if a checking account is to be used effectively.

10 You can prevent payment of a check you have written by placing a stop-payment order on that check.

11 A reconciliation of your checking account is complete when the adjusted cash balance per the bank equals the adjusted balance per your checkbook.

12 Selecting a checking account typically involves the search for a balance among minimum cost, range of services, and convenience.

13 Traveler's checks are a convenient and safe way to carry money and make payments when you are away from home.

14 A safe-deposit box is a convenient, safe storage place for your valuable effects.

15 Electronic terminals provide an added service for a financial institution's customers.

REVIEW YOUR UNDERSTANDING OF

Checking accounts
    Analysis account
    Special account
    Minimum checking balance
    Minimum savings balance
    Unrestricted free checking
    Package account
    NOW account
Postdating
Blank endorsement
Restrictive endorsement
Special endorsement
Overdraft

Certified check
Stop-payment order
Bank reconciliation
    Deposit in transit
    Outstanding check list
    Adjusted cash balance per the bank
    Adjusted cash balance per your checkbook
Cashier's check
Money order
Traveler's check
Safe-deposit box

DISCUSSION QUESTIONS

1   What services do you think a one-stop personal finance center should offer? Which financial institution comes closest to your description? Why?

2   What are the principal advantages to a NOW account? If all savings banks and S&Ls could offer an account resembling a NOW account, would it have an impact on commercial banks? Why? Could commercial banks offer a similar account? Why?

3   Sharon Swift is considering the following options for her personal checks:

Type	Fee
a Personalized with name	Free from the bank
b Personalized with name and address	$1.00 per 100 checks
c Personalized with name, address, and scenic landscape	$2.50 per 100 checks
d Personalized "totally"—name, address, and reproduction of famous art work	$4.50 per 100 checks

What are the advantages to each type of check? Which would you recommend?

4   What is the principal difference between a restrictive endorsement and a blank endorsement? Under what conditions would each be most appropriate?

5 How would you respond to the following advertisement: "Totally free checking when you maintain a $300 minimum balance"?

6 How does a certified check differ from a regular personal check? Why would a bank refuse to accept a stop-payment order on a certified check?

7 Ralph and Sandra North are evaluating three checking accounts:

   a Thrifty Check—no minimum balance; 50 cents monthly maintenance fee; checks cost $2.50 per 25 checks.

   b 200 Econo—minimum $200 balance in checking account, computed as average of daily balances; no check or monthly fee if balance is above $200, checks cost $1.25 per 100.

   c 190 Mini—required $190 checking account minimum is based on the lowest daily balance during the month; no other service fees if minimum is met; checks cost $1.25 per 100.

   The Norths currently keep their cash reserve fund in a 6 percent savings account at a credit union. If the Norths anticipate writing five checks per month, which account should they select? Why? If the Norths anticipate 20 checks a month, which would you recommend?

8 Don Smith has devised a simplified recording system for his checking account. He never records any checks; instead, he waits until the bank sends an overdraft notice. At that time he deposits $500 in the account. That $500 may last several weeks or more. His account has an automatic overdraft, so he is not assessed the regular $5 overdraft penalty. But the bank charges an 18 percent annual finance charge on the outstanding overdraft balance. What are the strengths and weaknesses of Don's system? Would you recommend any changes? What advantages do your revisions promise?

9 Does a stop-payment order eliminate the possibility of a check being cashed? Can you give several examples where such an order would be used?

10 Why are banks and financial service companies willing to offer traveler's checks with no set expiration date? If the seller of the traveler's check receives most of the $1 per $100 commission, how does the issuer of the traveler's check make a profit?

11 How is a deposit which is recorded in your checkbook, but not on the bank statement, handled in a reconciliation? In a reconciliation, how do you treat checks which have been written and entered in the checkbook, but have not been cashed?

12 After completing his reconciliation, Dick Smith found that his adjusted cash balance per the bank was $35.10 while the adjusted cash balance per his checkbook was $17.10. What would you recommend? Why?

13 Why should you always maintain an itemized list of your safe-deposit box contents? Would most banks replace those contents if an unscrupulous bank employee took off with the contents? Why would banks be reluctant to accept that responsibility?

14 Sally DiCassa is considering the following two alternatives:

   a Cash the $500 of traveler's checks she currently has. Deposit the proceeds in a $5\frac{1}{2}$ percent savings account. Purchase new traveler's checks in 180 days.

   b Retain the $500 of traveler's checks, thereby avoiding the $1 fee per $100 of checks.

   How should she decide? If she anticipates using the checks in 30 days, what would you recommend? How long a holding period (number of days) does it take to make the two alternatives equal? (*Hint:* Compute the daily holding cost.)

15 Why is it difficult to analyze the cost of a package checking account? Which people would benefit most with this account? Least?

CASE PROBLEM

Phil Fast has recently opened a personal checking account. Being new to the checking account world, he is having more than a few problems with his monthly reconciliation. To date, his reconciliation consists of:

Balance per bank statement	$142.50
Balance per checkbook	$121.00

The fact the two do not agree disturbs him, but he is unclear about how to proceed. His checkbook and bank statement are shown below.

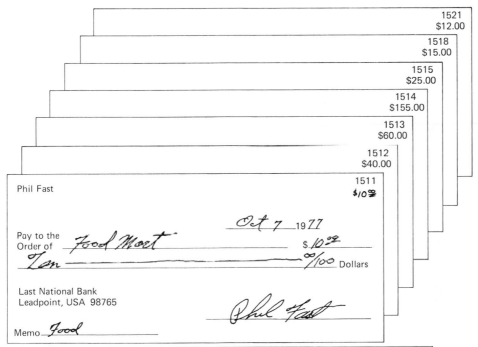

Phil Fast
1456 Deadend
Leadpoint, USA 98765

Last National Bank
Leadpoint, USA 98765

Statement Period: October 5 to November 5

Beginning Balance	Total Deposit		Total Charges		Ending Balance
51.00	410.00		318.50		142.50

Charges			Credits	Date	Balance
				10-6	51.00
10.00				10-11	41.00
			320.00	10-15	361.00
40.00	60.00	155.00		10-17	106.00
25.00				10-20	81.00
			90.00	10-22	171.00
15.00				10-24	156.00
12.00				11-4	144.00
SC 1.50				11-5	142.50

SC Service Charge   FC Finance Charge   DM Debit Memo

Check number	Date	Check issued to	Check amount	Deposit amount	Balance 51.00
1511	10/7	Central Food Mart	$ 10.00		$ 41.00
1512	10/14	Leadpoint Public Service	40.00		1.00
	10/14	Deposit		$320.00	321.00
1514	10/15	Ajax Retail Service	155.00		166.00
1515	10/15	Quick Charge, Inc.	25.00		141.00
1516	10/15	Ralph Smith, M.D.	10.00		131.00
1517	10/15	Red Dot Insurance	40.00		91.00
1518	10/18	Central Food Mart	15.00		76.00
	10/21	Deposit		90.00	166.00
1519	10/25	Fred's Auto Repairs	37.00		129.00
1520	10/30	Tony's Clothes	25.00		104.00
1521	10/30	Cash	12.00		92.00
1522	11/2	Central Food Mart	16.00		76.00
	11/4	Deposit		45.00	121.00
1523	11/6	Western Beverage Spot	13.50		107.50

a Why is the balance per bank statement, $142.50, different from the balance in Phil's checkbook, $121.00?

b What information is needed before the account can be reconciled?

c Using this information, compile an outstanding check list. Why is this needed?

d Are there any deposits in transit?

e Complete the reconciliation of Phil's account.

f What corrections, if any, should Phil make in his checkbook?

RECOMMENDED READINGS

Books

Cohen, Jerome B., *Personal Finance.* Homewood, Ill.: Irwin, 1975.
      Chapter 6 discusses the availability and use of bank services.
Wolf, Harold A., *Personal Finance.* Boston: Allyn and Bacon, 1975.
      Chapter 5 discusses using bank services.

Magazines

Money:

Main, Jeremy, "Putting Your Bank's New Look to Work." April 1974, pp. 27–30.
      Discusses the recent innovations in bank services.

Changing Times:

"Coming—A Shakeup in Banking." February 1974, pp. 37–38.
      Discusses the changes that are likely to be made in the area of personal banking services.
"Checkpointers on Checking Accounts." September 1974, p. 14.
      Discusses important points on checking accounts.
"Get Ready For Cashless, Checkless Living." October 1975, pp. 6–10.
      Discusses the emerging trend to electronic funds transfer which is expected to replace many cash and check transactions.

The Bankers Magazine:

Elias, Christopher, "Let the Bank Customer Beware." Winter 1974, pp. 49–54.
  Takes a candid look at the way some banks treat their small customers. Reveals
  some unscrupulous practices.
Brown, William J., "Get Ready to Pay Interest on Demand Deposits." Spring 1975, pp.
  33–36.
  Discusses the possible shift to paying interest on checking accounts.
Leff, Gary, "What Now with NOW Accounts?" Autumn 1975, pp. 29–31.
  Discusses the future role and prospects of NOW accounts.

Consumer Reports:

"A Guide to Banking Services." January 1975, pp. 32–33.
  Provides an overview of the general state of banking services.
"Picking the Best Checking Account." January 1975, pp. 34–38.
  Provides a good discussion of the types of checking accounts that are currently
  available.

Booklets

Using Bank Services

  A basic booklet discussing general bank services. A copy is available from The
  American Bankers Association, 1120 Connecticut Ave., NW., Washington, D.C.
  20036.

Chapter 6

Strategy of Tax Management

After completing this chapter you should be able to:

explain the basic income tax structure.

illustrate how taxes can reduce the effective cost of a deductible expense.

describe how "gross income" is computed.

recall the major "adjustment to gross income."

describe what items qualify as moving expenses.

recall which taxpayers qualify for a retirement plan deduction.

estimate a standard deduction.

recall the principal itemized deductions.

illustrate the tax treatment of medical and dental expenses.

describe the qualifications for deducting child and dependent care expenses.

illustrate the computation of a casualty or theft loss.

decide which deduction technique—standard, low-income allowance, or itemized—is best in a given situation.

use the five eligibility tests to decide whether a person qualifies as a "dependent."

judge whether an individual qualifies for income averaging.

decide who must file an estimated tax declaration.

assess whether outside tax assistance is necessary.

develop a strategy for surviving an audit by the Internal Revenue Service.

Income taxes are an unavoidable part of receiving income in the United States. With tax rates reaching 20 percent or more even in the lower income ranks, the federal government commands a sizable portion of your income. Therefore it is essential that you use every available legal means to minimize the taxes you must pay. Unfortunately, the task is not an easy one. Current tax regulations are written with voluminous, legalistic, tortuous, vague, and at times confusing, prose. And the tax forms do not make things clearer; sometimes they make them more confusing.

Despite a general recognition of the need for simplification, tax regulations continue to increase the myriad items that must be included or excluded, or that can or cannot be deducted. Since the regulations are not likely to change soon, we must make the best of the tax maze as it currently stands. And, while federal income taxes are a difficult subject, they are not an impossible one. Our intent is not to turn you into a professional tax advisor; instead, we strive to provide sufficient basic information so you can incorporate taxes into your total personal financial plan.

It is essential that you have at least a working knowledge of taxes. First, taxes can drastically alter the financial implications of a particular decision. Second, treating a tax item improperly can cost you hundreds of dollars of unnecessary taxes. Last, the quality of much of the professional tax advice that suddenly makes itself available to individuals around tax time is highly questionable. Consequently, it is doubly important that you be in a position to manage your own tax matters so you do not have to rely on outside assistance.

We will discuss the salient points about income taxes, but we will not use the "cookbook" approach; that is, we will not work through a complete set of tax forms line by line. Instead, we stress the basic concepts underlying each major point. When there are numerous qualifications and limitations, we present the major thrust without getting bogged down in the small detail. To obtain complete information, you should refer to the appropriate section in one of the tax reference books listed at the chapter's end. Nevertheless, we feel our discussion will signal the important points so you can consider their tax implications.

Avoidance, Not Evasion

While there are no hard statistics, it is likely that a sizable number of people overpay their income taxes either through oversight, confusion, error, or simple reluctance to claim an eligible deduction. We feel that this is an extremely poor way to spend your money. There is a significant difference between avoiding taxes and evading taxes. The latter practice involves ignoring taxes, understating income, or fraudulently maneuvering to lower the taxes you must pay. All such processes are illegal, and we certainly are not recommending evasion as a tax strategy. Taxpayers do, however, have every right to reduce their taxes as much as allowed by the tax regulations. In fact, the Supreme Court has affirmed that it is a taxpayer's right to avoid taxes. Too often, people are hesitant to use a deduction or an exclusion simply because they are afraid the Internal Revenue Service (IRS) may question it. Our recommendation is direct and simple: If you feel a particular item qualifies, then take it. If it is any consolation, very few taxpayers ever draw a criminal penalty, and those who do, have intentionally and willfully evaded taxes.

BASIC INCOME TAX STRUCTURE

It will be much easier to discuss the various income tax provisions if we first examine the basic underlying income tax structure. In particular, we want to review the computation steps that begin with gross income and end with taxes payable. Gross income is the total of a person's income from all sources— wages, tips, interest, royalties, profits, and so on. Exhibit 6–1 illustrates the basic steps in the tax computation and traces the flow of income through to the final tax computation.

The discussion of taxes in this chapter follows the pattern outlined in Exhibit 6–1. Note, in the center of the exhibit, the box emphasized—Adjusted Gross Income. The significance of adjusted gross income will be explained later, but for the moment, it is important to recognize that there are two distinct categories of deductions. One type is called *adjustments to gross income* and the result is adjusted gross income. The second type is called *deduction from adjusted gross income* and the result leads to taxable income. The qualifying items in the second category are available only to those taxpayers who itemize their deductions from adjusted gross income rather than take a standard deduction.

Progressive Tax Rates   The rate schedule shown in Exhibit 6–2 illustrates the progressive structure of federal income tax rates. For example, assume Ralph Smith is single and he expects his taxable income will be $16,000 for the current year. If he received an additional $100 bonus, the added tax on that bonus would be $34 (34 percent tax rate). Had his taxable income been $20,000, the added tax on a $100 bonus would be $38 (38 percent tax rate). Thus, the

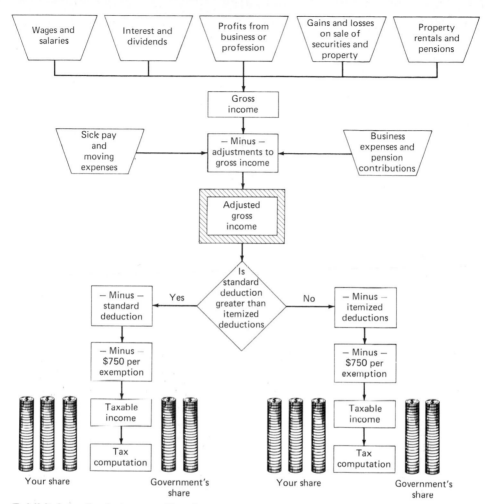

Exhibit 6-1 Basic Income Tax Structure

higher your income, the higher the tax rate on each dollar of additional income.

A frequent misconception is that moving into a higher tax bracket automatically entails a higher tax rate on the entire income. But the rate schedule does not operate that way. The higher rate applies only to the amount of income that moved you into the higher bracket; the preceding amount of income is still taxed at the preceding rate. Exhibit 6–3 illustrates our previous example where Ralph Smith received a $100 bonus in addition to his initial $16,000 of taxable income. Granted, Ralph's $100 bonus raised him to the 34 percent tax rate, but that 34 percent rate applies only to the income in excess of $16,000. The tax on his initial $16,000 of taxable income remains unchanged.

Marginal Tax Rate   Throughout this book we refer to an individual's marginal tax rate. That rate is the tax rate on the last dollar of taxable income the individual earned. Thus, if Sarah Brad's income was $11,500, her marginal

Exhibit 6-2   Federal Tax Rate Schedule

Taxable income		Unmarried		Married, joint return		Head of household	
					Amount of tax *		
Lower limit	Upper limit	Base	Tax rate on amount over lower limit	Base	Tax rate on amount over lower limit	Base	Tax rate on amount over lower limit
$ 6,000	$ 8,000	$1,100	24 percent	$1,000	19 percent	$1,040	22 percent
8,000	10,000	1,590	25	1,380	22	1,480	23
10,000	12,000	2,090	27	1,820	22	1,940	25
12,000	14,000	2,630	29	2,260	25	2,440	27
14,000	16,000	3,210	31	2,760	25	2,980	28
16,000	18,000	3,830	34	3,260	28	3,540	31
18,000	20,000	4,510	36	3,820	28	4,160	32
20,000	22,000	5,230	38	4,380	32	4,800	35
22,000	24,000	5,990	40	5,020	32	5,500	36
24,000	26,000	6,790	40	5,660	36	6,220	38
26,000	28,000	7,590	45	6,380	36	6,980	41
28,000	30,000	8,490	45	7,100	39	7,800	42

*Amount of tax = base + (tax rate X amount over lower income limit).
Source: Internal Revenue Service, *1975 Federal Income Tax Forms*, Washington, D.C., 1975.

federal tax rate would be 27 percent, assuming she is single. To obtain her combined state and federal marginal rate, we would take the above rate and add the appropriate state tax rate for her income level. Of course, if there is a city income tax where she lives, that would also be added to her overall marginal tax rate. Assume the state income tax rate for her income level is 11 percent and the city income tax is 3 percent. Combining these two rates with the 27 percent rate from Exhibit 6–2 gives an overall marginal tax rate of 41 percent (27 percent + 11 percent + 3 percent). Thus, if Sarah earned $1 of additional income, $.41 of it would go to pay her combined federal, state, and city taxes.

IMPACT OF TAXES ON FINANCIAL DECISIONS

Income taxes have a major impact on many of your personal financial decisions. Despite this, some people never incorporate taxes into their financial decisions process. Of course, it would be equally inappropriate to go to the opposite extreme of making taxes the controlling input to the decision process. We think a compromise between those two extremes is likely to be best for most people.

Timing of Financial Decisions   Income taxes can alter the timing of an individual's financial decisions. For example, assume John Fountin, a car salesman, earned $20,000 in commissions by December 1 of this year; that is nearly double his usual earnings. Since his income is already much higher than

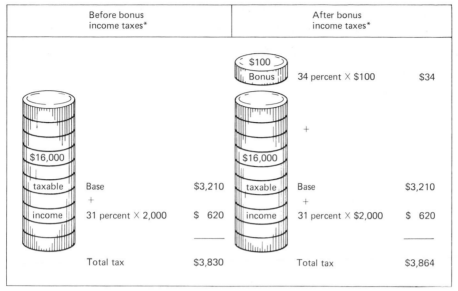

Before bonus income taxes*			After bonus income taxes*		
			$100 Bonus	34 percent × $100	$34
				+	
$16,000 taxable income	Base	$3,210	$16,000 taxable income	Base	$3,210
	+			+	
	31 percent × 2,000	$ 620		31 percent × $2,000	$ 620
	Total tax	$3,830		Total tax	$3,864

*Computed using Exhibit 6-2.

Exhibit 6-3 Impact of Moving to a Higher Tax Bracket

usual, he might want to defer selling some common stock whose price has risen sharply since he purchased it. Should his commissions drop next year, he could sell the stock at that time when his profit on the stock and lower commissions would combine to result in a lower tax rate. Of course, if the stock's price has declined sharply, he would likely want to sell it this year. That way, his loss on the stock would reduce this year's sharply higher commissions. Since the marginal tax rate on the income from commissions is high, lowering his gross income with the stock loss would substantially reduce the taxes he would have to pay. In short, to reduce income taxes, it is often highly advantageous for you to shift deductible expenses and qualifying losses to a year when your income is high. Likewise, in high income years you may want to defer additional income or gains until a year when your income is lower.

> **Strategy: If possible, consider shifting your deductible expenses and losses to years with unusually high income, and conversely, move added income and gains to low-income years.**

Deductible Expenses: A Tax Shield Because certain expenses can be deducted from income, they reduce taxable income and thereby shield you from taxes. For example, assume Steve and Elaine LaRosa's combined taxable income was $16,000; since they file a joint return, their taxes would be $3,260 (Exhibit 6–2). Included in their itemized deductions from gross income was $1,000 in property taxes and $2,500 in mortgage interest (both qualify as deductible expenses), in addition to other deductible items. Had they rented a house rather than owning one, they would not have had the property tax and mortgage interest deduction, so their taxable income would be $19,500 ($16,000 + $1,000 + $2,500). On that income, their taxes would have been $4,240 [$3,820 + (28 percent × $1,500)]. Granted the property taxes and mortgage interest cost the LaRosas an additional $3,500, but the deductibility of those items shielded them from paying $980 ($4,240 − $3,260) in taxes. Consequently, the effect of this income tax saving reduces the net cost of the property taxes and mortgage interest to only $2,520 ($3,500 − $980).

The same computation could be made more directly by using the appropriate marginal tax rate. For the LaRosas, the marginal tax rate on their $19,500 of taxable income is 28 percent (Exhibit 6–2). That means they pay 28 cents ($1 × 28 percent) in taxes for each dollar of added income over $18,000. But that works in reverse as well; reducing taxable income $1 reduces taxes 28 cents. Since the property tax and mortgage interest reduced the LaRosa's taxable income $3,500, their taxes were reduced $980 ($3,500 × 28 percent). That is the same result we obtained in the previous computation. The net cost would be the same $2,520 ($3,500 − $980) as before. The net cost could be computed directly as:

Net cost = deductible expense − (deductible expense × marginal tax rate)

For the above example, that would be:

Net cost = $3,500 − ($3,500 × 28 percent) = $2,520

We hasten to add that the above computation is more involved when the deductible expense drops the individual to a lower tax bracket. Had the LaRosa's taxable income been $14,000 ($17,500 without the tax and interest deduction), the $3,500 would be at two rates. The first $1,500 deducted (reducing income from $17,500 to $16,000) would involve a 28 percent rate, while the remaining $2,000 deduction (reducing income from $16,000 to $14,000) would involve a 25 percent rate. The net reduction in taxes would be $920 [($1,500 × 28 percent) + ($2,000 × 25 percent)]. Although the tax computation seems more difficult because it involves two rates, the logic remains unaltered.

In effect, what the tax shield means is that the real cost of the deductible expense is reduced by the amount of the tax savings. Returning to the first example in this section, the deductible expense cost the LaRosas $3,500, but, as a result, they saved $980 in taxes. Or, putting that on a dollar basis, for each $1 they spent on the deductible expense, they saved 28 cents in taxes, which means the deductible expense really cost the LaRosas only 72 cents. And the higher a person's marginal tax rate, the larger the reduction. This would apply to any qualifying deductible expense such as the finance charge on a loan, property taxes, a donation, or child care expense.

WHO MUST FILE

If you are a citizen or a resident of the United States and your gross income—wages, interest, dividends, capital gains and losses—equals or exceeds the amounts given in Exhibit 6–4, you must file a tax return. Two categories in Exhibit 6–4 require further comment. First, individuals under nineteen, or full-time students whose parents claim them as exemptions, must file if their gross income equals or exceeds $750 and if part of that income is unearned: interest and dividends. If they have no unearned income, the cutoff remains at $2,350. Second, self-employed people with earnings of $400 or more from that self-employment must file.

Individuals who have had taxes withheld from their wages should file, even if their gross income was less than the amounts shown in Exhibit 6–4, to obtain a refund of those taxes.

FILING STATUS

A taxpayer can file under four major categories: unmarried, married—joint return, married—separate returns, and "head of household."

Single Taxpayers who are not married at year-end qualify to use the unmarried rates shown in Exhibit 6–2. The tax rates for this category are the second highest of the four.

Married—Joint Return To qualify for a joint return a couple must be married at year-end. Tax rates for this category are the lowest of the four. For most married couples, filing a joint return usually minimizes their taxes.

Married—Separate Returns Even if they qualify for a joint return, a couple can elect to file separate returns. Tax rates for this category are the highest of the four. However, under special circumstances a couple may find it advantageous to file separate returns rather than a joint return.

"Head of Household" The tax rates for "head of household" are second lowest of the four categories. To qualify, a taxpayer must meet five tests. First,

Exhibit 6-4 Required Filing: Gross Income Cutoff

	Under 65	Over 65	Both over 65
Single	$2,350	$3,100	
Married	$3,400	$4,150	$4,900

Under nineteen or full-time student:
  with unearned income of $750*
  without unearned income $2,350†
Self-employed (net earnings) $400

*Applies to individuals who have unearned income—dividends, interest—and whose parents claim them as an exemption.

†Applies to individuals with no unearned income whose parents claim them as an exemption.

Exhibit 6-5   List of Qualifying Relatives

Child, stepchild, or adopted child	Brother- or sister-in-law
Grandchild or great-grandchild	Stepbrother or stepsister
Parent, grandparent, or stepparent	Half-brother or -sister
Aunt or uncle	Niece or nephew by blood
Son- or daughter-in-law	Foster child who resided in taxpayer's home
Father- or mother-in-law	the entire year and is a household member
Brother or sister	

the taxpayer must be unmarried at year-end. Second, the taxpayer must furnish over half the cost of maintaining a household—it can be a house, condominium, or apartment—for the entire year for any dependent relative on the list in Exhibit 6–5. Third, the household must be the taxpayer's home and the dependent relative's main residence. Fourth, the taxpayer must pay more than one-half the cost of the household: property taxes, mortgage interest, rent, utilities, property insurance, food eaten at the household. Last, the taxpayer must be a United States citizen or a resident alien during the entire year.

Gross Income

As Exhibit 6–1 indicated, taxpayers must include a wide range of items in their gross income. The major items are summarized in Exhibit 6–6. While most types of income are relatively straightforward, requiring little or no computation, the computation of capital gains and losses is more involved.

Capital Gains and Losses   Assets qualifying for treatment as a capital gain or loss includes such things as common stock, corporate bonds, municipal bonds, and real estate. Most taxpayers would compute their capital gain or loss as outlined in Exhibit 6–7. A few high-income taxpayers would likely elect to have their long-term capital gains taxed at a flat 25 percent (an accepted option) rather than complete the steps outlined in Exhibit 6–7.

There are several things that complicate the series of computations in Exhibit 6–7. First, we must decide whether the resulting capital gain or loss is short-term—assets held 6 months or less—or long term—assets held more than

Exhibit 6-6   Items that Must Be Included in Gross Income

Bonuses	Lottery winnings
Capital gains and losses	Partnership income
Commissions	Pensions
Contest winnings	Profits from business operations
Dividends in excess of $100 ($200 on joint return)	Salaries
Gambling winnings to the extent they exceed	Tips
losses	U.S. savings bond interest
Interest on savings and time accounts	Wages
Interest on corporate and U.S. treasury bonds and notes	

6 months. The top half of Exhibit 6–7 concentrates on that point. Having determined this, the next step is to decide what portion of the resulting gain or loss should be included in gross income. This is an important step because only one-half of long-term gains are taxed, whereas short-term gains are completely taxable. And the treatment is similar when deducting losses from gross income: short-term losses are fully deductible, whereas only one-half of long-term losses are deducted. The bottom half of Exhibit 6–7 illustrates the steps for determining how the net short-term gain or loss, ST, and the net long-term gain or loss, LT, would be included in gross income. It looks complicated, but it is not; just follow it a step at a time.

An example will illustrate how Exhibit 6–7 can be used. Assume Anne Monks sold the following two blocks of common stock during 1977: (*a*) XQ Corporation, net purchase price $1,000, net sale price $1,700, and it was held 15 months; (*b*) Specialty Products, net purchase price $3,000, net sale price $2,000, and it was held 3 months. According to the top half of Exhibit 6–7, the $700 gain ($1,700 − $1,000) on XQ would be a long-term gain. The $1,000 loss ($2,000 − $3,000) on Specialty Products would be a short-term loss. Since these are Anne's only capital transactions during 1977, ST would equal −$1,000 (a loss) while LT would equal $700 (a gain). Moving through the series of decisions shown in the bottom half of Exhibit 6–7, we find the events described in the fourth condition fit Anne's situation—ST is a loss and it exceeds the gain at LT. Consequently, she would reduce her 1977 gross income by the difference (−$1,000 + $700) = −$300, a $300 loss.

The maximum capital loss deduction (combined short- and long-term) is limited to $1,000 in any one year. But any excess can be carried forward and deducted in future years. That carry-forward loss would first be used to reduce the succeeding year's short-term gains, if any. Next it would reduce long-term gains, if any. And if the loss is not exhausted on these two items, up to $1,000 could be deducted from that year's gross income.

Selling a House   The gain from the sale of a house receives special treatment. If you sell your house for more than you paid, and buy a replacement home within 18 months, or you complete construction of your new house and occupy it within 24 months, all or part of the gain may be deferred. Notice we said "deferred" because the tax on that gain is not canceled but is only deferred. If the taxpayer suffers a loss on the sale, that loss cannot be deducted. And it cannot be offset against some other capital gain.

The computation of the gain from a house sale is not simple, but the tax reference books listed at the chapter's end discuss it in detail.

Exclusions from Gross Income   The list in Exhibit 6–8 shows the major items that can be excluded from gross income. The reference books have lists of additional minor exclusions.

Adjustments to Gross Income

As previously pointed out, these items are used to compute adjusted gross income.

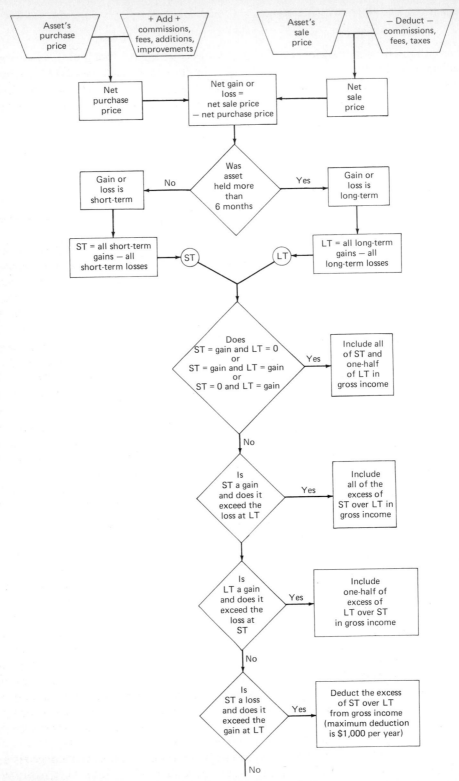

Exhibit 6-7 Computation of Capital Gains and Losses

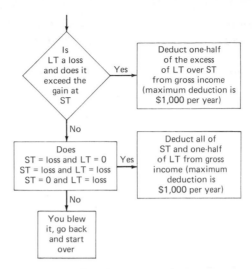

Sick Pay By meeting certain qualifications, you can exclude all or part of the income you receive while absent from work because of sickness or accident. In general, the qualifying standards eliminate very short-term illnesses unless accompanied by a day's hospitalization. Since the standards, limits, and computations are complicated, you should refer to one of the tax reference books to see whether you qualify.

Moving Expense If you accept a new job or are transferred to a new location for your present job, all or a portion of the moving-related expenses may be deducted from your gross income. You must meet two qualifications in order to take this deduction.

The first qualification concerns how far you move, and the distance is computed as follows:

Mileage difference = (distance from old residence to new job location) − (distance from old residence to old job location)

To qualify, that difference must be at least 50 miles. For example, assume your

Exhibit 6-8 Excludable from Gross Income

Annuity payments that are a return of your cost	Life insurance proceeds
Disability insurance benefits	Scholarship and fellowship awards
Dividends that are a return of capital	Social security benefits: disability, survivor, and retirement
Gifts and inheritances	Stock dividends and splits
Health and accident insurance proceeds	Unemployment benefits
Interest on debt instruments of states and municipalities	Welfare benefits

previous job was 13 miles from your old residence; if the new job were 65 miles from the old residence, you would qualify (65 miles − 13 miles = 52 miles).

The second qualification is that you must be a full-time employee at the new job location at least 39 weeks during the 12 months following the move. Those 39 weeks do not have to be consecutive, nor do they have to be with the same employer, but they must be in the same locality.

Traveling Expenses All costs incurred for transportation, meals, and lodging on the trip to the new job location can also be deducted as part of the moving expenses. If your own car was used, you can deduct either the cost of actual expenses (gas, oil, and repairs, but excluding depreciation) or a mileage allowance, which is currently 7 cents per mile.

Moving Costs Moving costs can be included for: packing, crating, transporting possessions, in-transit storage up to 30 days, costs of insuring your possessions in transit, cost of shipping an automobile, and charges for disconnecting and reconnecting household appliances.

House-hunting Trips The costs incurred on house-hunting trips (meals, lodging, and transportation) can be deducted. More than one trip is allowed and a trip does not have to be successful to qualify.

Temporary Living Costs If you do not have a permanent residence at the new job location, you are allowed to deduct the costs for meals and temporary lodging. This deduction is limited to costs incurred 30 consecutive days after you obtain employment. Furthermore, the total deduction is limited to $1,000 for the combined cost of house-hunting and temporary living quarters.

Expenses of Selling, Purchasing, or Leaving a Residence You can deduct the expenses of selling your old house, including real estate agent's commission, attorney's fee, and title fee. Likewise, the expenses of purchasing a new house can be deducted, including attorney's fee, appraisal cost, and title cost. When the move involves a house or apartment rental, you can include the expense of settling your old lease as well as the cost of acquiring a new lease. The combined cost of house-hunting, temporary living quarters, and the expenses of selling the old residence and purchasing a new one are deductible up to a limit of $2,500.

Employer Reimbursements When an employer reimburses an employee for a portion or all of the moving expense, the entire reimbursement is included in the employee's gross income. The employee then deducts all the moving-related expenses to compute adjusted gross income in the normal manner.

Employee Business Expenses In general, employees can deduct those business-related expenses incurred while performing their job and for which they were not reimbursed by their employer. Typical items would include transportation costs, meals and lodging while away from home, automobile expenses (actual or the current 15 cents per mile allowance), and certain entertainment expenses. The tax reference books listed at the chapter's end discuss the lengthy list of qualifications for an expense to be allowed as a deduction.

Contributions to Retirement Plans Self-employed persons and certain people who are not covered by a regular pension plan where they work can establish their own retirement plans if they meet certain qualifications. The principal advantage is that contributions to the plan are sheltered from income taxes until they are withdrawn from the plan. For example, suppose Carole Stein's marginal tax rate is 40 percent and she can establish a retirement plan. Without the tax-sheltering feature, she would only have $60 out of every $100 of income to invest in a retirement fund [$100 − (40 percent × $100)]. By contributing that $100 to a qualified retirement plan, she invests the full $100 because there is no tax to pay on it. Of course, there are limits on the amount she can contribute to a plan. And the taxes are only deferred. When she withdraws the money during retirement, that is the time she must pay the taxes. The real advantage is that, in all likelihood, her tax rate will be lower at that time. Because retirement plans are a complex and specialized area, you should consult a tax reference book for complete details.

Self-employed Pension Plans Self-employed individuals who meet the necessary qualifications can deduct up to $7,500 or 15 percent of their self-employment income, whichever is smaller. However, you can contribute $750 to your retirement plan even if your income is less than $5,000. Except in cases of total disability, there are penalties if the person withdraws funds before reaching 59½ years of age.

Individual Retirement Accounts (IRA) Beginning in 1975, individuals who do not participate in a qualified pension plan, profit-sharing, stock option or government plan, set up their own individual retirement account. The maximum contribution is $1,500 or 15 percent of income, whichever is lower. Withdrawal before 59½ years of age, unless the individual has become totally disabled, entails a penalty.

Deductions from Adjusted Gross Income

Taxpayers have three computational alternatives for determining their deductions from adjusted gross income: (1) they can take a standard deduction which is a fixed percentage of their adjusted gross income; (2) they can take a specified low-income allowance; or (3) they can itemize their qualifying deductible expenses and deduct the total of these expenses.

Standard Deduction   The standard deduction is computed as a flat percentage of the taxpayer's adjusted gross income. Currently, the rate is 16 percent with ceilings of $2,300 and $2,600 for unmarried and married taxpayers filing a joint return, respectively. Thus, if Grace Smith, who is unmarried, had adjusted gross income of $12,000, her standard deduction would be $1,920, ($12,000 × 16 percent). Given the ceiling, a single individual whose adjusted gross income exceeded $14,375 ($2,300 ÷ 16 percent) would be restricted to the $2,300 maximum. Likewise, a married couple whose adjusted gross income exceeded $16,250 ($2,600 ÷ 16 percent) could not claim more than the $2,600 deduction.

As this is written, the 16 percent rate is a temporary one. The 16 percent rate and the $2,300 and $2,600 ceilings are a temporary change from the previous 15 percent rate and a $2,000 ceiling for either single or married taxpayers. There has been a move to make the change permanent, but the issue has not been concluded at this time.

Low-Income Allowance   The low-income allowance is really a specialized standard deduction that is available to all taxpayers. Its principal intent was to eliminate, or substantially reduce, the tax liability of low-income taxpayers. The allowance is $1,600 for unmarried taxpayers and $1,900 for married taxpayers filing a joint return. Thus, for a single person with an adjusted gross income of $7,000, the $1,600 low-income allowance would be a better deduction than $1,120 ($7,000 × 16 percent) from the standard deduction.

Itemized Deductions   Rather than take either of the above flat rate deductions, individuals can itemize their qualifying deductions and deduct that total from their adjusted gross income.

Interest and Finance Charges   The interest and finance charges on home mortgages, consumer cash loans, credit cards, charge accounts, and most other credit transactions are deductible. Many creditors indicate the year's cumulative interest or finance charge on their January or December billing. Or you may be able to reconstruct the year's finance charge from the coupons for the payments you made during the year. If you are uncertain about the finance charge, ask the institution which granted the credit for assistance in computing the total amount you paid in finance charges during the year. Barring information from one of these sources, you can estimate the finance charge using a 6 percent annual rate; the actual computation is described in the tax reference books listed at the chapter's end.

Strategy: Always thoroughly exhaust all other possibilities before you use the 6

percent estimation technique; the 6 percent rate is generally much less than the actual finance charges you paid during the year.

Taxes   In general, the following taxes are deductible: state, local, and foreign real property taxes; state and local personal property taxes; state, local, and foreign income taxes; state and local sales and use taxes; and state and local taxes on gasoline and other motor fuels. Special assessments for improving streets, sidewalks, sewers, or water mains are not deductible even though they may be included with the regular property tax billing.

The United States Treasury has approved the use of optional tax tables to assist a taxpayer in computing sales and use taxes, as well as gasoline taxes. But the tables are strictly optional. Taxpayers can always substitute their own records and computation. The only requirement is that they can substantiate the deduction if asked to do so.

Strategy: When using the optional sales and use tax table, you are allowed to add the taxes on expensive items such as cars, boats, etc. If your actual sales tax payments exceed those shown in the table, by all means use the larger amount. Likewise, if your computations indicate you paid more gas taxes than the table allows, then substitute your own larger amount.

Contributions   A taxpayer can deduct donations to most religious, charitable, educational, and other philanthropic organizations. In addition, donations to federal, state, and local governmental units are also deductible. If you are unsure whether an organization qualifies, ask if it has been approved by the U.S. Treasury Department, or check the Treasury's list of approved organizations. Contributions to the following do not qualify as deductions: lobbying organizations, many fraternal groups, professional groups, social clubs, chambers of commerce, and civic leagues, and gifts to needy individuals.

Contributions are deductible in the year in which the cash was paid or the property was actually donated. If at all possible, obtain receipts or pay by check so you have the canceled check as a receipt. If you made a cash donation, by all means include it even if you do not have a receipt. The worst thing that could happen is that you would have difficulty supporting that donation should your return be questioned. However, most IRS auditors will accept some unsupported cash donations.

Donations of property—securities, books, furniture, clothes—are also deductible. In most cases, the allowable deduction is the property's fair market value. There are, however, several special cases. If you donate securities (stock and bonds) which you held more than 6 months, you can deduct their full market value at the time you donated them. This can provide a sizable tax benefit where the price of a common stock has risen sharply since you purchased it. Actually, you gain a double benefit: You pay no tax on the appreciation in market value (appreciation = market value − your cost); yet your deduction is the amount of the current market value of the security. On personal property—furniture, fixtures, jewelry, art objects—you can deduct the full market value if the receiving organization uses the property as part of its normal operations. For example, assume you donated an oriental rug (market value $1,500, your cost $700) to your church. If the church kept the rug and used it as part of their furnishings, you could deduct the full $1,500. On the other hand, if the receiving organization does not use the donated item, but immediately resells it, you can deduct your cost plus 50 percent of the appreciation. Thus, had the church immediately resold the rug in the above example, you could only deduct $1,100 [$700 + (50 percent × $800)]. Donations of handicraft and food items can be deducted at their fair market value.

The value of services donated is not deductible. But, in donating services, if you incur expenses such as postage, phone, stationery, and office supplies, they are deductible. In addition, when you use your automobile to travel to the charitable organization's office, or as part of the voluntary work, you can deduct a mileage allowance: currently it is 7 cents per mile.

Strategy: If you plan to make a donation near the beginning of next year, consider making it in December so you receive the immediate tax benefits from the deduction.

Medical and Dental Expenses   In general, deductible medical expenses include: professional services (doctor, dentist, nurse, etc.); medical equipment, medicines and drugs, laboratory tests, medical treatments, hospital services, and premiums for health insurance policies. Transportation expenses to the doctor's office or hospital are also deductible—either the actual cost of commercial transportation or 7 cents per mile for your personal auto.

There are, however, restrictions and special calculations to determine how much of the actual expenses are allowable as deductions. First, the expense must have been paid in the current tax year and it must be for yourself, your spouse, or a qualifying dependent. Second, you cannot claim any expense that has been reimbursed by insurance or other compensation. Third, only medical

Exhibit 6-9   Computation of Medical Deduction

Medical insurance premium		$ 450	
50 percent limit		225	
Maximum deduction			$150
Medical and dental expenses		$ 750	
Drug expense	$200		
Less: 1 percent cutoff* ($12,500 × 1 percent)	125		
Eligible as medical expense		$ 75	
Add: remainder of insurance premium		300	
Subtotal		$1,125	
Less: 3 percent cutoff* ($12,500 × 3 percent)		375	
Eligible deduction			$750
Total deduction			$900

*Adjusted gross income is $12,500.

expenses in excess of 3 percent of your adjusted gross income are deductible. Also drug expenses in excess of 1 percent of adjusted gross income can be included as a drug expense. Premiums for medical insurance—including insurance for contact lens replacement—are deducted in two stages. One-half the premiums are directly deductible up to a maximum of $150, and are not subject to the 3 percent limit. The balance of the premiums are included with regular medical expenses which, of course, are subject to the 3 percent limit. If your insurance provides disability coverage for illness or injury as well as medical care, only that part of the premiums allocated to medical care is deductible.

Exhibit 6–9 illustrates the medical deduction computation with an example. Assume the Jones family incurred the following medical expenses during the year: premium on medical insurance, $450; unreimbursed medical and dental expenses, $750; and unreimbursed drug expense, $200. The Jones's combined adjusted gross income was $12,500.

Child and Dependent Care Taxpayers may deduct household services and related child and dependent care costs which are necessary so they can work full time. Full time is defined as three-quarters or more of the typical workweek. This deduction is available to all taxpayers—unmarried, married, divorced, or separated—who meet the required standards. Deductible items include: cost of having someone care for your child in your home, cost of domestic service for your home, and child care costs outside the home (at day care center, nursery school, baby-sitter's house). In general, payments made to relatives, whether for child or dependent care in your house, care in their house, or domestic services, are not deductible. The maximum monthly deduction is limited to $400. Furthermore, the outside care component (day care center, nursery school, baby-sitter's house) is limited to $200 per month for one child, $300 for two, and $400 for three or more. Also, the total yearly allowable deduction is reduced 50 cents for each dollar by which the taxpayer's adjusted gross income exceeds $36,000. Thus, on an adjusted gross income of $37,200, the $1,200 excess reduces the maximum monthly deduction $50 [($1,200 × .5) ÷ 12 months]; the maximum monthly deduction therefore would be $350. Also, to qualify for the deduction, a married couple must file a joint return.

The limits governing deductions for qualifying dependent care are similar. But there are added restrictions on which relatives qualify and on how the dependent's income is treated. Most tax reference books discuss these restrictions.

Education Expense Taxpayers can deduct the cost of furthering their education provided three conditions are met. First, the person is currently employed or self-employed. Second, the person already meets the minimum education requirements of the present employment. That is, if the purpose of the education program is to qualify the person for the education minimums of the present position, the cost is not deductible. Third, the education program must maintain or improve the skills required for the person's present position. The fact the person eventually obtains a college degree does not void the deduction, as long as the above three qualifications are satisfied. Likewise, if the person qualifies for a job promotion during the education program, the deduction will be allowed as long as the job duties remain similar. Situations which typically would not qualify include: courses taken to qualify for a new profession or courses taken for general education or enrichment purposes.

Deductible expenses include: course fees, tuition, books, supplies, transportation costs from job to the course, travel expenses to a school away from home, living expenses incurred at a school away from home. Qualifying courses can be either at the basic, intermediate, or advanced level. And they can be taken at a university, vocational school, or adult education program, or by correspondence.

Job Search Expense   All expenses incurred while searching for new employment in a taxpayer's present trade or profession are fully deductible. This holds regardless of whether the search is successful or not. Typical qualifying expenses include: résumés, employment agency fees, telephone calls, travel expense for interviews, parking, and tolls. These items are not deductible, however, when the taxpayer is applying for a position in an area other than the present trade or profession.

Casualty and Theft Losses   A taxpayer can deduct unreimbursed property losses resulting from fire, storm, flood, earthquake, other natural catastrophes, riots, theft, and vandalism. Losses which do not involve a "sudden action," such as diseases of trees and shrubs, termite damage, and moth or insect damage, are excluded. Losses, however, are only deductible to the extent they exceed $100. And each qualifying loss during the year has a separate $100 deduction. Thus, if an individual had $250 of storm damage in June and $150 worth of plants and trees were stolen in December, both losses would be reduced by $100. The deductible loss would be $150 ($250 − $100) for the storm, plus $50 ($150 − $100) for the theft.

The essential steps in computing a loss are shown in Exhibit 6–10. Assume a choice oriental rug was stolen from Max Jones's house. Since his homeowners policy covered only part of the loss, the remainder is used to compute the loss deduction shown in Exhibit 6–10. If a professional appraisal was needed to establish the extent of the loss, the appraisal fee can be included as a miscellaneous itemized deduction without regard for the $100 deduction. Likewise, the cost of pictures taken to support the claim can be included in miscellaneous deductions.

Good supporting records are essential when claiming a casualty loss. Since

Exhibit 6-10   Computing a Casualty or Theft Loss

Market value at time of loss	$1,400
Taxpayer's basis—purchase cost plus improvements	$ 600
Lesser of market value or taxpayer's basis	$ 600
Less: Salvage value	0
Insurance reimbursement	100
$100 loss deduction	100
Eligible deduction	$ 400

Exhibit 6-11   Miscellaneous Deductible Expenses

Alimony—if it qualifies	Periodicals and books used in business or
Specialized clothing	profession
Dues—union, professional societies, trade	Political contributions
associations	Safe-deposit box
Investment counsel fee	Tax preparation fees
	Tools used in profession

the IRS often questions a casualty loss, you should have reasonable proof of the loss.

Miscellaneous Deductions   Because the list of miscellaneous deductions is extensive, we give only the more frequently used ones in Exhibit 6–11. For a complete list, consult one of the tax reference books listed at the chapter's end.

While many miscellaneous deductions are not large, it is essential that a taxpayer not overlook an eligible item. For example, a taxpayer in the 30 percent marginal tax bracket who overlooked $100 in miscellaneous deductions would pay $30 more in taxes than required.

Which Deduction: Standard? Low-Income Allowance? Itemized?   Compute all three deduction totals to decide whether you should itemize, take the standard deduction, or take the low-income allowance. Homeownership is probably the most frequent event that shifts taxpayers from taking a standard deduction to itemizing deductions. The combination of mortgage interest and property taxes generally shifts the balance toward itemizing. But you may still find itemizing advantageous even if you do not own a house.

Strategy: Rather than accept some generalization, compute all three deductions—standard, low-income, and itemized—to decide which is most advantageous.

Exemption

After you have deducted the total amount of your allowable deductions from your adjusted gross income, there remains one more step to arrive at taxable income. This final step concerns exemptions.

For each exemption, a taxpayer can reduce adjusted gross income by $750. Every person who files a tax form is allowed at least one exemption for himself or herself. Taxpayers who are sixty-five or over may claim an additional exemption. The taxpayer who is blind also is allowed an additional exemption. Thus, a single, blind, sixty-eight-year-old taxpayer would have three exemptions.

Married persons filing joint tax forms are allowed two exemptions. Similarly, they may claim additional exemptions for age (sixty-five or over) and blindness. Thus, if both partners are over sixty-five and blind, they may claim six exemptions on a joint return.

In addition, a taxpayer can claim an exemption for every person who qualifies as a dependent. Unlike taxpayers, dependents cannot qualify for the extra exemptions for age and blindness.

To qualify as a dependent, the person claimed as a dependent must meet the five tests detailed in Exhibit 6–12. There must be yes responses to at least one part of each test. A complication arises when the person receives support from several people, as shown in Test 2, Question 2. First, the entire group must provide more than 50 percent of the person's support. Second, the taxpayer claiming the dependent must provide at least 10 percent of the person's total support. And third, everyone involved in the multiple-support arrangement must agree on which one of them will claim the dependent. The support computation would include costs such as lodging, food, clothing, medical and dental care, recreation, entertainment, and education expenses. For the questions in Test 3, gross income includes the items discussed at the start of this section.

The total exemption deduction is computed by multiplying $750 times the number of exemptions claimed. How you take your previous deductions—whether you itemize, take the standard deduction, or the low-income allowance—has nothing to do with these exemptions. You take the total exemption deduction, no matter how you took the other deductions.

Strategy: Since an additional exemption can substantially reduce taxes, you should carefully consider every possible exemption.

Tax Computation

We have now nearly completed the income tax computation cycle outlined in Exhibit 6–1. We now have determined taxable income. All that remains is to compute the tax on the taxable income. The five major tax computation methods are summarized in Exhibit 6–13. We will cover the first three methods;

Exhibit 6-12 Checklist for Dependent Qualifications

	Yes	No
TEST 1: Relationship or Member of Household		
1 Is the person one of the relatives listed in Exhibit 6-5?	( )	( )
or		
2 Did the person reside in your home and was the person a household member during the entire year?	( )	( )
TEST 2: Support Test		
1 Did you pay more than half of the person's support?	( )	( )
or		
2 If the person received support from several people:		
a did combined support exceed 50 percent of total?	( )	( )
b and, did you provide more than 10 percent of total support?	( )	( )
c and, has everyone agreed to your claiming the dependent?	( )	( )
TEST 3: Gross Income Test		
1 Was the dependent's gross income less than $750?	( )	( )
or		
2 Is the dependent your child and under nineteen, or a full-time student? (If yes, the $750 gross income test does not apply.)	( )	( )
TEST 4: Citizenship or Resident Test		
1 Is the dependent a U.S. citizen or a resident of the United States, Canada, Mexico, the Canal Zone, or the Republic of Panama?	( )	( )
TEST 5: Joint Return Test		
1 If married, does the dependent file a separate, rather than a joint, return?	( )	( )

the final two methods have only limited application, so we leave their discussion to the tax reference books listed at the chapter's end.

Tax Tables The tax tables are specifically designed to ease the tax computation. The tables can be used when adjusted gross income is $15,000 or

Exhibit 6-13 Summary of Federal Income Tax Computational Techniques

Computation method	Qualifications or limitations
Tax tables	Adjusted gross income $15,000 or less *and* taxpayer does not itemize deductions
Tax rate: Schedule X, Y, and Z	Adjusted gross income exceeds $15,000 *or* deductions are itemized
Schedule G— Income Averaging	Current year's gross income is being averaged with 4 previous years
Schedule D	Generally advantageous to taxpayers with marginal tax rates over 50 percent and with sizable long-term capital gains
Form 4726	Generally applies to taxpayers with marginal tax rates over 50 percent

less and the taxpayer does not itemize deductions. There are separate tables for 1 through 12 exemptions. Once taxpayers know their own adjusted gross income, number of exemptions, and filing status, the tax amount is read directly from the table. The tables automatically incorporate the standard deduction or the low-income allowance, whichever gives the lowest tax.

Tax Rate Schedule X, Y, and Z   The tax rate schedules X, Y, and Z are for taxpayers whose adjusted gross income exceeds $15,000 or who itemize deductions. There is a separate schedule for each filing status: X for single taxpayers, Y for married taxpayers, and Z for heads of household. Excerpts from the three schedules are shown in Exhibit 6–2.

Income Averaging   Because tax rates are much higher in the upper-income brackets, an individual who has a highly volatile income pattern—high income for one or two years followed by low income for several years—would pay more taxes than would the taxpayer who received the same total income in a relatively steady stream. To partially redeem this situation, taxpayers can average their income over a 5-year period, provided they meet certain qualifications. Exhibit 6–14 details those qualifying standards.

For taxpayers who have not recently graduated from school or recently begun work, the computation is straightforward unless the taxpayer was married during the last 4 years and wants to file a joint return; most tax reference books discuss this in detail. For the recently graduated or new entrants to the work force, the qualifications are narrow and involved. To qualify, a taxpayer must meet one of the three exceptions shown in Exhibit 6–14. Many recent graduates and most new workers cannot fit one of those exceptions. This was no oversight. The rules are specifically formulated to exclude the majority of these two groups.

PAYMENT OF TAXES

Most individuals pay their income taxes through a combination of three methods: payroll withholding, tax estimates, or directly with their tax return.

Payroll Withholding   Most people pay their taxes through payroll withholding. That is, the employer withholds the amount of the taxes for each pay period and forwards it to the United States Treasury. The amount withheld is based on Form W-4 the employee files with the employer. The W-4 form lists filing status, number of exemptions, and any special withholding instructions. With the appropriate instruction, you can have additional tax withheld or you can claim a special allowance to reduce the tax withheld. You can file a new W-4 at any time.

Overwithholding: A Good Savings Plan?   Some people intentionally understate their exemptions on Form W-4. In this way, they pay more taxes through withholding than required. That ensures a refund when they file their tax return. While this payment method does force them to save, they receive no interest on the amount overwithheld: the Treasury does not even send a

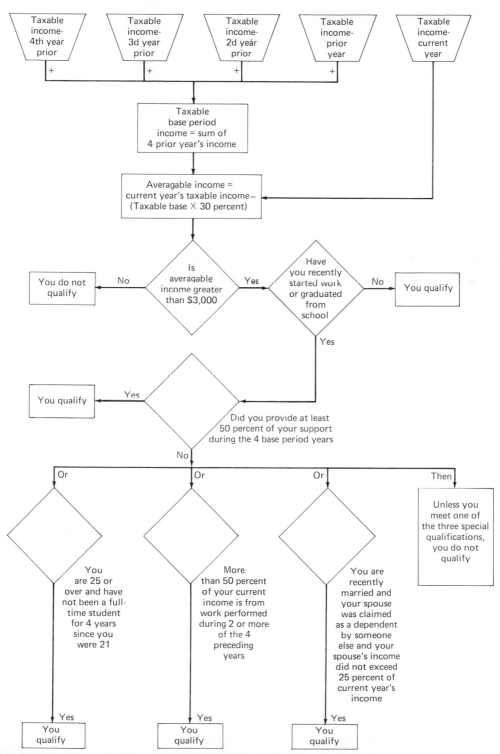

Exhibit 6-14 Income Averaging: Qualifying Standards

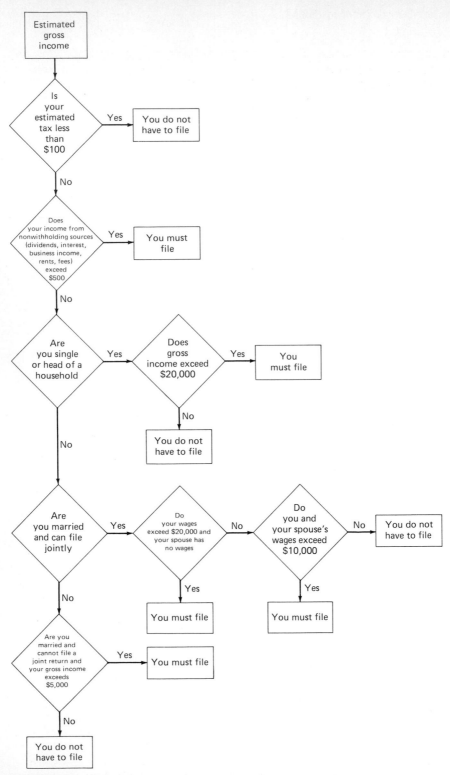

Exhibit 6-15 Estimated Tax Declaration: Who Must File?

thank-you note. If you are interested in forced savings, instead of overpaying taxes through withholding arrange to have a similar amount withheld and placed in a savings account where you will receive interest.

Estimated Taxes Self-employed people or those who receive substantial income over and above their regular wages are not subject to these withholding provisions. Consequently, they are required to file an estimated tax declaration. Essentially, the estimated tax must be paid in four equal quarterly payments: April 15, June 15, September 15, and January 15 of the next year.

The requirements for those who must file a declaration of estimated tax are summarized in Exhibit 6–15. Despite specific instructions about who must file, there is no penalty for not filing. Instead, taxpayers who fail to file are assessed the same penalty as when they underpay their estimated tax: 7 percent annual interest on the adjusted underpayment. That adjusted underpayment is the difference between estimated tax payments and 80 percent of the actual tax due. Thus an individual whose actual taxes were $6,000 but who had made estimated tax payments of $4,500 would have a $300 adjusted underpayment [$4,500 − ($6,000 × 80 percent)]. Under certain conditions, you are exempt from the penalty; tax reference books discuss these in detail.

FILING THE RETURN

Taxpayers who are on a regular calendar year, as most people are, must file their tax return by April 15. If you expect a refund, file your return as soon after December 31 as possible. If you owe taxes, wait until the last minute to file. But if you have not paid at least 80 percent of the taxes you owe, you may want to file early to avoid the 7 percent annual interest for underpayment of taxes.

Time Extension By filing the appropriate form, a taxpayer can obtain an automatic 60-day extension that moves the date the tax form is due to June 15. The extension does not change the date the taxes must be paid. That remains April 15. What you must do is estimate your tax and pay it when you file for the extension. Then, when you calculate your actual tax, any shortfall must be paid and interest is assessed at 7 percent per year. For those needing still more time, an additional 2- to 6-month extension can be requested. But the person must justify the need for additional time.

Do Not File Late The penalty for filing late is 5 percent of the tax due for each month the return is late, up to a maximum of 25 percent. And there is also an interest charge of 7 percent per year on the unpaid tax. Thus, filing 4 months late would entail a 22.3 percent penalty [(5 percent × 4 months) + (7 percent × 4 months/12 months)]. Even if you cannot pay the tax due, you should still file on time. In most cases the Treasury will bill you for the taxes together with a penalty of .5 percent of the tax due for each month the tax is unpaid (Maximum 25 percent) and interest at 7 percent per year. But that .5 percent monthly

penalty is only ¹⁄₁₀ of the 5 percent monthly late filing penalty. Where the Treasury decides the failure to pay resulted from "willful neglect," it may also assess 5 percent of the tax due as a penalty.

> **Strategy: Always file on time. The penalty for filing late is much larger than the penalty for filing on time although not paying the tax until later.**

ASSISTANCE ON TAXES

There is no general agreement on when a taxpayer should seek outside assistance.[1] The Treasury maintains that most taxpayers should be able to complete their own returns. The tax preparation industry, for obvious reasons, takes somewhat the opposite position. We believe the key factor is the taxpayer. Those willing to make a moderate time commitment can likely prepare a reasonably complex return without assistance. For those without the time, or for those unwilling to spend the time, even a basic return may be beyond their reach. The checklist in Exhibit 6–16 should help you decide whether outside assistance is warranted. If the majority of answers are yes, you may want to consider outside assistance.

The fee for tax assistance can be included as a miscellaneous itemized deduction. That deduction lowers the effective cost for people who itemize.

---

[1]A recent study suggests the quality of tax assistance is very poor. Errors were found in 70 to 80 percent of the returns that had itemized deductions prepared with outside tax assistance. And those high error rates applied to all tax services: certified public accountants, tax lawyers, commercial preparers, as well as the IRS's taxpayer service. "IRS Help on Taxes Unreliable," *Milwaukee Journal,* Dec. 16, 1975, part 2, p. 9, col. 1.

Exhibit 6-16   Checklist: Is Outside Tax Assistance Needed?

	Yes	No
Your qualifications		
1 Do you find reading tax rules and instructions extremely arduous?	( )	( )
2 Do you lack the 10 to 30 hours needed to prepare a simple to moderately complicated return?	( )	( )
3 Do you question your competence to do a satisfactory preparation?	( )	( )
4 Will you have sleepless nights worrying whether your return was correct?	( )	( )
Your tax return		
1 Has your filing status changed?	( )	( )
2 Has your current year's income increased substantially?	( )	( )
3 Do you anticipate a lengthy list of itemized deductions?	( )	( )
4 Will you have to file numerous supporting forms: sick pay, capital gains, business expenses?	( )	( )
5 Do you have major financial transactions with extensive tax ramifications: a move to a new job, sale of your house, a complicated capital gain or loss, an opportunity to use income averaging?	( )	( )
6 Did you use outside assistance last year?	( )	( )

But that does not mean every person should seek the most expensive, specialized tax assistance available. On simple returns, expensive, specialized assistance will likely accomplish little more than a cheaper service could do.

Unfortunately, too many people expect miracles from a tax service. True, in some cases they can substantially reduce a person's taxes. Yet, for everyone to expect a sizable reduction is simply unrealistic. Regrettably, some tax services have resorted to practices that border on fraud to outright tax evasion in their quest to convince the taxpayer they are doing great things. If you do not expect or demand that the tax service be the local miracle worker, you will be better satisfied and more likely to receive an honest preparation effort.

IRS Taxpayer Service   The IRS taxpayer service does not prepare tax returns. Instead, IRS people answer taxpayers' questions about how an item should be treated for tax purposes. This service is available in person at all IRS offices or through a telephone call. While it is a minimum service, it may be sufficient to permit you to complete your return without further assistance. Since the service is free, use it whenever you have a specific question.

> **Strategy: If you disagree or question the advice from this service, ask to speak to the person's supervisor for a confirmation of the advice.**

Commercial Preparers   Commercial preparers can range from an individual who prepares returns as a sideline to the large nationwide firms that specialize in tax preparation and advertise on TV and in the newspapers. The quality of the work varies tremendously. And the size of the firm is no guarantee of quality; some of the largest firms utilize part-time employees who typically have a minimal tax background.

The fee to prepare your tax return varies according to the complexity of the return. A $10 to $25 fee would be typical for a very basic tax return. We have several reservations about commercial preparers. For one thing, it is extremely difficult, if not impossible, to ascertain the competence of the preparer. For another, some preparers will take the easy way out and not encourage a taxpayer to take all the itemized deductions to which he or she is entitled, especially if the item is likely to be questioned. And then there are the preparers who will go to any length to lower taxes—legal or otherwise.

Strategy: Ask your friends if they know of a good preparer, or check with a local bank officer for a recommendation.

Tax Practitioners   Tax practitioners include certified public accountants (CPAs), lawyers who specialize in taxes, and those individuals who meet the Treasury's qualifying standards for an "enrolled agent." While most small to medium-sized CPA firms handle individual tax returns, the large national firms generally do not. The quality of service largely depends on how heavily the practitioner specializes in taxes. Unless the consultant has a strong tax background and keeps current, the quality will suffer. The fee varies over such a wide range that it is meaningless even to quote an average price.

Strategy: Check your friends to see if they can recommend a good practitioner. If they have no recommendation, consult the Yellow Pages in your area.

MAKE IT EASIER

Many people do little, if anything, about taxes during the year. Then a few days before April 15 they launch into taxes with several long, miserable night sessions. We make no claim to transform tax time into a period of joy. We do, however, feel some advanced work and planning can remove much of the drudgery from tax preparation.

Records   Too often, people never keep records during the year; consequently, they must reconstruct everything at the time they prepare their returns. The real risk is that they will overlook an item. A far better way is to set up a separate tax file at the beginning of the year. That way, tax-related material, whether it be an invoice, a check, a receipt, or a special note reminding you of some item, can easily be dropped in it.

Think Taxes   While you certainly do not have to think taxes continuously, you should consider the tax implications of your financial actions and decisions. For example, when making a contribution, note it in the memo space on the check. And pay it with a check rather than cash. When you receive a doctor's bill, place it in the current year's tax file. When you have a special tax situation—such as donating property or suffering a casualty loss—write out the details and put it in the tax file.

Reference Book A good tax reference book is essential to any tax preparation effort. Any of those listed at the chapter's end (there are many such publications) will be helpful. The examples and explanations in these books can vastly simplify the whole process. And the cost of the book can be included with miscellaneous itemized deductions.

Timing There are several advantages to preparing your tax return long before the April 15 deadline. For one thing, you have time to get answers on questionable items. Also, should you be missing an item in your records, you can obtain a duplicate. And, like preparing for exams, it is simply much easier and a lot less frustrating to work on taxes in several short sessions rather than a single crash session.

Before Filing Your Return If you have prepared your own return, double-check all your arithmetic before you mail in the return. It is best if you do this several days after preparing the return, so that you are less likely to overlook an obvious error. When you have the return ready to mail, make a copy of each page and retain it in your records. Should the IRS question an item, you will have a copy you can quickly refer to.

AN AUDIT BY THE IRS

Each year the Internal Revenue Service informs a number of taxpayers that their tax returns have been selected for audit. Too often, people are overly concerned about the implications of an audit. Some people do not use every opportunity to avoid taxes, just to ensure they will not be audited. We strongly

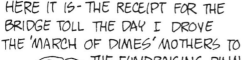

believe such measures are unwarranted; a tax audit should not present a major crisis.

Who Is Selected? A small percentage of the tax returns are selected on a random basis. But the majority are singled out by an initial computer audit which selects a return either because it is atypical of other returns in its income category or because the return has certain key features. Unfortunately, the IRS never reveals what those features are.

Exhibit 6–17 shows the averages for the various itemized deductions for different income groups. Your return will not inevitably be audited just because your return is above one or more of the averages shown in Exhibit 6–17, but an above-average deduction increases the likelihood.

What Is Examined Most audits are directed to just one or two specific items. It could be a particular deduction or a question about a gross income item. Rare is the audit that examines a return item by item.

Audit Procedure When a taxpayer is notified that his or her return is being audited, the notice specifies which item is under scrutiny. The notice will request that supporting details be mailed to the IRS office, or will suggest a date when the auditor would like to meet with the taxpayer. After this conference the auditor will explain whether additional tax is believed due and will explain why. At this point, the taxpayer can either accept the auditor's findings or appeal the decision to a higher level. That appeal can be made either to the upper administrative levels within the IRS or through the courts.

Preparing for an Audit When you receive the audit notice, carefully review your copy of your tax return for errors or omissions. Next, review your supporting documentation for the items under review. If anything is incomplete or missing, now is the time to put that file in order. The best evidence is documents from outside sources—invoices, canceled checks, appraisals.

Surviving an Audit When dealing with the IRS, remember that the auditor is neither questioning your integrity nor conducting an inquisition. The auditor

Exhibit 6-17 Average Itemized Deduction

Adjusted gross income	Type of deduction						
	Medical	Taxes paid	Contri-bution	Interest paid	Casualty loss	Child care	Miscella-neous
$ 5,000-$10,000	$552	$ 718	$305	$ 756	$648	$669	$204
10,000– 13,000	437	960	337	955	528	670	269
13,000– 15,000	418	1,164	391	1,083	535	710	294
15,000– 20,000	397	1,407	424	1,177	462	742	318
20,000– 25,000	396	1,781	553	1,338	520	685	384
25,000– 30,000	456	2,185	705	1,556	567	462	464

Source: Internal Revenue Service, *Statistics of Income—1972, Individual Income Tax Returns,* Washington, D.C., 1974.

is merely trying to determine whether additional taxes are due. Most auditors are easy to talk with: in fact, so easy that many people say far too much. The first rule is to discuss only the item being questioned. Do not volunteer information about other items on your return; it could encourage the auditor to extend the audit. By taking your supporting documents and your arguments justifying your position, you should be able to win your case. An audit is simply not the terrifying experience some people think it is. Just consider it as a way to liven up an otherwise dull Thursday afternoon.

SUMMARY

1   Taxpayers are entitled to use all legal means to reduce the taxes they must pay.
2   The rate structure for federal income taxes is progressive: the higher the income, the higher the tax rate.
3   The marginal tax rate is the tax rate on the last dollar of income that was earned.
4   Income taxes reduce the effective cost of a deductible expense: interest and finance charges, most taxes, donations, medical expenses, education expense, child care.
5   Ranked by decreasing size, the tax rates apply to: married couple filing separate returns, unmarried individual, head of household, and married couple filing a joint return.
6   The basic income tax structure is:

	Gross income
Less:	Adjustments to gross income
Equals:	Adjusted gross income
Less:	Deductions from adjusted gross
Less:	Exemptions
Equals:	Taxable income

7   The four frequently encountered adjustments to gross income are: sick-pay exclusion, moving expense, employee business expense, contributions to a qualified retirement plan.
8   A taxpayer has three options on deductions from adjusted gross income: standard deduction, low-income allowance, and itemized deductions.
9   Major categories of itemized deductions include: interest and finance charges, taxes, contributions, medical and dental expense, child and dependent care, education expense, job-search expense, casualty and theft loss.
10 To qualify as a dependent, five tests must be met: relationship test, support test, gross income test, residency test, joint return test.
11 Income averaging can substantially reduce the taxes for individuals with wide variations in income from year to year.
12 Individuals who receive substantial income that is not covered by withholding and those whose taxes withheld are significantly short of their tax liability must file an estimated tax declaration.
13 The penalty for filing late is 5 percent per month plus 7 percent annual interest.
14 The major sources of outside tax assistance are: IRS taxpayer service, commercial preparers, and tax practitioners.
15 Advanced planning, coupled with complete tax records and a good tax reference book, can substantially reduce the burden of tax preparation.
16 When the IRS audits an individual's tax return, the auditor generally concentrates on one or two items.

REVIEW YOUR UNDERSTANDING OF:

Progressive tax

Marginal tax rate

Married—joint return

Married—separate returns

Head of a household

Capital gain or loss, short-term

Capital gain or loss, long-term

Adjustments to gross income

Moving expense—deductible items

Employee business expense

Self-employed pension plan

Individual retirement account (IRA)

Deductions from adjusted gross income

Standard deduction

Low-income allowance

Itemized deductions

    Interest and finance charge

Taxes

Contributions

Medical and dental expense

Child and dependent care

Education expense

Job-search expense

Casualty and theft loss

Exemption

Tax table

Tax rate schedules X, Y, and Z

Income averaging

Withholding of tax

Estimated tax declaration

IRS taxpayer service

Commercial preparer

Tax practitioner

IRS audit

DISCUSSION QUESTIONS

1   Which of the following would be included in gross income: wages, proceeds from a life insurance policy, interest on United States savings bonds, a net long-term capital gain, interest on a municipal bond?

2   What are the major features that distinguish between adjustments to gross income and deductions from adjusted gross income? Why would an individual who claims a standard deduction want a particular item classified as an adjustment to gross income rather than as a deduction from adjusted gross income?

3   Wilma Smith is single and her taxable income is $17,000. What is the effective cost of the $950 of property tax on her house? What would her net cost be if she decided to donate $200 to her favorite charity?

4   Some people have suggested that a couple, because of certain tax laws, could actually save taxes if they had only joint residence rather than joint residence plus marriage. Can you list several examples of tax rules that support this position?

5   How would you react to the comment: "I cannot possibly earn that extra $500 because it would put me into the next tax bracket and my taxes would skyrocket"?

6   What are the specific requirements which would likely limit the number of individuals who could qualify as "head of a household"? What is the advantage to qualifying?

7   Fred and Becky Bear sold the following common stock during the year:

Corporation	QT, Inc.	Pioneer, Inc.	Imports Limited
Net purchase price	$1,200	$1,300	$ 950
Net sale price	$1,500	$ 700	$1,100
Holding period	7 months	5 months	3 years

a   What is their net short-term gain or loss? Long-term gain or loss?

b   How would they treat the amounts on their tax return?

c   If their marginal tax rate was 30 percent, how would their taxes be affected by these sales?

8 How does the low-income allowance differ from the standard deduction? When would it typically be used?

9 Do you agree with the comment: "The requirements for income averaging are such that most college graduates have difficulty qualifying"? Why?

10 What tests must be met to qualify moving expenses as a deductible item? What are the major types of expenses that can be included? Could most recently graduated college students qualify?

11 What are the key expense items that shift most taxpayers from claiming a standard deduction to itemizing their deductions? Why?

12 What tests must be met in order for a taxpayer to deduct education-related expenses?

13 Sharon Jones had the following medical expenses during the year: Health insurance premiums of $350, unreimbursed doctors' and dentists' bills of $400, and medicine charges of $125. Her adjusted gross income was $12,000 and she plans to itemize. What is her medical expense deduction?

14 What factor seriously limits the deductibility of child care expenses by middle-income couples where both people work full time?

15 Would the following individuals qualify as exemptions? Why?

   a The individual is the taxpayer's uncle; his gross income was $700; he is a United States citizen; the taxpayer paid $2,000 toward the uncle's total support of $3,500; the uncle is single.

   b The individual is a great-aunt; her gross income was $600; she lived the entire year in Canada; the taxpayer paid $1,000 toward her total support of $1,900; she is unmarried.

   c The individual is a brother; his gross income was $700; the taxpayer, together with four other brothers and sisters, paid $3,000 of the brother's total support of $4,000; the taxpayer paid $300; the brother is a United States citizen and is single; the other brothers and sisters agree the taxpayer should claim the deduction.

16 When the tax tables are used, do you have to make separate computations using a standard deduction and low-income allowance? Why?

17 What is the advantage to using income averaging? Why does it give lower taxes for qualifying taxpayers?

18 Under what circumstances might you want more tax withheld than necessary? When might you want to do the opposite?

19 Why is it better to file on time, even though you may not be able to pay your taxes, than to wait until you have the money to pay what you owe?

CASE PROBLEM

Herb and Grazelda Procrastinator are beginning their April 13 income tax marathon; it usually lasts well into April 14, if not April 15. They both work full time and have a young son. A perusal of their checkbook and scant records revealed the following for 1977:

Outflows

Purchase of new car	$4,000	Interest on home mortgage	$2,400
Medical expenses		Veterinary expenses for	
(unreimbursed)	$ 100	McKenzie, their dog	$ 100
Gasoline taxes	$ 75	Gifts for their parents	$ 300
Dental expenses	$ 100	Safe-deposit box rental	$ 10

Professional teaching dues for Grazelda	$ 150	Son's nursery school fee (monthly)	$ 200
Sales taxes	$ 360	Finance charges on various loans and	
Utility bills for the house	$ 450	credit cards	$ 400
Health insurance	$ 250	Medicine and drugs	$ 50
Contributions	$ 300	Tax reference book	$ 5
Property taxes	$1,050	Grocery bills	$2,300
Automobile insurance	$ 250		
Life insurance	$ 450		

In the past year the Procrastinators have taken a standard deduction on their joint return. Their combined adjusted gross income for 1977 will be $24,000.

1 On the basis of the information given, do you feel they should use a standard deduction on this year's return? Why? Should they use a joint return? Why?
2 If they itemized, what would their total deductions be? How does this compare with their other deduction options?
3 What would their taxable income be for the year? What would their total tax be?
4 Would you have any recommendations for Herb and Grazelda for next year's tax return? What advantages can they expect from your suggestions?
5 A review of Herb and Grazelda's combined taxable income for preceding years revealed: $13,000 for 1976, $11,500 for 1975, $10,000 for 1974, $8,000 for 1973, and $7,500 for 1972. Can they qualify for income averaging? Why?

RECOMMENDED READINGS

General Tax Reference Books

U.S. Treasury Department, Bureau of Internal Revenue, *Your Federal Income Tax—for Individuals*. Publication 17, Washington, D.C., published annually.
Your local IRS office will supply a copy at no charge. Reasonably thorough, but some parts are difficult to read. Several rereads will usually clarify the points. Given that it is free, it cannot be beaten.

J. K. Lasser's Your Income Tax. Simon & Schuster, New York, published yearly.
A very thorough treatment of the subject. Includes several sections with "tax-saving ideas." By mailing the request card, you receive an up-dated supplement together with a line-by-line example using the current year's tax forms. The example has excellent cross-indexing to the reference volume.

The Research Institute of America, Inc., *(Year) Individual Tax Return Guide*. Grosset & Dunlap, New York, published annually.
Not so complete as the two previous references, but easier to read. Has illustrations of complete tax returns using the appropriate forms for the year being covered.

Magazines

Money:

Leeds, Mark B., "How the IRS Looks at Your Tax Return." March 1973, pp. 33–36.
Discusses the selection criteria the IRS uses to pick returns for audit. Limited discussion of its techniques; some recommended strategies.

Randall, Robert M., "Eight Tax Saving Ways to Happier Returns." March 1974, pp. 32–35.
   Discusses eight frequently used techniques for reducing taxes.
"What IRS Auditors Will Overlook." April 1974, pp. 49–50.
   Reviews select parts of IRS audit handbook.
Comarow, Avery, "Your Tax Bracket's Hidden Heights." November 1974, pp. 90–92.
   Discusses state and local income taxes.
"Choosing The Right Help at That Taxing Time." February 1975, pp. 69–72.
   Discusses sources of outside tax assistance.
Snider, Don, "How To Survive A Tax Audit." February 1976, pp. 37–40.
   Outlines IRS audit procedure and gives suggestions for surviving an audit.

Changing Times:

"If Your Tax Return Is Audited." June 1973, pp. 21–23.
   Discusses timing and game plan for IRS audit. Reviews appeal process.
"Taxes: The Rules on Dependent-Care Costs." October 1973, pp. 16–17.
   Discusses its subject in some detail.
"Where to Get Help on Your Tax Return." February 1974, pp. 7–11.
   Discusses sources of assistance, mostly IRS taxpayer service. Reviews whether you need professional assistance.

Booklets

U.S. Treasury Department, Bureau of Internal Revenue, *Publication, Number, Title, Year, Edition (e.g., Publication 526, Income Tax Deductions for Contributions, 1976 Edition)*, Washington, D.C., published regularly.
   The IRS publishes a host of booklets that address specialized tax topics, including child care, contributions, casualty and theft losses, education expense, income averaging, medical expenses, moving expenses, sick pay, plus numerous others. Free copies of these booklets can be obtained from your local IRS office. All are very complete and most are reasonably easy to understand.

Chapter 7

Obtaining and Using Credit

After completing this chapter you should be able to:

explain the impact of varying a loan's finance charge and its maturity.

decide whether credit is appropriate in a particular circumstance.

develop debt limits based on disposable income and discretionary income.

estimate a loan's annual percentage rate (APR).

compute the finance charge refund when a loan is paid before maturity.

demonstrate how finance charges are computed on charge accounts and credit cards.

explain the impact of truth in lending legislation.

describe the criteria lenders use in deciding whether to grant credit.

develop a plan for obtaining credit for the first time.

identify the consumer's rights under the Fair Credit Reporting Act.

judge whether credit can be a hedge against inflation.

formulate a plan to correct a credit overextension.

Consumer credit has become so widespread and so generally available that nearly everyone uses it at some point. The extent of usage, however, varies widely among different people. Some restrict credit usage to periods when they need extra money for emergencies or unexpected expenses. Others use it for emergencies, but they also buy cars, appliances, furniture, and other major durable goods with credit. Still others use it not only for all the previous purposes, but they also use credit for many of their small day-to-day transactions. Regardless of usage, credit has become an integral part of nearly everyone's spending process.

Because of credit's importance, this chapter and the next discuss its various aspects in considerable detail. We think this discussion is essential for several reasons. First, you should know what credit sources are currently available. Second, you should have a basis for deciding whether credit is warranted in a given situation. Assuming you decide it is, you should be able to evaluate the merits and disadvantages of competing credit offers. Finally, like any service, credit can be overused. And while you are unlikely to do so, you should know what corrective actions are necessary should you be overusing your credit.

Our discussion centers on four principal credit categories: (1) consumer cash loans, (2) consumer sales loans, (3) open-ended consumer credit, and (4) education loans. (The discussion of mortgage loans is deferred until Chapter 12 because it is directly associated with the purchase of a housing unit.) Our emphasis in this chapter is on the general attributes of credit, and correcting a credit overextension. The next chapter builds on this base to explore each of the four credit categories. It examines the details for each one and reviews the available sources.

THE CONCEPT OF CREDIT

Whenever you use credit, whether it be a 12-month sales loan, a 30-day credit-card purchase, or a short 10-day cash advance on your checking account, you are temporarily borrowing money from some lender. By obtaining those monies now, you expand your current purchasing power. But that expansion is a temporary one because the money must be repaid in the future and that reduces purchasing power then. Your total purchasing power is not increased, only the timing is altered: if purchasing power in the current period is increased, purchasing power in future periods is reduced. In fact, in most cases, total purchasing power is actually reduced. Lenders not only expect to be repaid the money advanced; they also expect a finance charge during the period the money was borrowed. That fee is essentially similar to the fee for renting an automobile, the major difference being that it covers the rental of money rather than of an automobile. Because of the finance charge, the amount repaid exceeds the initial amount borrowed. Consequently, total purchasing power is actually decreased.

Finance Charge   The finance charge is an all-inclusive term that includes all costs associated with a particular credit transaction. When lenders quote their finance charge, it must include the interest charge and any other fee that is part of the credit transaction. For example, it would have to include the application fee, any processing fee, premiums on credit life insurance, or any other fee that is a required part of the credit offer.

Repayment Terms   There are really two separate, but related, provisions to a credit transaction's repayment terms. First, there is the total time between the point when the money is initially borrowed and the point when it is completely repaid: the maturity. With consumer credit, that maturity typically ranges from a few days to 5 years. Second, there is the timing and the size of the required repayments. They could be monthly, weekly, or annually; likewise, they may be equal in size or some combination of unequal amounts. Typically, most consumer cash and sales loans require equal monthly payments over the loan's maturity. Throughout the next two chapters we assume a loan requires equal monthly payments unless stated otherwise. With open-ended consumer credit, the user typically has considerable latitude on payment size and timing. Payments can range from a single lump-sum repayment to a small, lender-specified, minimum amount of regular payments. Likewise, the time can be as short as 30 days, or it can extend over several years.

Varying the Finance Charge or the Maturity

The total amount of the finance charge and the amount of the monthly payments are determined by the annual rate of the finance charge and the maturity. Using a $1,000 consumer cash loan that has equal monthly payments, we will illustrate the effect that a change in the finance rate or the maturity has on the total finance charge and monthly payments.

Finance Charge   Initially, we assume the $1,000 loan has a 24-month maturity. Exhibit 7–1 illustrates the results for six different finance rates between 9 and 30 percent. The vertical bars in Exhibit 7–1 show the total finance charge at each of the various rates. The required monthly payment for each rate is shown in brackets at the bottom of the exhibit.

As Exhibit 7–1 demonstrates, the monthly payment is not drastically increased by increases in the annual finance rate. But extended over 24 months, the small increase in monthly payments considerably increases the total amount of the finance charge. For example, the monthly payment on an 18 percent loan is only $2.85 larger ($49.92 − $47.07) than the payment for a 12

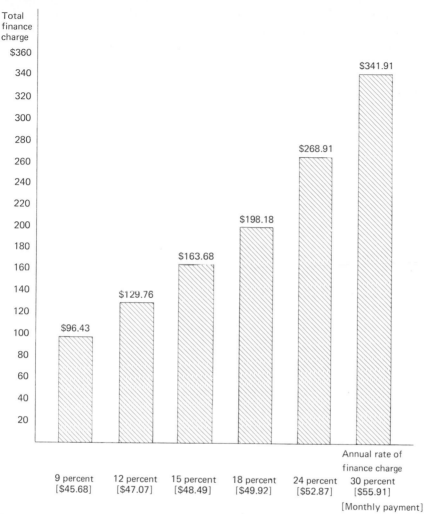

Exhibit 7-1 Total Finance Charge and Monthly Payment for a 24-Month $1,000 Loan

percent loan. Yet, extended over 24 months, the total amount of the finance charge for the 18 percent loan is more than 50 percent greater [($198.18 − $129.76) ÷ $129.76] than the amount of the 12 percent loan. The message from Exhibit 7–1 seems clear: a small change in the annual finance charge rate has a sizable effect on the total finance charge. Given that, a prospective borrower should carefully compare the annual rate on competing credit offers. The savings could be sizable.

Maturity Exhibit 7–2 illustrates the effect of different maturities on the monthly payment and total amount of the finance charge. We assume the $1,000 loan in Exhibit 7–2 has an 18 percent annual finance rate. Here, the vertical bars show the monthly payment while the total finance charge for each maturity is shown in brackets below the different maturities.

As Exhibit 7–2 illustrates, extending the maturity reduces the monthly payment; the reduction is especially pronounced in the shorter maturities. But the reduction does not represent a saving because the borrower's total finance charge rises rapidly as the maturity lengthens. For example, extending the maturity from 36 to 60 months reduces the monthly payment by $10.76 ($36.15 − $25.39), but it increases the total amount of the finance charge by $222.11 ($523.60 − $301.49). The extension has merely created the illusion of easing the payment. In reality, the burden has actually risen.

> **Strategy: If your only purpose in extending the maturity is to make the payments fit your budget, you probably should not be using that additional credit at all.**

USING CREDIT

There is no simple definitive answer to questions about when credit should be used or about how much credit is appropriate. Nor is there a standard rule for deciding those questions. In the end you must answer those questions for your own individual situation.

Credit: The Cost-Benefit Trade-Off

There are two cost elements that should be considered when making a credit decision. First, there is the direct cost of using credit: the finance charge. Because it reduces future purchasing power, your gain in current purchasing power is less than your sacrifice in future purchasing power. Second, there are the indirect costs of reduced flexibility and increased risk. Since most credit alternatives entail a fixed repayment schedule, the borrower might be unable to meet those payments. The consequences of that failure can be considerable:

JOHN, ITS TIME TO MAKE ANOTHER PAYMENT ON THE SKI EQUIPMENT... .JOHN?..

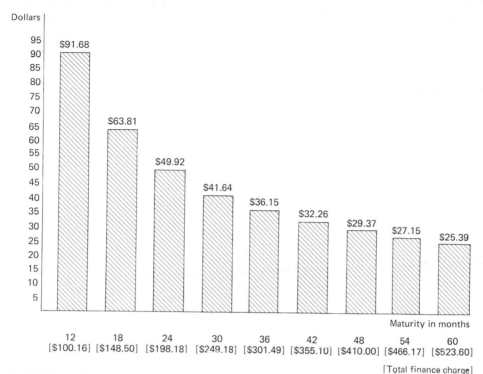

Exhibit 7-2 Monthly Payment and Total Finance Charge for a $1,000 Loan with 18 Percent Annual Charge

the lender's collection effort, garnishment of wages, repossession of goods. While it is difficult to place a cost on these possibilities, they must still be counted as a cost of using credit.

On the other hand, using credit can provide several benefits. First, by buying an item—car, appliance, furniture—on credit, the borrower receives the service from those items immediately. Second, by using credit, people can take advantage of a sale price on an item even if they do not have the money, providing the saving is greater than the total finance charge. Last, there are credit's convenience aspects: no large sums of money to carry, a single bill each month, and a record of purchases.

The decision to use credit essentially becomes one of deciding whether the benefits from today's increased purchasing power equals or exceeds the costs of reduced future purchasing power coupled with the decreased flexibility and increased risk that are part of every credit transaction.

Is Credit Justified?

The questions in Exhibit 7-3 provide a guide to help you decide whether a particular expenditure really qualifies as a proper use of credit. Although the questions seem rather basic, it is amazing how few people stop and ask: Is credit really justified in this circumstance? Many people seem so hypnotized by the lure of a "bargain" or the "easy" credit terms, they never ask whether they really need the item. Likewise, few people consider the alternatives to credit: delay the purchase, save the necessary money, decide not to purchase the item at all.

We are not suggesting credit be restricted only to major, long-lived, durable goods such as appliances, cars, or furniture. But when credit is used as a convenience, we believe the repayment period should be short. If you use credit for short-lived consumer goods, plan to repay the entire amount when billed. Extended repayment terms are rarely justified in this circumstance.

Obviously, if the item is essential to your daily living, then your choice is likely to be more limited. But that does not mean ignoring possible alternatives. Nor does it mean ignoring the item's useful life when setting the repayment period.

> **Strategy: If the majority of your responses in Exhibit 7–3 were yes, using credit is probably justified. On the other hand, if many questions drew a no, especially questions 2 or 3, further consideration is in order.**

Setting Debt Limits

Unfortunately, all too many people rely on the lender to set debt limits for them. If the lender is willing to extend additional credit, these people feel they are below their credit limits. True, most lenders are excellent judges of how much credit an individual can handle. But obtaining credit is so easy and so widespread that a lender may not be fully aware of how much credit a borrower currently has outstanding. Consequently, a person can become grossly overextended before a lender signals a halt. Even then, many people put off the inevitable by trying different lenders until they find one who will grant them

Exhibit 7-3   Guide to Deciding Whether Credit is Justified

	Yes	No
1 Do you really need the item?	( )	( )
2 Is the item a necessity that cannot be postponed?	( )	( )
3 Is purchasing on credit the only alternative?		
a Would it be impossible to draw down your savings instead of using credit?	( )	( )
b Is it impossible to defer the purchase and save the money?	( )	( )
4 When the credit has extended payment terms:		
a Is the item's useful working life reasonably long (3 to 5 years)?	( )	( )
b Does its life equal or exceed the loan's maturity?	( )	( )
c Is the item's price such that it cannot be fitted into the monthly budget?	( )	( )
5 When the credit has flexible repayment terms:		
a If the item is short-lived (food, entertainment, clothing), can you repay the entire amount when billed?	( )	( )
b If credit is used to meet a temporary cash shortage, can the amount be repaid when billed?	( )	( )

credit. At best, having the lender set your debt limits is imprecise, at worst it can be an invitation to disaster. In the end, you know your personal finances best, so you should set those limits.

Estimating Your Limits The questions in Exhibit 7–4 can provide a guide to whether you are nearing your debt limits. If nearly all responses are no, then you are probably within your debt limits. We think question 1 deserves special emphasis. If the new credit causes you constant worry or sleepless nights, they are a high price to pay. In general, if you can identify the source of the new payment and if it does not necessitate a major revamping of your present expenditure and saving plans, then you are probably within your limits.

Disposable Income A more direct test of your debt limit is to compare your monthly debt payments with your total monthly disposable income (gross income less withholdings). Your list of payments should include all consumer credit that has extended repayment terms: cash loans, sales loans, and open-ended credit. Do not include payments on credit cards, where you repay the entire balance each month. Also, do not include your home mortgage payment. Total disposable income should include income from all sources— wages, interest, dividends, etc.

To demonstrate the test, assume Gus and Dimitra Alevas are considering $2,500 of credit to purchase a boat. They want to know whether the amount will put them above their debt limit. Financed over 3 years, the monthly loan payment would be $83.04, if the $2,500 loan has a 12 percent annual finance charge. Their combined monthly income is $1,000 and their current debt payments are shown in Exhibit 7–5.

According to the guidelines at the bottom of Exhibit 7–5, the 17 percent debt percentage suggests that Gus and Dimitra are nearing their debt limit. Adding the new $83 loan payment would place them at 25 percent [($170 + $83) ÷ $1,000], which is above the general upper limit of 20 percent. Unless they are willing to make some major sacrifices in their present expenditures, they should avoid this new debt. Exhibit 7–5 is easily modified to fit any situation.

Exhibit 7-4 Checklist for Upper Debt Limit

	Yes	No
1 Will adding more debt make you feel uncomfortable?	( )	( )
2 Will you have difficulty fitting the new payment in your budget?	( )	( )
3 Will the new payment:		
a take money away from essential expenditures (food, clothing, housing, savings)?	( )	( )
b make it difficult to meet your current debt payments?	( )	( )
c reduce discretionary income (disposable income less essential expenditures) to a point where you must seriously restrict or alter your current spending pattern?	( )	( )
d reduce or eliminate your budgeted savings?	( )	( )
4 Will the added debt cause a serious imbalance (liabilities in excess of assets) in your personal balance sheet?	( )	( )

Exhibit 7-5 Estimating Debt Limits: Disposable Income

1 Monthly disposable income:*
 a Salaries $970
 b Interest and dividends   30
 c Total $1,000

2 Monthly debt payments:*
 a Automobile $110
 b Appliances   40
 c Cash loan   20
 d Total $ 170

3 Payments as a percentage of disposable income:
 line 2d ÷ line 1c ($170 ÷ $1,000) =   17 percent

General Debt Guidelines: Payments as a Percentage of Disposable Income

Percent	Current debt load	Additional credit usage
15 or less	Safely within limits	New credit could be undertaken.
15 to 20	Fully extended with present credit	Further use is possible, but care is required
20 to 30	Overextended on credit, corrective action recommended	Any further use is ill-advised
30 or more	Seriously overextended, drastic corrective action is imperative	Further use is out of the question

*All amounts rounded to nearest dollar.

The 20 percent mark is intended as a general guide, not an iron-clad rule. Some people spend 30 percent of their income on debt payments, yet they do so successfully. But recognize that such a commitment likely entails major reductions in other expenditures. This test's most serious shortcoming is that it makes no allowance for special situations. An individual with unusually high essential expenditures—medical expenses, child support, care of a dependent—would likely find 20 percent to be too high. On the other hand, where both husband and wife work full time, 20 percent might be too low.

Strategy: As a general guide, your monthly debt payments should not exceed 20 percent of your disposable income. Should you decide to push beyond 20 percent, you may have to make major reductions in some other monthly expenditures.

Discretionary Income   The objective of the discretionary income test is to compute how much of an individual's monthly income is available for debt payments. As the first step, essential expenditures are deducted from disposable income to give discretionary income. Next, discretionary expenditures are ranked with the highest priority items heading the list. One at a time, the discretionary expenditures are subtracted, in the order ranked, from discretionary income. Based on the outcome, the individual should be able to decide whether there is sufficient income remaining to carry some new debt payments.

To illustrate the computation, we continue our previous example of Gus and Dimitra Alevas. Their combined disposable income ($1,000 monthly) and current debt payments ($170) are unchanged. Likewise, they are still considering a $2,500 loan that requires $83.04 monthly payments. The top half of Exhibit 7–6 illustrates the computation of their discretionary income: $390. The bottom half of Exhibit 7–6 shows their discretionary expenditures in descending order of importance. As might be expected, repayment of present debts, savings, insurance premiums, and recreational expenses rank high on that list. The order of the ranking could vary, however, depending on an individual's preference.

According to Exhibit 7–6, Gus and Dimitra have approximately $30 that could be used for new debt. But this is far short of the $83.04 they need for the payments on the boat loan. Unless they can, and are willing to, reduce their other discretionary expenses by $50, they should not add the new debt.

The major advantage of the discretionary income test is that it forces you to identify where the new payment is to come from. Furthermore, the test is tailored to your specific income and expenditure pattern. For these reasons, it provides a more precise answer to the question: How much additional debt can your income support?

One final point: To be meaningful, your monthly expenditure estimates should be as accurate as possible, especially in the discretionary category

Exhibit 7-6 Estimating a Debt Limit: Discretionary Income

1	Monthly disposable income		
	a Salaries	$970	
	b Interest and dividends	30	$1,000
2	Less essential expenditures:		
	a Food	$250	
	b Housing*	240	
	c Transportation†	30	
	d Clothing	90	$ 610
3	Discretionary income (line 1 − line 2)		$ 390
4	Less discretionary expenditures:		
	a Present debts—automobile†	$110	
	—appliance	40	
	—cash loan	20	
	b Savings	85	
	c Insurance	40	
	d Entertainment and recreation	35	
	e Gifts and donations	30	$ 360
5	Available discretionary income (line 3 − line 4)		$ 30

*Includes utilities

†Transportation expenses are split between the loan payment at line 4a and other operating expenses at line 2c.

where many people tend to underestimate their expenditures. Likewise, be realistic when you estimate the amount you can trim from discretionary expenditures. Too often, people think these expenditures can be drastically reduced without fully appreciating the sacrifice such cutting entails.

Strategy: Before undertaking any new debt, estimate your discretionary income to see whether you have the money for the new payments.

Extended Repayment Periods   An earlier section demonstrated that an extension in the maturity can sharply reduce the required monthly payments. An immediate question is: Does that payment reduction expand your debt capacity? Certainly lower monthly payments would make both the previous debt tests appear more favorable. With lower monthly payments, debt payments as a percent of disposable income would decrease (disposable income test). And you would appear to have more discretionary income available (discretionary income test). But has debt capacity really expanded? In nearly all cases, we would say no. Extending the maturity reduces the payments, but it also prolongs them for several more years. About the only time an extension truly expands debt capacity is where the original repayment terms were abnormally short: for example, a car loan with a 6-month maturity. Under those circumstances, an extension to 24 months would generally be justified.

Strategy: Except for special circumstances, extending the maturity does not raise your effective debt capacity. If you must extend maturities to stay within your debt limits, then you are probably overextended on credit.

COST OF CREDIT

Most lenders must quote their finance charges in dollars as well as an annual percentage rate. And that finance charge must include any and all costs associated with the credit transaction.

Annual Percentage Rate (APR)   The annual percentage rate (APR) that a lender quotes expresses the annual finance charge associated with a credit transaction as a percentage of the amount borrowed. Thus, a $1,000 loan that had an APR of 12 percent would have a $120 ($1,000 × 12 percent) finance charge for one year if the loan was repaid in a lump sum at the end of the year.

The principal advantage to APR is that it is a relative-cost measure. That is, it gives the annual cost of credit as a percentage of the amount borrowed. Because it is a relative-cost measure, the APR on two competing credit offers can be compared directly to decide which is cheaper. And this holds regardless of whether the offers are identical in all respects or different in some respects. For example, we can compare a $500, 21-month loan with an APR of 14 percent to a $600, 24-month loan with an APR of 12 percent. Despite the fact that the loans are for different amounts and have different maturities, we would conclude that the first loan, because its APR is 14 percent versus an APR of 12 percent for the second loan, costs more per dollar borrowed.

Comparative Shopping

Too often, people accept the first credit offer they receive. They never check to see if the same amount is available from other lenders at a lower APR. Few people buy a car from the first dealer who quoted a price, yet they seem reluctant to shop for the lowest APR. When you borrow money, the lender is performing a service and you pay a finance charge for that service. So why not shop for the lowest cost? Assuming you have a good credit rating and are within your debt limits, you should be able to obtain quotes from a number of potential lenders. Probably some will quote a lower cost than others.

Exhibit 7–7 shows the range of APRs that are typically available from different lenders. Not only are there large differences in APRs among lenders, but there is also a considerable spread within each lender group as well. The intent of Exhibit 7–7 is not to single out any particular lender group as the cheapest. Rather, it shows that comparative shopping can provide sizable savings. For example, switching a $3,000 loan from an auto dealer who quoted an APR of 25 to a credit union with an APR of 12 would save $453 ($843 − $390) in finance charges. While some lenders—credit unions, savings and loans, and life insurance companies—restrict their lending to certain eligible borrowers, most people can qualify for several of the lenders shown in Exhibit 7–7.

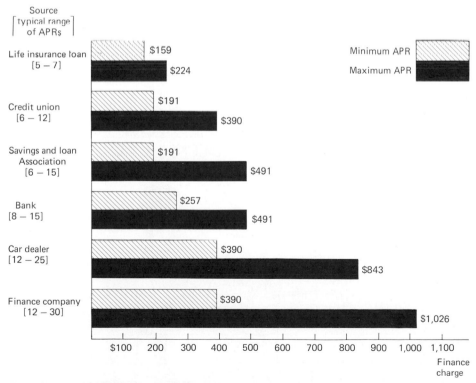

Exhibit 7-7   Finance Charges: $3,000, 24-Month Sales Loan

When comparing credit offers, make certain the lender is quoting you the APR. Some lenders will not quote their APR unless pushed, despite the fact they are required to do so. And some lenders may even quote the old-fashioned discount percentage—it is generally about one-half the APR—to make their rate look like a bargain. If you encounter a lender who is reluctant to disclose his or her rate, or if that rate seems too good to be true, insist on being quoted the true APR.

Strategy: Before deciding on a particular lender, check the rates of other lenders in your area. Compare the APR on competing credit offers to find the lowest cost.

Bargaining with the Lender Few people consider the possibility of bargaining with the lender for a lower APR. Yet the heavy competition in the personal consumer-credit market has made this a useful technique. Some lenders may be surprised when you ask them if they are quoting you the best APR they can offer. Go ahead and surprise them with the question. It could mean a lower rate. If another lender has quoted a better rate, you might mention that in the negotiations. But be honest when quoting a competitor's rate. Lenders know what their competitors are doing.

Finance Charge: Cash and Sales Loans

The requirement that finance charges be quoted as an annual percentage rate has removed much of the confusion that previously existed in this area. The confusion arose because most cash and sales loans require equal monthly repayments throughout the loan's maturity. That meant that if you borrowed $1,200 for 12 months, you repaid part of the loan each month, and therefore you

did not have use of the $1,200 for the entire year. In fact, the amount actually borrowed for the entire year was nearer $600. But lenders quoted finance charge rates based on the $1,200 figure, thereby understating the true cost. The APR has corrected this because it is based on the effective amount borrowed rather than the beginning loan balance.

Estimating the APR   Although computing a loan's exact APR is rather involved, you can make a reasonable approximation using this formula:

$$APR = \frac{200 \times F \times n}{L \times t}$$

where F = total dollar finance charge
n = number of payments each year
L = amount borrowed
t = total number of payments plus one

Assume we wanted to estimate the APR on a $1,200, 12-month loan with finance charges of $60. Using the above formula, the APR would be:

$$APR = \frac{200 \times \$60 \times 12}{\$1200 \times 13} = \frac{144,000}{15,600} = 9.23 \text{ percent}$$

The 9.23 percent estimate is reasonably close to the loan's actual APR of 9.11 percent. Do you need more practice? Turn back to Exhibit 7–1 and estimate the APRs for the loans in that exhibit. Your estimate should be reasonably close to the percentage shown on the horizontal axis.

Computing the Finance Charge   Lenders compute the finance charge on a sale or cash loan using one of three techniques. The computational methods vary partly because of lender choice and partly because some states restrict the method a lender can use. To illustrate the different methods, we use a $1,200 loan which is repaid in 12 equal monthly payments.

Add-on   Under the add-on technique, the finance charge is added to the amount borrowed to give the balance that is to be repaid. If the finance charge on the above loan were $60, the balance to be repaid would be $1,260 ($1,200 + $60). That would necessitate monthly payments of $105 ($1,260 ÷ 12). Because the finance charge is added to the balance, the borrower receives the full $1,200 when taking out the loan.

Discount   With the discount method, the lender deducts the finance charge from the amount borrowed. Consequently, the borrower receives only the difference. Continuing our example, the lender would deduct the $60 finance charge, leaving the borrower $1,140 ($1,200 − $60). Since the borrower is paying $60 to borrow $1,140 rather than $1,200, the effective cost of borrowing is higher under this method. The APR on the discount loan is 9.58

percent compared with 9.11 percent for the previous add-on loan. The borrower who wanted $1,200 would have to borrow approximately $1,263.

Simple Interest   With simple interest, the finance charge is based on the exact amount borrowed over the number of days the amount is outstanding. In the simplest case, assume $1,200 was borrowed at 10 percent annual interest, the entire amount plus the finance charge, $120 ($1,200 × 10 percent), to be paid back in one payment exactly one year after the date of the loan. But that is not the usual case. What generally happens is that the loan is repaid in monthly payments. Exhibit 7–8 illustrates the repayment schedule and finance charges for a simple interest loan of $600 with a 10 percent annual finance charge (APR of 10), to be repaid in six monthly payments of approximately $103.

The finance charge for the first payment is based on the entire $600 outstanding for a period of 25 days (June 15 to July 10). The balance outstanding during the second month is $501.11 ($600 + $4.11 − $103.00). Therefore the finance charge is based on $501.11 outstanding for a period of 31 days (July 10 to August 10). The finance charge for the remaining months was computed in a similar manner.

Exhibit 7-8   Finance Charge Using Simple Interest

Payment number	Date	Outstanding Balance for the period*	Finance charge for the period†,‡	Payment	Remaining balance §
1	July 10	$600.00	$4.11	$103.00	$501.11
2	Aug. 10	501.11	4.26	103.00	402.37
3	Sept. 20	402.37	4.41	103.00	303.78
4	Oct. 15	303.78	2.08	103.00	202.86
5	Nov. 15	202.86	1.72	103.00	101.58
6	Dec. 15	101.58	0.83	102.41¶	0

*Computation for a $600 loan with annual finance charge of 10 percent. Obtained on June 15 and repaid in 6 monthly payments.

†Some financial institutions would assume 360 days in the year to simplify computations.

‡Computed as follows:

Payment 1: Finance charge = $600 × 10 percent × $\dfrac{25 \text{ days}}{365 \text{ days}}$ = $4.11

Payment 2: Finance charge = $501.11 × 10 percent × $\dfrac{31 \text{ days}}{365 \text{ days}}$ = $4.26

Payment 3: Finance charge = $402.37 × 10 percent × $\dfrac{40 \text{ days}}{365 \text{ days}}$ = $4.41

Payment 4: Finance charge = $303.78 × 10 percent × $\dfrac{25 \text{ days}}{365 \text{ days}}$ = $2.08

The finance charge on the remaining payments would be computed in a similar manner.

§Computed as follows:

Payment 1: Remaining balance = ($600 + $4.11) − $103 = $501.11
Payment 2: Remaining balance = ($501.11 + $4.26) − $103 = $402.37
Payment 3: Remaining balance = ($402.37 + $4.41) − $103 = $303.78
Payment 4: Remaining balance = ($303.78 + $2.08) − $103 = $202.86
The computations for payments 5 and 6 would be similar.

¶ The final payment was determined by the outstanding balance remaining on the loan plus the finance charge for the final period.

The simple interest technique can provide several advantages. First, if a payment is made a few days early, the borrower receives credit because there is no finance charge for those days. Typically, a borrower receives no credit when a payment is made several days early with either an add-on or a discount loan. Of course, if the payment is several days late, the borrower pays interest for those days. But that is generally much less than the sizable late fee many add-on or discount loans assess for a late payment. In short, a borrower generally benefits with a simple interest loan. A word of caution. Check the lender's procedures for early and late payments; a few have instituted penalties and restrictions that effectively cancel the above benefits.

> **Strategy: Provided a simple interest loan's APR is competitive with other sources, it offers certain advantages over an add-on or a discount loan. But be sure you check the lender's provisions covering early and late payments.**

Rebate of the Finance Charge   When an add-on or a discount loan is repaid before maturity, for example, when a 12-month loan is repaid in 6 months, a portion of the finance charge is refunded. Most lenders compute the refund using the so-called "rule of 78" or some variant thereof. The 78 is computed as follows: (1) the months are numbered consecutively: the first month = 12, the second month = 11, the third = 10, etc.; (2) these numbers are added: for one year, the sum is 78 (12 + 11 + 10 + . . . + 1 = 78). The second step is to compute the sum of the months the loan has been outstanding. A loan outstanding for 2 months would equal 23 (12 + 11). This sum, taken as a percentage of 78, represents the finance charge on the loan; the balance of the finance charge would be refunded.

To illustrate, assume a $1,200, 12-month loan was repaid at the end of 6 months. Exhibit 7–9 illustrates what portion of the $60 finance charge would be refunded.

While the refund rule is reasonably equitable, the borrower is generally assessed a penalty for prepaying the loan. One way to avoid the repayment hassle is to match a loan's maturity to your anticipated repayment schedule. If

Exhibit 7-9   Refund of the Finance Charge

1 Sum of the months to the loan's final maturity: 12 + 11 + 10 + 9 + 8 + 7 + 6 + 5 + 4 + 3 + 2 + 1 =	78
2 Sum of the months the loan has been outstanding: 12 + 11 + 10 + 9 + 8 + 7 =	57
3 Percentage of the finance charge applicable to the time the loan has been outstanding: line 2 ÷ line 1	73%
4 Total finance charge	$60
5 Finance charge to date: $60 × 73 percent	$43.80
6 Finance charge refund: line 4 − line 5	$16.20

you plan to make larger payments, select a shorter maturity. Another way to avoid the refund issue is to select a simple interest loan, since most loans of this type permit prepayment with no penalty.

Estimating Monthly Payments   Exhibit 7–10 shows the approximate monthly payment required on a $1,000 loan at different maturities and APRs. Since they have been rounded to the nearest penny, they are not exact, but they are accurate enough for our purposes.

By using the appropriate maturity and APR, Exhibit 7–10 can be used to estimate the monthly payment on most loans. For example, assume we want to know the monthly payment for a 24-month, $2,000 loan that has an APR of 12 percent. Since the amounts shown in Exhibit 7–10 are for a $1,000 loan, the payment on the above loan would be $94.14 ($47.07 × [$2,000 ÷ $1,000]). Do you need more practice? Compute the payment on a $3,600, 18-month, 10 percent loan. (*Hint:* it should be $216.22.)

Exhibit 7–10 can also be used to estimate the total finance charge for a given loan. Previously, we determined that a $2,000, 24-month loan with an APR of 12 percent would have monthly payments of $94.14. Over its 24 months, the loan's total payments would be $2,259.36 ($94.14 × 24 months). Since $2,000 of that represents repayment of the initial loan, the difference, $259.36 ($2,259.36 − $2,000), is the finance charge. Do you need more practice? Work through the previous $3,600 loan; its finance charge is $291.96.

Finance Charge: Credit Card Accounts

This section examines the computation of finance charges on the credit card accounts offered by nationwide retailers, large department stores, oil companies, and bank-affiliated cards. Part of the complication in computing the finance charge arises because there is no single transaction date. That is, the credit card holder can use the card a number of times during any given month. The computation is further complicated because the holder typically has the option of repaying the entire balance, or only a part of the balance.

Billing Cycle   Before we illustrate the actual computation, we need to review the monthly billing cycle on which most credit card companies base

Exhibit 7-10   Required Monthly Payment on a $1,000 Cash Loan

Maturity in months	Annual percentage rate						
	9	10	11	12	15	18	24
12	$87.45	$87.92	$88.38	$88.85	$90.26	$91.68	$94.56
18	59.60	60.06	60.52	60.98	62.38	63.81	66.70
24	45.68	46.15	46.61	47.07	48.49	49.92	52.87
30	37.35	37.81	38.28	38.75	40.18	41.64	44.65
36	31.80	32.27	32.74	33.21	34.67	36.15	39.23
48	24.88	25.36	25.85	26.33	27.83	29.37	32.60
60	20.76	21.25	21.74	22.24	23.79	25.39	28.77

Note: Payments rounded to nearest penny.

their finance charge. There are two key dates in that cycle: (1) the billing or closing date, and (2) the due date. The sample monthly billing statement shown in Exhibit 7–11 contains the essential information needed to demonstrate the billing cycle.

Billing or Closing Date The billing or closing date is the last day that transactions (either credit purchases or payments) have been posted to the account. In Exhibit 7–11 this date is shown at point [A], 9-2-76. The September statement shown in Exhibit 7–11 includes all transactions posted to the account between August 3 and September 2. A purchase made on September 3 would appear on the October statement.

Whatever the billing date, it remains unchanged each month.

Due Date The due date typically falls 25 days after the billing date. In Exhibit 7–11, this date is shown at point [B], 9-27-76. The payment is due on or

Exhibit 7-11 Monthly Billing Statement

MONTHLY STATEMENT

Ralph Smith
456 Dead End St.
Nowhere

Account Number
123-4567-890

Date	Reference Number	Description	Amount	
8-23 76	305F-402319	Ajax Lumber Co.	100	00

Previous Balance	New Purchases	Finance Charge	Payments	New Balance	Past Due Balance	Minimum Payment
0	100.00	0	0	100.00	0	10.00

Annual Percentage Rate	Billing Date [A]	Payment Due Date [B]	Card Limit
18 percent	9-2-76	9-27-76	$500

before this date. In reality you usually can pay several days after that date and still be on time. Most credit card companies allow 4 to 5 days after the due date to process the customers' payments.

Grace Period   For regular purchases made during the current billing period, most credit card accounts consider the 25-day period between the billing and due dates as a grace period. If the card holder has no unpaid balance from the previous statement, has made credit purchases that were billed on the current statement, and, further, has paid the entire balance of the current statement by the due date, no finance charge is assessed. The card holder has effectively used credit during that period at no charge. We emphasize that the grace period applies only to regular purchases billed on the current statement. If the card holder had an unpaid balance from the previous month's statement, there would be a finance charge on this previous balance even if the entire balance was paid by the due date. The grace period for Exhibit 7–11 extends from September 2 through September 27. In Exhibit 7–11, Ralph's previous balance is zero. To avoid the finance charge on the credit purchase he made during the current period ($100 purchase on 8-23-76), he would have to pay the entire current balance of $100 by September 27. If Ralph Smith had had a $200 previous balance, he would have been assessed a finance charge on that $200 even if he paid the entire balance by September 27.

By concentrating purchases immediately after the billing date, the card holder can extend the effective grace period beyond 25 days. To demonstrate, assume Ralph Smith, in Exhibit 7–11, made a $400 purchase on September 3. Since his billing date is September 2, this item would not be billed until the October statement. Because that statement's due date is October 27, his effective grace period is 54 days: September 3 to October 27. That provides $400 of credit for 54 days with no finance charge.

Strategy: Concentrate your purchases immediately after your billing date to maximize your effective grace period.

Computing the Finance Charge   Most credit card accounts compute their finance charge using some variation of three techniques: previous balance, average daily balance, and adjusted balance. Their similarities and differences can best be illustrated by continuing the example from Exhibit 7–11. We assume Ralph Smith made a single $50 payment on September 17, leaving a $50 unpaid balance. Exhibit 7–12 summarizes the computations for the three basic techniques.

Previous Balance   The previous balance method gives no credit for partial payments. Unless the entire balance is paid by the due date, a finance charge is assessed against the unpaid balance as of September 2 (the unpaid balance includes the previous balance, plus all new purchases, less all payments), even though part of the balance was paid during the current period. In effect, this

Exhibit 7-12   Computation of Finance Charge: Previous Balance, Average Daily Balance, and Adjusted Balance

	Previous balance	Average daily balance	Adjusted balance
Closing balance, September 2	$100	$100	$100
Payments, September 17	50	50	50
Ending balance	50	50	50
Balance finance charge is based on	100*	75†	50‡
Finance charge for September (1½% per month)	1.50	1.13	.75
Credit for partial payment	None	Partial	Complete

*Represents unpaid balance on Sept. 2, 1976.

†Represents average daily balance during the period:

$$15 \text{ days } (9\text{-}3 \text{ to } 9\text{-}17) @ \$100 = \$1,500$$
$$15 \text{ days } (9\text{-}18 \text{ to } 10\text{-}2) @ \$ 50 = \underline{\ \ \ 750}$$
$$\text{Total} \qquad \$2,250$$

Average daily balance = $2,250 ÷ 30 days = $75

‡Represents unpaid balance on Oct. 2, 1976.

method ignores the fact that the unpaid balance was only $50 after September 17.

In most cases, previous balance has the highest finance charge of the three methods. Unfortunately, nearly one-half of all credit card accounts use this method. Its usage is declining, however, because it has been restricted or outlawed in many states.

Average Daily Balance   With average daily balance, the finance charge is based on the average outstanding balance during the period. This average is computed by taking the balance each day during the regular billing cycle. Since payments during the period reduce the unpaid balance, the finance charge under this method is less costly than the finance charge under the previous balance method. This method is the second most frequently used on credit card accounts.

Adjusted Balance   With adjusted balance, the finance charge is based on the unpaid balance at the end of the billing cycle. Because it provides full credit for all payments during the period, it generally has the lowest finance charge. Unfortunately, it is also the least used of the three.

Minimizing Finance Charges   Several things can be done to minimize the finance charge. First, you should concentrate on credit cards having the adjusted balance method. Second, you should always pay within the grace period. Third, make certain that your payment arrives in time. While most creditors allow several days past the due date, you are risking a finance charge. And paying an extra 1½ percent seems a high price for being 1 or 2 days late.

Strategy: When possible, pay the entire balance within the grace period and avoid the finance charge. If you are one or two days late, call the store and explain your oversight. It does not always work, but the store often will cancel the finance charges when you are that close.

SAVING: AN ALTERNATIVE TO CREDIT

Actually, the best way to minimize your finance charge is to reduce it to zero by not purchasing on extended credit terms. Rather than use credit, you can delay the purchase until you have saved the money to buy the item. This assumes there is no emergency or pressing need which necessitates your having the item immediately.

Cost Differential: Savings versus Credit The cost difference between saving for an item and purchasing it on credit is best illustrated with an example. Assume Fred and Becky Bear are considering buying new furniture costing $1,000. One option is to use credit and repay the $1,000 in 12 monthly payments. The lender has quoted an APR of 18 percent, so the total finance charge is approximately $100.16 (computed using Exhibit 7–10). Alternatively, they could wait 12 months until they have saved the required $1,000. We assume the savings account pays 5 percent interest. Exhibit 7–13 illustrates how to calculate the cost difference between saving and buying on credit.

The $1,100.16 cost of the credit alternative, shown in the top half of Exhibit 7–13, includes repayment of the loan and its associated finance charge. The computations for the savings alternative, while not difficult, are more involved. Because the account earns interest during the year the money is being saved, the full $1,000 does not have to be deposited in the account. By computing the interest earned on the account's average balance, we have a rough estimate of the interest. We know the account started at zero but had a $1,000 ending balance, so the average balance was near $500. At 5 percent, that $500 balance would provide $25 in interest ($500 × 5 percent). Given $25 interest, the required deposits would be $975 ($1,000 − $25). That estimate, while not exact, is reasonably close to the actual interest of $26.80.

Although finance charges are deductible on income taxes and earned interest is taxable, we will ignore these effects for the moment to keep this example simple. Therefore, it would cost the Bears $126.96 more to buy the furniture on credit ($1,100.16) rather than save ($973.20) for it ($1,100.16 − $973.20 = $126.96).

Impact of Income Tax Now we will consider the effect of taxes on this example. If Fred and Becky itemize deductions on their federal tax return rather than take a standard deduction, their cost difference should consider the tax effect. The bottom half of Exhibit 7–13 assumes their marginal tax rate is 30 percent. Since finance charges are included in itemized deductions, their taxable income is reduced $100.16. Since this reduction lowers the Bears' income taxes by $30.05 ($100.16 × 30 percent), the net cost of borrowing is $70.11 ($100.16 − $30.05).

Exhibit 7-13 Cost Differential: Savings versus Credit

	Alternative	
Cost elements	Credit	Savings
Loan repayments: loan + finance charge	$1,100.16	
Required account balance		$1,000.00
Less interest earned		−26.80
Total cost	$1,100.16	$ 973.20
Reduction in taxes due to finance charge		
$100.16 × 30 percent	30.05	
Added savings deposit needed to offset tax on interest		
$26.80 × 30 percent		+8.04
Net cost	$1,070.11	$ 981.24

Income taxes have the opposite effect on the savings alternative. Part of the benefit from saving is lost to taxes because interest is taxable. Since $8.04 ($26.80 × 30 percent) of the interest is lost to taxes, the deposits to the savings account must be increased by $8.04. While the comparison still favors savings over credit, the cost differential is narrowed to $88.87 ($1,070.11 − $981.24).

Estimating the Cost Differential Exhibit 7–13 can readily be modified to fit your specific situation. The interest that can be earned on the savings option is estimated along the lines outlined in the preceding section. Likewise, the total payment and the total finance charge for the credit option can be estimated using the payment details shown in Exhibit 7–10. The bottom half of Exhibit 7–13 can be completed using your marginal tax rate. But remember, the reduction in taxes due to the finance charge is available only if you itemize deductions.

Strategy: If you have some flexibility, consider savings as an alternative to using credit. Granted, you do not have immediate use of the item, but the savings can be considerable.

TRUTH IN LENDING

Prior to the passage of truth in lending legislation as part of the Consumer Credit Protection Act of 1968, potential borrowers generally lacked sufficient information to enable them to directly compare and evaluate competing credit offers. The information they did receive was generally fragmented and lacked uniformity. But the passage of truth in lending legislation has greatly improved this situation.

Coverage The act covers all credit transactions of $25,000 (or less) that are extended for personal, household, or agricultural purposes. Further, all noncommercial real estate transactions are covered, regardless of amount. The legislation covers any individuals or organizations that regularly extend credit: bank, credit union, savings and loan association, retail and service charge accounts, credit card issuers, doctors, and dentists.

Disclosures The act requires lenders to disclose specific information about their loans. The principal disclosures are outlined in Exhibit 7–14. Typically, these disclosures are contained in the credit agreement you sign. That makes it imperative that you read and understand the information contained in the agreement. If you have a question, ask the lender for an explanation before you sign.

Cancellation Privilege In addition, if the loan entails a lien on the borrower's house (except first mortgages), the borrower has 3 business days in which to cancel the loan at no cost. For example, assume Franz Overmeyer signed a home improvement contract on Monday to have the basement of his house remodeled. Part of that contract was an improvement loan that entailed a lien on his house. Franz would have to be informed that he had a 3-day cancellation period. If he changed his mind about the remodeling on Wednesday, he could cancel the loan transaction at no cost.

Strategy: When comparing competing credit alternatives, obtain complete information on every offer before you make that final choice. If you are unclear as to the meaning or the intent of a lender's disclosure, ask for an explanation. The disclosures required under the Consumer Credit Protection Act are only as good as your knowledge of what they mean and how they can be used.

Exhibit 7-14   Required Disclosures: Truth in Lending

Required disclosure	Type of credit		
	Home mortgage*	Cash and sales loans	Charge accounts and credit cards
Cost of credit			
Annual percentage rate (APR)	Yes	Yes	Yes
Total dollars of finance charge		Yes	Yes
Method of computing finance charge			Yes
Description of grace period			Yes
Payments			
Number of payments	Yes	Yes	Yes
Amount of each payment	Yes	Yes	
Due date of payments	Yes	Yes	Yes
Total amount of payments		Yes	
Minimum payment			Yes
Details of balloon payments†	Yes	Yes	
Penalties			
Fee for late payment	Yes	Yes	
Fee for prepaying before maturity	Yes	Yes	
Security			
Description of borrower's property held as security	Yes	Yes	Yes

*Applies to first mortgages. See Chapter 12 on homeownership for further discussion.
†Defined as any payment that is more than twice the size of the regular payment.

QUALIFYING FOR CREDIT

Lenders use two broad criteria to decide whether credit should be extended: the borrower's ability to repay, and the borrower's willingness to repay.

Ability to Repay   In considering ability to repay, the lender compares the borrower's current debt obligations with the individual's financial resources to decide whether the credit can be repaid. The top half of Exhibit 7–15 illustrates some typical questions used in this evaluation.

Willingness to Repay   Merely having the ability to repay does not necessarily mean the credit will be repaid. Consequently, lenders review a borrower's payment record to see if previous obligations were paid on time. The bottom half of Exhibit 7–15 illustrates some typical questions used in that review.

Applying for Credit

The best response to a lender's questions, such as those in Exhibit 7–15, is a candid, complete answer. The lender will not be impressed by later finding that you altered or omitted some important information. If you feel a question is too personal or not relevant, tell the lender. When discussing your credit application, emphasize your strengths and be positive about your ability to handle the new credit. After all, if you do not believe you deserve the credit, the lender is not likely to believe you do either. Before you apply for any form of credit, do your homework by answering the questions in Exhibit 7–15. In addition, decide in advance the amount, the maturity, and the reason you need the credit.

Exhibit 7-15   Evaluation of Credit-Ability

Ability to repay
1 Current income
   a Regular income?   c Length of present employment?
   b Outside income?   d Previous employment record?

2 Current obligations
   a Present debts?   c Unusually high expenses?
   b Number of dependents?   d Other fixed expenses?

3 Financial resources
   a Savings account?   c Stocks or bonds?
   b Regular deposits in that account?   d Homeownership?
                                          e Property other than a home?

Willingness to repay
1 Current and previous credit transactions
   a Were previous credit obligations repaid?   c Amount of prior credit experience?
   b If paid late, was it justified?   d Prior lenders' opinion of borrower?

2 Payment record on recurring monthly expenses
   a Payment record on rent, utilities, telephone, etc.?
   b If there were delays, were they reasonable and justified?

Your Application Is Turned Down   If your credit request is denied, ask why it was refused. Many lenders will discuss your application and point out why they denied your request. If the denial was based on a report from a credit bureau, you must be told the source.

Using the information the creditor has provided, reevaluate your situation. Ask yourself: Is the weakness in my application, or was the refusal unwarranted? If there is a weakness or shortcoming, how can I correct it? Will the situation be improved by waiting several months? Depending on your answers, you have several options. The first is to try a different creditor. One lender's refusal should not discourage you from trying a different source. Second, if your record has a serious weakness that should be corrected, correct it. You can then reapply for credit.

The First-Time Credit Request   Obtaining credit for the first time can be difficult and the possibility of being refused is fairly high. Much of the difficulty stems from the new borrower's lack of a previous payment record. Developing that record entails a search for a lender who is willing to take the first step. Once the first transaction is made, subsequent credit transactions are typically much easier.

There are several types of credit that you may want to consider if you are a first-time borrower. Often, one of these sources will extend credit when other sources would likely refuse you.

Secured Savings Account Loan   With a secured savings account loan, your savings account is pledged as security. Most savings institutions—banks, mutual savings banks, credit unions, and some savings and loan associations—will make this loan. Your savings account continues to earn interest, which offsets a portion of the loan's finance charge.

Loan with a Cosigner Often a lender will grant a loan if you have a cosigner. The cosigner promises to repay the loan if you fail to do so. Obviously, the stronger the cosigner's credit record, the more willing a lender will be to extend credit.

Charge Account Many department stores will open a charge account even though the individual's credit record is limited. Another alternative is a credit card from a large national retail chain; many are willing to accommodate a first-time credit applicant. By using the retail credit route, you can generally avoid a finance charge if you pay within the store's grace period.

CONSUMER CREDIT FILES

Every individual who has used, or applied for, credit probably has a personal data file at a local credit bureau. Typically, that file contains data on previous credit experience, payment record, employment, lawsuits, arrests, and personal bankruptcies.

Fair Credit Reporting Act

The Fair Credit Reporting Act was enacted to protect the consumer from possible damage resulting from misleading credit information. The reforms were directed toward two areas. First, the act was intended to protect the individual against the circulation of inaccurate or incomplete information. Second, it created redress procedures that individuals could use to correct or remove biased or bogus data from their files.

Your Rights If you are denied credit, or if your cost of credit was increased because a lender was influenced by information in a credit report, the

lender must disclose which credit bureau compiled that report. You can then request an interview with the bureau to learn the substance of the information in your file. A bureau representative must discuss the contents of the file and must reveal the bureau's sources except for certain personal interviews. In addition, the bureau must provide a list of people who have received your credit report during the past 6 months.

Incorrect Information   If the information is incorrect or incomplete, you can request that the bureau reinvestigate the item. If the alleged information cannot be verified, it must be removed. In addition, you can ask the bureau to send a correction to everyone who has received a credit report during the last 6 months; there is no charge for this service.

Disputed Information   When there is disputed information that cannot be resolved, you can request that your version be placed in the file. Future credit reports must contain your version of the dispute. For a nominal fee, you can request the credit bureau to send copies of your version to anyone who has recently received your credit report.

Obsolete Information   In general, all adverse information is considered obsolete after 7 years and therefore must be deleted at that time. Bankruptcy information, however, can be retained for 14 years.

Fees   If a credit bureau's report was the basis on which you were denied credit, the bureau must review your file with you, free of charge. But the review request must be made within 30 days of the denial. Even if you have not been refused credit, you can still review your file for a nominal fee: typically, $5 to $25.

CREDIT: A HEDGE AGAINST INFLATION?

During periods of rising prices, credit can provide an added benefit since it permits you to buy at today's price; if you wait until you have saved the money, the price may have risen. For example, assume Timothy O'Connor is considering a new $1,000 stereo. A lender has offered a 12-month $1,000 sales loan with an APR of 18 percent. We assume that Tim itemizes his income tax deductions and that his marginal tax rate is 25 percent. The top half of Exhibit 7–16 outlines the cost of this credit.

The bottom half of Exhibit 7–16 illustrates the impact of 3 percent and 6 percent inflation rates. Clearly, the results suggest that inflation reduces the effective cost of credit. That conclusion, however, needs to be qualified. Lenders know that a period of high inflation reduces the value of the finance charge they collect. Consequently, they may raise their APR to counter the effects of inflation; this could offset part, or all, of the cost reduction shown in the lower part of Exhibit 7–16.

Strategy: If you expect high inflation rates over the next several years, you may want to adjust the effective cost of a purchase when considering the use of credit.

Exhibit 7-16   Impact of Inflation on Cost of Credit

Cost of credit	
Finance charge on $1,000, 12-month loan with APR of 18 percent	$100.16*
Less: Tax benefit from finance charge ($100.16 × 25 percent)	25.04
Net cost of credit	$ 75.12
Impact of inflation	
1 At 3 percent annual inflation:	
a Cost of stereo in 1 year ($1,000 × 103 percent) $1,030	
b Savings from immediate purchase 30	
c Net cost of credit, corrected for inflation	
($75.12 − $30)	$ 45.12
2 At 6 percent annual inflation:	
a Cost of stereo in 1 year ($1,000 × 106 percent) $1,060	
b Savings from immediate purchase 60	
c Net cost of credit, corrected for inflation	
($75.12 − $60)	$ 15.12

*Computed, using Exhibit 7-10.

OVEREXTENDED WITH CREDIT

Recently there has been a sharp increase in the number of people who have become grossly overextended with credit. For many of these people, the wide availability of credit is just too enticing. They never stop and ask themselves how they are going to make the payments on the new credit they are considering. They just shrug off that question by telling themselves that the money will come from somewhere. Unfortunately, by the time they realize the full implications of the payment load, they are so overextended that only a drastic change can correct the problem.

Overextended?   The questions shown in Exhibit 7–17 can provide an early warning signal of impending credit problems. "Yes" responses to five or six questions suggest that the person might be approaching an overextension with credit.

Correction and Retrenchment

Before any correction plan can succeed, the individual involved must want to correct the problem.

Self-Study and Evaluation   Your first step is to stop using any more credit: you simply cannot borrow your way out of debt. Next, do a thorough self-study of your current debts together with their repayment schedules. If you do not have a detailed budget, make one immediately. It should be an emergency budget that reduces all discretionary expenditures to a minimum. You will then know how much money you have available for debt payments.

If the money you have available exceeds the amount needed to make the minimum payments on your debts, use that extra money to repay those debts

Exhibit 7-17   Early Warning Signals: Credit Problems Ahead

	Yes	No
Savings		
1 Have your cash reserves decreased sharply?	( )	( )
2 Are your forced to draw on your savings each month?	( )	( )
3 Do you rarely make deposits to your savings?	( )	( )
Monthly payments		
1 Do you only make the minimum payment on credit cards?	( )	( )
2 Has your bill paying slowed?	( )	( )
3 Are any of your debts delinquent?	( )	( )
4 Do you need overtime or an extra job to make ends meet?	( )	( )
5 Are you unclear where the money goes?	( )	( )
6 Are you always short before payday?	( )	( )
7 Do you need the overdraft on your checking account each month?	( )	( )
Use of credit		
1 Do you have many charge accounts and other debts?	( )	( )
2 Are you uncertain how much you owe?	( )	( )
3 Have you started receiving past due notices?	( )	( )
4 Do you have any debt consolidation loans?	( )	( )

that have the highest APR. If you do not have enough even to make the minimum payments, more drastic action may be in order. One possibility is to concentrate your payments on those debts having the highest APR, and to reduce, or defer if possible, your payments on debts with the lowest APR.

Once you have decided on a course of action, contact each creditor and explain your plan. A well-documented plan can convince your creditors that you recognize the seriousness of your situation and that you intend to correct it.

Debt Consolidation Loan   Some lenders tout debt consolidation loans as the answer to all debt problems. They suggest, "Consolidate all your payments into a single loan payment and the problem disappears." But does it? We think not. At best, you obtain breathing space to work out a long-term solution. But the cost is high: APRs of 30 to 40 percent are common. And you still have to repay that loan. If you use this source, you should absolutely not use additional credit until the consolidation loan is totally repaid.

> **Strategy: When considering a debt consolidation loan, ask yourself: Is it part of a viable correction plan? Should you decide on the loan, keep the maturity as short as your emergency budget will allow.**

Nonprofit Credit Counseling   Many medium- to large-sized cities have a nonprofit credit agency that assists people with credit problems. The fee is nominal, generally less than $10. The agency works with the individual to design a repayment plan. If the counselors feel they cannot help, they tell the person. Their role is strictly as advisor; they do not negotiate with the individual's creditors. The individual must contact the creditors and explain the plan. Your local United Fund, Legal Aid Society, or Community Chest can tell you whether there is a credit counseling agency in your area.

Debt Consolidators Debt consolidators are in business to make a profit and their fees reflect it. They do not advance money to pay off their customers' debts. Rather, they negotiate a repayment schedule between the customer and the creditors. We strongly recommend you avoid this group. Their service fee runs an astounding 10 to 20 percent of the customer's debts. And their reputation is generally poor among creditors. If you could afford that fee, you would do better by using it to pay off your debts.

Bankruptcy Proceedings Bankruptcy is not so much a solution as an end to your debt obligations. We consider bankruptcy as an absolute last resort. There are two courses of action open to the individual: "straight bankruptcy," and the "wage earner plan."

As part of the court proceedings under a straight bankruptcy, the debtor's assets (except for certain items which are excluded by state statute) are sold for cash and the proceeds are divided among the creditors. The debtor is discharged from all unsatisfied debts as part of the bankruptcy proceedings. But the debtor cannot file for bankruptcy again for 6 years.

The "wage earner plan" is intended to help the debtor repay the debts from future earnings. The debtor files a budget with the court that earmarks a portion of the debtor's future earnings to repay the debts. The "wage earner plan" is used much less frequently than straight bankruptcy.

If you decide this step is necessary, check with a local attorney for a detailed explanation of what is required.

SUMMARY

1 Borrowing increases your immediate purchasing power but simultaneously reduces your future purchasing power.
2 The finance charge includes all costs of borrowing: interest, collection costs, record keeping, required insurance, etc.
3 Extending the maturity reduces the monthly payment, but the total finance charge rises sharply.
4 The decision to use credit entails a comparison between the increase in today's purchasing power versus the reduction in future purchasing power.
5 The borrower can best judge whether credit is justified in a particular situation.
6 As a general rule, monthly debt payments, excluding mortgage payment, should be less than 20 percent of disposable income. Or, a more specific rule is: Debt payments should equal, or be less than, the available monthly discretionary income.
7 A borrower should shop for credit the same as for any other service.
8 The APRs on competing credit offers should be compared to decide which has the lowest cost.
9 The finance charge on credit card accounts is computed by one of three general techniques: previous balance, average daily balance, or adjusted balance.
10 Most credit card accounts provide a grace period with no finance charge.
11 Truth in lending legislation requires that lenders disclose information on the cost of credit, the required payments, and the penalties.
12 Lenders use two principal criteria to evaluate the credit worthiness of an individual: ability to repay, and willingness to repay.

13 Secured bank loans or retail credit can be a good place for first-time borrowers to begin their credit record.

14 Credit bureaus must take specific corrective action if some information in an individual's file is incorrect, unsupportable, or disputed.

15 A thorough self-study and evaluation is a key step in correcting an overextension on credit.

REVIEW YOUR UNDERSTANDING OF

Finance charge
Repayment terms
Credit: the cost-benefit trade-off
Your debt limits
    Disposable income
    Discretionary income
Annual percentage rate (APR)
Finance charge computation
    Add-on
    Discount
    Simple interest
Billing cycle
Grace period

Finance charge computation
    Previous balance
    Average daily balance
    Adjusted balance
Truth in lending
Ability to repay
Willingness to repay
Fair Credit Reporting Act
Inflation: effect on cost of credit
Debt consolidation loan
Nonprofit counseling agencies
Debt consolidators

QUESTIONS FOR DISCUSSION

1 How would you answer the criticism that borrowing encourages you to live beyond your means? Do you agree that borrowing is fraught with risks of eventual bankruptcy? Why?

2 What are some early warning signs of overextension on credit? Do you think some are more valid than others? Why?

3 What causes the cost differential between the borrowing and savings alternatives? How do taxes affect the differential? Would inflation widen or narrow the differential?

4 Comment on the statement, "Extending the repayment period expands your debt capacity."

5 What is the principal difference between the previous balance and the adjusted balance techniques of computing finance charges? Which would you favor? Why?

6 What benefits do you see in the truth in lending legislation? How can the consumer make maximum use of the disclosures?

7 Under what situation can income taxes reduce the cost of borrowing? Why? When do taxes have no effect on borrowing costs?

8 Susan Banks is considering two $4,000 loan alternatives for her new car: (a) a 36-month loan with an APR of 18 or (b) a 60-month loan with the same APR. The lender has stressed how much "easier" the payments would be on the second type of loan. What are the monthly payments on the respective loans? Is the 60-month loan cheaper? If Susan could make the payments on either loan, which would you recommend? Why?

9 Give an example of how the grace period on a credit card works. How can the effectiveness of that period be maximized?

10 How is the discretionary income test for debt limits computed? What are its major advantages?
11 Under what conditions does inflation reduce the effective cost of credit? Give an example.
12 Discuss your rights under the Fair Credit Reporting Act if you find inaccurate or obsolete information in your file.
13 What types of items do you feel best qualify for credit purchase? Which items do you feel least qualify?

CASE PROBLEM

Ralph and Grazelda Smith are currently deciding whether they should buy a $4,000 camping trailer. Although they have decided they would like the trailer, they still have reservations about whether their outstanding debts are becoming excessive. The Smiths both work full time and their combined annual disposable income is $18,600 ($1,550 monthly). Their normal monthly expenses (they have no children) average: rent, $265.00; utilities, $60; food, $250; clothing, $105; transportation (excluding their car loan payment), $200; entertainment, $100; donations, $40; insurance premiums, $30; and savings, $100. Their monthly debt payments include (the months remaining to the loan's maturity are shown in parentheses): car payment (30), $200; furniture (20), $100; and television and stereo (35), $70. Since their savings balance is limited, they plan to finance $3,645 of the trailer's $4000 cost. The dealer has offered a 36-month, $3,645 sales loan that carries an APR of 24 percent; it requires monthly payments of $143.

a Is the new credit justified? Would you recommend any alternatives?
b According to the disposable income test, are the Smiths nearing their debt limit? Does the discretionary income test give a similar answer?
c Basing your judgment on the above, what would you recommend the Smiths do? Do you feel the new debt will fit into their budget? Why?
d One of Ralph's friends has suggested a debt consolidation loan to clean up their old debts. He maintains that the longer maturity on that loan will ease their present payment burden and permit them to take on new debt. What are the strengths and weaknesses in that argument?
e Assuming the Smiths buy the new trailer, formulate an appropriate budget. (*Hint:* use the general guidelines given in the budgeting chapter.)

RECOMMENDED READINGS

Magazines

Money:

Herrera, Philip, "How Much Can You Borrow?" October 1972, pp. 60–68.
    Discusses criteria that lenders use to evaluate borrowers. Provides some guidelines on how lenders decide a borrower's maximum.
Pollack, Jack Harrison, "Advice to the Debt-lorn." January 1973, pp. 61–66.
    Discusses the services and cost of nonprofit debt counseling centers.
Carper, Jean, "The Reputation Merchants." February 1974, pp. 26–30.
    Examines the need for reform in credit bureau practices.

Changing Times:

"Are You Using All Your Truth-In-Lending Rights?" November 1973, pp. 17–18.
   Good coverage on that topic.
"Do You Owe Too Much?" June 1974, pp. 6–9.
   Good discussion of early signs of overextension on credit.
"What Happens If You Go Bankrupt." June 1975, pp. 39–42.
   A good discussion of that topic.
"Somebody Has a File on You." August 1975, pp. 41–44.
   Discusses major types of reports assembled by credit bureaus. Reviews your rights under Fair Credit Reporting Act.

Booklets

Credit Union National Association, Inc., *Using Credit Wisely.* Madison, Wis.: 1966.
   A good discussion of the truth in lending legislation in chapter 3.
Hawver, Carl F., *Basic Principles in Family Money and Credit Management. Washington, D.C.: National Consumer Finance Association, 1972.*
   Chapters 1 and 3, respectively, include a discussion of the role of credit and its proper use. Each chapter ends with a very useful glossary of credit terms.

Chapter 8

Sources of Consumer Credit

After completing this chapter you should be able to:

explain the principal attributes of a consumer cash loan.

compare a secured loan with an unsecured loan.

recall the major lending sources for consumer cash loans.

formulate a plan to obtain a cash loan with a low finance charge.

explain the major features of consumer sales loans.

describe the credit agreement for a sales loan.

outline a plan for comparing sales loans.

analyze the credit life insurance decision.

explain the major attributes of open-ended credit.

compare and contrast the three major charge accounts.

explain the "minimum payment rut."

formulate a plan to borrow money for college with favorable terms and a low finance charge.

During the past 10 years, more and more lending institutions have become actively involved in consumer lending. And not only has the number of lenders grown; many of them offer several types of consumer credit. Moreover, the amounts available, the repayment terms, and other features of consumer credit have been considerably liberalized and extended to fit a wide range of consumer needs. To choose the best loan for your needs, it is essential that you be well informed about what is available.

Selecting an inappropriate loan or an inappropriate lender could easily double the cost of credit. Or a wrong choice could subject you to repayment terms or other provisions that simply do not suit your intended purpose for the loan.

This chapter examines the four principal categories of consumer credit: consumer cash loan, consumer sales loan, open-ended consumer credit, and education loan. For each credit category, we discuss general attributes, principal sources, the advantages and disadvantages to each source, and the special features of that category.

CONSUMER CASH LOANS

With a consumer cash loan the borrower receives cash, not merchandise. Cash loans are available in amounts of as little as $10 or more than $10,000. Maturities can be as short as a few days or as long as 5 years. Generally, very small loans, or those with very short maturities, have the highest APR. The APRs on some cash loans can be as low as 5 percent, yet exceed 40 percent on other cash loans. Nearly all cash loans require equal monthly payments throughout the time the loan is outstanding.

Cash loans can either be secured or unsecured, depending on the amount and the borrower's credit record. The difference between the two centers on the loan's repayment provisions.

Secured Loan   A secured loan requires two things: the borrower's written promise to repay and the pledge of security in the form of collateral or a cosigner. The collateral can be part of the borrower's personal property, such as a car, household furniture, a boat, or similar personal property. Often it is the item the borrower plans to buy with the loan proceeds. The security can also be in the form of a cosigner who promises to repay the loan should the borrower fail to do so. Despite the added collateral, the borrower's ability and willingness to repay are still the principal criteria the lender uses to decide whether the loan should be granted.

If the borrower fails to repay the loan, the lender can repossess the collateral as complete or partial payment of the loan. Where there is a cosigner, the lender will proceed against the cosigner to force payment. A lender will insist the loan be secured when the amount is large, or the borrower's credit record is limited or questionable.

A secured loan does expose the borrower to the possibility that the collateral will be repossessed or that the cosigner will be forced to repay the loan. But that possibility should be remote if credit usage is held to a prudent level.

Unsecured Loan The borrower's promise to repay is the lender's only assurance behind an unsecured loan. Neither collateral nor cosigner is required. The borrower's ability and willingness to repay are the lender's sole assurance the loan will be repaid. Unsecured loans are typical when the amount is small or the borrower's credit record is top grade and well established.

> Strategy: Since the added risk with a secured loan is small, a secured loan would be justified if it offers a lower APR than an unsecured loan.

Summary of Major Consumer Cash Loans

Exhibit 8-1 summarizes the principal features of the major consumer cash loans. The principal advantages and disadvantages of each loan are discussed below.

Commercial Banks: Personal Cash Loan The notion that commercial banks lend only to upper-income people is simply not true. Banks offer personal cash loans of $500 to $5,000 to a wide range of borrowers. And they will lend larger amounts if the borrower meets the bank's credit standards. Maturities typically range from 6 months to more than 5 years where state banking regulations permit. Depending on the loan's size and the borrower's credit record, the loan can either be secured or unsecured. The APR of the finance charge ranges from 8 to 20 percent, although 12 to 14 percent is the most common rate. Some banks quote a lower APR on a secured loan than they offer on an equivalent unsecured loan. Credit life insurance is nearly always available as an option at extra cost; it generally is not required as a condition to obtain the loan.

Advantages The APR on most bank cash loans is generally very competitive with the APRs offered by other lenders. Also, by repaying the loan on time, borrowers can establish a credit record that may qualify them for the bank's other credit alternatives: home mortgage, credit card, overdraft on checking account.

Disadvantages Because banks restrict their lending to borrowers with strong, well-established credit records, some borrowers may find that this lending source is simply not available. Also, banks are reluctant to make loans for less than $500 or with maturities shorter than 6 months.

Exhibit 8-1   Summary of Major Consumer Cash Loans

Source	Finance charge (APR)	Available maturities	Range of loan amounts	Type of loan (unsecured or secured)
Commercial bank	8 to 20%	6 months to 5 years	$100 to $5,000*	Unsecured and secured
Credit union	8 to 12%	6 months to 5 years	$100 to $5,000†	Unsecured and secured (always secured if loan exceeds $2,500)
Consumer finance company	18 to 42%	1 month to 3 years‡	$50 to $1,000§	Unsecured and secured (generally secured on most loans)
Life insurance	5 to 7%	Flexible¶	95% of policy's cash value	Secured (insurance policy's cash value)
Savings and loan	Annual rate 1 to 1½% above rate on savings account	6 months to 2 years	90 to 100% of savings account balance	Secured (savings account)
Second mortgage	15 to 30%	6 months to 10 years	50 to 60% of borrower's equity in house	Secured (borrower's house)
Pawnshop	24 to 120%	6 to 12 months	50% of value of pledged property	Secured (pledged property)

*Borrowers that qualify can obtain larger loans.

†Larger amounts are available if borrower qualifies.

‡Maximum maturity varies according to the regulations of the different states.

§Maximum loan amount is higher when state regulations permit.

¶Loan has no set repayment schedule.

Strategy: When shopping for a cash loan, first check the commercial banks in your area.

Commercial Banks: Automatic Overdraft or Advances   Many banks now offer an automatic overdraft or cash advance on the checking accounts of customers who qualify for this feature. The qualifying customer can write checks exceeding the amount of money in the account. That is, the bank automatically provides a short-term cash advance to the customer to cover those checks which would overdraw the account. The amount the bank will make available ranges from $100 to more than $1,000, depending on the customer's credit record. Once approved, the customer does not have to notify the bank each time the overdraft is going to be used; hence the connotation "automatic."

Typically, the account holder does not have to pay any fee as long as the advance is unused. Once used, the finance charge is based on the amount of the advance and the number of days outstanding. The APR is generally 12 percent, although it can be as high as 18 percent. The daily finance rate is computed by dividing the APR by 365 days (some banks use 360 days). The daily rate times the amount outstanding gives the daily finance charge. Multiplying the daily finance charge by the number of days outstanding gives the total cost of the automatic overdraft. For example, the finance charge on a $200 advance outstanding 21 days with an APR of 12 percent would be $1.38 [$200 × 21 days × (12 percent ÷ 365 days)].

The size of the required repayment is based on the amount advanced. Most repayment schedules require complete repayment within 12 to 24 months. The mechanics of the repayment takes one of two forms. Either the repayment may be automatically deducted from the customer's next deposit to the account, or the customer may have to mail in the payment and specifically designate it as a payment on the advance. Of the two, the first is the most desirable because it eliminates the possibility of forgetting to make the payment.

With some overdraft plans, when the bank advances cash to an overdrawn account, the amount of the advance equals the amount of the overdraft. With others, the advance is made in multiples of $100. Thus, a $205 overdraft would signal a $300 advance to the account. With this plan, the finance charge is based on $300 rather than $205. Under the first method, the finance charge would be based on $205. Clearly, the exact advance plan is more desirable than the $100 multiple advance plan.

> **Strategy: When considering automatic overdrafts, try to find one that offers a cash advance exactly equal to the overdraft and automatically deducts repayment from the next deposit to your checking account.**

Advantages   An automatic overdraft is a convenient, emergency short-term cash source. As long as it is not used, it costs the customer nothing. And once the automatic overdraft has been authorized for your checking account, it can be used without the need for further negotiation. Further, its APR is competitive with other short-term cash sources.

Disadvantages   Because an automatic overdraft is so easy and painless to use, it can easily be misused. Because it is automatic, some people depend on their overdraft to carry them between paychecks. As long as the amount is small and the period outstanding is short, the finance charge is not very significant. Unfortunately, some people never completely repay one month's advance before they draw another one. Over a period of time, the outstanding balance continues to grow to the point where they are continually overdrawn; their temporary advance has become a permanent debt. Soon they find a growing portion of their repayment is needed just to cover the finance charge; repaying the balance becomes an increasingly difficult task.

Credit Union: Cash Loan   A credit union is a mutually owned, nonprofit financial institution that provides savings and lending services to members only. To be a member, you typically must be part of the common group that formed the credit union. Generally, that will be a group of people who work for the same company, or live in a particular neighborhood, or attend the same church, or have some other common bond.

Credit unions offer unsecured cash loans ranging from $25 to $2,500. For amounts larger than $2,500, or where the member's credit record does not meet their standards, the loan must be secured. The maximum finance charge is limited to 1 percent per month on the unpaid balance: an APR of 12 percent. Most credit unions, however, quote loan rates that are less than the allowable maximum. At some, the APR can be as low as 8 to 9 percent.

Maturities range from a few months to more than 5 years, depending on the credit union. Nearly all loans include credit life insurance as part of the loan; consequently, the premium is included as part of the quoted finance charge.

Advantages   The principal advantage to borrowing from a credit union is its low APR, generally one of the lowest of all lenders. Also, most credit unions will make cash loans for small amounts or short maturities.

Disadvantages   The principal shortcoming to borrowing from a credit union is that you must be a member. Unless you are part of a group that has established a credit union, this alternative may not be open to you. A few states do have a credit union that extends membership to residents who cannot qualify for membership at any other credit union. To find out if there is one in your area, write: Credit Union National Association, Inc., Public Relations, Box 431, Madison, Wisconsin 53701.

Some people feel that it is a disadvantage to deal with an organization comprised of their close associates. They maintain that their borrowing needs are not confidential when their loan request is submitted to the credit union's loan committee, which is typically staffed with fellow members.

Strategy: We strongly recommend that you consider a credit union as a potential lending source if you qualify.

Consumer Finance Company: Cash Loan   Consumer finance companies specialize in lending to a wide range of borrowers. Typically, they will extend credit to people with poor credit records who could not borrow from other lenders. Because consumer finance companies lend to weaker borrowers, their collection effort must be greater and their loss on uncollected loans is higher. Both problems boost their operating cost—which is then reflected in their higher finance charge. Most states heavily regulate and control the lending activities of consumer finance companies.

Consumer finance companies offer both secured and unsecured loans. Secured loans are the most common, especially when the amount is large or the borrower's credit record is very weak. Maximum loan amount is generally set by state statute, although some states are beginning to leave this to the lender's discretion. Loans of $50 to $1,000 are available in nearly all states. Maximum finance charges are almost always set by state regulation. Typical APRs range from 18 to 42 percent. Some states have a graduated APR schedule where the APR decreases for larger loan amounts. Thus, there might be a very high maximum APR on the first $150 borrowed, a lower rate on loan amounts between $150 and $300, and a still lower rate on amounts above $300. Other states specify a single maximum for all loans regardless of size. While the diverse state regulations make it difficult to generalize, an APR of 24 to 36 percent appears to be typical. Maximum maturities are 18 months to 5 years, depending on the lender and prevailing state regulations. Many states have removed these limits, leaving maximum maturity to the lender's discretion.

Advantages   Probably the most significant advantage to finance companies is their willingness to lend to borrowers with weak credit records and borrowers with no previous credit record. Finance companies process their loan requests quickly and many are willing to loan small amounts. (A word of caution about those small loans: The APR on many is so high that they are prohibitively expensive.) Most finance companies will accept a wide range of items as security for the loan.

Disadvantages   The major disadvantage to borrowing from a finance company is the high finance charge. Usually it is the highest among the lenders discussed thus far. In addition, if you live in a state with highly restrictive maturity or maximum borrowing limits, the available loan may not satisfy your needs.

> **Strategy: If your credit record is poor or unestablished, a finance company may be your only choice. Nevertheless, try a commercial bank or a credit union before you resign yourself to this source.**

Life Insurance: Cash Loan   Since we will discuss life insurance cash loans in Chapter 14, we will just summarize the key points here.

Advantages   The principal advantage to borrowing on your life insurance is the very low finance charge. With an APR of 5 to 7 percent, it is the lowest among lending sources. There is no credit investigation or qualifying standards; all policyholders automatically qualify for a loan up to 95 percent of their policy's cash value. An insurance loan has no set repayment schedule; that is left to the borrower's discretion.

Disadvantages   The most obvious disadvantage is that you must be a policyholder to qualify. Furthermore, your policy's cash value would have to be sizable if you are to obtain a large loan. Also, borrowing on your policy reduces your insurance coverage, since any outstanding loan reduces the policy's death benefit. Related to that is another disadvantage: The lack of a set repayment schedule could encourage the borrower to postpone repaying the loan indefinitely. Finally, the minimum payment you must make is the finance charge, and if you fail to make the payment, the entire policy could eventually be canceled.

> **Strategy: For those who qualify, this loan is an excellent emergency cash source when you expect to repay it within a short time. It can also serve as an extended payment cash loan. But it should be used only if you can discipline yourself to repay the loan in a timely fashion.**

Savings and Loan Association: Secured Savings Loan   Nearly all savings and loan associations offer a cash loan secured by a depositor's savings account. The loan can range from 90 to 100 percent of the depositor's savings account balance. Typically, the finance charge is 1 to 1½ percent more than the depositor is currently earning on the savings account. Even while the loan is outstanding, the savings account continues to pay interest, so the loan's effective cost is low.

Advantages   A secured savings loan can provide emergency cash where a depositor does not want to withdraw money from the savings account. For example, it would be advantageous where the money is held in a restrictive savings account that assesses a sizable penalty if a withdrawal is made before a certain date. Likewise, it can be used by a first-time borrower to establish a credit record.

Disadvantages   The requirement that the loan be secured by a savings account restricts its usage to short-term emergency situations. It is hard to imagine a situation where the borrower had sufficient money in a savings account, yet chose to use a long-term secured savings loan rather than draw the cash needed from the savings account.

Savings and Loan Association: Unsecured Cash Loan   To date, savings and loan associations (S&Ls) have generally been restricted to secured savings loans. A few states, however, have relaxed their regulations so that S&Ls chartered in that state can offer unsecured cash loans. Nevertheless, because unsecured cash loans among S&Ls are still rather limited, we cannot generalize about availability, maximum amounts, maturities, or annual finance charge. We recommend that you check the S&Ls in your area to see whether they make unsecured cash loans.

Second Mortgage: Cash Loan   A cash loan secured by a second mortgage on the borrower's home is a specialized type of cash loan. Such loans are offered by specialized finance companies as well as some consumer finance companies.

Generally the loan is limited to 50 to 60 percent of the borrower's equity in the house. That is, the maximum amount cannot exceed 50 to 60 percent of the amount the borrower has repaid on the house. For example, if your house cost $40,000 and you have repaid $20,000, you can borrow $10,000 or $12,000 (50 percent or 60 percent × $20,000) with a second mortage.

Finance charges range from an APR of 15 percent or more, depending on the amount borrowed, the lender, the loan's maturity, and the borrower's credit record. Typical maturities extend from 1 to 10 years. Some loans require that the amount be repaid in equal monthly payments over the loan's maturity. Other loans require small monthly payments that do little more than cover the loan's finance charge; at the loan's maturity, however, the borrower must make a very large lump-sum payment to repay the loan.

Advantages   The principal advantage to a second mortgage cash loan is that it can be easily obtained. Because the loan is well secured, most lenders will make the loan even if the borrower has a weak credit record.

Disadvantages   The principal shortcoming to this loan is the borrower's risk in pledging his or her home as security. We doubt many borrowers realize the seriousness of this pledge.

While the lump-sum repayment option may look appealing, we feel most borrowers cannot discipline themselves to save sufficient money for that final giant payment. As a consequence, they have to refinance the loan and continue the high finance charges.

Some lending practices in secondary mortgages border on the unscrupulous. To date, many states have been extremely slow and lax in providing adequate regulation; this lack has left the consumer with little or no protection. Consequently, it is imperative that you be extremely knowledgeable and cautious when considering this loan.

Strategy: Because of the risk, we strongly recommend that you investigate all other potential lending sources before you even consider a second mortgage cash loan.

Pawnshop: Cash Loan   A pawnshop makes a loan to a borrower who pledges personal property as security. And to make the pledge even more secure, the pawnshop takes possession of the property and returns it to the borrower only when the loan is repaid. Should the borrower fail to repay the loan, the pawnshop can sell the pledged item. Since the pawnshop's assurance of repayment is based on the sales proceeds from the pledged property, it rarely advances more than 50 percent of the property's market value.

By repaying the loan and its associated finance charge within the redemption period, typically 6 to 12 months, the borrower regains the pledged property. Finance charges average 2 to 3 percent per month, although monthly rates as high as 10 percent are not unknown. Repayment terms call for a single, lump-sum payment at the end of the loan.

Advantages   Since the value of the pledged property exceeds the loan, there is no credit investigation. Consequently, the borrower can obtain the money quickly and with minimal paperwork.

Disadvantages   One disadvantage to a pawnshop loan is that you must give up the pledged property until you repay the loan. Another disadvantage is that the amount of the loan is only half the value of the property pledged. Further, the finance charge is high and the maturity is short. Finally, if you fail to redeem the property, your borrowing cost is the loss of the item.

Strategy: At best, a pawnshop is a source of short-term emergency cash. If your intent in pledging an item is merely to get rid of it, you should sell it yourself for the full value rather than lose it as a pledged pawn item, thereby getting only half its value.

Questionable Lenders   Despite the wide array of legitimate lenders, there still seems to be room for the loan sharks who operate without license or regulation and usually illegally. Their speciality is loans that promise quick money, have low qualifying standards, and require a lump-sum payment at the end of their short maturity. But the cost can be devastating: annual rates range from 120 percent to 1,000 percent per year! And sometimes the loan sharks will not let you repay the loan amount but, instead, insist that you keep on paying the high finance charge: This is a crime called extortion. And should you fail to cooperate, their collection efforts will be quick, brutal, and unrelenting.

> **Strategy: Our recommendation is an absolute and unequivocal DON'T. There are plenty of other lenders to try. And if all those lenders have refused you, then your finances are probably in such dire condition that a loan shark is not going to rectify your financial problems. If this is your situation, see a lawyer or your legal aid society instead.**

Shopping for a Cash Loan

The checklist in Exhibit 8–2 can assist in your search for a suitable cash loan. You should answer the questions in the preliminary section before you visit any lenders. While this seems intuitively obvious, many borrowers fail to specify clearly what they are looking for before they begin their search.

The questions in the bottom half of Exhibit 8–2 should provide the key information you need to compare competing loan offers. To obtain this information, you will probably have to ask some direct questions. Many borrowers simply never ask because they do not use this information. Consequently, some lenders do not volunteer the information unless asked.

You should check at least three lenders, even if the first lender's offer seems attractive. Rare is the loan offer that is so good that it cannot stand a few hours of careful thought before being accepted. In making your decision, select the loan that has the lowest APR, yet whose terms match your needs.

If you are turned down by one lender, try others. Quite often, one lender will decide a loan is fully justified when another lender might reach just the

Exhibit 8-2   Checklist for Shopping for a Cash Loan

Preliminaries
1 How will the money be used?
2 How much money is needed?
3 How long do you need the loan?
4 If required, what security can you pledge on the loan?
5 Do you have current data on yourself: income, rent, present debts, monthly payments, savings, etc.?
6 Do you have a list of prospective lenders you have ranked by preference?

Questions to Ask Prospective Lenders
1 What is the APR of the loan's finance charge?
2 What are the repayment terms?
3 Does the loan require security? Is so, what?
4 Are there late payment penalties?
5 Is there a penalty for repaying the loan before maturity?
6 If repaid early, how is the finance charge refund computed?
7 Is credit life insurance required?

opposite conclusion. So check several sources before you decide the loan is unavailable. Of course, if you decide your credit record has a serious deficiency, you will have to take corrective action, as outlined in the previous chapter, before a lender will consider you eligible for a loan.

CONSUMER SALES LOAN

Consumer sales loans are always associated with the purchase of big-ticket durable goods, such as an automobile, furniture, a home appliance, or a recreation vehicle. With a sales loan, the borrower does not receive cash; instead, the borrower immediately receives the merchandise in exchange for a repayment promise. All sales loans are secured with a lien or pledge of the merchandise purchased. While most sales loans originate with the dealer who sells the merchandise, few stop there. Dealers generally have a standing agreement with a finance company or a bank to purchase the sales loans the dealer originates. By selling the loan, the dealer obtains immediate cash without waiting 12 to 60 months while the buyer repays the loan.

The price of the item purchased determines the size of the loan. Typically, the buyer pays a small fraction of that purchase price as a down payment and finances the balance with a sales loan. The loan could be as little as $50 when it involves a small household appliance, or it could exceed $10,000 for an expensive automobile or a large boat. Maturities range from 3 months to 5 years, but 2 to 3 years are common maturity periods. The increased availability of the longer 4- and 5-year maturities is a recent development. One reason for

the lengthened maturities is the recent sharp price increases on many big-ticket durable goods. By extending maturities, lenders have been able to keep the monthly loan payment within the reach of most consumers. The APR of the finance charge ranges from 12 to 36 percent, although the average is between 24 and 36 percent. All sales loans require equal monthly payments over the loan's maturity.

The Credit Agreement

The credit agreement for a consumer sales loan has two major components: the note, which specifies the amount of the loan and the repayment schedule, and the installment sales contract, which specifies all other terms and conditions for the loan.

Generally, the major points in the loan contract are specified by the bank or finance company that ultimately purchases the loan, although the dealer often sets the APR. Since many required disclosures are set forth in this agreement, it is essential that you read and fully understand it before signing. If you are unclear about a section, ask for an explanation. If you find some parts of the agreement favor the lender at your expense, look elsewhere for your merchandise and sales loan. Never rely on the dealer's verbal assurance that "we never enforce unfavorable parts of the loan agreement."

Disclosure   The minimum disclosure requirements for the sales agreement are set forth in the truth in lending legislation. Those requirements are summarized in Exhibit 8–3. Some states require additional disclosures beyond those outlined in Exhibit 8–3.

By standardizing the required information, truth in lending has made it much easier for the buyer to compare competing sales loans. At the same time, the sales loan can also be compared to a cash loan or to the extended terms available on bank credit cards. But that information is only as good as your understanding of it. Most of these disclosures are contained in the credit agreement and you should read them carefully.

Exhibit 8-3   Minimum Disclosure: Consumer Sales Loan

General
1 Name and address of buyer and seller
2 Transaction date

3 Description of merchandise
4 Explanation of creditor's security interest in merchandise

Financing detail
1 Cash price
2 Down payment: cash plus any trade-in
3 Unpaid balance (number 1 minus number 2)
4 List of charges not included in the finance charge

5 Amount financed (number 3 plus number 4)
6 Finance charge in dollars
7 Finance charge as an APR

Payment detail
1 Number, amount, and date of payments
2 Description of delinquency or default fee

3 Method of computing finance charge refund if loan is repaid early

Installment Sales Contract The installment sales contract describes the merchandise and gives details such as price, down payment, finance charge, and payment schedule. The contract takes one of three forms: conditional sales contract, chattel mortgage, or bailment lease. All are similar in that the buyer is responsible for any loss or damage to the merchandise. When you sign the installment sales contract, you are pledging the merchandise as security for the sales loan. Should you fail to repay the loan according to the agreement, the lender has the right to repossess the merchandise. The principal difference between the three types of contracts centers on the form of the lender's security interest in the pledged merchandise.

Conditional Sales Contract With a conditional sales contract, the buyer takes immediate possession of the merchandise, but title remains with the lender (the lender legally owns the merchandise) until the loan is completely repaid.

Chattel Mortgage When a buyer signs a chattel mortgage, the title to the merchandise passes to the lender as collateral for the loan. By filing the mortgage with the appropriate government agency, the lender can prevent the buyer from pledging the same item as security on a different loan.

Bailment Lease With a bailment lease, the buyer does not obtain title to the merchandise until the final payment is made. Up until that time, the buyer is considered to have rented the item. When the merchandise is completely paid for, the buyer can purchase title from the seller for a nominal fee.

The Note The note specifies the total amount due and the repayment details. When you sign the note, it constitutes your promise to repay the debt. In addition to your promise to repay, the sales loan is secured by one of the previously discussed installment sales contracts: conditional sales contract, chattel mortgage, or bailment lease.

Caution: Problem Clauses in Credit Agreements Despite considerable state and federal legislation, many credit agreements still contain several burdensome provisions which can be very costly to the buyer.

Balloon Note A balloon note has deceptively small monthly payments while the loan is outstanding. But at maturity the borrower must make a final giant payment to repay the loan. Most people simply are not prepared to make that payment. If you need a balloon note to be able to make the small loan payments, you probably cannot really afford to buy the item.

Add-on Clause An add-on clause gives the dealer a security interest in all the items the buyer purchases from that dealer until everything is repaid. For example, assume Olga Drobowski bought a television set in January and a new dishwasher one year later. Both items came from the same dealer and there was an add-on clause in the sales loan. Because of that clause, the dealer would have a security interest in both items until both were completely paid for. We recommend that you avoid any dealer who insists on an add-on clause.

Acceleration Clause An acceleration clause makes the entire loan due immediately, should the buyer fail to make a payment. If the buyer has to miss one payment, the individual obviously cannot suddenly repay the entire amount; therefore, the lender may repossess the merchandise. Many sales loans have an acceleration clause.

Wage Assignment and Confession of Judgment   With a wage assignment clause, if the borrower fails to repay the loan, the lender can request that part of the borrower's wages be forwarded to the lender. With a confession of judgment, the borrower waives any right to an attorney or to due legal process. Should you fail to repay the loan, the lender can make an admission of indebtedness for you in legal proceedings without your being present. If a loan has either clause, you should find another lender; the inclusion of these clauses is never justified.

Repossession   The exact steps a lender must take to repossess an item depends on the type of sales contract and the prevailing state regulations. Should a buyer fail to make the payments under a bailment lease, all previous payments are considered rental payments; the lender can repossess the item to handle in any way whatsoever.

With a conditional sales contract or a chattel mortgage, the lender can use any legal means to take physical possession of the item; having done this, the lender has several options. If the buyer has repaid less than 60 percent of the loan, most states allow the lender to keep the item as full satisfaction of the outstanding loan balance. But the borrower must be notified of the lender's intent. If, within 30 days, the buyer objects, the item must be sold; should the proceeds exceed the unpaid loan balance, the excess must be returned to the buyer. The lender can sell the item at a public or private sale. Most states require the item to be sold when the buyer has repaid more than 60 percent of the loan. If the sale proceeds exceed the unpaid loan balance, the buyer receives the excess. Should the proceeds be insufficient, the buyer is generally required to repay the difference.

In most cases, repossession is a poor way to repay a loan. First, you lose the services of the repossessed item; you might then be forced to purchase those services elsewhere at a higher cost. Second, if the sale proceeds are insufficient, you end up repaying a loan, although you no longer have the merchandise. Third, some lenders make only a half-hearted effort to obtain the highest price when they sell the repossessed item.[1] Finally, the tactics some lenders use to repossess an item range from questionable to illegal. In short, avoid repossession if at all possible.

Strategy: Discuss your problem with the lender. Most will not repossess an item as long as you continue to make even minimal payments. Since you cannot legally sell a pledged item until after the debt is repaid, you will need a temporary cash source to

---

[1]The Federal Trade Commission has charged that three automakers—General Motors, Ford, and Chrysler—have not refunded the surplus to some buyers whose car or truck was repossessed and ultimately sold for more than the buyer owed on the auto loan. "Cheating Alleged On Repossessions By Auto Firms," *The Wall Street Journal*, Feb. 12, 1976, p. 2, col. 1.

repay the debt. Obtain temporary cash, immediately resell the pledged item, and then repay that temporary cash source. You will generally find that it is less costly to do it this way rather than to have the lender repossess the item.

Sales Loan: Role of the Lending Institution That Purchases the Loan

While most sales loans have three parties—the buyer, the dealer, and the lending institution that provides the loan—they rarely participate simultaneously in the loan transaction. Typically, the buyer negotiates with the dealer and has no contact with the lending institution until after the loan has been sold. The indirect role of the lending institution in these negotiations has raised several questions.

Rebate   When a bank or finance company purchases a sales loan, it generally rebates a portion of the loan's finance charge to the dealer. In part, this rebate compensates the dealer for work on the required loan documents. In addition, it encourages the dealer to sell other loan contracts to that particular institution. Because dealers get these rebates, it is easy to understand why they actively push sales loans. It also creates a situation where dealers might be more interested in selling their loans to lenders offering the largest rebate rather than to lenders offering the lowest APR to the buyer.

> **Strategy: To be sure that the dealer is not getting a large rebate at your expense, make certain the APR on the dealer's sales loan is competitive with other credit alternatives.**

Redress against the Dealer   Prior to the recent Federal Trade Commission ruling (effective May 14, 1976), a buyer did not have much redress against the dealer once the loan contract was sold. Essentially, the lending institution that purchased the loan would claim that it was not liable to the buyer for unsatisfactory performance by the dealer. Clauses in the contract, called *waiver of defense* or *holder-in-due-course,* made the lender's stance perfectly legal. As a consequence, the buyer could not withhold payment from the lending institution to force corrective action from the dealer. But the new ruling has modified both the holder-in-due-course and waiver-of-defense clauses so that the financial institution cannot use them to avoid its responsibility. Now a buyer can withhold a loan payment to force corrective action from the dealer. This change has significantly improved the consumer's bargaining position when there is a dispute with the dealer.

> **Strategy: Even though you now have redress with the dealer, your best defense is to buy from a dealer you know to be reputable, either through previous dealings or your friends' recommendations.**

Shopping for a Sales Loan

The guidelines outlined in Exhibit 8–2 are equally applicable to sales loans, although the range of choices among sales loans is more limited. Once you have narrowed your choice to a particular brand of automobile, appliance, or furniture, your only sales loan options are those offered by the dealers who sell that brand. But there is no reason to restrict the choice to a sales loan; a cash loan will do as well. Obtain quotes on several cash loans and you will probably find a substantial saving over the dealer's sales loan.

> **Strategy: Compare the APR on the dealer's sales loan with other credit options. Then decide which loan to use.**

CREDIT LIFE INSURANCE

Credit life insurance is offered on most cash and sales loans either as a requirement for obtaining the loan or as an extra cost option. When it is required, the lender must include the premium in the loan's finance charge.

Coverage   Credit life insurance repays the loan should the borrower die before the loan is repaid. Generally, the amount of coverage declines as the outstanding balance on the loan decreases.

Cost   The maximum allowable rates are regulated by the individual states, and they are usually generous: 75 cents to $1 per year for each $100 of coverage. The rate most lenders charge is near the allowable maximums. This is very expensive insurance coverage when you realize that regular term life insurance (discussed in more detail in Chapter 14, Life Insurance and Income Maintenance) would provide the same protection, yet it usually costs less than

40 cents per $100 of coverage. Several studies have concluded that credit life premiums should average 43 cents per $100, or about half the current cost.[2]

Is Credit Life Necessary? Despite the lender's enticing arguments about "peace of mind" and "financial security," we remain unconvinced. If you plan your life insurance coverage along the lines that we will discuss in the life insurance chapter, then credit life likely duplicates the coverage you already have. Even if you decide you do want additional life insurance during the period of the loan, consider regular term life insurance instead of credit life insurance. Assuming credit life costs $1 per $100 and regular term 40 cents per $100, your savings on a $3,000, 3-year loan would be $54 {[($3,000 ÷ $100) × $1.00 × 3 years] − [($3,000 ÷ $100) × $.40 × 3 years]}. Of course, if credit life is a requirement for obtaining the loan, your choices are narrowed.

> **Strategy: Make certain you really need credit life insurance. If you feel it is needed, carefully consider purchasing that coverage from someone beside the lender.**

DISABILITY INSURANCE

Some cash and sales loans offer disability insurance as an extra cost option. This insurance covers the loan payments if the borrower becomes disabled during the period of the loan. Depending on the policy, the coverage may begin immediately when the borrower becomes disabled or not until after a waiting period. Obviously, policies with a waiting period have a lower premium.

Is Disability Insurance Necessary? We have the same reservations about disability insurance as we voiced in the previous discussion on credit life insurance. Purchasing coverage from the lender is generally more expensive than purchasing it from an outside insurance firm. Also, the coverage may duplicate the disability insurance that borrowers have through their employers. If you decide disability insurance is necessary during your loan, check several outside insurance sources to see if you cannot obtain the same coverage at a much lower cost.

OPEN-ENDED CONSUMER CREDIT

Open-ended consumer credit includes a wide range of charge accounts and credit cards. With most open-ended credit, the customer is assigned an upper credit limit. The customer can use any amount of credit within that limit. Most open-ended credit is intended for small, recurring transactions rather than the single transaction that typifies cash and sales loans. However, the extended payment terms on some credit cards and charge accounts have partially removed this limitation.

---

[2]"Credit Insurance: How You Can Get Soaked," *Changing Times*, August 1972, pp. 6–9.

Most open-ended credit has very flexible repayment terms. The customer generally has a choice of extending the repayment over several years, of repaying the entire balance within 30 days, or of repaying according to some schedule between these two extremes. When repayment extends beyond 30 days, the customer generally pays an annual finance charge of 12 to 18 percent. However, by paying the entire balance within the 20- to 30-day grace period, the customer generally avoids any finance charge. The latter feature is the major advantage to open-ended credit.

Charge Account

Charge accounts are offered by individual businesses such as a department store, drugstore, doctor, dentist, or utility company. The use of a charge account is restricted to the particular business that offers the account. Although there are variations, most charge accounts can be grouped into three general categories: regular charge account, revolving account, and option account.

Regular Charge Account   The regular charge account, or 30-day account, is the oldest and most common. When an item is charged on the account, the customer immediately receives title to the item in exchange for a promise to pay at a later date. Purchases are accumulated and billed monthly. The customer is expected to pay the entire balance within 30 days of being billed and there is no finance charge. Failure to repay within the 30-day grace period could entail a monthly service fee of 1 to $1^1/2$ percent on the past-due balance.

Revolving Account   The revolving account allows the customer to extend repayment. Typically, the account requires a minimum monthly payment which could be either a fixed amount, say $25 on a $300 account, or a percentage of the outstanding balance, say 10 percent of the $300. A monthly finance charge of 1 to $1^1/2$ percent is levied against the unpaid balance at the end of the month. As the balance is repaid, the customer can make new purchases up to the limit on the account. The revolving account is primarily intended as medium-term credit—12 to 24 months.

Option Account   The option charge account is a hybrid that combines features from the regular and the revolving accounts. With an option account, the entire balance can be paid within the 25- to 30-day grace period, thereby avoiding any finance charge. Or, the repayment can be extended over 12 to 24 months by paying a finance charge of 1 to $1^1/2$ percent per month on the unpaid balance.

> **Strategy: Match the charge account to the type of item you are going to purchase. Use a regular charge for short-lived and low-priced items. For longer-lived, more expensive items, the extended terms of an option or revolving charge would be appropriate.**

Credit Card Account

Credit card accounts vary from the very specialized cards used only at a single business to cards which are accepted by businesses nationwide and worldwide. A credit card is a very versatile and convenient type of credit. We discuss three major types of credit cards: (1) the two major bank cards (Master Charge and BankAmericard); (2) the credit cards of nationwide retail stores (J.C. Penney Co., Montgomery Ward Co., Sears, Roebuck and Co.) and major oil companies (Mobil Oil, Standard Oil, Shell Oil), and (3) the three travel and entertainment cards (American Express, Diners Club, and Carte Blanche).

Bank Credit Card   The two major bank credit cards are offered by a group of affiliated banks which extends across the United States. Although bank credit cards are accepted nationwide, the individual accounts are administered and controlled by the bank which issued the card. All card holders are assigned an upper credit limit based on their income and credit record: $300 to $1,000 is typical, although higher limits are available. Most banks allow a small overrun of that limit as long as the customer continues to pay the account promptly.

Except for a few states, bank credit cards have no annual membership fee and there is no transaction fee when the card is used. Provided the entire balance is paid within the 25- to 30-day grace period, there is no finance charge. If the balance is not paid within that grace period, there is a monthly finance charge of 1 to 1½ percent, based on either the previous balance, the average daily balance, or the adjusted balance (these were discussed in Chapter 7). Some accounts have a graduated finance charge: 1½ percent on the first $500 and 1 percent on everything over $500. All accounts require that the holder make at least a minimum payment each month.

Extended Payment Supplement   Recently, both bank cards have added an extended payment supplement. This supplement is directed toward large, expensive items that would exceed or largely exhaust the holder's regular credit limit. An item charged on the extended payment supplement has no set upper limit, but the merchant or dealer must obtain approval from an affiliated bank before accepting your purchase and charging it to your account. There is no grace period with the extended payment supplement; monthly finance charges of 1 to 1½ percent begin the day of the purchase. The card holder specifies the repayment period, usually between 6 months and 36 months. All activities in this supplement are shown as separate items on the holder's regular monthly statement. This supplement is similar to the traditional sales loan.

Strategy: Before deciding to use the extended payment supplement, compare its APR and other terms to several cash or sales loans.

Cash Advance   A card holder can obtain a short-term cash advance, but the amount cannot exceed the account's unused credit limit. There is no grace period; monthly finance charges of 1 to 1½ percent begin when the advance is made. The nearest competitor to this cash advance would be the automatic checking account overdraft we discussed in the cash loan section.

Strategy: Before using the cash advance, compare its APR with that for the overdraft on your checking account.

Using the Grace Period   As noted in the previous chapter, you can extend an account's grace period to 50 or 60 days by concentrating your purchases shortly after the billing or closing date. In those cases where you do not have sufficient money to repay on the due date, but where you expect to have the money in a few days, you should use the cash advance (overdraft) on your checking account to pay the balance. For example, assume Sandy Smith's average daily balance on her bank card was $300. Provided she pays the $300 balance by the due date, she avoids the $1^{1}/_{2}$ percent monthly finance charge. But she is short of money on the due date and she does not expect to have the $300 until 10 days later. Missing the due date will cost her $4.50 ($300 × $1^{1}/_{2}$ percent) in finance charges. Yet, if she drew $300 as a cash overdraft on her checking account for 10 days (we assume its APR is 12 percent), her finance charge would only be 99 cents [$300 × (12 percent ÷ 365 days) × 10 days]. The overdraft would save her $3.51 ($4.50 − $.99) in finance charges.

National Retail Store and Major Oil Company Cards   Credit cards of national retail stores and major oil companies provide immediate credit over a wide geographic area, but they can be used only for a limited range of products

and services. All accounts have a credit ceiling based on the card holder's income and credit record. The card holder can repay the entire balance within the 25- to 30-day grace period and thereby avoid any finance charge. Or the repayment period can be extended up to 36 months, but that entails a 1 to $1\frac{1}{2}$ percent monthly finance charge.

Travel and Entertainment Cards The three travel and entertainment (T&E) cards are widely accepted by hotels, motels, restaurants, airlines, major department stores, and other businesses in the United States and many foreign countries.

To qualify for a card, the holder generally must have an annual income of $10,000 or more. In addition, the holder pays an annual membership fee of $15 to $25. There is an upper limit on the account depending on the holder's income and credit record. Except for certain major purchases, the entire balance must be repaid within 30 days. Although there is no finance charge, there is a late payment fee if the amount is not paid within 60 days. Failure to repay the balance promptly can be grounds for canceling the card. While the cards provide cash advances, the terms are much more restrictive than those of bank credit cards.

The principal attraction of T&E cards is that they cover a wide range of products and services and are accepted nearly worldwide. Offsetting these advantages is their annual membership fee coupled with the limited repayment period.

Lost Credit Cards

Prior to an amendment to the truth in lending legislation, card holders were liable for the use of lost or stolen credit cards up to the time the credit card company was notified of the missing card. Now the holder's maximum liability is limited to $50 per credit card. Furthermore, the card holder has that liability only when all the following conditions exist: (1) the card holder has been supplied with a self-addressed form to notify the issuer of a missing card; (2) the unauthorized use occurred before the card issuer was notified; (3) a facsimile of the holder's signature is on the credit card; and (4) the holder was informed of the potential liability when the card was issued. The steps shown in Exhibit 8–4 should be followed if you lose a credit card.

Exhibit 8-4 Steps for Reporting a Missing Credit Card

1 Call the card issuer to report the loss.
2 Obtain the person's name with whom you discuss the loss.
3 Send a certified letter to the card issuer. Save the receipt as proof of notification.
4 Carefully examine subsequent monthly billings for any account charges that were made by someone else.
5 Should you suffer a loss, check your homeowner's or renter's policy. Many cover losses up to $500 or $1,000.

"Minimum Payment Rut"

The extended repayment terms offered by most credit cards substantially enhance their flexibility. Should the holder be temporarily short of cash, the major part of the balance can be deferred to a time when more cash is available to make a larger payment. Typically, most accounts require that the holder repay a percentage of the balance (for example, 5 percent of a $300 balance) or a small fixed payment (for example, $10 on a $300 balance). But some people abuse the minimum payment option to the point where it becomes a distinct liability.

Assume Fred Bear charged $280 on his credit card during the past month. His bill arrives, and since he is short of cash, he elects to make only the required $10 minimum payment. The finance charge is 1½ percent per month on the balance. We assume he continues to make the same $10 minimum payment each month. The details of how the repayment would proceed are shown in Exhibit 8–5.

As the details in Exhibit 8–5 illustrate, during the first several months, about $4 of the $10 monthly payment goes to pay the finance charge and only $6 goes toward repaying the account balance. Even after 12 months, $3 pays the finance charge, $7 repays the balance, and the balance is still nearly $200. By paying only the minimum required amount, it would take nearly 36 months to completely repay the balance. In effect, the credit card account has become a long-term loan. And with an APR of 18 percent (1½ percent for 12 months), it is an expensive source of long-term credit.

Exhibit 8-5   Repayment Schedule with Minimum Payment

Month	Opening balance	Payment	Finance charge*	Ending balance†
1	$280.00	$10	0	$270.00
2	270.00	10	$4.05	264.05
3	264.05	10	3.96	258.01
4	258.01	10	3.87	251.88
.	.	.	.	.
.	.	.	.	.
.	.	.	.	.
12	206.32	10	3.09	199.41
.	.	.	.	.
.	.	.	.	.
.	.	.	.	.
24	116.27	10	1.74	108.01
.	.	.	.	.
.	.	.	.	.
.	.	.	.	.
30	64.84	10	0.97	55.81

*Computed as: 1½ percent × opening balance. No finance charge in the first month since it was assumed to be the grace period.

†Computed as: ending balance = opening balance − (payment − finance charge).

It is not hard to imagine a situation where a credit card holder would never fully repay the account. That is, as soon as a portion of the balance was repaid, the holder would charge some additional items and run the account balance back up again. For those people, we probably could expand the old truism that the only sure things are death and taxes to include yet a third item: an outstanding balance in their credit card account!

> **Strategy: You should limit your use of the minimum payment option to periods of temporary financial emergency. If you need repayment terms of 24 to 36 months, consider a cash loan as a substitute. Often its APR will be much lower than the APR of a credit card account.**

BORROWING MONEY FOR COLLEGE

The best place to begin your search for education funds is the financial aids office (the typical title) at the college of your choice. It can generally provide information on whether you qualify and the general availability of funds from the large national loan programs as well as details on the rapidly expanding list of private, state-sponsored, and professionally supported loan and assistance programs. Because this latter group is so diverse and varied, we will concentrate our discussion on three national programs: direct government loans, government-guaranteed loans, and commercial sources.

Direct Government Loans

At its peak, this program funneled tremendous amounts of money to eligible students; but the program has been cut back to the point where it is only a shadow of its former self. Its most attractive features are still there: low cost combined with liberal repayment terms.

Limits Qualified students can borrow up to $5,000 during their undergraduate careers. Borrowing during the first two years cannot exceed $2,500. Since this loan is so attractive, student demand greatly exceeds available funds. So you should be prepared to accept substantially less than the cited maximums.

Qualifications To qualify, the prospective borrower must demonstrate financial need. But each educational institution defines "need" differently and it has the final word on who qualifies and for what amount. Application for a loan should be made directly to the financial aids office at the university of your choice.

Cost This loan's biggest attraction is its extremely low finance charge: 3 percent annually! Furthermore, borrowers are not required to begin repayments and are not assessed any finance charge until 9 months after they leave school. The maximum maturity is 10 years. Should the borrower join the Peace Corps, Vista, or the military service, attend graduate school, or work as a teacher, he or she may qualify for extended repayment terms and possibly a partial cancellation of the loan.

Strategy: Even if you can satisfy only part of your needs through a direct government loan, it is well worth your time to apply.

Government-guaranteed Loans

The guaranteed loan was designed to remove the federal government from the lending business. An outside commercial lender, such as a savings and loan association, bank, or credit union, extends the funds to the student; the federal government merely guarantees their repayment.

Limits   To qualify for this loan, the prospective borrower does not have to demonstrate financial need. But the borrower must find a financial institution that is willing to lend the money. The amount of the loan is limited to $2,500 per year or $10,000 during the undergraduate period.

Cost   The maximum APR for the finance charge is 7 percent. Repayment begins 9 to 12 months after the borrower leaves school, but the finance charge begins when the loan is granted. However, if the borrower can show "need," the federal government will pay the finance charge until graduation. Maximum maturities run between 5 and 10 years. With its low 7 percent APR, this loan ranks next to a direct government loan in desirability. Unfortunately, while a low APR is attractive to borrowers, it is unattractive to lenders. Because of the low APR, many financial institutions are reluctant to commit funds to this plan. Your search for a willing lender may be long, and the amount offered will likely be less than the maximum.

Commercial Sources

Traditional lending sources (banks, credit unions, finance companies) also grant loans for educational purposes. Unlike direct government loans and government-guaranteed loans, commercial education loans have fewer restrictions on amounts, but their finance charge is at current market rates, which makes them much more expensive. In reality, a commercial education loan is a consumer cash loan with a specialized purpose. The borrower must begin repaying the loan almost immediately and the finance charge ranges from 12 to 36 percent annually. The immediate repayment requirement, coupled with the heavy finance charge, makes this source much less suited to financing an entire undergraduate-degree program. But the commercial source can be a useful supplement if you need only temporary or partial financial assistance.

SUMMARY

1   Consumer credit transactions can be either secured or unsecured. With a secured loan, the borrower either pledges some personal asset or has some other individual(s) cosign the note.
2   A consumer cash loan involves two people, the borrower and the lender, and the loan proceeds are paid in cash.
3   A borrower should shop for credit just as if shopping for any large purchase: obtain price quotations, compare features, obtain an explanation when a feature is not fully understood.

4 The salient features of a sales loan are: (*a*) It is used to purchase large-ticket items; (*b*) the loan provides no cash; and (*c*) generally there are three parties—the borrower, the dealer, and the lender.

5 All sales loans are secured th·ough one of the following: conditional sales contract (widely used), chattel mortgage (less widely used), or bailment lease (only limited use). In nearly all cases, the lender can repossess the pledged asset should the borrower fail to repay the loan.

6 Buyers can now withhold payment on a sales loan to force corrective action from the dealer.

7 The decision to accept or reject credit life insurance should be based first on whether the coverage is needed, and second on whether the coverage can be obtained at a lower cost elsewhere.

8 With open-ended credit, the consumer has a fixed amount of credit available, but the consumer decides when and to what extent that credit will be utilized.

9 Credit cards offer more flexibility than charge accounts because they are accepted by a wide range of retail and service businesses.

10 Since the passage of federal legislation in 1971, credit card holders' maximum liability from the unauthorized use of their cards is set at $50 per card.

11 By making only the required "minimum payment" on a credit card account, the card holder greatly extends the repayment period, but the finance charge is high.

12 The best source of information on availability of education funds is the financial aids department at the college you wish to attend.

13 Direct government education loans or government-guaranteed loans offer attractive repayment terms coupled with low finance charges.

REVIEW YOUR UNDERSTANDING OF

Secured credit

Unsecured credit

Cosigner

Automatic advance or overdraft

Credit unions

    Membership requirements

    Open membership

Loan sharks

Conditional sales contract

Chattel mortgage

Bailment lease

Balloon contract

Add-on clause

Acceleration clause

Repossession

Credit life insurance

Charge accounts

    Regular

    Revolving

    Option

Grace period

Minimum payment rut

Education loans

    Direct government loans

    Government-guaranteed loans

DISCUSSION QUESTIONS

1 What advantages and disadvantages do you see for the lender in having a secured consumer cash loan rather than an unsecured loan? What about the borrower?

2 Compare and contrast a commercial bank with a credit union as a potential source of a cash loan.

3 What are the principal differences between a consumer cash loan and a sales loan? What key factors should be considered in deciding between the two loans?

4   What factors account for the fact that the APR on cash loans from consumer finance companies generally exceeds those from banks and credit unions?

5   What problems and potential pitfalls are associated with a cash loan using a second mortgage?

6   If a friend should ask for a checklist of things she should look for when shopping for a loan, what would you recommend?

7   Explain how you can maximize the grace period on most major credit cards.

8   Do you feel a borrower should always purchase credit life insurance? Why?

9   Do you agree with the following: "Allowing the lender to repossess the item that is pledged as security on a loan is a poor way to repay that loan"? Why?

10 What are the major differences between a charge account and a credit card account?

11 What advantages are there to the small minimum-payment feature that many credit cards offer? Are there disadvantages?

12 What factors account for the rapid expansion of bank credit cards? What future do you see for these cards?

13 What is the credit card holder's liability should a card be lost or stolen? Are there any special conditions?

14 What features make government-guaranteed education loans so attractive? Why are funds so hard to obtain?

15 How have the recent legislative changes improved the buyer's bargaining position with the seller once the sales loan has been sold to a bank or finance company? Why was this change necessary?

CASE PROBLEM

Eric and Ingrid Svensen have decided to replace the kitchen stove and refrigerator that came with their house. The stove and refrigerator they want are handled by the local appliance dealer. The dealer's price for the two units is $800 and he has assured them that he will handle all the financing problems. Eric and Ingrid think that the dealer's sales loan seems a bit costly: a 24-month loan with an APR of 30 percent, and credit life and disability insurance included as extra cost items. But they feel they are fortunate that the dealer will make the small loan. Both doubt that their bank or credit union would make an $800 loan. The Svensens' current monthly debt payments (excluding mortgage) are 10 percent of their monthly disposable income. Loan payment is $44.73 monthly.

a   Is a sales loan their only option? Could you recommend an alternative?

b   What is your opinion of the above loan? Do you see any problems with the dealer-arranged loan?

c   What would be the potential saving if the Svensens could find the same 24-month loan with an APR of 12? Of 9? (*Hint:* The loan payment exhibit in Chapter 7 may be helpful.)

d   The Svensens have considered charging the two units on their bank credit card (their limit is $1,000) and making the minimum monthly payment. What are the strengths and weaknesses in this option?

e   How should the Svensens decide about the credit life and disability insurance? If they decide the coverage is needed, what would you recommend?

RECOMMENDED READINGS

Booklets

Hawver, Carl F., *Basic Principles in Family Money and Credit Management.* Washington, D.C.: National Consumer Finance Association, 1972.
Chapter 2 includes a discussion of consumer sales loans. A useful glossary is provided at the end of the chapter.

Credit Union National Association, Inc., *Using Credit Wisely.* Madison, Wis., 1966.
Chapter 4 provides a comparative analysis of the major sources of consumer cash loans. Sections 1 and 2 of chapter 5, respectively, discuss consumer sales loans and open-ended consumer credit. The final section of chapter 5 concludes with an informative consumer credit glossary.

Magazines

Changing Times:

"Credit Insurance: How You Can Get Soaked." August 1972, pp. 6–9.
Good coverage of that topic.

"How to Pay Those College Bills." September 1973, pp. 17–20.
Discusses sources of college financing.

"The Big-Name Credit Cards and How They Compare." September 1973, pp. 25–28.
Discusses the coverage, cost, and extent of the credit services offered by the principal credit cards.

"When You Need to Borrow Cash." February 1975, pp. 33–34.
Discusses sources of cash loans and points to be considered.

"If Installment Contracts Said It in Plain English." July 1975, pp. 46–47.
Discusses needed revisions to installment sales contracts.

Money:

"An Owner's Manual for Financing a Car." December 1973, pp. 78–82.
Discusses that topic in detail.

Consumer Reports:

"How to Shop for Credit." March 1975, pp. 171–178.
Excellent discussion of the alternative sources for cash loans, sales loans, and open-ended credit.

CONSUMER EXPENDITURES

Chapter 9

Consumerism

After completing this chapter you should be able to:

explain the development of consumer protection legislation forward from *caveat emptor*.

discuss the advantages and disadvantages to consumer protection legislation.

recognize the problems and abuses the average consumer faces.

explain how consumer buyers' clubs operate.

recall the most frequently encountered consumer frauds.

compare various pricing practices and determine which ones are designed to confuse and mislead potential buyers.

explain how deceptive advertising presents a product or situation which differs from reality.

compare and **contrast** the two routes consumer protection legislation has taken.

develop an effective complaint.

design a recovery strategy for obtaining satisfaction with a defective product or inadequate service.

Consumerism is one of the buzz words of the 1970s. Everyone who uses the word does not agree on precisely the same definition. However, the word seems to denote the attitudes and activities related to consumer protection, consumer redress, and, in general, making known the consumers' needs to producers, manufacturers, dealers, advertisers, and government legislators. Before consumerism and the consumer movement, the relationship between the consumer and business was *caveat emptor*, a Latin expression meaning "let the buyer beware." Surely, that attitude did not favor the consumer; it protected business. And with that protection, deceptive advertising, fraudulent sales methods, shoddy products, and worthless warranties became standard business practices. The goal of consumerism is to change all that.

The origins of consumerism can be traced to the muckrakers of the 1920s who exposed the deplorable conditions in the meat-packing plants. The efforts of the muckrakers forced the institution of federal inspection of meat-packing operations, producing a substantial upgrading in food processing standards. However, with a few other exceptions, the early consumerism efforts made little impact until recently when Ralph Nader single-handedly brought General Motors to its knees. Nader, working alone and with no significant financial backing, spotlighted the unsafe conditions in autos which were being ignored by the manufacturers. As a direct result of Nader's efforts, manufacturers now announce defects in their autos and recall the cars for repairs, even after purchase. Nader demonstrated that the consumer voice can be heard by business and that business can be moved to provide satisfactory results.

The success of Ralph Nader seems to have ignited a pent-up need of consumers to have their grievances heard and acted on. Governmental agencies, which were long charged with consumer protection but did little about it, now feel the change in the nation's mood and have started vigorously championing the cause of the consumer. All this activity has produced an effort on the consumer's behalf which cannot be turned off.

Consumerism is not just Ralph Nader and government agencies trying to protect the consumer. It is also a wide-ranging effort directed at consumer education. There is no central power or authority responsible for consumer education. Instead, it is being provided by schools and colleges, magazines, newspaper reporters, and federal and state government agencies. The basic assumption underlying consumer education is that more knowledgeable consumers will make better use of their income.

There are two sides to consumerism, protection and education, and they both will be explored in this chapter. The specifics of either subject could fill volumes. Consequently, we will limit ourselves to a few typical examples which should help you in making decisions involving many different consumer situations.

CONSUMER PROTECTION

The English common-law phrase *caveat emptor,* "let the buyer beware," essentially means that the buyer is responsible for examining a product for possible defects and shortcomings before making the purchase. Under this doctrine, should the product prove defective or perform inadequately, the buyer typically has little recourse against the seller. But the increased complexity of products and services has pointed up weaknesses in this doctrine. First, the average consumer cannot be expected to possess the wide array of technical and engineering skills needed to judge complex products. Second, today's consumers are involved in a tremendous number of purchase decisions every year. It is not possible for them to fully evaluate and analyze each decision. Finally, *caveat emptor* was intended to protect the seller, not the buyer.

Consumers have become much more vocal and have taken a more active role in pushing new consumer legislation. In part, their interest has come from their increased awareness that they really do have a choice when selecting products and services. That is, they do not have to accept everything the seller offers. Further, they realize that a product or service can be reasonably trouble-free if the manufacturer or service firm makes a concerted effort. This consumer awareness has fostered legislation that specifies certain minimum quality and performance standards and establishes avenues of redress for the purchaser should the product be faulty.

To no small degree, the sellers' attitude of "the consumer be damned" indirectly encouraged additional consumer legislation. When a product proved faulty, their defense was *caveat emptor.* When customers complained, their complaints seldom got any results. Yet, sellers continued to advertise that this year's product was vastly better than last year's. "Buy this and your every problem, need, and desire will be fulfilled." Advertising that made false claims and products that failed to fulfill such claims started a trail of irate buyers who demanded increased consumer legislation.

Consumer Protection: A Necessity?

The consumer experience has suggested that consumer protection is indeed a necessity. The consumer as an individual is in a woefully inadequate position when confronting some of the corporate giants that are today's sellers. Consequently, consumer protection legislation has become an integral part of today's business world. While most would agree some protection is essential, the question of how much remains unresolved.

Benefits   Properly structured consumer protection legislation can provide some definite benefits. It can help the consumer receive fair value for the price paid. Further, it can set standards so that a product can be safely used for its intended purpose. Moreover, it can set minimums to ensure that a product is reasonably wholesome and will not injure the consumer's health.

Disadvantages   There are also some potential disadvantages to consumer protection laws, especially laws that are overzealous in their coverage. For one thing, legislation can seriously restrict free choice for both the seller and consumer. Excessive regulation can result in standardized products and inhibit the introduction of innovative products. Sellers may withdraw from the marketplace because they face an overwhelming array of complex rules and regulations. In the end, the laws that were intended to improve the consumer's lot may actually work in reverse.

There is also a question of whether these protection laws may eventually completely replace the consumer's responsibility in making buying decisions. After all, the seller still needs some protection from consumers. For example, there are consumers who have the time to make, and enjoy making, flimsy or fictitious complaints and claims to manufacturers. Also, there are consumers who do not properly maintain or service a product and who expect the manufacturer to honor their claim when the product eventually becomes faulty. Consumer protection laws should take these things into consideration.

A third potential disadvantage is that restrictive laws can substantially raise the cost of a product or service. Unfortunately, this possibility is all too often overlooked in the rush to pass consumer legislation. In the end, it is the consumer who pays for the added costs of incorporating the required improvements or safety features. Without question, there are times when the added burden is justified. But there are times when the added cost of meeting stringent new regulations can price a product out of the reach of most people. In those cases, consumers lose their right to a free choice.

Needed: A Balance   Consumer protection must balance the gains with the disadvantages. What is needed is careful consideration of each proposed consumer protection regulation to determine whether the gains match the costs. If not, the regulation should be modified until that balance is achieved.

Who should be charged with making that decision? The consumer? The producer? The seller? Some government agency? To be meaningful and balanced, the decision needs input from all four. Consumers should participate because the outcome has a direct impact on their welfare and satisfaction. The producer and the seller deserve a role because they can provide data on the cost of a proposed regulation. And their welfare, plus the welfare of their employees, is affected by the outcome. The government agency can coordinate and weigh the input from these three sources to make a decision. Furthermore, once a particular consumer protection provision is enacted, there should be an organization that will enforce it.

CONSUMER EDUCATION: "GOOD DEALS" MAY BE BAD DEALS

Perhaps a better name for consumer education would be consumer awareness. Consumers are too often duped not because the information is unavailable, but because they are not aware it is available. Pointing out what information is available and prodding the consumer to think about it should be the objective of consumer education.

Consumer Buyers' Clubs: What Are They?

Consumer buyers' clubs represent themselves as organizations to help the consumer buy big-ticket items, such as appliances and furniture, directly from the manufacturer or wholesaler at prices substantially below retail levels. The clubs publish sales literature that makes membership sound exclusive and desirable. Their sales pitch often maintains that to become a member, you must be recommended by another active member. If you turn down the offer of membership, you will never have the chance to join at a later date. The implication is that membership is too valuable to be passed up.

Consumer buyers' clubs are generally small regional operations. They may operate in one major city or in a number of medium-sized communities in a fairly small geographic area. Typically, the club has an office, a secretary, and a phone, and that is the extent of their operations. The catalogs of the merchandise available through the club are located in the office. The member may come in, select merchandise through one of the catalogs, and order the item through the club. The club advertises that savings of 10 to 50 percent or more are possible by buying directly from the manufacturer or wholesaler. The possibility of 50 percent savings certainly has a great deal of appeal for most people. As a result, membership in many of the clubs has reached 20,000 or more families.

What Are the Costs?   So far, the buyers' clubs look like a good deal; like all good deals, however, there is a cost involved. In the case of many buyers' clubs, that cost can be substantial. Membership in a typical club is offered for 10 years and calls for an initiation fee of $39.95. That really does not seem too bad. But the fine print in the membership form discloses that there are dues of $360, payable over 24 months. Thus, to join, the cost is $39.95 down and $15 per month for 24 months; total cost of the membership comes to $399.95, or almost $400. Other clubs may charge a bit more or less, but the total cost in this example is representative.

Even at this high cost, the clubs might be a bargain if they provided the savings which they advertise. But that seldom happens. For example, a club's claim of savings of 50 percent is based on the full retail cost; the club's claim fails to consider the possibility of sales or other price reductions which are generally available elsewhere.

For the purpose of evaluating the cost of membership, we will assume that 10 percent represents an achievable saving through a buyers' club. That means that an individual must buy $4,000 of merchandise just to recover the membership costs!

> **Strategy: Before considering a membership in a consumer buyers' club, be sure to compare the cost of the membership with the potential savings. If you do this, you will most likely not join the club.**

Limitations   Detracting further from the attractiveness of the clubs are a host of variables which are not apparent at first glance. Therefore, we will discuss some of them in the following sections.

Contractual Obligation   Often the buyers' club will introduce a third party to the contract by charging the dues to the member's Master Charge account. If the member does not happen to have a Master Charge credit card, the club opens an account for that individual. By transferring the dues to the individual's Master Charge account, the club obtains its money immediately. The member then must make payments to Master Charge, and now the membership dues payments are converted into a credit obligation. This means that a member who wants to withdraw from the club cannot do so by discontinuing the dues payments because that would be defaulting on a credit obligation. Thus, membership in a buyers' club could affect your credit rating.

Another thing to consider: When the dues payments are transferred to a credit card account, the finance charge further increases the total cost of membership in the buyers' club.

Minimum Order Size   Most clubs are unwilling to handle orders for less than $10. Thus, small purchases are impossible to make through the club.

Comparison Shopping   Since all purchases must be made through a catalog, the merchandise cannot be examined before you buy it. To be sure, you can go to a store and see the item before ordering. But stores do not always carry the items listed in a manufacturer's catalog.

Returns   When you buy a sofa or refrigerator through an established, reputable retail store, you can usually return the item with no difficulty. After the sofa is delivered, you may not like the color or there may be a small nick on the leg. A telephone call to the dealer is usually all that is needed to get proper return service. However, when buying through a club, you must handle all aspects of the return. For example, if the furniture factory is located in Greenville, South Carolina, and you live in Portland, Oregon, the burden of making this exchange is yours, not the manufacturer's, and there is no dealer to help you. For many people, just the annoyance of trying to handle such a situation far outweighs any potential savings.

Recommended Savings   Many of the buyers' clubs discourage members from ordering anything unless the saving is at least $30. It appears that the objective of the buyers' club is to sell memberships, not merchandise. In fact, since the clubs do not make a profit on sales, there is little incentive to assist members in purchasing goods.

Are There Any Advantages to Clubs?   From our investigation, we can find no reason for a person to buy membership (notice we did not say "join"!) in a consumer buyers' club. The limitations of buying through clubs should be enough to dissuade most potential members. To clinch your decision against membership, consider how little buying activity the clubs actually produce: According to state sales tax records, a club with over 20,000 members delivered only $25,000 of merchandise in a recent 3-month period. This is only $1.25 per member. At that rate, it would take the average member 800 years to recoup the cost of membership, assuming purchases through the club yield 10 percent savings over retail prices. The club in the meantime has collected dues of almost $8 million! Little wonder that the clubs have no interest in helping people after they join. Repeating: Clubs sell memberships, not merchandise.

OTHER HIGH-PRESSURE SALES GIMMICKS

Consumer buyers' clubs are not the only place where consumers are being bilked by high-pressure sales tactics. There are many other door-to-door, telephone, and even in-store schemes to defraud the unwary customer. A few examples should make you aware of such schemes.

Freezer Deals   First cousins of the buyers' clubs are the deals which sell freezers and frozen food. The deal goes something like this: If you buy a freezer from the dealer for $350, you will also be sold frozen food, including meat, at wholesale prices. But the deal is usually very unsatisfactory for several reasons. The freezer can often be purchased at any appliance store for

IT'S ALL YOURS FOLKS—
ONE FREEZER AND
500 POUNDS OF MEAT!

about $200. Like the buyers' clubs, the freezer dealers have little interest in selling the frozen food after the refrigerator sale. Often the bargain food turns out to be of inferior quality. Many people just forget about ordering any more food when they see how bad their first shipment is. This is precisely what the dealer wants them to do. After all, if dealers can sell a $200 freezer for $350 but do not make much profit on the frozen food, of course they are delighted when you discontinue your orders.

> **Strategy: Before signing a contract for a freezer, compare the price of the model being offered with the retail price available from a reputable retailer. If the freezer deal price is above the retail price, you can be almost certain that the freezer deal being offered should be rejected without further investigation. In any case, before committing yourself to a freezer deal, check the dealer's reputation by contacting a local better business bureau.**

Outright Frauds

Many door-to-door sales practices are fradulent. The buyers' clubs and freezer deals are within the letter of the law since they do deliver the service they sell. They may not be in the consumers' best interest, but they are not illegal. Other door-to-door operations actually overstep the bounds of legality.

The Furnace Game   Several classic schemes have swindled millions of dollars from unwary consumers. In one well-known ploy, a reputable-looking man posing as a city furnace inspector calls on a homeowner. After inspecting the furnace, he announces that immediate repairs must be made to prevent a serious explosion or fire. He just happens to know a repair service that can

INSPECTOR.. THIS IS THE WATER HEATER.. THE FURNACE IS IN THE OTHER ROOM...

complete the work that afternoon. Not wanting to see the family home burn to the ground, the homeowner jumps at the opportunity of getting an immediate repair. The repair job performed by the recommended firm is usually unnecessary, and often nothing is even done to the furnace. This operation is outright fraud. Cities do not send around furnace inspectors, and even if they did, they would be prohibited from recommending specific repair services.

The obvious question you are probably asking yourself is: Who would be stupid enough to fall for such a scheme? The answer is: many people. This type of fraud is particularly successful with older people and the poorly educated. But it has also bilked a lot of college graduates. The people that run these operations are skillful. They know the type of neighborhood to work in and they can sense when the homeowner is aware that the operation is not legitimate. They work in such a way that arrests and convictions are difficult. And that is why these people are still around, defrauding more and more unsuspecting customers.

> **Strategy: Beware of anyone who tries to rush you into costly repairs of technically complex items. Call the manufacturer of the item and ask for the name of a service shop to determine if you really need repairs.**

The Saturday Afternoon Special   Another widely successful scheme is the driveway reblacking ploy. There is a special product which can extend the life and improve the appearance of asphalt driveways. An unsuspecting homeowner will usually be contacted late on a Saturday afternoon by a man who claims to have been applying this product to driveways in the neighborhood. The man explains that he has a little of the blacking compound left and, rather than take it back to the shop, he offers to do the homeowner's driveway for a bargain price which may be as much as $50 below the standard cost. Usually these con men are not legitimate operators. In many instances, all they do is spread a gallon of old crankcase oil on the driveway. It immediately improves the appearance of the drive by making it blacker. However, it does nothing to prolong its life and may in fact harm the asphalt. As with the furnace repair fraud, arrest and conviction are difficult. The amount of money involved is not large, and since something was actually spread on the driveway, proving that a crime has been committed is virtually impossible.

Avoiding High-Pressure Sales Tactics

When confronted with a door-to-door sales agent or telephone solicitor, consumers should summon all the resistance they can muster. A few pointed questions can uncover the details of any deal. Do not be afraid to ask them. To evaluate any door-to-door or telephone offer, develop your questions from the following:

1   *Do* find out the total cost of the deal. Many offers are couched in terms of "pennies a day" or "less than the price of a Sunday newspaper." Remember, 50 pennies a day is nearly $200 per year.

2 *Do* insist that the salesperson explain all parts of the contract. Keep asking questions until you understand everything in the contract.

3 *Do* find out if the contract can be canceled, the merchandise returned, and your money refunded.

4 *Do* ask for references.

5 *Do* check with the better business bureau to make sure that the company is reputable.

6 *Do not* sign any contract without thinking it over for at least 2 or 3 days. There are no deals that are too good to pass up. If the salesperson pressures you to sign by saying the offer will be unavailable in a day or two, that assertion is a pretty good reason for refusing to sign a contract.

Finding Information

The examples we have discussed are situations where the consumer must make a buying decision based on an analysis of facts that are immediately available. That is, the situation itself presents the necessary facts to be evaluated. However, there are many situations where consumers can make better decisions if they carefully research the subject prior to making the purchase. In each of the chapters of this book, we have included recommended readings to assist you in making your financial decisions. We urge you as consumers to make use of the chapter bibliographies and to delve even more deeply into many of the subjects. It has been estimated that the difference between good and bad buying may run as high as $50,000 over a person's working lifetime. We think that a little additional reading is a small price to pay for such potentially large savings.

Deceptive Advertising

It can be argued that by its very nature, any advertising is deceptive. Companies obviously do not point out the negative aspects of their products. Stressing a product's positive features is generally accepted as an ethical practice. Advertising becomes deceptive when the product or service is represented as something other than its true self. It becomes unacceptable when the misrepresentation induces consumers to purchase a product they would otherwise reject.

Deceptive advertising is not limited to disreputable firms. Some of the largest companies engage in advertising which, on close examination, could be considered questionable. A few examples will illustrate what we mean.

The Soup with Marbles A leading producer of canned soups photographed its product on a well-set table to display its appetizing qualities. Since vegetables and meat are not very buoyant, they sink in soup. An honest photo of the soup would show only the broth, not the meat and vegetables (especially if there were not much meat and vegetables in the soup to begin with). To solve this problem, the manufacturer put marbles in the bottom of the soup bowl to make sure the camera would show the vegetables and meat.

Deceptive advertising? It certainly makes the product appear to be

THE SECRET OF THE BUSINESS IS THIS, KID—TOMORROW NEVER COMES!

something it is not. It does not cost the consumer much, but if truth is important, why does the company misrepresent the product this way?

The Extra-Strength Cold Remedy A leading patent medicine proclaims that it contains the pain reliever most prescribed by doctors. The advertisement does not say so, but that pain reliever happens to be aspirin, which is available at much lower cost. The manufacturer of this medicine goes on to say that it contains extra strength. The extra strength is the addition of caffeine, which has no known pain-relieving effect.

This advertisement misleads to the extent that the aspirin is purported to be some miracle drug prescribed by doctors and that a noneffective ingredient is said to add extra strength.

Other Heavily Advertised Products Many other products of questionable value are sold with the help of extensive advertising, often misleading or deceptive. However, it is difficult to correct such advertising because the deception must be proved and the litigation is a slow process. Examples of some of the products are given below.

Vitamins According to many medical authorities, vitamins are unnecessary in all but a few cases where a dietary deficiency exists. Americans still continue to consume millions of dollars worth annually despite such medical findings. In large part, we continue to buy vitamins because the advertisements lead us to believe that they will make us young and vibrant.

Mouthwashes The evidence is conclusive that bad breath is often caused by food particles between the teeth. Proper brushing and the use of dental floss are all that is required to eliminate this particular problem. Despite these facts, we continue to buy mouthwashes and other such products because of the way they are advertised.

Why Take Advertising to Task?

Why the stress on deceptive advertising? We feel that an awareness of some of the misuses and abuses of advertising can save you substantial amounts of money. If you are buying products which give you no benefits and you stop buying them, the result will be a net addition to your spendable income.

Pricing

Businesses have been guilty of using questionable pricing practices to make products appear to be more of a bargain than they really are. An awareness of some of the more blatant tactics can be helpful in avoiding the apparent but fictitious bargains being offered by some retailers.

Psychological Pricing   This involves the use of prices such as $4.97 rather than $5. Most consumers, seeing $4.97, think of the product as a $4 item, not the $5 that it really is. In a classic case of the use of psychological pricing, a merchant who was selling an item for 40 cents advertised the article as two for 99 cents. In total contradiction of economic theory, which contends that when prices are increased less goods will be sold, this merchant actually increased sales volume for the product over 50 times shortly after changing the price.

Inflated List Prices   Another way to make an item look like a bargain is to inflate the list price and then offer a large discount from that price. Of course, all that has really happened is that the product is being offered at a realistic price. Unfortunately, many consumers have a weakness for bargains, real or imaginary. The only way to avoid this type of deception is to be aware of product prices.

"Bait and Switch"

Unfortunately, the "bait and switch" routine is a prevalent sales tactic. Although it is illegal, it is still around, but in a restrained form. The routine goes something like this: First there is the "bait"—a heavily advertised product that entices the customer through its super low price—then comes the "switch"— the customer, once attracted, is switched from the bait to a more expensive product. The switch techniques are numerous and ingenious.

The salesperson may claim that the store is out of the "bait" (if it ever had any), but that it will "sacrifice" a more expensive product as a substitute (translated, that means the merchant's profit is slightly less than exorbitant). Alternatively, the salesperson expounds on the weaknesses and shortcomings of the "bait." Of course there always is a highly recommended substitute (translated, that means a higher price and more dealer profit). Another switch technique is to present the "bait" in the worst possible light. Pick a ghastly color, hide it in a corner, put no display lights on it, assemble it without a few parts; any and all of these deceptive presentation techniques may be used. Of course, the customer readily agrees it is a loser, at which point he or she is shown a "better model." The final technique borders on outright fraud. In advertising the "bait," the store grossly misrepresents it. For example, it might claim the item is full-sized when it is not.

Regardless of the exact switch technique used, you can protect yourself by just refusing to be switched. If you really are interested in the "bait," fine, but stick to your original plan. Should you decide that the "bait" is not what you want, or if you find it is unobtainable, look elsewhere; chances are that you will not be missing any great bargains by passing up the substitutes. If you encounter this practice, report it to your local better business bureau and the consumer protection agency in your state.

Strategy: Avoid being switched by demanding the "bait" if it really fits your needs. If it is not what you want, drop that store and shop a competitor.

Misleading Labels

What is the giant economy size and how does it compare with the family size or the regular size? Many of the products we buy have labels which do more to confuse than to provide information on size and price. Some help is available in the form of unit pricing. Products labeled on a unit-price basis show the cost of the item on a per ounce basis, permitting the consumer to compare the giant economy size directly with the regular package size.

CONSUMER PROTECTION LEGISLATION

Most consumer legislation has taken two decidedly different tracks to achieve increased protection. One approach has placed specific limits and controls on certain business practices. The other approach requires that a consumer be provided with sufficient information to evaluate a product or service.

Limits and Controls on Business Practices   Essentially this legislation assumes consumers are not in a position to judge and therefore rules and regulations are needed to protect them.

Product Quality   Probably the best examples are the regulations setting minimum product-quality standards on food items and drugs. These regulations set production standards, limit the materials used in production, and place controls on the final use of the product. The minimum quality standards for "all meat hot dogs" are an example of this type of legislation; the standards not only specify the maximum percentages of fat and cereal those hot dogs contain, but they also limit the type of meat that can be used.

Safety and Health   These regulations set specific safety minimums on certain products. The ban on children's toys that could inflict injury or present potential hazard is an example. The required safety equipment on new automobiles is another example.

Fraud and Deception   The legislation in this area is aimed at eliminating fraudulent and deceptive practices. Examples include the controls on door-to-door high-pressure sales, using the mails for illicit sales schemes, and the use of false and misleading claims to sell a product.

How Much Control?   While the spirit of consumer protection legislation is admirable, the reality is that it cannot cover every conceivable circumstance. Even though the coverage of early legislation has been reinterpreted and broadened, legislation cannot hold the consumer's hand through each and every transaction. New products and business practices arise too fast for legislation to regulate and control them all. Consumers must continue to assume a large part of the responsibility for their own protection.

Sufficient Consumer Information   Much of the recent consumer legislation has been directed toward requiring that consumers be provided with certain minimum information. Given this, they can make an informed decision.

Improved Labeling   Recent legislation requires that each product be accompanied with information that discloses the product's contents, its performance specification, its operating cost, its expected life, and similar facts. Even more important, the information disclosed must be reasonably understandable.

Truth and Fair Reporting   This legislation is primarily directed toward minimum disclosures on consumer services: credit cards, loan transactions, home purchases, and credit bureau reports. Since services are even harder to analyze than products, it is essential that the consumer have sufficient information to judge the cost and extent of the promised service.

How Much Information?   One well-documented fact has emerged from recent minimum disclosure requirements. Even if a manufacturer or a seller provides consumers with a mountain of understandable data, the information does not mean that the consumer will be well-informed. All that information means little or nothing to a consumer who lacks the skills and training to use it. For too long we have accepted the premise that consumers will somehow weld all the information they are given into a cohesive, intelligible decision. Present evidence suggests that the consumer is the weakest link in the consumer protection chain. This is not to say we should reduce the information that consumer legislation has finally pried loose from the seller. Instead, we must undertake the massive effort of training consumers to effectively use that information. Certainly, there is still a need for additional information in many areas, but what we need right now is a better-informed and better-trained consumer.

> **Strategy: If you are not clear about what a particular disclosure means, ask the seller for an explanation. Barring success there, research the topic at your local public library.**

Consumer Protection Agencies

There are many different agencies charged with the responsibility of protecting the consumer. Most of them are at the federal level. But consumer protection is moving closer to the people. State and local governmental units have taken a more active role in protecting the welfare of their constituents.

Federal Agencies   The majority of federal agencies are multifaceted operations. For most of these agencies, consumer protection is only one of their many responsibilities. They may also have close ties to industry or service groups. This connection has caused critics to charge that serving both consumers and industry produces results that satisfy neither. There are also agencies that have almost no input from consumers, yet consumer protection is supposed to be one of their principal duties.

Coverage   Most federal agencies limit their coverage to interstate transactions. That is, unless a transaction extends across a state boundary, it is not the responsibility of the federal agency. And, if there is a poor business practice going on only within your state, and your state has no consumer protection agency, you must protect yourself, all by yourself.

Consumer Access   Most of the federal agencies are not readily accessible to the individual consumer. Most of their findings, discussions, and agreements are never published, nor are they readily available to the individual. Furthermore, most agencies will not assist an individual consumer who is pressing a claim on a particular product or service.

State Agencies   The level of state involvement in consumer protection varies widely. The leaders, such as New York, California, and Massachusetts, have moved aggressively to provide increased consumer protection. Yet, at the opposite extreme, some states have made only a token effort in this direction. There does, however, seem to be an increased awareness among the state legislatures that they must accept a large part of the responsibility for protecting the state's citizens.

Coverage   It is difficult to generalize about the extent of state service efforts because they vary so widely. Nearly all cover the health, safety, and product-quality issues to some extent. Likewise, many have attempted to control fraudulent and deceptive sales practices within their states. But beyond that, the efforts are more mixed.

Unfortunately, many state enforcement agencies are so understaffed that even the best-designed regulation becomes ineffective through lack of enforcement. Finally, consumer protection is so fragmented in many states that the agencies involved often spend more time on jurisdictional disputes than on consumer issues. This problem can lead to duplication of effort in some matters and large gaps in coverage in others.

Consumer Access   Those states with well-developed consumer protection efforts generally respond quickly and aggressively to most consumer complaints. In other states the response is likely to be more mixed. Some respond after a lengthy delay; others actively discourage consumer complaints.

> **Strategy: If you have a complaint that you have not been able to resolve at the local level, call the consumer protection agency (the typical title) in your state capital.**

Local Agencies   Some large cities have established consumer protection agencies within the local governmental structure. Much of this work is still in its infancy, so it is difficult to say whether this trend will continue. Certainly, if you live in a large metropolitan area and have a problem, you should check to see whether your city has a consumer protection agency.

Voluntary Consumer Organizations   In many areas, groups of interested consumers have established voluntary consumer organizations. Many are affiliated with one of the national consumer groups, such as the Consumer Federation of America, National Consumer League, National Consumer Information Center, National Consumer Congress, and others. Their activities can range from assisting with local consumer complaints to an active role in lobbying for national and state consumer legislation.

Development of local consumer groups has been actively encouraged by many private and public groups. The Office of Consumer Affairs at the federal level encourages and assists in establishing local groups.

> **Strategy: If you are interested in developing a local voluntary consumer organization, you should write: Office of Consumer Assistance, 330 Independence Avenue, S.W., Washington, D.C. 20201.**

Recovering Your Losses: When, Where, How

Although a thorough analysis when buying a product or service will minimize the possibility of your having problems, it will not totally eliminate them. Even with a well-executed advance plan, you may encounter a product that needs to be returned or a service that is not totally acceptable. Consequently, an action plan is needed that will correct the particular problem or recover the loss suffered.

Compiling an Effective Complaint   To be effective, a complaint should be complete in every detail; leave nothing to your listener's or reader's imagination. The first step is to furnish purchase details: receipt, company's billing, guarantee, etc. Next, document your complaint with details on why you are dissatisfied and what you have done to correct the problem. Describe what you have received from the product or service and why it does not measure up to what you expected. Include copies of invoices for any corrective repairs made thus far. Although the statement seems obvious, your complaint should be made shortly after purchase. Many people wait weeks or months and thus reduce their chances of recovery. Finally, describe exactly what corrective action you want: repair of the product, rework of the service, replacement of

the product. *Important:* Keep copies of all letters you write. Send copies of supporting documents (invoices, receipts, guarantees) so that you can keep the originals in your file.

If there is no response within a week or two, follow up on your complaint. Much of the recent warranty legislation sets a definite time limit for the manufacturer to resolve a customer's complaint; failure to do so can make the customer eligible for a refund. These time limits should help because the manufacturer has an added incentive to take prompt action on your complaint.

Obtaining Satisfaction: The Selling Store or Service Firm Customers have one major thing in their favor in any complaint action: Most stores or service firms do not want dissatisfied customers. Consequently, most will try to correct the problem. The initial starting point is to take your documented complaint to the store or service firm where you made the purchase. Whenever possible, try to do this at a time when the staff is not too busy. That way, you are more likely to find a supervisor on duty. If the clerk cannot help, discuss the matter with the department manager. Barring success here, arrange for a conference with the store manager. Whenever you present your complaint to the next higher level, remember that the interviewer has not been privy to your previous discussions. So present your complete case to each person you see.

When the Local Store or Service Firm Balks If you are not satisfied with the response from the local store or service firm, there are several appeal routes. The decision of which one to pursue depends on the type of firm with which you are dealing.

Nationwide Retail Chain   When dealing with a large national chain store or a store that is part of an affiliated group, your best route is to appeal to the chain or group's central office. In some cases, that means arranging a meeting with the district supervisor who covers your local store. If the supervisor does not handle customer claims, you should appeal directly to the central office. Send your request to the customer relations office, if you know the firm has one. Otherwise, direct your letter to the president's attention. Check your warranty booklet for the address of the central office. If you cannot find it there, ask your local librarian for assistance.

Better Business Bureau   Most major cities have a better business bureau. While the bureau has a host of responsibilities, you are primarily concerned with its role in consumer complaints.

Traditionally the bureau's role has been as an independent third party which assists the customer and the business firm to reach an agreeable solution. It does not negotiate a settlement, nor are its recommendations binding on either party.

However, a number of these bureaus have established arbitration boards to hear consumer complaints and determine a solution.[1] The decision to accept arbitration is strictly voluntary for the consumer and the business firm. But if both agree to arbitration, the board's findings are binding and can be legally enforced.

Some bureaus provide the service without charge, while others charge a fee ranging from $20 upward. Typically, those without a fee have a voluntary arbitration board. Those charging a fee rely on professional arbitrators.

Some critics assert that bureaus have a conflict of interest because much of their financial support comes from local business organizations. Another frequently voiced criticism is that many bureaus are so swamped with work that there is a long delay before they take action on a complaint. Despite these negative points, we feel you should give the bureau in your area a try. Many have an excellent success record.

If you live in an area that does not have a bureau, give the local chamber of commerce a call. A few perform somewhat similar services in those areas that lack a better business bureau.

Manufacturer   If the local store has been unable to resolve your problem, you should contact the manufacturer. Most manufacturers have factory representatives who visit the various retail stores; this is especially true on large, expensive items—major appliances, furniture, and automobiles. If there is such a representative, have your local store arrange an appointment to discuss your problem. Or, write directly to the manufacturer's central office.

---

[1]Approximately 92 out of the 135 existing bureaus have established arbitration boards. "The Final Word—Arbitration for Consumer Is Spreading as Better Business Bureaus Offer It," *The Wall Street Journal*, April 21, 1975, p. 24, col. 1.

(Check your warranty information for the address or ask the local librarian to help you locate the firm's headquarters.) Direct your complaint to the customer relations office if there is one indicated on your warranty. Otherwise, send the letter to the attention of the president. If you have not received a reply within several weeks, send off a copy of your complaint with a new letter, saying that you received no reply to your first letter. Remember to keep copies of all correspondence for your file.

When the Manufacturer Balks A number of business and trade associations have formed consumer complaint panels to hear consumer problems. These panels will accept consumer complaints against any company which is a member of the association. They do, however, require that the consumer present the complaint to the local store and the manufacturer and exhaust all possibilities at those levels before they will accept the complaint. The panel's findings are not binding on either party. Several of these panels have released some impressive statistics on their success rate.

To date, panels have been established by the furniture, rug and carpet, appliance, and automobile industries. If you have tried all avenues up to this point, it would certainly be worth presenting your complaint to the appropriate panel. Addresses are given in the appendix to this chapter.

Legal Action: When? Legal action has to be considered one of the last steps in the complaint process. In most cases, it will be the last resort when all other approaches have been utilized.

Small Claims Court Most states have small claims courts that can provide a possible avenue of recourse if you have been unsuccessful in other appeals. This route has several distinct advantages over initiating action through a

regular trial court. The proceedings are informal, so you can often present your own case without the need for legal counsel. This approach helps to keep the cost low. In most states, you obtain speedy action on your complaint—a far cry from the 1- to 5-year wait that prevails in the regular court system. Most small claims courts will not handle cases that involve more than $200, although a few have higher ceilings. Since most consumer complaints are typically small, this is not a serious constraint.

> **Strategy: If you have been unsuccessful in the other avenues of redress, you should consider action in a small claims court.**

Regular Court Action Initiating action through the regular court system should be considered a last-resort measure. Often the amount involved does not warrant the high cost of such action. Further, the entire process can be extremely time-consuming. Given those sizable time commitments and the need for legal counsel, the costs can be very high.

In short, the legal system generally discourages most consumer action. Clearly, there is a need to revamp that system so it will be more accessible to the consumer. But there is no prospect for immediate action on this matter, so the consumer is left with only limited recourse through the legal system.

SUMMARY

1   Consumerism is concerned with protecting the consumer by eliminating dangerous products, strengthening warranties, and making redress possible. It is also concerned with educating consumers so that they will allocate their incomes more advantageously.

2   Increased product complexity, coupled with frequent product and service purchases, has made consumer protection legislation essential.

3   Consumer protection can help consumers obtain fair value for their money. Offsetting this benefit is the reduced choice and added production costs that protection legislation can entail.

4   Before deciding on a consumer buyers' club, the consumer should carefully weigh the benefits offered against the costs. To fully analyze these clubs, you should understand the costs they entail and make certain that you do not buy membership as a result of a high-pressure sales pitch.

5   Many of the undesirable sales practices are legal, although not in the best interests of the consumer. Other practices are outright frauds. Protecting yourself against both types of practices can save you hundreds of dollars.

6   To avoid high-pressure sales tactics, ask the salesperson to list all the costs. And then refuse to sign any contract for at least 2 or 3 days.

7   Deceptive advertising is the misrepresentation of a product or service as something better than what it is, thereby inducing the consumer to purchase a product that would otherwise be rejected.

8   There have been two distinct approaches to consumer protection legislation: (a) the regulation and limitation of certain business practices, and (b) the providing of sufficient information to the consumer.

9 State consumer protection agencies have taken an increasingly active role in the protection of their constituents.
10 The development of local voluntary consumer organizations has received both public and private support.
11 An effectively presented complaint should be sufficiently detailed so that it leaves little to the reader's or listener's misunderstanding.
12 When the local retail store is part of a national chain, the complaint can be appealed to the central office of the chain.
13 The better business bureau helps consumers obtain satisfaction when they have complaints against a local retail store or service firm.
14 Some manufacturers and trade associations have formed consumer complaint panels to resolve consumer problems.
15 Legal action to resolve a consumer complaint should be considered a last resort.

REVIEW YOUR UNDERSTANDING OF

Consumerism
    Consumer protection
    Consumer education
Caveat emptor
Buyers' clubs
State consumer protection agency
Voluntary consumer organization
Better business bureau
Consumer complaint panel

Small claims court
Freezer deals
Deceptive advertising
Pricing strategies
Consumer protection legislation
    Limits and controls on business practices
    Sufficient consumer information

DISCUSSION QUESTIONS

1 Under what circumstances do you feel the membership in a buyers' club might be worthwhile? How would you evaluate whether to buy a membership in one of the buyers' clubs?
2 What steps can a person take to avoid being trapped by the high-pressure tactics used to sell freezer deals and encyclopedias?
3 Which steps in the recommendations for avoiding high-pressure sales tactics do you believe would be most helpful in identifying whether the product or service being sold is fraudulent?
4 How would you suggest a person avoid the pressure associated with "bait and switch" advertising?
5 How can a consumer be sure a product's price is a "true" price and not one designed to make it appear a bargain?
6 What deficiencies do you see in *caveat emptor*? Does it provide true consumer protection? Has *caveat emptor* been completely replaced? Why?
7 What potential disadvantages do you see in the overzealous expansion of consumer protection legislation? What potential abuses arise when consumer protection legislation is inadequate? Would you favor a slight excess or a shortfall of protection legislation? Why?
8 What key points should be covered in a good consumer complaint? Why should that complaint have complete details?
9 What direction has recent consumer legislation taken? How has it differed from

earlier legislation? What do you feel will be the future trends in protection legislation? Why?

10 How do the better business bureaus help to resolve consumer complaints? How does their arbitration service differ from their earlier role?

11 What are the advantages of small claims courts for resolving a consumer complaint? What factors effectively make the regular court system a last resort for consumer problems?

12 Can you give an example of a federal agency that is so closely aligned with the industry it regulates that it would have difficulty performing its consumer protection responsibilities? What changes are needed? Are there moves to correct the conflicts?

13 Do you see any advantage in having state agencies assume a larger role in protecting consumers? Are there problems in that shift?

CASE PROBLEM

Fosby Jones, a recent college graduate, is in the process of furnishing an apartment for the first time. He is very much concerned with saving money since he will be contributing to the support of his parents and two younger brothers. Despite his budget constraint, he wants a nice place to live. A representative from a local buyers' club recently contacted him about a $400, 10-year membership. The representative has pointed out that Fosby will likely spend more than $1,000 on furniture and appliances. With the 50 percent saving the club promises, the representative maintains that Fosby will more than recover his membership fee. And, as an added bonus, Fosby still has his membership for another 10 years.

Fosby also wants to save money by doing all his own cooking. Consequently, he is about to sign up for a frozen food plan which promises him substantial savings if he buys a freezer through the supplier.

a Convince Fosby not to join the buyers' club.

b Should he buy the freezer?

RECOMMENDED READINGS

Books

Ross, Donald K., *A Public Citizen's Action Manual.* New York: Grossman Publishing Co., 1973.
  Recommends a number of community action plans for improving local business and service practices.
Aaker, David A., and George S. Day (eds.), *Consumerism: Search for the Consumer Interest.* New York: Macmillan, 1974.
  Robert O. Herrmann, "The Consumer Movement In Historical Perspective," pp. 10–18. Traces the development of the consumer movement.
  Ralph Nader, "The Great American Gyp," pp. 23–35. Discusses weaknesses in current consumer protection. Reviews possible corrective action.
  Ralph K. Winter, "The Consumer Advocate versus the Consumer," pp. 49–63. Discusses consumerism and its related problems.
Taylor, Jack L., Jr., and Arch W. Troelstrup (eds.), *The Consumer In American Society: Additional Dimensions.* New York: McGraw-Hill, 1974.

Helen F. McHugh, "Consumer Protection Against . . . What?" pp. 392–397.
Discusses the five federal agencies that accept consumer complaints.
Morton J. Simon, "The Fractured Legal Structure of Consumerism," pp. 399–410.
Discusses the overlapping structure of consumerism.

Magazines

Money:

Clark, Champ, "Better Business Bureaus Are Getting Better." April 1973, pp. 62–66.
Discusses recent improvements in bureau services. Gives a checklist to get the most from those services.
———, "Courts of First Resort." June 1973, pp. 32–36.
Discusses the working of small claims courts. Summarizes the different court systems by state.
Mead, William B., "Help from a Consumerist Congress." April 1975, pp. 50–57.
Discusses possible legislative moves for increased consumer protection.

Congressional Digest:

"Congress and Consumer Protection Proposals—Pro and Con." March 1968, pp. 67–70.
Reviews scope of present federal activity.

MSU Business Topics:

Barksdale, Hiram C., and Warren A. French, "Response to Consumerism: How Change Is Perceived by Both Sides." September 1975, pp. 55–67.
Surveys the impact of the consumer movement on the business practices of the firm.

California Management Review:

Sethi, S. Prakash, "Business and the Consumer: Wither Goes the Confrontation." Winter 1974, pp. 82–87.
Discusses the problems of consumer protection and how it should proceed.

Harvard Business Review:

Gregser, Stephen A., and Steven L. Diamond, "Business Is Adapting to Consumerism." September 1974, pp. 38–40.
Surveys business executives for their opinions of consumerism and its future direction.

Changing Times:

"Small-Claims Courts Aren't Doing Their Job." April 1973, pp. 41–43.
Reviews the problems with small claims courts and some possible relief.
"Does Consumer Arbitration Really Work?" July 1973, pp. 19–21.
Discusses merits of using arbitration to settle consumer disputes.
"Warning! Some Buying Clubs Are Traps." August 1974, pp. 21–23.
Discusses potential pitfalls in some buying clubs.
"The Power of Positive Complaining by Mail." December 1974, pp. 17–19.
Discusses techniques for writing effective complaint letters.

Booklets

Office of Consumer Affairs, *Forming Consumer Organizations.* 1972.
> Explains the steps involved in establishing a voluntary consumer organization. A copy can be obtained from Superintendent of Documents, U.S. Government Printing Office, Washington, D.C. 20402.

Office of Consumer Affairs, *Directory of State, County and City Government Consumer Offices.* July 1, 1973.
> Provides a directory of the offices established by state and local governments to assist the consumer. Check your local library for a copy.

Appendix: Consumer Complaint Agencies

Listed below are the addresses of the most frequently used agencies that assist consumers in resolving their product or service disputes.

Consumer Action Panels

Major Appliances Consumer Action Panel
20 N. Wacker Drive
Chicago, Illinois 60606

Carpet and Rug Industry Consumer Action Panel
Box 1568
Dalton, Georgia 30720

Furniture Industry Consumer Action Panel
Box 951
High Point, North Carolina 27161

Automobile Consumer Action Panel
U.S. Department of Health, Education, and Welfare
Office of Consumer Affairs
Washington, D.C. 20201. Write for address of nearest AUTOCAPS Office.

Federal Agencies

Automobiles and Automotive Safety
Department of Transportation
400 Seventh Street, S.W.
Washington, D.C. 20590

National Highway Traffic Safety Administration
400 Seventh Street, S.W.
Washington, D.C. 20590

Mail Service and Sales Schemes Using the Mails
U.S. Postal Service

475 L'Enfant Plaza, S.W.
Washington, D.C. 20260

Food and Drugs
Food and Drug Administration
U.S. Department of Health, Education, and Welfare
5600 Fishers Lane
Rockville, Maryland 20852

Broadcasting—Radio and Television
Federal Communications Commission
1919 M Street, N.W.
Washington, D.C. 20554

Product Safety
Consumer Product Safety Commission
1750 K Street, N.W.
Washington, D.C. 20207

Household Moving Problems
Interstate Commerce Commission
Twelfth Street and Constitution Avenue, N.W.
Washington, D.C. 20423

Unfair and Deceptive Business Practices
Federal Trade Commission
Pennsylvania Avenue at Sixth Street
Washington, D.C. 20580

Consumer Affairs—General
Office of Consumer Affairs
U.S. Department of Health, Education, and Welfare
New Executive Office Building
Seventeenth and H Streets, N.W.
Washington, D.C. 20506

State Agencies

Check with the attorney general's office in your state to see whether there is a separate consumer affairs office. Your local librarian can also help you find the address of the consumer affairs office for your state.

Local Agencies

Check your local better business bureau or chamber of commerce to see if there are any voluntary consumer groups in your area. The local librarian can also assist you in your search.

Chapter 10

Transportation: Your Automobile

After completing this chapter you should be able to:

describe the essential differences among the five major categories of automobiles.

recall the principal cost components in automobile ownership.

identify the areas of potential savings from owning a compact or subcompact model.

judge which model fits your budget.

describe how you would shop for an automobile.

explain the coverage and duration of automobile warranties.

propose a plan for obtaining satisfaction when you have a warranty claim.

compare and **contrast** leasing a car with owning a car.

The automobile has had a tremendous impact on the life-style of every American. The mobility it offers has changed living and working patterns to an extent undreamed of a generation ago. This increased dependence and reliance on one's car have created a strong bond between most owners and their automobiles. Unfortunately, in the process of developing this bond, many people have lost sight of why they really own an automobile: to provide transportation.

Despite the 50 years of concerted advertising by the manufacturers, the purpose of an automobile is transportation, not a symbol of status or sex. If you are willing to review cost figures and temporarily remove your ego from the decision process, we feel this chapter's information could save you hundreds of dollars annually in car expense. In the final analysis, we think the decision to buy or keep a car is strictly an economic one. That means owning a car that adequately meets your needs and at minimum cost.

OWNERSHIP: STATUS OR TRANSPORTATION

To better understand the current trend in the automobile market, we need a short review of recent history.

The Status Image of the 1950s and 1960s During the 1950s and early 1960s many people were infatuated with their automobiles. An automobile was an extension of themselves so it had to provide external evidence of their status in life. Consideration of such important things as operating costs, transportation efficiency, passenger comfort, safety, and pollution were relegated to minor importance. As a status symbol, the automobile had arrived.

The Transportation Image of the 1970s The recent continued increase in new car prices as well as the rapid rise in the whole range of operating expenses—insurance, gasoline, tires, maintenance, and repairs—has jolted consumers into asking: Does my present auto match my needs? Does it have to be so big? How many options and accessories do I really need? Does it make a difference if it is restyled every 3 years?

The Image for the 1980s Despite several flings with small cars during the past 20 years, interest in those models has always waned as people returned to full-sized models. An immediate question is whether the recent shift to small cars is a short-run phenomenon or is the beginning of a future trend. We feel efficiency will be the key concern during the seventies and eighties. The most successful cars will be those which combine adequate passenger space and comfort with good operating economy.

SELECTING AN AUTOMOBILE MODEL

There are five general types of automobiles: subcompact, compact, intermediate, full-size, and specialty models. They are differentiated by four major features: (1) passenger and luggage accommodations, (2) purchase price and operating costs, (3) driving ease and ride comfort, and (4) distance capability (whether short commuting trips or long trips). Exhibit 10–1 summarizes the principal strengths and weaknesses for the five automobile categories.

Finding Your Needs, Then Your Automobile To decide which model best fits your needs, you should consider four key areas: (1) accommodations; (2) operating costs; (3) travel needs—trip length, ride comfort, maneuverability; and (4) reliability and warranty. The decision process is illustrated in Exhibit 10–2.

The following sections develop a portion of the input to the decision process shown in Exhibit 10–2. Periodicals such as *Consumer Reports, Consumers' Research Magazine, Popular Science,* and *Road and Track* are other valuable inputs to the process. Your own critical analysis of the competing automobiles is the key factor to this whole process. The disparity between the best and worst examples within each auto category is tremendous. Only through a rigorous personal analysis can you decide which car has what you want.

Exhibit 10-1 Strengths and Weaknesses of Current Automobile Models

Attribute	Automobile model				
	Subcompact	Compact	Intermediate	Full size	Specialty
Passenger capacity	2–4	4–5	5–6	5–6	2–4
Luggage space	G	G	VG	E	F
General roominess	F	G	G	VG	F
Gas mileage	E	VG	F	P	NR
Routine maintenance costs	E	VG	G	F	NR
Insurance premiums	VG	VG	G	G	P
Annual decline in market value	E	E	G	F	G to P
Relative purchase price	E	VG	F	P	P
Maneuverability	E	VG	F	P	NR
Ride comfort	F	G	VG	E	NR
Handling	VG	VG	F	P	NR
Driving ease	E	VG	G	F	NR
Suitability for: commuting	E	VG	F	P	NR
long trips	F	VG	VG	E	NR

Key to ratings:
  E = Excellent   P = Poor
VG = Very good   NR = Not rated because range is so broad that a single rating is
  G = Good   meaningless.
  F = Fair

Select for Your Typical Needs   Trying to pick a model that can handle every conceivable demand you might face is not a good objective. Instead, pick a model that satisfies your typical needs rather than the infrequent extreme. For example, selecting a full-sized model for that 3-week camping trip you are planning within the next 4 years is ill-advised. For that trip it will be excellent, but what about the remaining 205 weeks? It is much more sensible to meet the needs of those 205 weeks and possibly suffer some inconvenience during that 3-week trip. Too often, people justify a full-sized car with the claim they need extra passenger or luggage space. Yet they rarely carry anyone in the back seat or use the luggage space.

> **Strategy: Select that model with an eye toward meeting your typical needs. Rather than selecting a model for infrequent special situations, match it to your daily demands throughout the entire year.**

Cost of Automobile Ownership

We group the costs of owning and operating an automobile into two general categories: a fixed component and a variable component. The representative costs used in this chapter were drawn from a 1976 Department of Highway Administration study.[1]

---

[1] L. L. Liston and C. A. Aiken, *Cost of Owning and Operating an Automobile—1976.* Washington, D.C.: U.S. Department of Transportation, 1976, passim.

Exhibit 10-2   Auto Decision: Finding Your Model

Based on that study, Exhibit 10–3 shows the fixed costs, and Exhibit 10–4 the variable costs, of owning and operating a subcompact, a compact, and a full-sized car. The exhibits show the cost per mile for such things as depreciation (fixed cost) and gas and oil (variable cost).

The study assumed each car was purchased new and held for 10 years, during which time it was driven 100,000 miles. The study was based in Maryland, and therefore the costs are considered typical for a medium-cost suburban area. Of course, costs such as state registration and gasoline taxes would be different in different states. Similarly, there would be a considerable difference between large cities and rural areas for costs such as insurance, parking, tolls, and maintenance (labor rates). Nevertheless, although the exact costs would differ, the point of the study and of these exhibits is that the cost

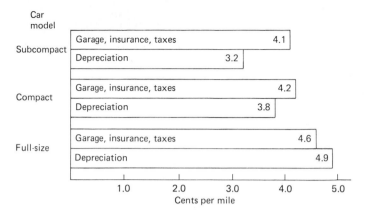

Source: L. L. Liston and C. A. Aiken, Cost of Operating an Automobile—1976, *Washington; U.S. Dept. of Transportation,*
1976.

Exhibit 10-3   Cost of Automobile Operation: Fixed Components

differential among models would remain relatively unchanged. For example, if
the cost of insurance is 100 percent greater in New York City and Chicago than
it is in Poland Spring, Maine, and Missoula, Montana, it is that much greater for
all models. The exhibits are still valid in either place for comparing the costs
among different models, although the exact costs would not be the same.

Although the study does not include an intermediate-sized car, the
omission is not a serious shortcoming because its operating cost would be
similar to a full-size one. Also, no specialty model is covered because that
group's range is just too broad to treat adequately with a single example.

Fixed Costs   One of the major costs of owning a car is its annual decline in
market value. As Exhibit 10–3 points up, this depreciation ranges from a high of

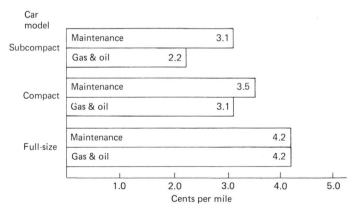

Source: L. L. Liston and C. A. Aiken, Cost of Operating an Automobile—1976, *Washington; U.S. Dept. of Transportation,*
1976.

Exhibit 10-4   Cost of Automobile Operation: Variable Components

4.9 cents per mile on a full-size car to a low of 3.2 cents per mile on a subcompact. For the most part, this cost component is unavoidable regardless of how few miles you drive. However, the point is that the cost of depreciation is less for a compact or a subcompact than it is for a full-size car. For the average driver who covers 10,000 miles per year, the depreciation cost for a full-size would be $490 (4.9 cents × 10,000); that is substantially more than a compact at $380 (3.8 cents × 10,000). Part of the lower cost is due to the compact's lower purchase price; given a lower price, the annual dollar decline is smaller. In addition, the rate of decline for the compact is less than for a full-size auto.

The second cost in the fixed group—parking, garage fees, collision and liability insurance, title fees, and registration taxes—is very nearly the same for all three models. This is not unexpected, since these costs are only slightly affected by differences in purchase price or size.

For a full-size car, these items cost 4.6 cents per mile; for a subcompact, 4.1 cents per mile. The savings for a subcompact driven 10,000 miles per year would be $50 [(4.6 − 4.1) cents/mile × 10,000 miles]. That is about the difference in yearly costs in insurance and registration fees between a full-size car and a subcompact.

Variable Costs   The variable-cost group includes those items which vary directly with the miles driven. The greater the number of miles traveled, the larger total variable cost becomes. Because of this direct relationship, these costs are crucial to people who drive many miles each year.

One variable cost is the cost of gasoline and oil plus their associated state and federal taxes. Turning to Exhibit 10–4, we note a considerable difference in gas and oil costs among subcompact, compact, and full-size cars. Subcompacts are tops in fuel economy. Gas and oil for a subcompact cost 2.2 cents per mile; for a compact, the cost is more than 40 percent higher, or 3.1 cents per mile; for a full-size car, the cost is more than 90 percent higher, or 4.2 cents per mile. Assuming you drive 10,000 miles each year, the saving between a subcompact and a full-size car is $200 annually ($220 versus $420).

The other variable cost is maintenance. It includes repairs, normal maintenance procedures, and tires. A review of Exhibit 10–4 shows a pattern similar to that for gasoline and oil: subcompacts have the lowest cost, compacts are second, and full-size cars have the most expensive maintenance. The maintenance cost on a subcompact is about 35 percent less than for a full-size car. A subcompact would save about $110 ($310 versus $420) each year over a full-size car if both were driven 10,000 miles annually.

Areas of Savings   A compact or subcompact produces significant savings over a full-size car in three areas: depreciation, gas and oil expense, and lower maintenance.

The savings from reduced depreciation expense arise from two factors. First, the annual rate of depreciation among the three models varies considerably: the subcompact declines in value slowly each year, the full-size declines in value much more rapidly. Second, the lower purchase price of a new small car means that the dollar amount of the annual decline will be less than for the larger cars. Exhibit 10–5 summarizes the annual percentage decline during the first 6 years of ownership. The chart demonstrates that in the early years, a full-size declines much faster than either a subcompact or compact.

Because of this rapid decline, a full-size can be extremely expensive during the early years of ownership. Exhibit 10–6 shows the estimated market value of three typical cars during the first 4 years of ownership. Each year's market price was estimated using the percentages given in Exhibit 10–5. Despite the large initial price differential between the three models, the rapid decline in the full-size quickly reduces that differential. In fact, for all practical purposes the market value is nearly equal after 4 years.

Strategy: If you trade your car every 2 or 3 years just to have a new car, switching to a compact could save you a tidy sum.

The second and third savings elements, reduced maintenance cost and lower gas and oil expense, result from the efficiency gains of the smaller size and lighter weight of the compact and subcompact models. Because they weigh less, it takes less energy to move them down the highway. That lighter weight also makes a smaller engine possible. Both things substantially improve the operating economy. The lighter weight also means that many of the power-assisted accessories, so essential to a full-size model, can be eliminated; their

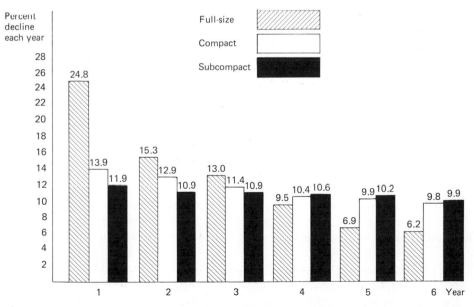

Source: L. L. Liston and C. A. Aiken, Cost of Operating an Automobile—1976, Washington; U.S. Dept. of Transportation, 1976.

Exhibit 10-5   Decline in Market Price for Each Year of Ownership

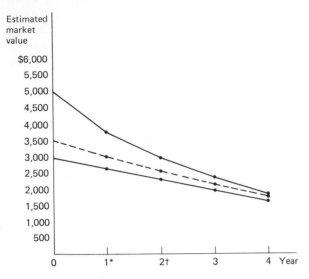

Full-size, new price = $5,000,
Compact, new price = $3,500,
Subcompact, new price = $3,000,

*Estimated market value for the full-size at the end of the 1st year:
$5,000 − ($5,000 × 24.8 percent per Exhibit 10-5) = $3,760. Other
models were computed in a similar manner.
    †Estimated market value for the full-size at the end of the 2d year:
$3,760 − ($5,000 × 15.3 percent per Exhibit 10-5) = $2,995. Other
models were computed in a similar manner.

Exhibit 10-6   Estimated Market Value at the End of Each Year of Ownership

absence improves economy and eliminates the maintenance and repair expense
on those accessories. In addition, most compacts and subcompacts have a
limited number of nonfunctional accessories and trim options. Not only does
this restriction keep the initial price lower; it eliminates maintenance and
repairs on these items.

   Total Operating Cost   In Exhibit 10–7, the fixed and variable costs are
combined to give an overall cost per mile. The three columns (*a, b, c*) of Exhibit
10–7 were constructed using three assumptions: column *a* shows a car held 10
years and driven 100,000 miles; in column *b*, the car was held 6 years and driven
68,800 miles; and column *c* shows the car was held 4 years and driven 49,000
miles. As such, Exhibit 10–7 not only provides a comparison of operating costs
among models; it also highlights the difference due to varying ownership
periods.
   The message seems clear. No matter how long the holding period, the
subcompact is less expensive; its operating cost per mile is significantly below
that of the compact or full-size car. Assuming a 10-year holding period, the
full-size annual costs would be $1,790, the subcompact would cost $1,260,

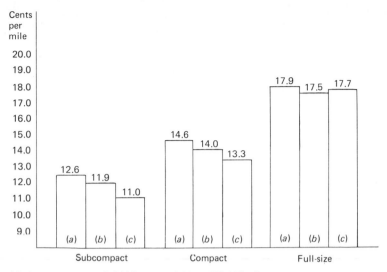

(a) Assumes auto was held 10 years and driven 100,000 miles.
(b) Assumes auto was held 6 years and driven 68,800 miles.
(c) Assumes auto was held 4 years and driven 49,000 miles.

Source: L. L. Liston and C. A. Aiken, Cost of Operating an Automobile—1976, Washington; U.S. Dept. of Transportation, 1976.

Exhibit 10-7   Total Cost of Automobile Operation: Fixed and Variable Costs

representing an annual savings of $530. The annual saving between a full-size model and a compact would be ($1,790 − $1,460), or $330.

> **Strategy: If you want to reduce automobile expenses, consider whether either a compact or subcompact will meet your needs.**

Optimum Holding Period

The optimum holding period is primarily determined by your recent and anticipated automobile repair expenses. However, you must also consider the age and mileage of your car. When the major components on your car require expensive repairs costing $200 to $500, or when there are indications they soon will need major repairs, you should carefully consider whether it is time to sell the car or trade it in for a new or used one. If your mileage is high and your car is getting old, it probably will not pay to continue having it repaired. On the other hand, if the mileage is low, it probably will be cheaper to make the repair and keep the car. The key question is: Will this repair expense likely be followed shortly by a continuing string of major repair bills? If the answer is yes, the car has probably reached its optimum holding period, and it is time to get rid of it and buy another.

Operating Costs, Given Different Holding Periods   Exhibit 10–7 provides a comparative analysis of the total operating costs for different holding periods.

The operating costs for a full-size are nearly equal for all three holding periods. While the early years of ownership have low repair expenses, they are offset by the high depreciation on a full-size during those years. In later years, when depreciation is more moderate, repair expenses have increased so that the total for those years is similar to the early years. Those for compacts and subcompacts are lowest for a 4-year holding period, second lowest for 6 years, and highest for 10 years. This difference arises because both models have moderate depreciation and very low repairs in the early part of their life. In later years, the depreciation declines slightly, but this is more than offset by the rise in repair expenses. Consequently, the overall cost per mile rises. This fact does not necessarily suggest you should trade a compact or subcompact every 4 years. Instead, repair expenses should still be your major indicator. As long as they are not serious and costly, you should continue to hold your present compact or subcompact.

> **Strategy: If your present car provides reliable transportation, hold on to it even if it is getting old.**

Transportation Cost in the Family Budget

Transportation expense is the third largest monthly expenditure in the family budget, exceeded only by housing and food. As a general rule, this expense should not exceed 12 percent of your annual disposable income. To illustrate, assume Anne Smith's disposable income is $10,800. To remain within that 12 percent limit, her transportation expenses should not exceed $10,800 × 12 percent) or $1,296. That total should include all automobile expenses plus any public transportation expenses.

Match the Car to the Budget   Your car should fit your budget—very basic advice. Yet, many people do it the other way around. First, they decide on the car, then they force their expenditure pattern to fit the transportation costs to which they have committed themselves. When the costs of automobile ownership rise, as they have recently, these people find that their automobile costs are gnawing away at an increasing portion of their income. In effect, many people have become "car-poor."

Our advice is: First budget your expenses, then select a car to match.

Before we can decide whether a particular car fits a specific budget constraint, we need to estimate its operating cost. That estimate requires two cost elements: total operating costs excluding depreciation, and depreciation. Exhibit 10–8 shows total operating cost excluding depreciation for three different holding periods for each of the three auto models. The depreciation cost is calculated separately, as will be shown in Exhibit 10–9.

The easiest way to illustrate how to determine whether a car fits a budget is to work through an example. Let us assume Anne Smith is considering a new compact that costs $4,000. She plans to hold it 4 years, during which time she expects to drive it 49,000 miles. Using this basic information, Exhibit 10–9 shows step by step how to calculate the estimated total operating cost per mile.

Based on the computations in Exhibit 10–9, the estimated total operating cost per mile would be 13.4 cents. Assuming Anne Smith averaged 12,250 miles each year, her annual cost would be (13.4 cents × 12,250 miles), or $1,642. Given her $10,800 disposable income, and based on the general rule of 12 percent for transportation, her budget will allow only $1,296 annually for this expense. Her costs would exceed her budget! At this point she has several options: (1) switch to a lower-priced compact; (2) switch to a subcompact; or (3) purchase the $4,000 compact and reduce her other discretionary expenditures accordingly.

The guideline that transportation expense be limited to 12 percent of disposable income is not meant as a rigid rule; rather, it is a recommended limit. There is no reason why an individual making $10,000 cannot drive a $6,000 full-sized car. But in so doing, the buyer should recognize that 20 percent of

Exhibit 10-8   Operating Costs per Mile excluding Depreciation for Different Holding Periods

Model	4 years, 49,000 miles	6 years, 68,800 miles	10 years, 100,000 miles
Subcompact	8.1¢	8.9¢	9.4¢
Compact	9.4	10.1	10.8
Full size	11.5	12.1	13.0

Exhibit 10-9 Estimating Operating Cost

Part A: Depreciation expense
Line

1 Purchase price	$4,000
2 Holding period	4 years
3 Estimated mileage	49,000 miles
4 Percentage decline in market value during holding period	48.6 percent*
5 Depreciation expense: line 1 × line 4	$1,944
6 Depreciation cost per mile: line 5 ÷ line 3	4.0¢
7 Total operating cost excluding depreciation	9.4¢†
8 Total cost per mile: line 6 + line 7	13.4¢

Part B: Calculating annual cost

9 Average annual mileage: line 3 ÷ line 2	12,250 miles
10 Annual cost: line 9 × line 8	$1,642

*Obtained by summing the appropriate depreciation percentages for years 1, 2, 3, and 4 from Exhibit 10-5: 13.9 + 12.9 + 11.4 + 10.4 = 48.6 percent.
†Obtained from the appropriate column and row of Exhibit 10-8.

annual income will be spent on automobile-related expenses, and that means some major sacrifices in other areas.

The details in Exhibit 10–9 could readily be modified to fit any auto category, holding period, or purchase price. When estimating the cost for a 10-year holding period, 100 percent should be used in line 4 rather than data from Exhibit 10–5 (which only goes to 6 years). Effectively, the 100 percent decline assumes the car is worthless after 10 years and 100,000 miles. That assumption seems reasonable.

Although there are no specific costs for an intermediate model, using the operating costs for a full-size model from Exhibit 10–8 will provide a reasonable estimate. Likewise, there are no specific costs for specialty models. Here, your best guide would be to use those operating costs from Exhibit 10–8 which best match the specialty model being considered. Thus, a compact-sized specialty model would use the operating costs for a compact, a full-sized specialty, those of a full-size car.

> **Strategy: We strongly recommend that you match your transportation costs to your disposable income. By computing those costs in advance, you can avoid ending up "car-poor."**

Operating Costs in Future Years

In our opinion, the recent rapid rise in operating costs is a harbinger of future trends. Certainly the costs of gasoline and oil will continue to rise as usage increases and reserves dwindle. Likewise, the continued increase in material costs and labor rates will raise new car prices, as well as boost repair costs.

The implications seem clear. First, as costs rise, matching your auto expenses to your budget will become even more critical. Second, those models which operate with top efficiency will become the best choice to obtain maximum utility from your transportation dollar. Last, as the costs increase, full-size cars are likely to become less attractive to the majority of consumers. This drop in popularity will likely cause the market price of these models to decline even more rapidly, thereby increasing the depreciation component of their operating costs.

SHOPPING FOR YOUR AUTOMOBILE

You should now have an idea which automobile category best meets your transportation needs. But several key questions remain: What brand? Which dealer? What is a fair price? How to bargain with the dealer?

Selecting a Brand   The central objective in the search for a particular brand is to find one that is dependable, that requires minimal maintenance and repairs, and that has a competent dealer network to provide service when it is required.

Owner Surveys   The best guide to the reliability and maintenance needs of a particular model are comments from its previous owners. While not infallible, their opinions give a general idea of what you can expect from a particular brand. Several monthly periodicals—*Consumer Reports, Popular Science*, and *Road and Track*—conduct surveys among their subscribers to obtain data on their ownership experience. *Consumer Reports* publishes an annual survey which covers all major brands; it requests information on each of the car's major systems: fuel system, engine, transmission, etc. The owners surveys published by *Popular Science* and *Road and Track,* by contrast, concentrate on a single model. Furthermore, their coverage is less systematic since they focus on recently introduced models. But their surveys are more detailed and include such things as best and least liked features, major and minor trouble areas, and dealer service. These evaluations can be a valuable input to your auto decision.

Car Advertisements   A car advertisement of 5 years ago provided many superlatives, glittering generalities, sweeping claims, but little if any hard facts. All that has changed. Now the ads contain considerable amounts of comparative data and performance statistics. That should be a big improvement. Right? Based on the advertisements we have seen, the answer is occasionally yes, but more likely no. True, the ads now provide some hard statistics, yet their validity is so questionable that they are at best of limited value and at worst fraudulent.

Personal Evaluation   While the comments of owners and professional testers are an essential input when compiling your list of potential cars, your own personal evaluation is the final analysis. That means visiting car dealers to thoroughly analyze competing models on your list. Be highly critical and demanding in your comparative review. Try out the passenger space for size, comfort, and convenience. Examine the trunk to see whether it meets your needs. Ask for a test drive in the car. And make it sufficiently long so that you can try the car under widely varying conditions: expressways, winding, hilly country roads, and city streets. In short, consider every aspect, then consider each one a second time. Since this is a preliminary review and you are still evaluating cars toward a final decision, there is no need to talk price with the dealer at this time.

> **Strategy: Use this personal evaluation to single out the model, or models, that exactly fit your needs.**

Selecting a Dealer Your best source of information here is to ask your friends whether they have had first-hand experience or whether they know of someone who has dealt with a particular dealer. Of special concern is how the dealer treats the customer after the sale. Questions you should ask are: Did the dealer handle warranty items quickly and fairly? Is the dealer's service department competent? Would your friends buy from that dealer again? Unless the savings are significant, picking a dealer that is 100 miles from where you live can be a poor choice if you have to make frequent trips to the dealer for warranty or adjustment work. Last, read those dealer advertising claims with the same skeptical eye as manufacturers' advertisements; claims of "lowest prices in the city," "rock-bottom prices," and "tremendous discounts" may in reality be full-truths, half-truths, or no-truths.

> **Strategy: Be your own judge. Select a dealer on the basis of what he or she has done for actual buyers rather than on claims of providing service. Try to find a dealer who is not only interested in you at the time of the sale, but even more important, who continues to be interested in serving you after the sale.**

Estimating a Fair Price When purchasing a new car, most people decide on a "fair price" by obtaining quotes from several dealers. We think our system is easier and more accurate. Implementing it requires three cost estimates: (1) current wholesale price of your present used car which you intend to trade in; (2) dealer's cost (invoice price) for the new car you intend to buy; and (3) an estimate of the dealer's profit margin.

Used Car Price The current wholesale price of the car you are trading in can be obtained from several specialized publications: the *Official Used Car Guide* from the National Automobile Dealers Association covers most areas of the United States; *Kelley Blue Book* concentrates its coverage on the West Coast; and third, many state dealer associations publish a price guide for their own state. Check your local credit union, bank, or public library for one of these publications. Barring success here, visit a used car dealer in your area; many will let you examine their copy at no charge.

Dealer's Cost for New Cars Several publications compile the dealer's invoice cost on new cars and optional equipment: for example, *Edmond's 1976 New Car Prices* and *Charlton's 1976 New Car Prices*. Check your local library or buy a copy at your local news store.

These publications give the dealer's cost for the different models and the cost of the optional equipment that can be ordered on each model. These prices are strictly the dealer's cost; they include no dealer profit.

The Dealer's Profit Margin   The final cost estimate needed to complete our computation is the dealer's profit margin. Depending upon how competitive the local market is, that margin can range from $100 to $500; a reasonable estimate is between $300 and $400.

Estimating the Net Cash Difference   Exhibit 10–10 illustrates how these three cost components are combined to estimate the highest and lowest prices you might expect to pay for a new car. It is for you to determine what is a fair price between these values. An example will demonstrate the computations.

Fred Bear has decided to trade his 6-year old compact for a new compact. A check of the used car prices disclosed that his old car was worth $850 wholesale. Checking one of the new car price sources, he found that the new model and options he wants cost the dealer $3,250. Using these costs in the system illustrated in Exhibit 10–10 shows that, depending on the dealer's margin, the low price for the new car would be $2,758, the high price, $3,070. Having done his homework, he could now visit a dealer, knowing that when trading in his old car for the new one, he would expect to pay a price somewhere between these two values. He probably would still want to get competing quotes from several dealers, but he will be doing that as an informed buyer.

Developing price information takes work, but the payoff is worth it. For one thing, you avoid running to a dozen different dealers to make sure you have a "fair price." Second, your negotiating position is strengthened because you have computed the various cost components before you visited the dealer.

Exhibit 10-10   Estimating a Fair Price for a New Car

	Low margin	High margin
Dealer cost*: new car	$2,850	$2,850
options	400	400
Total cost	$3,250	$3,250
Less: Current wholesale value of your used car*	850	850
Difference	$2,400	$2,400
Add: Dealer's profit margin*	200	500
Sales tax (if applicable)†	138	150
Title and license transfer (if applicable)‡	20	20
Net cash difference	$2,758	$3,070

*See discussion in the text for source.

†Assumed to be 4 percent: ($3,450 × 4 percent) and ($3,750 × 4 percent).

‡Assumed to be $20.

Bargaining with the Dealer   Before you visit any dealers to bargain about price, decide exactly what model and what optional equipment you want. If you want immediate delivery, you will have to accept a car the dealer has in stock. Chances are you will have to be flexible; you will have to (1) accept several options you would not normally order; (2) give up one or two accessories you would normally order, and (3) accept the color and trim combination the dealer has on hand. Do not, however, feel that you must accept what the dealer has in stock. Instead, we favor ordering a car exactly the way you want it. Sure, it will take 5 or 6 weeks longer, but then you have the model, options, and color you want. At the very least, do not let the dealer pressure you into accepting a car that is loaded with accessories and options you do not want. Likewise, do not be pushed into a full-sized car when you want a compact.

When visiting dealers, do not be misled by the dealer who quotes you an unusually high trade-in price on your present car, claiming that you will be getting "top dollar" (remember: "top dollar" is advertising talk and means nothing) on your trade-in, which probably is true. But chances are, the price on the new car will also be high, so that in the end, you still pay the same or a higher price. Just be sure that the dealer's offer for your used car and the price for the new car work out to the lowest price when you use the system in Exhibit 10–10. Do not be swayed by the dealer's claim of cutting several hundred dollars off the new car's list price. No doubt this is so, but it is because the list price is highly inflated. Knocking a few hundred dollars off merely makes that price a bit more realistic. Also, avoid the all-inclusive deal with just a single price for the car, insurance, financing, and credit life insurance. A variation on this theme is where the dealer quotes you the "easy" monthly payment on a 36-month sales loan that includes everything. It is fine if the dealer wants to quote a price on all those things, but ask for a separate price on each item.

Last, don't be rushed or pressured into accepting a dealer's offer. Rare is the offer that is so attractive or such a "bargain" that it cannot wait while you take time to think it over.

> **Strategy: Know exactly what you want and approximately how much it will cost before you meet the dealer. Stand firm on that decision. Second, ask the salesperson for a written offer that clearly breaks out each element of the deal and ask to have it initialled by the salesmanager. Last, take your time until you are convinced that the car fits your needs and resources.**

WILL A USED CAR DO THE JOB?

It is difficult to develop a definitive answer to the question of whether a used car will do as well as a new one. At its best, a good used car can provide tremendously economical transportation. The purchase price of a one-year old car with low mileage will be substantially less than that for a similar new car. And if its repair and maintenance expenses are relatively low, the total operating cost per mile will be lower than that of a new car. Unfortunately, a used car can sometimes require such extensive and frequent repairs that its operating costs exceed those on a new car.

Selecting a Used Car   Your greatest risk in purchasing a used car is the possibility of frequent expensive repairs. The checklist in Exhibit 10–11 will help you to minimize that possibility. If caution is required when buying a new car, then double or triple caution should be exercised when buying used cars.

The best place to begin your search is to ask your friends and coworkers whether they know of anyone with a car for sale. Familiarity might motivate the seller to give candid answers to your questions about the car. And do not be afraid to ask lots of questions. You can also try the ads placed by private sellers in local newspapers. If neither of these sources is successful, then you might explore dealers that specialize in used cars or new car dealers that handle used cars. Your friends can be a good source of information on the reputation of the various dealers in your area.

Pricing a Used Car   All three publications discussed in the previous section on used car prices are an excellent source of price information. If you are buying from a dealer, the quoted price will likely be near the suggested retail price. If the seller is a private owner, the price should be near the wholesale price.

Operating Cost: New versus Used   If you can buy a good used car at an attractive price and if the repair expenses are minimal, its cost per mile will likely be substantially less than that of a new car. But this statement has two major "if's." Purchasing an older used car does not necessarily guarantee lower total operating cost. True, depreciation expense declines, but it may be more than offset by increased repairs and maintenance.

Exhibit 10-11   General Guidelines when Purchasing a Used Car

Key feature	Rationale or explanation
1 Concentrate on brands with good repair records.	The owner surveys in *Consumer Reports, Road and Track*, and *Popular Science* are a good resource.
2 Stay with basic models rather than those loaded with options and accessories.	Initial cost is less and those extras can become a repair nightmare.
3 Look for a low-mileage car.	Recent legislation has improved, yet not guaranteed, an honest odometer reading in used cars.
4 Buy from a reputable dealer.	An unscruplous dealer can make a junker look and run great until the sale is complete.
5 The car should have a valid safety sticker if your state requires one.	Cost of correcting safety problems can be sizable.
6 Do an exhaustive check on the car's overall condition.	Several books discuss the key check points and tests in detail. Check your library for a copy. Have a mechanic you know and trust examine the car.

A 3- to 5-year-old, low-mileage used car is probably the best choice to minimize operating costs. The 3-year-old should have less than 30,000 miles and the 5-year-old less than 50,000 miles. This combination has two advantages. The purchase price should be moderate because a car's market price declines sharply in the early years. At the same time, the repair expenses should remain reasonably low provided the car's mileage is low. Nevertheless, the original owner may have sold that low-mileage car because it had so many problems.

Strategy: If you decide on a used car, exercise extra caution in the purchase decision.

CAR WARRANTIES

Car manufacturers provide warranties on their new cars for a specified number of months or a specified number of miles, whichever occurs first. The coverage period is typically 12 months or 12,000 miles, although some provide 24 months or 24,000 miles, and a few are even more liberal. During the coverage period, the manufacturer promises to repair or replace any covered component that proves defective.

Coverage: Components   Most warranties cover the major components in the car's drive train: engine, engine accessories, transmission, rear axle, and major running components. They exclude parts with a limited or short life—tires, hoses and belts, and brake pads—and cosmetic items—paint, trim, and upholstery materials.

Total Coverage   Several automobile companies now offer warranties that cover nearly every component. Generally, the owner must service the car according to the manufacturer's recommendations to keep this coverage in force. Some manufacturers offer total coverage warranties as an extra cost option.

Strategy: If the manufacturer offers a total protection warranty, we strongly recommend it even if it costs extra.

Evaluating a Warranty   The checklist shown in Exhibit 10–12 highlights important areas you should consider when evaluating warranties. Certainly a strong warranty with few restrictions has to be counted as a definite plus in favor of a particular car.

Using Your Warranty

Always file all warranty claims promptly. As soon as you are aware of a potential warranty problem, report it to your dealer. If it is not fixed the first time, ask the dealer to try again. Keep repeating your request until you are satisfied. Be highly skeptical of the dealer's claims that you must wait a few

Exhibit 10-12   Warranty Checklist

1 Warranty coverage period	_____ months _____ miles
2 What major components are covered?	_____
3 Are any of those components covered for an extended period?	_____
4 Does the manufacturer offer a total coverage warranty?	_____
5 Does the warranty cover all parts and labor?	_____
6 Does the dealer provide a replacement car during warranty repairs?	_____
7 Can warranty coverage be extended as an extra cost option?	_____

thousand miles. Under those circumstances, ask the dealer to put this commitment in writing.

When the Dealer Cannot Resolve a Warranty Problem   Make certain you have fully exhausted your efforts with the dealer before taking your complaint to some other agency. For one thing, the first question any other agency will ask is whether you have given the dealer an opportunity to correct the problem. Also, most dealers really want their customers to be satisfied with their service. If, however, your dealer is unable or unwilling to rectify the problem, your next contact is the company that made the car.

Manufacturer's Representative   The starting point here is to arrange a meeting with the manufacturer's representative who covers your geographical area. These representatives work in the manufacturer's zone office and are the contact link between the manufacturer and its dealers. Since they visit the various dealers on a regular basis, have your dealer set up a conference among the three of you to discuss your problem. Be prepared at the conference with complete details of your problem, copies of any repair bills, and a clear idea of what you want done. This can often prod some action out of a dealer who might be reluctant to contact the zone office about your problem.

Manufacturer's Central Office   Another way to notify the manufacturer is to telephone the customer relations department (it may also be called customer service, customer complaints, or some similar title) at the manufacturer's central office. Although the exact procedure varies, most manufacturers forward the information from these telephone calls to their zone office personnel. The zone office contacts the customer and tries to work out a solution. Despite a lot of initial fanfare in the auto manufacturers' ads about customer service, we have not heard much lately about these special contact people. Either they are working more quietly now, or the commitment by the manufacturer has waned and these departments have been eliminated or sharply curtailed. At the very least, it is worth a telephone call or letter to the manufacturer to see if the central office can expedite a solution to your problem. In writing, include a complete statement of your problem, details of what you have done, and a statement of what you want the manufacturer or dealer to do.

Automobile Consumer Action Panel (AUTOCAP)   The formation of consumer action panels (CAPs) is a recent development in the automobile area. These panels were formed by automobile dealer associations to help consumers with their automobile problems. To date, there are seven panels, with more in the process of forming. AUTOCAP is modeled directly after a similar, highly successful group within the appliance industry. Owing to its newness, AUTO-CAP has yet to establish a "track record" of successes or failures, so we have no idea how much clout this group is going to have with consumer automobile problems. If there is one in your area (the Appendix to Chapter 9 has details on locating one), we certainly urge you to give it a try after you have exhausted your avenues through the dealer and manufacturer.

CAR REPAIRS

The entire area of car repairs and service continues to cause considerable frustration and grief among consumers. In part, the problem stems from the lack of well-trained service personnel. And there is no immediate relief in sight, because there still are not enough people entering the automobile service trade. Another part of the problem is the lack of licensing or regulation of this major service industry. In most states, there is no examination or minimum experience requirement to establish an individual's competence in auto mechanics. Likewise, most states have few, if any, regulations that restrict or control who can open an auto repair shop.

Locating a Reputable Service Facility   Your friends and coworkers are your best information source on the quality of service facilities in your area. A second source is the local better business bureau, if your area has one. Not only can it tell you how many complaints it has received on a particular service facility, it also explains how those complaints were resolved. You could also ask the local voluntary consumer action group, if there is one, for its recommendations. We cannot give a blanket recommendation as to whether an independent repair shop or a dealer's service department is best. There are good and bad facilities in both groups; you will have to find out which one is best in your area.

Why Not Do It Yourself?   While major repairs are not within the competence of the weekend do-it-yourselfer, most routine maintenance can be performed by the average owner. This is especially true on most subcompacts and compacts; they are less complex and they are more easily serviced than larger cars.

Check with your local junior college, technical school, or high school to see whether it has an evening course in basic auto mechanics. Many schools offer such courses and the fee is generally nominal. The course will provide sufficient background so you can do most maintenance and minor repair work. You do not have to be a mechanic to do the routine service work and you can save a tidy sum. For example, you can change your oil and oil filter at home for $6; cost at the dealer would be $12.

You will have to buy some basic tools, if you have none, but you will need only a few, and they should be fairly inexpensive. Furthermore, they will last for years, so the annual cost is small. With the current standard labor rate for automotive service running between $10 and $25 an hour, you will save enough money in doing your first few repairs to cover the cost of your course in auto mechanics and your tools.

Strategy: If you have any interest in the subject, give your local evening course in basic automotive mechanics a try.

LEASING: AN ALTERNATIVE TO PURCHASE

Increasingly, consumers are being encouraged to lease their cars rather than purchase them. Before we can decide whether leasing or purchasing is best, we need to examine what leasing entails.

What Leasing Offers   Leases can cover any period the customer desires, although 24 to 48 months is the typical period. For a monthly payment, the customer has unrestricted use of a car during the lease period.

Unfortunately, some of the highly touted benefits claimed in some leasing advertisements are questionable. For example, some claim it ends the hassle of negotiating for the purchase of a new car every few years. But if you want to lease a car, you should negotiate with several leasing companies to determine whether you have been quoted a fair lease price.

Some advertisements would have you believe that, by leasing, you avoid all maintenance and repair problems. But the standard lease provides neither service. To obtain these services, you must purchase a separate maintenance contract at an added cost: a typical all-inclusive contract would cost $20 to $40 per month. Think of it in terms of the annual cost, $240 to $480, and it is a substantial added cost. No doubt the same amount would cover all your repairs and maintenance had you purchased the car.

Likewise, the standard lease does not include auto insurance; that also must be purchased as an added extra.

What the standard lease really covers is your depreciation expense and possibly your registration fee. You pay all other expenses—maintenance, repairs, gasoline and oil, insurance—the same as if you owned the car.

Types of Leases   There are two types of leases available to individuals: the net lease (closed-end, straight, walkaway, or flat rate are other names) and the open-end lease (participating or cost plus are alternative names).

Net Lease   The customer's obligation under a net lease is limited to the agreed-upon monthly lease payment. If, at the end of the lease period, the market value of the car is less than the company estimated at the beginning of the period, that is the company's problem.

Open-end Lease   The customer's obligation under an open-end lease includes not only the monthly payment, but also the difference between the estimated and the actual market prices of the car at the end of the lease. For example, assume the leasing company, in quoting the rate on a car, estimated the car would have a market value of $3,000 at the end of the lease. If the price actually was $2,500, the customer would have to pay the $500 difference. Of course, had the price been $3,500, the customer would have received a $500 refund.

Since the customer carries the risk of market price fluctuations, the monthly rate on an open-end lease should be less than a net cost lease. A potential problem with an open-end lease is that an unscrupulous leasing company could quote a very attractive monthly rate by using an unrealistically high price for the leased car at the end of a lease.[2] The customer would then face a large final payment. Be extra careful when dealing with an open-end lease.

Strategy: If you expect a period of stable used-car prices over the next 24 to 48 months, the cost savings generally justify an open-end lease. If, however, prices are likely to be volatile, you probably will be further ahead with a net lease.

Cost of Leasing versus Purchase   To compare the cost of leasing versus purchase, we have to consider only depreciation because all other operating costs are identical for the two alternatives. This cost comparison is illustrated in Exhibit 10–13.

The example used in Exhibit 10–13 was a full-size car that could be purchased for $5,000. To compute the cost of owning, in the top part of Exhibit 10–13, we assumed a $500 downpayment with the $4,500 balance financed over 24 months at an APR of 12 percent. Using the appropriate percentages from Exhibit 10–5, we estimated the car would be worth approximately $2,995 after 2 years. The lower half of Exhibit 10–13 illustrates the leasing alternative. It was assumed the lease payment included sales tax and license.

The message from Exhibit 10–13 is that leasing is substantially more expensive than ownership. The cost of leasing for the example is 21 percent higher ([$3,497 − $2,889] ÷ $2,889) than it is for ownership. In all likelihood, this cost differential would be less for a low-priced compact and larger for a

[2]"Truth-in-Leasing Law Is Urged by Fed, Cite Abuses in Car Rentals," *The Wall Street Journal*, Jan. 5, 1975, p. 3, col. 2.

Exhibit 10-13 Cost of Leasing versus Ownership

Costs of ownership — 2 years	
Down payment	$ 500
Lost interest on down payment, $500 @ 6 percent for 2 years	60
Payments on sales loan	
$4,500 loan, 24 monthly payments @ $211.83, APR 12 percent	5,084
Sales tax @ 4 percent	200
License, 2 years	40
Total costs	$5,884
Less: Wholesale value of car 2 years from today	− 2,995
Net cost of ownership	$2,889
Cost of leasing — 2 years	
Down payment (1 month's rental)	$ 145
Lost interest on down payment, $145 @ 6 percent for 2 years	17
Payments, 23 months @ $145	3,335
Net cost of leasing	$3,497

high-priced full-size. But the point is, the cost of ownership is almost always less than the cost of leasing.

One final word of caution: A few leasing companies offer comparisons between the monthly lease payment and the monthly payment on the auto loan and claim that leasing is cheaper because the monthly payment is less. This is an erroneous cost comparison. In Exhibit 10–13, the lease payment, $145, was less than the loan payment, $211.83. But at the end of the lease, you have 24 payment receipts, nothing more! After paying the higher loan payment for 24 months, you have a used car worth approximately $3,000. Comparing monthly payments is grossly inaccurate; you must make a cost analysis similar to Exhibit 10–13 to evaluate leasing versus purchasing.

CAR FINANCING

Since credit was discussed extensively in Chapters 7 and 8, we will comment here on only several key points with respect to automobile financing.

Maturity   The maximum maturity on your automobile loan should equal the time you expect to keep the car. Thus, if you plan to keep a car 3 years, a 36-month loan would be maximum. In fact, we recommend a 36-month maximum even if you plan to hold that car for 5 or 6 years. By having the loan repaid in the third year, you avoid the combined load of loan payments and the increased repair expenses that typically occur in the later years of ownership. We suggest that even after the loan has been repaid, you continue to deposit your monthly car payment in a special "car emergency fund." That fund can then be used to cover your automobile repairs; any balance remaining in the fund can be used when you purchase a new car.

The new extended auto loan maturities—they can reach 60 months in some cases—create several problems. First, the total finance charge is much larger. For example, the finance charges on a $4,000, 60-month loan with an APR of 12 percent would be $1,339, compared with $783 on the same loan over 36 months. Second, the rapid decline in a car's market price could mean that the car would be worth substantially less than the outstanding loan balance. If you should have to sell the car, it would not provide enough money to repay the loan. Yet you would still be responsible for any unpaid balance.

Strategy: If a car is so expensive that you need a 60-month loan to afford the payments, chances are it is much too expensive for your budget.

Comparative Shopping   When financing a new or used car, there is no reason to limit your choice to the dealer's loan offer. Many lenders—banks, credit unions, and finance companies—are eager to finance new or used automobiles. Given the wide availability of auto loans, you should shop for the one with the lowest APR. Financing through the dealer generally does not give you any added leverage. Most dealers immediately sell their finance contracts to some financial institutions.

Strategy: When shopping for automobile financing, consider all competing lending sources. Unless the dealer's offer has the lowest APR, there is no added benefit to be gained from financing with the dealer.

SUMMARY

1   Consumers' preference in automobiles has shifted dramatically during the early 1970s. Operating efficiency and passenger accommodations are receiving much more emphasis than was true in the late 1960s.
2   The transportation needs of most consumers can be served quite adequately by a well-designed and well-engineered subcompact or compact model.
3   One of the major costs of automobile ownership is the annual decline in the car's market value.
4   The total operating cost of a subcompact is substantially less than the cost of a compact; and the cost of a compact is significantly less than that of a full-size car.
5   The optimum holding period on most cars is that point when the car begins to require major, expensive repairs. Try to become knowledgeable enough about your car so that you can anticipate this point.
6   Transportation costs should not be more than 12 percent of the family budget.
7   Your transportation costs should be matched to your budget, not the reverse procedure.
8   You can estimate what constitutes a fair price on a new car when trading in your old car by determining (*a*) the wholesale value of your old car, (*b*) the dealer's cost on the new car, and (*c*) the dealer's profit margin on the new car.
9   The majority of car warranties limit their coverage to the car's major operating components. Further, that coverage is generally limited to 12,000 miles or 12 months, whichever occurs first.

10   When you have a warranty problem that your dealer cannot, or will not, correct, discuss the problem with the manufacturer's zone representative.

11   In most cases, the cost of leasing substantially exceeds the cost of ownership.

REVIEW YOUR UNDERSTANDING OF

Automobile models
    Subcompact
    Compact
    Intermediate
    Full-size
    Specialty
Cost of auto ownership
    Fixed costs
    Variable costs
Optimum holding period
Owner surveys
Net cash difference

Shopping for an automobile
    Selecting a brand
    Picking a dealer
    Estimating a price
Warranty coverage: time and components
Total coverage warranty
Customer complaints
    Manufacturer's representative
    Manufacturer's central office
    AUTOCAPS
Net lease
Open-end lease

DISCUSSION QUESTIONS

1   What group of consumers can be best served by a subcompact model? Least well served?

2   What are the two largest costs of automobile ownership? How do they vary among models? Why?

3   What factors account for the substantially lower operating cost of subcompacts and compacts?

4   What types of cars do you foresee in the 1980s? How will they differ from today's models?

5   What cost components are essential to determine a fair price for a new car when trading in your old car?

6   What are your greatest risks in purchasing a used car? How can they be minimized?

7   What added benefit does a consumer gain from a "total coverage" warranty?

8   What factors cause the entire auto repair area to be such a "can of worms"? What can you do to minimize your problems with auto repairs?

9   What are the advantages and disadvantages to leasing rather than owning an automobile? What groups would best be served by leasing? Do you think leasing will become widespread?

CASE PROBLEM

Fred and Becky Bear are considering replacing their current full-size station wagon with a new full-size wagon. Their combined disposable income, $16,000, stems from Fred's working fulltime and Becky parttime. They live in a medium-sized metropolitan area and most of their travel is within the city and suburbs. Their principal reason for considering a full-size wagon is not so much their need for passenger space—they have two children. Rather, they feel it would hold a lot of camping gear for their annual one-week summer camping trip. Second, they have never thought that a smaller car offered any significant savings. They anticipate holding the car for 6 years, during which time they will drive some 69,000 miles. The full-size wagon with the options they want costs $6,500.

a   Approximately how much would this car cost per mile? (*Hint:* Use Exhibit 10–9.)

b   Does their choice fit within the suggested budget guideline? Why?

c   Assuming they plan to drive approximately 11,500 miles per year, which model (full-size, compact, or subcompact) would you recommend? Why?

d   If Fred and Becky should decide on a compact station wagon that cost $4,800, what would be their ownership cost per mile (assume 6 years and 69,000 miles)?

e   Assuming they drove 11,500 miles annually, what annual savings will the compact wagon, costing $4,800, provide over the full-size they were originally considering?

f   Do you feel the full-size wagon is a good choice, given Fred and Becky's current status, income, and needs? Why?

RECOMMENDED READINGS

Booklets

American Automobile Association, *Your Driving Costs*. Falls Church, Va., 1975.
   Provides estimated operating costs for the four principal automobile categories: subcompact, compact, intermediate, and full-size. Check your public library or local AAA office for a copy.

Liston, L. L., and C. A. Aiken, *Cost of Owning and Operating an Automobile—1976*. Washington, D.C.: U.S. Dept. of Transportation, 1976.
   Discusses all aspects of the individual cost components connected with automobile ownership. It includes a separate table that summarizes estimated annual operating costs for three size categories: subcompact, compact, and full-size. The cost breakdown in those tables is excellent.

Magazines

Consumer Reports:

"How to Buy a Good Used Car." April 1975, pp. 256–258.
   A good discussion of the subject.

The annual "auto issue" of *Consumer Reports* (generally the April issue) is required reading for anyone who is considering the purchase of a new or used car. Provides information on repair records, body dimensions, selecting options, ratings and comments, etc.

Changing Times:

"Lease a Car Instead of Buying?" November 1973, pp. 21–23.
   Discusses the topic in detail.

"Ways They Can Cheat You When They Service Your Car." June 1974, pp. 11–14.
   Discusses common repair frauds. Includes recommendations for protecting yourself against them.

"At Last! Certified Repairmen to Fix Your Car." September 1974, pp. 31–33.
   Explains the development of the certification program and the implications for the consumer.

"Buying a Used Car." January 1975, pp. 25–28.
    Discusses the entire area: where to buy, what to buy, how to price it, how to check
    it out.
"The High Cost of Running a Car and What to Do about It." June 1975, pp. 25–28.
    Reviews potential areas of savings on car ownership.
"Knocking Down the Sticker Price of a New Car." October 1975, pp. 11–13.
    Presents guidelines for reducing the cost of a new car.

Money:

Mead, William B., "The Princely Sum of the Auto Parts." November 1972, pp. 32–35.
    Discusses high cost of automotive parts. Reviews causes and possible solutions.
"Car Makers' Promises." January 1973, pp. 12–16.
    Discusses problems of car warranties. Suggest avenues of redress.
"An Owner's Manual for Financing a Car." December 1973, pp. 78–82.
    Reviews potential lending sources for auto loans.
Moore, Oliver S., III, "The Limitations of Leasing." December 1973, p. 82.
    Discusses advantages and disadvantages of leasing.
"A Compact Guide to Trading Down." July 1974, pp. 37–39.
    Examines the potential savings from switching to a small car. Demonstrates the
    required computations needed to estimate those savings.
Randall, Robert M., "Getting Used to Used Cars." October 1974, pp. 36–40.
    Discusses checkpoints to be used when purchasing used cars. Suggests a number
    of tests and gives estimated cost of select repairs.
Boroson, Warren, "What New Cars Really Sell For." May 1975, pp. 30–33.
    Provides interesting statistics on actual car costs in a 10 city survey. Discusses
    bargaining techniques. Reviews some dealer abuses.

Chapter 11

Selecting Consumer Durables

After completing this chapter you should be able to:

describe the four criteria to evaluate when purchasing appliances.

explain the importance of service cost as part of total ownership costs.

develop a plan for selecting a service firm.

analyze the merits of service contracts.

explain the relative importance of operating cost in total ownership costs.

estimate the operating cost of competing appliance models.

decide whether the price of a particular appliance is reasonable.

evaluate whether an appliance's design features meet your needs.

describe the essential disclosures required in a warranty.

differentiate between a "full" and "limited" coverage warranty.

formulate a plan for obtaining action on a warranty problem.

Major consumer durables, such as refrigerators, air conditioners, dish-washers, television sets, clothes washers, and dryers, have become an integral part of today's life-style. Every year the average homeowner spends between $400 and $700 to purchase appliances, operate them, and have them repaired. Depending on income, these costs can easily represent 2 to 5 percent of a person's annual expenditures. Even people who rent a house or an apartment are likely to spend $100 to $200 annually on such things as a television, dishwasher, clothes washer, and dryer.

There are several reasons why it is important to carefully consider your purchase of consumer durables. Consumer durables, as the name implies, generally have a long life expectancy. For example, clothes washers and dryers are expected to last about 8 to 10 years, refrigerators and freezers, 12 to 15 years. Once you buy an appliance, you are stuck with it for a long time. A poor choice could easily double your total costs (including purchase, operation, and repairs) over that time. What could be worse is a poor choice that not only results in higher costs but also does not give you the service you want.

Of course, appliances can be repaired. Some repair service companies provide good repair service, others barely adequate service, and, unfortunately, many companies do repair work that is either incompetent or fraudulent. Although it is very difficult to evaluate precisely, one of your major goals in evaluating an appliance before purchasing it is your confidence that it will require minimum contact (better yet, none) with the repair service industry during its useful life.

For the balance of this chapter, we will use the term *appliance* when referring to any major consumer durable. We define appliance very broadly to include television, stereo, and air conditioner as well as the traditional range of major kitchen and laundry items (refrigerator, freezer, range, dishwasher, clothes washer, and dryer).

Evaluation Criteria

There are four criteria which should be incorporated in the appliance decision: service, operating cost, purchase price, and the unit's capabilities and features. The complete decision process is illustrated in Exhibit 11–1.

The relative importance of each criterion in a particular decision depends upon the appliance being considered. Too often people use purchase price as the sole criterion and do not consider the other three. On many appliances, operating cost or service cost can be a much larger part of total ownership cost than the initial purchase price. Over its lifetime, the cheaper appliance could

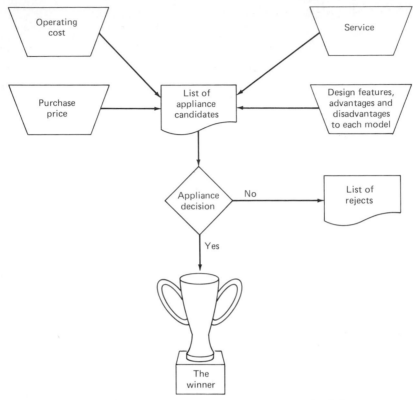

Exhibit 11-1   Evaluation Criteria for the Appliance Decision

easily be far more expensive because of service and operating costs. That is why every appliance decision should be based on joint consideration of all four criteria.

Service

On some appliances, service costs can represent more than 40 percent of the total ownership cost. The reliability of many appliances continues to improve so that they require fewer service calls during their lifetime. Unfortunately, this reduction has been largely offset by the increase in service cost. Consequently, the total lifetime service cost has changed very little.[1]

In general, the more mechanically or electrically complex the appliance, the more important it is to consider service when deciding on an appliance. Exhibit 11–2 illustrates two extremes on the service spectrum.

Service cost represents 35 percent of the total ownership cost of the color television set shown, for example, in the top half of Exhibit 11–2. Clearly, the service criterion should rank high for a complex appliance such as a television,

[1]Massachusetts Institute of Technology Center for Alternatives with the Charles Stark Draper Laboratory, Inc., *The M.I.T. Report Consumer Appliances: The Real Cost.* Cambridge, Mass.: M.I.T., p. 7.

Exhibit 11-2   Service: Relative Importance in the Appliance Decision

Appliance	Importance of service cost	Proportion of total ownership cost			
		Purchase	Service	Operation	Total
Color television:	High	53 percent	35 percent	12 percent	100 percent
$500 set*		$500	$330	$113	$ 943
Refrigerator:	Low	36 percent	6 percent	58 percent	100 percent
$400 unit*		$400	$ 67	$644	$1,111

*Author's estimates of costs.

Source: Massachusetts Institute of Technology Center for Policy Alternatives with The Charles Stark Draper Laboratory, Inc., *The M.I.T. Report Consumer Appliances: The Real Cost.* Cambridge, Mass.: M.I.T., pp. 6–7.

dishwasher, or clothes washer. The refrigerator cited in the bottom half of Exhibit 11–2 illustrates the opposite situation. Only 6 percent of its total ownership cost goes for servicing. For less complex appliances, such as refrigerators, gas and electric ranges, or dryers, the service criterion should receive less weight in the decision.

Strategy: On complex appliances, service should be a key factor when comparing competing models.

The service question has three aspects that need to be considered: the frequency of required service, the serviceability of the unit, and the availability of adequate service. Service frequency affects the total service cost because the more often an appliance must be repaired, the higher its lifetime service cost. Serviceability refers to how easy or difficult it is to repair a particular appliance. Obviously, the more serviceable an appliance, the less time and effort required to repair it, and therefore the lower the cost. The availability of adequate service affects not only service cost, but also your general satisfaction with an appliance.

Information Sources: Service Frequency and Serviceability

Where service is an important factor, the brand with a good service record will likely be the cheapest in the long-run. Even if it costs $50 to $100 more, the extra cost can be recovered if the unit requires fewer service calls than a lower-priced unit with a mediocre service record.

Information about a particular brand's service frequency and its serviceability can be obtained from two sources: your friends and their experience with their appliances, and the owner survey published by *Consumer Reports.*

Friends   Often the experience of your friends can help you evaluate which brands have a good or poor service record. To be meaningful, however, the model you are considering should be similar to the one your friend owns. In addition, your experience with a new model may not necessarily duplicate your friend's experience with the older model. Also, unless you have many friends with the same unit, this source of service research will probably be limited to the experience of a single owner. Nevertheless, try to learn the facts of their service experiences, not merely their impressions.

Owner Survey   The magazine *Consumer Reports* is an excellent source of service data. Its tests cover a wide range of appliances, models, and brands, so you can readily analyze and compare competing brands of appliances. Those tests generally cover serviceability and frequency of repair. *Consumer Reports* determines frequency of repair based on a questionnaire it sends its readers each year.

Service Organizations

Most appliances are serviced by three groups: factory service outlets, independent service firms, and the service departments of appliance dealers.

Factory service outlets   Factory service outlets are owned and operated by the appliance manufacturer. While they have expanded geographically, they are still primarily concentrated in medium to large metropolitan areas. Because they specialize in a single brand, their service personnel are generally well prepared to perform the latest repair techniques. Furthermore, the outlets generally carry all necessary replacement parts for the company's entire product line. However, despite a continual effort to upgrade their service staffs, their service quality may be no better than an independent or dealer

service department. The fact that they are factory-owned does not always guarantee top-quality repair service.

Independent service firms   There are two types of independent service firms. Neither type is company-owned, although one is somewhat associated with an appliance manufacturer, and the other is entirely independent.

In a geographic area where an appliance manufacturer has no factory service outlet, the manufacturer will franchise (appoint) a local independent firm as the authorized service representative to service its appliances. These franchised service shops can employ as many as 50 or as few as only several service technicians. The manufacturer may provide support to the franchised independents, such as training their personnel, sending service and repair bulletins, and providing access to the manufacturer's inventory of replacement parts. Franchised independent service firms are usually found in small and medium-sized cities. The quality of service they provide varies tremendously. At one extreme, there are service people with the latest technical training coupled with a good stock of replacement parts; they generally deliver good-quality service. At the other extreme, the personnel may be poorly trained and the stock of replacement parts may be minimal; here, the quality is usually not so good.

The other group of independents not affiliated with any manufacturer rely on free-lance service work on any and all appliance brands. The shops are usually quite small and it generally is harder to find a good one. For one thing, they cover a vast territory by taking on all brands. For another, appliance manufacturers are quick to franchise a good independent, which tends to leave the marginal and substandard service firms within the ranks of the unaffiliated.

Dealer service department   At one time most of the dealers that sold appliances also had their own service departments which did repair work. But as department stores and discount stores began to sell appliances, taking business away from dealers, the dealer service departments began to shrink. Dealers discontinued their service departments because they were usually unprofitable, especially when competing against the lower prices of department and discount stores that did not have service departments to support.

Dealers who still operate a service department generally receive good manufacturer's support—training seminars, service bulletins, access to replacement parts. In small cities and rural areas, usually only dealer repair service is available. Those areas simply do not have the service volume to support a manufacturer's service outlet or a large, franchised independent service firm.

Selecting a Service Firm   Investigate the service firms in your area *before* you need service. It is tough to be objective and deliberate in investigating a service firm when your washer is overflowing or the food in your freezer is turning to mush. The more critical it is for your appliance to operate continuously, the more important it is for you to locate a prospective service firm before a breakdown.

Your friends frequently have information on the quality and reputation of the service firms in your area. When they tell you about exceptional service, jot down the firm's name and keep it in your appliance file. Likewise, when they have had a bad experience, note that firm's name so you can avoid it.

Most better business bureaus (BBBs) keep a record of consumer complaints against service firms. This record can help you avoid firms with a poor reputation. It will not always guarantee high-quality service work, but it can minimize the chance of incompetent or fraudulent work. If there is no BBB in your area, try the local chamber of commerce; occasionally it performs this function in smaller cities.

Another guide to service quality is the length of time the firm has been in business and whether it is prospering. Your chances of receiving good service are likely to be better when the firm has been in business a number of years and has continued to expand. That does not mean all new service firms should be excluded; rather, you should use extra care when dealing with them. The checklist in Exhibit 11–3 should help you judge the reputation of a service firm you might use.

Minimizing Service Calls   Before calling a service firm, make certain the unit really needs service. Check to see that the appliance is plugged in, that a blown fuse or tripped circuit breaker is not the problem, or, if the unit requires water, that the water is turned on. Also, read your owner's manual to see whether you are using the correct operating procedure. Often, the manual describes basic operating procedures and related problems and provides simple instructions for correcting the problem yourself. Finally, be sure to use the unit only for the purpose for which it was designed. Although these recommendations are so basic they may seem not worth repeating, many service calls are directly attributable to improperly connecting the unit, using the wrong operating sequence, or simply misusing or abusing it.

Action on Your Service Complaint   When you feel you have received faulty or inadequate repair service, your first stop is the firm that did the work. Most service firms do not want irate customers and they will offer to correct a

Exhibit 11-3   Judging a Service Firm

	Yes	No
1 Have your friends used this firm?	( )	( )
2 If so, were they satisfied		
a with the work?	( )	( )
b with the cost?	( )	( )
c with the time the service work took?	( )	( )
3 Has the local better business bureau received relatively few customer complaints on the firm?	( )	( )
4 If numerous, were the complaints resolved to the customer's satisfaction?	( )	( )
5 Has the firm been established a number of years?	( )	( )
6 Does the firm look prosperous?	( )	( )

customer's service complaint when possible. If the firm you contact does not correct your problem the first time, ask it to make a second try.

In presenting your complaint, tell the firm exactly what repairs have been made, what the problem is, and what you want done. The best person to contact when dealing with a small independent firm is the owner. For factory outlets and larger independents, the service manager is the appropriate contact. And remember, one personal visit to the firm is often worth a dozen phone calls.

Better Business Bureau   When the service firm is unable or unwilling to correct the problem, you should file a report with the local better business bureau. It may or may not help you resolve your complaint. But at the very least, by filing your complaint, it will become part of the service firm's record; when other people call the bureau, they will have the benefit of your experience.

Service Contracts

A service contract provides complete or partial repairs for a specific appliance for a specified period of time. Total service contracts are the most popular type because they include all parts and labor.

A service contract covers appliance repairs after the initial guarantee from the manufacturer has expired. When considering a service contract, make certain the coverage under the contract does not merely duplicate the appliance's guarantee. Some dealers will sell a service contract covering repairs during the first year of ownership when a part, or all, of that year's service is covered by the appliance's guarantee.

What the Service Contract Does for the Owner   For a flat fee you can buy a service contract which provides complete appliance service regardless of how many service calls your appliance may need during the contract period. The service contract is like an insurance policy; for the set fee, the owner is protected against all appliance repair costs. One of the main advantages is that once you purchase a service contract, your cost of repairs does not rise during the contract period even if the costs of parts and labor rise. Unfortunately, you get the most out of a service contract only when the appliance is at its worst.

What It Does for the Service Firm   There are indications that contracts are very profitable for the seller. Service firms push contracts much too aggressively for them to be money losers. Aside from that, the main advantage to the service firm is that a large number of contracts guarantees it a certain amount of repair work. And since the cost of the contract effectively pays the firm in advance for the repairs, it can use that money for training personnel and buying necessary equipment and replacement parts.

Cost of Service Contracts   The two service contracts illustrated in Exhibit 11–4 are from a large nationwide retail store. We have rounded the costs to the nearest dollar (i.e., $59.99 became $60). We intentionally chose a color

Exhibit 11-4 Cost of Service Contract

Appliance	Annual cost by year of ownership							Total for 7 years
	1	2	3	4	5	6	7	
Color television	$60	$60	$80	$90	$100	$110	$110	$610
Clothes washer	$20	$20	$30	$30	$ 30	$ 40	$ 50	$220

television and a clothes washer because their service costs are an important component of their total lifetime ownership cost. Although the exhibit shows only the annual cost for each of the first 7 years, most firms offer annual contracts on older appliances.

Two things stand out in Exhibit 11–4: The annual cost rises sharply as the unit becomes older, and the total cost over a 7-year period is enormous. When selling a contract, salespeople frequently try to disguise the cost by quoting a daily rate. For example, they may point out that you can end your television worries for only 16 cents per day ($60 ÷ 365 days). Yet, buying a service contract for each year of the television's 11-year expected life would cost a staggering $1,050. That is about double the cost of a new set! And you cannot reduce that cost by waiting until the later years to buy a contract because most firms will not sell a service contract unless the appliance has been covered since it was new. Unfortunately, many people buy a contract in the early years of ownership when it is least needed; then, as the contract's price rises, they drop coverage at the very time they might benefit from it.

Why does the service contract cost so much? Probably for several reasons. The unlimited service feature makes it expensive; it tends to make people feel that they need not take proper care of the appliance or that they can call for service even when it may not really be necessary. Also, the high profit margins and sales commissions make it expensive.

> **Strategy: When considering a contract, always look at the cost of the contract over the lifetime of the appliance, not just the annual cost. Ask yourself if your service costs are likely to match that total lifetime contract cost.**

Fund Your Own   Rather than insuring against a small loss with a service contract, why not fund your own contract? By depositing roughly one-half the monthly cost of a service contract in a separate repair fund each month, you will have the money to pay for the service calls. And if you do not have many service calls, you will probably have a sizable balance in your repair fund to be used as a down payment when it is time to buy a replacement appliance.

The Hard Sell   High sales commissions and a lucrative profit have led to some high pressure sales tactics. Even if you decide against the contract when you buy the appliance, the store frequently follows up with a phone call or mail notice implying that your refusal must have been an oversight; of course the store is only too willing to correct your oversight. Often a second refusal is not enough; the seller continues the hard sell through the mails or further phone calls.

Strategy: If you decide not to purchase a service contract, stick to that decision. While some sellers are phenomenally slow learners, several flat refusals should convey the message.

COST OF OPERATION

In the past, operating cost generally was not very important in deciding what appliance to buy. The relatively low energy costs minimized the cost differential between the high, efficient models that performed a given task with a small amount of energy and the less efficient models that used a much larger amount of energy to perform the same task. At the same time, manufacturers designed appliances without much regard for operating efficiency. But the low-cost energy of the past is exactly that: the past! Consumers can expect steadily rising energy prices over the next decade. Consequently, operating cost will be an increasingly important criterion in selecting an appliance.

Estimating Operating Cost   There are many factors that affect the operating cost of an appliance; therefore it is not a simple task to estimate the operating cost. Nevertheless, by testing a number of equivalent units under similar conditions, it is possible to compare their relative operating efficiency; thus you have a good start toward estimating which one will cost the least to operate. The higher an appliance's operating efficiency, the less energy it will need to perform a given task. There are three sources for these comparative operating tests: consumer magazines, the Association of Home Appliance Manufacturers, and appliance manufacturers.

Consumer Magazines   *Consumers' Research Magazine* publishes operating cost data from comparative tests of refrigerators and dishwashers. Those cost estimates are made under controlled laboratory conditions so that the differences in operating costs among models are directly due to differences in their efficiency. Using these estimates, you can readily rank competing models according to their operating efficiency.

Because of the many factors which affect operating cost, *Consumer Reports* does not always provide exact operating cost estimates on all models of appliances. However, in its test data, the magazine generally does include its findings on relative operating efficiency among equivalent competing appliances and also points out which models are unusually efficient or highly inefficient.

Association of Home Appliance Manufacturers   The Association of Home Appliance Manufacturers (AHAM) publishes a directory showing the energy consumption of refrigerators and freezers the association has certified as to storage capacity and energy consumption. In addition, it publishes a directory showing the relative operating efficiency of room air conditioners it has certified for cooling capacity and electrical input. There are two shortcomings

IF IT'S OPERATING COST THAT YOU'RE
CONCERNED ABOUT— THEN THIS IS THE
MODEL FOR YOU!

to this directory: it rates only refrigerators, freezers, and air conditioners; and it covers only those manufacturers that have submitted their products for testing. If your local library does not have the directory, a copy can be obtained from the AHAM, 20 North Wacker Drive, Chicago 60606.

Manufacturer's Estimate   The federal government is considering legislation that would require all manufacturers to label their major appliances with some kind of data to indicate their operating cost. That requirement is long overdue. Currently, manufacturers of air conditioners label their products with a very useful and revealing energy efficiency ratio (EER). By selecting the unit with the highest EER, a buyer can obtain the lowest operating cost for a given cooling capacity. We think similar information is needed on all major appliances, and we hope that other manufacturers will follow the precedent of the air conditioner manufacturers and volunteer energy efficiency data on their product labels. But it will probably take a government regulation to get all manufacturers to comply.

Importance to the Decision Process   The operating cost of an appliance is basically determined by how much energy it consumes while operating and how many hours it is operated. Exhibit 11–5 shows estimated typical monthly and yearly operating costs for a refrigerator, a dishwasher, and a clothes dryer.

As might be expected, the operating cost of a refrigerator is high because it operates continuously. This fact is an important criterion in deciding what refrigerator to buy. Although a dishwasher operates less frequently, it consumes large amounts of energy (most of it to heat the water required) when it does operate. Consequently, operating cost is also an important criterion in

Exhibit 11-5   Operating Costs: Importance in the Appliance Decision

Appliance	Operating costs* (computed at 4 cents per kilowatt hour)	
	Per month	Per year
Refrigerator		
(rated volume, 17.5 to 20.5 cubic feet)	$9.70	$116.40
Dishwasher*	8.75	105.00
Clothes dryer	3.31	39.72

*Assumes unit is used twice daily. Includes author's estimate of the cost of hot water used.

Source: Data on refrigerator from Association of Home Appliance Manufacturers, *1975 Directory of Certified Refrigerators and Freezers.* Data on dishwasher from *Consumers' Research Magazine,* January 1972, p. 21, and November 1974, p. 20. (Costs of detergent and other products are not included.) Data on clothes dryer from Edison Electric Institute, *Annual Energy Requirements of Electric Household Appliances.*

selecting a dishwasher. For a clothes dryer, operating cost is less important because it is used less frequently and consumes less energy.

Potential Savings   You can minimize operating costs with an appliance that has a high efficiency rating. And the more the appliance is to be used, such as a refrigerator or freezer which must operate continuously, the more you can save in operating costs. Exhibit 11–6 illustrates the range of estimated operating costs for refrigerators and dishwashers. The refrigerator data represents the average for all models in that particular size range. The data on dishwashers are based on a representative model (brand names are omitted). The costs are given for three groups of dishwashers and refrigerators: least efficient, medium efficient, and most efficient. All models are matched on major features, so that the operating cost differentials are due only to differences in efficiency.

Exhibit 11–6 reveals a sizable cost differential among the three efficiency rankings. For example, selecting the high-efficiency refrigerator rather than the low-efficiency model would save you $68.40 in annual operating costs. Choosing even the medium-efficiency model instead of the low-efficiency one would produce an annual saving of $34.20. Over a refrigerator's typical 15-year life, the savings could range from $1,026 ($68.40 × 15 years) to $513 ($34.20 × 15 years). The point you should learn from this exhibit is that the annual operating cost can be substantially lower (and your savings higher) when you own a highly efficient appliance rather than a low-efficiency one.

High Efficiency: How Much Extra to Pay?   Recently several manufacturers have introduced high-efficiency models that cost less to operate but are more expensive to buy than standard models. As might be expected, manufacturers have concentrated their efforts on those appliances—refrigerators,

Exhibit 11-6   Operating Costs: Comparative Analysis

| | | | Cost differential | | | |
| | | | Annual | | 5-year savings | |
Appliance	Relative efficiency rank	Operating cost per year*	Top vs. low	Mid vs. low	Top model	Mid-model
Refrigerator	Top	$ 48.00				
(rated volume,			$68.40		$342.00	
17.5 to 20.5	Mid	$ 82.20				
cubic feet)†				$34.20		$171.00
	Low	$116.40				
Dishwasher	Top	$ 99.00				
(under counter)‡			$17.00		$ 85.00	
	Mid	$105.00				
				$11.00		$ 55.00
	Low	$116.00				

*Computed using 4 cents per kilowatt hour. Pontential savings would be larger in areas where the cost exceeds 4 cents (sometimes running as high as 8 cents).

†Assumed to be midway between the highest- and lowest-efficiency model.

‡Dishwasher costs include author's estimate of hot water used.

Sources: Data on refrigerator from Association of Home Appliance Manufacturers, *1975 Directory of Certified Refrigerators and Freezers.* Information on dishwasher from *Consumers' Research Magazine,* January 1972, p. 21, and November 1974, p. 20. (Includes cost of electricity at 4 cents per kilowatt hour but not costs of detergent and other products.)

freezers, dishwashers—where operating cost is an important consideration. That raises the question: Will the saving in operating cost make it worthwhile to pay the extra price of the high-efficiency model? The simplest way to answer would be to compare how much you expect to save in total lifetime operating costs with the difference in the purchase prices of the two efficiency models you are considering. If the saving exceeds the added purchase price, the more efficient model would be the choice. But this comparison is not entirely accurate because it assumes a dollar of savings 5 to 10 years in the future (when a dollar will be worth less) will be equivalent to a current dollar.

One way to compensate for this inaccuracy is to consider only part of the lifetime operating savings: Using the annual savings in operating costs, calculate how many years it will take to recover the extra purchase price of the more efficient model. If you can recover the extra cost through annual savings in 5 to 7 years, we feel the more efficient model is the best choice. Because most appliances generally have a lifetime of 10 to 15 years, an efficient model will have a lower total purchase plus operating cost. For example, assume a particular brand X appliance costs $450 and its annual operating cost is $120, and a similar brand Y appliance costs $390 and its annual operating cost is $135. Since brand X's added $60 purchase price would be recouped in 4 years ($60 ÷ $15 per year = 4 years), it would be the better choice. If both appliances have a 10-year lifetime, the purchase and operating cost of brand X will be $1,650

[\$450 + (10 × \$120)], and brand Y, \$1,740 [\$390 + (10 × \$135)] resulting in a lifetime saving of \$90.

> **Strategy: The most efficient appliance is the best choice if its added purchase cost can be recovered in 5 to 7 years through operating savings.**

Operating Cost: The Future

Over the next few years, energy costs (electricity, gasoline, and natural gas) are likely to increase 10 to 15 percent annually. As these costs rise, the penalty for owning an inefficient appliance will become much larger.

Exhibit 11–7 projects the annual operating cost for the top-efficiency refrigerator and the lowest-efficiency refrigerator from Exhibit 11–6. That projection assumes the cost of electricity increases 15 percent annually. At that rate, the cost differential between the two models would increase from \$68.40 (\$116.40 − \$48.00) to \$158.21 (\$269.24 − \$111.03) in 6 years. The message of Exhibit 11–7 is that operating efficiency will become increasingly important as energy costs rise.

APPLIANCE PRICES

Several practices in the appliance industry complicate the task of deciding what is a fair price to pay for a particular appliance. For example, manufacturers

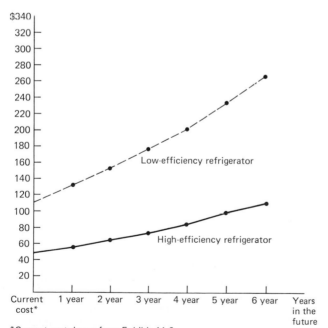

*Current cost drawn from Exhibit 11-6.
Assumes 15 percent annual increase in energy cost.

Exhibit 11-7   Projected Future Operating Cost

rarely indicate to the public the year an appliance was produced. The year of production is coded in the model number but the translation of that code is not general public information. Consequently, a buyer cannot determine the year a model was produced. Also, some appliance dealers heavily discount their prices while others charge full list price. And, further complicating the problem, many manufacturers do not publish a "suggested retail price." The net effect of all these practices is that buyers have limited price information and therefore must estimate the price that seems fair to both sides.

Estimating a Reasonable Price When shopping for the price on an appliance, you generally encounter two extremes. On the one hand, large department stores and nationwide retail chains typically have a tag on the unit showing its price, and their salespeople have little, if any, latitude to bargain with you on that price. On the other hand, small retailers frequently do not post their prices and their salespeople usually have some latitude in quoting prices to you. Usually, they are permitted to negotiate further if the customer resists the first price quoted. Because the large department stores and retail chains announce their prices, which are generally low but unbargainable, and the small dealers only quote their prices, which generally start high but are bargainable, it is difficult for shoppers to determine when they have obtained the lowest price, or even a reasonable price.

Average Price Estimating a reasonable price is much easier if you have an average price to use as a comparison point. The results of comparative appliance tests reported in *Consumer Reports* are a good source for price information. In addition to test data, *Consumer Reports* gives the price range for each model tested. Frequently the difference between highest and lowest price exceeds $100, so it is worth the time to get this information and to shop for the lowest price.

Haggling The choice of whether to haggle over price is a personal one. Some people thrive on it; others abhor it. Should you decide to haggle over price, do so from a position of knowledge. Be sure you know the average price of the appliance so that you can determine when the dealer offers a reasonable price. Otherwise, haggling will just be a waste of time and you may end up paying too high a price.

Trade-in Some people are happy only when the dealer quotes a high trade-in allowance on their old appliance. Unfortunately, dealers who give a higher trade-in allowance generally have a higher price on their new appliance; the net result is that the customer pays the same final price despite the higher trade-in. Since there is a ready market for serviceable used appliances, you will generally do better if you sell the unit yourself. A newspaper ad costs little, and you will likely sell the unit for more than the dealer's trade-in allowance. If you do not want that hassle, check local charities to see whether they accept old appliances as a donation. As a charitable donation, you can generally take the fair market value of the unit as an itemized deduction on your tax return (under Contributions). Of course, if the appliance is not operating, or if you expect it to have major problems soon, trade it in by all means. Otherwise you will have the expense and trouble of disposing of it yourself.

Method of Paying   Most dealers have two or three payment alternatives: straight cash, deferred payment same as cash, and consumer sales loan.

Cash   By paying straight cash the buyer avoids any and all finance charges. For the buyer who has the money, the cash payment is always cheaper than using credit since the cost of credit always exceeds the interest that money would earn in a savings account. There is no credit application or report, so administrative details are minimized. The principal drawback is that the customer has limited leverage with the dealer should there be a complaint. When the customer still owes a balance to the dealer, however, payment can be withheld until the problem is corrected. For that reason, we rank cash second among the three alternatives.

Under certain circumstances, customers can get an additional 4 to 6 percent discount by paying cash rather than charging the item on their bank credit card. If the transaction is charged, the credit organization assesses the dealer a 4 to 6 percent service fee, which you can be sure is buried in the price of the appliance. Depending on the dealer's willingness and your negotiating skill, you may be able to obtain this extra 4 to 6 percent discount for yourself.

Deferred Payments Same as Cash   With a deferred payment plan, the dealer generally allows the customer to pay part of the price at the time of the sale, with the remainder to be paid over the next 30, 60, or 90 days. Typically, there is no finance charge, so the terms are indeed the same as cash. Since there is an unpaid balance, the customer can use that to encourage corrective action from the dealer if necessary. Also, the 30- to 90-day payment extension may be sufficient for many people to fit the required payments into their monthly budget. We rank this option number 1.

Unfortunately, deferred payment terms are usually offered only by small and medium-sized appliance dealers; most large department stores and discount chains do not offer these terms. But always ask the seller whether or not this attractive payment option is available.

Consumer Sales Loan   Since we discussed sales loans in detail in the chapters on consumer credit, we will only summarize several important points here. Most dealers aggressively push sales loans. No doubt, part of their enthusiasm is due to the rebate the dealer receives when reselling the sales loan to a bank or finance company. Given this rebate practice, a dealer could easily be more concerned with maximizing the rebate than with minimizing the customer's annual percentage rate (APR). Comparative shopping among several lenders is essential before you accept the dealer's loan offer.

A sales loan provides the added advantage that a customer can withhold payment on the unpaid loan balance to force corrective action by the dealer. And this holds even when the dealer resells the sales loan to some financial institution. This was not always the case. Prior to May 14, 1976, the purchasing institution could generally force payment of the loan even if the dealer failed to correct a legitimate customer complaint. Chapter 8 discussed this change in detail. The principal disadvantage to the sales loan is the finance charge.

The two bank credit cards offer extended credit terms on major purchases which are essentially similar to a sales loan. Before you decide on these extended terms, compare their APR to your other credit alternatives: they may be convenient, but they are rarely cheapest.

> **Strategy: When offered, deferred payment, on the same terms as cash, is generally the best option if you can fit the payments into your monthly budget.**

DESIGN AND OPERATING FEATURES

Among the four criteria for evaluating appliances, design and operating features compose probably the most subjective category. That is true because manufacturers design appliances with many different minor or convenience features supplementing the basic service of the appliance. For example, refrigerators are available with such extra features as ice-water dispensers and crushed-ice dispensers. How important these features are is entirely up to you, given your needs and preferences. Rather than review specific appliances, we will suggest ways for you to evaluate whether you will need or use these extra features and whether they are worth the extra cost.

Information Sources   The results of comparative appliance tests reported in *Consumer Reports* and *Consumers' Research Magazine* provide a wealth of information on each model's essential and supplemental features. In addition *Consumer Reports* highlights the major advantages and disadvantages for each model. Test data cover how well each model performs the basic task it was designed to do as well as the model's various supplemental and convenience features. Both publications retest each major appliance every 2 or 3 years. Therefore, their information is reasonably up to date. Since nearly every library subscribes to one or both magazines, the information is readily accessible.

Evaluation   The reports in *Consumer Reports* and *Consumers' Research Magazine* generally group the models according to the extent of their supplemental features, and they recommend how useful these features are. Their lists of recommendations, advantages, and disadvantages are an excellent place to begin your evaluation. Frequently, they note things most people would overlook. But there is no need slavishly to follow their recommendations. Do not include their negative comments and lists of disadvantages in your evaluation of a model until you first ask yourself: Is that disadvantage important to me? Does that negative comment apply to my situation? Should you answer yes, the model should be downrated accordingly. Likewise, ask yourself whether the advantages reported in the publications will benefit you. We are not suggesting you summarily reject the findings; instead, we recommend that you decide whether these comments apply to your situation.

SHOPPING FOR APPLIANCES

This section discusses four considerations to keep in mind when shopping for appliances: (1) relative importance of price, service, operating cost, and design features; (2) selection of what you need; (3) judgment on whether you are buying at a sale price; and (4) timing of appliance purchases. Careful attention to each consideration should ensure maximum satisfaction at minimum cost.

Shopping Guidelines

Exhibit 11–8 shows the relative importance we attach to the four criteria in Exhibit 11–1. Because they are value judgments, the rankings are intended as general shopping guides rather than rigid rules. Our goal is to minimize total ownership cost, yet deliver adequate appliance performance. People who do not care about cost might rank the criteria differently. You may decide that some weights should be altered according to your own preferences.

> **Strategy: In shopping for appliances, the guidelines shown in Exhibit 11–8 should be satisfactory for most people.**

Selecting What You Need   The goal in selecting an appliance should be to find the one that just meets your needs. Too many people buy appliances that provide more features than they require. Maintain an attitude of "keep it simple" when shopping for an appliance. The first step should be to make certain the appliance you are considering will fit into your budget. Next, remember that options and extra features not only boost an appliance's price, but also increase its complexity. And complexity likely means more frequent breakdowns and higher repair costs when the appliance needs service. We are not suggesting that everyone buy the bare-bones model. Instead, we think the model should meet your needs and no more. When in doubt, ask yourself: Do I really need that added feature? Will I use it?

"Trading You Up"   In general, we think most people will be best served by the model midway between the manufacturer's most deluxe and simplest

Exhibit 11-8 Guidelines for Shopping for Major Appliances

Appliance	Criteria			
	Service	Operating costs	Minimizing purchase price	Design features, advantages, and disadvantages
Television	E	L	M	V
Range	L	L	V	V
Refrigerator	M	E	M	M
Clothes washer	V	L	M	M
Dryer	L	M	V	M
Dishwasher	V	V	M	M
Freezer	M	E	M	L
Air conditioner	V	E	M	M

Degree of Importance: E = extremely vital; V = very important; M = moderate; L = limited.

models. Unfortunately, the dealer and the salesperson both have an incentive to trade customers up to a higher-priced model: larger profits for the dealer, added commission for the salesperson. An executive of a large retail chain recently pointed out that much of its increase in sales came from trading up customers. Did the consumers benefit? We seriously doubt they did. A frequently used appliance sales tactic is "bait and switch," which we discussed in Chapter 9. Be wary of it.

Strategy: Before deciding on that deluxe model the dealer is pushing, ask yourself if you need it.

Judging Claims Regarding Price   *"Closeouts," "Manufacturer's Clearance"*—everyone has read advertisements announcing the "sale" of appliances using these or similar words. But when is a sale really a sale? We think it is much less often than the advertisements would have you believe. The best way to judge the legitimacy of a claimed sale is to know what a particular appliance should cost before shopping at the sale. Then you know how much prices have been reduced, if at all.

Floor Models   Generally, floor samples are true sale items that offer considerable savings. Examine the appliance carefully, however, to make certain that if there is any damage, it is of a minor cosmetic nature.

Last Year's Model   The saving on a prior year's model can often be substantial. Since the annual model change usually involves mostly cosmetic changes rather than many true design and performance improvements, you sacrifice little by buying last year's model. But let price be your guide. Dealers will often try to sell an old model without reducing its price.

Special Models   Some large dealers hold a sale on a "special" model. Typically the model differs only cosmetically—different trim, colors, control positions, etc.—from the manufacturer's regular line. Here are two statements of caution. One, try to find out which regular model the "special" is drawn from by comparing its features with the regular models; you will then have a means of analyzing what you are getting. Second, carefully check the price; just because the model is a "special" does not ensure a bargain price.

Strategy: Be skeptical when approaching a widely touted and highly advertised appliance sale.

Timing of Purchases   Most appliances have a seasonal sales pattern. That is, they sell better at certain times of the year than at others. By concentrating your purchases at the low points in those sales patterns, you can generally obtain the best prices. Typically, January and February are good months to shop for most appliances with the possible exception of a television set and an air conditioner. Summer is generally the best time for a television; late summer and fall are best for an air conditioner. Frequently, you can obtain a good price by buying a particular appliance just as its peak selling season is drawing to a close. Usually, the worst time to shop for an appliance is immediately before Christmas or Mother's Day.

Strategy: Buy your appliance in the off-season to obtain the lowest price.

WARRANTIES AND GUARANTEES

When a consumer buys an appliance with a full-coverage warranty or guarantee, the buyer should be able to depend on the guarantee to correct all problems, mistakes, defects, and design shortcomings that are directly attributable to the manufacturer. Unfortunately, the warranty or guarantee often falls woefully short of this mark. In large part, manufacturers are to blame. Many of them consider a warranty or guarantee as just one more sales tool; use it to clinch the sale, but then ignore it. On the surface, their warranty or guarantee seems to exude protection, yet there are so many restrictions, exclusions, and exceptions buried in the wording that coverage is nearly nonexistent.

Improving the Warranty Quagmire

The recently passed Magnuson-Moss Warranty–Federal Trade Commission Improvement Act gives the Federal Trade Commission (FTC) power to force meaningful changes within the warranty area. Most provisions in the act became law in June 1975, so that warranties after that date should be substantially improved. Its major provisions are detailed below.

Disclosure   Warranties must be stated in clear, concise terms that contain all relevant information. Warranties cannot contain excessive hedging and they must be free of misleading or fraudulent statements. They must disclose: (1) exactly what is covered; (2) who is covered; (3) the name and address of the warrantor; (4) a statement of the procedure for filing a claim; (5) a description

"THE NEW WASHING MACHINE IS MAKING THOSE FUNNY NOISES AGAIN!"

of the available procedures should the consumer have a complaint; and (6) the coverage period.

Coverage   Where an appliance warranty claims to be "full" coverage, it cannot limit the duration of the product's implied warranty. An implied warranty says that a buyer has a right to expect that the product will perform the specific task or purpose for which it was sold. Further, upon receiving notice from the buyer, the warrantor must fix the defective product within a reasonable time and at no cost to the consumer. Warranties which fail to meet these criteria must be clearly described as "limited." A manufacturer can, however, cover part of an appliance with a "full" warranty while providing "limited" coverage on the balance of the components; but that limitation must be specified in detail in the warranty.

Adjustment Procedure   Under a full warranty, the FTC can set limits on what constitutes an adequate opportunity for correction. Thus, should the warrantor be unable or unwilling to repair a product after a number of attempts, the buyer can request a free replacement or a cash refund. In the case of a refund, the warrantor can deduct a reasonable allowance to cover the wear on the unit. If the warranty has an informal settlement procedure, the details of what the consumer must do under the procedure have to be clearly set forth. For example, the informal procedure could require that the store which sold the appliance be given several opportunities to correct the problem. Or it may specify that the unit must be returned to the factory for corrective service work. Regardless of the exact form of the procedure, the consumer must first seek redress through this procedure. Where there is no procedure, or barring satisfaction there, the buyer can sue. If the buyer wins, the manufacturer must pay attorney's fees. When a group of consumers feel they have been defrauded through a manufacturer's warranty, they can bring a class-action suit. In short, the 1975 legislation opens up avenues of redress that were unavailable before.

Consumer's Responsibility   The buyer is responsible for maintaining the product and not abusing it. Also, the buyer must give the warrantor an opportunity to correct the problem. The buyer must read the warranty or guarantee; otherwise, the consequences are his or her responsibility.

What the Legislation Does Not Do   The act does not promise that the FTC will press the buyer's complaint against the manufacturer. That is still the buyer's responsibility. Nor does the FTC promise to prosecute manufacturers who fail to meet their warranty responsibility. That step still must be taken through the court system by the buyer.

Protect Yourself

The provisions of the Magnuson-Moss Act should do much to correct many of the glaring abuses that have prevailed in the warranty area. But the final

Exhibit 11-9 Warranty Checklist

	Yes	No
What Is Covered		
Does the warranty give "full" coverage?	( )	( )
Is there a single warranty?	( )	( )
If there are several, is the component coverage ("full" or "limited") specified?	( )	( )
Is that coverage reasonable?	( )	( )
If the warranty is "limited," do the exclusions and limitations seem reasonable?	( )	( )
Are both parts and labor covered?	( )	( )
Is the total repair charge covered?	( )	( )
Who Is Covered		
Does the warranty cover subsequent owners?	( )	( )
Does coverage remain in force when the unit is moved?	( )	( )
Is there a special registration requirement (e.g., card to be mailed in)?	( )	( )
Duration of Coverage		
Length of "full" coverage	_____	
Length of "limited" coverage	_____	
Is coverage equal to that of competing brands?	( )	( )
How Adjustments Are Made		
Is the adjustment procedure clear?	( )	( )
If the unit must be returned to the manufacturer, does the manufacturer pay the shipping?	( )	( )
Are there local service facilities?	( )	( )
Is the adjustment procedure reasonable and feasible?	( )	( )
The Adjustment Procedure		
Is there an informal settlement procedure?	( )	( )
Is the procedure explained?	( )	( )
Does it appear fair?	( )	( )
Is it feasible?	( )	( )
If there are other legal remedies, are they explained?	( )	( )

responsibility still rests with you. All the improvements in disclosure will be meaningless unless you read the warranty. Even with the improvements, it is imperative that a warranty be considered carefully. Exhibit 11–9 provides a checklist to help evaluate a warranty. A large number of "no" responses suggests a warranty that is restrictive and offers limited coverage.

> **Strategy: Compare warranty coverage of various brands to judge the relative merits of each. Downgrade any brand with heavily restrictive or limited coverage.**

Action on Warranty Claims

When you have a warranty claim, the first step is to discuss your problem with the contact person noted in the warranty; typically, the dealer or the nearest authorized service outlet. When presenting your claim, describe what the problem is, what has been done, and what you expect the contact person to do. Even if he or she is unsuccessful the first time, you should return the unit until this source has been thoroughly exhausted.

Manufacturer's Hot Line Many appliance manufacturers have established a special telephone number customers can call to register their complaints. If you have been unable or unsuccessful in obtaining corrective action at the local level, a call to this number may prod some further action. Since the cost is minimal, it is certainly worth the effort.

Major Appliance Consumer Action Panel (MACAP) This is one of the consumer action panels, discussed in Chapter 9, that essentially act as an intermediary between consumers and manufacturers to help resolve consumer warranty problems. If you are unsatisfied with the manufacturer's corrective action, you should contact MACAP; their address is given in the appendix to Chapter 9. When writing MACAP, include: (1) a statement of the problems, (2) details of what the manufacturer has done, (3) why that action has been inadequate, and (4) exactly what you want done.

SUMMARY

1 The four principal criteria for the appliance decision are: (*a*) service, (*b*) operating cost, (*c*) purchase price, and (*d*) design features.
2 Service should be the most important decision criterion on technically complex appliances.
3 Most service work on appliances is performed by (*a*) factory outlets, (*b*) independent service firms, and (*c*) dealer's service departments.
4 The local better business bureau can often aid in resolving disputes with a service firm.
5 Service contracts relieve the customer of service worries, but the cost is high.
6 Operating cost is critical on appliances that are used continuously or frequently, or that require large amounts of energy.
7 A high-efficiency appliance is the best buy if its added purchase price can be recovered through annual operating savings in 5 to 7 years.
8 Operating cost will become increasingly important as energy costs continue to rise.
9 The average price cited in *Consumer Reports* can be an excellent starting point when estimating a reasonable price on a particular appliance.
10 Deferred payments same as cash is the best payment option.
11 The terms of the dealer's sales loan offer should be compared with other credit alternatives.
12 The results of comparative appliance tests reported in *Consumers' Research Magazine* and *Consumer Reports* are excellent sources for a particular model's design features.
13 Individual preferences and needs are a key input when evaluating the design features on a particular appliance.
14 Select the appliance model that just meets your needs and no more.
15 Many dealers and salespeople try to trade customers up to a more expensive model.

16 Avoid the old "bait and switch" technique by refusing to be switched.
17 A good warranty or guarantee should correct the problems, mistakes, and design shortcomings that are directly attributable to the manufacturer.
18 Read and carefully analyze all sections of the warranty before purchasing any appliance.

REVIEW YOUR UNDERSTANDING OF

Appliance decision criteria
   Service
   Operating cost
   Purchase price
   Design features
Service organizations
   Factory outlet
   Independent service firm
   Dealer's service department
Service contract
Operating cost
   Sources of estimates
   Relative importance
High-efficiency appliances

Appliance prices
   Average price
   Haggling
   Trade-in allowance
Deferred payment same as cash
Trading up
Appliance sales
"Bait and switch"
Magnuson-Moss Warranty–Federal Trade Commission Improvement Act
"Full" coverage warranty
"Limited" coverage warranty
Major Appliance Consumer Action Panel

DISCUSSION QUESTIONS

1 What avenues of redress do consumers have when they have a warranty problem? In what order should they be used?
2 Do you agree with the comment that a service contract will end your service worries for only a few pennies per day? Why?
3 How would you decide what weight to assign to the service, operating cost, purchase price, and design features criteria when considering a particular appliance? Which criterion would be most important on a freezer? Why? Which would be most important for a kitchen range? Why?
4 What steps would you take to find a reputable service firm when you move to a new city?
5 What is "bait and switch?" Why do you think it is a problem in the appliance area? How can a consumer defend against this practice?
6 Why is it difficult to compare prices of appliances? What steps can be used to estimate a reasonable price?
7 Would you recommend that everyone rigidly follow the recommendations in *Consumer Reports* and *Consumers' Research Magazine*? Why or why not?
8 Fast Phil's Appliance Sales has recently announced the start of its "supercolossal clearance sale." How would you decide if it is legitimate?
9 What improvements has the Magnuson-Moss warranty bill brought to the warranty area? Does the Federal Trade Commission's role relieve the consumer of all responsibility? Why?
10 Susan McKenzie is going to replace the refrigerator in her condominium with one of three models:

Model	Purchase price	Estimated monthly operating cost
Standard, freezer on top	$400	$6.50
Standard, freezer on side	$390	$7.90
Superefficient, freezer on top	$445	$5.40

Which should she select? Why?

11 Service is an important consideration in buying what types of appliance? What steps would you use to assign a service ranking to the various competing brands? What service factors should be considered?

12 The dealer has quoted Ralph and Grazelda Swift two payment options on their new appliances costing $700: (*a*) 90-day deferred payment same as cash, and (*b*) a 24-month sales loan with an APR of 24 percent. Which would you recommend? Why? Which option would the dealer likely stress? Why?

13 What are the major types of service organizations? How do they differ? Which one usually gives the highest-quality service?

14 Herman Andrews is considering two color television sets:

Model	Purchase price	Annual operating cost
A, tube type	$470	$26
B, solid state	$500	$17

If energy costs rise 10 percent annually, what will the operating cost differential be in 5 years? 10 years? Which model should Herman buy?

CASE PROBLEM

Fred and Jan Smith need major appliances for their recently purchased home. A local dealer has quoted them $1,800 for a total package, which includes refrigerator, range, clothes washer, and dryer. The dealer has assured them the appliances are super deluxe models with numerous options and extras. The dealer maintains that all appliances are basically similar, so the only thing to consider is price (of course he quickly notes his price is the lowest available). Since the Smiths are short of cash, the dealer has offered an easy 2-year sales loan (APR 30 percent). The $100.64 monthly payment comes out to a low, low $3.31 per day. "Not much for all that service," the dealer notes. Because they are "good" customers, the dealer has offered a service contract covering all four units for only 20 cents per day. The Smiths combined annual income is $17,000.

a Do you agree with the dealer's point that price is the only consideration? Why?

b How would you recommend the Smiths shop for each of the appliances?

c What guidelines would you recommend they use to decide which model best meets their needs?

d How much will those "easy" terms cost the Smiths? How much is the finance charge?

e What credit alternatives would you recommend? Why?

f What is the annual cost of that service contract? Is it likely to remain at that level throughout the lifetime of the appliances? Assuming the service contract fee remains constant, approximately how much will those fees total over the next 15 years (a reasonable estimate of the appliances' life)?

RECOMMENDED READINGS

Magazines

Changing Times:

"Before You Sign That Appliance Service Contract." October, 1972, pp. 31–33.
  Discusses the preliminaries to signing a contract in reasonable detail.

Books

Garman, E. Thomas, and Sidney W. Eckert, *The Consumer's World: Buying, Money Management, and Issues: Resource.* New York: McGraw-Hill, 1974.
  Chapter 10 discusses the purchase of both furniture and appliances.
Klamkin, Charles, *How to Buy Major Appliances.* Chicago: Regnery, 1973.
  The first four chapters discuss the problems of purchasing appliances, practices in the appliance trade, minimizing purchase price, and problems with warranty claims and service work. The latter chapters outline a shopping strategy for each major appliance.

Booklets

Sears, Roebuck and Company, *How To Select Major Home Appliances.* Chicago: 1970.
  Contains a good checklist for each major appliance that can be used when selecting appliances. A copy can be obtained for a nominal fee from Consumer Information Services, Dept. 703— Public Relations, Sears, Roebuck and Co., Chicago 60611
Household Finance Company, Money Management Institute, *Your Equipment Dollar.* Chicago: 1973.
  A useful guide to selecting home appliances. Copies can be obtained for a nominal fee from: Household Finance Company, Money Management Institute, Prudential Plaza, Chicago 60601.

APPENDIX: Energy Requirements of Major House Appliances

The accompanying chart illustrates two important factors for determining the operating cost of major appliances: estimated kilowatt hours (kwh) consumed annually, and estimated annual cost, assuming 4 cents per kwh.

  The chart can readily be adjusted for the energy costs in your area. The first step is

Exhibit A11-1   Energy Consumption of Major Appliances

Appliance	Annual kwh consumed	Cost (at 4 cents per kwh)
Air conditioner, room (assumes 1,000 hours operation)	860	$34.40
Clothes dryer	993	39.72
Dehumidifier	377	15.08
Fan		
Attic	291	11.64
Circulating	43	1.72
Window	170	6.80
Freezer, 15 to 21 cubic feet		
Chest, manual defrost	1,320	52.80
Upright, manual defrost	1,320	52.80
Upright, automatic defrost	1,985	79.40
Heater, portable	176	7.04
Humidifier	163	6.52
Oven, microwave	190	7.60
Radio	86	3.44
Refrigerator/freezer, automatic defrost		
16 to 18 cubic feet	1,795	71.80
20 cubic feet and up	1,895	75.80
Television, black and white		
Tube type	220	8.80
Solid state	100	4.00
Television, color		
Tube type	528	21.12
Solid state	320	12.80
Vacuum cleaner	46	1.84
Washing machine, automatic	103	4.12

Source: Edison Electric Institute, *Annual Energy Requirements of Electric Household Appliances*, New York.

to estimate the cost per kwh, using your most recent utility billing. Most billings give the kwh consumed during the period, as well as the total cost. To compute the cost:

    Cost per kwh = Total cost ÷ kwh consumed

By multiplying this cost times the estimated annual kwh consumption, you will have the estimated operating cost for your area.

Chapter 12

The Housing Decision

After completing this chapter you should be able to:

judge whether renting or purchasing is superior for your situation.

estimate the cost of ownership.

recall income limitations on the size house you can afford.

compare FHA, VA, and conventional mortgages.

use a mortgage table to calculate monthly payments.

identify the primary sources of mortgage money.

recall the major mortgage provisions.

compare and **contrast** the advantages and disadvantages of new and old homes.

determine whether or not to use the services of a broker.

analyze the differences between mobile homes and conventional housing.

Among your most important personal decisions are career, marriage, and family. In the next rank of personal decisions and your most important one is the housing decision. It is the most important for several reasons: Most families spend about 25 percent of their gross income on housing, which is usually their largest expense. Also, the housing decision has a significant impact on your daily life because it determines the amount of time you will spend commuting to work or running errands, and it has a large part in determining your social contacts.

The housing possibilities include an apartment, a house, a mobile home, or a condominium. Each of these alternatives has advantages. At certain times in life, renting an apartment makes more sense than buying a house or condominium, especially when a person is just beginning a career. The biggest problem then is finding the best apartment for the cost. If a couple starts raising a family, ownership may be preferable to renting. At any time of life, however, the housing decision should be made with great care. The important factors to consider include determining the amount that can be spent for housing and an analysis of the relative costs of owning versus renting in each situation. If your decision is made to purchase a house, then you must carefully consider things such as location and quality, and you must be able to understand home financing in order to analyze the costs of various available home mortgage loans.

THE BASIC DECISION: RENT OR BUY

An understanding of the influential factors in renting or buying a home can help you decide which is the better choice for you. This section will cover the most important factors to be considered and develop some basic standards which can be used by families in deciding whether to rent or buy.

The Advantages of Ownership

Owning a home has some distinct advantages over renting, and the benefits are probably the reason approximately two-thirds of the homes in this country are owner-occupied. These advantages are both economic and psychological.

Tax Advantages   Homeowners can deduct real estate taxes and mortgage interest payments from their federal income tax return. The owner of a $35,000 home with a 9 percent, $28,000, 25-year mortgage and real estate taxes of $900 per year will have a tax deduction of approximately $3,420. That is, taxes plus interest, or $900 + 9 percent × $28,000, equals $3,420. Assuming a 30 percent marginal tax bracket, the tax saving will be $1,026 (30 percent × $3,420). To be sure, the amount of interest will decline a small amount each year. However, the deduction for interest expense will be quite large for many years. This is a distinct economic advantage of ownership which results directly from the tax laws. A similar deduction is not available to renters. A renter who pays $285 per month pays the same $3,420 each year but cannot deduct it on his or her tax return.

Inflation Hedge   Homeownership acts as an inflation hedge in two ways. First, when you buy a house, you pay for a large part of the cost with a mortgage loan of 20 to 30 years and your monthly mortgage payments remain fixed for that period even though utilities and taxes may rise in cost. Renters have no guarantee that their rent will not be periodically increased as prices rise.

The second way that homeownership acts as a hedge against inflation is the potential appreciation in the value of the property. How much the value of the property increases is subject to factors such as location, maintenance of the property, and increases in the price level of housing. Well-maintained properties have appreciated between 5 and 10 percent per year over the past decade. Everybody has stories of a relative or friend who bought a house for $25,000 and sold it 3 years later for $30,000 or $35,000. Cases such as this have become more the rule than the exception over the past few years.

Psychological Factors   Perhaps the major advantage of homeownership involves psychological rewards that cannot be measured in dollars. The psychological values of homeownership may include: the enjoyment of privacy, pride of ownership, a better place to raise children, more living space, or the need for status associated with owning. Your own psychological values may not be the same as these, but they are just as important to you.

Disadvantages of Ownership

Buying a house carries with it responsibilities for upkeep and maintenance that renters do not have to contend with. Economically, ownership can be very unsatisfactory if the home is of poor quality or is in a bad location.

Repairs and Maintenance   Many real estate advisors use 1 percent of the value of the property as a guide to the amount that will be required each year for upkeep. This figure will vary depending on the age and geographic location of your property, but it represents a good approximation of the yearly repair and maintenance costs facing the average homeowner.

Flexibility   A major drawback of ownership is the permanence of the commitment. The cost of disposing of property and the time required to do so usually makes moving difficult. This is particularly true if the home has been owned for only a short period of time. As a general rule, anyone planning to move in less than 3 years is probably financially better off renting than owning. If you expect to remain in one location for at least 3 years, you will probably come out ahead if you buy a house.

Advantages of Renting

In many instances renting has distinct advantages which far outweigh the economic and psychological advantages of ownership.

Life-style   The modern garden apartment and townhouse developments with swimming pools, tennis courts, and party rooms provide advantages which the average homeowner is unable to provide independently. Many people find these renter extras extremely desirable. This is particularly true for newly marrieds without children and many retired people.

Maintenance   Maintenance is a constant problem for homeowners. For renters these problems are taken care of by the landlord. From a cost standpoint, there is probably no difference between renting and owning since landlords certainly incorporate the cost of maintenance in their rentals. The major advantage is simply that you need not worry about maintenance and repairs. Somebody else has that responsibility.

Flexibility   When you move, it is a lot easier to terminate a lease, or even pay for the months remaining on the lease, than it is to sell a house. There are no realtor's fees to pay, and in most cases, a move from an apartment can be accomplished with less difficulty than the move from a house.

Disadvantages of Renting

The major disadvantages of renting are economic. Renting provides no tax advantages and no hedge against inflation. These two disadvantages ultimately push most people toward ownership. Also, for the same monthly costs, you usually get less living space from renting than from ownership.

Example, Rent versus Buy Exhibit 12–1 summarizes the economic differences of the rent-buy decision. The house selected for comparison is a typical $35,000 home, which is in the range of many people.

Most of the calculations in the exhibit are reasonably self-explanatory. The tax savings of ownership arise because of mortgage interest and real estate taxes which are deductible from federal income taxes.

Each monthly mortgage payment actually comprises two payments: the interest on the mortgage, and a payment to reduce the amount of the loan outstanding. The part of the payment that reduces the loan is called equity. During the early years of a mortgage loan, the interest portion is much larger than the equity payments; during the later years, the equity portion is much larger than the interest. During the early years, you can save more on your federal taxes because the interest paid is high. During later years, the interest paid is low and you do not save so much on federal taxes but your equity increases.

A homeowner, paying the same monthly costs as a renter, actually pays a lower net cost. The lower cost represents a substantial amount over a period of 20 or 30 years. But you must understand that much of the potential advantage

Exhibit 12-1 Monthly Cost Comparison of Buying versus Renting

	Rent	Buy[a]
*Payments**		
Rent payment	$335	—
Mortgage	—	$235[b]
Taxes	—	75
Utilities	35	40
Insurance	5	15
Maintenance	—	30
Monthly outflow	$375	$395
Adjustments		
Less:		
Tax savings	—	$ 86[c]
Appreciation	—	146[d]
Equity increase	—	25[e]
Plus:		
Interest on down payment	—	29[f]
Net cost	$375	$167

*All numbers have been rounded for computational ease.

[a]$35,000 home.

[b]$28,000 mortgage at 9 percent for 25 years.

[c]Interest $210 + taxes $75, with tax savings at the 30 percent marginal rate. ($295 × 30 percent = $85.50)

[d]Home appreciates at 5 percent per year.

[e]During the first year, $308 of the mortgage will be paid off.

[f]After tax interest on $7,000 at 7 percent per year. If this money were not used for a down payment, it could be invested [($7,000 × 7 percent) × 1 − 30 percent].

of owning is not realized until after the house is sold. Until then, the monthly cash outflows for owning and renting will be about the same.

Furthermore, you should view the exhibit with caution: If the home does not appreciate in value and the maintenance costs are higher than expected, the net cost of owning will be higher than shown in the exhibit.

> **Strategy: Purchasing a home is a wise decision if you plan to be in a location for more than 3 years and are willing to undertake the obligations associated with owning.**

Checklist for Renting

If, after careful analysis, you have decided to rent, you must select an apartment. The more you know about the apartment before you rent it, the less likely you are to have unpleasant surprises after you move in. Exhibit 12–2 is a

Exhibit 12-2 Checklist for Apartments

Building and grounds
- [ ] attractive, well-constructed building
- [ ] good maintenance and up-keep
- [ ] clean, well-lighted and uncluttered halls, entrances, stairs
- [ ] reliable building management and supervision
- [ ] attractive landscaping with adequate outdoor space for tenants
- [ ] locking entrances, protected from outsiders
- [ ] clean, attractive lobby

Services and facilities
- [ ] laundry equipment
- [ ] parking space (indoor or outdoor)
- [ ] receiving room for packages
- [ ] convenient trash collection and disposal
- [ ] adequate fire escapes
- [ ] storage lockers
- [ ] locked mail boxes
- [ ] elevators
- [ ] engineer on call for emergency repairs
- [ ] extras—window washing, decorating, maid service, shops, doorman

Living space in the apartment
- [ ] adequate room sizes and storage space
- [ ] convenient floor plan
- [ ] suitable wall space for furniture
- [ ] soundproof. Listen for talking, footsteps, plumbing, and equipment noise from other apartments or hallways
- [ ] attractive decorating and fixtures
- [ ] pleasant views
- [ ] windows located to provide enough air, light and ventilation
- [ ] agreeable size, type and placement of windows
- [ ] windows with blinds, shades, screens and storm windows
- [ ] easy cleaning and maintenance
- [ ] attractive, easy-to-clean floors
- [ ] furnished appliances in good condition
- [ ] clean, effective heating, thermostatically controlled
- [ ] up-to-date wiring
- [ ] conveniently placed electric outlets
- [ ] well-fitted doors, casings, cabinets and built-ins
- [ ] extras—air conditioning, carpeting, dishwasher, disposer, fireplace, patio

Source: This information taken from the Money Management Institute booklet *Your Housing Dollar*, printed by the Money Management Institute of Household Finance Corporation, Chicago.

checklist which you can use for evaluating an apartment. By analyzing each apartment with the checklist, you will be more likely to ask the important questions.

How Much Can You Afford?

There is nothing worse than being overextended when buying a home because it is a long-term commitment. Two basic rules traditionally have been used in determining the maximum that should be spent for a house.

Rule 1 The house should cost no more than 2½ times gross income.

This simple yardstick is widely used, even though it is a dangerous one. It fails to allow for the taxes, maintenance, interest rate, down payment, and utility costs in each situation. For example, Irving and Rocky, each with an income of $16,000, are considering $40,000 homes. Irving may be able to afford the house because he has a much larger down payment than Rocky, his taxes are lower, and the utility costs are less because the house is in a geographically temperate location. Exhibit 12–3 shows how the monthly payment can differ substantially because of these factors.

Rule 2 Spend no more than 25 percent of gross income on housing.

The factors to be included in this amount are: (1) mortgage, (2) taxes, (3) utilities, (4) insurance, and (5) maintenance. There is some debate about whether the 25 percent should apply to gross income or to take-home pay. In most situations it is appropriate to apply this percentage factor to gross income. Figures for the United States economy as a whole indicate that 25 percent of gross income is about what people spend for housing.

Returning to the example, Irving, with a gross income of $16,000, can

Exhibit 12-3 Comparison of Housing Costs under Different Conditions

	Rocky	Irving
1 Location	Milwaukee, Wisconsin	Houston, Texas
2 Price	$40,000	$40,000
3 Down payment	2,000	12,000
	(5 percent)	(30 percent)
4 Mortgage	38,000	28,000
5 Monthly payment	345.31	225.30
	(10 percent,	(9 percent,
	25 years)	30 years)
6 Taxes (monthly)	82	22
7 Utilities	60	45
8 Insurance	10	10
9 Maintenance	33	33
Total costs (lines 5 + 6 + 7 + 8 + 9)	$ 530.31	$ 335.30
10 Required income	$25,454.00	$16,094.00

afford to spend $333.33 per month for housing [($16,000 × .25) = $4,000 per year and $4,000 ÷ 12 = $333.33 monthly]. Since his costs for this house represent only $335.30 per month, he can probably afford the $40,000 price. Rocky would have difficulty buying a $40,000 home. In fact, to keep his payments at $333.33 a month, he must spend no more than $25,800 for a home. In view of this, it is very clear that housing costs must be related to income and monthly payments, not to the value of the property as Rule 1 assumes.

The same rule—25 percent of gross income—should be applied to the rental decision. Renters cannot afford more than owners. For some reason, renters sometimes overextend themselves with an apartment lease, thinking that they can pay more for housing than owners. They soon find that paying 40 to 50 percent of income for rent can be disastrous.

FINANCING YOUR HOME

Most people have to borrow a large portion of the purchase price of a home and pay it off over an extended period of time. Without mortgages, it would be virtually impossible for most people to buy a house. Because of the long-term nature of the commitment, the careful analysis and selection of a mortgage are very important. Mortgages are currently classified in four categories:

1 Conventional mortgages
2 FHA (Federal Housing Authority) insured mortgages
3 VA (Veterans Administration) guaranteed mortgages
4 Privately insured mortgages

The type that is best for each family depends primarily on the amount of down payment they can make.

Conventional Mortgages

Generally, conventional mortgages are those home loans made by a savings institution without a guarantee of repayment by a federal agency or private insurer. The contract is between the lender and the homeowner. The lender's protection for this loan is the value of the property and the equity or down payment the purchaser has been required to make in order to get the loan.

Terms   Conventional mortgages call for a down payment of 20 to 30 percent of the value of the property: the balance is provided by the lender. The loan has a maturity of 20 to 30 years. Usually, the larger the down payment, the more favorable the terms of the loan. For example, the interest rate for a down payment of 30 percent is usually 1/2 of 1 percent lower than the interest rate for a down payment of 20 percent.

Large versus Small Down Payment   In terms of whether or not you save on interest costs, it is not advisable to increase the down payment to achieve a lower interest rate. For example, assume you are thinking of buying a $40,000 home, making a down payment of $8,000 and taking a $32,000 mortgage loan. If you increased your down payment by $4,000, you could reduce your interest rate by $1/2$ of 1 percent, but the savings on the $28,000 mortgage would amount to only $140 the first year. The $4,000 could have been invested at 7 percent, yielding a return of $280 annually. The only thing you really gain by making a larger down payment is lower monthly mortgage payments, not a true saving of interest cost. Payments on a $32,000, 25-year mortgage at 9 percent are $268.55 monthly. For a $28,000 loan at 8.5 percent for 25 years, the payments are only $225.47. On an annual basis, you reduce your mortgage payments by $516.96 [($268.55 − $225.47) × 12] with the larger down payment.

The size of the down payment required by conventional mortgages is the major factor which forces many people to seek alternative financing. To purchase a $30,000 house with a required 30 percent down payment, the buyer must have $9,000. For many young people, it is very difficult to raise such a large amount. Fortunately there are alternatives.

FHA-insured and VA-guaranteed Mortgages

The Federal Housing Authority and the Veterans Administration have the authority to insure or guarantee mortgage loans made by savings institutions. In the event a borrower cannot make the payments and the property is repossessed, the federal government makes sure the lender does not lose any money as a result of the loan. The federal guarantees permit a savings institution to loan a larger percentage of the property's value than required under the terms of a conventional mortgage. Thus, the down payment is lower. Section 203(b) of the National Housing Act sets limitations on the amount of a loan the FHA or VA will insure. They are:

Single-family homes	$45,000
Two-family homes	47,000
Three-family homes	49,000
Four-family homes	52,000

Within these limits the FHA and VA set loan-to-value ratios which specify how much the agencies will guarantee or insure as a percentage of the property's value. For plans approved by the FHA or VA prior to construction or for a dwelling which was completed more than one year before the date of application for a loan, the loan-to-value ratios are:

	Veteran	*Nonveteran*
First $25,000	100 percent	97 percent
Next $10,000	90 percent	90 percent
Over $35,000	85 percent	80 percent

Using these figures, if Harry Schultz purchased a home for $25,000 and he was not a veteran, he could secure an FHA mortgage for $24,250 (25,000 × 97 percent). Thus, rather than the $5,000 to $7,500 down payment required under a conventional mortgage, he would need only a $750 down payment—a much more affordable sum for most people. If the plan had not received FHA or VA approval prior to construction and if construction was completed less than 1 year before the application date, the buyer, either veteran or nonveteran, could borrow 90 percent of the first $25,000. On amounts over $25,000, the ratios are the same as those shown above. In all cases, the mortgage term is 30 years.

The government limits the interest rates that lenders can charge on FHA and VA loans. Often the rate on conventional loans will exceed this maximum, making lenders unwilling to commit funds to FHA and VA loans. One way the lenders circumvent the interest ceiling is by charging points on the loan.

Points

A point represents an immediate repayment of 1 percent of the loan. By charging points, lenders can raise their effective return. This is possible because, even though the amount of the points has been paid immediately upon the loan, the full face amount of the loan must be repaid. On a $20,000 loan with 5 points, the effect for the borrower is the same as receiving $19,000 but having to repay $20,000. As if the situation were not confused enough already, the government has compounded the matter by ruling that points cannot be paid by the buyer. Consequently, the lender assesses the seller, who pays the points. The seller obviously raises the price of the house by an amount sufficient to cover the assessment. Therefore the buyer pays the points after all.

Privately Insured Mortgages

One of the weaknesses of the FHA and VA programs has been the red tape involved in processing the loan application. As a result, private insurance companies have entered the picture, insuring part of the loan and with less red tape. As with government-guaranteed loans, a much lower down payment is required.

These loans call for either a 5 or 10 percent down payment. The insurance company insures the first 20 percent of the loan. If the bank has to foreclose, it is, in effect, in exactly the same position as if it had a conventional mortgage. On a $40,000 home, the bank could thus sell the house for as low as $32,000 and still recover the amount of the loan.

The guaranteed loan offers advantages to the lender and the borrower: To the lender, assurance that he or she will not suffer a loss in the event of a default; to the borrower, the opportunity of buying a home with a much smaller down payment. The buyer pays the cost of the insurance premium: for 95 percent loans the premium is 1 percent of the loan plus $20 for the first year and $1/4$ of 1 percent each year thereafter; for 90 percent loans the premium is $1/2$ of 1 percent plus $20 for the first year and $1/4$ of 1 percent thereafter.

The cost of an insured mortgage is compared with the cost of postponing the purchase of a home in Exhibit 12–4.

Exhibit 12-4   The Cost of Using Guaranteed Mortgages versus Waiting 5 Years to Purchase a House

	Buy today		Wait five years
	95 percent loan	90 percent loan	Conventional loan
1 Price	$35,000.00	$35,000.00	$ 45,000.00*
2 Mortgage	$33,250.00	$31,500.00	$ 38,000.00†
3 Down payment (line 1 minus 2)	$ 1,750.00	$ 3,500.00	$ 7,000.00
4 Loan interest rate	9 percent plus insurance	9 percent plus insurance	9 percent
5 Duration	25 years	25 years	25 years
6 Monthly payment at 9 percent	$ 279.04	$ 264.35	$ 318.90
7 Total payments for mortgage	$83,712.00	$79,305.00	$ 96,670.00
8 First year's premium	$ 352.50 (1 percent) (plus $20)	$ 177.50 (½ of 1 percent) (plus $20)	—
9 Premium years 2 through 25 (¼ of 1 percent)	$ 1,647.36	$ 1,560.96	—
10 Total insurance premium (line 8 plus 9)	$ 1,999.86	$ 1,738.46	—
11 Total cost of home	$87,461.00	$84,543.46	$103,670.00

*Home appreciates approximately 5 percent per year (total is rounded for computational purposes).

†A 20 percent down payment is required.

From the exhibit, note that despite the mortgage insurance (line 10), costing almost $2,000, the total costs are nearly 20 percent greater as a result of waiting to save a down payment for a conventional mortgage. Very modest increases in the value of the house require much larger mortgages and monthly payments.

> **Strategy: Lack of a sufficient down payment should not prevent you from buying a home. Remember, monthly payments will be larger with a smaller down payment. But projected continuing inflation in housing costs makes it very important to consider buying a house as soon as possible. This means looking into FHA, VA, and guaranteed loans as well as conventional financing.**

Using a Mortgage Table

Exhibit 12–5 is a mortgage table for maturities of 20, 25, or 30 years, which are the normal maturities for home mortgage loans, and interest rates ranging from 7 to 12 percent, which are the prevailing rates of the last few years. For a particular maturity and interest rate, the body of the table shows the monthly payment for each $1,000 of the mortgage amount. Because the table gives the monthly payment for each $1,000 of the mortgage amount, it can be used for a mortgage of any amount. To figure out the total monthly payment, simply divide the mortgage amount by $1,000 and multiply the result by the monthly

Exhibit 12-5   Monthly Payment to Amortize $1,000 Loan for Different Interest Rates and Loan Maturities

	Years to maturity		
Rate (percent)	20	25	30
7	7.76	7.07	6.66
7½	8.06	7.39	7.00
8	8.37	7.72	7.34
8½	8.68	8.06	7.69
9	9.00	8.40	8.05
9½	9.33	8.74	8.41
10	9.66	9.09	8.78
11	10.33	9.81	9.53
12	11.02	10.54	10.29

payment for each $1,000 from the table. For example, to find the cost of a $25,300 mortgage at 9 percent for 25 years, divide $25,300 by $1,000 and you get 25.3, then multiply 25.3 by $8.40; the result, $212.52, will be the total payment per month correct to about 25 cents (differences are due to rounding errors).

In the early years of a mortgage loan, most of your monthly mortgage payment goes toward interest, with very little amortizing (paying off) the loan. Exhibit 12–6 shows for a $1,000 mortgage the amount outstanding at the end of each year for maturities of 20, 25, and 30 years. Note how slowly the mortgage is reduced in the early years and how rapidly it reduces as the maturity date approaches. Note particularly that when the 20-year mortgage is paid in full, there is still $404 unpaid on the 25-year loan and $635 on the 30-year obligation. On the 30-year loan, only 36.5 percent of the mortgage has been repaid at the time the 20-year loan is completely repaid.

Variable Rate Mortgages

The advantage of a fixed monthly payment for the duration of a mortgage may soon become a thing of the past. There is a strong move by the savings and loan industry to adopt variable mortgage interest rates as the standard loan arrangement. The proposal is to tie the mortgage rate to a more general interest rate in the financial market, and as it increases and declines, so would the mortgage rate. The effect would be to make mortgage payments subject to the same price changes of other goods and services.

The variable rates would be advantageous to the consumer if the general interest rate was dropping. However, variable rates would primarily benefit the savings and loan industry. In the recent past, the S&Ls have seen their money costs, which is the amount they pay on savings, actually exceed the rate they are earning on many of their existing mortgages. Consequently, to remain profitable the S&Ls have had to charge higher rates on new loans to help subsidize their previous loan commitments.

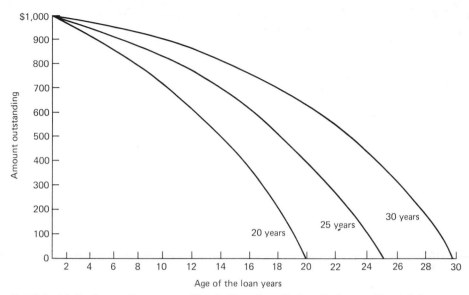

Exhibit 12-6 Loan Progress Chart Showing Dollar Balance Remaining on a $1,000, 9 Percent Loan for 20-, 25-, and 30-Year Maturities

Stretching Your Mortgage Dollar

Higher interest rates have sharply raised the monthly payment necessary to amortize loans of equivalent size. One of the ways to counteract this increase is by extending the maturity date of the mortgage. In this way the payments can be reduced by enough to compensate for the increased interest rate. Monthly payments for a $25,000 mortgage having different maturities and interest rates are shown in Exhibit 12–7.

From the information in Exhibit 12–7, it is evident that if mortgage rates move from 8 to 9.5 percent, monthly payments can be held almost constant by stretching the mortgage maturity from 20 to 30 years. The disadvantage, of course, is the increase in total payments for the home. An increase in interest rates from 8 to 9.5 percent increases the cost by $5,741.80, if the loan maturity is kept at 20 years. If the rate increases from 8 to 9.5 percent and you increase the maturity from 20 to 30 years to keep the monthly payment approximately the same, your total costs for a $25,000 mortgage will increase from $50,188.80 to $75,679.20; that is $25,490.40 more than you must pay. The total cost for the

Exhibit 12-7 Monthly Payment on a $25,000 Mortgage at Various Interest Rates and Loan Maturities

Years	7 percent	8 percent	9 percent	9.5 percent
20	$193.83	$209.12	$224.94	$233.04
25	176.70	192.96	209.80	218.43
30	166.33	183.45	201.16	210.22

$25,000 mortgage under differing interest and maturity assumptions is shown in Exhibit 12–8. The exhibit was constructed by multiplying the monthly payments shown in Exhibit 12–7 by the maturity of the loan.

> **Strategy: It is possible to decrease monthly mortgage payments by increasing the loan's maturity. However, the added cost over the life of the mortgage is so great that doing so is advisable only in special circumstances. It is probably most appropriate when the home will not be owned for an extended period.**

Finding Mortgage Money

After deciding which house you want to buy, you will have to obtain a mortgage to finance the purchase. The primary sources are: (1) savings and loan associations, (2) commercial banks, (3) mutual savings banks (primarily on the East Coast), and (4) life insurance companies.

During periods of tight money when mortgages are hard to obtain, some preliminary steps can be important in applying for a loan. Things that you can do to help you get mortgage money are:

1   Make sure the property is worth what you have offered for it.
2   Be able to make an adequate down payment.
3   Make sure your total payments will not exceed 25 percent of your gross income.
4   Be a customer of the institution where you are applying for money; have a savings and/or checking account with the bank.

Alternative Financing   Occasionally, adequate mortgage money is unavailable or interest rates may be extremely high. At such times there are several alternatives which are worth consideration.

Mortgage Assumption   Here, the buyer assumes the seller's mortgage and gives the seller a down payment equal to the difference between the selling price and the mortgage. This arrangement often offers low-cost financing. However, offsetting this advantage is the fact that the down payment may have to be quite large, especially if the seller's mortgage has been in existence for a long period of time. Assumable mortgages are becoming increasingly more difficult to find: In the last 5 to 7 years, most banks have specifically excluded assumable mortgages in their mortgage contracts.

Land Contracts   In this situation the seller finances the buyer, often requiring no down payment. A major disadvantage of the land contract is that

Exhibit 12-8   Total Payments for a $25,000 Mortgage at Different Interest Rates and Maturities

Years	7 percent	8 percent	9 percent	9.5 percent
20	$46,519.20	$50,188.80	$53,985.60	$55,929.60
25	53,010.00	57,888.00	62,940.00	65,529.00
30	59,878.80	66,042.00	72,417.60	75,679.20

in the event the buyer defaults, he or she loses whatever amount has been paid into the property. There are many cases where people have been paying on a land contract for 10 to 15 years, and lose everything they had put into the property.

Second Mortgages   In many instances, a seller will facilitate the sale of the property by giving the buyer additional financing in the form of a second mortgage. This enables the buyer to request a smaller first mortgage from a bank. The disadvantage of a second mortgage is that its maturity is usually very short and as a result, the second mortgage payments are quite large. Thus, during the period the second mortgage is in existence, the buyer may find that the sum of first and second mortgage payments exceeds 25 percent of income.

> **Strategy: A first mortgage from a reputable lending institution is the best way to finance a house. If you cannot obtain such financing, reassess whether you can really afford to buy a house. If you are convinced that you can afford a home, but market conditions have prevented you from getting financing, consider mortgage assumptions and second mortgages. Be aware of their pitfalls, however. Land contracts should be used only by the most knowledgeable buyers. They are extremely dangerous for most people.**

Mortgage Provisions

The standard mortgage calls for equal monthly payments over a specified period which will be sufficient to amortize, that is, retire the loan over the period, and pay all interest charges. There may be additional provisions which the borrower should be aware of. Some of the provisions may be worth trying to include in the mortgage, whereas others should be excluded, if possible.

Acceleration Clause   Most mortgages stipulate that if the loan is in default (payments are not made) for a period such as 60 or 90 days, the total amount of the loan becomes immediately due. The clause permits the lender to initiate foreclosure proceedings (repossess the property) in the event of default. It is not a negotiable provision.

Prepayment Penalty   Sometimes, during the period of a mortgage loan, the borrower may find it possible to pay off the balance of the original loan with a new loan at a lower interest rate from another lender (perhaps even the original lender). This procedure is called refinancing, and it would require prepaying the balance of the loan to the original lender. Many loan contracts stipulate that repaying the loan early for purposes of refinancing will be subject to an interest penalty. This provision is designed to make it unattractive for a borrower to repay the loan in the event interest rates drop. Try to have this provision excluded from the contract.

Escalator Clause   This provision permits the lender to increase the rate in the event interest rates increase. Until variable rate mortgages become standard, this is still a negotiable clause. It is to the borrower's benefit to have the mortgage contract written without an escalator clause.

Nonassumption Clause   This provision prevents a buyer from assuming payments of the seller's mortgage. It denies the seller the opportunity to use a low interest rate loan as a sales incentive during periods of high mortgage costs.

Open-End Mortgage   An open-end mortgage makes money available to the borrower at prevailing interest rates without requiring that the original loan be refinanced. If a borrower wants to make a major home improvement, an open-end mortgage will be more advantageous than a home improvement loan or refinancing an original loan.

Closing Costs

In analyzing how much to pay for a house, you must also include the costs which are incurred at the time the property is transferred from the seller to the buyer. These are called closing costs. Depending on geographic location, the closing costs may range from a low of approximately $100 to as much as $2,000, exclusive of realtor's commissions. These costs may be negotiable. They are set by law and precedent, but may vary depending on the situation.

The Department of Housing and Urban Development (HUD) of the federal government has listed 15 possible closing costs which may confront the buyer of a house. They are:[1]

1   Title search fee
2   Title insurance
3   Attorney's fees
4   Survey
5   Mortgage discount points
6   Appraisal fee
7   Recording fee
8   Mortgage insurance premiums
9   Preparation of documents
10   Credit report (on the buyer)
11   Termite inspection
12   Lender's origination fee
13   Escrow fees
14   Notary fees
15   Adjustment of prepaid items such as taxes

Each of these factors is quite technical. Since legal assistance should be obtained when buying a house, these items and their costs should be discussed with your attorney prior to the finalization of the sale. Recently enacted legislation requires that the closing costs be itemized and given to a mortgage

[1]U.S. Department of Housing and Urban Development, *Buying a Home? Don't Forget Those Closing Costs!* Washington, D.C.: 1973.

applicant at the time of application for the loan. This notification should enable you to negotiate many of the items before the sale is in the final stage. Doing so could easily save you hundreds of dollars.

Tax Escrow Accounts

Many mortgage lenders require that you make real estate tax payments with the monthly mortgage payment. The lender then accumulates these payments in a separate *non-interest-bearing* account and uses the money to pay the real estate taxes when they come due. The use of such accounts, called escrow accounts, effectively increases the interest cost to the borrower while raising the return to the lender because the lender has the use of the borrower's money at no cost.

Tax escrow accounts offer no advantage except that they force the borrower to pay tax obligations on a periodic basis. If there is any possibility of avoiding an escrow account, do so. A savings account will accomplish exactly the same thing for you, and at the same time earn interest.

Escrow accounts are also used to collect money for a homeowner's insurance. Again, if at all possible, make arrangements to pay the insurance personally. There is no reason to let the bank use your money without paying you to use it.

Some states have passed legislation requiring banks to pay interest on escrow accounts. Similar legislation is pending in other states. As yet, however, the majority of states do not have such requirements.

PICKING THE RIGHT HOUSE

If you decide to buy you must consider a number of factors in selecting the best possible home. You should consider factors such as location, construction, floor plan, and space utilization. This section briefly discusses some of the most important variables and summarizes the decision with a checklist which can be used to evaluate any home.

Location   One of the oldest sayings about real estate is: The three most important factors to consider in buying a home are location, location, and location. While this statement undoubtedly overstates the importance of location, it points out how crucial most real estate men and lending institutions consider it to be. A house that is structurally perfect could turn out to be a bad purchase if it is in a deteriorating neighborhood or close to industry or major highways.

Zoning   Zoning is the regulation by a community of the types of buildings which may be constructed in a given location.

Zoning may have a significant impact on a property's value. A home which appears to be in a good neighborhood could deteriorate in value substantially if industry is permitted to develop nearby. Nobody wants a meat-packing plant next door. In buying a home, make sure it is in an area where the zoning is for single-family or multifamily homes and excludes industrial buildings.

Value of Surrounding Property   The value of your home is, in a large measure, determined by its surroundings; therefore the emphasis on location and zoning. However, a $60,000 house in a good neighborhood of $40,000 houses will not be nearly as salable as a $60,000 house in a neighborhood of $80,000 dwellings.

> **Strategy: When buying a house, try to make sure that no more than 50 percent of the dwellings in the same neighborhood are of lower value.**

Convenience   Distance to shopping, schools, church, work, and other important places should be considered in the selection of a home. With rising transportation costs, you must think carefully about buying a home which increases commuting costs. Be sure to calculate the transportation time and costs you will incur if you buy a specific house.

New versus Old Home   Which is best—a brand new home or one that was built a number of years ago? Some people have a real fondness for older homes with their charm and grace. For the same purchase price, an older home provides more living space and many improvements such as trees and shrubs, and much of the major decorating will probably already have been done. The Department of Housing and Urban Development has suggested that you pay special attention to the following items before buying an older home.

   1   *Termite infestation and wood rot.* A check by a termite specialist is important, particularly in those areas of the country that have a history of infestation.

2 *Sagging structure.* Look carefully at the squareness of exterior walls.

3 *Inadequate wiring.* Be sure that there is sufficient electrical power (have an electrician check it out) and enough electrical outlets throughout the house. Request inspection by the local government for code compliance to make sure the wire is not dilapidated, exposed, and dangerous.

4 *Run-down heating plant.* Check the general condition of the heating system. What kinds of repairs are needed, what will they cost, and how long will the system last?

5 *Inadequate insulation.* Ask if the attic and the space between interior and exterior walls has been filled with an insulating material. What material was used and how was it installed?

6 *Faulty plumbing.* Choose a home that is connected to a public sewer system in preference to one served by a septic tank or a cesspool. Check with the plumber who last serviced the house to determine the condition of the plumbing and also to have the water pressure tested.

7 *Hot water heater.* Check the type and capacity of the tank to determine if there will be sufficient hot water for family needs. Look for any signs of rust or leaks. Obtain any guarantee held by the present owner, if it is still in effect.

8 *Roof and gutters.* What kind of roofing material was used and how old is it? Check inside the attic for water stains and discolorations. Ask the owner for a guarantee on the roofing if one exists.

9 *Wet basement.* A basement that looks dry in summer may be 4 inches under water in the spring. Are there signs around the foundation walls of water penetration?[2]

[2]U.S. Department of Housing and Urban Development, *Wise Home Buying.* November 1972, p. 11

Advantages of a new home are numerous. It does not need a new roof, a new furnace, or kitchen, a paint job, refurbished bathrooms, and a host of other items which deteriorate with age on any house. New homes are probably better insulated and have tighter windows and doors, thus reducing the cost of heating or air conditioning.

The location of a new home may be better. Older dwellings are often found in deteriorating neighborhoods. The ages of people in the neighborhoods may be vastly different, and if it is important for your children to have playmates, a newer home might be your best bet. Unfortunately, new homes are not without their pitfalls. The bulk of them hinge on the reputation and integrity of the builder. Will the builder live up to the construction contract? Even with a good contractor, it is wise to check the construction process regularly while the house is being built. A significant drawback to buying a new home is the necessity for landscaping. The cost can be substantial and it will be many years before the trees and shrubs reach the size that could be obtained when buying an older home.

Checklist for Homes   Exhibit 12–9 is a checklist which can help you systematically evaluate many of the additional features which are important in house selection. By answering all the questions on the checklist, you can avoid many of the unpleasant surprises that confront home buyers, such as leaking roofs and bad plumbing.

Should You Use a Broker?

Licensed real estate brokers earn their commissions by bringing sellers and buyers together. From the buyer's standpoint, the broker can show them many more homes of the type they want and can afford in a short period of time than they could hope to see by contacting sellers directly. Moreover, a seller who has listed property with a broker will have to pay a commission to the broker even if selling the house independently. For this reason, after listing with a broker, few sellers will be willing even to show the property themselves.

Brokers Are Agents of the Seller   As a buyer, remember the broker is an agent of the seller. His or her primary job is getting the best possible price for the client. Do not expect the broker to be of assistance to a buyer in getting a bargain.

From the seller's standpoint, a broker provides the widest possible exposure for the house in the shortest period of time. This is particularly true if the broker belongs to the Multiple Listing Service (MLS). MLS is a method where brokers share listings with one another. In a large suburban location, this permits a vast increase in the possible number of potential buyers. A good broker can also provide professional assistance in setting the best selling price for the property. Often sellers will be unsure of what their house is worth. Asking too low a price can be costly, and asking too high a price can prevent interested people from even looking at the property. The danger in overpricing a house is that it will be on the market too long. Buyers are very much aware of

Exhibit 12-9 Checklist for Houses

Outside house and yard
- [ ] attractive, well-designed house
- [ ] suited to natural surroundings
- [ ] lot of the right size and shape for house and garage
- [ ] suitable use of building materials
- [ ] compatible with houses in the area

- [ ] attractive landscaping and yard
- [ ] good drainage of rain and moisture
- [ ] dry, firm soil around the house
- [ ] mature, healthy trees— placed to give shade in summer
- [ ] convenient, well-kept driveway, walks, patio, porch

- [ ] yard for children
- [ ] parking convenience— garage, carport, or street
- [ ] distance between houses for privacy
- [ ] sheltered entry—well-lighted and large enough for several to enter the house together
- [ ] convenient service entrance

Outside construction
- [ ] durable siding materials—in good condition
- [ ] solid brick and masonry— free of cracks
- [ ] solid foundation walls—6 inches above ground level— 8 inches thick

- [ ] weather-stripped windows and doors
- [ ] noncorrosive gutters and downspouts, connected to storm sewer or splash block to carry water away from house

- [ ] copper or aluminum flashing used over doors, windows, and joints on the roof
- [ ] screens and storm windows or Thermopane glass
- [ ] storm doors

Inside construction
- [ ] sound, smooth walls with invisible nails and taping on dry walls; without hollows or large cracks in plaster walls
- [ ] well-done carpentry work with properly fitted joints and moldings
- [ ] properly fitted, easy-to-operate windows

- [ ] level wood floors with smooth finish and no high edges, wide gaps, or squeaks
- [ ] well-fitted tile floor—no cracked or damaged tiles— no visible adhesive
- [ ] good possibilities for improvements, remodeling, expanding
- [ ] properly fitted and easy-to-work doors and drawers in built-in cabinets

- [ ] dry basement floor with hard smooth surface
- [ ] adequate basement drain
- [ ] sturdy stairways with railings, adequate head room— not too steep
- [ ] leakproof roof—in good condition
- [ ] adequate insulation for warmth, coolness, and soundproofing

Living space
- [ ] convenient floor plan and paths from room to room
- [ ] convenient entry with foyer and closet
- [ ] convenient work areas (kitchen, laundry, workshop) with adequate drawers, cabinets, lighting, work space, electric power
- [ ] private areas (bedrooms and bathrooms) located far enough from other parts of the house for privacy and quiet

- [ ] social areas (living and dining rooms, play space, yard, porch or patio) convenient, comfortable, large enough for family and guests
- [ ] rooms conveniently related to each other—entry to living room, dining room to kitchen, bedrooms to baths
- [ ] adequate storage—closets, cabinets, shelves, attic, basement, garage
- [ ] suitable wall space and room size for your furnishings

- [ ] outdoor space convenient to indoor space
- [ ] windows located to provide enough air, light and ventilation
- [ ] agreeable type, size, and placement of windows
- [ ] usable attic and/or basement space
- [ ] possibilities for expansion
- [ ] attractive decorating and fixtures
- [ ] extras—fireplace, air conditioning, porches, new kitchen and baths, built-in equipment, decorating you like

Source: This information taken from the Money Management Institute booklet *Your Housing Dollar*, printed by the Money Management Institute of Household Finance Corporation, Chicago.

what is available and the prices asked. If they see a house advertised for months and then see the price reduced sharply, their first reaction is that something is wrong with the property. In many instances the seller is merely adjusting the asking price to market conditions. The image of inferior property is always present in such cases. In addition to pricing assistance, brokers can help facilitate sales by arranging financing for buyers. In times of tight money, brokers who deal regularly with banks and savings and loan institutions may receive favorable treatment not afforded unknown borrowers.

Broker's Fees   All these advantages have a cost. Broker's commissions average about 6 percent of the selling price of the house. A $40,000 home sold through a broker would have a $2,400 real estate commission. The seller would net $37,600. Undoubtedly both the buyer and the seller end up sharing in the cost of the commission. By dealing directly with the seller, a compromise price of $38,800 could be arranged; the seller would get a higher price and the buyer would pay a lower price. Thus, while there are advantages of dealing with a broker, the cost considerations make direct sales very attractive. They should be considered.

> **Strategy: When buying a home, try to find a direct purchase, if possible. When selling a home take the time to find a fair price and try to sell the property yourself. If you are unable to sell in some predetermined time period, then consider listing the property with a broker.**

Legal Aspects: The Actual Sale

Prior to, and at the time of the sale, there are a number of legal factors which should be considered. These involve: (1) earnest money, (2) legal assistance, (3) deeds and abstracts, and (4) title insurance, when necessary.

Earnest Money Example   Sam Splitlevel, after months of looking, found his dream house. He offered the owner $38,000 and accompanied his offer with a check for $1,000 as evidence of good faith. This advance is called *earnest money*. Sam later the same day found another house he liked even better and again offered the seller $38,000 with $1,000 earnest money. If both offers are accepted by the sellers, Sam just lost $1,000. Earnest money becomes the seller's if the buyer fails to complete the transaction. Unless Sam is ready to buy two houses, he will have to sacrifice the earnest money on one of them. There is one out, and it should be written into every offer to purchase. Make the earnest money contingent on obtaining satisfactory financing. If Sam had done this and then could not find a mortgage, both sellers would have had to return his earnest money.

Legal Assistance   Without exception, a lawyer should be retained to assist a home buyer. The lawyer represents the buyer when the actual title is transferred; this process is called the closing. The lawyer protects your interests in all aspects of the purchase and makes sure that you receive a clear deed to the property.

Strategy: Before signing any agreements for the purchase or sale of a house, be sure to retain legal counsel. Also be sure to see the lawyer's fee is agreed upon before using any attorney. Fees vary and it may be very worthwhile to shop for legal assistance.

Deeds, Titles, and Abstracts A written document called a deed is the instrument which conveys the title (right to ownership) to a piece of property from the seller to the buyer. In all states, the deed is recorded by the registry of deeds to notify any interested parties of the status of the property. There are four different types of deeds which can be used.

1   *Warranty deed.* This is the strongest deed. It guarantees that the title is good and unencumbered (all previous mortgages have been repaid).
2   *Special warranty deed.* Here the grantor guarantees that there are no mortgages on the property.
3   *Quitclaim deed.* Any interest the grantor (seller) may have is conveyed to the buyer. There are no guarantees.
4   *Deed of bargain and sale.* This deed conveys the property with or without guarantees.

An abstract consists of an historical record of all transactions and encumbrances involving a given property. If the title search raises questions as to the clarity of the title, the buyer can obtain protection by purchasing title insurance.

Title Insurance When Sam Splitlevel buys his dream house, he is concerned that somebody may later prove a financial interest in the property. This problem could result from faulty recording of liens (usually mortgages), or simply a poorly done title search which failed to disclose a lien. By paying a premium to a title insurance company at the time he buys the house, Sam ensures that if somebody with a beneficial interest does come forward, he will not lose his equity in the property.

The use of title insurance varies widely throughout the country. In most cases, the buyer has little choice of whether to buy title insurance or not. Insurance is used principally when a lender requires it. Surprisingly, such a requirement may vary within the same town. Some sections of town may be deemed title insurance areas, whereas in other areas a quitclaim deed is sufficient. The cost of title insurance is usually in the range of $100 to $300. The premium is paid only once, at the time the title is conveyed to the buyer, and the insurance protects the buyer for as long as he or she owns the property.

MOBILE HOMES

One of the fastest growing segments of the housing industry is the mobile home (MH) market. The "homes" are mobile only in that they are towed to their permanent location. Although called mobile, they barely resemble the trailers of a generation ago. Mobile homes are popular because of their relatively low

cost. A fully equipped mobile home can range in price from $6,000 to over $15,000. At the top of the price range, they provide over 1,000 square feet of comfortable, sometimes opulent, living accommodations. Many people who cannot afford, or do not wish to buy, a conventional home can obtain excellent living in a mobile home. This type of housing is most attractive to young married or retired couples, although more and more it is becoming an alternative for people with children as well.

Advantages of Mobile Homes

The single biggest advantage of a mobile home is its low purchase price. The low price means a lower down payment and lower monthly payments. Thus, many people who are financially unable to purchase a conventional house can afford a mobile home. Unfortunately, many of the seemingly apparent economic benefits of mobile homes are really very short term. Unlike conventional housing, mobile homes do not appreciate in value, and in many cases their value actually depreciates.

Disadvantages of Mobile Homes

Presently, the disadvantages of mobile homes are far more numerous than the advantages. The principal drawbacks are (1) resale value, (2) quality, and (3) location due to zoning restrictions.

Resale When you sell a mobile home, you will probably sell it for less than you paid for it. Because of this depreciation factor, total cost of ownership will often turn out to be greater than a single-family home costing 4 times the mobile home. Although the down payment and monthly payments on a mobile home are less than on a single-family home, the latter may be less expensive in the long run.

Quality   The quality of many mobile homes produced over the last 20 years has been extremely poor for various reasons. Materials are bad, workmanship is worse, and design is worse still. The industry and the government are aware of these problems. As a result, there has been a real effort to set minimum standards for safety and workmanship.

> **Strategy: When buying a mobile home, make sure to deal with an established manufacturer whose products are considered to be of high quality. To determine quality, try to contact a few people who have bought similar homes.**

Location: Mobile Home Parks   Although there are many well-operated and well-cared for mobile home parks, a vast number of them have become instant slums. The majority of mobile homes are in developments exclusively for mobile homes. Many park operators are also dealers and they often require that the home be purchased from them as a condition of residence in the park. This requirement takes away the power to bargain on price. The dealer who runs an attractive park is in an advantageous position.

Like single-family homes and for many of the same reasons, location, location, and location are the most important factors to consider in the purchase decision.

Financing Mobile Homes   Traditionally, mobile homes have been financed with consumer installment loans carrying a maturity of 5 to 7 years. Mobile home loans are now available with maturities of 10 to 15 years. The Federal Housing Authority, as of 1969, and the Veterans Administration, as of 1970, will insure and guarantee mobile home loans in the same manner as they provide FHA and VA mortgages on conventional homes. The maturities are still shorter than regular mortgages, however. Interest rates on mobile home loans run somewhat higher than regular mortgage loans; 12 percent is a typical rate.

Cost of a Mobile Home

Exhibit 12–10 details the costs of buying a $10,000 mobile home and compares it with the monthly cost of the $35,000 home presented in Exhibit 12–1. The comparison has one major limitation. It is valid only for a 7- to 10-year time span. But, even though home mortgages have much longer maturities, the comparison over this shorter time is reasonable because the average home in the United States changes owners every 7 or 8 years. One final note: The income tax savings shown in the exhibits are those for the first year of ownership. Just as with the single-family home, the tax saving decreases each year as the interest portion of the mortgage payment decreases. However, as

Exhibit 12-10 Monthly Cost of a Mobile Home versus a Conventional Home

	Mobile home[a]	Conventional home[b]
Payments		
Mortgage payment	$115[c]	$235[d]
Park rental	35	—
Taxes	10	75
Utilities	35	40
Insurance	5	15
Maintenance	5	30
Monthly outflow	$205	$395
Adjustments		
Less: Tax savings[e]	$ 27	$ 86
Appreciation	—	146[f]
Equity increase	35	25
Plus: Opportunity cost of interest on down payment after taxes[g]	8	29
Depreciation	41[h]	—
Net cost	$192	$167

[a]Mobile home costing $10,000.
[b]Conventional home costing $35,000.
[c]Mortgage of $8,000 at 12 percent for 10 years.
[d]Mortgage of $28,000 at 9 percent for 25 years.
[e]Tax savings at the 30 percent marginal rate.
[f]Home appreciation of 5 percent annually.
[g]Interest on the respective down payments after tax. If this money were not used for a down payment, it could be invested.
[h]Mobile home depreciation of 5 percent annually.

the interest declines, the equity increases. Consequently, the net benefit of these two items, tax savings plus equity increase, will remain about the same each year.

CONDOMINIUMS

Initially, condominiums were concentrated in large metropolitan areas and resort communities, but they have now spread to small and medium-sized cities as well. Condominiums are now available to most people. Some housing economists predict that more than 50 percent of the United States population will live in some form of condominium within the next 20 years.[3]

While a condominium has some attributes of a traditional house, it also has some unique features that need to be considered before making any purchase decision. For one thing, you must beware of the abuses which have occurred to some past condominium purchasers; abuses such as promised facilities that

[3]U.S. Department of Housing and Urban Development, *Questions about Condominiums: What to Ask before You Buy?* Washington, D.C.; 1974, p. 3

CONSIDER THE EXQUISITE VIEW... THEY CERTAINLY PICKED A LOVELY WALLPAPER FOR THEIR DINING ROOM ..

were never delivered, ownership costs that far exceeded original estimates, and units that were so poorly designed and constructed that they were nearly impossible to resell. Also, you must realize that living in a condominium development entails a different life-style from that of a traditional house. And another thing you must learn is that the cost of condominium ownership is not exactly the same as the cost of renting or home ownership. We will discuss the differences.

A Condominium Defined

Condominium ownership involves two different property areas: the individual living unit and the common property area.

Individual Living Unit   The individual living units are generally part of the larger multiunit building. But they are considered separate entities within the development, so purchasers each receive a deed to their specific living unit. Since it is an identified area, a condominium can be financed with a standard home mortgage. Real estate taxes are assessed on the living unit the same as on a house.

Individual owners are responsible for the taxes and mortgage payment on only their own living unit. Default by one owner on the mortgage or taxes has no impact on the other owners. Each individual owner is responsible only for his or her own debts and obligations and for no one else's.

Common Property Area The common property encompasses the land area where the condominium development is located and all property items not included in the living units. Normally this property includes structural parts of the buildings (exterior walls, stairways, roof, hallways), sidewalks, parking lots, and recreation facilities (swimming pool, tennis court, meeting hall). On some condominiums, however, parking lots and recreation facilities are owned by an outsider who leases them to the residents.

As part of the purchase, buyers receive an undivided interest in the common property area. By an undivided interest we mean that no owner can claim specific segments of the common property. For example, an owner cannot claim one corner of the swimming pool, or part of a tennis court, or a specific area of the lawn. Instead, each owner has an interest in the entire common property area and all owners must share the usage of that area. All owners share the maintenance and repair costs for the common property items. There are no real estate taxes on the common property; instead, all such taxes are assessed on the individual living units.

Economics Typically, land costs are substantially less for a condominium than they would be for a series of single-family homes. The reason is that the high-density design of most condominium living units takes less space. Since all the residents share the area surrounding the living units, the required amount of land is further reduced. The high-density design also provides some savings in construction cost. The net result is that a square foot of living space generally costs less in a condominium than it would in a comparable house.

Advantages and Added Features Since the maintenance of the common property area is contracted to an outside firm, a condominium owner avoids such things as yard work, painting, landscaping, snow removal, and similar tasks. This arrangement can be a definite advantage for the owner who lacks the time or the inclination to do this work. Contrary to the impression given by some condominium advertisements, all repairs, cleaning, and maintenance on the individual living units are still the owner's responsibility.

Many condominiums offer extensive recreational facilities. It would be extremely costly for an individual homeowner to duplicate such things as tennis courts, swimming pool, or a recreation building. Of course, the value of these added facilities to the owner depends upon how extensively he or she plans to use them.

Because of its intensive land use, a condominium can be located in an area near the downtown business section that would be prohibitively expensive for single-family homes. This added convenience feature can reduce the time and expense of commuting to work. And the larger the metropolitan area, the greater the potential benefit.

The checklist in Exhibit 12–11 should help a prospective buyer decide whether a condominium's advantages and features are important. If the majority of answers are yes, then a condominium should be high on the individual's list of housing alternatives.

Cost Comparison: Home Ownership versus Condominium Ownership

To compare the costs of house and condominium ownership, we will assume both have similar floor plans (3 bedrooms, $1\frac{1}{2}$ baths) and comparable living space. Exhibit 12–12 shows a comparison of the costs. The condominium's $35 monthly maintenance fee includes repair and maintenance of the common property area and unlimited use of the swimming pool. For both the house and condominium, we assumed a 20 percent down payment, with the balance financed over 25 years at 9 percent interest. Because of economic advantages of high-density living, the condominium costs $5,000 less than the house: $30,000 versus $35,000. A 30 percent marginal tax rate was used to compute the tax shield from the deductible property taxes and mortgage interest (this computation was discussed in Chapter 6, on taxes).

If we ignore the condominium's added features (reduced maintenance and swimming pool), the monthly cost differential between the two is only $10 ($167−$157).

For the house, there are larger mortgage and tax payments, but these are partially offset by the tax shield that results from these two items and the larger

Exhibit 12-11   Evaluating a Condominium's Added Features

Feature	Yes	No
1 Is the reduced maintenance feature		
a an appealing one?	( )	( )
b critical to you?	( )	( )
c eliminating work you dislike and exercise you do not need?	( )	( )
2 Are the recreational facilities		
a parallel to your interest?	( )	( )
b sufficient for the total development?	( )	( )
c such that you will use them extensively?	( )	( )
d such that you can eliminate your membership in a recreation club?	( )	( )
3 Will the unit's location		
a reduce your commuting effort?	( )	( )
b put you closer to social and cultural interests?	( )	( )
c benefit your family's interests and activities?	( )	( )

Exhibit 12-12   Monthly Ownership Costs: House versus Condominium

Cost element	House	Condominium
Payments[a]		
Mortgage[b]	$235	$201
Taxes	75	65
Utilities	40	35
Insurance	15	10
Maintenance fee	—	35
Maintenance, owner's responsibility	30	6
Monthly outflow	$395	$352
Adjustments[a]		
Add: Interest on down payment[c]	29	25
Less: Tax shield[d]	86	74
Equity increase[e]	25	21
Appreciation[f]	146	125
Net cost	$167	$157
Add: Cost of additional condominium features[g]	30	—
Net adjusted cost	$197	$157

[a] All amounts rounded to the nearest dollar.

[b] Payment on 25-year, 9 percent mortgage: $28,000 on the house and $24,000 on the condominium. Computed using Exhibit 12-5.

[c] After-tax interest that would have been earned had down payment been invested at 7 percent per year.

House:

([$7,000 $\times$ 7 percent] $-$ [($7,000 $\times$ 7 percent) $\times$ 30 percent]) $\div$ 12 months = $28.58.

Condominium:

([$6,000 $\times$ 7 percent] $-$ [($6,000 $\times$ 7 percent) $\times$ 30 percent]) $\div$ 12 months = $24.50.

[d] Tax shield using a 30 percent marginal tax rate.

House:

($210 [interest] + $75 [taxes]) $\times$ 30 percent = $85.50.

Condominium:

($180 [interest] + $65 [taxes]) $\times$ 30 percent = $73.50.

[e] Equity increase computed as

Monthly payment $-$ interest portion = equity

House: $235 $-$ $210 = $25

Condominium: $201 $-$ $180 = $21

[f] Assumes 5 percent appreciation each year on both home and condominium. But see discussion of appreciation potential in the next section.

[g] Estimated monthly cost of hiring yard work and external maintenance of house together with membership in a recreation club.

appreciation amount. When the additional cost of hiring the maintenance work and a recreation membership are added, the cost differential increases to $40 ($197−$157).

The lower down payment on the condominium could put it within reach of some people who lack the down payment for a regular house. In addition, the lower net cost of a condominium might fit the budget of some people who could not afford a regular house. But the differences are not large; people who find homeownership much too expensive will likely reach the same conclusion about condominiums.

Appreciation: The Unanswered Question While Exhibit 12–12 assumed the house and condominium both appreciated 5 percent annually, that may be an oversimplification. Recent history suggests that the value of a house will rise 5 percent each year. But condominiums have emerged so recently that it is difficult to estimate their rate of appreciation. Preliminary evidence suggests that their appreciation rate is likely to be substantially less than 5 percent. But that conclusion should be tempered by several factors. First, in some areas, condominium prices have been severely depressed because developers have built far more units than the area can absorb. Second, some early condominiums were so poorly built or ill-designed that they can be resold only with a sizable price concession. Last, the early abuses and questionable tactics have made buyers leery of condominiums!

If indeed condominiums are going to appreciate at a slower rate, that fact could easily negate much of the favorable cost differential we noted in Exhibit 12–12. To illustrate the impact of different appreciation rates, Exhibit 12–13 takes the cost data from Exhibit 12–12 and adjusts them for three different appreciation rates.

If homes and condominiums appreciate at the same rate, then the monthly cost differential favors condominiums. But if condominiums appreciate 1 or 2 percent slower than homes, then the monthly net adjusted costs will be about the same; that is, the monthly cost differential between a home and a condominium will be zero.

Cost Comparison: Apartment versus Condominium Ownership

Now we will compare the costs of renting an apartment with the costs of owning a condominium that is restricted to unmarried individuals and married

Exhibit 12-13 Ownership Cost with Different Appreciation Rates

	Net adjusted cost without appreciation*	Less monthly appreciation†	Net adjusted‡ cost
House:			
5 percent appreciation	$343	$146	$197
Condominium:			
5 percent appreciation	282	125	157
4 percent appreciation	282	100	182
3 percent appreciation	282	75	207

*Obtained from Exhibit 12-12. For the house: $197 + $146 = $343; for the condominium: $157 + $125 = $282.

†Computed as follows: Purchase price × appreciation rate ÷ 12 months.

‡Computed as: Net adjusted cost = net adjusted cost without appreciation − monthly appreciation.

couples without children. In this case, the condominium and the apartment each have two bedrooms and one bath and include extensive recreational facilities. We assume 10 percent of the condominium's $25,000 purchase price is made as a down payment, with the balance financed over 25 years at 9 percent interest. A 25 percent marginal tax rate was used to compute the tax shield from the deductible property tax and mortgage interest. The details of the cost comparison are shown in Exhibit 12–14.

If we ignore the appreciation factor, the net cost of the two alternatives is nearly equal: $155 + $63 = $218 for the condominium, and $215 for the apartment. On that basis, renting would be preferable because it requires no financial commitment and neither maintenance work nor costs.

When appreciation is considered, even at a conservative 3 percent rate, the net cost decidedly favors the condominium, $155 versus $215. But, until that appreciation potential is clearly demonstrated, we recommend that you compare only the nonmonetary advantages and disadvantages of renting an apartment and buying a condominium when deciding between them.

Caution! Problem Areas Ahead

Selecting a condominium is even more difficult than choosing a home. For a house, you must consider its construction and location. For a condominium, you must consider these factors and other factors like the common property area, the overall soundness of its high-density design, and the particular

Exhibit 12-14   Comparison of Monthly Cost: Apartment versus Condominium Costs

	Apartment	Condominium
Payments[a]		
Rent	$215	—
Mortgage payment[b]	—	$189
Taxes	—	54
Maintenance fee	—	35
Maintenance, owner's responsibility	—	5
Monthly outflow	$215	$283
Adjustments[a]		
Add: Interest on down payment[c]	—	$ 11
Less: Tax shield[d]	—	56
Equity increase[e]	—	20
Appreciation[f]	—	63
Net cost	$215	$155

[a] All amounts rounded to nearest dollar.

[b] Payment on a $22,500, 25-year, 9 percent mortgage. Computed using Exhibit 12-5.

[c] After-tax interest that would have been earned had the down payment been invested at 7 percent ([$2,500 × 7 percent] − [($2,500 × 7 percent) × 25 percent]) ÷ 12 months = $10.94.

[d] Tax shield assuming 25 percent marginal tax rate [$169 (interest) + $54 (taxes)] × 25 percent = $55.75.

[e] Computed as: Monthly payment − interest portion = equity portion.

[f] Appreciation assumed to be 3 percent per year. But see previous discussion of appreciation potential.

Exhibit 12-15 Judging a Condominium Development

	Yes	No
A General life-style		
1 Can you live where you		
a have limited control over external features (paint color, site layout)?	( )	( )
b may have to alter your life-style (noise, entertaining hours, pets)?	( )	( )
2 Are the neighbors		
a agreeable and financially able?	( )	( )
b from a socioeconomic background similar to yours?	( )	( )
c similar in status (single, young children, mature couples) to you?	( )	( )
B General development plans		
1 Does the overall development		
a appear attractive?	( )	( )
b seem well thought out and practical?	( )	( )
c provide adequate facilities and common area?	( )	( )
2 Is the design and construction suitable for the local climate?	( )	( )
3 When you want to sell,		
a are there restrictions?	( )	( )
b must you work through a particular realtor?	( )	( )
4 Have the maximum number of units and the final completion date been set?	( )	( )
C Common facilities		
1 Do the facilities meet your needs?	( )	( )
2 Are all recreation facilities part of common property?	( )	( )
3 If leased, are the fees reasonable?	( )	( )
4 If unfinished, is there a guaranteed completion date?	( )	( )
5 Are there penalties		
a for missing the deadlines?	( )	( )
b to force completion?	( )	( )
D Maintenance		
1 Are the units well built?	( )	( )
2 Do the budgeted expenses include replacement of major items (roof, painting, sidewalks)?	( )	( )
3 Is the estimated cost per unit based on a highly optimistic projection of the number of units that will ultimately be completed? (For example, estimate is 500 units, yet 50 units have been completed in 3 years.)	( )	( )
4 Does the developer have a record of creating high-quality, successful condominiums?	( )	( )
5 Can owners be forced to pay their maintenance charge?	( )	( )
6 If a new development, is the projected maintenance budget reasonable? (For example, how does the monthly fee compare to similar developments in the area?)	( )	( )
7 Does the budget include all common facilities?	( )	( )
8 Has the maintenance cost per unit remained stable each year? (It will rise by some amount.)	( )	( )
9 Are there many vacant units? Why?	( )	( )

life-style the condominium entails. The past abuses and questionable tactics that have characterized condominiums make it essential that a buyer exercise extra care in each and every aspect of the purchase. The major problem areas have centered on general life-style, general development plans, common area and facilities, and maintenance. The checklist in Exhibit 12–15 has sections for each of these areas. Too many "no" responses in a section may indicate problems ahead; consider and analyze that area further.

SUMMARY

1 Most people eventually buy a home because of the economic advantages of ownership.

2 Apartments, while economically less attractive, do have some important advantages, such as flexibility and convenience.

3 You should spend no more than 25 percent of your gross income on housing, whether you rent or buy.

4 Home financing is done through either conventional, FHA-guaranteed, VA-insured, or privately insured mortgages.

5 The cost of waiting and saving a sufficient down payment to purchase a home using conventional financing may far outweigh the cost premium on a privately insured mortgage, which permits a smaller down payment.

6 Mortgage periods range from 20 to 30 years. However, the longer the duration of the mortgage, the higher will be the total cost of the house.

7 Savings and loan associations represent the primary mortgage lenders. Banks and mutual savings banks should also be investigated. It is wise to discuss your mortgage needs with several different lenders before making a commitment.

8 Picking the right house can be an involved, complex process. A systematic evaluation can help in avoiding major pitfalls. Decide on the features most important to you and then analyze each house to make sure it meets your needs.

9 Using a broker can be advantageous. It gives wider coverage and selection to the buyer; for the seller, it can be beneficial in setting a fair market price for the property. The disadvantage of using a broker is the commission, which can be as high as 6 percent of the property's value.

10 Mobile homes represent an attractive alternative for many people. Advantages: They are less expensive, require a lower down payment, and lower monthly payments. Disadvantages: They entail depreciating value and potentially poor quality and location.

11 The cost per square foot of living space is generally less in a condominium than it is in a comparable house. The cost is less because less land is needed (more people living on a given plot of land) and slightly lower construction costs.

12 Ignoring possible differences in price appreciation, the monthly cost of a condominium is typically less than a comparable house.

13 Preliminary indications are that the price appreciation on condominiums will not match the 5 percent appreciation rate on houses.

14 Because condominium living includes both individually owned and jointly owned property, there are more considerations to evaluate when purchasing a condominium.

15 Potential problem areas that require careful evaluation when considering a condominium include (a) general life-style, (b) the general development plans, (c) common facilities, and (d) maintenance budget.

REVIEW YOUR UNDERSTANDING OF

Inflation hedge

Mortgages

    FHA, VA

    Conventional

    Privately insured

Amortization

Closing costs

Escrow accounts

Broker's fees

Conventional homes

Mobile homes

Title insurance

Deeds

Mortgage discount points

Titles

Abstracts

Common property area

Individual living unit

Monthly maintenance fee

DISCUSSION QUESTIONS

1   What are the economic advantages of ownership as opposed to renting?

2   Using Exhibit 12–5, calculate the cost of a 25-year, $23,000 mortgage at a rate of $9\frac{1}{2}$ percent. If you could reduce the rate to 9 percent by increasing your down payment by $3,000, would it be worth doing?

3   Using Exhibit 12–5, calculate the total interest cost for a $25,000 mortgage at 9 percent for 25 and 30 years. What is the monthly payment for these same mortgages? How much is the payment reduced by going from a 25- to a 30-year maturity? Is that extension justified?

4   Illustrate how taxpayers in the higher tax brackets, in effect, receive a higher housing subsidy than individuals in lower tax brackets. (*Hint:* What is the after-tax cost of real estate taxes of $1,000 for a 30 percent marginal tax-rate individual? For a 50 percent tax-rate person?)

5   Under what circumstances would you recommend that a person seek an FHA or privately insured mortgage instead of a conventional loan?

6   Are there any situations in which a mobile home is more advantageous than a conventional house or an apartment?

7   Discuss the comment, "Condominium living is always cheaper than a comparable house." What are the critical assumptions in that statement?

8   When comparing an apartment rental to condominium ownership, what nonmonetary factors should be considered?

9   Do you feel that condominiums will eventually house 50 percent of the United States population? Why or why not? Would you consider one?

10   Given your preferences, what advantages do you see in a condominium? What disadvantages?

11   Wilma Dixon is considering two housing alternatives:

    a   Apartment: $175 monthly rent.

    b   Condominium: $22,000 purchase price, $5,000 down payment, balance financed over 20 years at $9\frac{1}{2}$ percent, $540 property taxes annually, $30 monthly maintenance fee, approximately $134 of the monthly mortgage payment is interest.

    She will withdraw the down payment from a 6 percent savings account. Her marginal tax rate is 20 percent. She expects the condominium will appreciate 3 percent each year. Assuming both alternatives are acceptable, which has the lowest monthly cost? Which would you recommend?

12 In what ways would the selection of a reputable condominium developer be likely to minimize problems in the four major caution areas?

CASE PROBLEM

John Debit is a veteran who graduated from college 5 years ago with an accounting degree. He is currently working for a large national CPA firm at a salary of $17,000 per year, including overtime. He is married and has two children, ages three and one. John and his wife Symantha have been saving for the down payment on a home over the last 5 years, and they now have $6,000 for that purpose.

John and Symantha have found a ranch house in a good neighborhood which has the rooms and features they want. The asking price for the home is $34,000, although John is sure the owner will accept $33,000. Taxes on the home are $960 per year, insurance is $120, and utilities are estimated at $600. John is considering an FHA mortgage at 9.5 percent for 30 years. However, he would like to finance the home with a conventional mortgage at 9 percent for 25 years. The savings and loan institution requires a 25 percent down payment on this type of mortgage.

John has come to you for advice on what to do. How much of a down payment will he need with an FHA/VA loan? What will his monthly payments be? What will be his total monthly cost with an FHA/VA loan? If he elects a conventional mortgage, how much additional down payment will he need? What will his mortgage payment be under this alternative? Total payments? If the seller will give John a second mortgage for the difference between his $6,000 and the required down payment, should he take it?

RECOMMENDED READINGS

Booklets

U.S. Department of Housing and Urban Development, *Wise Home Buying.* Washington, D.C.: November 1972.
    A good guide to the essentials of buying, including a discussion of financing the purchase.
———, Washington, D.C.: *Questions about Condominiums. What to Ask Before You Buy?* June 1974.
    Discusses the basic condominium concept and points out the potential pitfalls in buying a condominium. Also considers the possible problems when a rental property is converted to a condominium. A bit technical in several places, but overall, it is a good treatment.

Magazines

Money:

"A Vacation Home That Helps Pay Its Way." November 1972, pp. 36–39.
    Examines the possibility of renting your resort condominium to reduce the costs of ownership. Worthwhile reading for anyone who hopes to rent his or her resort condominium.
Mead,William B., "Home Improvements for Love or Money." January 1973, pp. 24–27.
    Discusses how much of the cost of various home improvements you can expect to recapture at the time you sell the house.

———, "What's It Like on the Street Where You'll Live?" March 1973, pp. 28–32.
   Suggests ways for the prospective homeowner to decide what a neighborhood is
   really like and whether it fits his requirements.
Camarow, Avery, "Ins and Outs of Inspecting a House." July 1973, pp. 20–27.
   Through a series of pictures, this article highlights the frequently encountered
   structural problems of existing homes. The text discusses the implications and
   possible cost of the corrections. Good reading for the prospective house hunter.
Main, Jeremy, "Inflation Closes in on the One-Family Houses." September 1974, pp.
   28–32.
   Examines the causes for the recent shift to condominiums. Reviews the major
   features of the condominium concept and discusses its problem areas.
Changing Times:

"Facts to Know about Condominiums." October 1973, pp. 37–40.
   Has a good section covering the problem areas in condominium living.
"Suppose Your Apartment Goes Condominium." October 1974, pp. 45–47.
   Discusses the alternatives of buying your existing unit or moving on to a new
   apartment.

Books

Troelstrup, Arch W., *The Consumer in American Society: Personal and Family Finance.*
   5th ed., New York: McGraw-Hill, 1974.
   Chapter 9 covers some additional housing considerations, such as moving and
   insurance.
Brooks, Patricia, and Lester Brooks, *How to Buy a Condonminium.* New York: Stein and
   Day, 1975.
   A detailed discussion of that topic.

SAFEGUARDING *your* RESOURCES

Chapter 13

The Insurance Decision

After completing this chapter you should be able to:

analyze your insurance needs, using the principles of risk management.

explain how deductibles can be used to reduce insurance costs.

recall the primary reason insurance should be purchased.

recall the major ways to save money when buying insurance.

use the advice in the chapter to assist in selecting a good insurance agent.

recognize when claims for insurance should be submitted.

recall the types of documents which should accompany insurance claims.

Americans have come to accept insurance as a necessary evil. Few people understand the policies they buy, and most are not even sure why they are buying them. Insurance may be purchased when it is required, as with auto or homeowners policies; or worse, it may be purchased simply because of sales pressure. In any event, most people do not purchase insurance wisely. This is unfortunate, because insurance is important in maintaining a family's economic welfare. Without insurance, families may suffer devastating financial losses: the death of the breadwinner could impose severe financial hardship; or a fire could destroy the family's possessions. Insurance, tailored to the specific needs of the family or individual, can alleviate the financial consequences of such events.

To make an informed insurance decision you must ask yourself, and develop answers to, such questions as: What should be insured? How much should it be insured for? Where should the insurance be purchased? And, what policy provisions are best?

The technical name for answering these questions is *risk management*. It is the scientific approach to dealing with the pure risks which confront individuals. The idea of pure risk is important because it represents the only type of risk which can be insured. Simply defined: A pure risk has the possibility of loss, but absolutely no possibility of gain. Speculative risks, such as owning common stock, have the possibility of both gain and loss; it is impossible to insure them. You can purchase insurance on your home or car. You cannot buy insurance to protect you against losses in the stock market. Therefore, only the pure risks facing an individual will be discussed in this chapter.

UNDERSTANDING THE BASICS

An understanding of some basic concepts about insurance is important for making the best use of your insurance dollars. You should know the purpose of insurance and understand the fundamental ideas of risk management.

What Can You Insure?

Just about anything can be insured as long as the potential loss meets certain conditions and is a *pure* risk, not a *speculative* risk. The loss has to be financially measurable and it must be definite. It must be fortuitous or accidental, that is, resulting from something that may happen, not something that is certain to happen. Finally, the loss must be personal, not one affecting everybody at the same time. This is why flood insurance was impossible to buy until recently, when it was made available as a result of a government-sponsored program. Only those people in low lying areas would buy it—and everybody would be affected when a flood occurs.

In addition to the well-known insurance coverages such as auto, home-owners, and life, a wide variety of unusual insurance policies are sold. Although unusual, nevertheless they satisfy the conditions of an insurable risk. Examples of unusual insurance policies range from insuring picnics against rain to insuring critical parts of celebrities' anatomy.

INSURANCE: REIMBURSEMENT FOR LOSSES

Insurance is not designed to make money for you. All that it will do is return you to the same financial position you were in prior to the loss. This is called *indemnification.* The maximum a policy will pay is the loss that you suffer or the policy limit, whichever is less. If you own a home worth $30,000 and you insure it for $50,000, the maximum the insurance would pay is $30,000. There is no point to overinsuring a property because you will never collect more than its value.

Buying two or three policies will not help, either. Most insurance contracts contain a clause stipulating that in the event of multiple coverage, the insurers together will share the payments toward the total value of the loss.

Life insurance represents the one major exception to indemnification. Unlike the appraisal of a car or home, there is no satisfactory way to value a person's life. The insurance industry guards against the possibility of a person insuring his or her own life solely to provide immediate money for someone else. A suicide clause disallows claims by a beneficiary if the insured commits suicide within the first 2 years of the policy. And there are laws that prohibit beneficiaries from collecting life insurance proceeds when they are responsible for the insured's death. Protected as they are by these provisions, insurance companies place no limits beyond normal health standards on the amount of insurance they will sell to an individual. In fact, there are a number of people in this country who carry $10 million or more in life insurance.

Protect against Large Losses

Insurance should have the primary purpose of protecting against catastrophic losses which have a low probability of happening. These are the types of losses which can financially ruin an individual. For example, the probability of a $250,000 automobile accident lawsuit is very low. Yet, if it happened, it would be impossible for most people to pay such a judgment without insurance.

The idea of protecting against losses is central to the development of a sound personal insurance program. It means that policy limits should be set higher than most people would expect. Fortunately, the cost of increasing policy limits from $10,000 or $20,000, to $200,000 or $300,000, is very low.

Do Not Overinsure or Underinsure

The most common mistake people make in buying insurance is overinsuring or underinsuring. People are underinsured when they buy policy limits that are too low to protect against large losses. Overinsurance occurs when they are protected against even small losses which could be covered out of income or a small part of savings.

Buying $300,000 auto liability insurance is not overinsurance; it protects against a possible large loss. Buying only $10,000 of auto liability insurance is underinsurance because it does not provide sufficient protection against the size of settlements that are being awarded in many auto accidents.

Buying insurance to cover very small losses, as many people do, is overinsurance. For example, insurance to cover the loss of a contact lens represents a bad insurance buy. The cost of such insurance is high relative to the amount that can be recovered.

To avoid overinsuring, you must recognize which losses are most likely to occur and determine the amount of the potential loss. If the loss is small and its likelihood is quite high, you can probably afford to be self-insuring. Losses with a very low chance of happening, but having a high potential loss, are the types of risks where large amounts of coverage should be purchased.

PERSONAL RISK MANAGEMENT

Risk management, for the individual, involves four steps. Each of them is important in obtaining the right type of protection for the risks involved.

Step 1. Risk Identification   No insurance program can be implemented without listing what must be insured. Most people find they can relate their insurance needs to the following categories.

1   Loss of health, through either sickness or accident
2   Loss of financial assets, resulting from personal liability
3   Loss of property through theft, fire, or accident
4   Loss of life
5   Loss of income through sickness or accident

Each of these risks may be insured since it meets the criteria of insurable risks. The policies to protect against these risks are defined in basic terms below.

1   *Health insurance* protects a person against the expenses caused by an illness or accident. Reimbursement for medical expenses represents the most important and first insurance protection a family should buy.
2   *Liability insurance* protects a person from financial loss arising from his or her negligent behavior. It is included as a standard feature on both homeowners and auto insurance, although additional liability protection, called comprehensive personal liability, may be purchased separately.
3   *Property insurance* covers automobiles, homes, and personal property. It reimburses the insured for damages or theft of the property involved.
4   *Life insurance* pays a beneficiary a sum of money when the insured dies. In its purest form, life insurance is designed to replace a family's income when the breadwinner dies.
5   *Disability income insurance* provides a monthly income should the insured become physically disabled. The amount and duration of the payments are determined by the policy provisions.

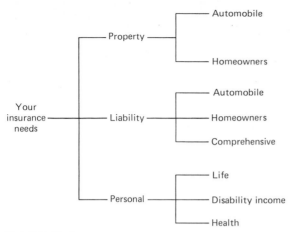

Exhibit 13-1

Exhibit 13–1 shows the breakdown of the major forms of personal insurance into their respective property, liability, and personal categories.

Step 2. Risk Evaluation   After determining the risks confronting you, a decision must be made as to how severely they would affect you if they should occur. A good way of doing this is by ranking the risks in terms of their potential loss and likelihood of occurrence. If you would be financially devastated by the loss, you should, by all means, buy adequate protection.

An example of the type of calculation needed to determine your risk exposure will illustrate the application of this data. Sam Jones is shopping for auto insurance and is trying to decide whether or not to purchase collision insurance. He owns a 6-year-old car with an estimated value of $650. Collision coverage with a $100 deductible would cost $87 annually. The calculation to determine whether he should buy the insurance is as follows:

Maximum loss		$650
Less: Deductible	$100	
Premium	$ 87	$187
Risk exposure		$463

Since Sam would be responsible for $100 even with insurance, and the insurance costs $87, his additional risk exposure is only $463. Viewed differently, Sam simply has to weigh $187 in insurance costs (premium plus deductible) against a maximum loss of $650. Sam figures that he can be self-insuring for this amount. In effect, as a self-insurer he has a policy with a $650 deductible, but he pays no premium.

You can use this calculation for all your insurance needs. Some protection is obviously a necessity, such as auto liability insurance and health insurance. Other protection, such as Sam's collision insurance, may not be so crucial. The value of this technique lies in its forcing you to make a systematic analysis of

your insurance needs. In this way, important coverages will not be overlooked and you can evaluate your needs more precisely so that you will be neither overinsured nor underinsured.

Exhibit 13–2 presents a simplified summary of risk evaluation for basic insurance policies and indicates who should buy the insurance. For most people, a sound personal insurance program should include all these coverages.

Step 3. Determining Whether to Buy Insurance   After evaluating potential losses, you are in a position to determine whether you should assume the risk yourself or buy insurance. There are three alternatives available. (1) Eliminate the risk entirely, thereby making insurance protection unnecessary. Selling an automobile or a boat to eliminate the need for insurance is an example of this strategy. (2) Reduce the risk, consequently reducing the cost of the insurance. Trading a high performance car, which carries an insurance surcharge, for a more conventional auto is an example of risk reduction. Risk reduction does not eliminate the need for insurance. (3) Transfer the risk without reducing or eliminating it. Risk transfer means transferring the risk from yourself to someone else, which is the insurance company. Hence, risk transfer simply means buying insurance. The purchase of life insurance is an example of this alternative.

Step 4. Selecting the Right Coverage   If you decide that the risk should be insured, you must then select a policy and an insurance company. Policies differ and rates of different companies vary considerably. The differences in coverages and rates may have a significant impact on the adequacy and total cost of your insurance program.

Exhibit 13-2 Risk Evaluation for Basic Insurance Contracts

Type of insurance	Maximum possible loss	Probability of loss	Individual who should buy
Life insurance	Depends on family's income (could be $250,000 or more)	Low; increasing with age	Head of family
Health insurance	$50,000 or more	Small losses almost certain; large losses less likely	Everybody
Disability income	Same as life insurance	1 chance in 10 before age 65	Everybody who earns a living
Auto, liability	$300,000 or more	Low	All auto owners
Auto, collision	Value of car	High	Auto owners who cannot be self-insuring
Homeowners, liability	$100,000 or more	Low	All homeowners and renters
Homeowners, property	Value of property plus contents	Low losses likely; total losses less likely	All homeowners and renters
Scheduled property (items, such as antiques, not covered by homeowners policy)	Value of property	Low	Owners of antiques, art, coins, etc.

Exhibit 13–3 depicts a flowchart approach to individual risk management.

MANAGING YOUR INSURANCE PROGRAM

The steps outlined under Personal Risk Management are only the preliminaries for a sound personal insurance program. After you set your priorities, you must evaluate the available agents and companies, make a selection, and buy the insurance. The job does not stop there, however. You should understand what steps must be taken to submit claims when such a submission becomes necessary. Also, the insurance program should be reviewed regularly.

Buying Insurance

You should have a good idea of what you need before contacting a sales representative. A good agent can certainly assist you in meeting your insurance needs, but you need to know enough about your needs to give the representative adequate information to work with. Most people find they need two insurance agents, one who specializes in life and health insurance, and another who specializes in property and liability insurance. We suggest that the following generalizations will be helpful in finding and dealing with agents of either type.

1 *Do not* buy from part-timers. Insurance is complex and should be

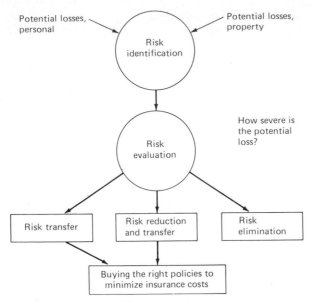

Exhibit 13-3   Risk Management

handled by somebody who knows what he or she is doing. The unemployed rock musician who is trying to make a few bucks selling insurance is a bad individual to entrust your insurance needs to.

2 *Do* make the agent work for you. Agents should be willing to answer your questions, quote rates on different policies, and offer advice in setting up a sound insurance program. If the agent makes these services sound like a favor—find somebody else. You are doing the person a favor by buying insurance from him or her—not vice versa.

3 *Do* make sure the agent works for a reputable, low-cost company. By and large, the better agents work for the better companies. Always make sure the company is sound before selecting the agent: do not select an agent without considering the company.

4 *Do* try to deal with agents who have demonstrated competence by passing professional examinations. The designation CLU, Chartered Life Underwriter, is a strong indicator that the life agent is a real professional. The same is true for the property agent qualifying as a Chartered Property and Casualty Underwriter (CPCU).

5 *Do* ask the opinions of friends and relatives. They may have some good ideas on whom to buy from. But be wary of overreliance on their recommendations—they may be making all the mistakes we are warning against.

Picking the Right Company   Thousands of companies sell insurance in this country. Like agents, some companies specialize in life insurance while others handle only property and liability insurance. Selecting the right company for each type of protection can save you a substantial amount on your insurance each year.

The first thing to recognize is that there are two basic forms of corporate organizations selling insurance and that they charge different rates. The two principal types are the stock insurance companies and the mutual insurance companies.

1   *Stock insurance companies.* Stock companies are organized like traditional corporations having stockholders and customers (policyholders). The profits made from selling insurance go to the stockholders.

2   *Mutual insurance companies.* The mutual companies differ from the stock firms in that the policyholders are the owners of the firm. Mutual companies would set their rates low enough to result in exactly zero profit each year if they could determine how to do that beforehand. But, since this is not possible, the mutual companies include a safety margin in their rates. Then, at the end of the year, the mutual companies calculate how much they overcharged beyond breaking even (zero profit), and return to each policyholder a share of the overcharge in the form of nontaxable dividends. As a result, the net insurance costs for the mutuals are usually lower than for the stock firms.

Another thing you must pay attention to is the firm's financial stability. *Best's Insurance Reports*, which is available in most public libraries, assesses the financial strength of most insurance companies.

Strategy: Selecting the lowest-cost company can produce significant savings when you buy insurance. Comparison shopping for low rates should start by concentrating on the mutual companies, restricting the search to those mutuals with the highest financial rating. Sources of information to assist you in narrowing the search for specific types of policies are included in the following chapters of this book.

Reducing Insurance Costs   The cost of a personal insurance program can be overwhelming unless you take care to keep expenses down. There are a number of things which can be done with all types of insurance to reduce costs. The most important ones are discussed in this section.

Use Deductibles   A deductible can be included in many types of insurance. The deductible you are probably most familiar with is the $50 deductible clause on auto collision insurance. With such a feature, an insured suffering $500 of auto damages would have to pay $50 and the insurance company would pay the remainder.

Deductibles are available on auto collision and comprehensive insurance, health insurance, and homeowners property insurance. The amount deductible can usually be increased or decreased at the policyholder's request. Increasing the deductible amount will lower the policy premium. It places the insured in the position of self-insuring against small losses. However, within 2 years, the amount saved from a higher deductible will usually cover a small loss.

For example, on auto collision insurance it is possible to reduce the premium by $35 annually when the deductible is increased from $50 to $100. You would have to have an accident every 1.42 years to be better off with $50 deductible collision. That, of course, assumes that with such a driving record you would still be able to get insurance at the same rates. Most likely, your coverage would be canceled or the rates increased substantially. If the driver who has a fender bender about every 10 years elects the higher deductible, the total insurance costs will be reduced by $300 over that period. While saving $35 annually for 10 years, or $350, the driver, out of that saving, will have to pay about $50 for the one accident that has occurred.

Analyzing the cost saving with deductibles applies to homeowners insurance as well as collision insurance.

Even higher deductibles, such as $250 or $500, may be appropriate in certain situations. You should evaluate your circumstances carefully to see whether you should specify a higher deductible for your policies. Do not expect a great deal of help from agents in this decision. The lower premium offered by the higher deductible will reduce the agent's income. An agent handling 1,000 auto insurance customers could conceivably see his or her commission income drop by $5,000, if every client changed from $50 to $100 deductible collision coverage. If you appear knowledgeable about your insurance needs, the agent will probably go along with your decision to increase the deductible. A bit of hesitancy on your part will give the agent a chance to extol the virtues of low deductibles. Stick by your decision to raise the deductible—it will save you money in the long run.

Exhibit 13–4 shows the relationship between the annual premium for a comprehensive health insurance policy and the amount of the deductible. A similar relationship exists for automobile collision insurance and homeowners

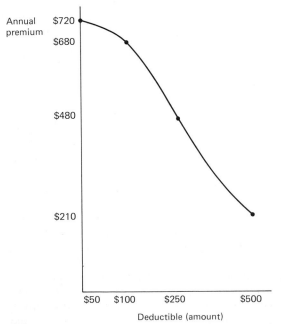

Exhibit 13-4   The Cost of Health Insurance with Various Deductible Provisions

insurance although the annual premiums and deductibles are not quite the same.

Be Self-Insuring Do not buy insurance for small losses; for example, do not buy coverage on contact lenses. A typical policy to reimburse for the loss of a lens costs about $25 per year. The replacement cost of a lens is about $25. Unless you lose more than one lens a year, you will be better off insuring yourself, that is, paying for a new lens yourself when you lose one.

The extent to which you can self-insure will be directly determined by the amount of money you have in your emergency reserve and short-term savings program. Until you build up your savings, you should probably overinsure to be protected against losses you cannot readily pay for yourself. However, in general, if you can afford the cost of the insurance for small losses, you can probably afford to self-insure against those losses. After accumulating an adequate emergency fund, it may be possible to stop buying auto collision insurance and to increase the deductible on your homeowners policy to $500.

Pay Premiums Annually Insurance premiums are set as annual rates. Often the company will bill you semiannually, or even monthly. It may seem like a good idea to spread out your payments. By doing so, however, your insurance will always cost more. Insurance companies add to the premiums a service charge if you make payments semiannually, quarterly, or monthly. The interest you might earn by not paying the full premium in one payment really does not offset the charge levied for the more frequent billings. By paying premiums annually, you could save several dollars or much more, depending on the total amount of the insurance premiums involved.

Try Buying Direct There are a number of places where you can save money by purchasing insurance directly from a company, rather than going through an agent. The companies which deal directly do not have agents, so you must seek them out. Sometimes dealing directly will not save you money; many times, however, it will, and it is worthwhile investigating.

1 *Life insurance.* In Wisconsin the state runs a life fund and amounts up to $10,000 may be purchased at very low rates. In Massachusetts, Connecticut, and New York, low-cost life insurance is offered through savings banks. For educators, the Teachers Insurance and Annuity Association (TIAA) offers low-cost life insurance on a direct basis. Also, many professional associations and college alumni groups are making insurance available to their members at extremely competitive rates.

2 *Health insurance.* Blue Cross–Blue Shield is a direct writer of health insurance. The rates may be higher than some competing private carriers. However, the policies are well designed and represent good health insurance coverage for most people. As your age increases, the rates on Blue Cross–Blue Shield become even more favorable. Some insurance experts suggest that when you are under thirty-five, private carriers may be more competitive, while after 35, you will find it advantageous to buy your health insurance from Blue Cross–Blue Shield.

3 *Auto insurance.* A few companies sell insurance through their own

salaried sales personnel. The rates for these direct policies may be below the rates for companies selling through commission agents.

An innovation in auto insurance is group coverage. Several insurance companies have started selling group auto insurance and a number of employers are making it available as an employee fringe benefit. The cost of group auto insurance can be substantially below the cost of individual policies. If it is available to you, strongly consider it.

Use Group Insurance Group insurance is usually less expensive and better than individual policies. As just mentioned, many companies provide group insurance programs for their employees as part of a fringe-benefit program. If the employee contributes to the cost, he or she has the option of accepting or rejecting the coverage. Probably the only reason to reject available group coverage is lack of need. A woman may not need health insurance if she is covered by her husband's policy, or a bachelor may find little need for life insurance. If you need insurance, the group plan will undoubtedly be less expensive and you should buy it.

Nevertheless, there are a few words of caution about group insurance. The principal drawback is termination of coverage when you leave the group, that is, when you leave your job. Your new employer may not have a group insurance program, or if so, you may not be eligible to participate in the plan until after a specified period. Therefore, you may be left with serious gaps in your insurance program which could be difficult to fill. The danger can be minimized if you take a few precautionary steps before you change jobs. Make sure you understand the group plan's provisions for converting to individual policies. Then, before leaving an employer, you can take the steps to convert your group coverage to an individual policy and/or purchase coverage to fill the gaps created by the termination of the group insurance.

Buy Big Policies Quantity discounts are available on some types of insurance. Life insurance is a prime example where savings can be realized by buying large policies. A $50,000 life insurance policy will cost less than five $10,000 policies. Look into the possibility, when buying insurance, of getting preferred rates by buying high-limit coverages.

When to Review Your Insurance

Your insurance program is not static. It should change as your needs change. As a good rule of thumb, you should contact your life insurance agent or property insurance agent, depending on the insurance affected, when you do any of the following things: (1) get married, (2) get divorced, (3) have children, (4) buy a house, (5) move, (6) buy a boat, a car, or other major purchase, or (7) change jobs. In addition, it is wise to reassess insurance needs every 2 or 3 years, even if no major changes have taken place.

Collecting Insurance Claims

The ultimate purpose of insurance is to reimburse you for loss or damages. But you must make a claim to collect the reimbursement. Paradoxically, one of the best pieces of advice that can be given is, do not submit all claims. Technically, you may be entitled to reimbursement for small losses, but in the long run you will be better off ignoring them. For example, if you have $100 deductible collision insurance and you find your car in the parking lot at the supermarket with fender damage that costs $135 to repair, the insurance company will pay $35 of the loss. If you collect the $35, you will have a claim on your record which may boost your premium by more than the amount you received. Another area where people often make claims they should ignore is for small losses covered by their homeowners policy. If $120 of lawn furniture is stolen, they submit a claim for $20 ($100 deductible for theft). The companies consider these to be nuisance claims and will cancel the policy of someone who submits such claims too often. Think twice before you make a claim. Is it worth the possibility of higher rates or a canceled policy? If the answer is no, absorb the loss yourself.

Any claim should be accompanied with complete documentation. Auto claims are the ones which require the greatest care since the accident may involve some measure of legal negligence. In the event of an auto accident, care should be taken to get the names and addresses of all witnesses; they can be crucial to whether or not you collect.

Health claims should be supported with receipted bills for services. It is also important to know when the claim should be submitted directly by the doctor or hospital.

Disability income claims depend heavily on statements by attending physicians. The start of the disability should be clearly documented since benefits will not start until a waiting period has expired. Without an accurate record which precisely determines the beginning of the disability, the start of the waiting period will be difficult to determine.

Life insurance claims must include the death certificate for the insured, and, surprisingly, some proof of birth, preferably a registered birth certificate. This is necessary since premiums for life insurance are based on a person's age at the time the policy was issued. An understatement of age means that policy benefits are overstated and ultimately must be reduced. The companies are willing to accept questionable proof of birth when selling the policy, but require accurate proof when paying the proceeds.

SUMMARY

1   Insurance may be purchased to protect against the possibility of loss from a pure risk. A pure risk is one which does not have the possibility of gain. Speculative risks possess the possibility of both loss and gain.
2   Insurance indemnifies against loss. That is, it will only pay benefits up to the amount of the loss. It is not possible to make money by overinsuring a property.
3   If you own more than two policies for the same purpose, any reimbursement will be paid on a prorata basis (shared according to the amount they have insured) by the insurers.
4   The primary purpose of insurance is to protect against large losses.
5   The most common mistake people make is overinsuring or underinsuring. It is possible to be both underinsured and overinsured at the same time.
6   Personal risk management has four steps. They are: (a) risk identification, (b) risk evaluation, (c) determination of whether to buy insurance, and (d) selection of the right insurance coverage.
7   When buying insurance, care should be taken in selecting qualified agents and buying from financially sound insurance companies.
8   Insurance companies are organized as either stock insurance companies or mutual insurance companies. Stock companies distribute profits (the overcharge of premiums) to the stockholders. Mutual companies distribute the overcharge to the policyholders, thus reducing the cost of insurance.
9   Deductible clauses (an amount you must pay before collecting) can be used to substantially reduce insurance costs.
10   Other ways to save insurance dollars are: (a) be self-insuring, (b) pay premiums annually, (c) buy insurance directly from the companies, (d) rely heavily on group insurance, and (e) buy large policies.
11   Your insurance program should be reviewed both periodically and when you experience a major event, such as a major purchase, marriage, or the birth of a child.
12   The ultimate purpose of insurance is to reimburse you for loss. Paradoxically, there are many instances where claims for small losses should not be submitted.

REVIEW YOUR UNDERSTANDING OF

Pure risks	Risk management
Speculative risks	Risk identification
Indemnification	Risk evaluation
Deductibles	Risk retention
Risk exposure	Risk transfer
Self-insurance	Policy selection

DISCUSSION QUESTIONS

1 What are the four basic steps in risk management? Which of them do you feel is the most important? Why?
2 What are deductibles? How can they be used to minimize insurance costs?
3 What factor is the most important in determining whether a risk should be retained or transferred? Give an example of a risk that may be retained, then one of a risk that should be transferred.
4 What insurance protection should be purchased first by most people? List the coverages, in order of importance, that you believe a young family man should have.
5 What impact does increasing the deductible have on total risk exposure?
6 What are the specific factors you feel are most important in selecting insurance agents?
7 What are the two most important factors in selecting an insurance company?
8 Under what conditions should your insurance program be reviewed? Name specific events that would make you reassess your life insurance program; your homeowners insurance; your health insurance.
9 When should you not submit a claim for insurance even though you are entitled to do so?
10 How would you analyze a situation to determine whether a claim should be submitted?

CASE PROBLEM

Gus Zorba has decided to reevaluate his insurance program. He is particularly concerned with his auto and homeowners policies. Currently, he has $50 deductibles on both and feels that may be excessive. Gus has a savings account of $4,000, which is equal to about 4 months' take-home pay, and a checking account with a $500 balance. These are his total financial resources. His homeowners insurance could be reduced by $20 annually with a $250 deductible; his auto policy would show a $35 saving with a $100 deductible; a $40 saving with a $250 deductible and an $85 saving if the deductible is eliminated. Gus owns a 7-year-old car with a book value of $500. He has a good driving record. He had one accident 5 years ago with total damage of $250.

a Evaluate Gus's risk exposure on both policies.
b Evaluate his new risk exposure if he takes (1) the $250 homeowners deductible and $100 auto deductible, (2) the $250 auto deductible, or (3) elimination of the auto deductible.
c What course of action do you recommend for Gus?

RECOMMENDED READINGS

Books

Deneberg, Herbert S., *The Insurance Trap*. New York: Western Publishing Company, Inc., 1972.
 This is a nontechnical, well-presented discussion of the family insurance decision. It spells out the need for insurance and the major pitfalls in buying insurance, exposes insurance schemes and frauds, and advises how to avoid them.

Chapter 14

Life Insurance and Income Maintenance

After completing this chapter you should be able to:

explain the differences among the major types of life insurance contracts.

decide which type of insurance policy is most appropriate for your circumstances.

recall the standard provisions of the most commonly purchased insurance policies.

decide which of the optional policy provisions you should consider when buying life insurance.

recall the differences between participating and nonparticipating insurance contracts.

recall the different ways insurance proceeds can be paid to beneficiaries.

explain the major tax features of life insurance contracts.

explain the technical details of the beneficiary and ownership provisions of an insurance contract.

develop an insurance program for yourself which accurately reflects the amount of protection you actually need.

illustrate how to coordinate social security benefits with a life insurance program.

explain the impact of inflation on an individual's insurance program.

explain why disability income protection is often more important for an individual than life insurance coverage.

select a good insurance agent.

recall the misleading and unwarranted claims and advice about insurance protection.

recall the sources of life insurance cost rankings.

Life insurance is one of the most misunderstood, poorly managed, and often wasteful uses of a family's income. Many people who should have substantial amounts of protection are underinsured, unfortunately. And there are others who have too much life insurance and do not need it. What makes it so difficult for people to evaluate life insurance properly is the existence of so many different forms of life insurance offered by more than 1,800 companies. Some policies are excellent, whereas others provide very poor insurance protection. Moreover, the cost of competing life insurance contracts varies substantially among companies.

The purposes of this chapter are to explain the basics of life insurance, to develop a framework for calculating the amount of insurance you need (if any), and to provide guidelines for buying the protection at the lowest possible cost.

TYPES OF INSURANCE CONTRACTS

Much of the confusion about life insurance arises from the many different types of policies. Some life insurance policies provide only insurance protection. Other types provide protection and also build a cash value, which is similar to a savings account. The term of a life insurance policy can be a person's lifetime or a specific period, such as 20 years.

By understanding the characteristics of the different insurance contracts, you will find it much easier to decide which policy provides the best protection for your specific circumstances.

Term Insurance   Term insurance is the most basic form of life insurance and the easiest to understand. A simple example will show how it works. Assume that 1,000 people get together and agree that, as a group, they will pay $1,000 to the closest relative of each group member who dies that year. If each member is 30 years old, then, based on past experience, three of the people can be expected to die during the year. In order to pay the $1,000 to each of their three relatives as agreed, $3 must be collected from each individual at the beginning of the year, making $3,000 available for the payments. Now assume another group of 1,000 40-year-olds makes the same agreement. But because the members of this group are older, the likelihood of their death is higher. Consequently, the charge for the insurance for this group will be higher. A policy based on this type of calculation is known as *term insurance*; in this example, the term is 1 year.

Term insurance contracts are offered for terms of 1 year, 5 years, 10 years, 20 years, and term to 65, that is, insurance from the individual's current age until 65 years of age. This type of insurance is also available as decreasing term insurance where the face amount of the policy declines during the period the insurance is in force. Term insurance should be automatically renewable (except for term to 65 and decreasing term) and convertible into whole life insurance (which is explained next) at the option of the insured. Term insurance is often sold as a supplement to other insurance policies. When it is attached to another contract, it is referred to as a *rider*. The rider may be either level term (1 year, 5 years, etc.) or decreasing term insurance.

Term insurance is the best life insurance buy for most people. It provides the maximum amount of protection at the minimum cost during the period when insurance is most important.

Whole Life Insurance   Whole life insurance, or straight life or ordinary life as it is often called, is the policy familiar to most people. Under the basic whole life policy, premiums are payable during the insured's lifetime and protection at the face amount of insurance continues as long as the premiums are paid.

Unlike term insurance, whole life policies build a cash value. Therefore, the policy provides both insurance protection and a method of forced savings. Unlike term insurance, the premium on whole life policies remains constant during the life of the insured.

For the same amount of insurance, the premium for term insurance will be less than the premium for whole life until the insured person is about age 55. After age 55, the cost of term insurance escalates quite rapidly.

The buildup in the cash value for a whole life contract occurs because the premium exceeds the insurance costs during the early years of the policy. For example, at age 25 the premium for whole life may be $14 per year and the premium for term insurance $2. The difference ($12) represents the amount of "overcharge" on the whole life policy. Most of the overcharge goes into the cash value or savings element of the whole life policy. It is this overcharge in the early years which permits the insurance company to charge the same premium during the entire life of the insured. In effect, the policyholder pays more than the insurance cost at the beginning of the policy and less than the insurance cost during the later years.

Exhibit 14–1 shows the relationship between the whole life premium and the cost of term insurance for a man 25.

Term versus Whole Life   Insurance advocates recommend whole life policies for a number of reasons: The premium remains level over the life of the contract; insurance protection continues after age 65; and the policy builds a cash value. However, we feel that none of these is a particularly good reason to buy whole life insurance. The premium for term insurance is less than for whole life, through age 55. Most people will have a sharply reduced need for insurance after that age. Thus, the fact that term premiums increase at that age is of little concern. If you buy whole life solely to obtain a level premium, you will pay far more for your whole life premiums than you would for term premiums up to age 55 (see Exhibit 14–1). After that age, when the whole life premiums will be lower than the term premiums, you probably would not need the insurance. The need for life insurance after reaching age 65 is even more questionable. Insurance is meant to replace a person's earning power: few people over 65 need that protection. Finally, a whole life policy has a cash value only because the company has overcharged you for the insurance. In most cases, you would be better off buying term insurance and investing the money you save through its lower cost. The savings feature of whole life policies represents a bad investment. Even with better policies, the return over an extended period from cash value insurance is about 4.5 percent. Many policies have returns which fall below this modest level.

Limited Pay Life Policies   An apparent disadvantage of whole life policies is that the insured must pay premiums for his or her entire lifetime. People

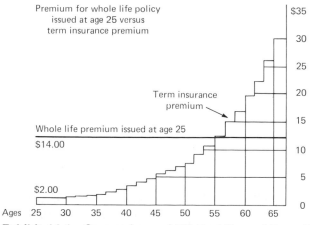

Exhibit 14-1   Comparison of Whole Life and Term Premiums for $1,000 Insurance

wanting protection after reaching age 65 would like the premiums to stop at that point. The industry has developed policies, such as "20 pay life" and "life to 65," where the premium is payable for a shorter period while protection continues until the insured reaches one hundred years of age or dies. In order to build the cash value and provide protection, the company must charge higher premiums during the abbreviated premium period. Because the premiums are higher for a limited pay life policy than for whole life for the same face amount of insurance, limited pay life policies represent an unwise insurance purchase. People who want continued protection until after they reach age 65 without having to continue to make premium payments can lapse a whole life policy for paid-up insurance. This is discussed under the nonforfeiture options in the next section of this chapter.

Endowment Policies　　Endowment insurance provides that the face amount be paid at the end of a definite period, such as 20 or 30 years or at the time of the insured's death, whichever occurs first. The policy rapidly builds a cash value which equals the face amount at the maturity of the contract. Because of the limited-term nature of the policy and the need to build a large cash value in a short time period, the cost of protection with endowments is extremely high.

An endowment policy is an inappropriate insurance choice for most people. The primary purpose of insurance is to provide maximum protection. Endowments really provide maximum savings and minimum protection. Endowments have been sold to fund specific objectives, such as providing for a college education. If the insured (the family's breadwinner) dies prematurely, the face amount payable at death will provide the funds. If the insured survives, the cash value payable at maturity will provide the funds. Yet, the insured can obtain more protection with a modest reduction in cash value by purchasing a whole life policy. Even more protection, at a lower cost, could be obtained by purchasing term insurance.

Comparing the Four Types of Insurance　　The major differences between the four basic types of insurance contracts are summarized in Exhibit 14–2.

Exhibit 14-2　Features of Basic Life Insurance Policies

Type	Duration	Cash value	Cost
Term	1 year, 5 years, 20 years; usually renewable	None	Increases each time policy is renewed. Initially, it is very low.
Whole life	Until age 100, or death	Yes	Level premium for life of contract.
Limited payment life	Until age 100, or death	Yes	Level premium for specific period. Policy is paid up at end of premium period.
Endowment	10 years, 20 years, to age 65	Yes	Level premium, much higher than cost of whole life or term insurance.

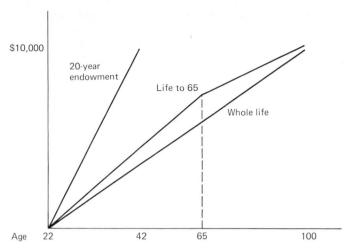

Exhibit 14-3   Buildup of Cash Surrender Values for Typical Policies

The difference in cash surrender values for whole life, life to 65, and a 20-year endowment all issued at age 22 is shown in Exhibit 14–3. For the same face amount, life to 65 builds a cash value faster than whole life, and 20-year endowment builds its cash value even faster. That is why life to 65 costs more than whole life, and 20-year endowment costs the most.

Exhibit 14–4 shows the typical cost for a $10,000 policy issued to an insured person between ages 20 and 25 for different types of coverage. The important thing to note from this table is the low relative cost of the term and whole life policies. Also, it should be emphasized that these are approximate rates. There is a wide variance in actual rates among insurance companies.

Term or Whole Life Is Best   Term offers the maximum protection at the lowest cost. Whole life provides both insurance and savings. You can create

Exhibit 14-4   Approximate Annual Premiums for $10,000 of Insurance*

Type of policy	Age at which policy is issued					
	20	21	22	23	24	25
5-year term (renewable and convertible)	$ 52.80	$ 52.90	$ 53.00	$ 53.10	$ 53.20	$ 53.50
Straight life	115.00	118.70	122.20	125.70	129.50	133.50
Life paid up at 65	126.60	130.50	134.60	139.00	143.70	148.60
20-payment life	198.40	202.60	206.90	211.30	215.90	220.70
Retirement income at 65	176.90	184.10	191.70	199.70	208.20	217.20
20-year endowment	425.60	425.70	426.00	426.20	426.60	426.90

*Rates shown are approximate premium rates for $10,000 of life insurance protection for men. Rates of "participating" policies would be higher, but the cost would be lowered by annual dividends. "Nonparticipating" policy premium rates would be somewhat lower than those shown and no dividends would be paid. Measured in cost per $1,000 of insurance, policies under $10,000 would be a little higher in premium rates and lower for $25,000 and over. Policies for women are at lower rates in recognition of their mortality rates.

Source: Institute of Life Insurance. New York, 1974.

Exhibit 14-5   Cost and Investment Comparison of Term and Whole Life Policies Issued at Age 25 and Held to Age 65

Policy	Amount	Annual premium	Cash value at 65
Whole life	$25,000	$346.25	$14,250
Term (to 65 with level premium)	$25,000	$146.50	$0
Savings account at 7 percent	—	$199.75 (difference between premiums)	$41,256

your own whole life policy by purchasing term insurance and investing the difference between the costs of term and whole life policies. The advantage of doing so may be substantial. Results comparing a typical term and whole life policy are shown in Exhibit 14–5.

By investing the difference in cost, you will have almost 3 times more cash at age 65 than the cash value of a whole life policy ($41,256 versus $14,250). Or, if you invest one-third the annual difference in cost between whole life and term and you buy term insurance, then, through age 65, you will have about the same coverage and same cash value as with whole life, but at less total cost. However, you must save automatically and faithfully to accumulate the cash value.

> **Strategy: Term and whole life represent the best insurance buys. Limited pay life and endowment policies are a bad insurance buy for most people. The primary purpose of insurance is protection. Term and whole life provide the greatest protection for the lowest dollar outlay. Of the two, term is preferable because it provides the maximum protection at the lowest cost.**

Special Policy Forms

Most insurance contracts represent combinations of the three basic policies discussed previously. In this section we will outline the provisions of the more common package life policies offered by the insurance industry.

Family Income Policy   This is a combination of whole life and decreasing term insurance. For example, assume the decreasing term part of the policy is for 20 years and the insured dies after 10 years. Under the term portion of the policy, the insurance company will make regular payments to the beneficiaries for the remaining 10 years. Each payment consists of principal from the decreasing term portion of the policy and interest from the face amount of the whole life portion of the policy. At the end of the 10 years, the entire face amount of the whole life portion of the policy is paid to the beneficiaries.

Family Income Rider   The family income rider is virtually the same as the family income policy, except that the face amount of the whole life policy is payable at the time of the death of the insured. Since the face amount has been paid and is no longer available to earn interest, to have income payments from the family income rider equal to those under the family income policy, the amount of the term rider must be larger, and consequently requires a larger premium.

Family Maintenance Policy   With the family income policy and family income rider, the length of time the beneficiaries receive payments is determined by the length of time between purchase of the policy and the death of the insured. For example, if the decreasing term is for 20 years and the insured dies after the first year, the payments will be made for 19 years; if the insured dies after 18 years, payments will be made for 2 years. With the family maintenance policy, the payments are made for a specified length of time beginning with the insured's death. To accomplish this, the term rider is level term, not decreasing term, and it means that the premiums are even higher than for the family income rider. The face amount of the policy is payable in one entire sum at the end of the income period. A pictorial representation of these three types of policies is given in Exhibit 14–6

> **Strategy: Of the three family income type policies, the *family income policy* probably provides the best insurance buy for most people. If there is the need for a lump-sum settlement, then the *family income rider* is the next best buy. The *family maintenance policy* represents the least attractive alternative and should be considered only under unusual circumstances.**

Family Protection Policy   As the name implies, this policy provides insurance coverage on all members of the family. The coverage on the husband is whole life, and on the wife and children it is term insurance. The policy seems to be attractive in insuring the whole family. Remember, though, the

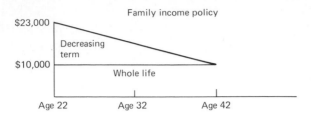

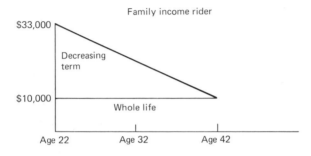

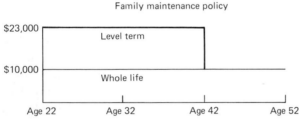

**Exhibit 14-6   Family Income Policy, Family Income Rider, and Family Mainte-
nance Policy**

primary purpose of insurance is to replace the breadwinner's income. There is
little economic reason to insure the lives of children. In buying the family
protection policy, premium dollars which should be concentrated on coverage
to replace lost income are spread over more lives, thus giving less protection
where it is most necessary. A family protection policy should be considered
only when the breadwinner is fully insured. If the breadwinner cannot afford
adequate insurance, the family protection policy should never be purchased.

There are many other policies which a sales agent may try to sell. The
provisions may seem extremely attractive. In all cases the benefits have a cost.
A good rule of thumb in buying insurance is, "Keep it simple." Adequate
protection is available with either term or whole life or a combination of the
two. Retirement income policies, "return of premium" policies, "modified
whole life" or "juvenile insurance" are getting away from the basic purpose of
insurance. In general, the more complex the policy, the more inappropriate it is
for most people.

MAJOR POLICY PROVISIONS

The insurance policy is a very technical instrument which has a number of important provisions that affect the insured and beneficiaries protected by the contract. There are two basic types of provisions that you must consider: provisions that affect the policy while it is in force, and those that take effect at the termination of the insurance.

Beneficiaries, Ownership, and the Insured

Insurance policies have at least two, and often three, people designated in the contract: the insured, the beneficiary, and sometimes the owner of the policy. The insured is the person whose life is covered by the policy. Those individuals who will receive payments at the time of the insured's death are the beneficiaries. The owner of the policy is the person who may change the beneficiary or make any other changes permitted by the insurance company. Most commonly, the person who owns the policy is the insured. But the beneficiary, or some other individual, may be the owner. Ownership often involves tax considerations because the proceeds of the insurance will be in the insured's estate if he or she is the owner. Often, a husband will transfer ownership to his wife (the beneficiary) to avoid these tax consequences.

Every policy should have a primary and a secondary beneficiary. If children are named as beneficiaries, some sort of guardianship or trustee arrangement is also necessary. This is done outside the provisions of the insurance contract. Also, if children are named as beneficiaries, the beneficiary clause should include any unborn children of the marriage. Without this provision, if a policy is issued naming only Johnny and Susy as beneficiaries, and Billy is subsequently born, he will be excluded from benefits. For most people, deciding on the beneficiaries is relatively uncomplicated. However, it is a decision which should be reevaluated every few years to make sure that as circumstances change, the beneficiary is still appropriate.

Nonforfeiture Options

Included in whole life contracts are nonforfeiture provisions which assure the cash value of the policy to the insured in the event of nonpayment of premium. The three basic nonforfeiture options are: (1) to surrender for cash, (2) to convert to paid-up insurance, and (3) to use the cash value to purchase extended term insurance. Some contracts also have automatic premium loans which can be considered a nonforfeiture option.

Cash Surrender Value   With this option the owner receives a check for the cash value of the policy upon surrendering the policy. The advantage of this option is the receipt of the cash. The disadvantage is the fact that the insurance protection ceases with the surrender of the policy. Only when the need for any protection has ceased should this option be selected.

Paid-up Insurance   The owner has the option of converting any whole life policy to paid-up status. The company takes the accumulated cash value from the current policy and uses it as a single premium to purchase a new policy requiring no additional payments. By electing this nonforfeiture provision, the insured continues to receive protection, although it is reduced, and no longer pays any premiums. This option represents a good compromise between receipt of the cash surrender value and purchase of extended term insurance, described in the next section.

Extended Term Insurance   Under this option the cash value is used to purchase term insurance equal to the policy's face amount for as long as the cash will permit. For example, a person age 45 with a $10,000 policy having a cash surrender value of $3,000 may be able to purchase extended term insurance in the amount of $10,000 for 20 years without additional premium payments. This option is desirable when maximum protection must be continued. Its disadvantages are the use of the cash value and the limited duration of the protection. Once the extended term period is over, the policy expires with no value.

In most instances, extended term is selected by individuals who know they are going to die in a short time; they withhold payments on their whole life policies and exercise the extended term option. The insurance companies are faced with the problem of adverse selection. That is, poorer risks select this cheaper form of insurance. Consequently, the rate per $1,000 is somewhat higher for extended term insurance purchased under this option than it is for term insurance purchased under ordinary circumstances.

Exhibit 14–7 gives approximate values for the three nonforfeiture options at various ages for a whole life policy issued to a person age 20.

Automatic Premium Loan   The automatic premium loan is sometimes considered a special nonforfeiture option. With this feature, when a premium payment is missed, the insurance company automatically borrows the amount of the payment from the cash value of the policy to keep the contract in force. For example, a $10,000 policy with a $200 annual premium and $3,000 of cash value would borrow the premium from the cash value. After one such automatic premium loan, if the insured should die, the company would pay $10,000 less the $200 loan, or $9,800, or if the insured should cash in the policy, the cash value would be about $2,800.

Exhibit 14-7 Approximate Nonforfeiture Values per $10,000 of Insurance for a Straight Life Insurance Policy Issued at Age 20

Premiums paid to age	Cash value	Paid-up insurance	Extended term insurance
25	$ 210	$ 810	6 yrs.—219 days
30	760	2,520	20 yrs.—106 days
40	2,180	5,370	24 yrs.—349 days
65	5,910	8,570	15 yrs.—348 days

Source: Institute of Life Insurance. New York, 1974.

Policy Loan Provisions

A supposed benefit of cash value insurance is the provision permitting the policyholder to borrow up to 95 percent of the cash value at 5 percent or 6 percent simple interest. The benefit is somewhat misleading, since the insured is, in fact, borrowing his or her own money. For example, an individual who has a $10,000 policy with $3,000 of accumulated cash value may borrow $2,850 without a credit investigation, and with no stipulated payment schedule. If the insured should die while a loan is outstanding, the face amount will be reduced by the amount of the indebtedness. In this example, the beneficiary would receive $7,150 in the event of the insured's death.

Special Policy Provisions

Buying a whole life insurance policy is similar to buying a new car. You can buy a stripped-down model or one having special options which will cost substantially more. Unlike the special options on a car which are paid for only once, the special features on a life insurance policy must be paid for every year for as long as you have the policy. As a result, it is very important to analyze the options carefully when buying a policy. The most common extra provisions are: (1) waiver of premium, (2) guaranteed reinsurability, and (3) accidental death benefit.

Waiver of Premium By paying for this option, you obtain the additional protection that should you become disabled and no longer can work, the insurance company will pay the premiums on your policy. The cost of this benefit is not large and is probably worthwhile for most people.

Guaranteed Reinsurability This option guarantees you the right to purchase additional life insurance, at specified intervals for some multiple of the face amount of the original policy, without providing evidence of insurability. Thus, if you become incurably ill after buying the initial policy, you will still be able to purchase additional insurance at standard rates in the future. The feature is most valuable for younger people who are beginning an insurance program by purchasing a portion of their needs and who expect to increase their insurance later when they can afford it. There is no need to elect this option if you are buying all the insurance you will ever need.

Accidental Death Benefit This feature, also referred to as double indemnity or triple indemnity, stipulates that if, prior to a certain age (usually 65), the insured is killed in an accident, the company will pay double the face amount of the policy. Moreover, if the accident occurs on a regularly scheduled common carrier, such as a plane or bus, the company will pay 3 times the face amount. For example, the beneficiary of a person with a $10,000 policy who is killed in a plane crash on a regularly scheduled flight would receive not $10,000 but $30,000.

This option has a great deal of appeal. For a very small extra premium, the face amount of the policy can be doubled or tripled. However, with a soundly constructed insurance program, the extra coverage is unnecessary. The gamble may seem pretty good, yet most people should not purchase this policy extra.

> **Strategy: Waiver of premium and guaranteed reinsurability represent worthwhile additions to your insurance program. The accidental death benefit is not appropriate if the basic coverage of your policy provides all the necessary protection.**

Participating and Nonparticipating Insurance

The life insurance industry consists of two major types of organizations: stock insurance companies, which are owned by stockholders, and mutual companies, which are owned by the policyholders. Any profit earned by a stock company accrues to the company's shareholders, whereas, with a mutual company, the profit belongs to the policyholders. Generally, stock companies issue nonparticipating policies; mutual companies issue participating contracts.

Participating policies are insurance contracts which return any premium overcharges to the policyholders in the form of *nontaxable* dividends. Since the premiums for insurance are based on estimates, it is impossible to set the premium in advance at the exact figure the insurance will finally cost. Interest earnings, actual mortality experience, and expense of operations, the three factors that determine insurance costs, are unknown and only approximately estimated at the time the insurance is sold. Mutual companies approximate these costs with an overestimate, and when the actual costs are determined at the end of the year, the overcharges are returned to the policyholders in the form of dividends.

Nonparticipating policies do not rebate any overcharges to the policyholder. Any charges in excess of the true cost of the insurance accrue for the benefit of the stockholders of the insurance company, not the policyholders.

Usually, the initial premium will be lower for a nonparticipating policy. However, in the long run, the participating policies usually have a lower net cost, resulting from the dividend payments. In selecting an insurance company, you should be careful not to be misled by the seemingly lower cost of the nonparticipating policies.

Dividend Options   The dividend paid on participating policies can be used in a number of ways. The available alternatives are: (1) payment in cash, (2) reduction of premium for the next period, (3) deposit with the company to earn interest, (4) purchase of paid-up additional insurance, and (5) purchase of 1-year term insurance to cover the cash value.

The last option is not available from all companies and the firms which offer it may impose different limitations. Consequently, it is important to be sure of the provisions before electing option 5.

While each of the options has something to recommend it, the only ones which should be seriously considered are options 2, reduction of premium, 3, purchase of paid-up additional insurance, and 5, purchase of term insurance. By using the dividend to reduce the premium, insurance costs can be minimized. This is desirable as long as adequate insurance has been purchased. By utilizing the dividends to purchase "paid-up ads" (the technical nickname) or term insurance, you can obtain increased insurance protection without additional cost.

Settlement Options

At the time a life insurance contract matures, either by death or surrender of the policy, the settlement can be made in a number of ways other than a lump-sum payment. Each of the alternatives has something to recommend it, but care should be exercised in selecting the best method for the individual situation.

Interest Option The proceeds are left on deposit with the insurance company and the company periodically pays the interest to the beneficiary. This is usually a temporary settlement until the beneficiary has had time to select the best option. Note: In the event the policy was surrendered rather than maturing as a result of the insured's death, the recipient of the income would be the owner.

Installments for a Fixed Period Under this settlement, the company agrees to make payments for a specified number of years or months until the total amount of the proceeds is exhausted. With a participating policy, this settlement option provides an additional advantage—during the payment period, company profits are added to the remaining balance to be paid.

This option would be appropriate for a beneficiary who can determine that the proceeds will provide sufficient regular income to support the family during the payment period. For example, a middle-aged widow must attend to several young teenage children and support their education. In 5 or 6 years when the children's education is complete and they are working, the widow, with a skill or trade, can return to work and support only herself. This option would not be appropriate for a beneficiary who needs an income for life because she or he cannot earn an income; the proceeds could be depleted while the beneficiary is still alive.

Installments of a Fixed Amount Installments of a fixed amount are just a minor variation of the previous option. Instead of specifying the number of periods, the beneficiary specifies the amount of each periodic payment and the payments will be made until the proceeds are depleted.

We cannot see any circumstances where this option would be superior to the installments for a fixed period.

The Life Options The previous three options are not designed to guarantee an income for the life of the beneficiary. Insurance companies using the same principles of risk sharing that are applicable in all other kinds of insurance can guarantee a life income for a beneficiary even if the beneficiary lives longer than the funds would provide. This is the case simply because some people will die before they have exhausted their funds. Some form of a life income option is desirable for people who need the security of a guaranteed lifetime income.

A straight life option guarantees the income for as long as the recipient lives. If an individual were to start receiving payments of $100 per month under this option, and should die after receiving one payment, most of the money would be lost. If the initial principal were $10,000, then $9,900 would revert to the insurance company upon the recipient's death. While this option provides the maximum monthly benefit of all settlement options guaranteed for an individual's lifetime, there is a distinct possibility that the recipient may die before payment of the original principal is completed. To avoid this, the life options can also be written with guaranteed payments for a stated period, such as 10 years, or with a lump-sum cash refund feature. With a guaranteed installment period, the monthly payment would continue to be made to another designated recipient for the duration of the 10 years. In the case above, if a lump-sum option is elected, $9,900 would be paid to the recipient's heirs.

The payment under the refund options is slightly smaller than would be received from a straight life option. It is advantageous, however, in that if the income recipient dies shortly after payments start, the principal amount will not be sacrificed but will be distributed to the recipient's heirs.

> **Strategy: Most individuals at or near retirement age should select one of the life options with a refund or guarantee feature. The nonlife options are suited for younger families to provide income for specific time periods, such as when children are in school.**

Taxes and Life Insurance

At the time of the insured's death, proceeds paid to the beneficiaries are exempt from federal and state income taxes. The proceeds are exempt from federal estate taxes if the policy was not owned by the insured. For example, if Harry Smith died leaving his children $100,000 of life insurance and his children owned the policy, estate taxes would not have to be paid. If Harry owned the policy, the $100,000 would have to be included in his gross estate for estate tax purposes.

If an insured surrenders a whole life policy for its cash value, there is no tax payable on the proceeds unless the cash value exceeds the gross premiums paid on the policy; then, only the excess would be taxable. For example, if Harry surrendered a policy and received $10,000, on which he had paid $300 per year for 30 years ($9,000), he would have a tax liability on $1,000 to be treated as ordinary income.

If Harry elected to convert the cash value to one of the settlement options, a portion of each payment he received would be considered taxable. Calculating how much is taxable is fairly complex. But, using the previous example, roughly 10 percent of each payment would have to be declared as ordinary income.

During the period that a policy is in force, the interest earnings that build up cash value are not subject to taxation. Only if the policy is surrendered and its cash value exceeds cost will there be a tax on the excess. However, in the event of the insured's death, those interest earnings will never be subject to income tax. The tax contingencies are summarized in Exhibit 14–8.

Strategy: If taxation is an important consideration in your insurance program, obtain the assistance of a qualified insurance agent and tax attorney or CPA. The issues are far too complex and changing to be handled by a nonprofessional.

DETERMINING INSURANCE REQUIREMENTS

How much insurance you decide to buy depends on your individual needs and value judgments. Sometimes value judgments override needs. If you decide that your family can manage without help if you die, the decision is your prerogative. Your family's needs may indicate otherwise, but you are still free to make such a choice.

In deciding how much insurance to buy, however, the decision should be based on sound calculations, not on simplistic rules such as "Buy insurance which is 2 times your annual income." There are now two generally accepted methods for calculating insurance requirements: the life value method, and the needs approach. Of the two, the needs approach is the better technique. However, both methods are discussed so that you will be aware of the limitations inherent in the life value method.

The Life Value Method

The value of a person's expected earnings until age 65 is termed the person's life value. These expected earnings are reduced by an interest factor to account for the fact that money received in future years is not equivalent to money received today. This calculation is known as present value. For example, at a 5

Exhibit 14-8   Tax Status of Life Insurance Proceeds

Event	Policy owned by	Income tax	Estate tax
Death of the insured	Insured	No	Will be included in insured's gross estate
Death of the insured	Beneficiary	No	No
Surrender for cash value	Anybody	On difference between total premiums paid and proceeds received	No
Surrender under settlement option	Anybody	Payments subject to tax if proceeds exceed premiums	No
Interest earned when policy is in force	Anybody	No	No

AS A MATTER OF FACT,
I WAS JUST THINKING
ABOUT NEEDING TO GET
MY LIFE INSURANCE
PROGRAM ORGANIZED...

percent annual interest rate, the life value of a man of 30 earning $15,000 per year is $245,610. Over the 35 years, the man actually earns $525,000. However, it would only take $245,610 invested at 5 percent annually to provide an income of $15,000 annually for 35 years. Looking at this another way, if he should die at age 30 and leave his family $245,610, the family members could invest the money in a savings account at 5 percent annual interest; they could have $15,000 each year for the next 35 years, at which time the initial $245,610 would be depleted. A portion of the payment they receive each year would come from interest and a portion would come from the principal amount.

The life value approach is an oversimplification of determining the right amount of insurance to buy because it does not relate insurance to the unique needs of the individual. There may be two people at the same age with exactly the same income whose insurance requirements are substantially different because of unusual family circumstances. For example, if John Smith, age 35, is making $15,000, has an invalid wife and four children including a handi-capped child, he will have vastly different requirements from those of Jim Brown, age 35, making the same salary and having one child and a wife who earns $11,000 per year as a truck driver.

The only useful purpose in looking at the life value approach is to get a quick approximation of insurance needs. A more valid approach to building an insurance program is based on determining your specific needs and the amount necessary to cover those needs.

The Needs Approach

The needs approach lists specific items which can be covered by life insurance. For most people these needs involve seven broad categories: (1) cleanup expenses, (2) mortgage redemption, (3) the family income period, (4) income for the middle years, (5) retirement income for your spouse, (6) an emergency fund, and (7) a college education fund. Insurance coverage for any specific needs not included in this list can be developed for each unique situation.

Using this list, we will develop a program of the insurance needs for Arnie Average. Arnie is 34 years old, his wife is 32, and he has two children ages 6 and 4. His current income is $18,000.

The level of protection he needs will be determined by his present standard of living and how much he feels he would like to provide for his family. The upper limit for this protection is determined by the amount that he can afford to spend for insurance premiums. Listed below are the amounts of insurance that Arnie feels are necessary in each of the seven categories.

Cleanup Expenses   Money should be readily available for the payment of (1) funeral expenses, (2) outstanding debts, and (3) medical bills incurred during the last illness. Since the family's income will stop with the death of the breadwinner, it makes a great deal of sense to provide a fund to cover both any outstanding consumer debts and the expenses directly related to the death of the insured.

Arnie has adequate health insurance to cover any medical expenses, and he estimates that $5,000 will be sufficient to pay off a bank loan of $3,500 for his car and to cover any funeral expenses.

Mortgage Redemption   In Arnie Average's case, this is the portion of his total insurance coverage which should be earmarked for paying off the outstanding home mortgage. Decreasing term insurance lends itself nicely to this need, although any part of his insurance could be set aside for this purpose.

Arnie currently owns a $35,000 house with $25,000 left to pay on the mortgage over the next 20 years. Thus, his need is for $25,000 of life insurance, decreasing over the next 20 years at a rate equivalent to the reduction in his mortgage.

Family Income Period   The family income period is the time when the children are under 18 and will qualify for social security payments. It is the time in a family's life when the need for insurance is most crucial. In most young families, when the breadwinner dies without life insurance, the wife would have to work and hire outside help to care for the children, or even worse, the family would have to go on welfare.

Being a prudent man, Arnie is concerned with seeing that his wife and children are sufficiently provided for in case of his death. He estimates that they can maintain their present standard of living with an income of $1,000 per month. This is somewhat below their present income. But since the family will have one less member (Arnie) and much of the income will be tax free, the $1,000 per month from his insurance is quite comparable to his present taxable income of $1,500 monthly.

Middle Years   The middle years are the period between the time when social security payments stop as the children reach age 18 and the time when social security survivors' benefits are available at age 60. All income during this period must be provided from life insurance or other investments.

With the increasing liberation of women in our society today, the need for insurance during the middle years is somewhat reduced. If a woman can work, there may be little need for any insurance. The most conservative plan would be to provide some income for this period in the event a wife cannot work because of a future disability or is unable to earn an adequate income for herself. Arnie feels that $600 per month is sufficient for his wife during the 13 years when social security is unavailable. Social security payments to his wife will stop when his youngest child reaches 18 years of age. At that time his wife will be 47 years old and her social security income will begin when she reaches 60.

Retirement Years   The retirement period starts at the point social security benefits are again available. The survivor's income during this period will come partially from the insurance program and partially from social security.

For young families, planning for the retirement years is probably the most difficult part of setting up their insurance program. It is always difficult to plan 30 years into the future. Circumstances may change so much that many of today's decisions will be of little value at a later date. However, this clearly illustrates the point that successful financial planning is a continuous process. Tough as making decisions may be, they must be made about future events. But they can be revised in light of changed circumstances. With this in mind, Arnie estimates that, under present conditions, $600 per month should provide sufficient retirement income for his wife. He recognizes that this figure will undoubtedly change. Presently, however, it seems like a prudent estimate.

His family's income needs, should Arnie die tomorrow, are graphically shown in Exhibit 14–9. The dashed line in Exhibit 14–9 shows the amount ($620) that we assume social security will contribute as survivors' benefits to

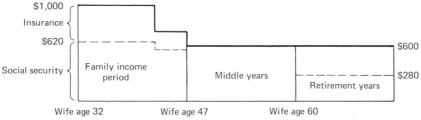

Exhibit 14-9   Arnie Average's Insurance Needs for Family Income Purposes

the income Arnie has specified for his family. (The amount available for each person is dependent on his or her income and the number of years worked under social security.) The remainder of the $1,000 per month specified for the family income period, $380, must be provided by insurance. The total amount for the middle years must be provided by insurance or investments.

Emergency Fund Good planning dictates that a family should have a liquid fund for emergencies. Arnie currently has $1,000 which he considers his emergency fund, but he believes that $3,000 would be a more prudent fund to leave his family. Consequently he should earmark $2,000 of insurance to the fund.

College Education Fund The need for a college education fund has diminished sharply now that social security benefits can be paid to full-time students between the ages of 18 and 22.

Arnie feels that both his children have the interest and capability to complete college successfully, and he would like them to be able to attend one of the better schools. With tuition and fees now running at around $5,000 per year, he needs a $40,000 education fund to see both of his children through 4 years of college. Since social security, at current levels, will provide benefits of approximately $22,000 to his children while they are in college, Arnie needs an additional $18,000 of insurance.

Exhibit 14–10 summarizes Arnie's insurance requirements for each of the categories listed in this section. Arnie's monthly requirements have been converted into total insurance amounts based on tables (called annuity tables) which show the amount of money required to provide a specified monthly income.

> **Strategy: In selecting insurance coverage, be sure to tailor the level of coverage directly to your needs. A good life insurance agent can assist you to determine your insurance needs.**

Warning: Problem Area Many companies have computer programs to calculate insurance requirements using the needs approach. However, if the amounts are specified by the agent, not by yourself, the amounts of insurance recommended by different firms may vary as much as 100 percent. One company may recommend $75,000 while another calculates that $150,000 is needed. If you use a computer analysis to determine your insurance requirements, make sure you specify the amounts in each needs category. By doing this, you will be able to directly compare costs and recommended coverages from several different companies.

Reassessing the Needs Approach The insurance program developed by Arnie Average makes assumptions which are crucial in determining how much coverage should be purchased. Perhaps such full coverage as Arnie's may be

Exhibit 14-10   Insurance for Arnie Average Based on His Stated Needs

Need	Amount	Amount currently provided	Social security benefits	Excess	Face amount of insurance
Cleanup fund	$ 5,000 (total)	—	$ 255	$ 4,745	$ 4,745
Mortgage redemption	25,000 (total)	—	—	25,000	25,000
Family income prior to age 45 (oldest child is 18)	1,000 (monthly)	—	620	380	} 35,000
prior to age 47 (youngest child is 18)	1,000 (monthly)	—	531	469	
Income for middle years	600 (monthly)	—	—	600	20,000
Retirement income	600 (monthly)	—	280	320	30,000
Emergency fund	3,000 (total)	$1,000	—	2,000	2,000
College fund	40,000 (total)	—	22,000	18,000	18,000
		Total insurance needs			$134,745
		Less: Current group insurance			15,000
					$119,745

unnecessary or too expensive for some families. Probably the wisest course is to develop the needs program with the full knowledge and agreement of both the husband and wife. Many couples will probably agree that certain portions of the insurance program could be eliminated or reduced without severe financial hardship. Perhaps the children can attend a local university and live at home, thus substantially reducing the need for a college fund. Or, a couple may feel that moving into a smaller house would not be a hardship in the event of the husband's death; thus, the need for mortgage redemption insurance could be reduced. All these are individual decisions which should be fully discussed.

Insurance and Inflation

A frequently raised question about insurance is whether the amount of insurance should be increased from time to time because of the impact of inflation on the purchasing power of the dollar. This is difficult to answer precisely for each situation, although there are two answers which may apply in general.

For the first answer, consider a case where an insured dies sometime after middle age, leaving the survivor $30,000 in insurance proceeds. The survivor may need regular income of $6,000 per year from the proceeds for only 5 years. Each year, inflation will reduce the purchasing power of the $6,000 income, but not drastically during the 5 years. Furthermore, the interest on the proceeds will tend to offset the effects of inflation over this short period. Therefore, for such cases an insured might not need to consider how inflation will affect the survivor's income.

For the second answer, consider a case where a young insured dies shortly after setting up an insurance program, leaving the survivor with $100,000 in proceeds. The survivor may need income from the proceeds for 30 years. A fixed income plan from the proceeds would provide roughly $8,000 (annual interest plus a portion of the principal amount) each year for 30 years. But here is a case where the purchasing power of the $8,000 would be drastically reduced, especially in later years. For any level of inflation, amounts that were adequate at the start of the period will be woefully small in 30 years. Increases in social security will provide some protection and maybe the new variable insurance contracts being pioneered by some companies will solve the rest of the problem. Nevertheless, short of initially providing extremely large—and costly—insurance, at the present time there seems to be no adequate solution to the problems imposed by inflation.

DISABILITY INCOME PROTECTION

Most people who buy life insurance seldom consider the need for also purchasing disability income protection. The possibility of being disabled during your working lifetime is extremely high: As many as one in three wage earners suffers some period of disability before reaching age 65. Just as much income can be lost because of disability as can be lost because of death. And

besides lost income, disability incurs costs which death does not: Medical costs may be high, and expenses for food and clothing will continue for the disabled person.

A calculation to determine disability income requirements is easier than the comparable calculation for life insurance. Benefits under disability income policies are stated in terms of monthly payments. Total family needs can be expressed as a monthly income requirement. Disability income protection can then be purchased for that amount. Just as with life insurance requirement calculations, value judgments must be made in determining how much monthly income a family will need.

Disability income protection can be purchased as a rider (option) on a whole life insurance policy or as a separate policy. When disability insurance is issued in conjunction with life insurance, the company agrees to pay a monthly disability benefit which is some percentage of the policy's face amount. A typical policy would provide a payment of $10 per month per $1,000 face amount of insurance. Thus, an individual with a $10,000 policy would receive $100 per month from that policy in the event he or she becomes disabled.

Whether disability income protection is obtained through life insurance or a separate disability income policy, there are three important factors in addition to cost which should be considered.

1   *The definition of disability.* Defining disability involves precise legal terminology which can vary widely among companies. Some policies specify that disability is the condition when a person cannot perform his or her normal occupation. Other policies are not so liberal, specifying disability as a condition in which a person cannot perform any kind of gainful employment.

2   *Duration of the benefits.* Is the policy designed to pay income for 1 year? 5 years? or for as long as the disability persists? or to age 65? A policy with a benefit period to age 65 does not cost much more than a policy with a 5-year benefit period, yet provides much better protection.

3   *The waiting period.* Do benefits start after 31 days—or 61, 91, 181, or 366 days—after the disability is incurred? The longer the waiting period, the smaller the cost of the policy for equivalent monthly income payments. The waiting period in effect acts as a deductible. With a longer waiting period, fewer benefits are payable. Moreover, because many disabilities are brief, a long waiting period will eliminate many of them.

Each of these three factors affects the cost of the policy. Generally, the more liberal the provisions, the greater the cost. Another factor which influences cost is the occupation of the insured. The cost of a policy providing $500 per month is substantially higher for a construction worker than for a high school teacher because the chance of disability is much higher in construction jobs.

John Swenson is an attorney, age 33, who has investigated disability income insurance for himself. A large life insurance company quoted him the cost for a straight disability income policy that would pay him 60 percent (the maximum) of his monthly salary of $1,800. The cost of the policy is $275 per year. The policy calls for a 366-day waiting period; that is, he would have to be considered disabled for a year before benefits would start. Payments would continue for as long as the disability lasts up until he reaches 65. A policy with payments for only 5 years would cost $232. Thus, for an additional $43 per year, John can increase his potential benefits by as much as 26 years.

> **Strategy: Disability income protection should be considered by everyone. If the decision is made to purchase a disability income policy, the benefit period should run to age 65. The waiting period should be the maximum time that you could live without the income from your job. It will depend on your emergency reserve and other investments.**

Coordinating Insurance and Social Security

The social security system, in addition to paying retirement benefits, also provides survivors and disability income payments. Coordinating an insurance program with social security payments is not complicated. All that you need to know is the benefit payable in the event of the insured's death or disability. An approximation of the amounts payable in various situations can be obtained from Exhibit 14–11. Because of eligibility provisions and different levels of earnings, the exact amount available to any individual should be determined with the assistance of a local social security office. It is important to determine the amount payable for your own situation because it will determine the amount of additional insurance which must be purchased to provide the total monthly income to meet your needs.

Selecting an Insurance Agent

The complexity of life insurance makes professional assistance very important. To determine the amount of your insurance, a competent life insurance agent should complete a questionnaire with the essential characteristics of the needs approach. The agent who fails to delve deeply into the client's personal financial affairs is more interested in selling a policy than in developing a total insurance program. Remember, the agent is not paid a salary but receives a commission on the amount of insurance sold. Sales will obviously be the agent's primary objective. Nevertheless, a good agent working for a good company will admit that additional insurance is unnecessary when that is true. Finding a good agent requires more than recommendations from friends and relatives. Remember they may be making the same mistakes you are trying to avoid. Some of the most important things to consider in selecting an agent are discussed in this section.

Affiliation with a Large, Reputable Insurance Company   Good agents seem to gravitate toward the better and larger companies simply because it is easier to sell for a well-known firm than for a small unknown organization, and as a result, they earn more.

Exhibit 14-11 Examples of Monthly Social Security Benefits

Qualified beneficiary	$923 or less	$3,000	$4,200	$5,400	$6,600	$7,800	$9,000	$10,800	$12,000
					Average yearly earnings after 1950*				
Disabled worker	$ 84.50	$174.80	$213.30	$250.60	$288.40	$331.00	$354.50	$384.50	$404.50
Wife under 65 and one child	42.30	92.50	157.40	217.30	233.90	248.30	265.90	288.40	303.40
Widowed mother and one child	126.80	262.20	320.00	376.00	432.60	496.60	531.80	576.80	606.80
Widowed mother and two children	126.80	267.30	370.70	467.90	522.30	579.30	620.40	672.90	707.90
One child of retired or disabled worker	42.30	87.40	106.70	125.30	144.20	165.50	177.30	192.30	202.30
One surviving child	84.50	131.10	160.00	188.00	216.30	248.30	265.90	288.40	303.40
Maximum family payment	126.80	267.30	370.70	467.90	522.30	579.30	620.40	672.90	707.90

Source: U.S. Department of Health, Education, and Welfare, Social Security Administration, June 1974.

CLU Designation   To become a chartered life underwriter (CLU), agents must pass a series of examinations which are designed to test their competence in all aspects of life insurance. Designation as a CLU is not a guarantee that the agent will be helpful, but it is a measure of some achievement in the field.

Membership in the Million-Dollar Roundtable   Agents selling $1 million of insurance in a year are honored by the industry with Roundtable membership. It indicates a certain degree of ability. Usually agents do not sell $1 million of life insurance without providing the type of financial assistance that is necessary in building a sound insurance program.

The Agent's Sales Presentation   If the agent will not spend an hour assessing your present financial condition and discussing what your needs are, he or she is doing a poor job. (Remember that just because you ask an agent to make a sales presentation, you are not obligated to buy insurance from the same individual.)

The Agent's Willingness to Sell Term Insurance   Because the commissions for term are lower than for whole life policies, most agents are extremely reluctant to sell term insurance. This is unfortunate because term represents the best alternative for most people. An agent who is really interested in your welfare should be willing to sell you term insurance and not pressure you into whole life contracts when you express a preference for term insurance.

Strategy: After listening to the sales agent's presentation, never sign a policy application for at least two days, or until you have completely thought over your decision and what it means. The agent can wait, and so can you.

RUSES AND ABUSES

In this section we will examine some of the common misunderstandings, questionable sales pitches, and outright misrepresentations which make buying life insurance such a complicated task.

"Buy Life Insurance When You Are Young"   Sales representatives point out that if you buy whole life when you are young, you will obtain a lower premium than if you buy it at a later age. This is very true, but it also means that you are paying for life insurance when you may not need it. If you do not need the insurance, do not buy it just to realize a lower premium.

"Do Not Drop In-Force Policies"   The insurance industry has aggressively promoted the idea that there is something sinful about dropping a life insurance policy. If you do not need the insurance, there is no reason to keep the policy in force. If you have insurance, but find a policy which is less expensive, then take it and drop your current insurance.

"Insurance for College Seniors"   Several major companies aggressively try to sell policies to graduating seniors. The sales pitch makes the policy look like an excellent bargain. In fact, it is one of the poorest insurance buys on the market. The attraction of these policies lies in the company's offer to sell a $15,000 whole life policy for a $10 first-year payment. As part of the sale, the insured must sign a note for the difference between the payment and the actual premium due. Typically, the premium for such a policy is about $170. A year later, the second year's premium must be paid and the interest on the loan must also be paid or the contract is canceled. In the event the policy is canceled, the loan, plus accrued interest on the loan, must be paid. Since the total cost is about the same under either alternative, most people pay the premium.

On a cost basis, these policies are very poor relative to other insurance contracts. Moreover, most college seniors do not even need insurance.

"Insurance for Children"   Children do not need life insurance. Insurance agents may stress the need for insurance to cover the cost of a funeral if the child should die. To purchase insurance for such a remote possibility represents a very poor way to spend money. Remember, the basic purpose of insurance is to replace income; children do not earn money.

"Insurance for Nonworking Wives"   Although many women work, there are still millions of women homemakers who do not produce income. The insurance industry aggressively promotes the idea that these women should be insured so money will be available for baby-sitters and household help, should they die. In most cases insurance is unnecessary. A family's expenses will drop if the wife and mother dies. The reduction in expenses should be sufficient, in most situations, to provide money for needed services.

SHOPPING FOR INSURANCE

There is absolutely no doubt that a substantial amount of money can be saved by carefully shopping for your insurance protection. According to a study done by the Commissioner of Insurance for the State of Pennsylvania, there is a cost variation of at least 140 percent between many term insurance policies. Therefore, careful selection could produce savings of over $3,000 (interest adjusted) on a 20-year $25,000 term policy.[1] The potential saving on whole life policies is even larger; it is possible to save $5,000 on a $25,000 life policy over 20 years.

Studies done by *Consumer Reports* for a limited sample of 125 insurance companies showed a 20-year difference of as much as $4 per year per $1,000 face amount, based on a $10,000 5-year term policy issued at age 25.[2] If you were to buy $40,000 of the least expensive policy, your saving over the most expensive contract would be $160 annually, or $3,200 over a 20-year period.

[1]Pennsylvania Insurance Department, "A Shopper's Guide to Term Life Insurance." Harrisburg: 1972, p. 1.
[2]*Consumer Reports*, "A Guide to Life Insurance." January 1974, p. 42.

Strategy: Since the cost differentials on life insurance can be substantial, check the adjusted net cost for several policies before making a purchase. Sources of information are *Consumer Reports*, *Changing Times*, and *Best's Insurance Reports*.

SUMMARY

1 Life insurance is designed to cover the financial needs of a family in the event of the premature death of the principle breadwinner.

2 The life insurance program can be set up using policies which include (*a*) term, (*b*) whole life, and (*c*) endowments.

3 Additional features which can be purchased include (*a*) waiver of premium, (*b*) guaranteed reinsurability, (*c*) accidental death benefit, and (*d*) disability income. Each of these provisions should be considered according to the individual's needs.

4 Life insurance is either participating or nonparticipating. The participating policies return overcharges to the policyholder in the form of dividends. These dividends can be (*a*) received as cash, (*b*) used to reduce the premium, (*c*) left on deposit with the company to earn interest, (*d*) used to purchase paid-up additional insurance, and (*e*) used to purchase 1-year term insurance.

5 The proceeds of a life insurance policy may be paid to the beneficiaries in a variety of ways. The exact settlement option will depend on the needs of the individual.

6 Cash values are protected through the nonforfeiture options. They are (*a*) cash surrender value, (*b*) reduced paid-up insurance, (*c*) extended term insurance, and (*d*) automatic premium loan.

7 Tax consequences of insurance should be determined with a good agent and/or tax attorney.

8 The total amount of life insurance you need depends on (*a*) cleanup expenses, (*b*) mortgage redemption, (*c*) family income period, (*d*) income for the middle years, (*e*) retirement income for your spouse, (*f*) an emergency fund, and (*g*) a college education fund.

9 Life insurance planning should be an ongoing process with needs and coverages reexamined at least every 2 or 3 years as circumstances change.

10 Cost of life insurance varies so widely from company to company that a substantial amount of money can be saved by comparison shopping.

REVIEW YOUR UNDERSTANDING OF

Term
Whole life
Limited payment life
Endowment
Family income policy
Family income rider
Family maintenance policy
Family protection policy
Dividends
Cash value
Loan value
Nonforfeiture options

Accidental death benefit
Guaranteed reinsurability
Waiver of premium
Participating policies
Settlement options
Beneficiary
Ownership
The insured
The needs approach
Disability income
CLU

DISCUSSION QUESTIONS

1   Under what circumstances should a person buy whole life insurance? Term? Endowment?
2   How do whole life and limited pay life policies differ? How are they the same?
3   How can you guarantee a college fund for your children through the use of life insurance?
4   What is the advantage of participating, rather than nonparticipating, life insurance? The disadvantage?
5   How does extended term insurance differ from decreasing term?
6   Under what conditions is the use of extended term insurance appropriate?
7   When should a person be advised to select a straight life income settlement option?
8   Formulate an insurance program for yourself or the principle wage-earning member of your family, using the needs approach. How closely does it match the amount of insurance now carried?
9   Can life insurance be beneficial even while you live? How?
10   Is it worthwhile to purchase cash value insurance merely to obtain a set lifetime premium? Why or why not?
11   How are the proceeds of life insurance policies taxed? Are they ever subject to income taxes?

CASE PROBLEM

Jason Smith (J.S. for short) is a 25-year-old mechanical engineer earning $21,000 a year. He is married and has four children, two by a previous marriage and two with his present wife. As part of the divorce settlement, he must maintain a $50,000 term policy until his youngest child (by his first wife) is 21. That will be in 15 years. Since his first wife has remarried a successful rock musician, J.S. feels no obligation to purchase additional insurance for his first family.

He is concerned about the welfare of his second family. An agent for the You Bet Your Life Insurance Company has recommended that J.S. buy a $25,000, 20-year endowment policy at an annual cost of $1,080. J.S. is concerned that he needs more protection than $25,000 and he is not sure that he can afford $1,080 per year in insurance premiums.

He feels that he needs $2,000 for an emergency fund, $20,000 for mortgage redemption, $22,000 for a college fund, and $75,000 to provide income for his family. Develop an insurance program for J.S. that will keep his cost below $600 per year and still provide the protection he needs. (*Hint*: Use Exhibit 14–4.) He also wants some forced savings with cash value insurance. Can he afford it? If so, how much can he afford and still get total protection?

RECOMMENDED READINGS

Booklets

Kelsey, R. Wilfred, and Arthur C. Daniels, *Handbook of Life Insurance*. New York: Institute of Life Insurance, 1966.
    A simplified reference detailing the major features of life insurance.
Cohen, Jerome B., *Decade of Decision*. New York: Institute of Life Insurance, 1974.

An excellent source for helping you figure how much, and what types of, insurance you should buy.

Magazines

Consumer Reports:

A three-part series on a guide to life insurance, appearing in the January, February, and March issues, 1974. Rates both term and ordinary life policies for 125 major companies.

Chapter 15

Health Insurance

After completing this chapter you should be able to:

recognize the five basic types of health insurance policies.

explain how deductibles and coinsurance clauses on health insurance policies operate.

recall the major provisions of typical health insurance contracts.

explain the difference between Blue Cross–Blue Shield and private insurance carriers.

recall the advantages of group insurance programs over individual coverages.

analyze an insurance policy to determine whether it is appropriate for your needs.

recognize the inherent limitations of most mail-order health insurance policies.

decide whether or not you should purchase dental insurance.

explain the differences between health insurance and prepaid medical plans.

You cannot afford to get sick in America. That simple statement tells why health coverage is the first insurance policy everybody should own. Long before you consider life insurance or property insurance, you should have insurance to protect you in the event of sickness or accident.

Medical costs have risen so fast in the last decade that a 1- or 2- week hospital confinement could prove financially catastrophic for most families without health insurance. Two weeks in the hospital for surgery can easily cost $3,000 to $4,000 or more. That expense would wipe out most families' total financial resources. An extended illness would be even more devastating. In such cases medical costs in excess of $50,000 are not unusual.

The best insurance against high medical costs is good health. You have heard all the advice: do not smoke, do not drink to excess, eat a balanced diet, get regular exercise, etc. Unfortunately, even these precautions do not eliminate the possibility of sickness or accident. The objective of this chapter is to convince you that health insurance is an absolute necessity, and to discuss the provisions, advantages, disadvantages, and costs of standard health insurance programs. Even if you already have some form of health insurance, this chapter can be valuable. It will explain the coverages and limitations of standard policies which will help you decide if your current policy provides adequate protection. If not, it can be supplemented with additional coverage.

HEALTH INSURANCE POLICIES

Health insurance contracts fall into five distinct categories. Three are referred to as basic plans; they have modest limits on the amount of coverage and are designed to cover specific items such as hospitalization. Two offer extended limits which supplement the basic policies. In addition, there are special accident insurance policies and dental insurance policies which are becoming popular.

This chapter will not cover disability income insurance. Many people view this type of insurance as a form of health insurance since it replaces a family's income when the breadwinner is disabled. But our view is that disability income insurance should be analyzed in the same framework as life insurance. Its purpose is to provide family income when the breadwinner is unable to work. This is precisely the purpose of life insurance. The basic difference between the two is the breadwinner's disability or death. Health insurance requires a different, and at times more complex, type of analysis. Consequently, this chapter will cover insurance designed to reimburse an individual for incurred medical expenses, not to replace income.

Hospital Expense Insurance

This insurance covers the hospital's room and board charges and may also cover additional expenses such as operating room fees, lab work, x-rays, and medication. Limits are usually stated in terms of dollars per day and maximum number of allowable days. For example, the policy may allow up to $100 per day for 45 days. Any charges that exceed this amount would have to be paid by the policyholder. The hospital expense insurance is the most basic form of health insurance available. The important things to consider when purchasing this type of coverage are the limitations imposed by the policy. They will be discussed more fully in a later section.

Surgical Expense Insurance

This policy pays the doctor's fee for surgical procedures. It is a separate policy and is usually sold with the hospital expense policy. Together, they form the foundation for most health insurance programs.

Policy limits on the surgical expense coverage vary according to each specific surgical procedure. For example a typical limit for an appendectomy might be $300. Should the surgeon charge $600, the difference would have to be paid by the policyholder. There are also surgical expense policies which provide a service benefit to the policyholder. Here, there is no set limit for each surgical procedure. Instead, the company agrees to pay all necessary and *reasonable* fees for surgical procedures. This latter policy is preferable since the company pays the entire cost, no matter what the surgeon charges. A flat-fee schedule may leave the policyholder liable for a large amount above the insurance coverage. From a cost standpoint, there does not appear to be a difference between the policies, making the service benefit policy even more attractive.

Regular Medical Insurance

Regular medical insurance pays part or all of the physician's fees for nonsurgical care. Since many procedures do not require surgery, but can nevertheless be very expensive, the need for regular medical insurance to supplement the hospital expense and surgical expense insurance is obvious. In fact, most health insurance policies combine all three types of insurance.

Basic Policy Limits

For each of these three basic health insurance plans—hospital, surgical, and regular medical—the policy specifies a limit on the amount that will be paid. Each maximum may apply either during any one calendar year or for any one illness. The latter is the more liberal policy. For example, if the limitation is applied to each illness, it would be possible to collect the maximum more than once in a calendar year. If the limitation were on a calendar year basis, the insurance company would pay the maximum only once during the year. In either case, the policy maximum is modest; for example, the hospital expense policy may cover only 30 days confinement. Consequently the basic health insurance plans provide only minimal protection. For this reason, the supplemental contract known as major medical insurance has been developed.

Major Medical Insurance

Major medical (MM) coverage takes over where the basic policies end. It protects against the large expenses arising from a serious accident or a prolonged illness. Coverage under major medical usually includes all the items—hospital, surgical, and regular medical—that are protected by the basic contracts, but for larger amounts.

The main feature of major medical insurance is its sizable upper limits. The customary range is $25,000 to $50,000, and many policies are now being written with $100,000 limits. Like the basic plans, major medical can be written with a calendar year or occurrence limitation. Again, the more liberal form applies the limits to each illness or accident.

After the basic policy limits are paid, the insured can collect for costs above these limits from the major medical insurance. However, the insured does not collect the full amount above the basic limits, for there is a deductible feature.

The deductible may range from $100 to $1,000. That amount is deducted from the amount claimed under major medical, and the insurance company pays 80 percent of the difference. Hence, there are two amounts the insured must pay—the deductible amount and 20 percent of the costs above the deductible amount.

Let us consider an example: A serious accident results in total medical costs of $12,100. The basic policy pays $2,000. The remaining $10,100 is claimed under the major medical insurance. The deductible amount is $100. Under the major medical plan, the insurance company pays $8,000. Thus, the insured pays only $100 + $2,000, or $2,100 of the total $12,100 medical costs.

From this example you can see that despite the deductible and 80 percent–20 percent features, major medical is an important protection against the high costs of prolonged illness or serious accident.

Incidentally, this feature, whereby the insurance company pays 80 percent of the cost and the insured pays 20 percent, is called coinsurance. This type of insurance is used because it costs much less than insurance that pays the entire 100 percent. So, in a way, the insured is sharing the risk with the insurance company.

Comprehensive Medical Insurance

Comprehensive medical insurance is simply a single policy which combines the three basic contracts and the major medical policy. Comprehensive policies are becoming the primary health insurance offered through group insurance plans. As more people bought both basic and major medical coverage, the logical step was to combine the policies into one inclusive contract. The combined program eliminated much of the confusion about the coverages and deductibles which applied to each of the separate policies.

Under the terms of most comprehensive policies, there is a single deductible which applies only to the basic coverage and not to the major medical coverage. The more liberal comprehensive policies pay 100 percent coverage after the deductible instead of 80 percent. Comprehensive policies may be subject to the same exclusions, such as cosmetic surgery, which apply to other forms of health insurance.

Strategy: Most people should have the three basic health policies supplemented by a major medical contract. The policies can be purchased individually through the same company, or they can be obtained as a single comprehensive contract. In most cases, a comprehensive contract is the better alternative, although there are numerous exceptions to this advice. For wealthy individuals who do not need the basic coverage or for people who cannot afford a high premium, a major medical policy represents a good compromise. It protects against the large losses, but because of its high deductible and its reimbursement to the insured of only 80 percent of medical costs, it can be purchased for about one-quarter the cost of a comprehensive plan.

Accident Insurance

Originally, health and accident insurance were sold as separate policies. The health policy covered illnesses; reimbursement for medical costs due to accidents was made under the accident policy. Commonly, the provisions of the accident policy specified the benefits for each potential injury. An insured might receive $500 for the loss of a leg, $1,500 for an eye and so on, with a maximum of $10,000 if the insured died. Surprisingly, even though health insurance policies now reimburse for medical costs arising from injuries and life insurance is available to most people, accident policies are still being sold.

They represent a bad insurance buy. The medical costs of dismemberment should come from health insurance, and if the injury is disabling, a disability income policy will provide the best benefits. A life insurance policy would be a more efficient way of protecting against the economic consequences of the insured's death.

Dental Insurance

The fastest growing segment of the health insurance industry is dental insurance. Traditionally, health insurance policies have excluded normal dental work including dentures and other structural dental work. Treatment for diseases of the mouth and gums, however, is usually covered.

Normal dental work, particularly for dentures and orthodontia (having your teeth straightened), can be extremely expensive. As a result, dental insurance is becoming more common. Impetus for its adoption has come from the labor unions as part of their contract bargaining. As union members become covered under dental plans, many companies, as a matter of policy, extend the benefits to their nonunion employees. At the same time, companies writing the group dental policies have entered the market with individual plans.

The cost of dental coverage, like the cost of health insurance, is subject to numerous variables. Deductibles, coinsurance clauses, and exclusions vary widely in dental policies. Consequently, it is impossible to give representative examples of the costs of dental insurance.

Should You Buy Dental Insurance? Health insurance is certainly a must. Is dental insurance? The answer to that question is a qualified no. If dental insurance is part of a group plan your employer subsidizes, by all means take the coverage. However, if you are thinking about buying an individual policy, consider the decision carefully. Remember there is little likelihood of catastrophically expensive dental problems. Major oral diseases or structural repairs resulting from accidents should be covered by your health insurance.

The dental insurance is designed to cover normal fillings, dentures, and orthodontia. Fillings are relatively inexpensive. While dentures may be expensive, it is a procedure that can be anticipated and budgeted for. Even though orthodontia can be expensive, it is a procedure that is administered over a fairly long period. Thus you should be able to pay its cost out of current income.

Dental insurance, like other coverages designed to pay small, highly likely losses, represents little more than a prepayment plan. In the long run, most people will find their dental expenses will be about the same whether they pay them or buy insurance coverage.

> **Strategy: Individual dental insurance should be considered only by people who cannot budget the costs required for dental care.**

Policy Provisions

There are no standard health insurance contracts. Policy provisions vary widely, making direct comparisons very difficult. Nevertheless, it is important to understand the major features of a contract before you buy it. This section discusses the most important provisions of a health insurance contract: deductibles, coinsurance, coverages, renewal terms, exclusions, and waiting periods.

All policies, be they hospital expense insurance, major medical insurance, or comprehensive plans, incorporate some or all of the provisions discussed in this section. The details of each provision may vary with different policies, but these specifics should be considered in evaluating any policy.

Deductibles Many health insurance contracts are written with a deductible provision. Typically, the deductible will range from $100 upward. The policyholder must pay that amount; the company pays the balance. The objective of the deductible is to eliminate many small claims. Without it, people would make claims for reimbursement every time they went to the doctor for a cold or sore throat. If all medical expenses were paid by insurance, there would be little incentive for people not to see a doctor at the first sign of a sore throat or cold.

The deductible forces policyholders to be self-insuring for at least the first $100 of their medical expenses. Elimination of the deductible would increase the cost of the insurance by more than $100, since the companies must collect an amount sufficient to pay these small claims as well as cover their administrative costs. Consequently, it is conceivable that health care costs would increase dramatically if deductible provisions were dropped or substantially reduced.

Deductibles vary widely among companies. Things to watch for are: First, how long does the policy allow you to accumulate bills to reach the deductible amount? Some policies put a 3- or 6- month limitation on the deductible. For example, if in the 3- month period you did not have enough bills to exceed the deductible amount, you would have to start accumulating expenses from zero at the start of the next 3- month period.

Second, check to determine whether the deductible may be accumulated against the charges for one family member for only one illness, or for any number of illnesses within the deductible period. Obviously, if you are restricted to accumulating expenses for only one illness, the policy will be less beneficial than if it covers all illnesses for a family member. An even better deductible permits you to accumulate expenses for all family members. If one member has high medical expenses, the deductible can be reached for the entire family through the expenses of that one person. Likewise modest expenses for each member will also fulfill the deductible provision.

> **Strategy: When selecting a health insurance policy, the use of a deductible provision can be helpful in reducing the cost of the policy. The larger the deductible you select, the lower will be the premium for a given amount of insurance. A deductible of as much as $500 would not be unreasonable in certain situations.**

Coinsurance Clauses Many health insurance contracts are also written with a coinsurance feature. A typical coinsurance clause calls for the insurance company to pay 80 percent of all claims, after the deductible; the insured pays the remaining 20 percent. Another frequently used breakdown is 75–25 percent. Exhibit 15–1 shows the relationship of the deductible and the coinsurance provision for a typical policy.

The objective of the coinsurance clause, in addition to reducing the cost of claims, is to give the insured an incentive to minimize the medical expenses that exceed the deductible provision. Theoretically, it should make the insured try to get well faster—if that is possible! Whereas the deductible discourages trivial claims without causing financial hardship on the insured, the same cannot be said for the coinsurance feature. The economic impact of the coinsurance clause can be quite severe. For example, if a person incurred $10,000 of medical expenses, after the deductible, the insured with a 75 percent 25 percent coinsurance feature would have to pay $2,500 of the costs. In a situation such as this, the insurance fails to provide the protection against large losses, which is its primary purpose.

The amount that will be reimbursed by a health insurance policy depends on the limits, excludable expenses, the deductible, and the coinsurance percentages. Exhibit 15–2 gives an example of the amount that may be recovered for a typical illness. Note that even with a low deductible and a high coinsurance breakdown, the insured still pays a substantial amount. This provides further evidence that the coinsurance policies should be avoided if at all possible.

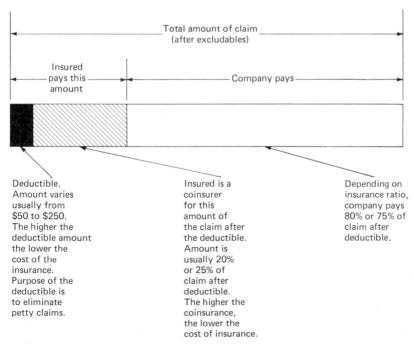

Exhibit 15-1   Deductibles and Coinsurance

Exhibit 15-2 Sample Claim Calculation for a Comprehensive Medical Policy with a $100 Deductible and an 80–20 Percent Coinsurance Clause

Expenses	$4,280
Less: excluded expenses (phone, TV rental)	235
Allowable expenses	$4,045
Less: deductible	100
Amount subject to coinsurance	$3,945
20 percent coinsurance	789
80 percent reimbursed	3,156
Total paid by insured ($235 + $100 + $789)	$1,124
Total paid by insurance	3,156
Total	$4,280

Strategy: If at all possible, try to purchase a policy which does not have a coinsurance clause. Since you want protection against large losses, the coinsurance clause is not a desirable feature of an insurance contract.

Policy Exclusions   Before buying a health insurance policy, make sure you know whether certain illnesses and procedures are excluded from coverage. Many policies do not cover normal pregnancy, but do cover any complications which arise from childbirth. For an additional fee, most companies will also cover maternity costs. But it is reasonably expensive coverage since people electing it are undoubtedly contemplating having children. Consequently, the insurance companies must charge everybody a premium which is about

I'M AFRAID I HAVE SOME BAD NEWS FOR YOU, MR. DIPPLE...

equivalent to the actual cost of the benefit. As a result, you may be better off self-insuring for maternity expenses. After all, you should have at least 9 months to save for the cost of maternity expenses.

Some exclusions are more acceptable than others. For example, a policy which does not cover elective cosmetic surgery may be perfectly adequate in all other respects. But, policies that exclude treatment of mental illness and coverage for convalescent expenses may not suit the needs of some people. Some states have enacted legislation to force insurance companies to broaden their coverage. For example, in Wisconsin, health insurance policies must contain a provision allowing up to $500 in claims for psychiatric care. The trend seems to be toward extending policy benefits. Nevertheless, there are still major differences between policies. For this reason, the exclusions of a contract should be carefully examined before it is purchased.

Waiting Periods   Most policies are written to include a waiting period—the insurance company will not pay for a claim for certain illnesses or maternity until a period of time after the date the policy was purchased. Policies which cover maternity benefits are invariably written with a 9- or 10-month waiting period. Illnesses such as tonsilitis may have shorter waiting periods.

Imposing a waiting period on illnesses where treatment could be postponed for a short period forces people to have insurance prior to those illnesses. The waiting period prevents people from postponing medical treatment until they buy insurance. It is an equitable provision in a system that is designed for risk sharing.

Renewability   A contract which is cancelable at the option of the insurance company is a far less desirable policy than one which guarantees continued protection for the policyholder. Guaranteed renewable policies are usually more expensive than policies which may be canceled by the company. Some policies may be canceled only if all policyholders in the same state are dropped at the same time. The danger in buying a policy renewable at the company's option is that the company may cancel at just the time you most need the insurance. At that point, it may be difficult to qualify for health insurance, and you may be left unprotected and unable to replace the coverage.

> **Strategy: In shopping for health insurance, renewability is among the most critical features to consider. If you are faced with the choice between a cancelable and an automatically renewable policy at a much higher price for equivalent coverages, you should have a very compelling reason for not taking the renewable policy.**

Policy Limits   What is the maximum amount the policy will cover? Is it for any one illness, or is it for the life of the policy? The policies which apply the limit to each illness are more desirable than ones which apply a limit to all claims. Obviously, the higher the policy limits, the better the policy.

Policy limits of $50,000 or more are not extravagant with today's high medical costs. Many advisors are now recommending that individuals should have coverage of at least $100,000 and that $250,000 is not unreasonable. Fortunately, the cost of increasing the policy limits is very small. To increase from $25,000 to $100,000 in major medical coverage may cost only $10 more per year. The additional cost is a small price to pay for protecting against the possibility of catastrophic medical costs.

Usually, the basic plans are written with low limits, such as $2,000 to $5,000, while the higher limits apply to the major medical policies. A comprehensive policy will usually carry the limits associated with the major medical coverage. It is important to recognize that different limits may apply to the basic and major medical plans. Failure to realize this could result in severe underinsurance.

Analyzing Policy Provisions

Exhibit 15–3 is a checklist for systematically evaluating provisions of health insurance policies. It points out the most important things to look for in the contracts and suggests the features which the better policies contain. Undoubtedly, the closer a policy comes to meeting the suggested standards in this checklist, the more expensive the policy will be. If cost is a major drawback, then some of the features will have to be sacrificed to obtain a lower premium.

Group Insurance—Individual Policies

Most people in the United States are covered under group insurance contracts provided by their employer. In fact, approximately 70 percent of the people having health insurance receive their protection this way. Group insurance, in most cases, is far superior to individual policies. The cost is usually lower, even if the employer does not contribute to the payments, although many companies pay a substantial percentage of the premium. Coverage under a group contract is immediate, and often there is no waiting period for existing illnesses or conditions, even pregnancy. Benefit limits are usually higher and there are fewer policy exclusions.

Because of all these advantages of group insurance, if you are eligible for such a plan, take it. Make sure you understand the provisions, however. There may be gaps in the coverage, such as an inadequate number of hospital days covered, that should be supplemented with individual insurance.

For the 30 percent of the people not covered by group plans, selecting a health insurance plan is probably their most difficult insurance decision. Evaluating the major policy features and requirements will help make it less difficult.

WHERE TO BUY INSURANCE

Health insurance is sold by private insurance companies through salesagents and by mail order. Nonprofit service organizations provide coverage for

Exhibit 15-3 Checklist for Analyzing Policy Provisions

Area of Concern	Recommendation

Hospital Expense Insurance

1 How many days are covered? — Best policies cover 365 days.

2 What is the daily benefit? — Benefits should be adequate to cover the full daily cost of hospitalization.

3 Are additional services such as x-ray, lab, and medication covered? — Better policies have broad coverage in these areas.

4 Is there a deductible? — The deductible should fit your needs.

5 Is the policy automatically renewable? — Better policies are renewable at your request.

6 Is there a waiting period for certain illnesses? — Better policies have few illnesses subject to waiting periods and have very short waiting periods.

7 Are there policy exclusions? — Better policies have few exclusions. Some, such as elective cosmetic surgery, are acceptable.

Surgical Expense Insurance

1 Does the policy pay a stated amount or all reasonable charges? — Better policies pay all reasonable charges rather than a flat fee schedule.

2 Does the policy pay for office procedures as well as hospitalized surgical care? — Since many surgical procedures can be done in a doctor's office, these should be covered.

3 What are the policy limits? — If limits are low, such as $1,000, buying additional major medical insurance is a must.

4 What are the exclusions? — Better policies have few exclusions.

Regular Medical Insurance

1 What is covered? — The policy should pay all nonsurgical medical care expenses except routine office visits, subject to a deductible, if any.

2 Are prescription drugs covered? — Coverage for drugs is important for people with chronic conditions requiring prolonged medication.

3 What are the policy limits? — Low limits should be supplemented with major medical insurance.

Major Medical—Comprehensive Insurance

1 What is the policy maximum? — The maximum should be at least $25,000; limits of $100,000 are recommended.

2 Does the maximum apply only once or to each occurrence? — The maximum should apply to each condition.

3 Is there a deductible? — Deductibles that apply to all bills in a calendar year are preferable; less desirable are per occurrence deductibles and deductibles which must be met in less than one year.

4 Is there a coinsurance clause? — Better policies will not have a coinsurance feature.

5 Is the policy renewable at your request? — It should be.

millions of individuals. The best known nonprofit plan is the group collectively known as Blue Cross–Blue Shield. The private companies provide cash benefits to indemnify policyholders, whereas the nonprofit plans provide a service benefit. The difference between a cash benefit and a service benefit is the amount that will be paid. Service contracts pay all necessary and reasonable charges. Cash benefits, paid to the policyholder, are flat rates for each procedure. Usually the payments under service contracts are made directly to the hospital or physician rather than to the insured.

The federal government has also become a major factor in health insurance through the Medicare program. Finally, there are also health maintenance organizations, or prepayment plans, which do not pay a benefit for the cost of medical attention but, instead, actually provide the medical services through their own facilities. These plans now serve over 8 million Americans.

To assist in deciding which type of company will provide the insurance you need, this section discusses each major insurance plan and offers some suggestions.

Blue Cross–Blue Shield

The largest writer of health insurance is a group of nonprofit organizations known as Blue Cross and Blue Shield (BC-BS). There are currently 71 Blue Shield plans and 80 Blue Cross plans scattered throughout the United States. Among the unique characteristics of the Blues, as they are often called, is the fact that everyone in the same geographic location may join, either on a group or an individual basis. The protection provided under Blue Cross–Blue Shield is among the best available. As a nonprofit organization, the sole objective of the plans is to act as a risk-sharing pool. Premiums are set to just cover claims and administrative expenses.

A good measure of how well an insurance company protects its policyholders is the ratio of the company's claims paid to premium income. Blue Cross–Blue Shield has averaged 97.5 percent claims to premiums. In other words, almost 98 cents out of every $1 that is collected is returned to the policyholders in the form of benefits. Many private insurance companies have ratios of between 60 and 80 percent and some companies are as low as 20 percent.

Blue Cross   Blue Cross is the hospital expense insurance portion of Blue Cross–Blue Shield. In addition to paying for room and board charges, the insurance also covers lab fees, x-rays, operating room charges, and prescription medication.

The rates for Blue Cross vary, depending on the geographic location and the policy limits. Costs for hospital care show wide regional differences. The larger cities are usually more expensive than small towns and the Northeast and California have higher costs than the South and the Midwest. The insurance rates must be set to recognize these differences. Other differences include limits on the number of hospital days allowable (anywhere from 30 days to 1 year) and a limit on the daily hospital cost payable. These factors are also incorporated in the company's insurance rate structure.

These wide variations in policy limits and reimbursement schedules permit Blue Cross to write contracts with annual premiums which may be as low as $100 to as high as $1,000, or more. Depending on the amount of insurance protection you want and can afford, you should be able to find a contract through Blue Cross.

Blue Shield   Blue Shield is the surgical expense coverage of the Blue Cross–Blue Shield plans. It is really broader than just surgical expense coverage since it also reimburses for some physicians' fees which do not involve surgery.

Blue Shield contracts generally state that payment will be made for all reasonable and necessary charges. This permits the physicians some latitude in setting their fees without forcing the policyholder to pay the difference between the actual charge and some maximum reimbursement by the company.

In those cases where benefits are stated as a flat payment, most physicians agree to accept the stated benefit as full payment for services. They do this because Blue Shield is an organization originated and supported by doctors, and in many states 90 percent of the physicians are sponsoring members of the plan. Nonparticipating MDs may charge more than the set fee; however, they must collect the difference from the patient, not from Blue Shield. Many Blue Shield plans urge their policyholders to refrain from signing supplemental fee agreements (promises to pay more than the insurance coverage) and to refer any doctor's charges in excess of stated levels back to Blue Shield for negotiation.

Private Insurance Companies

Much of the blame for the confusing and treacherous nature of health insurance rests with the private insurance industry. There are many reputable private companies writing very acceptable health insurance policies, although sometimes the legalistic garble can confuse lawyers. Unfortunately, there are also companies which seem to be writing policies designed specifically to defraud the policyholder and enrich the firm's stockholders.

The difficulties start with the policy itself. Exclusions may be so broad that there exist dangerous gaps in the insurance protection. For example, many policies cover dependent children from fourteen days to nineteen years old. By excluding the first 14 days, the company potentially shifts the costs of congenital birth defects to the parents. The costs of such illnesses can be unbelievably high, and such possibilities are quite likely since many children are born with some problem. State legislatures are not unaware of these problem areas and corrective legislation is being enacted. Recently, Wisconsin passed a bill which requires all family health policies sold in the state to provide immediate coverage at birth.

Other private plans either may have a 2-year waiting period for certain conditions or totally exclude existing conditions from being covered at any time.

All the policy provisions we discussed earlier should be very carefully scrutinized when you are considering a policy sold by a profit-making insurance company. With the wide differences between policies and companies, uninformed insurance buyers can be woefully underprotected if they select a poor contract or buy from a bad company.

Prepaid Medical Plans

An intriguing and successful variation of health insurance is available in a few geographic locations. Often called prepayment or health maintenance organizations (HMOs), the plans provide direct medical care for their members. The largest HMO is the Kaiser Permanente plan, which was formed in 1945. This organization now provides prepaid health care for over 2.5 million people.

Under the terms of a typical HMO, a family pays a flat amount for its total annual health care needs. Here the similarity between the HMOs and conventional health insurance ends. The HMO provides the medical care by owning hospitals and employing doctors. The member simply goes to the plan's clinic or hospital whenever in need of medical attention. The annual prepayment covers any services provided during the year.

The HMOs have been both praised and damned. Praise has come from groups which see the plans as an effective way of delivering health care services. Opponents of the plans claim that they remove the individual's freedom of choice in selecting a personal physician. They further argue that doctors should work on a fee-for-service basis and that working for a salary reduces the physician's incentive to provide good medical care. Despite these arguments, the HMOs appear to be providing sound medical care for their members. By and large, the members are satisfied and there are no statistics to indicate that the care is inferior to traditional medical services.

> **Strategy: If you live in an area which has a prepaid medical plan in operation, investigate membership as an alternative to health insurance. The services are sound and the exclusions under the HMOs are far less numerous than under many health insurance policies.**

Mail-Order Hospital Insurance

The Sunday supplements of many newspapers carry appealing ads for supplemental hospitalization insurance available by mail. The ads promise $600 or $1,000 per month without explaining under what conditions the payments will be made. The large print also promises that payments will be made up to a maximum of $50,000 or more.

These policies are a poor insurance supplement. Many of these mail-order contracts require that you be hospitalized to collect benefits. Assuming a maximum benefit of $600 per month, you would have to be in the hospital for almost 7 years to receive the $50,000 the policy promises. Another deceptive thing about these policies: They will not start paying benefits until the hospital stay reaches 6 days. The average hospital stay in the United States is 5 days! Finally, a 1- or 2- year waiting period for many conditions is included in the fine print. This stipulation effectively eliminates many claims that a policyholder might make during the first year or two the contract is in force.

Further proof of the inferiority of mail-order insurance is the claims-to-premium ratio. As we mentioned, Blue Cross has about a 98 percent ratio; the mail-order insurers operate with ratios as low as 20 percent—that is good business for the company, bad insurance for people.

Although these plans are not doing anything illegal, they do a real disservice to many people. The policies seem attractive because of their low cost. Many people who should be purchasing insurance that may cost $600 to $1,000 annually buy mail-order insurance instead. When they ultimately need to collect for medical costs, they find the coverage is inadequate for their needs.

Exhibit 15–4 shows a comparison of five typical mail-order health insurance policies. While the premiums are low, ranging from $42 to $75.60 per year, the benefits are also low. The advertised benefits of $14.28 to $33.33 per day do not really provide adequate hospital coverage.

Government Programs

The United States is undoubtedly moving toward some system of national health insurance. An initial step in that direction was made when health insurance was included as a part of the social security program. The program consists of both mandatory and voluntary coverages for eligible individuals.

Medicare   Medicare coverage under social security is divided into health insurance, part A, and medical expense insurance, part B. Everyone over sixty-five drawing social security benefits is automatically covered under part

SAY AAH!

Exhibit 15-4 Comparison of Five Sample Mail-Order Health Insurance Policies

Company	Advertised benefit claim	Total maximum benefit	Daily benefit	Beginning of illness coverage	Preexisting conditions covered after	Annual premium, age 35
National Home (Art Linkletter)	$1,000	Unlimited	$33.33	6th day	2 years	$64.20
Physicians Mutual (Doctors Hospital Plan)	None	$5,000	$14.28	1st day	1 year	$47.20
Stern's (Beneficial Standard)	$25,000	Unlimited	$20 for 1st year, $10 afterward	Not covered (accident coverage only)	Not covered	$42.00
Commercial Travelers	$200 a week	$10,400	$28.57	1st day	2 years	$72.00
American Express	$36 a day	500 days	$30 a day plus $6 a day in lump sum on discharge	1st day	2 years if treated in year prior to policy; 1 year if no treatment needed for 12 consecutive months after purchase of policy	$75.60

Source: The Record, Hackensack, N.J., 1973.

Exhibit 15-5   Medicare, Part A Benefits

After $92 deductible, full cost of hospital room for first 60 days
Cost of a semiprivate room for the 61st through the 90th day. The patient's share is $23 per day
Up to 60 "reserve," or additional, days over person's lifetime. The patient's share is $46 daily
The 21st through 100th days in a nursing facility. The patient's share is $11.50 daily
Meals
Regular nursing services
Intensive care unit costs
Drugs
Laboratory fees
X-rays and radiology services
Operating room fees
Medical supplies, such as casts
Use of medical appliances, such as a wheelchair
Physical, occupational, and speech therapy services

A, and may voluntarily enroll for part B by paying a small monthly premium. Individuals receiving disability income payments are also covered under the same provisions; and a special category has been included in the law to extend benefits to individuals with kidney disorders requiring dialysis treatments.

Benefits under Medicare, Part A   Part A covers the hospital, nursing home, and some at-home medical expenses. Specific benefits covered by part A are shown in Exhibit 15–5.

Benefits under Medicare, Part B   Part B of Medicare must be elected by the individual and an additional monthly premium must be paid to obtain the coverage. Benefits under part B can help pay for physicians' services and other medical expenses. Medicare, part B, operates with a $60 calendar year deductible and an 80–20 percent coinsurance clause. Thus, after the insured person has incurred $60 of expenses in a given year, Medicare B will pay 80 percent of the reasonable charges for covered services. Exclusions include routine physicals, foot care, eyeglasses and hearing aids, and cosmetic surgery. Specific services covered under Medicare, part B, are shown in Exhibit 15–6.

Medicaid   The Medicaid provision of the social security health care program pays for the medical services of low-income individuals. Eligibility for

Exhibit 15-6   Medicare, Part B Benefits

Doctors' Services Covered
Medical and surgical fees
Diagnostic tests and procedures
Other services such as x-rays, drugs, medical supplies, and therapy billed by the doctor

Medical Services Covered
Emergency-room services or outpatient clinic services
Laboratory fees ⎱
X-rays   ⎰ billed by the hospital
Medical supplies
Drugs

Medicaid benefits is determined by a person's income and liquid assets. For example, the maximum income is $150 monthly and maximum assets, $400, for a person to be eligible for Medicaid. These ceilings effectively limit the number of eligible individuals. For a person also eligible for Medicare A, Medicaid will pay the costs not covered under Medicare.

The important thing to remember about Medicaid is that it provides supplemental benefits to the Medicare coverage and that eligibility is determined on a need basis. You can determine your eligibility by contacting a local social security office.

Summarizing Health Coverages

The principal types of health insurance coverages discussed in this chapter are summarized in Exhibit 15–7. The exhibit shows the policy type, indicates whether it is sold on a group or an individual basis, and tells which type of insurance company writes the contract.

Updating Your Health Insurance

Since your personal and financial position may change, all your insurance needs may change. Health insurance, like all other insurance plans, should be reviewed periodically to make sure that coverages are adequate. This is true even if you are covered under a group health contract. In addition to reviewing coverage at least every 2 years, you should take a careful look at your policy under the following conditions.

Exhibit 15-7   Summary of Health Insurance Policies and Insurance Carriers

Type	Group or individual	Available from
Basic: Hospital expense, surgical expense, regular medical } Inclusive / Major medical / Comprehensive	Both	Service organizations such as Blue Cross—Blue Shield or private insurance companies
Prepaid	Both	Health maintenance organizations
Mail order	Individual	Private companies
Accident insurance	Individual	Private companies
Dental insurance	Both	Service organizations or private insurance companies
Medicare	Individual	U.S. Government
Medicaid	Individual	U.S. Government

Change of Jobs   If you are covered under a group plan, your protection will stop when you leave your current employer. If you may be out of work for a while, or will not be covered under a new plan during a waiting period, see if you can convert your former group insurance to an individual policy for a term equal to the new policy's waiting period. If this is impossible, consider buying a major medical policy to fill the gap. You will need some protection.

If you are covered under an individual policy and you go from a dangerous to a safe job, contact your agent. You may well qualify for a reduced rate as a result of your new occupation.

Change in Family Status   Make sure your employer knows when you have children so they can be covered under the group policy. If you have an individual policy, make sure to notify your agent of any family change.

Children Nineteen or More Years Old   Most health policies protect dependent children only until age nineteen. After than at individual policy will have to be purchased for dependent children over nineteen. College students can often buy adequate low-cost protection through their school. If they are under nineteen, do not consider additional insurance as long as they are covered under a family policy. It would unnecessarily duplicate the coverage.

Retirement   Protection under an employer's group plan may stop with retirement, or some form of reduced protection may continue as a part of the retirement benefits. It is important to be sure whether you will be covered, since inadequate health insurance after sixty-five can prove particularly devastating because of the increased medical needs which often accompany old age.

Costs of Health Insurance Policies

Generalizations about the cost of health insurance policies are impossible. Premiums vary depending on the company, the coverages, the insured's geographic location, and whether the policy is for an individual or a family. About the only thing that can be said is that adequate health insurance protection is very expensive: a good family policy with maternity benefits can cost between $600 and $1,000 a year; identical coverage for a single person (excluding maternity benefits) may cost as little as $200 annually.

To complicate matters further, it is almost impossible to compare health policies. Coverage under auto insurance policies has been standardized to the extent that direct cost comparisons are possible (see Chapter 16). Unfortunately, the same situation does not exist with health insurance.

Which Program Is Best?

Perhaps the simplest and best way to obtain good health coverage is to work for a company which provides its employees with a comprehensive group insurance program. If you do not have the good fortune of being protected by a group plan, you can still take some steps to evaluate different individual policies. The strategy summarized below should go a long way toward helping you find adequate health insurance.

> **Strategy: Rules of thumb for selecting good health insurance are:**
> 1   If possible, buy from a reliable nonprofit organization.
> 2   Buy a policy without a coinsurance clause or with the most favorable coinsurance ratio for its cost.
> 3   Do not buy supplemental health insurance policies.
> 4   Reduce the cost of the insurance by increasing the deductible up to the maximum you can afford to self-insure.
> 5   Get the longest period allowed to accumulate the deductible.
> 6   Buy a major medical or a comprehensive policy with at least a $25,000 limit, preferably $50,000.
> 7   Make sure the policy is automatically renewable.
> 8   Make sure the policy exclusions and waiting periods are minimal.
> 9   Make sure you understand the exclusions and that they are reasonable.

HEALTH CARE—A BROADER LOOK

Selecting and buying good health care insurance is not enough. As a consumer, you should know some of the deficiencies in America's health service system so that changes can be started with grass-roots support. There are many reasons for escalating health care costs and they should come under hard scrutiny. A few examples might make you wonder why some methods of control have not been initiated before now.

Prescription Costs   Most states have laws forbidding drug stores from advertising prescription prices. Prices among stores may vary by as much as 500 percent, but without readily available published price lists, it is virtually impossible for the consumer to find the bargains. The laws certainly are not protecting the consumer. Whom are they protecting?

Unnecessary Medical Procedures   The amount of surgery varies widely in different regions of the United States. The only factor that seems to explain this disparity is that high surgery areas have lots of surgeons and low surgery areas have fewer surgeons. Unnecessary surgery makes the cost of health insurance higher than it should be.

Excessive Medical Procedures   Physicians tend to order extensive tests, which are often of questionable value, and to keep patients confined longer than they need be. These tendencies also contribute to higher insurance costs. Comparison with the HMOs shows that the average hospital stay for an HMO patient is shorter and the cost is less. Somehow the patients seem to get better at about the same rate.

Overconcentration of Physicians Doctors are not spread evenly throughout the country. Some areas, such as New York City, have 3 to 4 times as many doctors per 100,000 population as rural Southern areas. Is there any way society can get doctors to service rural areas, or must America continue with this gross imbalance?

Inadequate Health Insurance Policies The confusing nature of health insurance could be reduced if state insurance commissioners would do their job. The commissioners in all states are authorized to approve policies before they can be issued. With the exception of the Pennsylvania insurance commissioner, the state commissioners have made little visible effort to reduce the confusion surrounding health insurance.

Underutilized-Overspecialized Equipment Modern specialized equipment, such as therapeutic x-ray machines, can cost hundreds of thousands of dollars. Yet, two or three hospitals in the same city will each buy the equipment when one would do for the entire community. Until very recently the hospitals have shown little cooperative effort to reduce this excessive duplication of facilities. The equipment has to be paid for and it is done by increasing your hospital bill.

There are many more examples of ways the American health care delivery system is inadequate and overly expensive. Reform in many cases is starting to be felt, but any major changes which will reduce the cost or significantly improve the system seem to be far in the future—unless the patient starts to rebel at the current practices.

SUMMARY

1   Health insurance is the most important and first insurance policy that everyone should own.
2   There are five standard health insurance policies: (a) hospital expense insurance, (b) surgical expense insurance, (c) regular medical insurance, (d) major medical insurance, and (e) comprehensive major medical insurance.
3   The most important policy provisions to be considered when buying health insurance are: (a) deductibles, (b) coinsurance, (c) renewal terms, (d) exclusions, (e) coverages, and (f) waiting periods.
4   Insurance can be purchased from a nonprofit organization such as Blue Cross–Blue Shield, private insurance companies, or prepaid health maintenance organizations. The federal government also provides insurance through Medicare for the elderly and Medicaid for the poor.
5   Mail-order health insurance usually represents a poor insurance purchase. While costs of such coverage may seem low, the benefits provided are usually inadequate.
6   As a general rule, the "best" health insurance buys are provided by the non-profit organizations. Those organizations return to their policyholders a high percentage of premiums in the form of benefits; that is a sign of an effective insurance program.
7   The cost of health insurance varies greatly depending on the policy provisions.

Geographic factors also influence the premium. One thing is certain, adequate coverage is expensive. A family policy providing good protection can cost as much as $1,000 per year.

8   Dental insurance is one of the fastest growing areas of the health insurance industry. It is not as essential as health insurance because it is more of a prepayment plan than protection against catastrophic losses.

9   Group insurance usually provides more comprehensive benefits at a lower cost than comparable individual policies.

REVIEW YOUR UNDERSTANDING OF

Hospital expense insurance	Limits
Surgical expense insurance	Blue Cross
Regular medical insurance	Blue Shield
Major medical	Medicare
Comprehensive	Part A
Deductibles	Part B
Coinsurance	Medicaid
Exclusions	Mail-order insurance
Waiting periods	Dental insurance
Renewability	

DISCUSSION QUESTIONS

1   List the five principal types of health insurance contracts. What coverages are provided by each of the policy forms?

2   Sam Smith has a basic health insurance policy with a $100 deductible and an 80 percent–20 percent coinsurance clause. Sam incurs $2,000 of hospital expenses. How much will the insurance company pay?

3   What is the rationale of the insurance companies for having deductible provisions and coinsurance clauses?

4   Which of the policy provisions discussed in the chapter do you feel is most important?

5   Under what conditions should a person consider purchasing dental insurance?

6   What is the difference between health insurance and so-called accident policies?

7   Supplemental health insurance contracts seem to provide attractive benefits for a modest premium. What features make these policies such a poor insurance purchase?

8   Health maintenance organizations (HMOs) are designed to provide medical assistance for plan members. How do the benefits differ from those offered by traditional health insurance policies? What features of the HMOs make them an attractive alternative to health insurance?

9   List and discuss the features which should be thoroughly investigated before buying any health insurance contract.

CASE PROBLEM

Bill Robinson is a self-employed manufacturer's representative. Since he is not eligible for a group health insurance plan, he has been investigating individual policies. He has narrowed the choice down to two policies.

Option one is to purchase a basic policy which has hospital expense, surgical expense, and regular medical expense coverages. The limits for the hospital expense portion are $80 per day for 30 days. The surgical expense portion of the policy indemnifies with a schedule that is adequate for the surgeons' fees currently being charged. Limits on the regular medical expense policy are $3,000 in any calendar year subject to a $100 deductible. The annual premium is $360.

Option two is to purchase a comprehensive policy with a $500 deductible and an 80–20 coinsurance clause. The policy limit is $25,000 and the annual premium is $220. Both policies would be issued by a private insurance that is considered reputable.

What are the pros and cons of these policies? Which contract should Bill purchase? Why?

RECOMMENDED READINGS

Books

Most basic insurance textbooks devote one or two chapters to health insurance. The discussion is more technical than this chapter has been. However, they really do not provide additional insights which would be helpful in evaluating individual policies.

Booklets

Health Insurance Institute, *Policies for Protection.* New York, 277 Park Ave., 10017. The booklet discusses how life insurance and health insurance work. Each section concludes with review questions and case studies to illustrate important points.

Magazine Articles

Money:

Margolis, Richard J., "Group Therapy for Runaway Medical Bills." May 1973. The pros and cons of health maintenance organizations are discussed in this article. A checklist for evaluating HMOs is included at the end of the discussion.

Boronson, Warren, "Diagnosing Your Health Insurance." September 1974. The article gives a well-balanced discussion of the important provisions to look for in health insurance coverage. Excellent advice is given on whether to buy from a private company or a nonprofit organization.

Chapter 16

Property and Liability Insurance

After completing this chapter you should be able to:

recognize the major provisions of homeowners insurance.

decide which form of homeowners policy is appropriate for your needs.

recognize the major provisions of the family auto policy.

develop an auto insurance policy which provides adequate protection at reduced costs.

recognize those factors which influence the cost of your homeowners and automobile insurance policies.

explain how the use of deductibles can help minimize the cost of homeowners and automobile insurance.

select a property and liability insurance agent on the basis of logical and systematic analysis.

Property insurance reimburses an individual for damage to or theft of such personal possessions as a car, home, or furniture. Liability insurance protects the policyholders from financial loss resulting from law suits brought against them for negligent behavior. In the event someone suffers injury caused by an insured's property or automobile and a judgment finds the insured was negligent, liability insurance would pay the claims up to the policy limits.

Technically, property and liability insurance are two distinct types of insurance. However, they are commonly sold as a combination policy to protect either a person's home or automobile. Rather than treat property and liability coverages separately, this chapter discusses two kinds of insurance policies which combine these coverages. These are the standard homeowners policy and the family auto policy. However, keep in mind that they really are combination policies which offer two very different kinds of insurance protection.

HOMEOWNERS INSURANCE

Homeowners insurance is sold as a combination policy to cover both personal property and personal liability. The coverage is available to anyone who owns a one- or two-family home. There is also a special policy designed exclusively for renters. In most states, the homeowners policies are designated as HO-1, HO-2, HO-3, and HO-5 for owner-occupied dwellings and HO-4 for renters. The policies differ primarily in the number of perils (causes of loss) which they insure against.

Homeowners Property Insurance

Exhibit 16–1 summarizes the perils covered by the different forms of homeowners insurance. Examine this exhibit and you will note that there are three forms: basic, broad, and comprehensive. The basic form covers loss or damage due to 11 specified perils. The broad form includes these plus 7 additional perils. The comprehensive form includes all 18 perils plus all perils not specified, except for certain specifically excluded catastrophic perils.

HO-3 is not shown on the exhibit, although it is a very commonly issued

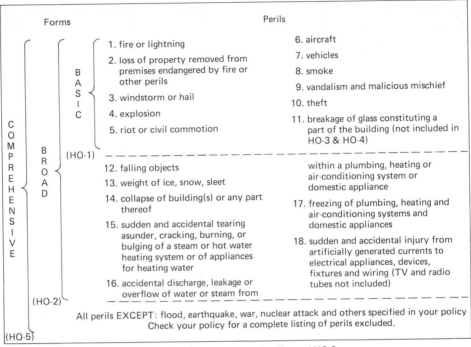

HO-3 is a combination policy providing HO-5 coverage on a dwelling and HO-2 coverage on the contents.

HO-4 provides coverage for renters. The property coverage is the same as HO-2.

Source: Insurance Information Institute, New York.

Exhibit 16-1   Perils against Which Properties Are Insured

policy. It is a combination of the comprehensive policy and the broad form policy. It provides comprehensive coverage on the dwelling and broad form coverage on the personal property. In effect, it has some of the features of HO-5 and some of HO-2.

The confusion in understanding the limitations on the homeowners policies arises because each type has evolved from an earlier property insurance policy. The basic contract's ancestor was the standard fire insurance policy. Policy types HO-2, HO-3, and HO-5 evolved from contracts which expanded on the basic fire insurance policy.

Property Coverages   Section I of the homeowners policy, which covers the insured's property, has four separate provisions which describe the coverage on the property of the policyholder.

Provision A   The coverage under this provision pertains to the building itself. Minimum coverage for the dwelling is $8,000, except for HO-5 where the minimum is $15,000. (Renter's insurance, HO-4, does not provide any coverage on the building.) The insured determines the amount to be covered for. There is no point in overinsuring, however, since the maximum amount an insurance company will reimburse is the replacement value of the property in case of total loss. The limit selected under this provision is referred to as the face amount of the policy.

Provision B   Garages, tool sheds, and similar outside buildings are referred to as appurtenant structures in insurance policies. Appurtenant structures are covered for an amount equal to 10 percent of the policy limits. If a home were insured for $20,000, the garage would automatically be covered for $2,000. In the event both structures were destroyed by fire, the policyholder would collect $22,000.

Provision C   This is the portion of the policy which specifies the amount of coverage on the contents of the building, such as furniture and clothing. This is usually specified at 50 percent of the policy's face amount. For a home insured for $20,000 the contents would be covered for $10,000. Coverage for the renter's policy, HO-4, is $4,000. Beyond that, policyholders can raise the limits to suit their needs.

Under HO-1, HO-2, and HO-3, property away from the premises is also covered. The limitations are 10 percent of the basic contents coverage. Thus, if you had an HO-3 policy with limits of $20,000 on the dwelling, the contents would be covered for $10,000 and property away from home would be protected up to $1,000. Examples of property away from the premises would be your son's or daughter's possessions in a college dormitory or the luggage in your car. An HO-5 policy covers property away from home to the same limits as property in the dwelling.

Provision D   Living expenses for you in the event your home cannot be occupied because of fire or other perils are defined in this provision. Limits are 10 percent of the face amount for HO-1 and 20 percent for HO-2, HO-3, and HO-5. HO-4 is limited to 20 percent as well. However, in HO-4, since there is no coverage on the dwelling, the additional living expenses are based on the coverage on the contents. Since this is always significantly less than a building would be insured for, the reimbursement for living expenses will be quite limited.

The 20 percent limitation is somewhat misleading, since the insurance company will pay only one-twelfth of the 20 percent in any one month. Thus if your home was insured for $30,000 under an HO-3 policy, the additional living expenses would be a maximum of $6,000. Only one-twelfth, or $500, could be paid in any one month.

Summary of Policy Coverages

Exhibit 16–2 summarizes the standard coverages under the five types of homeowners policies. This summary is for both the property and liability features of the policy. In using this table, it is important to note that all the property coverage limits depend on the amount that is specified for the basic dwelling. (The liability features will be discussed in a separate section.)

> **Strategy: The best insurance buy for most homeowners is either HO-2 or HO-3. The coverage under HO-1 is too limited and the more extensive coverage under HO-5 is appropriate only for very wealthy individuals.**

Exhibit 16-2 Summary of Homeowners Policy Coverages

Coverage on	Policy type				
	HO-1 Basic form	HO-2 Broad form	HO-3 Special form	HO-4 Renter's form	HO-5 Compre- hensive form
Dwelling	Stated	Stated	Stated	None	Stated
Appurtenant structures	10% of dwelling	10% of dwelling	10% of dwelling	None	10% of dwelling
Trees and shrubs	5% of dwelling	5% of dwelling	5% of dwelling	None	5% of dwelling
Personal property on premises	50% of dwelling	50% of dwelling	50% of dwelling	Stated	50% of dwelling
Personal property off premises	10% of property on premises	10% of property on premises	10% of property on premises	10% of property on premises	50% of dwelling
Additional living	10% of dwelling	20% of dwelling	20% of dwelling	20% of pers. property	20% of dwelling
Personal liability	$25,000 or more	$25,000 or more	$25,000 or more	$25,000 or more	$25,000 or more
Damage to others' property (per occurrence)	$250	$250	$250	$250	$250
Medical payments (per person)	$500 or more	$500 or more	$500 or more	$500 or more	$500 or more

How Much Insurance?

One of the major misunderstandings about homeowners insurance is the fact that policy limits must be at least 80 percent of the replacement value of the property; otherwise, the insured becomes a coinsurer with the company. That is, in the event of a fire, the policyholder will collect only a certain percentage of the loss. The percentage will be determined by the ratio of the amount of insurance required to the amount actually purchased.

For example, Sally Baker owned a home with a replacement value of $30,000. To meet the 80 percent requirement Sally needs $24,000 of insurance. However, she had not reviewed her insurance for several years and as a result the face amount was still only the $15,000 for which she originally insured the house. On a bitterly cold night this past winter, her furnace overheated, causing a fire which resulted in $12,000 of damages. Despite the fact that Sally had $15,000 of insurance, she collected only $7,500. Her coverage was figured by the insurance company as follows:

$$\frac{\text{Actual insurance}}{\text{Required insurance}} \times \text{amount of loss} = \text{payment}$$

In Sally's case, then,

$$\frac{\$15,000}{\$30,000 \times 80 \text{ percent}} \times \$12,000 = \$7,500$$

If Sally had maintained $24,000 of coverage on her home, she would have received the full $12,000 for the fire damage. With a face amount of $24,000, Sally would have received full payment for any damages up to that amount. Any loss in excess of $24,000 would not be covered, even if the 80 percent coverage factor were maintained. To receive full compensation for a total loss, Sally would have to insure her house for its full value of $30,000.

Despite the fact that complete compensation will not be received for a total loss unless full value insurance is carried, it is generally recommended that homes be insured for 80 percent of their replacement value. This coverage will afford full protection for any partial losses up to the face amount of the policy. Since most fires result in only partial losses, this should provide adequate protection. Moreover, even with a "total loss," the foundation and other below-ground portions of the home should still be usable.

> **Strategy: Insurance needs should be reevaluated every year and limits increased as necessary to maintain at least 80 percent protection. The insurance company does not bother to determine whether a house is insured for 80 percent until a loss has occurred. At that point, if the house is underinsured, it is too late to rectify the situation.**

Compensation for Loss of Personal Property

A home insured for $30,000 will cover personal property up to $15,000. That should be adequate coverage for most people. Unfortunately, the actual protection often falls far short of the amount stated in the policy. This occurs because standard items of personal property are covered at replacement cost less accumulated depreciation. This stipulation often substantially reduces the amount that can be collected from insurance, particularly when the insured item is close to the maximum age allowed for insurance purposes. For example, a dresser may have a useful life of 20 years for insurance purposes. Depreciation is calculated so that the item's value declines an equivalent amount each year. Thus, for a dresser with a 20-year life, the annual depreciation, or decline in value, is 5 percent of the article's replacement cost. A dresser which is nineteen years old and has a replacement cost of $600 would be covered for only $30 in the event of fire or theft. The calculation is:

Replacement cost − accumulated depreciation = settlement

or

$600 − ($30 per year × 19 years), or $600 − $570 = $30

The $570 depreciation is based on the item's age, which represents 95 percent of its useful life. The calculation is: $600 × 95 percent = $570. Or another way of looking at it is that only 5 percent of the dresser's useful life remained at the time of its loss.

The fact that the settlement for loss of personal property can be such a small percentage of the property's true value is an unpleasant surprise to many people. It is not something that is within the power of the policyholder to change. About all that can be done to realize maximum reimbursement is to make sure that your personal property inventory is up to date and accurate. An example of the type of inventory which should be maintained was discussed in Chapter 3. In addition, certain items should be insured separately for their fair market value. These are discussed more fully in the next section.

Additional Limitations   Special types of personal property which actually appreciate rather than depreciate in value are always underinsured by the standard homeowners policy. Articles such as antiques and art, unless identified and specified in the insurance policy, will be evaluated as ordinary furniture and pictures. Thus, in the event of loss, compensation would be limited to the depreciated value of the item. Since these items really appreciate in value, standard treatment would grossly underestimate their true value. Other articles, such as jewelry and furs, carry a $500 loss limitation on the homeowners policy.

The types of property which are underinsured by the homeowners policy and which should be separately insured include:

Jewelry	Art and antiques
Furs	Musical instruments
Silverware	Guns
Cameras	Stamps and coins

Coverage can be obtained by purchasing a special personal property policy, known as a personal property floater policy, or by adding the coverage to your homeowners policy: The items must be identified, which is known as scheduling, and added to the policy by endorsement. No matter what method is selected, it will be necessary to have authoritative verification of the item's value. An independent appraisal by a qualified individual is the best way to authenticate an article's value. The item should be reappraised at least every 5 years.

Recreational Vehicles   Coverage of boats, motors, snowmobiles, and campers is limited to $500 under the terms of the standard homeowners policy. Consequently, separate policies should be purchased to cover these items. The insurance agent who handles your homeowners and auto insurance policies can take care of this for you.

Mobile Homes and Farms   These types of homes cannot be insured under a standard homeowners policy. However, there are policies which are designed specifically for such residences. The provisions will differ somewhat from the homeowners policies. The important thing for you to do, if you live in a mobile home or on a farm, is to recognize that the coverage may be different and that it is important to read your policy to be aware of the differences.

Homeowners Liability Insurance

The liability portion of the homeowners policy provides coverage for personal liability, medical payments to others, and damage to others' property. Whether you rent or own, you are subject to the threat of financial loss if someone is injured in your home or on your property. Similarly, if you do something which results in damage to somebody else's property, you can also be held financially liable. In fact, in certain instances even if you can prove that someone was injured on your property through his or her own negligence, you could still be financially liable. Such would be the case if a child was injured on your property even though trespassing.

Personal Liability   The standard homeowners policies have liability limits of $25,000, although this can be increased substantially for a small additional premium. The liability coverage includes protection for legal judgments against you and the legal costs incurred in your defense.

The cost of an adverse liability settlement could be financially devastating to most people. For example, if a neighbor's child, while climbing your apple tree, should fall and sustain severe injuries, an award of $25,000 or $100,000 would not be uncommon. Could you afford to pay a settlement of that magnitude? Most likely, the answer is no. Even a $4,000 or $5,000 damage suit would be financially disastrous for most people. This is why the liability portion of the homeowners policy is so important.

> **Strategy: Given the small additional cost, as low as $4 annually, of increasing the liability limit on the homeowners policy, we feel that most people should purchase $50,000 or $100,000 of protection, rather than accept the standard coverage.**

Medical Payments   In addition to providing protection against liability judgments, the liability portion of the homeowners policy provides medical payments to persons other than the insured and his or her family. These payments are made whether or not the insured is found to be negligent. For example, if a woman slipped on your sidewalk, she could receive medical compensation from your insurance company without proving you to be at fault. The payments are made without recourse, so that if subsequent investigation proves you to be innocent of negligence, the payments will not have to be returned.

Property Damage Liability   If you, or another member of your family, should accidentally cause minor damage (under $250) to somebody else's property, this portion of the policy will pay the claim. In the event a child under thirteen causes the damage, the claim will be paid even if the damage was intentionally caused. If the child is over thirteen, claims will be paid only in the event that the damage was accidental.

Cost of Homeowners Insurance

Numerous factors influence the cost of the insurance coverage. As a property owner, you should be aware of them and, as a result, get the necessary coverage for the least cost.

The Policy Type   Policies covering a greater number of perils are always more expensive. For example, HO-5 is more costly than HO-2 since it covers more potential losses.

The Amount of Coverage   Insuring a $30,000 house will cost more than insuring a $25,000 house. Also insuring for full value will cost more than insuring the same property for 80 percent of full value.

Location of the Property   Some cities and portions of cities will have higher insurance costs because of higher fire and crime rates. Proximity to fire stations will also affect the insurance premium.

Construction of the Dwelling   Certain types of construction will cost more to insure simply because the potential for fire loss is increased with some materials.

Sample Costs   The Insurance Information Institute has calculated some typical costs for a $25,000 home insured under the basic, broad, and comprehensive policy forms. The range is from $88 to $182 per year depending on policy type and on whether insurance is for full value or for 80 percent of full value. The specifics of these calculations are given in Exhibit 16–3. The reader is cautioned that these are sample costs. Actual costs will depend on the previously discussed factors. The Insurance Information Institute suggests that the best place to get a quote for your particular needs is from a qualified insurance agent.

AUTOMOBILE INSURANCE

A major expense confronting automobile owners is the annual premium on the auto insurance policy. The cost of the policy is determined by two groups of factors: those over which you have no control, such as your age and place of residence; and those which you can influence, including your driving record and the type of automobile you own. Each of these factors will be discussed later in this chapter. Careful selection of the coverages in your auto policy can also reduce your cost substantially. In this section, we will look at the provisions of the standard family auto policy (FAP) and highlight the areas which can be of most importance to you in tailoring the policy to your needs. It is possible to be able to save $25 to $150 per year through careful insurance selection.

Exhibit 16-3   Typical Costs for Homeowners Insurance
Coverage (broad form policy)

	Amount of coverage	
	Insured to value	Insured at 80%
Property coverages		
Dwelling	$25,000 (full value)	$20,000 (80% of full value)
Appurtenant private structures	2,500 (10% of dwelling)	2,000 (10% of dwelling)
Unscheduled personal property	12,500 (50% of dwelling)	10,000 (50% of dwelling)
Additional living expenses	5,000 (20% of dwelling)	4,000 (20% of dwelling)
Liability coverages		
Personal liability	$25,000 (each occurrence)*	$25,000 (each occurrence)*
Medical payments to others	500 (each person)*	500 (each person)*
Physical damage to property of others	250 (each occurrence)	250 (each occurrence)

	Annual cost			
	Insured to value		Insured at 80%	
Coverage	Cost per year	Cost per month	Cost per year	Cost per month
Basic form, 11 perils†	$111	$ 9.25	$ 88	$ 7.33
Broad forms, 18 perils†	$126	$10.50	$ 99	$ 8.25
Comprehensive form, "all risks"†	$182	$15.17	$144	$12.00

*Larger amounts are available.
†$100 deductible.
Source: Insurance Information Institute, New York.

The Family Auto Policy

The principal auto insurance policy issued in this country is the family auto policy. The provisions of the policy are standard from company to company and, for the most part, from state to state. The FAP is designed only for the protection of privately owned vehicles, and is available only to individuals who satisfy stringent standards designed to eliminate high-risk drivers. Coverages under the policy fall into the following four sections: (1) liability, which covers both bodily injury and property damage; (2) medical payments; (3) property damage, both collision and comprehensive; and (4) uninsured motorists. Exhibit 16-4 summarizes the coverage under each of these policy provisions.

Liability Coverages   The primary need for auto insurance is to protect yourself against legal liability arising from negligence on your part. Section 1 of the policy gives limits for the maximum payment which will be made in the event of an accident. For example, a policy with limits of $100,000/$300,000/$25,000, often stated as 100/300/25, will pay $100,000 to any one accident victim, a maximum of $300,000 to all victims in one accident, and $25,000 in property damages. If you hit another car with four occupants, the maximum personal liability coverage would be $300,000 even though the policy will pay

Exhibit 16-4   Automobile Insurance

	Principal applications	
Bodily injury coverages	**Policyholder**	**Other persons**
Bodily injury liability	No	Yes
Medical payments	Yes	Yes
Protection against uninsured motorists	Yes	Yes
Property damage coverages	**Policyholder's car**	**Property of others**
Property damage liability	No	Yes
Comprehensive physical damage	Yes	No
Collision	Yes	No

Source: Insurance Information Institute, New York.

up to $100,000 to any one victim. Exhibit 16–5 shows these liability coverages.

Personal injury liability coverages begin at $5,000/$10,000 and increase to a maximum $100,000/$300,000. The cost differential between minimum coverage and maximum coverage is usually very small: the difference in cost could be as low as $16 annually. This is one place you should not try to save on insurance. You should purchase the maximum coverage you can obtain.

In addition to the basic liability coverage, the insurance company also agrees to defend the insured in any accident case. This promise to defend is separate from any liability settlement. Thus, if the judgment were for $300,000, the maximum under the policy, the insurance company would pay all court and defense costs as well as the $300,000 judgment.

The property damage liability portion of section 1 covers damages to other people's property in an accident caused by the insured. Running into another car, going through a storefront or knocking down a telephone pole would all be covered up to the policy limits. With the cost of many cars running $6,000 to $7,000, property damage liability limits of $10,000 or even $25,000 are not unreasonable. The incremental cost of $25,000 versus $10,000 is so small that you should purchase the larger amount, if you qualify.

Exhibit 16-5   Automobile Liability Insurance Limits

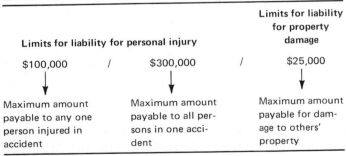

Medical Payments   Section 2 of the family automobile policy provides medical payments to the insured and passengers in the insured's car. The limits begin at $500; for a small additional premium cost, the limits can be increased to $5,000. If you have regular health insurance and you are injured in your car, you will receive medical payments from your auto insurance, and these payments will not affect any payments due you under your health insurance. The important thing about section 2 of the auto insurance is that the medical payments provide immediate coverage for the insured (there is no waiting period as in health insurance) and it provides coverage for the passengers who may not have health insurance.

Protection against Uninsured Motorists   One of the dangers confronting drivers is that of being involved in an accident where the other driver is at fault but does not have automobile insurance. The uninsured motorists section of your own FAP is designed to reimburse you for personal injuries if you are involved in an accident with an uninsured driver. It is important to realize that this protection covers only personal injury liability, not property damage liability. In addition, your reimbursement will be subject to the minimum limits for personal injury liability imposed by your state of residence. For example, in the state of Wisconsin the minimum limits are $15,000/$30,000. Even if you had maximum coverage, you would not collect more than the minimum. Limited as the protection may be, it is a worthwhile addition to your insurance policy. The cost is minimal, often as low as $2 per year. Most companies will automatically include this feature on the policy. And in some states it is a mandatory coverage on the FAP.

Collision Insurance   This portion of the FAP reimburses you for damages to your car resulting from an accident where you are at fault. Collision coverage is always written with a deductible provision. That is, you must pay a specified amount and the insurance company pays the rest. Standard deductible amounts are $50, $100, and $250. With a $50 deductible, if you suffered $1,000 of collision damages you would collect $950, provided your car was worth at least $1,000. The maximum the insurance company will pay is the wholesale price of the car. Thus, if a car valued at $500 is damaged but repairs would cost $1,000, the maximum compensation would be $450. Since the car could not be repaired for $450, the insured would probably have to buy a new car, or pay the difference between the compensation and the cost.

Collision insurance is extremely costly protection. Therefore the proper use of deductibles can be important. Tailoring the policy to your needs through careful selection of deductibles can save you a significant amount of money. This will be discussed thoroughly in a later section.

Comprehensive Property Coverage   The comprehensive provision reimburses you for damage to your car resulting from fire, theft, vandalism, hail, windstorm, flood, smoke, and similar perils. Unfortunately, many people

believe that the theft provisions of their comprehensive coverage also include personal articles in the automobile. This is not true. Only the automobile itself is covered by this portion of the policy. If luggage or other personal items are stolen from you car, any reimbursement must come from your homeowners or renter's insurance.

Comprehensive insurance coverage can be written either for the full value of your car or with a deductible feature. Like the collision insurance, the use of a deductible can reduce the cost of your insurance. However, the cost saving from using a deductible with the comprehensive provision will be substantially lower than the savings from a deductible with collision coverage.

Choosing Your Policy Limits

A great deal of attention has been paid to advising people on how to calculate how much liability protection they should purchase. Complex formulas calculating a person's future earnings potential plus their net worth have been developed to determine policy limits. Other advice suggests analyzing the size of settlements awarded in the area in which you live and selecting coverages adequate to meet the maximum judgments made in the last few years. Undoubtedly, accident awards vary according to the economic status of the negligent party and the geographic location. But it is nearly an impossible task to accurately pinpoint the upper accident award you may face.

In light of the complexity of determining upper limits, we believe a more simple standard is in order. Our advice is to purchase the maximum auto liability coverage you qualify for. As we previously pointed out, the differential between minimum and maximum limits is very small. But those few extra dollars spent on higher coverage will protect you against the possible catastrophic losses from a large damage award.

Who Is Covered?

The most important technical aspect of the FAP is the definition of who is covered by the insurance. The FAP is designed to provide protection for the insured when driving both owned and nonowned automobiles.

Owned Automobiles   An owned automobile is one owned by the insured. The coverage for an owned automobile is extensive. For example, if Mary Stone lends her car to Thelma Rock, Thelma would be covered by Mary's policy since she is driving with Mary's permission. Thelma would also be covered under her own FAP if she has one. The car, as defined by the insurance companies, qualifies as an owned automobile for Mary and a nonowned automobile for Thelma. The specific situations where an owned automobile will be covered are listed in Exhibit 16–6.

Nonowned Automobiles   A nonowned automobile is one not owned by the insured or by residents of the insured's household, nor is it an automobile provided for the regular use of the insured. The coverages for nonowned automobiles are also outlined in Exhibit 16–6.

A car which does not qualify for coverage by an individual's FAP is one owned by another resident of the same household. For example, if you own a car, are living with your parents, and lend the car to your father, his FAP will not protect him because the car does not meet the definition of either an owned or a nonowned vehicle. However, your father would still be insured under your policy, since he was driving with your permission. Of course, if your car were uninsured, there would be no protection in the event of an accident. This occurs, despite the fact that you father has an FAP, because of the way owned and nonowned autos are defined.

Items 4 and 7 in Exhibit 16–6 are not as clear as the others. Vicarious liability refers to a situation where a person or group becomes liable for the negligent acts of another person. For example, if a friend asks you to run an

---

Exhibit 16-6   Coverage Provided under the Family Auto Policy

For owned automobiles
1   The named insured and the named insured's spouse, if a resident of the same household
2   Residents of the same household
3   Anybody using the insured's automobile with the permission of the insured
4   Any person or organization having potential vicarious liability resulting from negligence by the insured, residents of the insured's household, or persons driving with permission of the insured

For nonowned automobiles
5   The named insured
6   Residents of the same household operating the nonowned vehicle with permission
7   Groups or persons who could be held vicariously liable

errand and an accident occurs, the owner of the damaged property can take legal action against both you and your friend. If you are uninsured, your friend is legally obligated under the concept of vicarious liability. In this case it would be the friend's FAP which would provide the coverage. In essence, then, protection for vicarious liability means that your policy will protect you for actions of others where those actions can be traced to you, such as your lending your car or even your asking a friend to run an errand in his car.

In summary, it is safe to assume that your FAP policy will cover you if (1) you are driving your car, (2) somebody else is driving your car with your permission, and (3) you are driving a borrowed car with permission, provided it meets the definition of a nonowned automobile. If you have a unique situation where there is a question about whether you or another person will be protected by your insurance, check with your agent.

Policy Cancelation

You may, of course, cancel your family auto policy at any time. The company may also cancel the policy at any time under certain conditions and you should be aware of those conditions. Under the provisions of the FAP, once the policy has been in force for 60 days, the company may not cancel unless any of the conditions listed in Exhibit 16–7 occur. Items 4 and 7 in Exhibit 16–7 are probably of greatest concern to most people. It is really important to make sure that your driving record is clean. You should be aware that even if your driving offenses are insufficient to warrant suspension or revocation of your license, they may be grounds for canceling your insurance.

Shopping for Auto Insurance

Coverages offered by two insurance companies may be identical, yet the costs can vary substantially. Exhibit 16–8 summarizes insurance costs for 12 representative insurance companies doing business in Milwaukee, Wisconsin. It is striking how much money can be saved by carefully shopping for insurance. For example, the 6-month premium for a person with two cars and a seventeen-year-old male driver in the family, living in Milwaukee, can run from a low of $176.65 to as high as $588. To be sure, this example is somewhat biased since the company charging $588 specializes in high-risk insurance. Even so, rates for similar companies may vary by as much as $75 for a 6-month

Exhibit 16-7 Grounds for Cancellation of the Family Auto Policy

1 The premium is not paid as agreed
2 There was fraudulent misrepresentation in obtaining the insurance
3 There is a violation of any of the terms or conditions of the policy
4 The driving license of the insured or a resident of the same household is suspended or revoked
5 The operator of the vehicle is subject to epileptic seizures or heart attacks
6 The named insured, or any other operator, has been convicted or has forfeited bail in the preceding 3 years for any felony, drunken driving, vehicular criminal negligence, hit and run, or misrepresentation in the application for a driver's license
7 Three moving traffic violations in an 18-month period

Exhibit 16-8 Insurance Costs for Representative Companies

Company	Best's rating	Premium group 1	Premium group 2
Aetna Casualty & Surety*	A+	$ 63.00	$246.00
Allstate†	A+	$ 76.70	$176.65
American Family†	A+	$ 64.80	$201.01
Classified	B	$ 80.60	$244.75
General Casualty*	A+	$ 79.00	$182.50
Heritage Mutual	A	$ 72.30	$193.40
Milwaukee Mutual	A	$ 86.25	$247.50
Mutual Service	A	$ 86.00	$223.30
Sentry*	B+	$ 80.00	$221.00
State Farm†,§	A+	$ 83.80	$269.07
American Standard‡	A+	$152.00	$376.00
Dairyland‡	B	$234.00	$588.00

Group 1—one car. Minimal 6-month auto insurance for a Milwaukee adult with a clean driving record on a 1970 Chevrolet Impala driven under 10 miles one way to work, under 7,500 miles a year.

Group 2—two cards. Minimal 6-month auto insurance for a Milwaukee family, with a seventeen-year-old male who drives occasionally, on a 1973 Ford Galaxie and a 1971 Chevrolet Vega, each driven under 10 miles one way to work, each under 7,500 miles a year. All drivers have clean driving records.

Rates were computed by the State Insurance Department at the request of *The Milwaukee Journal*. They can be doubled to obtain an annual rate.

The companies chosen are the top 12 in terms of sales dollars in Wisconsin in 1972, latest figures available. They account for 55 percent of the auto insurance sold.

The coverage is 15/30/5 liability, 15/30 bodily injured by uninsured motorist, $1,000 medical payments, $100 deductible collision, and full comprehensive coverage.

Note that Best's Insurance Reports rate insurance companies according to their financial stability.

*Aetna, General Casualty, and Sentry are for $35,000 single-limit liability, meaning they pay a maximum of $35,000 whether one or more persons are injured and for property damage.

†Some companies charge more for issuing bills on a monthly, quarterly, or 6-month basis. Allstate, for instance, charges $1 each time it bills. American Family and State Farm have an additional fee when a policy is begun.

‡The drivers, who have clean driving records, would not normally insure with American Standard or Dairyland. Rates at the two companies are higher because they specialize in high-risk insurance—insuring drivers with bad driving records. The examples are included to illustrate that the cost could be higher for a driver with a bad record than for the good driver who does not bother to do comparison shopping.

§State Farm lowered its rate May 1, 1974 and pays a variable dividend which would reduce its cost. Other rates also may change.

Reprinted with permission of The Milwaukee Journal Company, from *The Milwaukee Journal*, April 7, 1974, p. 13.

premium. Over a 30-year period the savings could amount to $4,500. Moreover, the careful insurance buyer who places that $150 annual saving in a 6 percent savings account will have $12,211 at the end of 30 years. That $150 per year may not seem like much, but those little savings accumulated over a long period of time can be substantial.

Getting the Most for Your Insurance Dollar

For each of the coverages under the FAP, it is possible either to save money or to purchase much more insurance for a small increase in the premium. Exhibit 16–9 illustrates some of the possible savings and protection increases. Specific suggestions for maximizing protection while minimizing cost are discussed in this section.

Liability   The difference in premiums between minimum and maximum liability protection will run as low as $8 every 6 months. Thus, for an additional annual premium of $16, you will be receiving added insurance of $270,000.

Medical   Purchase medical payments coverage of $5,000, or as much as you qualify for. Hospital costs are now running close to $200 per day in many sections of the country. If you have only $500 medical payments coverage, you will be lucky to get beyond the waiting room in most hospitals. Again, the added cost of increasing the coverage is small relative to the benefits which are provided.

Collision   Reduce the cost of your collision insurance by increasing the deductible or dropping the coverage altogether. For example, the cost of $50 deductible collision may run as high as $160 per year. By increasing the deductible to $100, it is possible to save $25 or even $30 per year. Thus, to have $50 deductible rather than $100, you are really paying $25 annually for $50 of insurance protection. That is expensive protection.

Many people continue to carry collision insurance on their automobiles long after the car has a value high enough to warrant such coverage. If you have a 6-year-old car which cost $4,000 when new, it is probably worth about $500 today. In the event of a total wreck or an accident with damages in excess of $500, you will collect a maximum of $450, assuming you have the $50

Exhibit 16-9   Representative Premiums for Family Auto Policy Coverages

Coverage	Limits	Percentage increase in limits	Annual premium	Percentage increase in cost
Liability	$15/$30		$ 75	
	$50/$100	233%	$ 89	18%
	$100/$300	100	$121	35
Medical payments	$ 500		$ 8	
	$1,000	100	$ 13	62
	$5,000	400	$ 22	69
Collision	$50 ded		$160	
	$100 ded	NA	$125	NA
Comprehensive	Full	—	$ 25	
Uninsured motorists	$15/$30	—	$ 10	

Within the next several years these premiums will probably increase about 30 percent or more, judging from increases over the past few years.

deductible. Is it worth $160 of insurance premiums each year to have $450 of insurance protection? Unless you have a major accident more than once every 2.8 years, the answer is no. If you had an accident every 2.8 years, you would be recovering your insurance costs. However, you probably could not get insurance at reasonable rates with that kind of driving record. In fact, you would be lucky still to have a driver's license.

> **Strategy: For most people, a careful look at their collision coverage may show that they are spending money foolishly. Review your coverage and purchase a $100 or $250 deductible if you currently have a $50 deductible. If your car is worth less than $1,000, seriously consider dropping the collision coverage.**

Comprehensive   You can use a deductible in lieu of full comprehensive coverage to lower your premium. The savings are not usually quite so great as they are with the collision insurance, but the use of deductibles is still worth looking into.

Rates for Automobile Insurance

In each locality, insurance companies determine a base rate for all drivers, as shown in Exhibit 16–10. Young drivers are divided into four groups, and within each group, the cost of the insurance varies depending on the age of the insured. Exhibit 16–10 shows the relationship of premiums to the base rate for the four principal rating groups. A dollar scale has not been used in this figure since the exact cost will vary according to geographic location.

Insurance rates are also adjusted for factors such as automobile usage and driving record. The major factors are discussed below. It is important to realize that it is possible to lower premium costs by paying attention to each of these special rating factors.

Type of Car   If you own a "hot" car, you will have to pay a substantial surcharge to obtain insurance coverage. The surcharge may run 30 or 40 percent annually. Thus, if the insurance costs $250 for an ordinary car, and you decide to buy a high-performance car, it will add $100 per year to your insurance costs. You should ask yourself: Can I afford the extra insurance cost to drive a high-powered car? In addition to the insurance costs, do not forget that the other ownership costs for this type of car are also likely to be higher.

Driving Record   Many automobile insurance companies offer a discount to safe drivers and impose a surcharge on drivers with a poor record. Their definition of a poor record includes not only drivers who have accidents, but individuals with moving violations as well. Your next speeding ticket may add $50 or more to your insurance costs in addition to the $50 fine. The moral is to keep that record clean and to save by avoiding a fine and a premium surcharge.

Automobile Use   The less you use your car, the lower your rates. Using your auto for commuting and/or business purposes can add substantially to

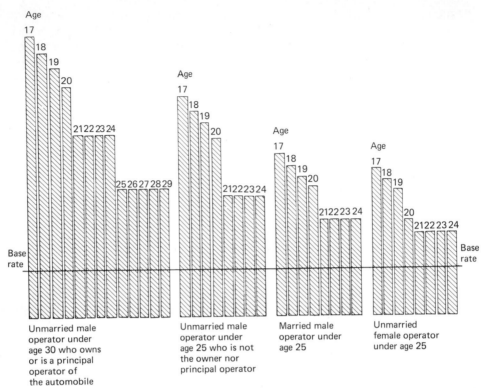

Source: Insurance Information Institute, New York.
Based on a driver classification plan used by a large segment of the business in many states. These comparisons of gradations are for private passenger cars used for pleasure where all operators have "clean" driving records. Adjustments in premiums are made for cars used to drive to work, for business, or on a farm. Adjustments are also made for youthful operators with driver-training credit, drivers with "unclean" driving records, and owners of more than one car. In many states, premium discounts are available to students with outstanding scholastic records.

Exhibit 16-10   Rates Go Down as Young Drivers Grow Older

your premium. The longer the distance you commute to work, the more costly will be your insurance. Given this, you may want to include auto insurance as one of the added variables that you should consider when selecting a place to live.

City of Residence   Auto insurance companies include your place of residence in calculating the insurance premium. In communities where drivers have fewer accidents, the insurance costs less than in communities where drivers have more accidents. This will be the case even if the communities are adjacent. For example, it may cost only one-half or even one-third as much to insure a car in Needham (a suburb of Boston) as it does in Boston proper. Again, selecting where you live can have a big influence on your insurance costs.

Two-Car Discounts   If you own two cars you should insure them with the same company. Most companies offer a second-car discount of as much as 10 percent. It could save you $20 or even $30 per year.

Driver Education Credits The premium surcharge imposed on young drivers can be reduced if they have completed a recognized driver-training program. It is evident from the material shown in Exhibit 16–10 that the costs for young drivers is high and that driving training will help reduce their costs.

No-Fault Insurance

Two long-standing complaints about auto insurance have been the delays and the costs of settling claims. Under the law, to collect in an auto accident, one party must prove the other to be at fault. Often this procedure requires lawyers on both sides and bitter legal action. In some cases, such as multicar chain collisions, it is virtually impossible to prove negligence by any one driver. As a result of the weaknesses and inequities in the current application of legal principles to auto insurance, there has been a gradually accelerating move to a system known as no-fault insurance.

Under no-fault insurance an insured collects from her own insurance company for injuries and damages sustained in an automobile accident. No-fault does not rule out litigation to collect from the other person's insurance carrier. Rather, it places limits on the amount of damages which must be sustained before lawsuits are permitted. The intent of no-fault legislation is to reduce the costs of insurance by eliminating the costs, primarily the legal costs, of settling claims. And the way no-fault does this is simply for the insurance company to pay the claim without determining who is at fault. If the claim exceeds the no-fault limit (usually between $2,000 and $5,000), lawsuits would be permitted just as they are under current insurance law.

A number of states have enacted no-fault legislation. Results to date indicate that the plans have great potential for reducing insurance costs. Presently there is no uniform system of no-fault insurance in this country. If you live in a state which has adopted no-fault, it would be wise to familiarize yourself with the major provisions of the program. Probably, within the next few years, a unified national no-fault system will be enacted by Congress.

Exhibit 16-11   Rules for Buying Insurance

Do get price quotes from four or five different agents. Any agent who is not competitive should be eliminated on the basis of price alone.

Do ask friends and relatives to recommend a good agent. Many people have a satisfactory long-term relationship with an agent and their experience can be invaluable in helping you find a good insurance agent.

Do contact four or five agents and ask them to help you plan an insurance program. Many agents just want to take orders and are not interested in advising clients. A good agent should be willing and able to do so.

Do not buy insurance from the car dealer. The insurance sold by dealers is, in most cases, not competitive with insurance you could purchase elsewhere.

Do not finance your automobile insurance through a dealer.

Do consider buying group auto insurance if it is available through your employer.

Selecting an Agent and Buying Insurance

It is generally good practice to purchase your homeowners and auto insurance through the same agent. The agent will be more inclined to get the lowest possible rate for you if he is handling all your property insurance needs. Some specific suggestions for selecting an agent and buying insurance are listed in Exhibit 16–11.

SUMMARY

1 Both homeowners and automobile insurance policies are combinations of personal liability and property insurance designed to provide protection for most perils facing a homeowner and auto owner.

2 There are four forms of homeowners insurance designed exclusively for owners and one form for renters. The selection of the policy form will depend on the amount and extent of protection desired.

3 To be fully protected for a partial loss to a dwelling, the dwelling must be insured for at least 80 percent of its replacement value. In the event that 80 percent coverage is not maintained, the insured becomes a coinsurer. The ratio for calculating the amount of the loss which will be reimbursed is:

$$\frac{\text{Actual insurance}}{\text{Required insurance}} \times \text{amount of loss} = \text{payment}$$

4 Compensation for loss of personal property is determined by deducting accumulated depreciation from the item's replacement cost.

5 Many items of personal property, such as jewelry, antiques, art, silverware, and furs, will be underinsured by the standard homeowners policy. Additional coverage can be obtained by identifying and specifying (scheduling) the items on the policy or purchasing a separate (floater) policy.

6 Recreational vehicles, such as boats, snowmobiles, and campers, are covered only

to a maximum of $500 under homeowners insurance. Separate policies should be purchased to protect these possessions.

7 The liability portion of the homeowners policy protects against financial judgments arising from injuries to people on the insured's property with or without negligent behavior on the part of the insured.

8 The cost of homeowners insurance is quite modest. The cost is influenced by the type of policy, the policy limits, the construction of the building, the location of the property, and the amount of the deductible feature.

9 The family auto policy (FAP) is the primary automobile insurance policy sold in this country. Its primary feature is liability insurance which can be supplemented with property insurance.

10 The primary reason for automobile insurance is for protection against large lawsuits arising from negligent behavior by the insured.

11 The insurance company can cancel a FAP if the insured has three moving traffic violations in 18 months or is convicted of any felony, drunken driving, vehicular criminal negligence, or hit and run. Other factors which may cause cancelation include nonpayment of premiums and revocation of the drivers license of any resident in the insured's household.

12 Auto insurance should be selected for maximum protection at minimim costs.

13 You may not need all the coverages offered under the standard family auto policy. Especially, carefully consider whether or not you need collision insurance.

14 You can reduce the cost of your insurance by using a deductible with the comprehensive insurance, and by increasing the deductible on the collision portion of the policy.

15 Rates among companies may vary by $150 or more per year for identical automobile insurance coverage.

16 Your driving record, the type of car you drive, and whether you use the car for business or pleasure, can have a major impact on your auto insurance costs.

REVIEW YOUR UNDERSTANDING OF

Perils

Property coverages
    Appurtenant structures
    Personal property
    Additional living expenses

Coinsurance

Personal property floaters

Liability coverages

Family auto policy
    Bodily injury liability

Medical payments

Property damage liability

Comprehensive physical damage

Collision

Liability limits

Deductibles

Vicarious liability

Owned automobiles

Nonowned automobiles

No-fault insurance

DISCUSSION QUESTIONS

1 Why should a person buy homeowners insurance? What does the owner have to lose if no insurance is bought?

2 Sam Smith told a friend that since he did not own a house, there was no reason to purchase insurance. Do you agree or disagree with this statement? Why?

3 John Smith owned a home with a replacement value of $36,000. His insurance policy was written for $18,000. John's home was hit by lightning and the resulting

fire caused $11,000 of damages. How much would John collect under the terms of his policy?

4   Tom Tillman had an HO-3 policy with liability limits of $25,000. A neighbor tripped on Tom's front walk and broke his ankle. He sued Tom for $25,000. There was no visible evidence of cracks or other imperfections in the sidewalk. Will the neighbor be able to collect? Can he collect under any provision of the homeowners policy?

5   Tom's son threw a baseball through the neighbor's picture window. Will Tom's policy pay for damages? Does it make any difference that his son is fourteen years old and admits that he tried to break the window?

6   Under what conditions is it advisable for individuals to drop the collision coverage on their automobile? Work out an example to prove your answer.

7   Is it advisable for a person to buy maximum liability coverage? Why?

8   What provisions of the family auto policy are of greatest importance for most drivers? Of least importance?

9   You have borrowed your mother's car for the evening. You loan the car to a friend who proceeds to smash into a new storefront, injuring three pedestrians in the process. Are you covered? Why or why not?

10 Phil Swensen owns a 1973 Belchfire Eight. His insurance policy has the following limits and annual costs:

Liability 15/30/5	$ 87
Medical payments $500	8
Collision $50 ded	160
Comprehensive full	25
Uninsured motorists	10
	$290
Performance car surcharge	125
Total	$415

Advise Fast Phil on how he can reduce his insurance costs. (Hint: See Exhibit 16–9.)

CASE PROBLEM

Jim Johnson is a typical two-car suburbanite. His automobiles are a one-year-old, full-size station wagon that is used primarily by his wife. He commutes 15 miles a day to work in a 5-year-old compact. Jim has just made an offer to purchase a $35,000 home. He estimates that the value of the land is approximately $5,000. Jim and Ann have collected antiques for a number of years and they now have articles which are valued at approximately $7,200.

   Jim has not reviewed his auto policies for a number of years. He does not have renter's insurance, but realizes that he will have to purchase a homeowners policy to satisfy the bank that is lending him the mortgage money for his home. He has come to you for advise since he knows that you have a great deal of expertise in property and liability insurance. Specifically, advise Jim on the amounts and coverages he should purchase for his cars and new home. What would you advise him to do about insuring the antique furniture? What advice could you give Jim about agents, companies, and policy forms?

RECOMMENDED READINGS

Books

Elliott, Curtis M., and Emmett J. Vaughn, *Fundamentals of Risk and Insurance.* New York: Wiley, 1972.
Chapters 19 and 20 contain a complete description of the family auto policy and a discussion of the differences between the family auto policy, special auto policy, and basic auto policy.

Booklets

Insurance Information Institute, *A Family Guide to Property and Liability Insurance.* New York, 1973.
This booklet is a well-presented treatment of the principal features of both homeowners and automobile insurance. It adequately covers most of the important details in each policy. It does not contain advice on selecting coverages.

Magazines

Money:

Mead, William B., "A Precrash Course in No-Fault Auto Insurance." June 1974, pp. 31–32.
The article discusses no-fault insurance and potential areas that may or may not yield lower premiums.

Chapter 17

Formulating Your Investment Goals

After completing this chapter you should be able to:

explain the workings of compound growth.

illustrate the impact of extending the compounding period.

decide which investment alternative provides the highest effective return, given different multiple compounding periods.

recall what is included in an investment's effective return.

define the following types of risk: business risk, risk of financial collapse, market price risk, interest rate risk.

describe the risk-return trade-off.

illustrate the impact of inflation on an investment's return.

analyze the strengths and weaknesses of lending investments and ownership investments as potential hedges against inflation.

explain the following criteria for judging investments: risk exposure, annual yield, maturity, flexibility, minimum-size limitation, tax features, hedge against inflation, and general availability.

develop your own investment goals.

design a plan for implementing your investment goals.

Investments should be a part of everyone's personal financial program. They are the second step of the savings process which we introduced in the budgeting chapter (Chapter 4) and have discussed in succeeding chapters. Although the traditional passbook savings account is one investment choice, we discuss a much broader range of alternatives in Chapters 18, 19, and 20. Most of these investments provide a higher rate of return to the investor, but, as might be expected, they also entail more risk. The more you know about the available alternatives, the better equipped you will be to select appropriate investments that meet the investment goals you have established.

People who can afford to invest large amounts of money have more to gain or lose from their investments than small investors. But small investors should be just as concerned about investments, if not more so, than their moneyed counterparts. Because small investors have less to invest, it is even more critical that their investments earn an adequate return. Furthermore, the return should be appropriate for the risk that investment entails.

There are many investment opportunities available to small investors, and indications are there will be even more opportunities in the future. As a small investor, you generally must be your own investment advisor. To be effective in that role, you need to have some basic background on investments. We think that Chapters 17 through 20 can help you achieve this objective.

Investment is not an easy area of study. Much of the area is complex, involved, and difficult to master. But we think every small investor can acquire the basic tools and skills necessary to effectively manage his or her personal investments. Furthermore, we hope that, after completing these chapters, you will find managing your personal investments an interesting, challenging, and satisfying pursuit.

These next several chapters will not provide you with a formula guaranteeing to make you rich. No book and no author can guarantee to bring you great wealth through investments even though many make such a claim. We stress guidelines and strategies that will provide a respectable investment return, yet will do so with relatively limited risk. While that goal is less ambitious, we believe it is quite achievable. That is more than can be said for most rapid-road-to-riches schemes.

SOME FIRST STEPS

To decide on a particular investment goal, you first need a detailed description of exactly what that goal is. It is not enough to say: I want to earn all the money I possibly can. If you really invested toward that goal, it could take you into such heady investments as the common stock of companies like Lost Horizons Gold Mines, Boom or Bust Oil Wells Incorporated, and Last Flight Airlines. Granted, the potential returns may be sizable, but there is also the possibility of a complete loss. The degree of risk may far outweigh the potential return, making the investments totally unacceptable to most people. What is needed is a set of specific goals which can assist you in deciding the important questions: How much to invest? Where to invest? When to invest? What are the risks? We will help you answer these and other questions in these chapters.

Do It Now   Even a modest annual investment will accumulate to a sizable sum over a period of years. For example, suppose Becky Bimstein decided she wanted to accumulate half-a-million dollars by her seventieth birthday. She could achieve that $500,000 goal by saving $1,722.15 each year, beginning at twenty years of age, and placing that money in an investment that earned 6 percent annually. Although few people aspire to a half-million-dollar goal (how could anyone possibly enjoy it when seventy years old!), it does demonstrate that even limited savings invested at a modest return will accumulate to a sizable amount over an extended period.

Let us work through a second example. Suppose Winthrop Adams wants to accumulate $10,000 to finance his daughter's college education. Assuming the same 6 percent return, he will have to save $1,774 per year if he does not start the investment program until 5 years before he needs the $10,000. Had the program been begun when his daughter was born, giving him 20 years to accumulate the money, he would have to save only $271.85 each year. This example illustrates a key point. Once you identify an investment goal, it is essential that you begin working toward that goal immediately, especially when the dollar amount is large.

A Tool for Every Purpose   Small investors have a number of investment alternatives; some are appropriate for certain investment goals, others are not. For example, the common stock of large corporations might be ideal for a long-range investment goal. However, it is likely to be inappropriate if the money is going to be invested for only 6 months. Our objective in this chapter is to provide the basic guidelines so you can match your investments to your goals.

INVESTMENT ALTERNATIVES

Individuals have basically two investment alternatives: They can lend their money to some borrower, or they can use their money to purchase partial or

full ownership in some income-producing asset. While the array of potential investments—savings account, government bond, common stock, real estate, corporate bond, etc.—is wide, each one can be classified as either a lending investment or an ownership investment.

Lending When you lend money, your return comes from the interest the borrower pays for using those funds. Most lending investments have a fixed income and a fixed maturity. *Fixed income* means the borrower promises to pay a set interest rate for use of the funds. *Fixed maturity* simply means that the borrower promises to repay the loan at some set point in the future. The principal attraction to lending is that the investor knows what the return will be, how long that return will continue, and when the amount borrowed will be repaid. Of course, if the borrower suffers a major financial crisis, it could alter that return or timing. The principal shortfall is that the lender's return is limited to the agreed-upon contractual rate.

Ownership There are several ways a person can invest through ownership. Examples include: partial ownership of a corporation by buying its common stock; buying mutual fund shares (the proceeds from the mutual fund shares are used to purchase the common stocks of many different corporations); ownership of a small business; a business partnership; ownership of real estate; ownership of some investment property, such as gold, art objects, and stamps. (Appendix C provides a list of recommended readings dealing with these specialized investment properties.) Regardless of the investment medium, your return is determined by the profitability of the income-producing asset. If it does well, you, as partial or complete owner, will share in its earnings. But the blade cuts both ways. Should the investment fare poorly, your return will be poor. Although there is no guaranteed return with ownership, neither is there an upper limit on the potential return. Because the potential return is unlimited, ownership is an attractive investment for many people. However, its principal disadvantage is the possibility the return could be very small, zero, or negative. A sizable negative return could mean the total loss of the investment. Furthermore, in some business and real estate ventures you, as an owner, could be liable for part of the business's debts.

IMPACT OF INFLATION

We are reminded of inflation's impact every time we purchase an item. The question is rarely whether the price went up; instead, the question is how much the price increased. Although the effect of inflation on investments is less obvious, it is just as damaging. For example, assume we deposit $100 in a savings account paying 5 percent annual interest. At the end of 1 year, the account balance will be $105 ($100 + $5 interest). Yet, if prices have risen 3 percent during the same year, our purchasing power has increased only 2 percent. Because prices have risen, it now takes $103 to buy the same thing $100 bought one year ago. Despite its promised 5 percent return, the savings account's real return (annual return rate minus the inflation rate) is only 2 percent. And it is not hard to imagine a situation where inflation could reduce an investment's real return to zero or even a negative rate. For example, the 11 percent inflation rate during 1974 reduced the typical 5 percent savings account real return to −6 percent. Thus, if you had $100 in a 5 percent savings account during 1974, your purchasing power would have actually declined by $6. It would take $111 to buy the same goods $100 bought a year earlier, but your savings increased to only $105 during the year. Therefore, your investment return actually lost 6 percent in purchasing power because of the 11 percent inflation rate.

Clearly the impact of inflation must be incorporated in any investment decision. An immediate question is: Were the high inflation rates of the past several years unusual, or are they the inflation wave of the future? The top half of Exhibit 17–1 shows the inflation rate during recent years. The bottom half of the exhibit traces out the effect of those inflation rates on the purchasing power of $1. However, you should be aware that the inflation rate is cumulative. Therefore, the 4 percent inflation rate of 1968 made the $1 worth only 96 cents in 1968; the 5 percent inflation rate of 1969 made 96 cents worth only 91 cents with respect to $1 in 1967; the inflation rate of 5 percent in 1970 made 91 cents worth only 86 cents with respect to $1 in 1967; and so on. Beginning at $1 in 1967, a dollar's purchasing power has shrunk to the point where it was worth only 68 cents in 1974. That means it took approximately $147.06 [($1.00 ÷ $0.68) × $100] to purchase the same goods that $100 would have bought in 1967.

An example can illustrate how inflation would have affected an investment

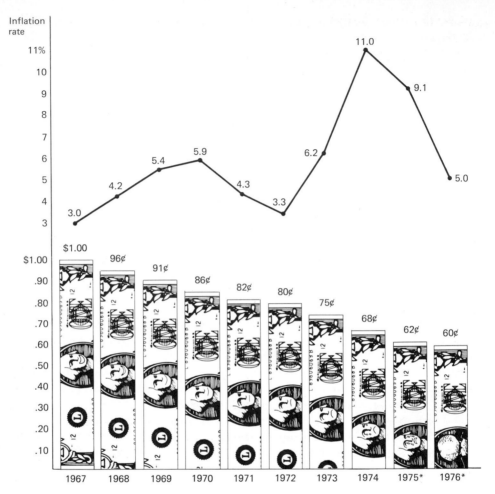

*Author's estimate.

Source: Annual inflation rates are authors' estimates. Purchasing power of $1 is from U.S. Department of Labor, Bureau of Labor Statistics *Handbook of Labor Statistics*, 1975, p. 316.

Exhibit 17-1 Consumer Prices: Annual Inflation Rate and Purchasing Power of $1

during that period. Assume an investor had $100 in a 5 percent savings account from 1967 through 1974. At the end of the period the amount invested plus interest would have totaled $147.75. Yet, in 1974 it required $147.06 to purchase the same thing that the initial $100 would have bought in 1967. To hold an investment for 8 years and do little more than break even is disheartening and depressing!

Future Prospect During the past 30 years, inflation has averaged 3½ percent annually. However, for the recent 10 years shown in Exhibit 17–1, the average inflation rate is approximately 6 percent. Unfortunately, we believe most preliminary evidence suggests that the annual rate during the late 1970s is likely to be closer to 6 percent than to the historical 3½ percent. This probability points up the need for continued concern about the impact of inflation on investment return.

Hedge against Inflation

If inflation rates are to continue at their recent high levels, we need an investment strategy that can partially, or completely, offset inflation's effect. While there is little, if anything, individual investors can do to slow inflation, they can concentrate on investments that offer some hedge against inflation.

Lending Investments   Because the return on a lending investment is fixed, its real return declines as inflation increases. Thus, the return on a 6 percent, 10-year bond remains at 6 percent regardless of inflation. If inflation ranges from 4 to 14 percent annually during those 10 years, the bond's real return could range from 2 percent to −8 percent. For this reason, many people maintain that fixed-income investments offer no protection against inflation and therefore are a poor investment.

We take a more sanguine view. We feel that interest rates do contain an inflation factor; the higher the inflation rate, the higher that factor will be. For example, during the early 1960s the interest rate on prime-quality bonds was approximately 4.3 percent. During that period, inflation averaged nearly 1.3 percent annually, so the bond's real return was roughly 3 percent (4.3 − 1.3). Despite inflation's sharp increase to 4.6 percent annually during the early seventies, the real return on prime-quality bonds still averaged nearly 3 percent because prevailing interest rates had risen to 7.4 percent. Because prevailing interest rates do increase in response to higher inflation rates, it is inappropriate to say that fixed-income investments do not respond to changes in the inflation rate. Unfortunately, the investor receives the higher interest rates only on recently purchased fixed-income investments. Where the investor had purchased a fixed-income investment several years prior, the interest rate received on that investment continues fixed at the prevailing rate that existed at the time the investment was purchased. That upward interest rate movement does, however, generally lag behind the inflation rate change. Given a 1 percent rise in inflation, it may be several years before interest rates fully reflect that rise. But the lag is shortening as investors are increasingly aware of the havoc rapid inflation inflicts on their real returns.

The fact remains, however, fixed-income investments perform poorly when inflation rates are fluctuating widely or when inflation rates rise to 9 percent or higher. Interest rates simply do not adequately compensate for a fluctuation of inflation rates at 3 percent for a period, rising to 9 percent in a subsequent period, and then returning to 3 percent. Obviously, interest rates have not risen sufficiently to offset recent periods of 10 to 15 percent inflation.

Despite these shortcomings, we believe most investors should carefully consider fixed-income investments. As this book is written, prime-grade corporate bonds are offering 9 percent annually. That means a 3 percent real return even if inflation averages 6 percent annually. Of course, if inflation averages 8 to 10 percent, and that is a possibility, the real return would be near zero.

Ownership Investments   Theoretically, an ownership investment should provide a better hedge against the ravages of inflation. In large measure, this assertion arises because most such investments involve an income-producing asset or some real property. As prices mount with inflation, the market value of those assets or property should also rise.

For example, assume Fred Fontana purchased some rental property for $20,000. If over the next 20 years all prices doubled, the property's market value should rise to at least $40,000. Assuming it had done so, Fred would not have a true $20,000 gain because, with prices doubled, that $40,000 would buy the same thing that only $20,000 bought 20 years earlier. Nevertheless, he would be in a much better position than had he held $20,000 in cash during that 20-year period. The cash would have lost half its purchasing power. Ignoring any income Fred may have earned from the property, owning the property itself has provided a hedge against inflation.

Analyzing a common stock investment during inflationary periods is a bit more involved. Assume Angela La Capria recently purchased 100 shares of XQ Corporation's common stock. Angela can reasonably expect that the market value of XQ's real property—its land, buildings, machinery, etc.—should rise with inflation. She can also expect that as XQ's production costs rise, so should the sale price of its products, maintaining or even increasing XQ's profit level. Increased profits, combined with the rise in the market value of the company's property, should help boost the market price of XQ's common stock. That rise in market price should offset all, or a part of, inflation's effect. But we hasten to add that each statement has been prefaced by the comment that this is what "should" happen.

An immediate question is: Have ownership investments worked in reality the way theory says they should? Unfortunately, there is no single definitive answer. Some ownership investments, such as real estate, have fared reasonably well during recent inflationary periods. Others, such as common stock and mutual funds, have not fared well. In fact, common stocks and mutual funds have performed best when inflation was low and poorest when it was high.

What can we conclude from this mixed picture? Ownership investments provide no guarantee as total protection against inflation. They do provide at least partial protection. For that reason they should be seriously considered by most investors.

COMPOUND RETURNS

The principle of compound growth centers on the fact that not only does the initial balance continue to grow, but the growth segments also increase each period. For example, assume that Ye Olde National Bank promises to pay interest at 10 percent[1] compounded annually. The top line in Exhibit 17–2 illustrates how an initial $1,000 deposit would grow over a 20-year period if the interest was left in the account. As can be seen from Exhibit 17–2, the deposit not only continues to grow each year; it grows at an ever-increasing rate. Although you cannot read the exact figures from the graph, the balance increased $147 between years 4 and 5, yet during a similar 1-year span between years 19 and 20, the balance rose by $612. Clearly a substantial increase in growth. Why the marked rise? It all centers on the fact that the account pays interest on the initial balance and also on all accumulated interest to date. Thus the $612 of interest for year 20 comes from two things: (1) the $100 interest on the initial $1,000 balance ($1,000 × 10 percent), and (2) the $511.60 interest on the $5,116 of interest that has accumulated during the previous 19 years ($5,116 × 10 percent)

The results in Exhibit 17–2 reemphasize our earlier point about an early

[1]Although we realize that 10 percent is not comparable to current bank rates—they are closer to 5 or 6 percent—using 10 percent simplifies the computations.

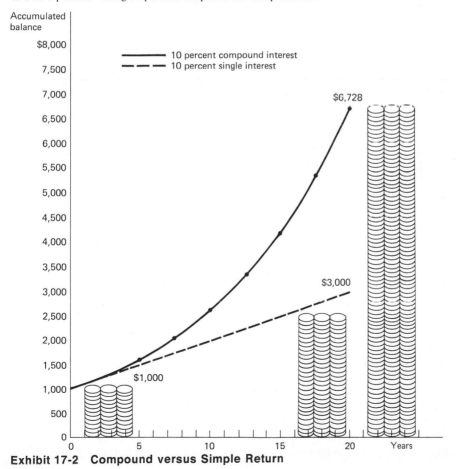

Exhibit 17-2   Compound versus Simple Return

start toward an investment goal. By having the funds on deposit for an extended period, the ending account balance becomes sizable. For example, in roughly 7 years the initial balance has doubled, yet in another 7 years the balance has nearly quadrupled. Appendix A at the end of this chapter demonstrates the steps needed to compute a compound return for various interest rates and different investment periods.

Simple versus Compound Return   The bottom line in Exhibit 17–2 illustrates how a $1,000 investment would grow with 10 percent simple interest. With simple interest, any interest earnings left in the account do not earn interest. Thus, given a $1,000 initial balance, the account continues to earn $100 interest ($1,000 × 10 percent) each year. By the end of year 20, the account would total only $3,000 [$1,000 + ($100 × 20 years)]. A comparison between the two examples in Exhibit 17–2 demonstrates the benefits of compounding.

Impact of Different Returns and Years of Compounding

The details in Exhibit 17–3 show the results from investing $1,000 for 5, 10, 15, and 20 years at annual compound interest rates of 5, 7.5, and 10 percent. The first thing that stands out in Exhibit 17–3 is the substantial impact a small increase in interest rate can have on an investment's terminal value. While switching from a 5 percent investment to a 7.5 percent investment increases the first year's interest by only $25 [$1,000 × (7.5 percent − 5 percent)], over a period of 5 years the total earnings are 58 percent [($436 − $276) ÷ $276] larger. For an investment period of 20 years, the total return on a 7.5 percent investment is nearly double the total return on a 5 percent investment ($3,248 ÷ $1,653 = 1.96).

The results in Exhibit 17–3 illustrate two points. First, a small increase in an investment's rate of return can have a sizable impact on its terminal value. Second, the longer the investment period, the greater the impact a higher rate of return has on the terminal value.

> Strategy: Because the benefits from compounding are especially pronounced when the investment period is long, you should begin working toward your investment goals as early as possible. And when considering comparable investments, the one with the higher rate of return should have preference even if the differential is small.

Compounding More than Once Each Year

The return on many investments is compounded more than once each year. To see how this alters the effective annual return, we return to our previous $1,000 savings example. We still assume the account pays 10 percent annual interest, but now we assume interest is paid every 6 months, or every half-year. For the first 6 months (which is one-half year), the interest is equal to ($1,000 × 10 percent) × 1/2 = $50. The interest is left in the account with the initial balance, so that for the second 6 months (or second half of the year), the interest is equal

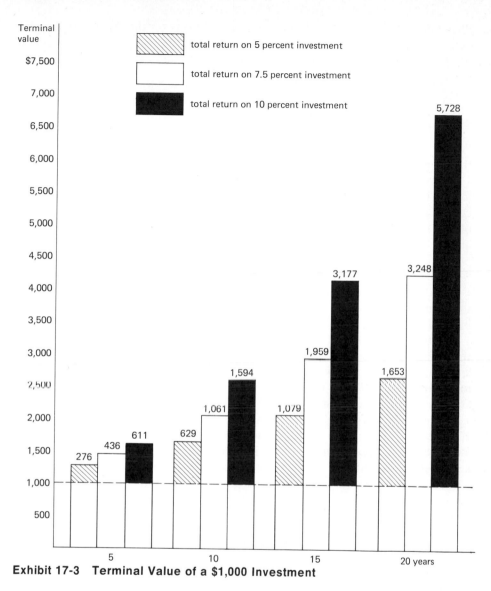

Exhibit 17-3   Terminal Value of a $1,000 Investment

to ($1,050 × 10 percent) × ¹/₂ = $52.50. During the second 6 months the account not only pays $50 interest for the initial $1,000 deposit; it also pays $2.50 ($50 × 10 percent) × ¹/₂ for the reinvestment of the first 6 months' earnings. At the end of the first year, the account balance is $1,102.50 ($1,000 + $50 + $50 + $2.50). That 10 percent return, compounded semiannually, provides an effective 10.25 percent [($1,102.50 − $1,000) ÷ $1,000] annual return. Would you expect the effective return for a 10 percent return compounded quarterly (every 3 months) to be: (1) greater than 10.25 percent, (2) less than 10.25 percent, or (3) equal to 10.25 percent? Not certain? Well, work it through. Exhibit 17–4 gives effective annual returns for different compounding periods. Those results can be summarized in a short rule: For any rate of return, the more frequent the compounding, the higher the effective return.

Strategy: Given two comparable investments with identical rates of return, choose the one offering the most frequent compounding.

EFFECTIVE RETURN ON AN INVESTMENT

Whenever you make an investment, you forgo the current purchasing power of the money you invest. In exchange for that, you expect to receive a return on your investment. Either that return can be annual income on the investment, or it can be an increase in the investment's market value, or it can be some combination of income plus increased market value. Regardless of the source of the return, it must be included when computing an investment's effective annual return. We use the combined effective return—annual income plus possible change in market price—to compare competing investments.

Income on Investments   In Chapters 18, 19, and 20 we will frequently use the following special terms to describe the different types of investment income.

Interest   When you lend someone money, the borrower pays interest for the use of your money. The borrower could be a bank, savings and loan association, credit union, corporation, municipality, the United States government, an individual, or a host of other borrowers. Generally, interest income is stated in terms of an annual percentage return.

Dividend, Common Stock   When a corporation pays a portion of its earnings to its common stock shareholders (the owners), that payment is called a dividend. A corporation is not required to pay its owners a fixed percentage of its earnings as dividends. A corporation may decide to retain 100 percent of its earnings for corporate purposes and pay no dividends at all. And it could continue that policy for years even though its earnings may be sizable. A corporation's dividend policy is determined by the size of its earnings and management's decision as to how those earnings should be used. Dividends are usually stated as a dollar amount per common share.

Exhibit 17-4   Effective Annual Rate of Return with Multiple Compounding
(In Per Cent)

Stated annual rate of return	Effective annual rate of return by compounding period				
	Annually	Semiannually	Quarterly	Monthly	Daily
5	5	5.06	5.09	5.12	5.13
6	6	6.09	6.14	6.17	6.18
7	7	7.12	7.19	7.23	7.25
8	8	8.16	8.24	8.30	8.33
9	9	9.20	9.31	9.38	9.42
10	10	10.25	10.38	10.47	10.52

Dividend, Preferred Stock Unlike the holders of common stock, preferred stock shareholders typically do not share in the ownership of the corporation. Common stock shareholders are owners; preferred stock shareholders are lenders. Most preferred shares specify that, given certain qualifying conditions, each share must receive a fixed annual dividend. The annual dividend may be stated as a fixed dollar amount—for example, $7 per share—or as a fixed percentage—for example, 7 percent of the share's $100 face value.

Rent When someone uses property you own, he or she is expected to pay rent. The rental agreement may be a formal lease that specifies the monthly payment and the exact length of the rental period. Or the rental agreement may be a more informal one whereby the person continues to rent the property on a monthly basis with no maximum or minimum rental period being specified.

Change in an Investment's Market Price The investments discussed in Chapters 18, 19, and 20 are subject to varying degrees of market price changes. At one extreme is the balance in a bank savings account. Barring the bank's collapse, that balance will not change except for the addition of interest earnings on the account. The market price of a savings account balance is highly stable. At the opposite extreme is the common stock of Last Ditch Gold Mines. Should the company strike it big, each share's market price would likely skyrocket. Of course Last Ditch may go bust and find nothing; in that case the share's price would likely plummet. The point here is that the market price of a share of Last Ditch Gold Mines could fluctuate widely.

Capital Gain A capital gain is the difference between an investment's sale price and its initial purchase price plus any selling expense. For example, if 40 shares of XQ Corporation were initially bought for $20 per share and later sold for $24, the capital gain would be $160 [($24−$20) × 40 shares]. To keep the example simple, we assumed zero selling expense. Capital gains on investments held more than 6 months qualify as long-term gains; for periods 6 months or less, they are short-term gains. As Chapter 6 discussed, the tax treatment is more favorable for long-term gains.

Capital Loss Although it would be nice if an investment's market price always increased, it does not always do so. Selling an investment for less than the combined total of its initial purchase price and the associated selling expenses results in a capital loss. Thus, if the shares of XQ from our previous example had been sold for $15, the capital loss would be $200 [($15−$20) × 40 shares]. Like the previous gain, a holding period greater than 6 months means a long-term capital loss; a period 6 months or shorter means a short-term loss.

RISK

Risk is defined as the variability in an investment's expected return. The greater the variability, the higher an investment's risk. For example, United States government securities would be at the lower end of the risk spectrum because the variability in their expected return is nearly nil. If they promise an 8 percent return, the possibilities of their paying more or less are nearly zero. So we would conclude they have extremely low risk. The upper end of the risk spectrum might include common stock in a small company that is searching for scarce minerals or petroleum. Depending on the success of that search, its return could range from a large profit to a large loss. Because the variability in its expected return is so large and the possibilities of those extremes actually occurring are so large, we would conclude that this investment has high risk.

Type of Risk   Every investment is exposed to one or more types of risk. We will describe these different types of risk exposure, so that by identifying the sources of an investment's risk, we can better judge and predict whether that risk will occur.

Business Risk   Business risk arises because there are fluctuations in the production and sales activity within any particular industry. The cause of the fluctuation could be a temporary slack in demand for that industry's products, competition from another product, a lack of essential raw materials, or a host of other reasons. Regardless of the exact cause, it results in fluctuations in the sales levels of the firms within that industry.

In general, the more susceptible an industry's production and sales activity to possible fluctuations, the higher its business risk. And this increased volatility is likely to be reflected in the earnings for the firms within a high-risk industry. During slack periods, they are likely to find their earnings seriously reduced, if not totally eliminated, by the costs associated with unused production capacity. Even in peak periods, their profitability could be reduced because of the added costs—overtime, excessive maintenance, old, inefficient production machinery, etc.—associated with trying to produce at 100 percent capacity. The opposite situation would likely prevail in industries with low business risk. Firms within those industries have little fluctuation in production and sales, and therefore should have reasonably stable earnings.

Thus, the common stock of a recreational motor-home manufacturer will have considerable business risk. Yet the common stock of a public utility company will have much lower business risk because of the stability of that industry.

Risk of Financial Collapse   The recent financial problems of many large cities have shown that financial collapse can occur in the public sector as well as the business sector. Evaluating the risk from financial collapse, whether in the business or public sector, requires a two-part analysis: How prone is the business or public sector to serious financial difficulty? How would a specific investment in that area fare, given financial difficulty?

Market Price Risk   An investment's market price may decline because investor preferences change. Such changes in preference create market price risks. In general, the more specialized an investment, or the more limited its resale market, the higher the market price risk. Thus, the common stock of XQ Corporation could decline because investors are no longer enthralled by XQ or its products. Or it could be that investors have developed some psychological barrier to investing in that stock. Specialized investments—coins, stamps, art pieces—can have considerable market risk because investors' whims and tastes can cause wide swings in their market price.

Interest Rate Risk   Fluctuations in the prevailing rate of interest can cause considerable interest rate risk on certain lending investments. For example, suppose Sue Fine paid $1,000 for a $1,000 face-value bond; it pays 5 percent interest each year—$50—for 20 years, and at the end of that period it matures and repays its $1,000 face value. Now assume for some reason the prevailing interest rate on this type of bond increased from 5 to 10 percent shortly after she bought the bond. Since current investors could obtain 10 percent interest on new bonds—annual interest of $100—they would be unwilling to pay $1,000 for Sue's bond because its annual interest is only $50. In fact, the 5 percent bond's market price would have to decline to approximately $500 before it is competitive with a $1,000 bond paying 10 percent. At $500 the 5 percent bond's effective return approaches 10 percent ($50 interest ÷ $500 price). In actuality, the price would not decline all the way to $500, but the example does clearly illustrate a general investment principle. When interest rates rise, the market price of fixed-income lending investments declines. Conversely, when interest rates decline, the market price of fixed-income investments rise.

Furthermore, the longer an investment's maturity, the wider its price swing. Thus, if the prevailing interest rates rise 2 percent, the price change for a 20-year bond will be much larger than a 1-year bond. For example, assume we have two bonds: a $1,000 bond that pays 6 percent interest ($60 per year) and matures in 1 year, and a $1,000 bond also paying 6 percent interest but maturing in 20 years. If the prevailing interest rate increases from 6 to 8 percent on this type of bond, the market price of the 1-year, 6 percent bond will decline to $981.49, while the 20-year, 6 percent bond will drop substantially more to $803.64. In addition, the size of the interest rate change also has a direct impact on the investment's price change. The larger the change, the larger the rise or decline in market price.

Interest rate risk does not, however, affect the investment's final redemption value. At maturity, the borrower repays the full face value regardless of what the interest rate is at that time.

Given a rise in prevailing interest rates, interest rate risk creates two potential loss situations. One is the loss of reduced market price: If an investor decides to sell an investment that pays lower interest than prevailing interest rates, the market price (i.e., selling price) could be substantially lower than its original purchase price. The other is the loss of interest income: If this same investor decides to hold the investment until maturity, he or she avoids a loss from reduced market price. But during that holding period, the investor has accepted an interest rate below the rates that could have been obtained on another investment of the same quality that pays higher interest.

Risk-Return Trade-Off

As compensation for accepting higher risk, investors expect and demand a higher return. That is, the more uncertain the return from an investment, the higher the return must be in order to attract investors. This risk-return trade-off is illustrated in Exhibit 17–5.

The five points along the risk-return line in Exhibit 17–5 are used merely to demonstrate where several typical investments might fall. There is very little risk exposure on United States government securities. Therefore, the chart shows that these securities have low risk and low expected return. Investments further out on the line provide a higher potential return, but they also entail higher risk exposure. We can generalize from Exhibit 17–5: The higher an investment's potential return, the higher its risk exposure.

Suitable Investments for You   Every investor must decide where he or she wants to be along the line in Exhibit 17–5. People who thrive on risk and can afford it would select investments far up the line. People who are very conservative and unwilling to accept risk would want to select investments on

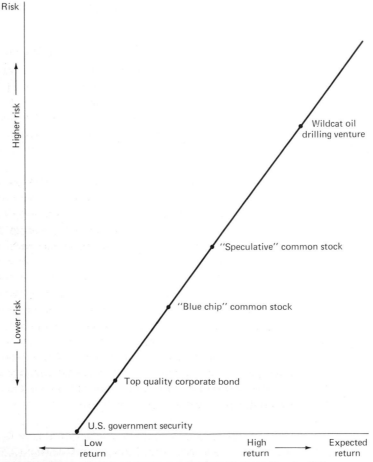

Exhibit 17-5   General Pattern of Risk-Return Trade-Off

SOME JERK TRIED TO SELL ME
THE BROOKLYN BRIDGE BUT I REMEMBERED
THE ADVICE TO 'START SMALL'...
SO I BOUGHT THE QUEENSBOROUGH BRIDGE!

the low end of the line. All other people would elect some intermediate point along the line.

Regardless of your particular risk preference, you should strive to maximize your investment return at that risk level. Unfortunately, not all high-risk investments necessarily have a high return. To be a wise investor, you should compare an investment's return to the returns from other investments in the same risk class.

All your investments do not, necessarily, have to be grouped about a single risk-return point. You may well decide that certain investment goals are so critical that safety is foremost. For those goals, investments that provide low returns at low risk are probably best. At the same time, you may decide that some other investment goals are less crucial. For these, accepting higher risk to obtain a potentially higher return seems fully justified.

Strategy: Decide which risk-return level is appropriate for you and your goals. Critically evaluate competing investments at that level to ensure that the one you are considering offers a return appropriate to the risk involved.

CRITERIA FOR INVESTMENT EVALUATION

Throughout the next three chapters our discussion of investment alternatives will concentrate on nine criteria: (1) exposure to risk, (2) annual return, (3) maturity, (4) flexibility, (5) minimum-size limitation, (6) investor involvement, (7) tax features, (8) hedge against inflation, and (9) general availability. By evaluating any investment in terms of these nine criteria, an investor should be able to decide whether a particular investment is suitable for a specific investment goal. A summary table of the alternatives and their criteria appears in Appendix B, at the end of the chapter.

Risk Exposure   Each investment entails various combinations of the four risk categories—business, financial collapse, market price, and interest rate risk—and the total risk exposure varies widely among different investments. When describing the degree of risk, we primarily rely on qualitative rather than quantitative measures. Not only are quantitative measures highly technical and complex, but also some professional investment analysts feel they are neither appropriate nor effective for evaluating investment risks. Therefore, for our purposes in these chapters, qualitative measures of risk will be appropriate and sufficient.

Annual Return   An investment's annual return not only includes the investment's annual income, such as interest, dividends, or rent. It also includes any loss or gain resulting from a change in the investment's market price. For investments such as some common stock, the change in market price may be the major source of its annual return. For others, such as savings accounts, there is no change in market price and the entire return comes from annual interest payments.

On some investments the annual return is determined by the current supply and demand for investment monies. That is, the return is determined by how badly borrowers need money (demand) and how willing the lenders are to invest (supply). When the supply of money is plentiful or the demand is light, the price (the annual rate of return) is likely to be moderate to rather low. On the other hand, if the supply of money is scarce or the demand is heavy, then the price will likely be high. Because the market determines the returns on these types of investment, the returns will fluctuate through a wide range. Examples of this type of investment include bonds and notes of corporations, new issues of common stock from corporations, bonds of municipalities, and bonds and notes of the United States Treasury.

On other investments, such as savings accounts, time accounts, and savings bonds, the return is not determined by the market (supply and demand of money) but, instead, the return is set by a regulatory board or agency. Typically, those returns (rates of interest) change very infrequently; consequently, there is usually a sizable time lag before they reflect the general trend of the market-determined returns. Although these returns are regulated by virtue of a maximum rate, any financial institution offering these investments is free to set their rates at or below the regulated maximum.

Maturity   Traditionally, an investment's maturity is the time span between its date of purchase and the date a borrower has agreed to redeem it at face value. In some cases, however, the borrower may be willing to redeem the investment at face value, but only if the investor accepts a rate of return substantially below the amount originally promised. For example, a 1-year, 6 percent time certificate can be redeemed at face value in less than 1 year, but the return would be less than 6 percent because early redemption entails a penalty of 90 days' interest. In cases such as this, we will quote the investment's minimum effective maturity. We define minimum effective maturity as the time an investment must be held to achieve its promised annual rate of return. Thus for the above 1-year time certificate, it would be 1 year because it must be held that long before it yields a 6 percent return.

Maturities are grouped into three broad categories: short term (1 year or less), intermediate term (1 to 5 years), and long term (5 to 30 years).

Flexibility   An investment's flexibility depends on how easily it can be converted into cash. One aspect of flexibility is the speed with which the investment can be turned into cash. If a borrower agrees to redeem an investment at any time the lender requests, that is fast convertibility and the investment is highly flexible. For example, the time for a savings account is fast because banks generally permit withdrawals without advance notice. Likewise, investments with a well-developed secondary market also have a short conversion time. A good secondary market is one where there are a number of buyers who stand ready to buy a particular investment should an investor decide to sell. (We discuss secondary markets further in Chapter 18.)

Other factors affecting the flexibility of converting the investment to cash are: price concession, transaction cost, and penalties.

Price Concession   Price concession is the amount an investor must reduce the selling price of the investment in order to attract a prospective buyer. Price concession is another measure of an investment's flexibility. At one extreme is a specialized investment like rental property. If an investor wanted to sell the property in a hurry, the selling price might have to be substantially below what the market price would bring with more time to wait for buyers. At the opposite extreme are United States Treasury notes. The resale market on these notes is so broad and extensive that they can be sold with little or no concession below the current market price.

Transaction Cost   Some investments can be converted to cash only through an outside sales agent. The agent's selling commission is a relevant cost that must be considered when determining an investment's flexibility. In general, the higher the transaction cost, the lower the investment's flexibility.

Penalty   A few investments assess a penalty fee when they are redeemed before their final maturity date. Again, a high penalty fee tends to reduce an investment's flexibility.

Minimum-Size Limitation   Many investments cannot be purchased in fewer than a minimum quantity or for less than a minimum amount. The reason is that some investments are available only in specific denominations, for example $1,000 or $5,000 blocks. For other investments, the commission to buy and the commission to sell are so large that small transactions simply are not

economical. The minimum-sized transaction for an investment is the smaller of
(1) its minimum denomination, or (2) the smallest number that can be bought
and sold without incurring prohibitive transaction costs.

Investor Involvement   The degree of investor involvement is defined as
the amount of time an investor must spend to effectively manage an investment. For individuals who are extremely busy or who consider investment
management an arduous task, an investment requiring minimal involvement is
essential.

Tax Features   The discussion of tax features centers on federal income
tax regulations. State income and personal property tax regulations are not
discussed here in any detail because they are so diverse they cannot be covered
in the limited space of this book.

The most important question about taxes and investments is whether an
investment's return is exempt from federal income tax. Depending on the
investment, some returns are taxable, some are not. And even where returns
are taxable, some portions of the returns are taxed at a lower rate. Of course,
the higher an investor's marginal tax rate, the more important tax considerations become.

Hedge against Inflation   An earlier section of this chapter examined the
impact of inflation on lending and ownership investments in general. The
discussion in succeeding chapters examines the potential of each type of
investment as a hedge against inflation. The discussion also reviews steps that
can be taken to minimize inflation's impact on each type of investment.

General Availability   Under the heading of general availability, for each
type of investment we examine the questions: Where can the investment be
obtained? Who sells or handles the investment? How is an investment
obtained?

YOUR INVESTMENT GOALS

Many people think that a suitable investment goal is merely to accumulate
money. The problem with that kind of thinking is that it does not provide the
necessary guidelines to help the investor to decide how that goal should be
achieved. Every goal should have five basic guidelines. First, a specific dollar
amount, so that you can measure the investment against the goal. Second, a
specific reason or purpose, so that you can decide whether an investment
entails too much or too little risk for the goal. And third, a set time horizon, so
that you can decide what maturity your investments should have to reach your
goal. In addition to these three basic guidelines, each goal should also clearly
specify the expected return and the required dollar contribution.

Purpose of Goal Investment goals can encompass a broad range of purposes. By specifying a separate goal for each purpose, it is easy to rank them as to their respective importance and to match potential investments accordingly.

Dollar Amount Once the purpose is specified, it should be relatively easy to estimate the dollar amount of the goal. Where a goal extends a number of years into the future, the estimate should include an allowance for price increases due to inflation. For example, assume that your goal is a 10 percent down payment, 3 years from now, on a house that currently costs $30,000. If the price of houses is expected to rise 10 percent annually during the next 3 years, you will need $3,993 ($39,930 × 10 percent), because of the price rise during those 3 years. At the end of 1 year the house will cost $33,000; after 2 years it will cost $36,300; and $39,930 after 3 years. Appendix A, at the end of this chapter, illustrates how the compound rate-of-return tables included there can be used to estimate the future price.

> **Strategy: The longer the time span of a goal, the more critical it is to estimate the dollar amount needed in the future.**

Time Horizon The time horizon for each investment goal is the period you set to achieve that particular goal. For some, this will be relatively short (as when you plan to purchase a new car); for others, it may be fairly long (if you plan for a son's or daughter's college education).

Expected Rate of Return The expected rate of return should include annual income plus any capital gains or losses. When you estimate the rate of return, be realistic. Currently, the typical return on short- to intermediate-term investments is 5 to 7 percent; on longer-term investments a typical return is 9 to 12 percent. Also remember the risk-return trade-off: high returns equal high-risk exposure. You should temper your expected return depending on the relative importance of a particular investment goal. A critically important goal may dictate low-risk investments and therefore a low expected return.

Required Dollar Contribution Based on (1) the dollar amount, (2) the time horizon, and (3) the expected return, we can estimate the required amount needed to achieve a specified goal. The goal may be achieved either by a single lump sum invested at the start of the investment period or by small amounts invested at regular intervals during the period.

Exhibit 17–6 shows the amounts that must be invested each month at various interest rates and different investment periods to provide $500 at the end of the period.

The monthly investments in Exhibit 17–6 can be readily modified for investment goals greater or less than $500. For example, assume that you want $3,000 to buy a car in 5 years and that you expect to earn 6 percent annual return on your monthly amounts invested. How much should your monthly amounts be? You need $43.02 [($3,000 ÷ 500) × $7.17] each month.

Exhibit 17-6   Monthly Investment Needed to Accumulate $500, Given Various Interest Rates*

Available time period	5%	6%	7%	8%	9%	10%
3 years	$12.90	$12.71	$12.52	$12.33	$12.15	$11.97
5 years	7.35	7.17	6.98	6.80	6.63	6.46
10 years	3.22	3.05	2.89	2.73	2.58	2.44
15 years	1.87	1.72	1.58	1.44	1.32	1.21

*This table assumes that the monthly amount is invested in time so that interest is earned on the monthly deposit.

The amounts in the exhibit can also be modified for rates of return between the rates shown. For example, to accumulate $500 during a 5-year period at $5\frac{1}{2}$ percent annual return, how much should the monthly investment be? Since $5\frac{1}{2}$ percent is midway between 5 and 6 percent, the monthly amount is midway between $7.35 and $7.17, or $7.26.

$$5 \text{ percent} \qquad 5\frac{1}{2} \text{ percent} \qquad 6 \text{ percent}$$
$$\$7.35 \qquad\qquad X \qquad\qquad \$7.17$$
$$X = \$7.17 + \frac{1}{2}\,(\$7.35 - 7.17) = 7.26$$

Appendix A, at the end of this chapter, shows how to use the compound return tables to estimate lump-sum and annual amounts needed to achieve a specific dollar amount at the end of an investment period.

Implementing Your Goals

Implementing your investment goals entails two separate steps: (1) ranking the goals according to priority, and (2) selecting investments suitable for a specific goal.

Ranking Your Goals   The initial starting point is to list your investment goals according to decreasing importance. By comparing your budgeted savings amount to the required monthly amount for each goal, you can decide how many goals you can implement. Do not be surprised if you exhaust your budgeted savings before you reach the end of your list of goals: Most people do!

If that is the case, you may want to review the specifications for each of your goals. In particular: Is the dollar amount accurate? Is the time horizon realistic? Is the expected investment return appropriate for the goal? After reviewing, you may have no major changes in specifications and you may have to defer the investment goals at the lower end of your list.

Matching the Investment to the Goal   Some people never really consider which investment is best suited to a specific goal. For example, they may select a savings account as their major investment vehicle for a long-term goal.

Granted a savings account has good flexibility and low risk, but flexibility is not what they should be concerned about on a long-term goal. Had they chosen United States Treasury notes (we discuss these later) rather than a savings account, their return would likely be much higher, the risk would be identical to a savings account, but the flexibility would be lower. At the opposite extreme, using a common stock as the principal investment for an emergency fund would be inappropriate. For an emergency fund, flexibility and low risk are paramount, yet a common stock lacks both.

Time Horizon and Flexibility   An investment's maturity and flexibility are somewhat interrelated, and the interrelationship should match your investment goals. For example, if you have an investment goal with a short time horizon (maturity), it is very likely that you may need the money from the investment on short notice (flexibility). Therefore, for goals having short time horizons, the flexibility of the investment is rather important. For goals with longer time horizons, flexibility is less necessary.

There is one other essential consideration with respect to time horizons, and that is inflation. Long-term goals should consider the effects of inflation; for short-term goals, it is not so important to consider inflation.

Risk-Return Decision   The starting point for the risk-return decision is: How much risk are you willing to accept? In deciding on the degree of acceptable risk, you also answer the amount of the return you will get. Nevertheless, there are differences in returns available from investments within a particular risk group. Once you decide on the risk you can accept, you should carefully compare the returns available from the investments within that risk group, and, of course, take the investment with the best return.

> **Strategy: Regardless of which risk-return combination you decide upon, select the investment that offers the highest return for that level of risk.**

GENERATING THE SAVINGS TO MEET YOUR INVESTMENT GOALS

Saving is difficult. But you cannot meet your investment goals without savings. There are several things you can do to make saving less agonizing and less haphazard.

Have Savings Withheld   Arrange with your employer to have a fixed portion of your pay deposited directly in a credit union account. Or, have your paycheck deposited directly in your checking account (an increasing number of companies are willing to do this). You can then instruct your bank to transfer a portion of your paycheck periodically to your savings account. In this way, you save regularly and your savings earn interest. When you accumulate enough money, withdraw it and make the investment of your choice.

Do Not Overpay Withholding Tax   We are adamantly opposed to the practice of understating the dependents you claim for federal income tax

withholding purposes. Although you receive a tax refund at year-end, the government pays no interest on the amount of taxes you overpaid. Instead of overpaying your taxes, have the same amount withheld and deposited in a savings account where it can earn 5 to 6 percent interest.

> **Strategy: Have your savings withheld and deposited in an interest-earning savings account (or similarly flexible investment) until you decide where you want to invest the money for your specific goals.**

SUMMARY

1. There are two basic ways to invest: Lending money to some borrower, and purchasing ownership in some income-producing asset.
2. Inflation reduces an investment's real rate of return.
3. The recent bouts of high inflation have reduced the real return on many investments to zero or negative returns (losses).
4. Investments which involve lending provide only a partial hedge against inflation.
5. Investments which involve ownership should, in theory, provide a better hedge against inflation. But recent experience has shown mixed results. Certainly there is no guarantee that they are completely effective in coping with high inflation rates.
6. With a compound return, the initial investment earns a return, and any earnings that are reinvested also earn a return. In effect, the investor receives earnings on previous earnings.
7. The benefit of compounding increases as the investment period lengthens.
8. With a compound return, even a small increase in the rate of return can substantially increase the value of an investment at the end of the investment period, especially for a long period.

9 The greater the frequency of compounding during the year, the greater effective annual rate of return.

10 The total effective return on an investment includes the annual income on the investment plus any difference between the investment's purchase and sale price.

11 An investment's risk exposure can be divided into four categories: business risk, risk of financial collapse, market-price risk, and interest-rate risk.

12 All investments involve a risk-return trade-off. The higher the potential return, the higher the investor's exposure to risk.

13 To properly evaluate the suitability of an investment, an investor needs information on nine criteria: risk exposure, expected rate of return, minimum maturity, flexibility, minimum size, investor involvement, tax features, hedge against inflation, and general availability.

14 A well-specified investment goal includes: reason for the investment, estimate of the dollar goal, time horizon, anticipated rate of return, and required dollar contribution.

15 Direct payroll-withholding is one of the least painful and easiest ways to implement a savings plan.

REVIEW YOUR UNDERSTANDING OF

Investment alternatives
   Lending
   Ownership
Real rate of return
Hedge against inflation
Compound return
Effective return
   Annual income
   Change in market price

Business risk
Risk of financial collapse
Market price risk
Interest rate risk
Flexibility in investments
Investment goal
   Specifying
   Implementing

DISCUSSION QUESTIONS

1 Do you think investment planning for small investors is more or less important today than it was 10 years ago? What reasons can you give to support your position? What trend do you see over the next 10 years?

2 If you have $1,000 invested at 10 percent, compounded annually for 15 years, during which of the following periods will your earnings increase the most: (a) the 5-year period from 5 to 10 years, or (b) the 5-year period from 10 to 15 years? Since both periods are the same—5 years—why are the earnings different? Would the same be true if the investment earned simple interest?

3 Using the details in question 2, what would the investment be worth after 5 years? 10 years? 15 years? (Assume the interest is reinvested.)

4 Assume Fred Bear wants to accumulate the money to purchase a vacation retreat. What steps will be involved in formulating an investment goal for that purpose?

5 If Fred (question 4) decides that he needs $5,000 just 10 years from today, what reasons can you give for starting that program early? How much will he have to save each month over the next 10 years to meet his goal, assuming a 7 percent return? How much will he have to save monthly if he wants the $5,000 in 5 years?

6   Why have many banks and other financial institutions switched to more frequent compounding? Why is the effective rate higher with more compounding?

7   Can you give examples of investments that derive most of their return from annual income? What investments derive most of their return from the change in market price?

8   Which of the two investment categories, lending or ownership, is likely to provide the steadiest return? Why?

9   Which of the following is likely to have the highest and the lowest business risk: (a) a manufacturer of pleasure boats, (b) a utility company that provides electricity and natural gas services, (c) a soft-drink manufacturer, and (d) a chain of high-fashion clothing stores? Why?

10 Why have investors become more concerned with an investment's "real rate of return"? Do you think this concern will diminish or intensify over the next 5 years? Why?

11 Many people maintain that ownership investments can better offset the impact of inflation. Do you agree? Why?

12 If you invested in a 6 percent bond several years ago, and suddenly the prevailing interest on comparable new bonds rises to 10 percent, what happens to the market price of your 6 percent bond?

13 What is meant by the statement, "You should pay yourself first"? How can you implement such a plan?

14 What investment criteria are most important when selecting investments suitable for short-term investment goals? How will the criteria differ for long-term investment goals?

CASE PROBLEM

Carlos and Carla Zapata have been married 4 years; they both work full time and they have no children. Despite the fact that their combined annual salaries total $21,000, they have accumulated only $500 in a savings account. They own their furniture and have completely paid off one of their cars, but still owe a sizable balance on the other. They would like to buy a house, but the prospect of accumulating the required 5 or 10 percent down payment on a $40,000 home has them worried. In addition, they think it would be nice to have a new boat, and possibly a travel trailer to keep by the lake when they go boating. Of course, they could also use the trailer in the winter if they were to buy a pair of snowmobiles. They agree they could put all these things to good use when they start their family next year. After looking at their long list of needs, they realize they will have to save more. They decide that if they try to spend less, there should be more left at the end of every month for savings. Also, they feel they must earn the highest return possible if they are ever going to get ahead.

a   Would you have any recommendations for Carlos and Carla as to how they should organize their projected purchases?

b   Do you think their strategy for implementing a new savings plan is a good one? Why?

c   Which of their future goals is going to be the easiest to achieve? The hardest?

d   How do you feel about their goal of "earning the highest return on their investment"? How would you go about setting the anticipated return for each goal?

e Do you feel that a single investment will meet all the Zapatas' goals? Why? What features are likely to differ among their various goals?

f How much will the Zapatas need each month to accumulate the desired house down payment of $4,000 in 5 years, assuming a 6 percent return?

g Based on the guidelines presented in the budgeting chapter (Chapter 4), what do you think their savings potential could be?

RECOMMENDED READINGS

Magazines

Changing Times:

"To Save or Invest Successfully, Make a Money Plan." May 1974, pp. 15–18.
  Discusses 10 basic guidelines for organizing a successful savings and investment program.

Books

Bailard, Thomas E., David L. Biehl, and Ronald W. Kaiser, *Personal Money Management*, Chicago: Science Research Associates, 1973.
  Chapter 13, (pp. 291–296) provides a 12-step procedure for planning investments and achieving one's goals. Has several numerical examples to illustrate how the procedure works.
Dougall, Herbert E., *Investments*, 9th ed., Englewood Cliffs, N.J.: Prentice-Hall, 1973.
  Chapters 19 and 20 discuss basic investment principles. The book includes a discussion of investment planning and determining investment objectives. The types of investment risk are reviewed and possible ways to minimize those risks are explained.
Malkiel, Burton G., *A Random Walk Down Wall Street*, New York: Norton, 1973.
  The first half of chapter 8 (pp. 179–193) presents an excellent discussion of the preliminary points an investor should consider when formulating investment objectives.
Amling, Frederick, *Investments: An Introduction to Analysis and Management*, 3d ed., Englewood Cliffs, N.J.: Prentice-Hall, 1974.
  Chapter 2 discusses the different methods of obtaining investable funds, covering the range from savings to borrowing. It also reviews the prerequisites an investor should meet before beginning an investment program.

Booklets

The Language of Investing. New York Stock Exchange, 11 Wall Street, New York, N.Y. 10005.
  Provides a glossary of financial terms. A copy may be obtained by sending a request to the above address.
How to Invest. Merrill Lynch, Pierce, Fenner & Smith, Inc., One Liberty Plaza, 165 Broadway, New York, N.Y. 10006.
  Provides a basic discussion of investing in stocks and bonds. A copy is available from the firm's advertising department.

Appendix A: Compound Rate-of-Return Tables

The two tables in this appendix present the effects of interest compounded annually. To illustrate how each of the tables can be used as a financial planning tool, the introduction to each table is followed by examples which demonstrate several applications.

Table A17–1 shows the terminal value of $1 invested at rates of return ranging from 4 to 15 percent and for periods ranging from 1 to 40 years. While the factors in the table are for $1, they are easily modified for any amount. For example, a $500 investment would be exactly 500 times the results shown for $1. You can also find the terminal value of $1 for rates of return between the rates shown in the table; e.g., rates such as $4^3/_8$ percent, $5^1/_2$ percent, or $6^3/_4$ percent. To illustrate, assume you want to know the terminal value of $1 invested at $6^3/_4$ percent for 12 years. The terminal value is between the values for 6 percent and 7 percent at 12 years on the table. The amount is $(2.01 +]^3/_4 \times (2.25 - 2.01)]) = 2.19$

Terminal Value of an Investment   Table A17–1 can be used to find the terminal value of a lump-sum investment. Assume we invest $525 as a lump sum today at 6 percent compounded annually. We want to know the terminal value of that investment after 5 years. Going to the 6 percent column and moving to 5 years, we find that $1 will be worth $1.34. The $525 investment will be approximately $703.50 ($525 × 1.34).

Required Lump-Sum Investment   Table A17–1 can be used to estimate the dollar amount we need to invest today to achieve some future goal. Assume we want to accumulate $3,000 to trade for a new car 4 years from today. We would like to know how much we must invest today at 5 percent to have $3,000 in 4 years. From the table we know that $1 invested at 5 percent today will equal $1.22 in 4 years. To accumulate the $3,000, we would have to invest $2,459.02 ($3,000 ÷ 1.22) today. Want to check that? Estimate how much $2,459.02 will be worth in 4 years at 5 percent.

Estimating the Required Return   Table A17–1 can be used to estimate what return we must earn on a given investment to reach a specific terminal value. Assume we need $10,000 to finance a son's or a daughter's college education. We currently have $5,000 to invest, and it will be 12 years before we need the $10,000. Since our initial $5,000 must increase approximately 2 times ($10,000 ÷ $5,000) to accomplish our goal, our investment must effectively double in 12 years. Going to the row for 12 years, we find that $1 at 4 percent grows to $1.60, which is too little. But at 6 percent, $1 is worth $2.01, which is very close to the 2.0 factor we need. Based on this, we conclude that we need at least a 6 percent return on our $5,000 investment if we are to accomplish our $10,000 goal.

Estimating Inflation's Impact.   While Table A17–1 is primarily intended for use in investment computations, it can be used whenever we have a compound growth situation. For example, assume we expect the price of houses to rise 7 percent each year over the next 4 years. We want to know how much a house that costs $36,000 today will cost in 4 years. First, we know that $1 invested at 7 percent will grow to $1.31 at the end of 4 years. Our inflation computation is much the same, the only difference being that we have a house whose price is growing at 7 percent per year rather than an investment that is growing at the same 7 percent rate. Thus, our $36,000 house will cost $47,160 ($36,000 × 1.31) 4 years from today, assuming a 7 percent price rise each year.

Table A17-1   Value of $1 at Various Rates of Compound Interest

Investment period in years	4%	5%	6%	7%	8%	9%	10%	11%	12%	13%	14%	15%
1	1.04	1.05	1.06	1.07	1.08	1.09	1.10	1.11	1.12	1.13	1.14	1.15
2	1.08	1.10	1.12	1.15	1.17	1.19	1.21	1.23	1.25	1.28	1.30	1.32
3	1.13	1.16	1.19	1.23	1.26	1.30	1.33	1.37	1.41	1.44	1.48	1.52
4	1.17	1.22	1.26	1.31	1.36	1.41	1.46	1.52	1.57	1.63	1.69	1.75
5	1.22	1.28	1.34	1.40	1.47	1.54	1.61	1.69	1.76	1.84	1.93	2.01
6	1.27	1.34	1.42	1.50	1.59	1.68	1.77	1.87	1.97	2.08	2.20	2.31
7	1.32	1.41	1.50	1.61	1.71	1.83	1.95	2.08	2.21	2.35	2.50	2.66
8	1.37	1.48	1.59	1.72	1.85	1.99	2.14	2.31	2.48	2.66	2.85	3.06
9	1.42	1.55	1.69	1.84	2.00	2.17	2.36	2.56	2.77	3.00	3.25	3.52
10	1.48	1.63	1.79	1.97	2.16	2.37	2.59	2.84	3.11	3.40	3.71	4.05
11	1.54	1.71	1.90	2.11	2.33	2.58	2.85	3.15	3.48	3.84	4.23	4.65
12	1.60	1.80	2.01	2.25	2.52	2.81	3.14	3.50	3.90	4.34	4.82	5.35
13	1.67	1.89	2.13	2.41	2.72	3.07	3.45	3.88	4.36	4.90	5.49	6.15
14	1.73	1.98	2.26	2.58	2.94	3.34	3.80	4.31	4.89	5.54	6.26	7.08
15	1.80	2.08	2.40	2.76	3.17	3.64	4.18	4.79	5.47	6.25	7.14	8.14
16	1.87	2.18	2.54	2.95	3.43	3.97	4.60	5.31	6.13	7.07	8.14	9.36
17	1.95	2.29	2.69	3.16	3.70	4.33	5.05	5.90	6.87	7.99	9.28	10.76
18	2.03	2.41	2.85	3.38	4.00	4.72	5.56	6.54	7.69	9.02	10.58	12.38
19	2.11	2.53	3.03	3.62	4.32	5.14	6.12	7.26	8.61	10.20	12.06	14.23
20	2.19	2.65	3.21	3.87	4.66	5.60	6.73	8.06	9.65	11.52	13.74	16.37
25	2.67	3.39	4.29	5.43	6.85	8.52	10.83	13.59	17.00	21.23	26.46	32.92
30	3.24	4.32	5.74	7.61	10.06	13.27	17.45	22.89	29.96	39.12	50.95	66.21
35	3.95	5.52	7.69	10.68	14.79	20.41	28.10	38.57	52.80	72.07	98.10	133.18
40	4.80	7.04	10.29	14.97	21.72	31.41	45.26	65.00	93.05	132.78	188.88	267.86

Table A17–2 shows the terminal value of investing $1 every year for periods from 1 to 40 years and at rates of return ranging from 4 to 15 percent. The basis of this table is the following: One dollar is invested at the end of the first year. One year later (the end of the second year), the investment grows by an amount equal to the yearly interest on that dollar, plus another dollar is then added to the original investment. The total amount thus far earns interest during the third year, and another dollar is added to the investment at the end of the third year. And so on. The principle difference between Tables A17–1 and A17–2 can best be illustrated with an example. If we had a $100 lump sum to invest once at the beginning of a specified period, Table A17–1 would be the appropriate one. On the other hand, if we were going to invest $100 each year over a specified period (we assume it is invested at the end of each year), Table A17–2 would be the appropriate one. Since Table A17–2 was constructed assuming $1 per period, it is easy to modify for other amounts. Likewise, Table A17–2 can be modified for fractional percentage rates of return by dividing the difference between the two nearest whole percentage returns in exactly the same way we illustrated for Table A17–1. For example, the factor for $5\frac{3}{4}$ percent for 5 years would be $(5.53 + [\frac{3}{4} \times (5.64 - 5.53)]) = 5.61$.

Future Value of an Investment   We can use Table A17–2 to find the future value of a particular investment. Assume we plan to invest $100 at the end of every year for the next 5 years. The investment's rate of return is 8 percent. Going to the 8 percent column and dropping to 5 years, we find that $1 per year for 5 years would be worth $5.87. Thus, our $100 annual investment would be worth $587.00 ($100 × 5.87) after 5 years.

Required Yearly Investment   Table A17–2 can also be used to estimate the amount that must be invested each year for a specified period to accomplish an investment goal. For example, assume we want to accumulate $6,910 over the next 10 years. We plan to make equal annual year-end contributions and expect to earn a 7 percent return, compounded annually. From Table A17–2 we know that $1 invested each year at 7 percent for 10 years will grow to $13.82 at the end of 10 years. Now, if we need $6,910 at the end of 10 years, we would have to invest $500 ($6,910 ÷ 13.82) at the end of each year to achieve that goal.

Estimating the Required Return   We can also use Table A17–2 to determine what rate of return we must earn on an investment if we are to achieve a set goal. Assume we plan to invest $900 at the end of each year for the next 4 years. We want to know what return we must earn on that investment in order to have $4,000 after 4 years. First, we know that our annual $900 investment must increase by a factor of 4.44 ($4,000 ÷ $900) if it is to equal $4,000 in 4 years. Going across the 4-year row, we find that investing $1 per year at 7 percent will provide $4.44 at the end of 4 years. Using this figure, we conclude that we would have to earn at least 7 percent if we are to accomplish our $4,000 goal.

Appendix B: Summary of Major Investment Alternatives

Table B17–1 summarizes nine criteria that describe the principal features of the major investment alternatives. Each investment is discussed in considerable detail in the succeeding three chapters.

Table A17-2 Compound Values of $1 Invested at the End of Each Year at Varying Rates of Interest

Investment period in years	4%	5%	6%	7%	8%	9%	10%	11%	12%	13%	14%	15%
1	1.00	1.00	1.00	1.00	1.00	1.00	1.00	1.00	1.00	1.00	1.00	1.00
2	2.04	2.05	2.06	2.07	2.08	2.09	2.10	2.11	2.12	2.13	2.14	2.15
3	3.12	3.15	3.18	3.22	3.25	3.28	3.31	3.34	3.37	3.41	3.44	3.47
4	4.25	4.31	4.38	4.44	4.51	4.57	4.64	4.71	4.78	4.85	4.92	4.99
5	5.42	5.53	5.64	5.75	5.87	5.99	6.11	6.23	6.35	6.48	6.61	6.74
6	6.63	6.80	6.98	7.15	7.34	7.52	7.72	7.91	8.12	8.32	8.54	8.75
7	7.90	8.14	8.39	8.65	8.92	9.20	9.49	9.78	10.09	10.41	10.73	11.07
8	9.21	9.55	9.90	10.26	10.64	11.03	11.44	11.86	12.30	12.76	13.23	13.73
9	10.58	11.03	11.49	11.98	12.49	13.02	13.58	14.16	14.78	15.42	16.09	16.79
10	12.00	12.58	13.18	13.82	14.49	15.19	15.94	16.72	17.55	18.42	19.34	20.30
11	13.49	14.21	14.97	15.78	16.65	17.56	18.53	19.56	20.66	21.81	23.04	24.35
12	15.03	15.92	16.87	17.89	18.98	20.14	21.38	22.71	24.13	25.65	27.27	29.00
13	16.63	17.71	18.88	20.14	21.50	22.95	24.52	26.21	28.03	29.99	32.09	34.35
14	18.29	19.60	21.02	22.55	24.22	26.02	27.98	30.10	32.39	34.88	37.58	40.51
15	20.02	21.58	23.28	25.13	27.15	29.36	31.77	34.41	37.28	40.42	43.84	47.58
16	21.83	23.66	25.67	27.89	30.32	33.00	35.95	39.19	42.75	46.67	50.98	55.72
17	23.70	25.84	28.21	30.84	33.75	36.97	40.55	44.50	48.88	53.74	59.12	65.08
18	25.65	28.13	30.91	34.00	37.45	41.30	45.60	50.40	55.75	61.73	68.39	75.84
19	27.67	30.54	33.76	37.38	41.45	46.02	51.16	56.94	63.44	70.75	78.97	88.21
20	29.78	33.07	36.79	41.00	45.76	51.16	57.28	64.20	72.05	80.95	91.03	102.44
25	41.65	47.73	54.86	63.25	73.11	84.70	98.35	114.41	133.33	155.62	181.87	212.79
30	56.08	66.44	79.06	94.46	113.28	136.31	164.49	199.02	241.33	293.20	356.79	434.75
35	73.65	90.32	111.43	138.24	172.32	215.71	271.02	341.59	431.66	546.68	693.57	881.17
40	95.03	120.80	154.76	199.64	259.06	337.88	442.59	581.83	767.09	1013.70	1342.03	1779.09

Table B17-1   Summary of Investment Alternatives

Investment	Risk exposure	1974–1975 annual yield range (percent)	Maturity	Flexibility
Savings account	None if account is insured	5 to 6	Instantly available	Extremely flexible; no fees or penalties for withdrawal
Time account (including limited-withdrawal account and certificate of deposit	None if account is insured	5½ to 7¾	90-day to 6-year minimum	Easily converted; 90-day interest penalty and reversion of rate to regular savings rate make early re-demption costly
United States Treasury:				
bills	Nonpayment risk is nil, but	5 to 8¾	90 days to 1 year	Easily converted; sales commission
notes	longer maturi-ties have	6 to 8¾	1 year to 10 years	when sold prior to maturity
bonds	interest-rate risk	6½ to 7½	More than 10 years	
Corporate bonds	Low to moder-ate, depending on the firm's business risk; longer maturities have interest rate risk	8¼ to 9 (Aaa); 9 to 10½ (Baa)	Notes, 5 to 10 years; (bonds, 20 to 30 years)	Bonds of large com-panies easily con-verted, those of small firms can be a problem; sales com-mission on all trans-actions
Municipal bonds	Low to moder-ate, depending on the govern-mental unit or revenue project backing the issue; interest rate risk on longer maturities	5½ to 6½ (Aaa); 6 to 7½ (Baa)	2 to 30 years	Moderate in large issues, increasingly limited on smaller issues, sales commis-sion on all trans-actions
Common stock	Moderate to high, depending on company's business line; market risk can be substantial on "high fliers"	9 to 10 (historical rate for large, top-notch firms); 10 to 12 (histori-cal rate for aggressive growth firms)	Open	Readily salable; sales commission on all transactions; in a market downturn, a stock's price can drop 25 to 50 per-cent, so the loss on a forced sale can be staggering

Minimum-size limitations	Investor involvement	Tax features	Hedge against inflation	Availability
None	None	Fully taxable	Very limited; regulated interest ceilings change only infrequently	All banks, credit unions, savings and loan associations
None to $5,000, depending on financial institution	None	Fully taxable	Very limited; regulated interest ceiling changes only infrequently	Most banks and savings and loan associations, some credit unions
$10,000 $1,000 to $5,000 $1,000	Very limited	Fully taxable, but exempt from state and local income taxes	Partial protection; rates move in response to market forces	All Federal Reserve banks and branches, many large commercial banks, most brokerage firms
$1,000; $5,000 on most new issues	Limited	Interest is fully taxable; capital gains tax on qualified long-term gains and losses from sale	Limited protection on short maturities; rates determined by market forces	Most brokerage firms, some banks
$1,000 to $5,000	Limited	Totally exempt from federal income tax; generally exempt from state and local taxes if bonds originated in state where investor lives	Limited protection on short maturities; rates determined by market forces	Many brokerage firms, a few banks
$300 to $400; sales commissions on lesser amounts become prohibitively high	Moderate to extensive	Dividends above $100 ($200 for joint return) are taxable; capital gains tax on qualified long-term gains and losses from sale	Reasonably complete	Brokerage firms

Table B17-1 Summary of Investment Alternatives (continued)

Investment	Risk exposure	1974–1975 annual yield range (percent)	Maturity	Flexibility
Mutual fund holding common stock or combined common stock plus bonds	Moderate to high, depending on the fund's objective	7 to 8 (11-year average for balanced income-growth funds); 9 to 12 (11-year average for growth funds)	Open	Readily salable; commission on purchase of "load" funds; in a declining market, share price can drop 20 to 50 percent, depending on how heavily the fund is invested in common stock, so a forced sale can cause a devastating loss
Mutual fund holding only				
money market	Limited to non-existent; very small interest-rate risk	5 to 9; most funds charge a management fee ranging from ½ to 1½ percent	Open	Readily converted; may entail a sales commission
municipal	Limited; most funds concentrate on top-quality issues; some interest-rate risk if holdings have lengthy maturities and fund must liquidate	6 to 7; most funds charge a small management fee	Open	Convertibility ranges from easy to limited, depending on the fund's rules

Appendix C: Investment Alternatives

Several investment alternatives, not covered in the next three chapters, are cited here. The Recommended Readings list is not meant to be all-inclusive. Instead, it samples the available materials in the various areas.

Real Estate

Mair, George, *Guide to Successful Real Estate: Investing, Buying, Financing, Leasing.* Englewood Cliffs, N.J.: Prentice-Hall, 1971.

Smith, Halbert C., Carl J. Tschappat, and Ronald L. Racster, *Real Estate and Urban Development.* Homewood, Ill.: Irwin, 1973.
Chapter 5 discusses the measurement of real estate value. Chapter 6 discusses how to estimate a justified investment price.

Minimum-size limitations	Investor involvement	Tax features	Hedge against inflation	Availability
A $500 to $1,000 initial investment typically required	Limited to moderate	Dividends are taxable; capital gains tax on qualified long-term gains and losses from sale	Partial to reasonably complete; the higher the percentage of common stocks held, the more complete the protection	Brokerage firms sell "load" funds; directly from fund managers for "no-load" funds
$100 to $5,000	Very limited	Fully taxable	Reasonably complete; concentration is on short-term instruments with highly responsive open-market interest rates	Directly from fund managers and from some brokerage firms
$1,000 on up	Limited	Exempt from federal income taxes	Limited protection on short-maturities; rates are determined by market forces	Directly from fund manager and some brokerage firms

Raw Land

Moral, Herbert R., *Buying Country Property.* New York: Bantam, 1972.

Benke, William, *Land Investor's Profit Guide and Negotiating Manual.* Englewood Cliffs, N.J.: Prentice-Hall, 1973.

Watkins, Arthur Martin, *Buying Land.* New York: Quadrangle/New York Times Book Co., 1975.

Futures

Hieronymus, Thomas A., *Economics of Futures Trading.* New York: Commodity Research Bureau, Inc., 1971.

Options

Chicago Board Options Exchange Clearing Corporation, *Understanding Options,* 1974. A free copy of this prospectus may be obtained from the corporation at 141 West Jackson, Chicago 60604.

Art

Rus, Richard, *Art as an Investment.* Englewood Cliffs, N.J.: Prentice-Hall, 1961.
Reitlinger, Gerald, *The Economics of Taste.* New York: Holt, 1961.
Loria, Jeffrey H., *Collecting Oriental Original Art.* New York: Harper, 1965.
Wraight, Robert, *The Art Game.* New York: Simon & Schuster, 1965.
Eagle, Joana, *Buying Art on a Budget.* New York: Hawthorn, 1968.
Taylor, John Russell, and Brian Brooke, *The Art Dealer.* New York: Scribner, 1969.
Keen, Geraldine, *Money and Art.* New York: Putnam, 1971.
Goodrich, David L., *Art Fakes in America.* New York: Viking, 1973.
Dorn, Sylvia O'Neill, *The Insider's Guide to Antiques, Art and Collectibles.* Garden City, N.Y.: Doubleday, 1974.

Antiques

Scott, Amoret, and Christopher Scott, *Antiques as an Investment.* New York: International Publications Service, 1967.
Rush, Richard, *Antiques as an Investment.* Englewood Cliffs, N.J.: Prentice-Hall, 1968.
Mebane, John, *The Poor Man's Guide to Antique Collecting.* Garden City, N.Y.: Doubleday, 1969.
Kovel, Ralph Mallory, *Know Your Antiques.* New York: Crown, 1973.
Mackay, James, *Turn of the Century Antiques: An Encyclopedia.* New York: Dutton, 1974.
Kovel, Ralph Mallory, and Terry Kovel, *The Kovel's Complete Antiques Price List.* New York: Crown, 1975.
Peterson, Harold Leslie, *How Do You Know It's Old?* New York: Scribner, 1975.

Oriental Rugs

Jacobsen, Charles W., *Oriental Rugs: A Complete Guide.* Rutland, Vt.: Tuttle, 1962.
Jacobsen, Charles W., *Check Points on How to Buy Oriental Rugs.* Rutland, Vt.: Tuttle, 1969.
Formenton, Fabio, *Oriental Rugs and Carpets.* New York: McGraw-Hill, 1972.
Eiland, Murray L., *Oriental Rugs a Comprehensive Guide.* (rev. ed.) Greenwich, Conn.: New York Graphic Society, 1975.

Gold

Hoppe, Donald J., *How to Invest in Gold Coins.* New York: Arco, 1970.
Cobleigh, Ira, *Buy Gold and Coin Money.* New York: Goldfax, 1972.
Green, Timothy, *How to Buy Gold.* New York: Walker, 1975.

Fixed-Income Investment Alternatives

After completing this chapter you should be able to:

describe the principal attributes of traditional savings and share accounts.

judge which savings or share account offers the highest effective return.

explain the strengths and weaknesses of investing in savings and share accounts.

formulate a plan for matching savings and share accounts with suitable investment goals.

minimize the interest penalty when a time account is redeemed prior to maturity.

explain the strengths and weaknesses of time accounts.

decide the investment goals for which time accounts are suitable.

describe the principal attributes of Series E and H savings bonds.

appraise the investment merits of savings bonds.

describe the major investment attributes of U.S. Treasury securities.

explain a secondary bond market transaction.

develop a plan to invest in Treasury securities using the secondary market.

decide on the investment goals for which Treasury securities are suitable.

describe the major investment attributes of corporate bonds.

analyze the advantages of purchasing corporate bonds in the primary or secondary market.

formulate a plan for matching corporate bonds to suitable investment goals.

describe the principal investment attributes of municipal bonds.

This chapter discusses the specific details of the various fixed-income investments. All the fixed-income investments we will describe involve lending arrangements whereby the investor lends a specific amount of money in exchange for two things—the borrower's promise to repay at some future date and the borrower's promise to pay a fixed rate of return during the period of the loan. Both of these promises are specified to the investor when the investment is made.

There are several reasons why an in-depth review of the various fixed-income investments is essential. One reason is that many people underestimate the range of investments available to them. Too often, investors accept an investment that has a low return or excessive restrictions and limited flexibility because they failed to fully investigate other investment options. For another reason, the range of fixed-income alternatives continues to expand through either new investment options or the repackaging of existing investments. Before investors can select which investments best match their specific investment goals, they need fairly complete information on what is available. One more reason is inflation: The ravages of inflation and taxes make it essential that investors obtain the highest return commensurate with the risk level they are willing to accept. Finally, we feel it is important to know about all the fixed-income investments because investing is an integral part of your personal financial planning.

The fixed-income investments covered in this chapter are suitable for most people—typical investors with $500 to $2,000 to invest each year. We will concentrate on investments with moderate to low risk. They provide a reasonable return without exposing the investor to the possibility of losing the entire investment should something go wrong. We will not cover highly specialized investments (those entailing a large minimum purchase, limited availability, or special tax features) or high-risk investments, because we believe they are suitable only for a small number of investors.

The investment alternatives we will examine are: savings and share accounts, restricted time accounts, United States savings bonds, United States Treasury securities, corporate bonds, and we shall give limited coverage to municipal bonds. We will review each of these fixed-income investments, using the previously cited nine basic criteria for evaluating any investment: risk exposure, yield, minimum maturity, flexibility, minimum size, investor involvement, tax features, hedge against inflation, and availability. Where special features or criteria apply to a particular investment, we will discuss them. We will also examine the major strengths and weaknesses of each investment, and we will suggest the goals for which the investment seems most appropriate. Our objective is to give you a working knowledge of all these fixed-income investments so that you can decide how each one relates to your specific investment goals.

SAVINGS ACCOUNTS OR SHARE ACCOUNTS

Savings or share accounts are offered by a wide array of financial institutions: commercial banks, mutual savings bonds, savings and loan associations, and credit unions. When the financial institution is mutually owned (all the depositors sharing in the ownership of the institution), the account is generally called a share account. Typically, share account earnings are called dividends rather than interest.

Financial institutions can pay a return on their savings and share accounts because they relend the money they take in as deposits. By consolidating the monies of small depositors, they can loan large amounts to a major borrower, such as a corporation, a small business, a home buyer, a local municipality, or even the United States government.

General Investment Criteria

The principal attributes of savings and share accounts evaluated according to the nine criteria are:

Risk Exposure   A savings or share account's principal risk exposure comes from the possibility that the financial institution may encounter serious financial difficulty. But there are several reasons why that is a remote possibility. One, the financial institution's operations are heavily regulated at both the state and federal levels. Two, financial institutions have long been the bastion of conservative financial management. Furthermore, most financial institutions have deposit insurance, so that even if they fall into difficulty and are unable to redeem depositors' accounts, the insurance will repay all depositors.

The institution pays the cost of the deposit insurance premiums; the depositor pays nothing. In most savings institutions, the deposit insurance coverage is limited to a maximum amount of $40,000 for each savings account or share account. However, if you have, say, $100,000 to deposit and you want to be covered for the entire amount by the institution's insurance, you can expand the maximum coverage by opening accounts for less than $40,000 at three different institutions. Or, at the same institution, you can open accounts in different names: for example, individual accounts for the husband and wife, a joint account, and certain trust accounts.

Commercial Bank   Nearly all bank savings accounts are insured with the Federal Deposit Insurance Corporation (FDIC) up to $40,000 per account.

Savings and Loan Association   The majority of savings accounts at savings and loan associations (S&Ls) are insured up to $40,000 through the Federal Savings and Loan Insurance Corporation (FSLIC).

Mutual Savings Bank   Most savings accounts at mutual savings banks are insured either through the Federal Deposit Insurance Corporation or through a state-sponsored insurance plan. The limit on the FDIC insurance is $40,000, but the state plans vary; so ask before you open an account.

Credit Union   Not all credit unions have deposit insurance. The ones that do are insured through either the National Credit Union Administration or a state insurance plan. Most plans cover at least $20,000 per account, but the limits vary.

Insurance: Is It Necessary?   While a well-managed savings institution should be able to repay its depositors in most situations short of a total financial catastrophe, it can be difficult for an outsider to judge whether an institution is properly managed or not. For that reason we feel deposit insurance is essential.

> **Strategy: When considering savings or share accounts, insist on an insured account. If it is a state or private insurance plan, make certain the maximum will cover the amount you intend to deposit.**

Yield   Maximum interest rates for savings accounts and share accounts are set by federal or state regulatory agencies. However, institutions can pay any rate they choose up to the ceiling rate. During the past 5 years, the increased competition for savings deposits, coupled with the upward movement of all interest rates, has forced many institutions to pay the maximum allowable interest rate. But that move has not been universal. Some large financial institutions in major metropolitan areas continue to offer less than the maximum rate. Certainly, an institution's size or the extent of its advertising promotion is no guarantee that it pays the highest rate. Likewise, some institutions in less populated areas, especially where there is little competition for depositors, continue to pay less than the maximum interest rate. In some cases it is substantially less.

Exhibit 18–1 presents the current maximum interest rates for savings and share accounts. While these rates apply directly to federally chartered and federally insured savings institutions, nearly all the other institutions have similar maximums. The maximum interest rate is slightly lower in commercial banks than in savings banks and S&Ls, but the differential has narrowed recently and may well disappear soon.

> **Strategy: Compare the interest rates among competing types of accounts rather than assume all accounts pay the same return. An interest rate that is $1/4$ to $1/2$ percent more can be significant when compounded over a long period.**

Frequency of Compounding   Most savings institutions now compound

Exhibit 18-1   Interest Rate Ceilings on Savings and Share Accounts

Institution	Percentage rate
Commercial bank	5
Savings and loan association	5¼
Mutual savings bank	5¼
Credit union	7

their interest payments quarterly (every 3 months), and some have switched to daily or even continuous compounding. As Exhibit 17–4 demonstrated in the previous chapter, the more frequent the compounding, the higher the account's effective yield. Some institutions have hedged their shift to daily compounding by requiring the money be on deposit for the entire 3-month quarter before the depositor receives daily compounding.

Computing Interest   Several different methods are used to compute the earnings on savings accounts. The differences depend on which account balance the institution uses when computing the interest.

The major difference between the four frequently used computation techniques can best be illustrated with a numerical example. Assume the initial balance in our savings account was $50. At the beginning of the second month, we deposited $75 in the account. At the beginning of the third month, we withdrew $50 from the account. The account pays 5 percent interest annually and uses a 3-month quarter to compute interest. To simplify the example, we assume there are 30 days in each month and 360 days in the year. Exhibit 18–2 summarizes the activity in the account.

Some accounts pay interest only on the lowest balance during a specified interest period (typically, a 3-month quarter). For our example, the lowest balance was $50. Consequently, the interest for the 3-month period was only 63 cents (computation is shown in Exhibit 18–2). For accounts having considerable deposit and withdrawal activity, the earnings in a minimum balance account can be very limited. Rather than use the lowest balance, some accounts require that the money be on deposit for the entire quarter in order to earn interest. The resulting interest payments would be identical to the above lowest balance computation.

Other institutions use a first-in, first-out (FIFO) technique with their accounts: Withdrawals during the period are considered as coming from the earliest deposits of the period, hence the first-in, first-out. For the example in Exhibit 18–2, the $50 withdrawal at the start of the third month would be considered to have come from the initial $50 balance in the account. Consequently, the account would pay interest only on $75 for the 60 days it was in the account. The resulting interest for the 3-month period would be 63 cents (computation is shown in Exhibit 18–2). When a withdrawal is made immediately before the end of the 3-month quarter, the account holder loses a sizable amount of interest. Thus, had the $50 withdrawal been made several days

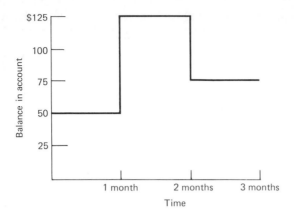

Minimum balance
   $50 × 5 percent × 90 days/360 days = $ .63
FIFO balance
   $75 × 5 percent × 60 days/360 days = $ .63
LIFO balance
   $50 × 5 percent × 90 days/360 days = $ .63
   $25 × 5 percent × 60 days/360 days =   .21
                                        $ .84
Day of deposit to day of withdrawal
   $50 × 5 percent × 30 days/360 days = $ .21
   $125 × 5 percent × 30 days/360 days =   .52
   $75 × 5 percent × 30 days/360 days =   .31
                                        $1.04

Exhibit 18-2   Computation of Interest on Savings and Share Accounts

before the end of the quarter, the account holder would receive no interest on
that $50 even though it had been in the account for nearly 3 months.

Some institutions modify this technique and assume last-in, first-out
(LIFO): Withdrawals are assumed to come from the most recent deposit. For
the example in Exhibit 18–2, the $50 withdrawal would be charged against the
$75 deposit made in the second month. Consequently, the account pays interest
on the initial $50 balance for 90 days and the remaining $25 balance ($75 deposit
− $50 withdrawal) for 60 days. Total interest for the period is 84 cents (shown
in Exhibit 18–2). While less onerous than the previous FIFO technique, the
account holder still suffers a sizable penalty for making withdrawals near the
end of the quarterly interest period.

The final and most equitable computation method pays interest on money
from the day it is deposited in the account until the day it is withdrawn. For our
example in Exhibit 18–2, the account balance during the first 30 days was $50,
for the second 30 days it was $125, and for the final 30 days it was $75. Total
interest for the period would be $1.04 (computation is shown in Exhibit 18–2).

The principal advantage of the "day of deposit to day of withdrawal" technique is that the account holder receives full credit regardless of the withdrawal and deposit activities during the period. Fortunately, an increasing number of institutions are switching to this computational technique.

> **Strategy: Your top priority should be a savings or share account which pays interest from day of deposit to day of withdrawal. Your second priority should be an account with frequent compounding.**

Minimum Maturity   While most savings and share accounts specify that the financial institution can require 30 days' prior notice for withdrawals, very few commercial banks, mutual savings banks, or savings and loan institutions enforce that requirement. Essentially, these accounts have no effective minimum maturity. The single exception is credit unions. Some of them enforce the advance withdrawal notice requirement because of their small size, limited deposit inflows, or specialized reinvestments.

Flexibility   Savings and share accounts can readily be converted to cash with little difficulty. Because the institution promises to repay the entire balance, the depositor (the investor) has no exposure to market fluctuations. Most accounts have no transaction fee for deposits, although some do charge a fee for withdrawals, especially when the number of withdrawals during a period exceeds a specified limit. But you should be able to find accounts with no fees for withdrawals.

Minimum Size   Most savings or share accounts do not require a minimum-sized deposit or withdrawal, but a few institutions request they be in multiples of $5 or $10. Many institutions close out an account, or transfer it to inactive status, when the balance drops below a prescribed minimum; typically, from $1 to $25.

Investor Involvement   By selecting an insured savings or share account, an investor is spared the need to investigate the soundness or management efficiency of the institution holding the investment. Also, with savings and share accounts, interest is automatically credited to the account. Therefore, with this type of investment, there is little or no investor involvement.

Tax Features   All interest on savings accounts and dividends on share accounts is fully taxable under federal tax regulations.

Hedge against Inflation   Because of their fixed-income feature, savings and share accounts are a poor hedge against inflation, especially when the inflation rate has increased sharply. Even when the inflation rate is steady, such as during the late 1960s, these accounts provide only a limited hedge against inflation. This is the case because the regulatory agencies do not change the interest rate ceilings on savings and share accounts often enough and quickly enough to keep pace with changes in general interest rates. As a consequence, the real return—the promised interest rate minus the inflation rate—has been near zero, and more often it has been negative. Unfortunately, the real return from savings and share accounts is likely to continue this way unless inflation rates slow down considerably or the interest ceilings are more immediately responsive to the general open-market rates on other investments. Otherwise, the real return will be substantially less than the $1\frac{1}{2}$ to 2 percent we believe these accounts should earn.

Availability   The standard savings and share account is widely available at many financial institutions. There are many commercial banks and savings and loan associations in nearly every city, although there are fewer S&Ls in small cities. Mutual savings banks are concentrated primarily in the northeastern section of the United States. In those areas, savings banks far outnumber S&Ls, but the services of the two are similar.

Special Features

Many institutions have special features and services that can substantially enhance their savings or share accounts.

Deposit and Withdrawal Options   Many institutions offer mail service for deposits and withdrawals. Obviously, this is a great convenience, saving you time, travel, and postage to make deposits and withdrawals. As a minor economy, try to find an account where the institution pays the postage.

Carrying this convenience one step further, some institutions will make a transfer between a depositor's savings and checking accounts with only a phone call. In addition, upon your instructions, many institutions will automatically transfer a set amount from your checking account to your savings each month. By using these services effectively, you can minimize the noninterest-earning cash balance in your checking account.

Transfers Many institutions will not only transfer a depositor's money between their own savings and checking accounts; they will also make transfers to accounts in other financial institutions. Thus, an S&L would transfer money from a depositor's savings account to the depositor's checking account in a commercial bank.

Bill-paying Service Many institutions offer a bill-paying service whereby the account holder can specify certain expenses that are to be paid automatically from the savings or share account each month. While this service was initially limited to housing-related expenses, many institutions have received authority to expand it to all recurring monthly expenses. This feature has special appeal for institutions which cannot offer a checking account such as S&Ls and many mutual savings banks. This service is not only a convenience; it offers account holders the opportunity to obtain interest on their money right up until the payment is made, assuming interest is paid on the daily balance.

Special Club Accounts Many institutions offer special-purpose savings accounts: Christmas, gift, or travel savings accounts. In general, these accounts require a set weekly deposit over a period of months. At the end of the period, the holder presumably withdraws the balance for some special purpose. Although some institutions now pay interest on these accounts, the rate they pay is still less than that paid on a savings account. We have no objection to the goal of most special accounts, but we do object to the fact that their interest rate return is less than the interest paid on a savings account. A well-chosen savings account has the flexibility of a special account without sacrificing any interest earnings.

Savings and Share Accounts: Strengths and Weaknesses

The major strengths and weaknesses of savings and share accounts are summarized in Exhibit 18–3.

Savings and Share Accounts: Suitable Investment Goals

Given their low risk exposure, savings and share accounts are ideally suited to investment goals where safety is of uppermost importance. The continuous liquidity and high flexibility of a savings or share account make it ideally suited for the emergency fund we discussed in the budgeting chapter (Chapter 4). With its daily interest feature, a savings or share account is a good temporary investment while the investor accumulates the necessary money for a larger,

Exhibit 18-3   Savings and Share Accounts — Strengths and Weaknesses

Strengths	Weaknesses
Extremely high liquidity	Very limited rate of return
Tremendous deposit and withdrawal flexibility	Adjustments to interest rate ceiling that lag far behind general market interest rates
Very low risk; near zero for insured deposits	Very poor hedge against inflation
No serious limits on transaction size	
Once established, no need for investor involvement	
Widely available	

more restrictive investment. Because most accounts require no advance withdrawal notice and have no size limits, they are well suited to all short-term goals, especially goals with considerable deposit and withdrawal activity.

Their relatively low interest rates make them a poor choice for medium- to long-term goals. For a 6-month goal of $500 they are perfect, but for a 5-year goal of $5,000 there are better investments.

TIME ACCOUNTS

Time accounts are offered by many of the same institutions which offer savings and share accounts. Their distinguishing and principal feature is that the depositor agrees not to withdraw the funds for a prescribed period that ranges from 90 days to 6 years. In exchange for accepting this withdrawal restriction, time accounts pay a higher interest rate. The longer the commitment period, the higher the return.

In general, a time account with a maturity of 1 year or less is designated as a special passbook account; typical names include golden passbook, major income account, and income plus account. The investor receives a passbook as evidence of the account. On maturities longer than 1 year, the account is evidenced by a certificate of deposit. The certificate indicates the maturity date, amount, and interest rate. Commercial banks also issue another type of certificate: large negotiable certificates of deposit. We will not discuss these; their minimum denomination is $100,000!

General Investment Criteria

Continuing the pattern from the preceding section, we shall examine time accounts, using the same nine criteria.

Risk Exposure   The risk exposure of time accounts is essentially the same as the risk exposure for savings or share accounts because they are offered by the same financial institutions. Where a financial institution has deposit insurance, that coverage extends to time accounts as well, and the coverage limits are identical to those on savings and share accounts; typically, $40,000.

Exhibit 18-4   Time Account Interest Rate Ceilings

Maturity of time account	Commercial bank	Savings and loan association	Mutual savings bank
90 days to 1 year	5½ percent	5¾ percent	5¾ percent
1 to 2½ years	6	6½	6½
2½ to 4 years	6½	6¾	6¾
4 to 6 years	7¼	7½	7½
6 years or more	7½	7¾	7¾

Yield   The interest rate ceilings on time accounts are set by the same federal and state regulatory agencies that control savings and share account rates. But the institution is under no obligation to pay the maximum rate. The current ceilings for federally chartered or insured institutions are shown in Exhibit 18–4. The maximum interest rates offered by institutions not chartered or insured by the federal government or its agency would closely parallel the rates shown in the exhibit.

Frequency of Compounding   Because the interest rates are generally higher for time accounts, multiple compounding can substantially boost the account's return. For example, a 4-year time account of $1,000 at 6½ percent with interest compounded quarterly, will total $1,294.22 at the end of 4 years. Had interest been compounded daily, the same account would be worth $1,301.51.

> Strategy: As with any kind of account, invest in a time account offering the highest interest and most frequent compounding, even if it means dealing with an institution which is some distance from where you live. You will deal with the institution only twice over the period—when you invest and when you redeem the account.

Minimum Maturity   Time accounts are available in five maturity ranges: 90 days, 1 year, 2½ years, 4 years, and 6 years. To earn the quoted rate, the funds must be on deposit for the entire maturity period. Most accounts permit early withdrawal, but as a penalty for early withdrawal, the interest rate is reduced.

Flexibility   Time accounts are readily redeemed at face value when they mature and any time thereafter. There is no service fee for this redemption. The only thing to consider with respect to flexibility is the penalty in reduced interest for early redemption.

Caution: Interest Penalty Ahead   The penalty for early redemption is effected in two ways: (1) the interest rate for the account reverts to the regular savings or share rate, and (2) 90 days' interest is deducted from whatever interest is payable. The top half of Exhibit 18–5 illustrates the impact of redeeming a 1-year, 6 percent (compounded quarterly), $1,000 time account

after 270 days. As the example demonstrates, the penalty for early redemption is substantial.

The bottom half of Exhibit 18–5 illustrates how much interest could have been earned, had the $1,000 been in a regular savings account at 5 percent for 270 days or in a time account at 5½ percent for three consecutive 90-day time periods. Clearly, the interest from both these alternatives is much better than

Exhibit 18-5   Time Accounts: Impact of Interest Penalty

Lost interest	
Regular earnings on $1,000 account: 270 days at 6 percent	$45.68*
Earnings on account after penalty: 180 days at 5 percent	25.16†
Interest lost due to early redemption	$20.52
Interest potential	
Regular savings account: 270 days at 5 percent	$37.97‡
Three 90-day time accounts: 270 days at 5½ percent	$41.82§

*Given a 6 percent annual rate, the quarterly rate is 1½ percent (6 percent ÷ 4 quarterly periods). Interest for three quarters (270 days) would be: ($1,000 × 1½ percent) + ($1,015 × 1½ percent) + ($1,030.23 × 1½ percent) = $45.68.

†The 90-day interest penalty leaves 180 days (270 − 90 days) at the regular 5 percent rate. At 5 percent, the quarterly rate is 1¼ (5 percent ÷ 4 quarterly periods). Interest for two quarters (180 days) would be: ($1,000 × 1¼ percent) + ($1,012.50 × 1¼ percent) = $25.16.

‡Interest for 270 days at 1¼ percent (5 percent ÷ 4 quarterly periods): ($1,000 × 1¼ percent) + ($1,012.50 × 1¼ percent) + ($1,025.16 × 1¼ percent) = $37.97.

§Interest for 270 days at 1⅜ percent (5½ percent ÷ 4 quarterly periods): ($1,000 × 1⅜ percent) + ($1,013.75 × 1⅜ percent) + ($1,027.69 × 1⅜ percent) = $41.82.

the $25.16 that the 1-year time account actually paid after all penalties for early redemption.

> **Strategy: Unless you can hold a time account for a long maturity, you should either accept a shorter maturity or consider regular savings.**

Avoiding Early Redemption One way to avoid early redemption is to borrow the money you need. Most financial institutions which offer time accounts will make cash loans, using the account as security. For such loans, the finance charge is typically 1 to $1^1/_2$ percent above the time account's interest rate.

When is a loan more advantageous than early redemption? The answer depends on the maturity of the time account and the finance charge of the loan. Exhibit 18-6 shows, for each time account maturity and two typical finance charges for time account loans, that point in time when it makes no difference whether you redeem the time account or take a loan to continue it. If you have held a time account for a period longer than shown in Exhibit 18-6, it is best to take a loan to continue the account. For example, if you have held a $2^1/_2$-year time account for 191 days, rather than redeem it at that point, it would be better to take a loan at a finance charge costing 1 percent above the time account rate. For holding periods shorter than shown, early redemption is better than taking a loan. For example, assume you have a $2^1/_2$-year time account and the loan's finance charge is 1 percent above the time account's rate. If the account was held for only 189 days, it would be advantageous to redeem the account rather than take the loan.

Minimum Size In general, the longer the maturity, the larger the minimum initial deposit.

Most 90-day accounts have no minimum deposit, although a few still require $100 to open an account. Since most 90-day accounts are in passbook form, an investor can make subsequent deposits to the account. But each

Exhibit 18-6   Minimum Holding Period for Cost of Cash Loan to Be Less than Penalty on Early Redemption of Time Account

Maturity on time account*	Differential above time account rate	
	1 percent	1½ percent
90 days	13 days	19 days
1 year	52 days	73 days
2½ years	190 days	310 days
4 years	312 days	465 days
6 years	500 days	710 days

*Assumes time account pays the maximum commercial bank rate shown in Exhibit 18-4. Because the effect of compounding would be small in these computations, it was disregarded. Holding periods for S&Ls and savings banks are similar.

deposit must remain in the account for 90 days to qualify for the quoted return. Any deposit in the account for 90 days can be redeemed with full interest.

For 1-year accounts, the picture is mixed; some require no minimum deposit, others require an initial deposit between $100 and $500.

A passbook time account offers the advantage that once the initial minimum deposit is made, subsequent deposits can be any amount, even amounts much smaller than the initial minimum deposit. Time accounts in the form of certificates of deposit do not offer the same advantage; the initial and all subsequent deposits must be for the same minimum amount and a new certificate is issued for every deposit.

Nearly all the longer maturity accounts—$2^1/_2$ years, 4 years, and 6 years—have minimums ranging from $500 to $5,000 and even higher. Generally these accounts are certificates of deposit. Obviously, the smaller the minimum, the more flexible the account.

Investor Involvement By selecting an insured time account, the investor avoids the need to evaluate the institution's management policies and general soundness.

Since most institutions will automatically renew their shorter-term time accounts for a period similar to the original account, an investor does not have to actively manage this type of account. Some institutions notify the investor prior to renewal, while others renew unless the investor instructs them otherwise. This feature presents no problem as long as the investor wants to recommit the money. A few institutions renew time accounts at the original rate rather than at the current interest rate. Thus, if rates have risen since the original investment, as is often the case, renewing a time account will yield a lower return than a new account. Nearly all the longer maturities require the investor to initiate the renewal. Since a time account pays no interest after its maturity, prompt action is necessary.

> **Strategy: Keep a list of your time account maturities so you will not be inadvertently locked into a new maturity period or end up with an expired account that earns no interest.**

Tax Features The interest on all time accounts, whether it is redeposited in the account or paid directly to the investor, is fully taxable for federal income tax purposes.

Hedge against Inflation The performance of time accounts as a hedge against inflation has ranged from poor to mediocre. Despite their high return, medium-term time accounts have barely matched price increases during the past 10 years. Even as other interest rates moved up in response to higher inflation, time account rate ceilings have changed infrequently and only by small amounts. In our opinion, extending the maturity to obtain a higher return is not the answer. If the interest ceiling on time accounts is raised during a long maturity, you would be locked into the original lower return until the end of the maturity period. And with the prospect of continued high inflation, the ceiling is likely to be lifted. Furthermore, the longer maturities—especially the 4- and 6-year categories—substantially reduce your flexibility and reinvestment options. In our opinion, the added return is not commensurate with that sacrifice. We think an investor should remain as flexible as possible given the future inflation prospects.

Strategy: We recommend that time account maturities not exceed 1 year or at most 2¹/₂ years because of the likelihood of high inflation rates during the late 1970s.

Availability   Short-term and medium-term time accounts are offered by nearly all commercial banks, savings and loan associations, and mutual savings banks. Many also offer 4- and 6-year accounts.

Time Accounts: Strengths and Weaknesses

The major strengths and weaknesses of time accounts are shown in Exhibit 18–7.

Time Accounts: Suitable Investment Goals

The range of maturities makes time accounts suitable for short- to medium-term investment goals. An added convenience of 90-day accounts is that many institutions will redeem them not only at the end of 90 days, but also at the end of their 3-month financial quarters without penalty. Thus, an account which was opened midway through the institution's 3 month financial quarter would never be more than 45 days away from a penalty-free redemption point.

Because there is no minimum deposit requirement, an investor can use a 90-day account to accumulate sufficient money for a larger or longer-term investment. For example, it can be used to accumulate the minimum deposit for a 1-year or 2¹/₂-year account. The time horizon for your investment goal should coincide rather closely with the maturity of a time account: if your time horizon is shorter than the maturity, there is the penalty for early redemption.

UNITED STATES SAVINGS BONDS

This section discusses Series E and Series H savings bonds. Both bonds are nonnegotiable instruments. That means that investors cannot sell or transfer their bonds to other individuals. Instead, a bond must be redeemed at a

Exhibit 18-7   Time Accounts — Strengths and Weaknesses

Strengths	Weaknesses
Risk that approaches zero for insured accounts	Limited rate of return
Small or no minimum denominations on shorter maturities	Poor hedge against inflation
Widely available	Sizable interest penalty for early redemption, making long maturities inflexible
Little or no investor involvement	

commercial bank or other financial institution. Consequently, there is no secondary market for bonds held by investors. The available denominations are extensive for Series E and H bonds and they are specially tailored to small investors. Series E bonds are more widely distributed and more readily available than Series H bonds.

General Investment Criteria

Unless specifically noted, the comments describing the attributes of savings bonds apply to both bond series.

Risk Exposure   Since savings bonds are backed by the credit and full faith of the United States government, they are effectively risk-free investments. The possibility that the government would fail to redeem the bonds is extremely remote.

There is no risk that a savings bond's market price will fluctuate with changes in open-market interest rates. A bond's redemption price is set by the government.

Yield   Both bond series currently promise a 6 percent return compounded semiannually. To receive that rate, however, Series E bonds must be held for 5 years and Series H bonds for 10 years.

Series E   A Series E bond is purchased at a discount from its face value. After a specified period, currently 5 years, it can be redeemed at face value. For example, an investor can purchase a $100 face value bond today for $75. Five years from today the bond can be redeemed at its $100 face value. In effect, the difference between purchase and redemption price is the interest payment. The promised 6 percent return (compounded semiannually) actually yields slightly more than full face value. Thus, a $25 bond gives $25.20 after 5 years, a $50 bond gives $50.40, a $100 bond gives $100.80, and so on.

Historically, Series E bonds have continued to pay interest after their designated maturity date. Also, when the interest on new E bonds was increased, the interest on older outstanding bonds was raised to the same rate as the new bonds. For example, when the most recent rise to 6 percent became effective in December 1973, the return on older Series E bonds was also raised to 6 percent. Since all bonds, new and outstanding, earn identical returns, there would be no point in swapping an outstanding E bond for a new one.

Series H   The differences between H bonds and E bonds are that interest on Series H bonds is paid twice each year and that investors pay the full face value of the bond to buy it and receive the same full face value when they redeem it.

The maturity of H bonds is 10 years, and, in the past, outstanding bonds have been extended for another 10 years. Like their Series E counterparts, whenever the rate on new bonds is raised, the interest rate on outstanding H bonds is also increased. Thus, a 5½ percent H bond purchased in 1971 began earning 6 percent in December 1973 when the rate on new bonds was increased to 6 percent.

Minimum Maturity   A Series E bond cannot be redeemed until 2 months after purchase: therefore 2 months is the minimum maturity. But E bonds have a graduated interest schedule which raises the effective minimum closer to 5 years. Because the redemption price rises slowly in the early periods, the bond's yield is substantially less than 6 percent if it is redeemed before 5 years. The middle column of Exhibit 18–8 shows the approximate annual yield for redeeming E bonds early.

Series H bonds cannot be redeemed until their minimum maturity, which is 6 months after purchase. The interest schedule on H bonds specifies small, semiannual payments during the early years followed by much larger payments in the later years. While those larger payments raise the yield to 6 percent, the return is much lower if the bond is redeemed early. The third column of Exhibit 18–8 shows the effective yield at various early redemption points.

Flexibility   Once past the minimum holding period—2 months for E bonds and 6 months for H bonds—both bonds can readily be converted to cash. Series E bonds can be redeemed at most commercial banks, many savings and loans, many mutual savings banks, Federal Reserve banks and branches, and the Department of the Treasury (Washington, D.C. 20226). Series H bonds can be redeemed at the last two locations plus the Bureau of Public Debt (536 S. Clark St., Chicago 60605).

There are no transaction fees for redeeming either bond. But the flexibility of savings bonds is substantially reduced by the early redemption penalty. Unless an investor plans to hold the bonds until maturity, both make poor short-term investments. For example, the return from holding an E bond 1 year is only $4^{1}/_{2}$ percent, which is substantially less than the 6 to $6^{1}/_{2}$ percent currently available on 1-year time accounts.

Strategy: To invest in E bonds or H bonds, you should be sure that you will hold them for the entire maturity period.

Minimum Size   Series E bonds can be purchased at their discount price in denominations of $18.75, $37.50, $56.25, $75, $150, $375, $750, and $7,500.

Exhibit 18-8   Effective Yield on Series E and H Bonds, Given Early Redemption

Bond redeemed after	Yield (in percent)	
	Series E	Series H
6 months	3.7	4.2
1 year	4.5	5.0
1½ years	4.7	5.3
2 years	4.8	5.4
3 years	5.0	5.5
4 years	5.1	5.6
6 years	—	5.8
8 years	—	5.9

Series H bonds are purchased at their face value in denominations of $500, $1,000, $5,000, and $10,000. The range of denominations makes it quite convenient for an investor to put together a combination of denominations to match nearly any investment goal.

Both bond series limit the amount of bonds that can be purchased in a calendar year: $10,000 of E bonds (their face value), or $10,000 of H bonds. But that upper limit poses few problems for most people.

Investor Involvement   After purchasing a bond, an investor really has no further involvement until the bonds are redeemed. Further, with the automatic maturity extension, the bonds do not have to be redeemed on the day they mature. And since the interest rate on older bonds is automatically increased to match that of new bonds, there is no advantage to redeeming the old bonds.

Tax Features   The interest on both bonds is fully taxable for federal income tax purposes. But with E bonds, where the interest accumulates until the bond matures or is redeemed, the investor can either recognize the interest each year or when the bond is redeemed. Since the latter option defers the tax, someone who expects to have a much lower marginal tax rate at some future time will find it advantageous to recognize the interest when the bond is redeemed. Since H bonds pay interest semiannually, it must be recognized and reported on your income taxes each year; there is no option to defer interest with H bonds.

The interest from E and H bonds is exempt from all state and local income taxes. One way of looking at this feature is that it increases the effective return. For example, if an investor's marginal state and local income tax rate is 10 percent, a 6 percent return from E and H bonds would be equivalent to 6.67 percent on a fully taxable investment (6 percent ÷ [100 percent − 10 percent]).

Hedge against Inflation   As with most fixed-income securities, savings bonds have not fared well during recent periods of high inflation. The rate on savings bonds has been increased twice in the past 6 years, so, in a way, the rate is responsive to inflation. But those increases were small and lagged far behind the upward movement in open-market interest rates. In fact, it was only after the rush to redeem old bonds had turned to a stampede, and after the sale of new bonds had fallen to a trickle, that rates were increased.

Availability   Series E bonds can be purchased from most commercial banks, a number of other financial institutions, select post offices, Federal Reserve banks and branches, and from the Department of the Treasury. In addition, many employers have a payroll plan whereby an employee can purchase bonds through payroll withholding. Some banks perform a similar service: Depositors instruct the bank to withdraw a fixed amount regularly from their checking or savings account and to use it to purchase a bond.

Series H bonds are available from Federal Reserve banks and branches and the Department of the Treasury. Either agency will sell the bonds by mail if the investor includes instructions for registering, a social security or taxpayer number, an address where the bond and the interest checks are to be sent, and a personal or cashiers check payable to either the Federal Reserve Bank or United States Treasury for the purchase price.

Savings Bonds: Strengths and Weaknesses

The principal strengths and weaknesses of savings bonds are summarized in Exhibit 18–9.

Savings Bonds: Suitable Investment Goals

Because the interest rate schedule is heavily biased against early redemption, savings bonds are poorly suited to short-term investment goals. Although their 5- to 10-year maturity suggests they are more appropriate for longer-term goals, the interest rate is simply not competitive with comparable time accounts, and inflation reduces their real return.

DANGER: Authors' Bias Ahead!   Our overall impression of savings bonds can be summed up in a single word: underwhelming! While we think patriotism is an admirable and worthy pursuit, we recommend you declare your money neutral territory. We have several reservations about savings bonds: The most important one is that an insured time account provides a higher return and a shorter minimum maturity. While we agree that savings bonds have slightly lower risk, we do not think it justifies sacrificing the difference in interest.

UNITED STATES TREASURY SECURITIES

United States Treasury securities differ from savings bonds in three ways:

One: They are marketable securities. That means they can be sold or transferred any time. And there is a well-established secondary market for them.

Two: Because these securities are sold in the open market, their interest rates can fluctuate in relation to the supply and demand for Treasury and other fixed-income securities. For example, if there were many investors with a lot of

Exhibit 18-9   Savings Bonds — Strengths and Weaknesses

Strengths	Weaknesses
Virtually risk-free	Limited rate of return
Wide availability in small denominations	Rates not competitive with comparable time accounts
Automatic maturity extensions and interest rate adjustments that make investor involvement minimal	Sizable interest penalty that discourages redeeming the bonds before they mature
	Poor hedge against inflation

money to invest and the volume of new Treasury and other fixed-income securities coming into the market was small, the interest rates on those securities could be fairly low, yet they would have no trouble attracting buyers. If, however, the conditions were exactly opposite—large volume of securities and few investors—the interest rates would have to be high to entice buyers.

Three: Unlike the rates of previously discussed investments, open-market interest rates are not regulated or controlled. Because these rates are determined by prevailing market forces, wide swings are not uncommon. For example, in January 1974 a 3- to 5-year Treasury security offered a 6.9 percent return; by August the return had risen to 8.6 percent; by January 1975 it had fallen to 7.3 percent, only to rise to 7.5 percent by May of that year. In short, the interest rate on Treasury securities can fluctuate through a considerable range in a relatively short time.

Principal Types of Securities   There are three major types of Treasury securities: Treasury bills, Treasury bonds, and Treasury notes.

Treasury Bills   The maturity on Treasury bills is 1 year or less and the minimum denomination is $10,000. The 90- and 180-day bills are sold at an auction every week; the 270- and 360-day bills are sold less frequently. All bills are sold at discount; that is, the investor buys the bill at less than face value. The discount amount becomes the interest earnings when the bill is redeemed for face value at maturity.

Treasury Bonds   Maturities on Treasury bonds are longer than 10 years, usually 20 to 30 years. Most bonds are available in $1,000 denominations. They pay a fixed interest rate and pay interest twice yearly.

Treasury Notes   The maturity on Treasury notes ranges from 1 to 10 years. The minimum denomination is either $1,000 or $5,000. New issues of notes are sold as the Treasury deems necessary either to meet its cash needs or to refund a maturing security issue. Treasury notes specify a fixed interest rate and the interest is paid twice yearly.

Because their maturities match the needs of many investors, and, further, since most investors can meet the minimum denomination, our discussion will concentrate on Treasury notes.

Secondary Market   All the other investments we have discussed so far are nonmarketable. If an investor wants to redeem a time account or a savings bond before it matures, she obtains the money from the original borrower. It works differently for Treasury securities. The United States Treasury will not redeem a Treasury security before maturity. But the investor is free to sell the security to another investor who is interested in buying it. And the Treasury will transfer ownership so the new owner receives the interest payments and the face value at maturity. Of course, investors could run want ads announcing: "For sale. One slightly used Treasury security. Mint condition, only handled once each month." They do not have to do this, however, because a number of bond dealers have already established a secondary market in Treasury securities. That market matches investors who have securities to sell with prospective investors who want to buy. As in any good market, the prevailing price changes in response to the influx of buyers and sellers.

Reading a Secondary Market List   Understanding Treasury securities requires that you be able to read a secondary market listing. Exhibit 18–10 shows a hypothetical secondary market listing. Listings showing similar information can be found in *The Wall Street Journal, Barron's*, and many major metropolitan newspapers. The only difference is that the actual newspaper listings include substantially more securities than the few examples shown in Exhibit 18–10.

The prices in Exhibit 18–10 in the columns headed High, Low, and Last are given as a percentage of the security's face value. The numbers to the right of the decimal point represent the fractional part of 1 percent, but it is not a decimal fraction. Instead, the fractional part is given in thirty-seconds. For example, a price quoted as 100.27 is really 100 and $27/_{32}$ percent; the decimal

Exhibit 18-10   Listing of Treasury Issues in the Secondary Market

Rate	Maturity	Type	Price			Change	Yield
			High	Low	Last		
6⅞s	May 1977	Note	99.11	99.3	99.10	+.6	7.28
9s	May 1977	Note	102.27	102.21	102.24	−.2	7.37
7¼s	Nov. 1977	Note	100.31	100.23	100.30	+.5	7.31
6¼s	Feb. 1978	Note	97.18	97.13	97.17	+.3	7.31
7½s	Aug. 1978	Note	100.11	99.30	100.8	+.4	7.52

equivalent is 100.84375 percent. Thus the price for a $1,000 note quoted at 100.27 would be approximately $1,008.44 ($1,000 × 100.84375 percent). The price in the "High" column is the highest price paid for the security during that day's trading. Likewise, the "Low" column lists the lowest price paid. And "Last" means this was the price paid for the security the last time it was traded during the day. The "Change" column shows the change in price between yesterday's "last" price and today's "last" price.

We will use the "6$\frac{1}{4}$s, Feb. 1978," to illustrate how the information in Exhibit 18–10 can be utilized. The security is a 6$\frac{1}{4}$ percent Treasury note maturing in February 1978. Under the "Last" column the price is shown as 97 and $^{17}/_{32}$ percent, or 97.53125 percent. If the note's face value is $1,000, the price on the last trade would be $975.31 ($1,000 × 97.53125 percent). If the note's face value is $5,000, the price would be $4,876.56 ($5,000 × 97.53125 percent).

Typically, the first column of the listing gives the fixed interest rate the security pays. Thus, the 6$\frac{1}{4}$s of February 1978 notes pay 6$\frac{1}{4}$ percent interest. But this is only one part of the total yield on the security. To find the total effective yield, both the effect of any change in the price of the security and the interest earnings must be considered. Most listings provide this information in a "Yield" column (shown at the extreme right in Exhibit 18–10). For the 6$\frac{1}{4}$s, Feb. 1978, note, the yield is 7.31 percent (unlike the price columns, this one is typically a decimal fraction). One part of that yield comes from the note's 6$\frac{1}{4}$ percent interest rate. The other part comes from the difference between the note's current market price $975.31, and its $1,000 redemption value in 1978.

Do you need practice? Look at the 6$\frac{7}{8}$ percent notes of May 1977 and the 9 percent notes of May 1977. Although their interest rates are different, their yields are similar, 7.28 percent versus 7.37 percent. The 9 percent note pays more interest, but its price, 102 and $^{24}/_{32}$ percent, is more than its face value. Since the note's redemption price is face value, the 2 and $^{24}/_{32}$ percent premium (102 and $^{24}/_{32}$ percent − 100 percent) is lost, the yield is thus reduced to 7.37 percent. While the 6$\frac{7}{8}$ percent note pays less interest, its price, 99 and $^{10}/_{32}$ percent, is less than face value, increasing the yield to 7.28 percent.

Primary versus Secondary Market   An investor can purchase either a new Treasury security in the primary market or an existing security in the secondary market. Which market is best? Certainly there is no difference in quality between the two. By buying in the primary market, the investor avoids all purchase fees. The advantage to the secondary market is the wide range of available maturities; even the partial listing in Exhibit 18–10 shows how extensive that choice would be. Further, an investor can purchase in the secondary market at any time, where the primary market offerings are more irregular, and the Treasury gives only limited notice on upcoming new issues. In the final analysis, the investor's needs generally dictate which market is best.

General Investment Criteria

We use the same nine criteria to describe the principal attributes of Treasury securities as were used for the three previous investments. Unless otherwise noted, the comments apply to bills, notes, and bonds.

Risk Exposure   Treasury securities are backed by the credit and full faith of the United States government. The risk is virtually nil, as discussed for savings bonds.

Interest Rate Risk   The change in the price of fixed-income securities is opposite to the change in their interest rates: as interest rates rise, security prices fall, and conversely, as interest rates decrease, security prices increase. If an investor decides to sell her Treasury security in the secondary market, she faces a potential loss if interest rates have risen since she bought the security. Of course, if interest rates have declined, she has a potential gain. To the extent that future interest rates may rise, a purchaser of Treasury securities is exposed to possible risk with respect to interest rates. And the longer the security's maturity, the larger the potential price change. For a $1/2$ percent change in interest rates, the price change on a 20-year bond would substantially exceed that of a 3-year note.

> **Strategy: Because of the prospect for continued sharp swings in interest rates, you should concentrate on 1- to 5-year maturities. Although doing so will not eliminate interest rate risk, it will reduce the impact.**

Yield   The yield for Treasury notes and bonds reflects both interest income and any difference between purchase and sale price. The yield for Treasury bills reflects only their price change, since Treasury bills do not pay interest. Computing a security's yield can be a bit involved, but a prospective investor rarely has to do this computation because most secondary market lists show each security's yield. And the yield on a newly issued Treasury note or bond is usually very close to its fixed interest rate.

Generally the longer the maturity, the higher the yield. But several times during the past 5 years, securities with maturities of 1 to 2 years have had the highest yield. And besides, the difference in interest rates between medium maturities (2- to 4-year) and long maturities (10- to 20-year) generally was much smaller during that period than in previous periods. Consequently, an investor could get just about the same yield from the shorter maturities as from the longer ones.

> **Strategy: We recommend maturities of 1 to 5 years unless you have investment goals with a very long time horizon. Even then, you should consider only long maturities if they have significantly higher yields.**

Current State of the Market   An investor can easily determine prevailing market yields by examining a current secondary list, such as the one in Exhibit 18–10. By comparing yields on the list, the investor can determine the spread between different maturities.

Minimum Maturity   An investor can purchase Treasury securities with maturities ranging from several months up to 20 or more years in the secondary market. However, the short maturities of 6 months or less are not practical because the $20 to $40 purchase fee on secondary market transactions substantially reduces their effective yield. With new issues, the choice of maturity is limited to the Treasury's current offering. Historically, the Treasury offers a fairly wide array of maturities during a 6- to 12-month period, so most investors can find a suitable maturity. Most of the recent maturities have been 1 to 5 years, which is the range that interests most investors.

Flexibility   Because the secondary market for Treasury securities is large and well developed, a security can be sold very quickly. Further, the security can be sold at, or very close to, its quoted market price.

Selling in the secondary market always entails a transaction fee because you must go through either a brokerage firm or a commercial bank which deals in Treasury securities. One of the banks in your area will very likely handle the sale of Treasury securities.

There is no penalty fee for selling prior to maturity. But remember, the price could be low if interest rates have risen since you purchased the note or bond. Of course, if interest rates have fallen, you might be able to sell at a gain.

Minimum Size   Most of the recent note issues have had minimum denominations of $1,000 or $5,000. Generally, the shorter maturities carry the $5,000 minimum. Nevertheless, an investor can almost always find a $1,000 denomination in a suitable maturity in the secondary market. The fee for buying a security in the secondary market is a flat $20 to $40, regardless of denomination or maturity. By purchasing in the primary market, you avoid this fee.

Exhibit 18-11   Reduction in Yield* Caused by Secondary Market Transaction Fees

Time to maturity	Transaction fee on a $1,000 investment		
	$20	$30	$40
6 months	4.00 percent	6.00 percent	8.00 percent
1 year	2.00	3.00	4.00
1½ years	1.33	2.00	2.67
2 years	1.00	1.50	2.00
3 years	0.67	1.00	1.33
4 years	0.50	0.75	1.00

*To simplify, effects of compounding were ignored.

Because the purchase fee reduces the security's yield, very small investments become uneconomical. Exhibit 18–11 illustrates the amount these transaction fees reduce the yield on a $1,000 investment. For a $2,000 investment, the yield would be reduced by one-half that shown. Thus, the yield on a $2,000, 2-year investment with a $20 fee is reduced .5 percent (1 percent $\times$ $^1/_2$).

While not presented as a rigid rule, our general guidelines are: (1) For maturities of 6 months to 1 year, the minimum secondary market purchase should be $4,000 to $6,000; (2) for $1^1/_2$- to 2-year maturities, the minimum drops to $2,000 or $3,000; and (3) for 3 to 4 years, the minimum can be as low as $1,000.

Investor Involvement   Investors who decide to purchase Treasury securities in the secondary market must decide which maturity, and therefore which issue, matches their specific needs. On the other hand, the investor electing to purchase a security in the primary market will have to monitor the new issues the Treasury is bringing out to find one that meets his or her needs. Consequently, the investor's involvement is moderate at the time the note or bond is purchased.

Redemption   Treasury securities are not automatically redeemed at maturity; instead, the investor must submit them for collection. Most commercial banks will redeem Treasury securities without charge. Or, they can be submitted by registered mail to a Federal Reserve bank for redemption. The Treasury does not give formal notice of a security's upcoming maturity. But, as a reminder, it does not mail the investor's final interest check. That interest payment is included in the proceeds when the security is redeemed.

Strategy: Since a Treasury security pays no interest after its maturity date, it is imperative that the securities be redeemed promptly.

Tax Features   The interest on a Treasury security is fully taxable at the investor's regular federal income tax rate. If the security has been held at least 6 months, the difference between the purchase and sale prices qualifies as a capital gain (or loss). Since the tax on gains is lower than the tax on interest, high-income investors could reduce their taxes by purchasing securities paying low interest but selling substantially below face value. Since most of the security's return is treated as a gain, the investor's tax burden would be lower. The interest and price appreciation on Treasury securities are exempt from state and local income taxes.

Hedge against Inflation   During the 1970–1973 period, the real return—effective yield less the inflation rate—on 3- to 5-year Treasury notes averaged 1.6 percent. While that was less than the 2 percent real return these securities should provide, it was better than many other investments offered.

As a hedge against inflation, Treasury securities have several advantages over other fixed-income investments. For one thing, their interest rates are not regulated at a ceiling but move in response to supply and demand for credit in the open market. If inflation increases, the open-market interest rates should also increase. For another thing, the lag between changes in the inflation rate and changes in the interest rate has become much more narrow for Treasury securities. And indications are that the lag will shorten further. Given that, we feel 1- to 5-year Treasury securities will provide a better partial hedge against inflation in future years. We are not so strongly convinced that the same will hold for 20- and 30-year securities. Locking into a long maturity may provide a slightly higher initial return, but should interest rates rise, you have two options: Hold the security and earn a substandard return for many years, or sell the security in the secondary market at a sizable loss.

Strategy: Because of the mixed outlook for inflation, we strongly recommend maturities be limited to 1 to 5 years.

Availability   New issues of Treasury securities can be purchased directly from any Federal Reserve bank or branch. Generally, the Treasury announces the new issue 1 to 2 weeks before it comes to the market. During that period, an investor can submit a noncompetitive bid in person or by mail to the nearest Federal Reserve bank or branch. With a noncompetitive bid, the investor does not bid a specific price but, instead, offers to pay the average selling price. To obtain further information on submitting a noncompetitive bid, call your nearest Federal Reserve bank or branch. Announcements of upcoming issues usually appear in *The Wall Street Journal* and the financial sections of some major metropolitan newspapers.

Outstanding issues can be purchased at any time in the secondary market through many commercial banks and most brokerage firms. If your bank does not handle Treasury securities, or handles only large purchases, check the other banks in your area.

Special Features

Treasury securities have several special features that warrant further discussion.

Developing a Switching Strategy   Because the interest rates on Treasury securities can fluctuate through a wide range within short periods, investors must decide the best time to buy. Certainly if the prevailing interest rate is near or below the interest rate of a 90-day time account, the investor should temporarily invest in a savings account or 90-day time account until the rate on Treasury securities rises. When it rises to about 1 to 2 percent greater than the rates for savings accounts or time accounts, pull out your money and buy Treasury securities. Some investors, instead of using this 1 or 2 percent guide, wait until open-market interest rates have peaked before they shift their money from savings or time accounts to securities. The problems with this strategy are: Even professionals are not sure when the market is at a peak; interest can be lost while waiting for a peak; investors must spend time analyzing interest rate trends.

Registration   An investor has three options for registering and holding Treasury securities. (1) Investors can register the securities in their name and hold them in a safe-deposit box. With this option, interest checks are mailed directly to the investor. (2) A security can be registered to "the bearer" and held in the investor's safe-deposit box. To obtain the interest, a small coupon must be snipped from the security and submitted to a bank for payment. The bearer form is a risky way to hold a security because it can be readily negotiated by anyone. (3) Some banks will hold the security in safekeeping and credit the interest directly to the investor's savings or checking account. Unfortunately, many banks have begun to charge for such safekeeping.

Treasury Securities: Strengths and Weaknesses

The principal strengths and weaknesses of Treasury securities are summarized in Exhibit 18–12.

Treasury Securities: Suitable Investment Goals

The maturities on Treasury securities make them perfectly suited for medium- to long-term objectives. Their low risk makes them ideal for any goal where safety is critical. Securities with maturities of 1 to 5 years can provide a partial hedge against inflation.

CORPORATE BONDS

Most corporations find it necessary to borrow money to meet a variety of needs. One way they obtain the money is to sell corporate bonds to a large number of investors, ranging from individuals who may have only small amounts to invest to large institutional investors which invest sizable amounts.

Exhibit 18-12   Treasury Securities — Strengths and Weaknesses

Strengths	Weaknesses
Virtual freedom from risk	Longer maturities exposed to interest-rate risk
Moderate rate of return	Transaction fee that makes small, short-term investments uneconomical
Interest rates that can fluctuate at any time and without limit	
	Sizable minimum denomination
Short maturities provide a partial hedge against inflation because rates are market-determined	Moderate investor involvement required, especially when purchasing new issues
Rates that reflect underlying open-market credit conditions	

The bonds specify a fixed interest rate and maturity date at which time the corporation will redeem the bond at face value. The corporation must pay the interest and retire the bonds at maturity regardless of whether or not it makes a profit. Should the firm fail to redeem at maturity, the bondholders can force payment even if it means the firm must cease operation and be liquidated. As creditors, the bondholders must be fully repaid before the owners (the common stock shareholders) or the preferred stockholders receive any income. But we hasten to add that few bondholders have to go to court to collect their interest. Nor are many involved in a corporate liquidation. Investors can minimize the possibility of these problems by selecting the bonds of a strong corporation which is both profitable and likely to continue operations.

The principal types of corporate bonds include (1) mortgage bonds—the corporation pledges specific property as security for the bonds; (2) convertible bonds, which can be converted into the corporation's common or preferred stock; (3) debentures—the corporation's unsecured promise to repay is the bond's security; and (4) subordinated debentures—the same as debentures except that the corporation's obligation to repay them ranks behind (is subordinated to) the obligation to repay other debt holders. Our discussion concentrates on the debenture category, although most comments are applicable to all four groups.

Corporate bonds are sold in the open market where they compete with other investments for the investor's money. Therefore, the interest rate on corporate bonds moves in response to underlying market forces. The spread in interest rates between a top-quality issue and a lower-quality issue is sizable. Investors recognize that lower quality entails higher risk; consequently, they demand an increasingly higher interest rate. We will concentrate on issues which offer moderate- to low-risk exposure.

Secondary Market   Once a corporate bond is sold in the primary market, the corporation's only obligations are to make interest payments and to redeem the bonds at maturity. The corporation is not obligated to repurchase the bonds prior to maturity. Should bondholders want to sell prior to maturity, they must use the secondary market. A secondary market exists because there are always bondholders who want to sell prior to maturity, and likewise, there are buyers who are interested in buying those bonds if the price is right.

Reading a Secondary Market Listing   Reading a secondary market listing of corporate bonds is not difficult once you are familiar with its features. The one in Exhibit 18–13 is a hypothetical one with only a few issues illustrated. More extensive lists showing similar information are published in *The Wall Street Journal, Barron's,* and the financial sections of most large metropolitan newspapers. Some corporate bonds are listed and traded on the New York Bond Exchange, others are listed and traded on the American Bond Exchange, and many more are listed and traded on the informal over-the-counter market. The secondary market for corporate bonds is enormous.

As an example, we use the All American Truck $7^3/_4$s 82 bonds shown in Exhibit 18–13. All the prices quoted in the listing are shown as a percentage of face value. The "high" price is the highest price for the bond on that trading

Exhibit 18-13   Secondary Market Listing of Corporate Bonds

Bond	Current yield	Volume	Price			
			High	Low	Close	Change
All American Truck 7¾s 82	7.8	164	97⅞	98½	98⅝	+¼
Anzo Steel 8¼s 75	8.2	15	100¼	100	100⅛	−⅛
Aston Power 9½s 82	9.3	92	101¼	101⅛	101⅛	−⅛
Blazo Finance 11s 90	10.0	20	101⅛	101	101	+⅛
Blecho Foods 4¼s 88	cv	15	61⅝	61¼	61½	+¼

day. Likewise, the "low" price is the lowest price of the day. And the "close" is the price on the last bond traded that day. The "Change" column shows the change in price between yesterday's "close" and today's "close." For the All American Truck bond, the closing price was 98 ⁵/₈ percent, or 98.625 percent. Thus, the market price on a $1,000 face-value All American Truck bond is $986.25 ($1,000 × 98.625 percent).

The numbers following the company's name (frequently abbreviated or identified by initials) represent the bond's fixed interest rate and maturity, respectively. The All American Truck 7³/₄s 82 bond pays 7³/₄ percent interest and matures in 1982. The current yield (second column) is based solely on the bond's interest earnings; unlike the yield on the preceding Treasury securities, it does not include any gain or loss due to a difference between current market price and the bond's face value. The 7.8 percent yield on the All American Truck bond was computed by dividing the bond's interest payment by its current market price ([$1,000 × 7³/₄ percent] ÷ $986.25). A small "cv" in the "Yield" column indicates a convertible bond, so no yield is estimated. The "Volume" column shows the number of bonds traded that day. Thus, 164 All American Truck bonds were traded according to the details in Exhibit 18–13.

Primary versus Secondary   The secondary market gives the prospective purchaser a tremendous array of bond issues: a broad maturity range, a wide risk-exposure range, and a choice between a bond with a low interest payment and a market price far below face value, or a bond with a high interest payment and a price which is close to face value. A secondary market purchase or sale always entails a sales commission: typically $7.50 to $10 per $1,000 bond on small transactions.

No commission is paid for new issues sold in the primary market. In addition, the yield on new issues is generally ¹/₄ to 1 percent above the yield on a comparable bond in the secondary market. The primary market's major shortcoming is that the new issue offered may not match an investor's needs. That can mean a wait of several weeks or months until the proper issue comes along.

General Investment Criteria

Let us now examine the principal attributes of corporate bonds according to the nine investment criteria.

Risk Exposure   Corporate bonds expose the investor directly to the possibility of financial collapse and the firm's business risk. The firm's ability to meet its bond obligations depends directly on its profitability.

Appraising Risk Exposure   The quality of corporate bonds is evaluated by two major rating agencies—Moody's and Standard & Poor's (S&P). In rating an issue, they analyze the strengths and weaknesses of the issuing corporation as well as compare its operations and financial position with those of other firms in the same industry. Exhibit 18–14 summarizes their quality ratings.

We believe bonds rated Baa or better by Moody's, or those rated BB or better by S&P, are appropriate for most investors. Investors who are extremely averse to risk should limit their choice to either triple A or double A bonds. But the investor who can accept a bit more risk may well buy a medium-grade bond (BB, A, or Baa) since it will pay more interest.

> **Strategy: Unless you are highly averse to risk, consider bonds rated A, Ba, or Baa by Moody's and A, BBB, or BB by S&P.**

Interest Rate Risk   Because the interest rate on corporate bonds responds to the open-market forces for investors' money, the prices of existing corporate bonds decrease as interest rates on new bonds increase, and prices increase as rates on new bonds decrease. If you want to sell a bond before maturity and interest rates have risen since you bought it, you will most likely sell the bond at a loss. And the longer the bond's maturity, the greater the bondholder's exposure to this kind of interest rate risk.

> **Strategy: Because of the prospect of continued wide swings in interest rates, we suggest that you consider only maturities of 5 years, or 10 years at most.**

Yield   When an investor plans to hold a bond for an extended period, the most meaningful measure of return is the bond's effective yield to maturity. For corporate bonds, the yield includes the yearly interest payments and the

Exhibit 18-14   Summary of Bond Ratings

Moody's		Standard & Poor's	
Rating	Description	Rating	Description
Aaa	Best quality	AAA	Highest grade
Aa	High quality	AA	High grade
A	High medium grade	A	Upper medium grade
Baa	Lower medium grade	BBB	Medium grade
Ba	Possesses speculative elements	BB	Lower medium grade
B*	Generally lacks characteristics of desirable investment	B*	Speculative

*Both agencies have lower ratings than B. But they are not shown here because few investors are interested in such low-quality bonds.

difference between purchase price and full face value at redemption. Unfortunately, computing the yield is quite involved and secondary market lists rarely include it. But most brokerage firms have this information and will readily volunteer it.

Recently, the dual effect of a large number of new corporate bond issues, coupled with high inflation rates, has pushed bond yields to new highs. As this is written, the yield on top-ranked Aaa bonds averaged 9 percent and the yield on Baa bonds average $10^{1}/_{2}$ percent. And there is every likelihood these high interest rates will prevail over the next few years, barring a sharp, prolonged economic recession.

Although the yield is higher on a bond with longer maturity, we have serious reservations about long-term bonds. For one thing, you will not sacrifice much yield by investing in the 3- to 10-year maturity range, rather than 10- to 20-year maturities. Many corporations have begun issuing bonds (frequently referred to as notes) in these short to medium maturities. And, for another thing, a long maturity pays a higher return *now*, but it can lock an investor into that return in the future when other investments will likely pay higher returns.

Minimum Maturities   Most new bond issues come in two distinct maturity ranges: either intermediate (3 to 5 years) or long term (20 to 30 years). Nearly any maturity can be obtained in the secondary market, although maturities shorter than 2 years are scarce. Maturities less than 2 years are uneconomical because the commission sharply reduces the yield.

Flexibility   Most corporate bonds can be sold through the secondary market. However, the effort required and the price concession vary. The bond issues of well-known corporations have the greatest flexibility because there is likely to be much more secondary market activity. The figures listed under the "Volume" column, such as shown in Exhibit 18–13, indicate how actively a bond is traded in the secondary market.

Minimum Size   Although most corporate bonds come in $1,000 denominations, bond dealers are generally reluctant to deal in amounts less than $3,000. On new issues the effective minimum is $5,000 because dealers are reluctant to go smaller. However, even if the minimum denomination were lower, we feel it represents a lot of money for most people and we do not recommend they invest it in only a single firm. Unless you have sufficient money to purchase several issues, we believe that you should consider a no-loan mutual fund specializing in corporate bonds (discussed in Chapter 20).

Investor Involvement   An investor should not invest in corporate bonds without expecting to become involved in deciding what bond to purchase and regularly reviewing it afterward. On secondary market transactions, the investor must decide on an appropriate maturity and quality. Even after deciding on a specific bond rating—AA, BBB, A—there is still the problem of selecting a specific bond from the wide array of available issues within the rating group chosen. In the primary market, an investor must consider all these things and, in addition, monitor new issues coming to market.

The bond interest may be mailed directly to the investor, or the investor may have to initiate payment by clipping a small coupon from the bottom of the bond and presenting it to the corporation to obtain the interest. A bond should be exchanged promptly at maturity because it pays no interest after that date.

Tax Features   All interest payments are fully taxable for federal income tax purposes. Any difference between purchase and sale prices qualifies for the lower capital gains tax rate, provided the bond has been held more than 6 months. Consequently, investors with high marginal tax rates should invest in bonds whose current price is substantially below face value and that pay low interest.

Hedge against Inflation   The real return—yield less inflation—on medium-grade (BBB) corporate bonds has averaged 3 percent in the late 1960s and early 1970s. This return is below the $3^1/_2$ to 4 percent return we think these bonds should provide. Nevertheless, corporate bond rates have moved up sharply in response to higher inflation rates and will probably continue to do so.

Availability   Corporate bonds are available from most brokers and some commercial banks. Announcements of forthcoming new bond issues regularly appear in *The Wall Street Journal.* In addition, most brokers will inform you of new issues that may meet your needs. Some brokers are more accommodating and helpful than others. So be prepared to check several.

Special Features

Corporate bonds have several special features that require a short explanation.

Diversification   One problem with corporate bonds is that the success of your investment depends heavily upon the fortunes of the issuing corporation. When you have only $4,000 or $5,000 to invest, there is little choice but to concentrate on a single issue. If, however, you have $7,000 to $8,000, you should probably split it between two issues. By diversifying among several issues, you reduce the risk exposure. While one firm may experience financial difficulty, it is doubtful that both would have difficulty.

> **Strategy: When selecting diversification candidates, select companies from different industries.**

Industrial versus Utility   Bonds of utility companies currently yield 1 to 2 percent more than comparably rated bonds of industrial companies. In part, this higher yield reflects investor disenchantment with the utilities' skyrocketing fuel costs, the slow, cumbersome procedures that set utility rates, and their sizable money needs over the next few years. Although utilities have problems, we think their current higher yield more than compensates for the risk posed by their problems.

Strategy: An investor should seriously consider high-quality utility company bonds—A or better—because they provide a better yield than comparable industrial bonds.

Call Protection Most corporate bonds can be called prior to maturity. That is, a corporation can request that investors redeem their bonds prior to maturity. To encourage investors to respond to such a recall, the corporation ceases interest payments on the bonds. Why would a corporation call its bonds? If interest rates have fallen, a corporation would find it advantageous to call an existing bond issue and replace it with a new issue at the new lower rate. Given this possibility, the bond should have a clause protecting the investor from a call for at least 5 years.

Corporate Bonds: Strengths and Weaknesses

The major strengths and weaknesses of corporate bonds are summarized in Exhibit 18–15.

Corporate Bonds: Suitable Investment Goals

The maturities on corporate bonds make them a natural for medium- to long-term investment goals. Their suitability for this purpose is enhanced by their attractive returns. When your investment goal involves a sizable amount of money, the yield on corporate bonds provides a reasonable hedge against inflation. However, corporate bonds are more suitable for people with a fair amount of money because the minimum purchase is sizable. Even then, most investors will need a temporary investment while they accumulate the money to buy additional corporate bonds. Although corporate bonds entail some risk, the risk can be kept in the low to moderate range by selecting bonds which have good ratings.

The large minimum purchase and long maturities render corporate bonds

Exhibit 18-15 Corporate Bonds — Strengths and Weaknesses

Strengths	Weaknesses
Attractive yield	Risk exposure ranging from moderate to high
Interest rates that are unregulated and move in response to open-market forces	Long maturities having sizable interest rate risk
Real return providing a reasonable hedge against inflation	Large minimum denomination
	Investor involvement that can be moderate to considerable
	Commissions that make frequent transactions uneconomical

unsuitable for short-term investment goals. Further, they do not have the desired flexibility if the investor expects to sell them on very short notice.

MUNICIPAL BONDS

Municipal bonds are a specialized, tax-free investment which appeals primarily to people in the upper income brackets. Because municipal bonds represent a special investment, we will only summarize their major points.

The interest on municipal bonds is fully exempt from federal income tax. An investor with a 40 percent marginal tax rate would have to earn $12^1/_2$ percent ($7^1/_2$ percent ÷ [100 percent − 40 percent]) on a fully taxable issue to match a $7^1/_2$ percent return on a municipal bond. And the higher the investor's marginal tax rate, the more appealing these bonds become.

The range of institutions and organizations that issue these bonds is enormous: small and large cities and special agencies within those cities; individual states and specialized agencies within those states. The bonds can be grouped into two categories: (1) general obligation bonds—backed by the general taxing authority of the issuing organization, and (2) revenue bonds— backed by the revenues generated by the facilities the bonds financed. There are fewer issues in the first group, but the investment community gives them a higher-quality ranking. The size of the bond issues ranges from very small to giant. As with corporate bonds, the strength of the secondary market varies directly with the size of the bond issue. The market is reasonably strong on most large issues, but on the smaller ones it ranges from weak to nonexistent.

Municipal bonds compete with other investments for the investor's dollar in the general credit market. But, given their tax exemption, they are primarily competing for money from high-income investors and certain financial institutions. As a consequence, interest rates on municipal bonds not only respond to regular market forces, but they also shift because of events that are unique to this market. Between 1973 and 1976, the interest rates on municipal bonds have approached new historical highs. There are two reasons for this: Large commercial banks have reduced their purchases of municipal bonds and so the bonds must attract other investors. But an even larger factor has been concern among investors about the financial viability of the institutions and organizations issuing these bonds. Certainly New York City's problems have exacerbated these concerns.

The principal risk exposure with municipal bonds is the possibility that the issuer will encounter serious financial difficulty. Increasingly, many investors are asking some penetrating questions about the safety of municipal bonds. While many revenue bonds have long been regarded as relatively risky, many general obligation bonds are now being grouped into those higher-risk categories as well. Most medium and large municipal bond issues are rated by Moody's and Standard & Poor's according to the rating scale illustrated in Exhibit 18–14. Given the increased concern about safety, investors should concentrate on issues rated A or above. Like other fixed-rate bonds, municipals with long maturities have considerable interest rate risk.

Municipal bonds come in $1,000 denominations, but most brokers will not deal in orders of less than $5,000. Nearly all municipal bonds have serial maturities. That is, the first group of bonds matures in 1 to 2 years from date of issue, the second group in 3 to 4 years, and so on right on out to the last group maturing in 20 to 30 years. We continue our previous recommendation, however, that maturities be limited to 10 years or less.

As a general guide, an investor's combined state and federal marginal tax rate (Chapter 6) would have to be 30 percent or more before the after-tax return on municipal bonds exceeds those available on comparable, fully taxable corporate bonds.

SUMMARY

1 A fixed-income investment promises a fixed return over a specified time period.
2 With deposit insurance, the risk exposure on savings and time accounts is minimal.
3 Federal and state regulations set the maximum interest rate that can be paid on savings and time accounts.
4 The major strengths of savings accounts are high flexibility, continuous liquidity, and extremely low risk.
5 With time accounts, the money cannot be withdrawn for a prescribed period.
6 The longer the minimum maturity of a time account, the higher its interest rate.
7 Redeeming a time account before maturity entails a two-part interest penalty: reversion of the interest rate to the regular savings account rate, and loss of 90 days' interest.
8 Principal strengths of time accounts are low risk, small minimum denominations, and wide availability.
9 United States Series E savings bonds mature in 5 years, and Series H bonds in 10 years.
10 If held to maturity, both savings bond series pay a 6 percent return, compounded semiannually.
11 Early redemption of savings bonds reduces the yield substantially below 6 percent.
12 Major strengths of savings bonds include freedom from risk and wide availability in small denominations.
13 The prevailing interest rate on Treasury securities is determined by supply and demand in the general credit markets.
14 Treasury securities have an active secondary market; an investor can readily sell a security at any time.
15 There is no fee to purchase a new Treasury issue.
16 Treasury securities with short maturities provide a partial hedge against inflation.
17 Principal strengths of Treasury securities are extremely limited risk exposure and interest rates that reflect open-market conditions.
18 Corporate bonds expose the investor to all three risk categories: financial collapse, business risk, and interest rate risk.
19 Larger corporate bond issues have an extensive secondary market, so the bond can be sold at any time.
20 The large minimum denominations make corporate bonds unsuitable for some investors.
21 Major strengths of corporate bonds are attractive yields and interest rates that reflect open-market conditions.

22   Municipal bonds appeal to high-income investors because their interest is exempt
     from all federal and many state income taxes.

REVIEW YOUR UNDERSTANDING OF

Savings account
Interest rate ceilings: savings and time
   accounts
Time accounts
Interest penalty: time accounts
U.S. savings bonds
U.S. Treasury bills
U.S. Treasury notes
U.S. Treasury bonds
Secondary market list: Treasury securi-
   ties

Corporate bonds
Corporate bond ratings: Moody's and
   Standard & Poor's
Call protection
Diversification when investing in corpo-
   rate bonds
Municipal bonds
Tax exemption on municipal bonds

DISCUSSION QUESTIONS

1   Frequently an advertisement claims a particular savings account pays the highest
    interest rate in the area. How much validity do such claims have? Why? What
    specific features are most likely to vary among savings accounts?

2   What specific features should be checked before deciding on a Christmas Club
    account? Why? Can you outline an alternative savings plan as a substitute?

3   Why should you concentrate on savings and time accounts that have deposit
    insurance? Is the typical $40,000 insurance ceiling a major problem?

4   What are the major shortcomings of a savings account as your sole investment
    vehicle?

5   Why is a time account unsuitable for a very short term, 1- to 3-month, investment
    goal?

6   Many people maintain that interest rates on savings and time accounts lag behind
    the interest rates in the open credit markets. Why is that true? How does it affect
    the performance of savings accounts during inflationary periods?

7   Janice Smith has a $500, $6\frac{1}{2}$ percent compounded quarterly, 1-year certificate of
    deposit (CD) at a local savings and loan association. Although the CD still has 270
    days to maturity, Janice needs the money now. The savings and loan institution has
    offered to lend her $500 for 270 days at 8 percent interest, with repayment in a lump
    sum at the end of the period. Should she take the loan or redeem the CD? Support
    your answer with the net cost of both options. (*Hint:*The effective annual rate for
    6.5 percent, compounded quarterly, is 6.66 percent. The regular savings rate is 5
    percent.)

8   Why is a time account superior to a savings account for a 5- to 10-year investment
    goal?

9   Why are U.S. savings bonds unsuitable for a medium-term, 1- to 3-year investment
    goal?

10 What advantages do U.S. Treasury securities have over U.S. savings bonds? What
    are the disadvantages?

11 What are the advantages of buying "used" Treasury securities in the secondary

market? *Optional*: Obtain a current secondary market list of Treasury securities. What maturities and rates are available? How much return do you sacrifice to remain in the 1- to 5-year maturities?

12 Why have investors in Treasury securities fared better than their counterparts in savings and time accounts during recent inflationary periods? What prospect do you see for the next 2 to 4 years?

13 Why are corporate bonds unsuitable for many small investors?

14 Ralph Right is considering the following two corporate bonds:

a XQ Corporation, S&P rating A, 1-year maturity, 10 percent annual interest rate, price $1,000, and 10 percent annual yield (10 percent annual interest return and 0 percent annual return from price appreciation).

b Specialities Plastics, Inc., S&P rating A, 1-year maturity, 5 percent annual interest rate, price $954.55, and 10 percent annual yield (5 percent annual interest return and 5 percent annual return from price appreciation).

     If his marginal tax rate is 40 percent, which bond should he select? Why? What is his after-tax rate of return? (*Hint:* Assume that capital gains are taxed at one-half the regular tax rate.)

15 What are the benefits from diversifying among several corporate bond issues? What are the limitations on diversification?

16 How has the real return on corporate bonds performed during recent inflationary periods? To what specific factors would you attribute this?

17 What investment strategy will minimize the impact of inflation on fixed-income investments? Which investments are best suited to that strategy?

18 Why is there investor interest in municipal bonds when their yield is 2 to 4 percent below that of comparable corporate bonds? Which group of investors is attracted to them?

CASE PROBLEM

Anne Jones is reviewing her present investments to see whether any change is needed. Her current position as a secondary school teacher pays $18,000 annually. She saves approximately $3,000, accumulated through regular savings during the year. So far, she has accumulated $3,000 in a savings account and $900 in savings bonds. At present, her major investment goals include: (*a*) to return to graduate school in 9 months for the summer semester: cost, $1,000; (*b*) to take a European trip in 2 years: cost, $2,000; (*c*) to replace her present car in 5 years at a cost of $3,000; (*d*) to accumulate a 15 percent down payment for the purchase of a $20,000 summer home in 10 years. She expects to devote $2,000 of her annual savings to these goals; the remaining $1,000 will cover smaller expenditures and general investment needs.

    Each month she invests $75 in U.S. savings bonds and $175 in a regular savings account. She plans to concentrate on fixed-income investments because she does not want the risk or involvement of common stocks or mutual funds. She wonders, however, about the interest on the savings account; it pays 3 percent, compounded yearly and computed on a LIFO basis. She selected the account because the bank was near her school.

    After a search, Anne found the following fixed-income alternatives:

Investment	Maturity	Minimum balance	Effective annual rate of return (percent)
Commercial bank, insured			
Savings account	1 day	$ 10.00	5.10
Time account	90 days	$ 25.00	5.61
Time account	1 year	$ 100.00	6.14
Savings and loan, insured			
Savings account	1 day	$ 1.00	5.36
Time account	90 days	$ 10.00	5.88
Time account	1 year	$ 50.00	6.66
Credit union, noninsured			
savings account	5 days	$ 5.00	5.10
U.S. savings bond, Series E	5 years	$ 18.75	6.10*
U.S. Treasury note	2 years	$1,000.00	7.75+
	3 years	$1,000.00	8.00+

*If held to maturity.
+Net return after deducting commission for $3,000 secondary market purchase.

a What are the strengths and weaknesses of Anne's present investments?
b What investments, if any, would you recommend as substitutes? Why?
c What investment(s) would you recommend for each investment goal? Why?
d How would you implement the plan you outlined in (c)?
e What annual return will your recommendations provide? Is it significantly better than her present return?

RECOMMENDED READINGS

Books

Dougall, Herbert E., *Investments*, 9th ed., Englewood Cliffs, N.J.: Prentice-Hall, 1973.
    The entire spectrum of fixed-income investments is reviewed in chapters 4 through 7.
Sauvain, Harry C., *Investment Management*, 4th ed., Englewood Cliffs, N.J.: Prentice-Hall, 1973.
    Chapter 2 has a good discussion of fixed-income investments.

Magazines

Money:

"Investing for Income." October 1974, pp. 55–64.
    Discusses the basics of investing for income. Reviews the essential features of different bonds.

Changing Times:

"Managing Your Savings for the Highest Return." December 1973, pp. 15–17.
    Discusses different compounding techniques used to compute interest on savings accounts.
"Are Tax Exempt Bonds Right for You?" February 1974, pp. 42–43.

Compares return on tax-exempt bonds with their fully taxable counterparts for different income brackets.

"Put Some of Your Money into Government Securities." April 1974, pp. 21–23.
Summarizes the major features of U.S. government securities. Discusses purchase details.

"Take Another Look at U.S. Savings Bonds." March 1975, pp. 25–27.
Reviews advantages and disadvantages of savings bonds.

Consumer Reports:

"How to Pick the Best Savings Account." February 1975, pp. 90–97.
Excellent discussion of the basic differences among savings accounts. Also examines some fixed-income alternatives.

Booklets

Tax-Exempt Bonds and the Investor
Describes the investment features of municipal bonds. A copy can be obtained from Securities Industry Association, 120 Broadway, New York 10005.

Understanding Preferred Stocks and Bonds
Describes the function of these investments. A copy can be obtained from New York Stock Exchange, 11 Wall Street, New York 10005.

How to Invest
Discusses the buying and selling of bonds and common stocks. A copy can be obtained from Merrill Lynch, Pierce, Fenner & Smith, Inc., 70 Pine Street, New York 10005.

Common Stock: Selection and Purchase

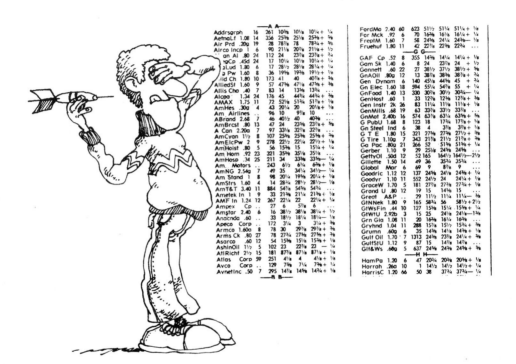

On completing this chapter you should be able to:

explain the underlying principle of common stock ownership.

describe the two components of shareholder return: dividend yield and market price change.

assess the value of a stock dividend and a stock split.

appraise the impact of inflation on common stock.

utilize the information given in a secondary market listing of common stocks.

describe the difference between selecting a common stock using the fundamental value approach and selecting one using the technical analysis approach.

develop a list of industries with attractive investment appeal.

formulate selection criteria for choosing a company within an attractive industry.

describe how common stocks are purchased.

describe the use of dollar-cost averaging to time your investment in common stock.

formulate criteria to decide the holding period for a common stock.

describe the major strengths and weaknesses of investing in common stocks.

judge whether common stock is suitable for your investment goals.

The introductory sections of many investment books contain a series of success stories about common stocks. They usually go like this: "Had your father invested $1,000 in the common stock of McDonald's (the hamburger spot) in mid-1965, it would be worth $42,310 in mid-1975 after allowing for all stock splits!" The stock's price appreciation, coupled with its dividends, provided an average annual compound return of 45 percent. Impressive performance? Definitely. Or suppose your father invested $1,000 in Hewlett-Packard Company (a manufacturer of electronic data, measuring, and test equipment) in mid-1965; it would total $8,500 in mid-1975 after including all stock splits. That works out to an average compound return of 25 percent annually. Again, that is impressive performance. Sounds almost too good to resist, does it not? Well, resist for a few more sentences because we have some more stories of "impressive" performance.

Suppose your father had decided to invest $1,000 in National Systems, Inc. (specializing in correspondence courses) in late 1968. He could sell that investment for $20 in mid-1975 after allowing for stock splits. Or maybe he decided to invest $1,000 in Polaroid Corporation in late 1965. In mid-1975, that investment would be worth $587 after allowing for dividends and stock splits. But maybe he liked the "special concept" stocks that were in vogue in the late 1960s. Had he invested $1,000 in National Student Marketing Corporation when it was at its zenith, as a lot of market professionals did, he could now take those ornate stock certificates and use them as a wall decoration since they are just about worthless. All three of these stories illustrate "impressive" performance, but in much different directions.

Unfortunately, the books that lead off with great success stories never complete the picture with the disaster stories.

We are not implying that common stock investors always end up giant winners or giant losers. In fact, many stocks have fluctuated but performed adequately, their overall investor return averaging 7 or 8 percent during the period 1965 to 1975. For example, had you invested $1,000 in Eastman Kodak in late 1965, that investment would be worth $1,560 in mid-1975. After including dividends and stock splits, the compound annual return averaged $9^{1}/_{2}$ percent. Likewise, had you invested $1,000 in Proctor and Gamble in 1965, that investment would be worth $2,000 in 1975. After dividends and stock splits, that is an average 10 percent annual return.

In our discussion, we stress a balanced view of the stock market. Although fortunes have been made in the stock market, we think it is totally unrealistic to invest in common stocks with that expectation. On the other hand, we do not think the stock market is so fraught with risk that you should expect either to make a spectacularly successful investment or to lose it all. Frankly, we think that with a moderate amount of background work, a large measure of common sense, and possibly a little luck, most people can avoid the market's major pitfalls. We think investors can realistically expect to average 8 to 15 percent annually, depending on how much risk they are willing to accept.

After reading this section, you may decide that investing in common stocks is not for you. Certainly there are some excellent fixed-income investments which provide a reasonable return with minimal risk. Our discussion on the analysis, selection, purchase, and management of common stock will be highly condensed and simplified. We have attempted to cover the major points without becoming bogged down in the detail. For the prospective investors who want to know more, we urge continuing study via the recommended readings list.

COMMON STOCK

The corporate business form has several appealing features. It exists as a separate entity, so the owner's liability for the corporation's debts and liabilities is limited to the owner's investment in the corporation. The common stock that is evidence of ownership in the corporation can be sold to a

subsequent investor without affecting the activity of the corporation. That is, an ownership change does not require dissolution of the corporation. Corporations can have anywhere from one to thousands of shareholders. How much of the corporation a shareholder owns depends on how much of the corporation's total common stock the shareholder owns. Thus, a person who holds 10 percent of the stock owns 10 percent of the firm. For most large corporations, the number of shares outstanding is very large; consequently, most shareholders own only a small fraction of the corporation.

Ownership

As an owner, the shareholder has an input into the management of the corporation. Because of a corporation's size and specialization, ownership is separated from control. The shareholder's management role is limited to the election of a board of directors who set the corporation's broad policy and goals. The board selects the management team whose members implement the policy and goals on a day-to-day basis.

Corporate Earnings   As owners, common stock shareholders are entitled to the corporation's earnings. Those earnings may be paid as a cash dividend, or they may be retained by the corporation to finance its continued expansion and growth. Typically, rapidly expanding corporations need large amounts of expansion money, and therefore pay very small or no dividends. Corporations whose expansion is slower have smaller reinvestment needs; consequently, a higher proportion of its earnings are paid as dividends. Either way, the shareholder should benefit. On one hand, a cash dividend gives the shareholder money to spend or reinvest. On the other hand, when the earnings are reinvested in earning assets, the shareholder ultimately receives a portion of the earnings from those new assets.

The board of directors decides how to use the corporation's earnings, basing their judgment on the firm's expansion needs and on its past history of dividend payment. Most firms believe it is important to pay dividends to stockholders regularly. That is, once they begin paying a certain dividend per share, they attempt to pay the same dividend every year even though the firm's earnings may fluctuate from year to year. If the earnings increase sharply one year, the corporation will probably not increase the dividend. Should the earnings remain at the same increased levels in subsequent years, the corporation will most likely raise the dividend. If earnings fall, the corporation may even borrow just to keep up its record of paying the same dividend each year. Of course, if the the earnings decline permanently, the dividend will ultimately be cut.

Liquidation   Should the corporation's operations be terminated, all the corporation's debts, loans, and bonds must first be repaid, and the shareholders get what is left. But as a practical matter, the shareholders generally receive little when a corporation is liquidated because of financial problems. The way to avoid the results of liquidation is to select a strong on-going corporation which has good future potential. You should not be overly concerned about liquidation, however, because only a small number of corporations are liquidated each year.

Time Horizon   Unlike most fixed-income investments, common stock has no set maturity period. That is, a share of stock generally remains outstanding until the corporation ceases operations. The firm does not promise to redeem the share at some future point in time, nor will it repurchase the shares should a shareholder want to sell.

Shareholder Return

The shareholder's return on common stock is a combination of its dividend yield and the change in its market price. Both must be considered to obtain the total effective return.

Cash Dividend   The annual cash dividend is typically quoted as a dollar amount per share. Generally it is paid in four equal quarterly payments, although a few companies pay an unequal amount each quarter. Thus a firm could pay 50 cents each quarter. Or it might pay 25 cents for the first two quarters and 75 cents the last two quarters of the year. When a firm's earnings are unusually good, it may declare a special year-end dividend in addition to its regular dividend. Thus, a firm may supplement its regular $2 dividend with a special nonrecurring $1 year-end payment.

The total dividend paid during the year can be converted to an annual percentage rate by dividing the dividend by the market price. For example, if XQ Corporation's current market price were $40, the annual dividend yield from its $2 payment would be 5 percent ($2 ÷ $40).

The first column of Exhibit 19–1 shows the annual dividend yield on a broad cross section of common stocks; that column considers only dividend

Exhibit 19-1   Dividend Yield and Price-Earnings Ratio on a Broad-based Common Stock Average

	Average dividend yield*	Price-earnings ratio*
1965	3.00 percent	12.04 times
1966	3.40	14.88
1967	3.20	17.51
1968	3.07	17.73
1969	3.24	16.45
1970	3.83	15.48
1971	3.14	18.48
1972	2.84	18.18
1973	3.06	14.04
1974	4.47	8.65
Average for the 10 years	3.33 percent	15.34 times

*Dividend yield and price-earnings ratio is for the 500 common stocks included in the Standard & Poor's Stock Index; it has been derived from yield series as published in the *Federal Reserve Bulletin* (various issues). Price-earnings ratio is explained on pp. 503–504.

yield, ignoring any return due to a change in market price. As can be seen, the dividend yield has varied over a considerable range during the 10 years shown. Most of that variance is due to a change in the market price used to compute the yield rather than changes in dividend payments. That is, the dollar amounts of the annual dividend payments have been reasonably stable, but because the market price has varied, the annual dividend yield has fluctuated widely. There is no "typical" or "expected" dividend yield. Dividend yields can be as high as 9 to 11 percent or as low as zero.

Market Price Change   Since a common stock share entitles the owner to a portion of the corporation's earnings, if the outlook for higher earnings is favorable, the market price of the stock will increase. (Of course, the converse also may occur.) In addition, there is a host of other factors that can affect market price. Regardless of the exact cause, changes in the price of a stock affect total return. Should XQ's common stock rise from $40 to $42 during the year, the shareholder's potential return from the change in market price would be 5 percent [($42 − $40) ÷ $40]. We say potential because a market price return is not realized until the share is sold.

The total yield for XQ is then 10 percent: 5 percent from the dividend return and 5 percent from the potential market price return.

The potential return from the change in market price can vary tremendously. In a good year it could increase 20 or 30 percent; yet the following year it could decrease 20 or 30 percent. And there are no general guidelines on what is considered typical. Usually, price appreciation is the major source of investor return on stocks which pay little or no dividends because the earnings are reinvested to finance the firm's growth. Conversely, the market price of stocks paying high dividends typically does not change very much.

Stock Dividend   Instead of paying a cash dividend, some corporations at times will issue stock as a dividend to shareholders. Typically, a stock dividend is quoted as a percentage of total shares outstanding. For example, if Fred Bear held 10 shares of XQ Corporation and the corporation declared a 10 percent stock dividend. Fred would receive 1 new share (10 shares × 10 percent). If Fred held 65 shares, he would receive 6.5 or 6$^1/_2$ shares (10 percent dividend on 65 shares). In this case, Fred could either take the cash equivalent of the half-share and receive 6 full shares, or he could pay the difference of a half-share and receive 7 full shares.

Although some investors feel a stock dividend increases the value of their holdings, that is not usually the result. To illustrate, assume ZAP Corporation had 100 common stock shares, and there are 10 shareholders, each holding 10 shares of ZAP's common stock. At some point, the firm pays a 10 percent stock dividend so that each shareholder now has 11 shares. The immediate question is: Have the shareholders gained from that dividend? To answer the question, consider the following: Before the stock dividend, each shareholder owned 10 percent of ZAP and was entitled to 10 percent of its earnings. After the stock dividend, ZAP was divided into 110 shares, each shareholder now holding 11 shares. But 11 shares out of a total of 110 shares is still 10 percent. Therefore, after the stock dividend, each shareholder owns 10 percent of ZAP and is entitled to 10 percent of its earnings—exactly the same as before the stock dividend!

Is the corporation worth more because it is divided into 110 shares rather than 100? No, of course it is not. The net effect of the stock dividend was to create more shares, but each share is smaller than before the dividend. Since the firm's earnings are divided among 110 pieces, the price per share will be less than before the dividend. In all likelihood, 11 of the new shares will be worth exactly the same as 10 of the old shares. Consequently, after a stock dividend the total value of each shareholder's stock holdings will probably remain unchanged.

Stock Split   A stock split is similar to a stock dividend except that it involves more shares. A stock dividend always increases the total number of shares by less than 25 percent. A split can be two new for one old share, three new for one old, or some other combination. Thus, if a corporation declared a 2 for 1 split, the number of shares outstanding would double. The effect of a stock split is similar to the effect of a stock dividend—more shares but a drop in the price per share. The net effect is to leave the value of the investor's common stock holdings basically unchanged.

The principal reason a corporation declares a stock split is to reduce the price of the corporations stock back to a price range that management considers optimal. Thus, if the management of XQ Corporation believed that the market price of XQ stock should be $20 to $30 per share and it currently stood at $50 per share, it could declare a 2 for 1 stock split so that, after the split, the price would be in the $20 to $30 range.

Common Stocks and Inflation   Common stocks are frequently referred to as a good hedge against inflation. As noted in the investment objectives chapter (Chapter 17), ownership investments such as common stock should fare reasonably well during inflationary periods.

One reason is that inflation generally increases a firm's sales prices and costs at the same rate, and this should increase the firm's earnings; increased earnings usually result in a higher return to the investor. Another reason is that the firm's assets should rise in value as the price of all items rises with inflation. The net effect should be increased dividends, or a rise in share price, or some combination of the two.

Although theory suggests that common stock is a good hedge, an immediate question is: Has common stock really been a good hedge in the past? To answer that question, Exhibit 19–2 charts stock prices from 1913 through 1975. The stock index charted there is the Dow Jones Industrial Average, which represents the average share price of 30 large industrial companies for each year during the 62 years on the chart.

THE 'CONSTANT-DOLLAR DOW'

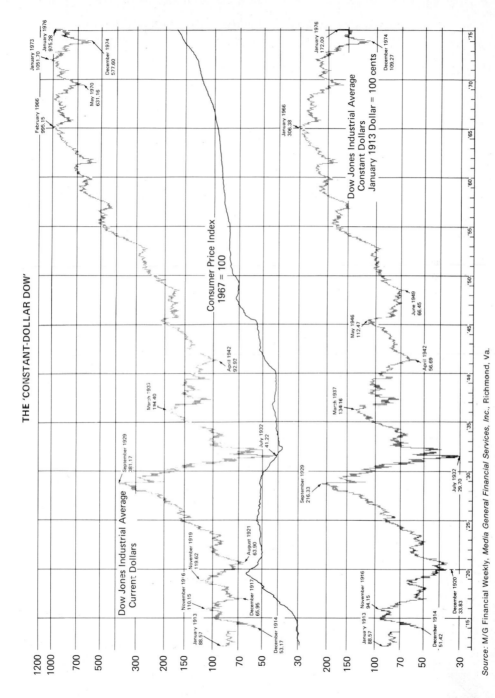

Source: M/G Financial Weekly, *Media General Financial Services, Inc.,* Richmond, Va.

Exhibit 19-2 Inflation and Common Stocks: Dow Jones Industrial Average in Current and Constant Dollars

The exhibit shows three things: (1) The average stock price index is charted in "current dollars" at the top of the exhibit. By current dollars we mean that the price of the stock between 1913 and 1975 is represented in the value of whatever a dollar was worth in each year during that period. That is, the index charted at the top simply follows the average price of the stock each year—it tells us nothing about the price of the stock with respect to inflation. (2) The index charted in the middle of the exhibit is the consumer price index—the telltale of inflation. (3) The index at the bottom is the average stock price index charted in "constant dollars." The constant dollar used in this index is the value of $1 in 1913.

By graphically adjusting the top index with the consumer price index (for this course, you need not be concerned about exactly how this graphical adjustment is made), the result is the bottom index, which does tell us something about the average stock price and inflation during the 62 years of the exhibit.

The constant dollar index in Exhibit 19–2 is the one we are interested in because it shows the real performance—current dollar performance less inflation's effect—of stock prices. The first thing that stands out is that real stock prices in the mid-1970s are about equal to those of the mid-1950s. In the 1950s the index was in the 150 to 175 range, and although it rose to 300 in the mid-1960s, it fell back to the 150 to 175 range by the mid-1970s. Essentially, real average stock price appreciation over those 20 years was zero. Those investors who purchased stock when prices were near their peak in the mid-sixties and held the stock to the mid-seventies lost money. The value of their stock declined at approximately −7 percent annually. Of course, some stocks outperformed those included in the Dow Jones Industrial Index, but there were many which failed even to match the index.

We can see some things clearly from Exhibit 19–2. Look at the consumer price index and note periods where inflation tends to increase more rapidly than in other periods. Then look below at the constant dollar index, and you will see that the average stock prices declined during the same periods that inflation increased rapidly. For example, note the increase in the consumer price index and the fall in average stock prices during the late 1960s to the mid-1970s. Another thing you can observe is that when the average stock price rises, inflation tends to offset much of that rise.

Real Investor Return   Since total investor return includes both a stock's dividend yield and its price change, we need to add dividend yield to the price performance shown in Exhibit 19–2. Over the 20 years from the mid-1950s to the mid-1970s, an investor's annual real return—total return (dividends plus price change) less inflation—was approximately 3.5 percent. That is less than the 4 to 4.5 percent real return we feel a top-grade common stock should provide. During the 10-year span between the mid-sixties and the mid-seventies, the real return was negative (investors lost money, on the average), in large part because of the dismal price performance of common stocks.

The best answer we can give to the question of whether common stocks are a good hedge against inflation is that, historically, they have done well when inflation rates were low, have provided a partial hedge during moderate inflation, and have done miserably during high-inflation periods. We believe stocks will be a fairly good hedge during low to moderate inflationary periods. But at inflation rates around 10 percent, stocks will not represent a good hedge.

Historical Investor Return   Over the 40-year span from 1926 to 1965, investor return on common stocks has averaged 9.3 percent.[1] But within that period the returns vary tremendously, ranging from the steep negative returns (losses) following the 1929 market crash to the large positive returns of the 1950s. How much of this historical experience will be repeated over the next few years? We believe that stock prices will not fluctuate through the wide extremes seen during the 1926–65 period. Likewise, we expect the dividend yield will be more stable over the next 10 years. In the period from 1950 through 1975, it ranged from an annual high of 6 percent to less than 3 percent. These two trends should dampen the swings in investor return over the next 10 years. Nevertheless, investor return could exceed 25 percent when prices are recovering from a sharp decline. And investor return could represent a loss of 25 percent when prices are declining. Overall, however, we expect the average return on top-grade common stocks to be about 8 to 9 percent during the next 10 years. Medium-quality stocks should return about 9 to 11 percent on the average. But, we hasten to qualify these statements: Our forecasts assume an annual inflation rate of 4 to 5 percent. Also, we assume corporations will not be encumbered with price controls or other economic limitations. If controls are installed for any significant period, investor return will likely be substantially less.

Stock Valuation

There are many factors which determine the price of a particular common stock. However, at this point, we are more interested in explaining several measures that can be used to evaluate a particular stock.

Earnings per Share (EPS)   Earnings per share is computed by dividing the firm's after-tax earnings by the number of shares of common stock outstanding. Thus, if XQ's earnings were $1.5 million and it had 300,000 shares, its EPS would be $5 ($1.5 million ÷ 300,000 shares). Sometimes the EPS represents the firm's earnings for the past year; sometimes EPS represents the firm's expected future earnings.

Price-Earnings Ratio (P/E)   The price-earnings ratio is computed by dividing the price per share by the earnings per share. The price-earnings ratio indicates the relationship between the price of a share and how much of the firm's earnings are represented by that share. Thus, a stock selling for $10 and

[1]L. Fisher and J. H. Lorie, "Rates of Return on Investments in Common Stock: The Year-by-Year Record, 1926–65," *Journal of Business*, July 1968, pp. 291–316.

having EPS of \$1 is selling at 10 times earnings (\$10 ÷ \$1 = 10 times). As such, it gives investors a way of evaluating a particular stock. At any point in time, there are stocks selling at 30 to 50 times earnings while others are selling at 3 to 5 times earnings. Why the big difference? It could be a number of things, such as future earning's prospects, highly respected company management, a glamorous product line, more publicity, or many other factors.

The fact that a stock has a high P/E does not necessarily mean it is overpriced. The high P/E may mean that its earnings are unusually low during a particular period. If earnings increased during a later period, the price-earnings ratio would appear more normal for that period. Likewise, a stock with a low price-earnings ratio may be no bargain. For example, its current earnings per share may be unusually high.

Often a stock's projected earnings are used to calculate the expected price-earnings ratio for a future period. The problem with this is that the expected P/E is based on that earnings estimate. To determine whether a projected P/E is reasonable or not, compare it with the actual P/E for the stock in the recent past.

The second column of Exhibit 19–1 shows an average P/E ratio based on 500 common stocks. Over the past 10 years, the ratio has varied through a wide range. As a consequence, it is nearly impossible to say what constitutes a "normal" level.

Common Stock Categories

To group all common stocks into a few summary categories would be difficult, and in the end some placements would be arbitrary. Nevertheless, a stock is often labeled either a "blue chip," a "growth stock," or some other title. While there is no universal definition, we provide our definition of three frequently used lables: blue chip stock, growth stock, and speculative stock. Of course, many stocks are not classified in any of the three categories.

Blue Chip Stock   A blue chip stock is generally from a large, well-regarded corporation. Examples include DuPont, American Telephone and Telegraph, General Foods, RCA, Exxon Corporation, and Sears, Roebuck and Company. Most have a long history of reasonably consistent earnings and steady dividends. Their earnings continue to grow, although the growth rate is generally not spectacular. The financial community regards these firms as well managed and prudently financed. Blue chip stocks typically have the lowest risk exposure of all common stocks.

Strategy: Concentrate on blue chip stocks if you are highly averse to risk.

Growth Stock   A growth stock is generally from a corporation whose earnings have grown at above-average rates during recent years. Examples include International Business Machines, McDonald's Inc., Hewlett-Packard Co., Xerox System Corporation, and S.S. Kresge Company. A true growth stock must also represent continued above-average growth in the future.

Merely increasing sales is not enough; the firm must also increase its earnings. With an earnings growth rate of 10 to 15 percent or more, you should expect that a firm cannot continue to grow at that rapid rate forever. For example, a firm growing at 15 percent annually would double in size every 5 years. Even if it started small, the firm would be 4 times its original size in 10 years.

Most growth firms pay only limited dividends because they need most of their earnings to pay for the costs of expansion. The P/E ratio on growth stocks, especially the large, well-known firms, tends to be well above the market average. The prices of growth stock are very volatile because they are highly sensitive to changes in the overall market of common stock. Typically, prices drop sharply when the general market declines, and, conversely, they rise sharply when the market advances.

Many factors can contribute to a firm's above-average growth: unique product, good industry prospects, superior management, or some combination of these or other factors. Regardless of the cause of growth, many investors are continually searching for "undiscovered" growth stocks. They hope to purchase the shares before the price of the shares reflects the firm's rosy future. Once a stock is recognized as a growth stock, its price rises sharply and early investors pick up a tidy profit. But identifying an "undiscovered" growth stock is no small task. Unfortunately, many promising candidates turn out to be the work of the accountant's creative pen, management's financial maneuvers, or just plain unsupported rhetoric. The market usually recognizes these for what they really are, so the price rarely skyrockets.

Speculative Stock   A speculative stock is from a company that may, or may not, have good future potential earnings. Examples include Pan American World Airways, Alcoa Corporation, National Semiconductor, Avon Products, Chrysler Corporation, and Champion Homes. In general, the stock sells on the prospect of its future earnings rather than its past accomplishments. The company could have a new or revised product that may revolutionize the industry. Or, the firm could have been highly successful in the past, but is currently experiencing difficulty. If these problems can be resolved, the firm may be highly successful once more. But investors have no guarantee that a speculative stock will succeed in increasing its earnings and eventually in boosting its price per share. For every stock that succeeds, there are dozens that looked equally promising but never worked out, so that investors received little or no return.

THE MARKETS WHERE STOCKS ARE TRADED

Common stocks can be purchased in the primary market directly from a firm issuing the stock. Once issued, the stock is bought and sold in the secondary market.

Primary Market   New issues of common stock are sold in the primary market. The actual sale is handled by a specialized selling group called the underwriters; the corporation receives the sale proceeds less a small commission for the selling group. A new company sells a new issue simply to obtain funds to begin operation. An existing firm may sell a new issue to finance a major expansion. Since most firms meet their capital needs out of retained earnings, the number of new issues each year is small.

Secondary Market   The secondary market is the one where most investors buy and sell stock; it is what most people mean when they say "the stock market." Stocks traded in this market are existing issues that have been outstanding for various lengths of time. Secondary market transactions involve a shareholder who decides to sell a particular stock and a prospective investor who decides to buy that stock. The corporation has no role in the transaction, nor does it receive any of the proceeds. A transaction always involves a stockbroker, and both the seller and the buyer must pay a commission to the broker. A stock's price at any point in time reflects the supply and demand for the stock at that precise time. If a large number of shareholders want to sell but not many investors are interested in buying, the price will decline and will continue to do so until prospective investors are attracted and will buy or until some existing holders are discouraged from selling. Conversely, a heavy demand with limited supply will cause the price to rise.

Reading a Secondary Market List   Exhibit 19–3 is a hypothetical example of a typical secondary market listing of common stocks. While the actual lists that appear in *The Wall Street Journal* and in other metropolitan newspapers may differ in format, their information content is similar to Exhibit 19–3. A company's common stock may be listed on one or more of the following stock exchanges: (1) New York Stock Exchange, (2) American Stock Exchange, (3) regional exchanges—Midwest, Pacific, Boston, and so on, and (4) the over-the-counter market. In general, the largest companies are traded on the New York Stock Exchange, medium-sized firms are traded on the American Stock Exchange and some regional exchanges, and smaller firms are traded over the counter.

To illustrate the information given in the listing, we will use as an example Atwood Chemical, which is near the middle of Exhibit 19–3. The first two columns show the stock's high and low prices for the year. The highest Atwood

Exhibit 19-3   Hypothetical Example of a Secondary Market Listing of Common Stocks Traded on October 28, 1976

| 1976 | | | | | | Price | | | |
High	Low	Stock	Div	Sales 100's	P/E ratio	High	Low	Close	Change
24⅛	21⅞	Algoma Products	1.00	13	10	23¼	23⅛	23⅛	−⅛
19⅜	18¼	American Power	2.50	3	6	18⅝	18½	18½	−
26⅜	18⅞	Atwood Chemical	.95	78	11	23⅜	22⅛	23	¼
9⅜	9	Azoor Finance	.04	17	12	9⅛	9	9	−⅛
75¾	70⅛	Baker Foods	2.75	6	5	71¼	71⅛	71¼	½
78⅛	45¼	Beeker Oil	.10	33	45	47½	47⅜	47⅜	−⅜

sold for was 26³/₈ ($26.375), and the lowest price was 18⁷/₈ ($18.875). The amount following the name of the stock—$.95—is the annual dividend. Following this, under "Sales 100's," is the number of shares traded that day in 100's. Thus, 7,800 shares of Atwood were traded on October 28. Next comes the stock's P/E ratio, based on its current price and its most recent annual EPS. Following this are the day's price range: high, low, and closing prices (the closing price is the price of stock at the last transaction on that day). Last comes the net price change between the previous and the current day's closing prices. A blank in the P/E column can mean that the stock either is a preferred stock (which has no earnings per share) or is that of a firm that had a loss last year, in which case the firm had no earnings and therefore the stock has no P/E ratio.

Stock Market Indexes   The widely publicized stock market indexes show the current state and recent performance of the total market. All stock indexes are based on the market price of a sample of selected stocks, but the sample varies widely for different indexes. Some indexes concentrate on industrial stocks: Dow Jones Industrial Average (30 firms), Standard & Poor's 425 Industrials (425 firms). Other indexes, such as the Standard & Poor's 500 Index, New York Stock Exchange Index, and American Stock Exchange Index, cover a much broader cross section of stocks. Because the indexes include different stocks, they all do not change the same amount in a given day. But the direction of change for the different indexes is usually the same.

None of the indexes consider dividends; the changes in stock indexes are due only to changes in stock prices. Also, a 1-point change in an index does not mean a $1 change in the average price per share. A separate statistic, usually preceding the stock listing in a newspaper, shows the dollar amount that an average share's price has advanced or declined between the previous and the current day.

Danger! Here Come the Bulls and the Bears   When stock prices are rising, the trend is typically referred to as a "bull market." On the other hand, declining prices indicate a "bear market." When these terms are translated to an individual, a "bear" is generally a pessimist who expects stock prices to decline; a "bull" is an optimist who expects stock prices to rise. So the next time someone begins discussing whether the current market is bullish or bearish, you can either pass the "bull" back or "bear" it.

SELECTING A COMMON STOCK

Despite some glowing success stories that are frequently repeated by investors and market professionals, there is an increasing body of evidence that suggests stock prices move in a random fashion. That is, an investor, even a hardened professional, cannot accurately predict the direction of a stock's future market price, certainly not with the accuracy and speed needed to earn an extraordinary return. Carrying this idea further, we could select stocks successfully by

merely putting the stock listing on a board and making a choice by throwing a
dart at it. This approach is sometimes called the random walk theory.
According to the supporters of the idea, stock prices move in a random fashion
so stocks selected using a dart board will do as well as stocks selected after
an elaborate investigation and analysis. What are the implications for the investor who selects a stock in this way? For one thing, it means the investor
must have skill and accuracy; after all, you have to hit the board with the dart.
For another thing, it takes the suspense and excitement out of investing. Seriously, it raises a real question about whether the time spent searching for
undervalued or undiscovered stocks is really worthwhile. Maybe an investor
would do equally well, albeit with less suspense, using a random selection
technique.

Certainly the dismal performance of most mutual funds that invest heavily
in common stocks provides considerable support for the random walk theory.
(The next chapter discusses mutual funds further.) Despite their claim to
professional expertise in the stock market, most mutual funds have not
consistently outperformed the average return for the stock market. An
immediate question is: If professionals cannot do better than the market
average, what can the average investor do? Our feeling is that most investors
cannot consistently beat the average. Nevertheless, we believe the possibility is
not entirely remote and the rewards can be substantial. Besides, trying to beat
the market can be fun for investors who want to get involved in their
investments.

We do, however, offer several cautions. First, we cannot stress enough
that our recommendation for picking a common stock carries no guarantee of
success. Second, we define a "successful" common stock as one whose return

is commensurate with the risk assumed. Because the range of risk exposure is so large, we cannot suggest a single rate of return which somehow represents an acceptable average. But we believe investors who expect to double their money every 6 months are not being realistic. Finally, our selection procedure requires a considerable amount of unglamorous detail work. Even after an investor—say, Ms. Brayns—has made her initial investment decision, she will still have to continue her analysis, searching out promising new investments and reviewing the progress and future prospect of her current investments. In short, many prospective investors will simply not have the time, or possibly the interest, to become immersed in the task of searching out a promising common stock. For those investors, we recommend they consider one of the mutual funds discussed in Chapter 20.

Picking a Specific Stock

Although our discussion about selecting a promising common stock will be brief, we feel it will give prospective investors sufficient background so they can decide whether they want to become involved in selecting common stock or whether they will leave the selection to someone else. The recommended readings at the chapter's end give additional information on implementing a selection plan for those who want to pursue the subject.

Fundamental Value Approach   Our selection technique stresses the underlying fundamental values of a prospective stock. Those fundamental values include factors unique to the firm as well as the industry: the firm's management capabilities, its current product line, its present earnings, its past earnings growth, its future earnings growth, its current dividend yield, its future dividend policy, investors' perception of the stock as reflected in its P/E ratio, future industry prospects, and competition within the industry. The fundamental value technique assumes a stock's price is determined primarily by its underlying fundamental values. Consequently, it stresses a careful examination and analysis of the factors affecting those values.

Technical Factors Approach   Not everyone subscribes to the fundamental values approach; some feel that only over a long term do the fundamental values affect a stock's price; but over the short term, only the supply and demand factors determine its price. These investors, called technical advocates, maintain that an investor can successfully invest in common stocks by studying the technical factors of supply and demand. Since several references are given at the chapter's end, we pursue technical analysis no further.

Selecting an Industry   Selecting the proper industry can be more important than singling out a specific stock in that industry. The first thing an industry should have is a good growth record, preferably over a period of 5 years or more. The industry's growth rate should equal, or preferably exceed, the 6 to 8 percent average growth of the total economy during the past 8 years. In addition, the industry should have similar growth prospects for the future and a product or service that will be in demand for the next few years.

Also important, but not so critical in selecting an industry, is its image—how do investors regard the image of that industry? This aspect is harder to define, but it should be an industry investors can identify with and become enthusiastic about. For example, the cement industry can have a promising future if construction activity is rapidly expanding. But if most investors view it as a stodgy, nongrowth industry, it is not likely to generate a large investor following. But we hasten to add that growth is much more important than a good investor image because a rapidly growing industry will eventually be recognized as having good investment potential.

When considering an industry, examine its production pattern to see if it goes through a pronounced cycle. The feast or famine patterns of the construction and automobile industries are good examples of cyclical industries. All cyclical industries need not be automatically excluded, but you need extra caution in determining when to buy their stocks. These stocks can be an excellent investment at the beginning of an expansion phase because their prices rise sharply. But as the contraction phase approaches, their prices usually fall off as sharply. When evaluating cyclical industries, investors should carefully consider the industry's current phase.

Information Sources   Exhibit 19–4 presents the major information sources for the recent performance, current status, and future prospect of different industries. Public libraries generally have most of these sources. In addition, there are usually one or more trade journals which discuss each industry's current developments and special topics.

Selecting a Company   Once a promising industry has been identified, the investor must evaluate the companies within that industry. When reviewing

Exhibit 19-4   Information Sources: Industry Data

Title	Publisher	Comment
Industry Surveys	Standard & Poor's Corporation	Analyzes, in detail, major industries, wealth of operating statistics, updated with quarterly supplements. Completely revised every 1 to 3 years.
Value Line Investment Service	The Value Line Investment Survey	Each weekly issue analyzes the current state and future prospects of four to six industries.
The Outlook	Standard & Poor's Corporation	Highlights several industries in each week's issue.
Stock Survey	Moody's Investor Services, Inc.	Highlights several industries in each week's issue.
Business Week	McGraw-Hill, Inc.	Summarizes recent performance data on major industries on a recurring basis.
Monthly Economic Letter	Citibank	This monthly letter surveys the major industries and publishes the results each quarter.
Forbes	Forbes Inc.	Analyzes the past and prospective performance of major industries in one issue each year.

specific stocks, we stress that you examine the fundamental factors underlying the value of that stock.

Earnings Growth   The company you are considering should have a consistent history of above-average earnings growth, preferably during the most recent 5 years. Even more important, that growth should be expected to continue in the future. Yesterday's growth may have benefited current shareholders, but it is tomorrow's growth that will benefit new shareholders. The previously discussed industry statistics can provide a good benchmark in analyzing a company's earnings performance.

P/E Ratio   As a beginning step, compare the company's P/E ratio with that of other firms in the industry. If the ratio is significantly higher, ask yourself: Do the underlying fundamental factors justify that ratio? The P/E ratio is likely to rise when a firm's earnings are rising sharply because increased earnings will cause stock price to increase sharply. But considerable skepticism is justified when considering a P/E ratio that is far above the industry average. A stock with a P/E of 50 or 60 may be overpriced, or it may be a great buy. Only its future earnings will determine the truth here.

Look for a stock that has all the marks of a winner—good industry, above-average earnings growth, good future prospects—but one whose P/E has not yet fully reflected those favorable characteristics. Firms with these attributes, but with P/E's that are near or below the industry average, should be good candidates for above-average returns in the near future. As the firm's earnings continue to grow, the market will recognize the firm's potential, causing a dramatic rise in the price of the stock.

In addition to comparing the prospective company's P/E ratio with those of other firms in the same industry, you should also compare that ratio with the current P/E ratio for one of the broad-based stock indexes: S&P's 425 Industrials or the Dow Jones Industrial Average. That comparison protects you against the possibility that all P/E's within an industry have been bid up to unwarranted heights; if that has happened, comparing the company's P/E ratio with industry statistics will not show the P/E ratio to be unusually high.

Will Second or Third String Do?   We believe investors should look beyond the leading firm in a given industry. Too often, investors concentrate on the top firm without investigating the second- or third-rank firm. Of course, it may be that the leading firm excels all others, but carefully consider the investment merits of the lower-ranked firms before you decide.

Current Shareholders   Extra caution is necessary when most of the firm's common stock is held by a few large shareholders. This generally occurs when the firm has previously been owned by a single family. While some of the shares are held by the public, the family group retains sufficient shares to exercise effective control—very often, only for its own benefit. Then the small shareholder may suffer.

There are two schools of thought about whether it is an advantage or a disadvantage that a sizable block of a firm's stock is held by large institutional investors, such as mutual funds, corporate pension funds, and insurance companies. On the one hand, institutional ownership could indicate that there will be increased interest in the future and that may bid up the price. But if the institutions decide to sell their shares, their action could substantially depress the price. Probably the best advice is to go with your convictions; if you feel you want to invest in a stock, go ahead regardless of whether its institutional following is strong or limited.

Information Sources   Exhibit 19–5 lists some of the major sources where you can find data and information on individual corporations. Nearly all these sources can be found in the large public libraries. In addition, there is a mass of newsletters and other investment data published by investment advisory services.

DEVELOPING INVESTMENT IDEAS

There is no easy, sure system for generating investment ideas. The ones we know about require hard work, some deft timing, a large quota of self-confidence to go with your convictions, and just plain luck. Nevertheless, there are several things investors can do to improve their search for investment leads.

Exhibit 19-5   Information Sources: Individual Corporations

Title	Publisher	Comment
Stock Reports	Standard & Poor's Corporation	Detailed data on corporations listed on the New York and American stock exchanges plus major issues from the over-the-counter; updated regularly.
Moody's Manuals	Moody's Investor Services, Inc.	In-depth historical sketch together with current data on all major corporations; updated regularly.
Corporation Records	Standard & Poor's Corporation	In-depth historical sketch and recent operating data on major firms; updated frequently.
Value Line Investment Service	Value Line Investment Survey	Comparative analysis of major firms within major industries; each industry's review is updated every 13 weeks.
The Outlook	Standard & Poor's Corporation	Reviews of major current events that affect an industry or specific stock; also comparative analysis of a major industry and its firms.
Stock Survey	Moody's Investor Services, Inc.	Comparative analysis and review of firms within select industries; also reviews of current events that affect a specific stock.
Forbes	Forbes Inc.	The industry analysis issue, appearing early in the year, covers the major firms within each industry; in addition, each issue discusses a number of companies.
Business Week	McGraw-Hill, Inc.	Regular summaries of the performance of major firms within each industry.

"Hot Tips"   Unfortunately, the hot tip from the barber, mail carrier, or taxi driver, is likely to have no substance. A hot tip means nothing by itself. You must evaluate the firm's fundamental factors to determine whether the stock does indeed represent a sound investment. You can usually stop a hot tip and turn it cold merely by asking the tipster whether he or she has invested in the stock.

Broker's Recommendations   We think many brokers are poorly prepared and equipped for their profession, despite their claims otherwise. The recent sharp market contractions seem to have driven out some of the more incompetent brokers. There are some good brokers, but they often deal with institutional clients rather than small investors. Too many brokers merely subscribe to the latest market fad without generating any new investment ideas. There is nothing wrong with asking your broker's suggestions, but do a detailed analysis of his or her recommendation before you act on it.

BUYING COMMON STOCKS

All purchases and sales of common stocks, whether in the primary or the secondary market, require a stock broker to execute the order.

Selecting a Broker   The purpose of a broker is to fulfill your order to purchase a stock. But we think you can and should expect more from a broker. Although we do not believe you should rely on most brokers' recommendations, they do represent a good source of information. Brokers can furnish you with research reports on those companies their firms have recently analyzed. Also, they can discuss the ideas that are currently making the rounds in the market.

When selecting a broker, examine the firm where the broker works to see if it has an active, competent research department which issues frequent reports. Unfortunately, many firms with the most respected research capabilities do not encourage small investor accounts. One possible step is to open an account with a firm and request some of their research reports. If they give you nothing but a simple data summary rather than a true analysis of the company's strengths and weaknesses, you should switch to a different firm.

Another place to begin your search is to ask your friends whether they know a good broker. The first time you talk to a broker, ask what he or she recommends. If you are immediately given a long list of stocks, chances are the broker will sell you anything to make a commission. On the other hand, if he or she takes time to discuss your investment goals before trying to sell, you should undertake further consideration. You should also ask what type of investment situations the broker spends most time on: short-term profits, long-term investments, steady income, or other investment features. If his or her experience and interests in stocks parallel your investment goals, you should definitely consider using this broker as your advisor.

Do not feel compelled to stay with a broker if you are unhappy with the individual's performance. Request that the brokerage house assign you a new representative, or switch to a different brokerage firm altogether.

Strategy: Select a broker who can deliver the investment information you need and whose investment experience and interests parallel your needs.

Churning Your Account   We define churning an account to include any transaction where the broker's primary motive is generating a commission. Your best protection is to resist your broker's attempts to switch you in and out of an issue unless you are convinced the switch is justified. If you feel your broker is churning your account, it is time to change brokers.

Brokerage Commissions   While brokerage firms are no longer required to charge identical commissions, most of their commissions are similar on small transactions. Commissions vary depending on the number of shares, share price, and the exchange involved in the transaction. But you can expect to pay a 2 to 3 percent commission when the amount invested is approximately $1,000; 3 to 5 percent on $500 investments; 5 to 7 percent on $350 investments; and 6 to 10 percent on $100 investments. These commissions apply on buying or selling stock. Thus, for a round-trip trade—purchasing and reselling the shares—the commissions would be double these rates. The commission is higher on an odd lot purchase (less than 100 shares) than on a 100 share round lot. Clearly, the commission structure is heavily weighted against small transactions. Unless a stock's performance is spectacular, it is uneconomical to invest $100 or $200.

Because commission rates are similar, shopping different brokers is not likely to save much. But to protect yourself, you should check several brokers to be sure you do not get one who discourages small investors by charging exorbitantly high commissions.

Timing of Stock Investments

Because common stock has no set maturity, investors face two questions: When should they buy? When should they sell? The old Wall Street axiom to "buy low and sell high" offers no guidance: Who says what is "low," and at what point is "high" reached? Investors must first decide whether they are pursuing a buy-and-hold strategy or whether they are trading for short-term profits.

Buy and Hold   With the buy-and-hold strategy, a common stock is held as long as it continues to provide a return commensurate with the risk it entails. Of course, should the stock's future prospects decline or appear doubtful, it should be sold. Likewise, the investor who has identified a substitute stock that appears to have more potential should definitely switch stock. For the great majority of small investors, the buy-and-hold strategy is probably the best.

Short-Term Trading   With short-term trading, the investor's objective is quite different. For one thing, the time horizon is days and weeks rather than years. For another, the potential profit is likely to center on a small, but definite, change in the stock's price. And that change does not have to be an increase. With a suitable strategy, a profit can be made on a price decline as well. Short-term trading requires heavy investor involvement because identifying potential profit opportunities is time-consuming and the time to react is short. There are several references given at the chapter's end which discuss this complicated and lengthy topic.

Is the Price Right?   Deciding what price you should pay for a particular stock is no easy matter. Nobody wants to buy and then watch the price go even lower than the purchase price. Likewise, it is frustrating to watch a stock's price increase after you have held off buying it because you thought the price was too high and would go lower. Nevertheless, an investor who has done sound homework on evaluating a particular stock should be able to decide whether to buy at the current price.

Dollar-Cost Averaging   Dollar-cost averaging avoids the question of whether the price is right. Rather than invest a single large amount, the investor puts a set amount of money into buying a particular stock at regular intervals. If the plan is followed consistently, the investor buys more shares when the price is down and fewer shares when the price is high. An example is the best way to illustrate dollar-cost averaging. Assume that Wilma Swift decided to invest $600 in XQ Corporation every 3 months. Exhibit 19-6 shows the details of investing in this way for one year.

Had Wilma purchased 24 shares each quarter at the price for that quarter, her average price for 96 shares purchased during the year would be $22.50. But by investing a set dollar amount at each quarter, she purchased 114 shares at an average cost per share equal to $21.05. One advantage to dollar-cost averaging is that it forces the investor to buy when prices are low even though overall market prospects may seem bleak at that point. For most people, buying stock when the total market is in a decline is far more difficult than buying when it is rising. Remember, if it was a good buy at $30 per share, it should be a great buy at $20, and one hell of a buy at $15. Of course, if a particular stock's future prospects have reversed, the investment should be discontinued.

Exhibit 19-6   Dollar-Cost Averaging: $600 Invested Each Quarter

Quarter	Share price	Amount invested	Shares purchased	Total shares	Cumulative investment	Average share price*
First	$25.00	$600	24	24	$ 600	$25.00
Second	$30.00	$600	20	44	$1,200	$27.27
Third	$15.00	$600	40	84	$1,800	$21.43
Fourth	$20.00	$600	30	114	$2,400	$21.05
Average†	$22.50					

*Cumulative investment divided by total shares.

†Average price is the simple average of the price for the four quarters: ([$25 + $30 + $15 + $20] ÷ 4 quarters) = $22.50. If you purchased an equal number of shares each quarter (e.g., 24 shares), your average cost would be $22.50.

Strategy: To make dollar-cost averaging work, stick to your investment schedule during rising markets—when it's easiest—and during declining markets—when it takes courage and conviction.

Systematic Investment Plans   Some large brokerage firms offer systematic investment plans that are specifically tailored to small investors who want to invest a small amount regularly. Typically, the investor can select from a wide range of different stocks. Investors can either have their payments invested quarterly or monthly. An investor's account is credited for the full and fractional shares. For example, a quarterly investment of $236.50 ($250 before commissions) would purchase 23.65 shares ($236.50 ÷ $10) if the stock was $10 per share. Typically, dividends are reinvested to purchase additional shares.

A plan's major advantage is its "forced savings" feature, since the investor makes a monthly payment, but there is no penalty for a missed payment. Another advantage is that the investor can buy fractional shares. Further, because it is a regular investment, it has the benefits of the dollar-cost averaging. The major disadvantage is the typical 5 to 10 percent commission if the amount invested is small. Investing quarterly, rather than monthly, lowers the commissions, but you receive no return on your money during the quarter while you are building up money in your account.

Holding Period on a New Investment   Investors should closely monitor the performance of their stock during the first 6 months of ownership. During those first 6 months you can deduct any loss you have on the investment from income for income tax purposes. Beyond 6 months, only one-half the loss can be deducted, since it has become a long-term capital loss. To determine the stock's performance, compare it with the overall market as well as with stock of other firms in the industry. If your stock has declined while both the market and the industry have advanced, you should seriously consider selling it. Of course, if you decide the stock still has good potential, you may want to hold it.

We have only one recommendation when you decide the stock is going nowhere: Take a deep breath and repeat the following short statement, "I blew it and will take my loss immediately." Then do it. The old statement "The first loss is the smallest" is distinctly true in stocks. A bad stock rarely recovers; it is usually a question of how large the loss will be. So take the loss and move to something with some upward potential.

Sell Signal for a Winner   Picking the time to sell a stock can be as difficult as deciding when to buy. The best guide for deciding when to sell is to analyze the same fundamental factors you examined when you bought the stock. As long as those factors remain positive, we think investors should hold the stock unless they have a replacement that looks more attractive. At times, however, a stock's price rises to very high but questionable levels. The events listed in Exhibit 19–7 can signal a time to sell. If a stock rates a yes on several questions, it may be time to consider selling.

Exhibit 19-7 Sell Signals

	Yes	No
1. Is the firm's P/E substantially above others in the industry?	( )	( )
2. Has the P/E increased markedly during the last 6 months, even though the earnings are basically unchanged?	( )	( )
3. Has the spread between the average P/E for the industry and that for an overall stock market index widened sharply?	( )	( )
4. Has the number of shares traded each day increased significantly?	( )	( )
5. Has the stock appeared on several stock advisory services' buy list?	( )	( )

Reaction to a Declining Market Certainly no one enjoys watching the price of his or her common stocks decline as the total market enters a downtrend. But it can be foolhardy and costly to panic and sell during an overall market downturn. Before you decide to switch to a different investment, consider the total cost of selling and possibly repurchasing a short time later. Of course, if you feel a different stock has better potential, you should switch to that stock. But if you are merely hoping a different stock will somehow not decline so much, it is likely all the switch will do is cost you commissions.

COMMON STOCKS: ARE THEY FOR YOU?

Because they are a specialized investment, common stocks are not for every investor. The price volatility of common stocks is just too high for some

AN INVESTMENT SCOUT IS CAUTIOUS, HARD WORKING, SELF CONFIDENT AND LUCKY!..

investors. Even if common stocks match an individual's investment goals, the investor may not be able to spend the considerable time needed to select potential investment candidates and regularly review their performance.

How Do You Measure Up? Some people are much better suited than others for investing in stocks. The checklist in Exhibit 19–8 should help you determine your own fitness for this type of investment. These questions stress the qualitative and psychological aspects of investing in stocks rather than the financial points.

Most of your answers should be yes if you are to consider yourself suitable to be a common stock investor; if your answers are mostly no, you should seriously consider other investment alternatives. If the prospect of sharp variations in your rate of return will cause you sleepless nights and possibly ulcers, you should restrict yourself to fixed-income investments. If you want to invest in common stocks, yet do not want to be involved in managing them, you should consider a mutual fund (Chapter 20).

Exhibit 19-8 Judging Your Common Stock Fitness Score

	Yes	No
Time commitment		
1. Will you spend 10 to 15 hours each week to keep abreast of current business developments?	( )	( )
2. Will you spend the 10 to 40 hours needed to fully evaluate an investment idea?	( )	( )
3. Will you spend 1 to 2 hours each month to reevaluate each of your previous investments?	( )	( )
Investor interest		
1. Will you find financial reports and brokerage research reports interesting?	( )	( )
2. Will you have sufficient confidence to raise questions if a research report concluded with a series of glowing, but unsupported, conclusions?	( )	( )
3. Do you find the prospect of picking a winner exciting?	( )	( )
4. Will you have sufficient interest to thoroughly analyze a particular stock?	( )	( )
Stock selection		
1. Do you think an average investor can pick successful stocks?	( )	( )
2. Do you think good investment opportunities exist in industries that may not have a lot of glamour?	( )	( )
3. Would you purchase a stock which appears to have good potential even though it is not a current market favorite?	( )	( )
4. Do you think a thorough analysis is a better way to pick investment candidates than someone's hot tip?	( )	( )
Anticipated rate of return		
1. Would you be satisfied with an average annual return of 8 to 12 percent?	( )	( )
2. Do you think it is unrealistic to expect a 20 to 30 percent annual return?	( )	( )
3. Could you accept without panicking a price decline of 20 to 50 percent in a market downturn?	( )	( )
4. Can you sleep nights while knowing this year's return might be a 20 percent increase or a 20 percent loss?	( )	( )

General Investment Attributes

At various points in this chapter, we have discussed all major investment attributes of common stocks except risk exposure and taxes.

Risk Exposure   Common stock exposes the shareholder to three of the four risk categories: business risk, risk of financial collapse, and market price risk. Business risk arises from the particular industry in which the corporation's business activity is concentrated. Fluctuations in the level of activity within that industry are reflected in the corporation's operations and, therefore, also in the shareholders' return. In general, business risk is highest when the corporation is in an industry which is subject to wide swings in its activity levels. For example, the common stock of automotive companies would have high business risk because their industry is highly cyclical. On the other hand, the stock of electric utility companies should have relatively low business risk because that industry has a stable demand pattern.

The shareholders' exposure to the risk of financial collapse arises not only from fluctuations in the firm's operations, but also from the way the firm is financed. In general, the more heavily a firm relies on fixed payment debt instruments—loans, bonds, and notes—as its source of financing, the higher the possibility of financial collapse. A firm with heavy debts in a volatile industry would represent a high risk level. Yet, the same debt in a stable industry would give moderate risk. Your best guide to estimating a firm's financial risk is to compare the firms within the industry. A firm whose debt (bonds, loans, and notes) as a percentage of its total assets is far above the average percentage for the other firms in that industry should be rated as high risk.

Market price risk arises because the stock market is subject to fads. If a particular stock, or even an entire industry, comes into vogue, the prices can rise to dazzling heights. But what goes up can also drop just as rapidly. Unfortunately, when a stock or industry is no longer in vogue, prices often drop to unjustified low levels. And recovery from those low prices can take a long time. To the extent a stock experiences wide swings in popularity, investors can be exposed to considerable market price risk.

Diversifying Your Stock Holdings   By splitting your investments among several stocks (diversifying), you can reduce your risk exposure. In particular, we are trying to reduce the high variability in investor returns which characterizes common stocks. Most investors are averse to sharp swings in the return on their investments. That is, most prefer to avoid a situation where the return is sharply positive one period, then is decidedly negative in the next period.

Selecting stocks for satisfactory diversification is a complicated process which involves considerable work. While the actual process is beyond the scope of this book, we can give a highly simplified description to help you understand the central goal of diversification. First, by spreading your investment among several companies, you reduce the possibility of losing the entire investment should a major financial crisis occur because it is unlikely that all the companies would simultaneously encounter financial difficulty. Second, by selecting companies from different industries, the success of the investment is not solely dependent upon the fortunes of a single industry. Even more important, by selecting companies from industries that have different expansion and contraction cycles, the return on the total investment will be more stable. When one industry is contracting, providing low returns, another industry may be expanding, providing high returns. The more "opposite" the industries, the more stable the combined return will be. The greater the variety of industries in a diversified investment program, the more stable the combined return.

Diversifying among a number of stocks has several implications for investors. To benefit from diversification, an investor would have to buy 5 to 10 different stocks. The investor who lacks a sizable amount to invest will not be able to purchase the required number of different stocks. Also, investors must realize that the selection process is extremely complex because of the tremendous number of available companies. Another thing investors must understand is that spreading the investment among many issues may provide a stable return, but the return will probably not exceed the average return for the total market. For some investors, this possibility may offset the benefits of diversification.

Tax Features   When a stock has been held more than 6 months, any difference between its purchase and sale prices qualifies for the long-term capital gains tax rate, which is lower than the tax on short-term gains. This can be an attractive tax benefit on stocks which pay low dividends but have a good potential to appreciate in price.

The cash dividends on common stocks are taxed at the regular rate except that an investor can exclude the first $100 of dividends as tax-free ($200 on a qualifying joint return). When the dividend represents a partial liquidation of the firm (the firm is ceasing all or a portion of its operations), part of the dividend is not taxable. In addition, a portion of some utility companies' dividends are not taxable. (The sources in Exhibit 19-5 discuss this feature.)

Common Stocks: Strengths and Weaknesses

The principal strengths and weaknesses of common stocks are summarized in Exhibit 19–9.

Common Stocks: Suitable Investment Goals

Although common stocks have no set maturity, they are suitable for medium- to long-term investment goals. Theoretically, an ownership investment such as common stock should provide a reasonable hedge against inflation. However, the dismal performance of common stocks during the recent periods of double-digit inflation (10 percent or more) raises serious doubt about their ability to offset such inflationary periods. Unfortunately, the real return on fixed-income investments has also been poor during those same times. Until a definite pattern emerges, investors may be well advised to split their invest-

Exhibit 19-9   Common Stocks — Strengths and Weaknesses

Strengths	Weaknesses
Historically, return has averaged 9 percent; but during the most recent 5 years it has been much less than 9 percent.	Highly volatile return can have wide extremes.
Theoretically, stock is well-positioned as a hedge against inflation.	The minimum investment is high, owing to the sizable commission on purchase and sale.
A sizable part of the investor's return may qualify as long-term capital gains for income taxes.	The potential of a sharp price decline seriously limits flexibility, especially during a down market.
	Heavy investor involvement is required in initial purchase and ongoing management.
	Risk exposure ranges from moderate to substantial, depending on firm size, the industry involved, market trends, the firm's financing mix, management's capabilities, and other factors.

ments between common stocks and fixed-income securities when providing for their large medium- and long-term goals.

Common stocks expose the investor to considerable risk from several sources. Even with careful diversification, there will still be some risk exposure. Consequently, common stocks are not suitable for an investment goal whose outcome is critical.

The high cost of purchasing and selling small amounts of common stock make them better suited to investors who have already accumulated a reasonable amount of money (generally $1,000 or more). The flexibility of common stock investment depends on the current state of the market. Without question, you can always sell your stock, but if the total market is in a steep decline, you might have to sell at an enormous loss. You can often avoid having to sell when stock prices are heavily depressed if you anticipate your money needs. That is, if you will need money for one of your investment goals (purchase of a home, start of a college education) in the next few months, you may want to sell some common stock before the final due date, thereby avoiding a possible loss should prices decline over the next several months.

AVOIDING THE PAST EXCESSES IN THE STOCK MARKET

Perhaps we can learn from some of the things that happened in the stock market during the "swinging sixties."

Growth Stocks   In the early 1960s, growth stocks emerged as the route to stock market profits. No doubt some of the early electronics and technology stocks were true growth investments. But the investing public's thirst for growth stock, especially undiscovered ones, soon encouraged abuses. The heavy emphasis on scientific research during that period spilled over into the stock market. Investors would buy a corporation's stock if its name hinted of technology. Firms would change their names just to give the illusion of sophisticated technology and new scientific horizons. Thus, a firm which made electric toasters would change its name from Reliable Toaster Company to the more dynamic one of Electronic Heat-Centers Unlimited and continue to make toasters. Only later did it become painfully obvious that a toaster manufacturer, by any label, is still a toaster manufacturer. Investors who paid inflated prices for highly touted stock soon discovered how rapidly those prices could plummet.

New Issues Mania   The mid-1960s also saw a rush to invest in new, unknown, and oftentimes not yet operating companies. The emphasis was on investing in a small company, or a recently founded firm, which had good future potential. Here a vague, inspiring, and eye-catching name was absolutely essential. Thus, a company such as Thermo-Dytonics Research Specialities, Inc., would be warmly embraced by investors wanting to make a killing. It made little difference that no one had the foggiest notion of what Thermo-Dytonics really meant (it probably had no real meaning), that the company had no past record and probably no assets, and that the company's major product was not even ready to be marketed. Investors were convinced that if they bought the stock on the initial offering and waited, the price would rise to dazzling heights. And many early issues did exactly that. While not identical to the proverbial lemmings' rush over the cliff, investors' rush to their own investment destruction had some similarity. The whole speculative rush suddenly came to an end. Yesterday's hot issue became today's dreg. The price correction was quick, sharp, and ruthless. Investors who had entered the game late paid a high price and got nothing.

Conglomerate Boom   The new issue rage had hardly cooled before a new hot game opened down the street (Wall Street, of course). Its scheme for fame and fortune was plotted by a group of companies that launched an extensive acquisitions program. Their ploy was to acquire a host of widely different companies and combine them into a single giant conglomerate corporation. The buzzword of the time was synergism: by mixing the right parts, you made the whole larger than the sum of the individual parts. Contrary to the old math rule, 2 + 2 + 2 was going to equal 7. At least, that is how the game was supposed to work. Evidently a lot of investors had forgotten the new issues game because they lined up in droves to be sheared once more. By the middle 1960s, the game was moving faster and faster, yet the line of players who wanted part of the action continued to swell. Finally, in the late 1960s it all tumbled down in a massive correction. Prices on conglomerate stocks plunged more than 40 percent in less than 6 months.

Concept Stocks   The concept stocks came into vogue in the mid-1960s when everyone was searching for performance. Earning a steady, respectable return was not enough—everyone wanted a "superstar" stock. To qualify as a concept stock, the issuing company had to have an appealing concept coupled with an exciting story about the firm's great future. Most investors were never overly concerned about whether the company had demonstrated an ability to capitalize on the new concept. Good, hard, financial data gave way to glowing superlatives which kept investors captivated. The concept stock era came to an end when people began to ask: If it looks so great in theory, why has the company not demonstrated some of that superior performance?

The Moral?   If there is one thing that emerged from the 1960s, it is that investor's greed is truly insatiable. Most investors are willing to believe nearly anything as long as it promises to make them a lot of money. How could investors have protected themselves against these excesses? Apparently, they did not ask such searching questions as: What makes this stock worth its dazzling price? How long will it take before the firm's performance justifies the inflated price? Why is it worth several times what it was a few weeks ago? In short, a good measure of just plain common sense would have been enough protection. Certainly the market professionals would not have protected the investor. Most have the herd instinct: They will charge over any cliff as long as they think everyone else is going the same way. In the end, there is but one person who protects the investor from the current excess: a look in the mirror reveals that person.

SUMMARY

1 The ownership of a corporation is evidenced by its common stock. As owners, the common stock shareholders are entitled to the corporation's earnings.

2 The shareholder's return is a combination of the stock's cash dividend and any change in the stock's market price.

3 The real return—current return less rate of inflation—on common stock has been highest during periods of moderate inflation and lowest during periods of high inflation.

4 During the recent 10 years, common stocks have provided only a partial hedge against inflation.

5 Earnings per share and price-earnings ratio are frequently used to describe the valuation of a stock.

6 Most common stock purchases and sales involve previously issued shares that are currently traded in the secondary market.

7 The widely publicized market indexes—Dow Jones Industrial Average, Standard & Poor's 500, New York Stock Exchange Index—show the current state and the recent performance of a large, representative segment of the overall stock market.

8 There is considerable evidence that stock prices move in a random fashion. Thus, even a professional investor cannot predict changes in price with sufficient accuracy to earn a better-than-average return.

9 One possible stock selection technique is first to concentrate on identifying an industry with good future potential. Next, examine the companies within that industry to find a promising investment candidate.

10 Key factors that should be considered when evaluating a common stock include

earnings growth, price-earnings ratio, and relative ranking within its respective industry.

11 A good stockbroker should not only handle your transactions but also should furnish you with purchase recommendations and research reports on selected companies.

12 Under dollar-cost averaging, the individual regularly invests a set amount of money in a specific common stock.

13 By diversifying among different common stocks, investors can reduce their risk exposure.

14 Investing in common stock generally involves a sizable time commitment, exposes the investor to considerable risk, subjects the investor to potentially sharp price declines, and often provides a volatile rate of return.

REVIEW YOUR UNDERSTANDING OF

Common stock shareholders' rights
    Corporate earnings
    Liquidation
Cash dividend
Market price change
Stock dividend
Stock split
Earnings per share (EPS)
Price-earnings ratio (P/E)
Stock market indexes
Blue chip stock
Growth stock
Speculative stock

Markets for common stock
    Primary market
    Secondary market
Fundamental value approach
Technical factors approach
Earnings growth
Round lot
Churning
Buy and hold
Short-term trading
Dollar-cost averaging
Systematic investment plans
Diversification

DISCUSSION QUESTIONS

1 If the general public were asked what annual rate of return a common stock investment should yield, do you think the most frequent answer would be: (a) less than 10 percent, (b) between 10 and 20 percent, (c) more than 20 percent? Do you think those expectations are realistic? Why?

2 Are there advantages to the corporate form of organization? How do they affect the corporation's shareholders?

3 While Susan Smith was commuting to work, her seatmate recommended she buy Last Ditch Gold Mines stock because it was a sure thing. What suggestions would you have for Susan? How could she check this "hot tip"?

4 What is the difference between a blue chip stock and a growth stock? Which investors would likely be best satisfied with a blue chip stock? With a growth stock?

5 Who is entitled to a corporation's earnings? Who decides what part of the earnings is paid as dividends? What factors affect the pay-out decision?

6 During the past 5 years, XQ Plastics has grown rapidly and has paid no cash dividends. But it has paid a 10 percent stock dividend each year. In addition, there was a 2 for 1 stock split 3 years ago. How do these actions affect the shareholder?

Has the shareholders' dividend return been 10 percent? Why? Why would a company declare a stock dividend or split?

7 Why should a common stock be a good hedge during an inflationary period? Has recent experience supported this contention? Why?

8 How would a current shareholder benefit from the earnings retained in the company? How would the benefit be reflected in the shareholder's return?

9 Assume the evening newscast reported the Dow Jones Industrial Average rose 5 points that day. What does that mean? How could you use that information? What is the reason for having a Dow Jones Industrial Average?

10 Specialty Products' earnings per share was $5 and its price-earnings ratio was 8.0 for the current year. What do those two numbers mean? Would you need further information to use them effectively? Why?

11 What is meant by the statement that stock prices move randomly? What implication does this theory have for an investor? How does it affect stock selection techniques?

12 Compare and contrast selecting a common stock by using fundamental values with selecting one by using technical factors.

13 How can an investor develop potential investment opportunities? What factors would you examine when evaluating an industry?

14 What should you look for when selecting a stockbroker? How can you judge whether a broker is doing a good job?

15 What are the advantages to diversifying your stock investments? Are there disadvantages and constraints?

16 When selecting a company from an industry, should the emphasis be on the largest firm? Why? What information sources could be used to help you decide which firm you should select?

17 What are the advantages of dollar-cost averaging? Are there disadvantages? What investors should use dollar-cost averaging?

18 During the two years Ralph Keep has held Zip Products stock, its price has risen from $6 per share to $23; its price-earnings ratio started at 6 and now stands at 24. Ralph is uncertain whether he sould sell or hold. How should he decide? Why?

CASE PROBLEM

Bill and Jan Stien are considering investing their $2,000 savings account in common stocks. While they earn $26,000 annually, their savings have averaged only $500 each year because they have needed much of their income to pay the high rent on their luxury apartment, to cover their extensive travel, and to trade one of their two cars each year for a new one. Bill and Jan have heard that common stocks are where the action is. And they feel the breathtaking stock returns will encourage them to save more. They have identified three investment goals they will use common stocks for:

a A temporary cash fund of $500

b A $2,000 fund for Jan to complete a graduate degree beginning 2 years from now

c Accumulate $4,000 for a down payment when they purchase a house in 4 years

Given their limited savings, they feel they need to earn 25 to 30 percent a year on their stock investments. Based on that return, they have estimated the following 4-year savings plan:

	1st year	2d year	3d year	4th year
Beginning investments balance	$2,000	$3,000	$2,250	$3,313
Earnings on balance (25 percent)	500	750	563	828
Total	$2,500	$3,750	$2,813	$4,141
Add: New savings for the year	+ 500	+ 500	+ 500	+ 500
Less: Withdrawals	− 0	−2,000	− 0	−4,000
Ending investment's balance	$3,000	$2,250	$3,313	$ 641

The Stiens are undecided about which stock they should select. Bill favors conservative stocks while Jan believes they should aim for the highest return by selecting stocks which might have a high return. Their current list of stocks includes the following (all "hot tips"):

Stock	Earnings growth, 5-year average	Price range over past 3 years	Current information per share			Business activity
			Price	Earnings	Dividend	
A	5 percent	$15–$25	$20	$3.33	$2.00	Gas and electric utility
B	No record; firm has operated 3 years	$5–$42	$40	$1.00	0	Franchisor for gambling casinos
C	10 percent	$50–$85	$75	$3.75	$2.25	Soft-drink manufacturer
D	6 percent	$30–$90	$50	$3.33	$2.50	Auto manufacturer
E	Not meaningful; firm had no earnings	$0.25–$1.35	$ 1	0	0	Gold mining

a What are the strengths and weaknesses of the Stiens' plan to begin investing in common stock?

b Do you feel certain types of stocks are more suited to each of their three investment goals? (You need not restrict yourself to their list.) Why?

c Is their projected savings plan a good one? Are any changes needed? What impact would those changes have?

d While the information in their list of stocks is extremely limited, what strengths and weaknesses do you see in each one? Do these stocks match their goals? Why?

e What other information, if any, should they have on the stocks in their list? Where can it be obtained?

f What parts of the Stiens' investment plan need major revision? Why? What changes would you recommend?

RECOMMENDED READINGS

Books

Engle, Louis, *How to Buy Stocks*, 5th ed., New York: Bantam Books, 1971.

A basic book that covers all aspects of investing in common stocks. Written for easy reading by anyone. A free copy can be obtained by writing: Merrill Lynch, Pierce, Fenner & Smith, Inc., 70 Pine Street, New York 10005.

Cohen, Jerome B., Edward D. Zinbarg, and Arthur Zeikel, *Investment Analysis and Portfolio Management*, Homewood, Ill.: Irwin, 1973.
Chapter 13 has a good discussion of technical analysis.

Malkiel, Barton G., *A Random Walk Down Wall Street*, Norton, New York, 1973.
A well-written, frequently witty introduction to the stock market. The book is easy to read, even for nonbusiness types. It discusses the major problem areas and pitfalls to avoid when investing in common stocks. For a reader short on time, chapters 5, 6, 7, and 8 are highly recommended.

Sauvain, Harry C., *Investment Management*, Englewood Cliffs, N.J.: Prentice-Hall, 1973.
Chapter 18 has a good discussion of diversification.

Amling, Frederick, *Investments*, 3d ed., Englewood Cliffs, N.J.: Prentice-Hall, 1974.
Chapter 6 discusses common stocks as a potential investment. A broker's function, responsibility, and general operation are covered in chapter 9.

Bellemore, Douglas H., and John C. Ritchie, *Investments*, Cincinnati: South-Western Publishing Co., Inc., 1974.
Chapter 12 contains a good discussion of fundamental analysis. Chapter 30 discusses several investment strategies for selecting common stocks.

D'Ambrosio, Charles A., *Principles of Modern Investing*, Palo Alto, Calif.: Science Research, 1976.
Chapter 13 has a good discussion of how to place a value on a particular common stock. Technical analysis and the random walk are discussed in chapter 14.

Magazines

Money:

Quint, Barbara, "What Your Broker Doesn't Know Can Hurt You." September 1973, pp. 39–41.
Reviews the problems and damages an inadequately trained broker can cause.

Malkiel, Burton, "An Unacademic Course in Stocks." October 1973, pp. 48–53.
Describes the author's four basic guidelines for investing in common stocks.

"It's a Bond, It's a Stock, It's a Convertible." July 1974, pp. 72–74.
Reviews the basics of convertible bonds.

Changing Times:

"How Do Brokers Treat Small Investors?" July 1973, pp. 25–28.
Examines how brokers treat small investors.

"10 Ways to Buy Stock a Little at a Time." November 1973, pp. 39–42.
Examines 10 ways for buying common stock in small amounts.

"Stocks: There's a Time to Sell, Too." March 1974, pp. 10–13.
Discusses possible reasons for selling.

"Which Stock Market Index Do You Read?" June 1974, pp. 43–46.
Examines the different stock market indexes.

"Do You Belong in the Stock Market?" June 1975, pp. 7–11.
Discusses the preliminaries to entering the stock market. Provides guidelines for investors to decide whether they belong in the stock market.

Booklets

How to Understand Financial Statements
   Discusses key points of financial statements. A single copy can be obtained from:
   New York Stock Exchange, 11 Wall Street, New York 10005.
How to Invest
   Discusses the buying and selling of bonds and common stocks. A copy is available
   from: Merrill Lynch, Pierce, Fenner & Smith, Inc., 70 Pine Street, New York
   10005.
How You Get More Out of Financial News
   Reviews the basic knowledge needed to interpret financial news. A copy can be
   obtained from: Dow Jones & Company, Inc., The Educational Service Bureau,
   P.O. Box 300, Princeton, N.J. 10854.

Chapter 20

Mutual Funds and Professional Investment Management

After completing this chapter you should be able to:

define the different types of mutual funds.

explain the advantages and disadvantages of mutual funds as investments.

select a mutual fund which is compatible with your investment objectives.

recognize the impact of the load or commission charge on the net investment.

recall the major reference sources for evaluating mutual funds.

explain how mutual funds can be used to reduce federal income taxes.

illustrate under what conditions mutual fund redemption insurance is worthwhile.

identify the services offered by mutual funds.

analyze mutual fund performance data to determine which are the better performing funds.

compare mutual funds and investment clubs to decide which investment alternative is best for your purposes.

recall the advantages and disadvantages of the investment services of a bank trust department.

During a subcommittee investigation of the mutual fund industry, a United States senator introduced a portfolio he had selected by throwing darts at a page of stock listings from *The Wall Street Journal*. The "portfolio" selected by the darts outperformed nearly all the funds being investigated by the subcommittee. This example of random stock selection was a dramatic and humorous way of saying something about the investment research of institutional investors. The evidence shows, conclusively, that randomly selected portfolios will do as well as carefully selected ones.

Investors in mutual funds pay a management fee for the privilege of having their money invested by professionals who cannot seem to do as well as somebody throwing darts at a page from *The Wall Street Journal*. The fee is generally about ½ of 1 percent of the value of the fund, whether or not the fund performs well. And the manager still collects. Despite these negative aspects, total assets of the mutual fund industry now exceed $35 billion, and over 10 million people own shares in mutual funds. The industry has diminished somewhat in the last few years, but mutual funds still represent a significant investment alternative for many people.

To be precise, a mutual fund is an investment company and the terms are sometimes used interchangeably. In this chapter, we will use the more commonly accepted name, mutual funds, in all instances.

WHAT ARE MUTUAL FUNDS?

Mutual funds are an indirect way of investing in the stock market. Rather than buy common stocks directly, investors entrust their money to a manager who will do the investing for them. Evidence of ownership is shares in the mutual fund, which in turn are backed by the fund's investments. If the fund's investments fare well, the mutual fund shares will perform equally as well, less the management fee which must be paid to the fund's advisors.

The value of a mutual fund share is determined by the fund's net asset value (NAV), or the total sum of the value of each of the fund's investments. The value of a share is found by dividing the total value by the number of shares issued by the fund. For example, if a fund is divided into 1,000 shares and the fund owns 100 shares of General Motors, 100 shares of Gulf Oil, and 100 shares of General Foods, the net asset can be calculated as follows:

Portfolio of XYZ Mutual Fund

Number of shares	Stock	Price per share	Total
100	General Motors	$45	$ 4,500
100	Gulf Oil	25	2,500
100	General Foods	30	3,000
		Total	$10,000

$$\frac{\text{Total Value of Fund}}{\text{Number of Shares Issued}} = \frac{\$10,000}{1,000} = \$10 \text{ per share net asset value}$$

Each person buying shares in the mutual fund has a prorata interest in each of the fund's investments. That means a person who owns 1 percent of the fund in effect owns 1 percent of the fund's General Motors stock, 1 percent of the fund's Gulf Oil stock, and 1 percent of the fund's General Foods stock. If those stocks increase in value, the fund's net asset value will rise and the fund's shares will increase proportionately.

For open-end funds (to be discussed later), the first price shown in the newspaper is the fund's net asset value. The second is the net asset value plus any sales commission. An example of the price quotations for mutual funds is shown in Exhibit 20-1.

Distributions to Shareholders

Investors purchase mutual funds expecting to earn a return on their investment. The return from mutual funds can come in three ways: dividends, capital gains distributions, and price appreciation.

Dividends By law, to retain their tax-exempt status, mutual funds must distribute to their stockholders 95 percent of all the income they receive. Either semiannually or quarterly, a mutual fund will pay its holders a dividend from the income received from its investments. The amount of income depends largely on the objective of the fund—the growth funds generally pay far less in dividends than funds which seek high current income. Dividends from mutual funds are usually treated exactly as corporate dividends for tax purposes. That is, they usually qualify for the $100 dividend exclusion. Any exceptions to this must be noted by the fund on the tax information statement sent to the fundholders annually.

Capital Gains Distributions If a mutual fund sells securities at a higher price than it paid for them, the gain will be distributed to the fundholders and is called a "capital gains distribution."

If the securities were held for more than 6 months, fundholders pay taxes on capital gains distributions at the capital gains tax rate, which is generally half the rate on ordinary income. If the gain was short term, it will be distributed as a dividend, but it is entirely taxable as ordinary income; no part of it is excludable from the first $100 of taxable dividends as corporate dividends are.

Price Appreciation Any changes in a fund's investments will be reflected in its net asset value and consequently in its market price. The potential that a fund's market price will appreciate substantially is what makes funds an

Exhibit 20-1   Typical Mutual Fund Newspaper Price Quotations

Mutual Funds, Friday, December 31, 1976

	Buy	Sell	Change
Allied Fund	10.23	11.17	+.03
Arctic Investors	5.21	5.21	+.08
Baloney Fund	23.81	26.02	+.83
Broadway Fund	11.02	11.02	−.05
Go For Broke	3.21	3.21	−.83
Zilch Fund	4.25	4.64	+.15

attractive investment. However, it is a two-way street, and the market price of funds can fall just as easily as it can increase in value.

The increase in a fund's price per share is realized at the time an investor redeems her or his shares. If the fund shares have been held more than 6 months, the difference between the redemption price and the cost of the shares is treated as a long-term gain. If the fund has been held less than 6 months, the gain is short term and thus taxable at ordinary income tax rates.

Types of Mutual Funds

For our purposes in this book, we will classify mutual funds according to two things: their investment objectives, and whether they charge a commission or sell their shares direct to the investor. Since there are over 600 active mutual funds, it is important to be able to differentiate the funds in order to select the best one to meet your objectives.

Investment Objectives   Mutual funds are required by law to state their investment objective. If you decide to purchase a fund, your first step is to narrow the choices to funds which have objectives consistent with your own goals. Mutual funds can be divided into three main categories on the basis of their stated objectives: funds that stress income; funds that attempt to provide both income and growth; and funds that stress only growth.

Balanced or Income Funds   A balanced fund typically holds one-third of its invested assets in bonds and preferred stocks. The other two-thirds of the fund's investments are usually diversified across more than 100 different common stocks. Balanced funds seek to minimize risk and conserve principal. These funds are conservatively managed and do not seek high-return investments which are risky.

Income and Growth Funds   The income and growth funds take a middle-of-the-road approach in selecting between high returns and low risks. As their name implies, these funds seek income from capital gains and dividends, but they do not invest in high-risk situations even though the returns may be higher.

Growth Funds   Growth funds, which are also called "go-go" or "performance" funds, seek to maximize their returns at high risk. The prospectuses of these funds usually refer to the fact that risks will be assumed in pursuit of high capital gains. Of course, these funds also seek income from dividends, but that is secondary to their main objective of growth through capital gains.[1]

Other Types of Funds   In addition to these three basic types of funds, there are a number of funds with unique characteristics and objectives.

Bond Funds   Bond funds invest exclusively in corporate bonds rather than common stocks. Their objective is high income accompanied by small risk. Bond funds represent a possible investment vehicle for people who need high current income and are not concerned with the possibility of price appreciation.

[1]Jack Clark Francis, *Investments: Analysis and Management*, New York: McGraw-Hill, 1972, p. 475.

Preferred Stock Funds   The objectives of the preferred stock funds are similar to those of the bond funds. The major difference is that these funds restrict their investments to preferred stock rather than corporate bonds.

Specialized Funds   Rather than hold a diversified portfolio of common stocks, the specialized funds concentrate their investments in one or two industries. For example, there are specialized funds which hold primarily gold stocks, and others which restrict their investments to shares of stock of companies that produce chemicals and drugs. The specialized funds have shown remarkable results from time to time. They do so, however, at the expense of violating the basic investment objective of diversification. Consequently, owning a specialized fund is advisable only if it represents a small portion of an individual's total investment portfolio. Placing all your money in a specialized fund is the same as buying stock in only one industry. It is like speculation, rather than investing.

Money Market Funds   The high interest rates of the past few years provided the incentive for the development of funds which invest exclusively in short-term, high-yielding securities. Examples of the securities they buy are Treasury bills and commercial paper. These types of securities cannot be purchased by the average small investor since the minimum transaction is usually $100,000. Although interest rates on savings accounts are controlled by regulation, the rates on money market investments are freely determined by supply and demand. At one point, when the rate on passbook savings accounts was limited to 5 percent, commercial paper was yielding 13 to 14 percent.

Money market funds permit small investors to realize the returns ordinarily realized only by wealthy individuals or institutional investors. Most money market funds will open an account for as little as $500 or $1,000. They provide immediate access to the money by giving investors checks which they can write against the balance in their accounts. These features give the investor the ability to participate in high-yielding, short-term investments, and, at the same time, they provide the same liquidity that is available in passbook savings accounts. There is undoubtedly a bit more risk in these funds than there is in a savings account because savings deposits are insured and funds are not. To date, however, that risk has been only theoretical since none of the funds has defaulted on shareholders' accounts.

> **Strategy: The money market funds are appropriate for investors needing high current income without the risk of losing their principal. They also are an attractive investment for the short-term portion of an individual's savings program. They can be used in lieu of a passbook savings account or certificates of deposit for all but the emergency reserve portion of savings.**

Exhibit 20–2 summarizes the types of mutual funds, based on their investment objectives. The exhibit shows the kinds of investments the funds purchase to achieve their objectives, and indicates the type of investor who may find them appropriate.

Exhibit 20-2   Mutual Funds: Their Objectives, Investments, and Recommended Investors

Type	Objective	Investments	Type of investor
Balanced	Conservation of principal	One-third bonds, two-third stocks	Older, income-oriented
Income-growth	Moderate growth with income	Common stocks (blue chip)	Middle-aged, conservative
Growth	High growth, low income	Common stocks (speculative)	Younger, aggressive
Bond	Income	Bonds	Older, income-oriented
Preferred stock	Income	Preferred stock	Older, income-oriented (bond funds are better)
Specialized	Various	Gold stocks, specialized industry stocks, convertible bonds, etc.	Depending on objective, but should be only a small portion of investments
Money market	Income and safety of principal	Money market instruments	Anyone needing income and safety

Other Ways of Classifying Funds   Mutual funds may also be classified according to whether they charge a sales commission (commonly called a loading charge) or sell the shares with no sales charge. Mutual funds are further classified as closed-end funds, which have a fixed number of outstanding shares, or as open-end funds, which will continuously sell shares as long as there are buyers. A final type is the dual purpose fund, which tries to realize both income and capital appreciation objectives. Each of these types of funds is discussed more fully in this section.

Load versus No-Load—or Don't Give Your Money Away.   The biggest mistake you can make in buying a mutual fund is paying a commission, or "load." The mutual fund industry comprises funds which are sold by sales agents who receive a commission for their efforts, and funds which are sold directly to the investors. No-load funds do not charge a commission. Thus, every dollar you invest will go toward investment, not toward an agent's commissions.

The standard commission is $85 per $1,000 investment. This works out to a true rate of 9.28 percent, since the commission is actually charged on a net investment of $915 ($85 ÷ $915 = 9.28 percent). The commission is reduced for larger purchases, but for most investors who will be investing small amounts, the rate will remain at 9.28 percent. If paying a commission would help you realize better investment results, it would certainly be worthwhile. Unfortunately, there is no evidence that load funds provide higher returns than no-load funds. Consequently, if you decide to buy a load mutual fund you are, in effect, throwing money away.

EXCUSE ME, MR. HARRIS...
COULD I ASK YOU A QUESTION
ABOUT THE AMOUNT OF COMMISSION
YOU GET FROM MY MUTUAL FUND?

If you decide to buy a mutual fund, the burden of finding a no-load fund is yours. Brokers who handle mutual funds will not provide assistance since they do not receive a commission from the transactions. Specialized mutual fund sales agents are also reluctant to help people save money for the same reason.

Information on no-load funds may be obtained from the sources listed at the end of this chapter. In addition, there will quite often be small ads for no-load funds in *The Wall Street Journal*, *Barron's*, and the financial pages of major metropolitan newspapers. Some idea of the range of funds available can be obtained by sending for the prospectuses (formal offering statements) for the funds that advertise in this manner.

> **Strategy: There are virtually no situations where a load mutual fund should be purchased in preference to a no-load fund. The addresses of all no-load mutual funds can be obtained from the sources listed at the end of this chapter under Recommended Readings.**

Front-End Loads   One of the most sharply criticized practices of the mutual fund industry has been the use of front-end loads, in conjunction with contractual investment plans. Under the terms of a contractual plan, an individual agrees to invest a set amount for a 10-year period. If the plan calls for a $1,000 annual payment, the investor signing an agreement commits himself to a $10,000 plan. The contract is nonbinding and may be broken by the investor at any time. To make the plans attractive for the salesforce to sell, the funds agree to pay the salespersons 50 percent of the total commission in the first year. The total commission on a contractual plan such as this would be $850. Thus, an investor paying $1,000 into the plan during the first year is actually paying $425 of that amount for the salesperson's commission. This amount is called the "front-end load." An investor stopping the plan after one year will have paid an effective commission of 73.9 percent. The calculation is as follows:

$$\frac{\text{Commission}}{\text{Net Investment}} = \frac{\$425}{\$575} = 73.9 \text{ percent}$$

The major problem with contractual plans has been that the majority of investors fail to see the plan through to completion. Therefore, in most cases, the effective commission rates on these plans are very high, making them an extremely poor investment.

> **Strategy: If you want to start a regular mutual fund investment program, do it on a voluntary basis with a no-load fund. With a contractual plan, you risk the loss of the front-end load if you are forced to drop out of the plan.**

Open-End and Closed-End Funds   Another way of dividing the mutual fund industry is based on the fund's policy toward issuing and redeeming shares.

Open-end funds continuously offer to sell and redeem shares. The shares are sold at net asset value plus commission, if any, and are redeemed at net asset value minus a service charge, if any. Open-end funds predominate in the industry.

Closed-end funds have a set number of shares. After a closed-end fund has been organized and its shares have initially been sold to investors, the fund will neither sell any more shares nor redeem its outstanding shares. Transactions do not take place between the investor and the fund. Rather, if you want to buy shares in a closed-end fund, you will have to purchase them from a person who is willing to sell. If you would like to redeem shares, you will have to find a buyer. The process is not as difficult as it seems, since most of the closed-end funds are traded on the New York Stock Exchange or in the over-the-counter market.

Strategy: Most investors should limit their purchases to no-load open-end mutual funds. You must pay a commission to buy closed-end funds and they have no distinct advantage over the open funds.

Dual-Purpose Funds   Dual-purpose funds try to achieve two investment objectives simultaneously—income and capital growth—and they offer investors the opportunity to participate in either objective. The funds' total shares are divided into two groups.

Exactly one-half the shares are designated income shares. Investors buy these shares with the understanding that (1) the fund will redeem them in the future, say 10 or 15 years, at a certain value (e.g., the original purchase price); and (2) all the entire fund's dividends during that period are distributed only to one-half the fund's shareholders—the capital shareholders.

The other half of the shares are designated capital shares. Investors buy capital shares with the understanding that they will receive no dividends during the 10- or 15-year period, but that the fund's entire capital growth, that is, the increase in the fund's total asset value, at the end of the time will be distributed only to one-half the fund's shareholders—the capital shareholders.

A numerical example should help to clarify these relationships. Assume the XYZ Fund sold 1 million shares at $10 per share; one-half were capital shares and one-half were income shares. Thus the fund started out with total asset value at $10 million and 500,000 income shares and 500,000 capital shares. Every year for 10 years the fund received $500,000 in dividends. This is a 5 percent annual dividend yield on the fund's total asset value. But, remember that all income goes to the income shareholders. Therefore they will receive $1 per share, which is a 10 percent return on their investment of $10 for each share. Now we will also assume that during the 10 years, the value of the fund's total assets increased by 100 percent. At the end of the tenth year the fund had $20 million. At that time the income shares were redeemed at $10 each, for a total of $5 million. That leaves $15 million for the capital shareholders. The capital shares, originally purchased for $10, now have a net asset value of $30. The total fund has increased in value by only 100 percent, but the capital shareholders' investment has grown 200 percent.

The magnification of gains by using others' money is called "leverage." In effect, both the shareholder groups had twice the amount of money working for them that they had originally invested. In this example, both the income shareholders and the capital shareholders had others' money working for them for different purposes. Leverage benefited both groups. It could have worked the opposite way, however. That is the danger in investing in dual-purpose funds.

ADVANTAGES OF MUTUAL FUNDS

Mutual funds provide investment services and record-keeping services which many investors find quite valuable. The more important ones are discussed in this section.

Diversification   The primary reason to buy mutual funds is to obtain diversification. Chapter 19 stressed that adequate diversification was critical to protecting your investment dollars. For a person with limited resources, such diversification is virtually impossible to achieve. Since it takes between 10 and 15 different stocks to approximate reasonable diversification, a small investor would have to purchase fewer stocks or stocks in lots of less than 100 shares. The commission on small purchases is much higher as a percentage of the transaction than when larger amounts are involved. As a result, commission costs would increase to the point that an adequate return would be impossible to achieve.

Mutual funds achieve diversification by holding 30 to 50 or more stocks. Consequently, unless the fund is concentrated in volatile, risky securities, its investment performance should not be too much different from a randomly selected stock portfolio. It is important to be aware of the type of fund that is being purchased, since the more aggressive funds will tend to perform better than the market in up markets—and worse than average in down markets.

Diversification is nothing more than the adage of "Don't put all your eggs in the same basket." If you would prefer not to be so conservative and, instead, to concentrate your money in one or two investments, this advantage of mutual funds is of little value.

Professional Management   Despite the lackluster performance of most mutual funds, some of them can make a strong argument that the professional management an investor receives is worthwhile. A conservatively managed fund will never make you rich, but most likely it will do a reasonably good job of preserving your capital. The fund managers usually avoid the major mistakes which investors make, such as overconcentration in a few stocks.

Investing in a mutual fund frees investors of the daily worry of managing their portfolios. The money can simply be turned over to the fund and then ignored. For many people, this aspect of mutual funds is well worth the management fee levied on each account. It relieves them of making investment decisions and ensures avoidance of disastrous outcomes.

Dollar-Cost Averaging   Regularly investing a fixed amount in a mutual fund will give the investor the benefits of dollar-cost averaging. Dollar-cost averaging means that each dollar you invest will buy more shares when the price is low, thus effectively lowering the average price of each share you hold. Dollar-cost averaging is advantageous no matter whether the market is falling or rising. Exhibit 20–3 shows the results of hypothetical investments made in each type of market.

Note that the effective average price per share is $5.92 in the declining market and $10.53 in the rising market. These prices represent the break-even points; by comparing these average prices with the current market price, you can determine how much profit or loss your investment represents. The secret of dollar-cost averaging is investing the same dollar amount each time, not buying the same number of shares.

Exhibit 20-3   Examples of Dollar Cost Averaging in Declining and Rising Stock Markets

	Declining market	
Amount invested	Price per share	Number of shares purchased
$100	$10.00	10
$100	8.00	12.5
$100	5.00	20.0
$100	4.00	25.0
Total $400		67.5
Average price during period	$ 6.75	
Average price paid = $400 ÷ 67.5 = $5.92		

	Rising market	
Amount invested	Price per share	Number of shares purchased
$100	$ 8.00	12.50
$100	10.00	10.00
$100	12.00	8.33
$100	14.00	7.14
Total $400		37.97
Average price during period	$11.00	
Average price paid = $400 ÷ 37.97 = $10.53		

Continuing a dollar-cost averaging program requires self-discipline. Most people tend to be very enthusiastic when the stock market is rising (a bull market), but lose the courage of their convictions in a declining market (a bear market). Actually, they should be more enthusiastic in a declining market because the investments made near the bottom of the market are the ones that ultimately produce the satisfactory returns.

Reduction in Record Keeping   Buying a mutual fund instead of a diversified list of common stocks substantially reduces an investor's record-keeping chores. Instead of having to record information for 10 to 15 different securities, you need to keep records for only one fund. Moreover, most of the mutual funds perform the record keeping for you. A typical mutual fund statement shows total shares held, the price paid for each share, and the date acquired. Annually, the fund reports the amounts paid as dividends and capital gains distributions. All the investor must do is keep the statements filed, chronologically, to have all the information needed for tax returns. Many investors find this simple record keeping is an advantage offered by mutual funds.

Automatic Reinvestment   Mutual funds will automatically reinvest all dividends and/or capital gains distributions of the fund for investors. Many funds have a minimum investment requirement, such as $250, which limits an investor's ability to make small increments to her or his holdings. The fund waives this requirement when a shareholder elects the automatic reinvestment feature. Thus, when the fund declares a dividend, it is automatically reinvested to purchase shares for the investor; the investor gets the benefit of immediate reinvestment with no additional paperwork and transaction costs.

This feature is particularly attractive to younger fundholders trying to accumulate capital. It will be inappropriate for older investors, such as retired people who rely on dividend income as one of their principal sources of support. For these people, the systematic withdrawal plan may be more appropriate.

Systematic Withdrawal   With systematic withdrawal, the mutual fund will pay a fixed amount each month to the shareholder. A typical withdrawal arrangement calls for a $50 monthly payment for each $10,000 in the fund. Each monthly payment is paid from whatever dividends and capital gains distributions are due to the investor. If the dividends and capital gains are not enough to make up the fixed payments, the difference is taken from the investor's principal. Theoretically, the fund should grow in value by an amount that is sufficient to cover the invasion of principal. In rising markets, this has been true. Investors have been able to receive a 6 percent return and still have their investments grow in value. In declining markets, the systematic withdrawal plans have not been nearly so successful. Over a 10- or 15-year period, however, a systematic withdrawal plan should produce favorable results.

Systematic withdrawal is not a good plan for people who must maximize income while minimizing risk or who must preserve their capital. The possibility exists that the invasion of principal, coupled with a declining stock market, could seriously erode the investor's capital.

Special Uses for Funds

Mutual funds may be used for two special-purpose investments which you should consider because they provide unique tax advantages.

Accounts for Children   Shares may be purchased for children under the Uniform Gifts to Minors Act. Since the child owns the fund, any dividends and capital gains distributions are paid to the child. In most cases, the child will not have sufficient income, either from these payments or other income, to have a tax liability. Thus, fund shares held in this manner provide a good way to build a college fund by avoiding taxes. If enough money is put in the fund to provide $1,000 per year in income, the tax savings would be $300 for parents in a 30 percent marginal tax bracket. Investing thus for several children can substantially reduce family taxes while helping to build money for college educations.

Retirement Accounts   Self-employed people may now contribute 15 percent of their income up to a maximum of $7,500 each year to a tax-sheltered retirement fund. The contribution is made before taxes and reduces adjusted gross income. These self-employed retirement programs may be invested in mutual funds.

Employed individuals who are not covered under a pension plan may set up an Individual Retirement Account (IRA) and contribute a maximum $1,500 per year on a tax-sheltered basis. These accounts may also be invested in mutual fund shares.

For both types of retirement accounts, the initial contribution is exempt from income taxes, and all dividends and all capital gains are exempt from income taxes while the plan is in existence. When the person retires, all payments are subject to taxes.

Summary of Mutual Fund Advantages   These advantages and services of mutual funds are summarized in Exhibit 20–4. Each of the items in the exhibit has some value for any investor. In total, they make a strong case for individuals to consider mutual funds as an investment alternative.

THE PAST RECORD

Mutual funds' recent performance record is disappointing compared with general stock market averages. However, it is superior to investments in savings accounts, bonds, or other fixed-income securities.

Individual Fund Performance

A good place to start your investigation for a fund is by comparing the past performance of individual funds. An example of the information available on funds is shown in Exhibit 20–5. This exhibit is a page from *Forbes* magazine,

Exhibit 20-4   Summary of Mutual Fund Advantages and Services

Advantage	Accomplishments	Advantageous for (type of investor)
Diversification	Spreads the risk	Small (under $50,000)
Professional management	Removes the burden of watching individual investments	Nonsophisticated
Dollar-cost averaging	Removes wide price fluctuations	Younger; trying to accumulate capital
Record keeping	Provides periodic, up-to-date reports to the fundholder	All
Automatic reinvestment	Reinvests dividends and capital gains at no transaction costs	Younger; trying to accumulate capital
Systematic withdrawal	Permits a high monthly income using dividends, capital gains, and principal value	Older, income-oriented
Custody accounts	Money may be invested for minors, thus reducing family tax liability	All with children, trying to save for college
Retirement accounts	A method of accumulating tax-sheltered retirement funds, when the individual qualifies	Self-employed and people without pension plans

Exhibit 20-5 Fund Ratings—1975

| Performance ratings | | | Dollar results | | | Total assets | | Maximum | Annual |
In UP markets	In DOWN markets		Latest 12 months	9-year average annual growth rate	Dividend return	6/30/75 in millions	% change 1975 vs. 1974	sales charge	expenses per $100
—	—	Standard & Poor's 500 Stock Average	10.7%	0.1%	4.0%				
C	C	FORBES Stock Fund Average	13.8%	−0.5%	3.1%				
		STOCK FUNDS (NO-LOAD)							
C	B	Energy Fund..............	29.6%	2.0%	3.1%	$154.7	32.9	none	$0.79
D	D	Farm Bureau Mutual Fund....	9.3	−2.7	3.0	10.6	17.8	none	1.04
·C	··F	Financial Dynamics Fund .... (started 9/67)	30.8	—	1.8	37.0	30.3	none	0.90
C	D	Financial Industrial Fund	13.0	−0.4	4.1	247.0	13.7	none	0.68
C	B	Financial Industrial Income Fund.	26.8	3.8	5.6	98.2	26.9	none	0.73
·D	··B	First Multifund of America ... (started 10/67)	12.0	—	3.6	14.0	11.1	none	2.13
·C	·B	Fleming Berger Fund (started 4/69) .	5.1	—	none	2.4	−17.2	none	1.50
··A	·F	44 Wall Street Fund (started 7/69) ...	57.5	—	none	5.0	284.6	none	2.36
C	D	Foursquare Fund............	13.1	−2.3	2.4	6.2	3.3	none	2.60
··B	·C	Fund for Mutual Depositors........ (started 8/69)	17.2	—	2.1	20.4	20.7	none	0.81
D	C	General Securities............	29.4	−4.0	3.3	7.5	41.5	none	1.46
B	D	Growth Industry Shares	12.1	0.9	1.2	37.3	9.1	none	0.86
C	A	Guardian Mutual Fund.........	21.1	2.6	4.5	57.7	20.0	none	0.76
·B	··F	Hartwell Growth Fund (started 1/67) .	22.6	—	none	5.1	10.9	none	2.90
··C	··D	Hartwell Leverage Fund (started 9/68).	40.7	—	none	6.7	21.8	none	3.70
··D	··F	Hedge Fund of America (started 2/68).	16.2	—	none	8.4	6.3	†	3.01

·Fund rated for one period only; maximum allowable rating A.

*Formerly Side Fund.

†Fund no longer selling new shares; existing shares traded over-the-counter.

··Fund rated for two periods only; maximum allowable rating A.

#Fee paid to fund.

Exhibit 20-5 Fund Ratings—1975 (continued)

| Performance ratings | | | Dollar results | | | Total assets | | | |
In UP markets	In DOWN markets		Latest 12 months	9-year average annual growth rate	Dividend return	6/30/75 in millions	% change 1975 vs. 1974	Maximum sales charge	Annual expenses per $100
B	F	The Heritage Fund	36.8%	—	none	$ 0.7	40.0	†	$7.00
C	D	Herold Fund (started 3/68)	17.6	—	1.6%	4.2	−2.3	1.00%#	1.32
C	C	Investment Guidance Fund (started 6/68)	22.1	—	2.2	2.3	21.1	none	1.57
A	F	Ivy Fund	10.5	3.6%	2.0	40.1	11.1	none	1.40
B	A	Janus Fund (started 2/70)	12.3	—	5.3	37.3	32.3	none	1.48
A	D	The Johnston Mutual Fund	12.9	3.7	2.2	303.8	19.2	none	0.65
A	D	Loomis-Sayles Capital Development Fund	6.9	2.3	1.4	57.8	7.8	none	0.78
A	F	Magellan Fund	37.0	—	1.6	6.1	27.1	†	1.68
A	F	Magnacap Fund (started 1/70)	23.8	—	1.1	7.7	24.2	none	1.50
A+	D	Mairs & Power Growth Fund	18.5	3.8	2.4	12.1	22.2	none	0.83
D	F	Mates Investment Fund (started 7/67)	8.5	—	none	1.0	0.0	none	4.19
A+	F	Mathers Fund	28.7	7.8	3.0	72.6	36.5	none	0.82
C	B	Mutual Shares	29.4	6.5	4.1	5.6	9.8	†	1.48
B	B	Naess & Thomas Special Fund (started 1/68)	30.3	—	2.3	14.1	17.5	none	1.14
D	C	Nassau Fund	15.7	−1.1	4.2	4.8	6.7	none	1.57
B	F	National Industries Fund	20.9	−1.3	3.0	18.8	51.6	none	1.00
D	D	NEA Mutual Fund	10.3	−2.8	3.8	39.1	25.7	none	0.77
C	D	Neuwirth Fund (started 2/67)	17.3	—	4.0	22.7	43.7	†	1.77
A	F	Nicholas Fund (started 7/69)	28.2	—	0.8	44.0	39.7	none	1.08
D	C	Oceanographic Fund (started 5/68)	15.8	—	4.2	11.8	15.7	none	1.69
D	D	The One Hundred Fund (started 11/66)	−6.6	—	1.6	15.1	−14.7	none	1.40
D	A	The One Hundred & One Fund (started 12/66)	9.1	—	5.3	1.8	−10.0	none	1.50

Exhibit 20-5 Fund Ratings—1975 (continued)

Performance ratings			Dollar results			Total assets			
In UP markets	In DOWN markets		Latest 12 months	9-year average annual growth rate	Dividend return	6/30/75 in millions	% change 1975 vs. 1974	Maximum sales charge	Annual expenses per $100
B	C	The One William Street Fund	11.5%	2.3%	2.7%	$254.3	9.0	none	$0.55
·· D	·· A	Partners Fund* (started 7/68)	18.7	—	3.0	23.4	18.2	none	1.89
D	B	Penn Square Mutual Fund	22.3	-0.4	4.5	146.6	25.2	none	0.61
·· C	·· F	Pennsylvania Mutual Fund (started 6/67)	56.1	—	none	6.3	142.3	none	5.50
D	A	Pine Street Fund	17.6	2.5	4.3	48.1	14.5	none	0.48
		Price Funds							
A	D	T. Rowe Price Growth Stock	10.7	2.4	2.0	1,214.6	20.2	none	0.55
·· C	· B	Rowe Price New Era (started 5/69)	13.6	—	2.5	266.5	20.5	none	0.72
A+	F	Rowe Price New Horizons	19.3	8.4	1.2	369.3	31.0	none	0.64
·· B	·· D	PRO Fund (started 9/67)	3.7	—	1.0	35.7	15.9	none	0.91
A	F	Scudder Special Fund	6.1	-0.4	2.1	100.4	0.2	none	0.74
C	D	Scudder Stevens & Clark Common Stock Fund	10.2	-2.7	3.4	132.5	15.3	none	0.77
D	D	Selected American Shares	6.9	-2.7	4.5	133.7	18.2	none	0.80
·· C	·· C	Selected Special Shares (started 1/68)	29.5	—	2.3	60.3	37.4	none	0.96
·· C	·· C	Sherman, Dean Fund (started 2/68)	40.9	—	none	6.3	103.2	none	1.30
·· B	·· C	Smith, Barney Equity Fund (started 8/68)	18.1	—	2.9	56.9	14.3	none	1.00
·· D	·· B	Smith, Barney Income & Growth Fund (started 6/67)	11.0	—	6.2	2.9	11.5	none	1.51

Source: Forbes, August 15, 1975.

which devotes its August 15 issue each year to analyzing and ranking most mutual funds. The letter rankings are for the fund's performance in both rising and declining markets. An A+ rating in either an up or a down market is the highest a fund can achieve. Lower letter ratings indicate worse performance during the period being evaluated. Results, in percentage terms, are given for the most recent 12 months, and 9-year performance comparisons are also given. All these can be compared with a representative stock index and with mutual fund averages, which are shown at the top of the exhibit.

Past performance is a reasonable yardstick, but not an infallible one to use in selecting a mutual fund. Funds which perform well in one year may turn in a dismal performance in the next year. Luck helps a great deal in picking the fund which will consistently outperform the market.

One way to increase the possibility of finding a superior fund is to restrict your selection to smaller funds. It is difficult for funds having total assets of $500 million or more to outperform market averages. There are several reasons why this is so. A small fund can buy 10,000 shares of a $15 stock which may make a significant impact on its performance. A fund that is, say 10 times larger would have to purchase 100,000 shares to achieve the same overall impact from the same stock. But buying this much stock may not be possible because it could violate securities laws. Funds are restricted to the percentage of a firm they may control. Smaller funds also have more flexibility than larger funds in adjusting their portfolios. It is extremely difficult to sell 200,000 shares of a stock without severely depressing the market. Smaller transactions do not suffer this handicap, so more aggressive trading strategies are open to the managers of small funds.

ARE MUTUAL FUNDS FOR YOU?

If you have decided that you can afford to put some of your investment dollars in equity securities (common stock), how do you decide whether to buy stocks directly or let a mutual fund manage your money? The answer depends on three things: (1) your investment objectives, (2) the amount of time you can devote to your investments, and (3) the amount of money you can invest. Exhibit 20–6 is a somewhat broader checklist of questions which should help you in determining whether to buy a fund or go it alone.

"Yes" answers to the first four questions and "no" answers to questions 5 and 6 indicate that you should invest directly in stocks. If your answers to questions 1 through 4 are predominantly no, you should seriously consider investing in mutual funds.

What Fund?

After deciding to buy shares in a mutual fund, you are still confronted with the problem of selecting a fund. With over 600 funds to choose from, it is not an easy job. There are a few suggestions which can help the process, however.

Match Fund to Goals Make sure the fund's objectives match your

Exhibit 20-6   Checklist for Assessing Mutual Fund Ownership

	Yes	No
1. Can you devote adequate time to managing your investments?	( )	( )
2. If you do not have enough money to diversify adequately are you willing to assume the extra risks of concentrating your stock holdings in one or two stocks?	( )	( )
3. Do you feel comfortable taking risks?	( )	( )
4. Do you have enough training in finance, accounting, and economics to understand what you are doing?	( )	( )
5. Are the advantages of mutual funds, such as record keeping, accumulation plans, and automatic reinvestment plans, important to you?	( )	( )
6. Do you plan to invest regularly, usually in small amounts such as $200 to $500?	( )	( )

investment goals. It does not make sense for a young person seeking long-term capital growth to buy a balanced fund. Yet this is often just what happens because an investor may not know the fund's objectives. The prospectus issued by the fund must disclose the fund's objectives. Read it to find out the fund's goal.

Buy No-Load Funds   Limit your selection to no-load funds. There is no sense in paying commissions when you do not have to. There are many well managed no-load funds to choose from. By limiting yourself to no-load funds, you will eliminate about two-thirds of all funds. You will thus have to select from only about 200 funds.

Buy Small Funds   If your goal is capital appreciation, buy a small fund. The smaller funds seem to perform the best in rising markets, although some of the price fluctuations on the way can give all but the hardiest investor heart failure. If your goal is income or capital preservation, it probably is best to stick with the large funds. They will generally not perform as well, but they will not scare you with their fluctuating prices.

Invest Only Risk Capital   Since investing under the best of circumstances involves considerable risk, make sure that money you put in mutual fund shares is a part of your long-term investment funds. Mutual funds and the stock market are no place for your short-term savings.

Invest Regularly   Investor enthusiasm seems to peak at the same time the market is about to drop through the floor. Therefore, by all means, try to invest in mutual funds regularly. You will benefit from dollar-cost averaging. Otherwise, if you wait to invest in one lump sum at the "right" time, you might invest it all on the day the market reached an all-time high.

Buy More than One Fund   Buy shares of two or three funds. It may seem strange to diversify among funds since that is precisely what the funds are trying to do. Nevertheless, from the performance results shown in Exhibit 20–5, it is clear that the results can vary markedly from fund to fund. There is no guarantee that the fund you pick will be a winner or will do even as well as the market averages. But, by buying two or three funds, you should be pretty sure of coming out with at least an average return. If you can achieve this with mutual funds, that is about the best you can expect.

Mutual Fund Insurance—Have Your Cake and Eat It Too?

In 1970 the Securities and Exchange Commission (SEC), regulator of the investments industry, approved a plan where the redemption value of mutual fund investments can be insured. The insurance, called Insured Mutual Fund Redemption Value (IMFRV), guarantees that fundholders will at least recover their initial investment, including sales charges, the insurance premium, and administrative expenses.

There are a few hitches in the plan. The insurance must be purchased for a 10-year period at least. All dividends and capital gains must be reinvested and they do not count as a protected investment. This aspect is what makes the insurance viable. Over 10 years it is quite likely that dividends and capital gains distributions may be 70 percent or more of the original investment. For example, if you invested $5,000 in a fund and the value of your investment at the end of 10 years was $5,000, of which $2,000 was the value of the original shares and $3,000 was the value of the shares purchased by dividends and capital gains, you would not collect under the terms of the IMFRV. In true economic terms, you have suffered a substantial loss since the original value of your investment has declined by $3,000. However, your total investment, including dividends, has not declined. Consequently insurance will not reimburse you for any loss.

Is the Insurance Worthwhile? The cost of the insurance is certainly modest at about 0.6 percent annually. The insurance can be canceled at any time and a new policy initiated at a higher value, again for the 10-year duration. Thus, if you bought $5,000 of a fund and the investment increased to $7,500, you could insure that new value. The insurance seems to have some attraction despite its shortcomings and is certainly worth considering by anybody buying fund shares. The main drawback right now is that few funds offer the insurance. Psychologically, it goes against the idea of equity investments to insure against loss. Quite likely, though, the insurance will catch on with the buying public and more funds will be forced into offering it to remain competitive.

INVESTMENT CLUBS

Investors who are seeking the diversification offered by mutual funds but are reluctant to give up control of their money may want to consider joining an investment club. There are thousands of clubs, and if you cannot join an existing one, you could start one yourself.

The clubs are small groups of people—usually less than 10—who have joined together to pool their investment dollars and knowledge. Often, the clubs consist of coworkers, neighbors, or people from the same professional group. Typically, the clubs meet once a month to make their investment decisions. Monthly contributions by members may be set at $50 per month or any multiple of $10. All these things will be determined by the club's by-laws, which are approved by the membership.

The primary advantage of joining an investment club is learning something about the stock market. The $300 to $500 you might invest each year will not make you rich. Nor should you put much more than that into a club. But sitting down with a group of friends once a month to discuss the market and individual stocks can be of immeasurable help in your other investments. You may find, after working with a club for a few years, that you feel comfortable enough with the market to make your own decisions and not to leave them up to a mutual fund.

The National Association of Investment Clubs (NAIC) has a complete packet of information to assist you in starting a club. The information includes well-developed accounting forms to keep track of the club's finances. A booklet gives advice on stock selection and there is a monthly magazine devoted to investments and the activity of investment clubs. The cost of these aids and an annual membership is quite modest and well worthwhile for anybody seriously interested in starting a club. Information can be obtained from: National Association of Investment Clubs, 13th Floor, Washington Boulevard Building, Detroit, Michigan 48231.

Some stockbrokers may also be willing to assist you in setting up a club. Since you will be investing through a broker, it is necessary to find one who is willing to work with your club. This should not be difficult because many brokers feel the people in the club may also open individual accounts.

> **Strategy: Before joining or starting an investment club, seriously consider the obligations. As a club officer, you will be required to file tax returns and provide accounting records of the members' money. Clubs are successful only when they meet regularly, invest a reasonable amount each month, and sustain the interest of the members. If you recognize these conditions, club membership can be a good way to learn about the stock market. Remember, however, much of the club's value is informative and social rather than financial.**

BANK TRUST DEPARTMENTS

An alternative to mutual fund management is available through the trust departments of many commercial banks. The banks have handled accounts for large investors for many years. Recently they have been more willing to take on small investors. The minimum amount a bank will manage depends on the individual bank. Generally the minimum is $10,000, although a few banks will accept smaller amounts.

There are several advantages to bank management over mutual funds. The relationship is far more personal and the trust officer assigned to your account can be consulted at any time. With a management account, the trust officer advises you, but you exercise final control over all investment decisions. The bank performs the investment research, recommends purchases and sales, but leaves the decision up to you. Amounts may be withdrawn or added to the account with ease.

Offsetting the more personalized approach of the banks is the cost of the service. For example, the agreement may call for a minimum annual fee of $250 or a fee of 1 percent of the total amount invested. An investor with only $10,000

will therefore pay $250, or, effectively 2$\frac{1}{2}$ percent for the service. The account must reach $25,000 before the fee drops to 1 percent. Conclusive proof that the high fee is justified by superior performance is not available. As a result, investors weighing a bank-managed account against a mutual fund should do so on the basis of the increased flexibility and additional personal attention given to the account. These features are certainly worth the extra cost to many investors, but are of little value to others. The decision is one which should be considered with care before it is made.

SUMMARY

1 Mutual funds represent an indirect way of investing. Money invested in a fund is used to purchase shares of common stock, or other investments such as bonds or preferred stock. Consequently, every fund shareholder owns a part of those investments; how large a part is owned depends on the amount invested in the fund.

2   Holders of mutual funds may benefit from dividends, capital gains distributions, and price appreciation. The opportunity for substantial gains exists, but large losses are also possible.

3   The investment objectives of mutual funds can be classified as growth, income with growth, and income. In addition, there are bond funds and preferred stock funds designed for high income. Specialized funds invest in the securities of one or two industries. There are also money market funds which invest in short-term liquid assets for the purpose of high current income and safety of principal.

4   Mutual funds are classified as load or no-load depending on whether they charge a sales commission. There is no reason for anyone to buy a load fund.

5   Open-end mutual funds stand ready to sell and redeem their shares continually at net asset value. Closed-end mutual funds have a set number of shares; after their initial sale, investors must buy and sell them in the secondary market, just like common stock.

6   Dual-purpose funds are a form of closed-end fund with a limited life span, usually 12 to 20 years. These funds issue an equal number of income shares and capital shares. All income goes to the income shareholders; any capital appreciation is distributed to the capital shareholders at the time the fund is liquidated.

7   The principal advantages of mutual funds are their provision of professional management, diversification of investments, and record keeping. Secondary advantages arise from services offered, such as automatic dividend reinvestment, systematic distribution plans, and dollar-cost averaging of investments.

8   The past record of mutual funds has shown that, on average, they will outperform a fixed savings account but may not do as well as a diversified portfolio of common stocks.

9   You should consider mutual funds if you cannot devote adequate time to investing, if you lack a strong background in finance, accounting, and economics, if you feel uncomfortable taking risks, and if you feel the clerical advantages of funds, such as record keeping and automatic reinvestment of dividends, are important.

10 You should select a mutual fund having objectives that are consistent with your own personal investment objectives. For example, a young person seeking long-term capital gains should not purchase a fund whose objective is high current income.

11 Membership in an investment club is a good way to learn about the mechanics of stock market investments.

12 The trust departments of commercial banks will handle an individual's investments. The principal advantage is the personalized service offered by the banks. A severe drawback is the cost, which can be extremely high for small accounts.

REVIEW YOUR UNDERSTANDING OF

Dollar-cost averaging
Investment objectives
    Balanced funds
    Growth and income funds
    Growth funds
    Bond funds
    Preferred stock funds
    Special-purpose funds

No-load
Front-end load
Open-end
Closed-end
Dual-purpose funds
Systematic withdrawal
Automatic reinvestment
Capital gains distribution

Money-market funds
Load
Mutual fund redemption insurance

Investment clubs
Trust department management

DISCUSSION QUESTIONS

1 Under what circumstances would it be advisable for a person to purchase a mutual fund instead of directly buying common stocks?
2 John J. Smith invested $500 every 3 months for a year in the Go For Broke Mutual Fund. The first time each share cost him $20. Subsequently, the shares were purchased at $15, $10, and $5 each. Calculate the average cost per share for John. (Shares can be purchased in fractional amounts.)
3 What is a load? How much is the load as a percentage of the net investment? Can you think of any reasons when a load fund should be purchased in preference to a no-load fund?
4 In view of your answers to question 3, how do you explain the fact that there are more load funds than no-load funds, and that the load funds have more assets than the no-load funds?
5 What is the difference between open-end and closed-end funds?
6 What types of investors should invest in the income shares of a dual-purpose fund? Who should invest in the capital shares? Into which of the three main categories of mutual funds do you feel the dual funds best fit?
7 Why do small mutual funds often outperform larger funds? Are the small funds appropriate for all types of investors?
8 Based on the information in Exhibit 20–5, which of the funds had the best long-term overall performance? If you felt the future market direction was uncertain, which fund would you consider buying? Why?
9 Front-end loads have come in for a lot of criticism lately. What are they? How can an investor avoid them? Do they have any advantage for investors?
10 How can mutual funds be used to obtain income not subject to federal income taxes?

CASE PROBLEM

Tom Trask has decided that he is now in a position to invest a maximum of $100 monthly in some form of equity securities. He talked with a broker who recommended that he buy shares of the XYZ Fund. The load is 9.28 percent, but the broker assures Tom that the commission is justified by the superior performance of the fund.

Tom is an independent manufacturer's representative. As such, he is not covered by any pension plan. His income last year was $18,000, and he expects that to increase several thousand a year during the foreseeable future.

In addition to investing for himself, Tom has two children seven and three years of age, and he would like to start building a college fund for them. He has thought of investing the money in a passbook savings account in his name, and plans to put $50 monthly for each of the children in the account.

a Evaluate Tom's investment plans.
b How can he reduce his taxes and still make investments in a mutual fund?
c Should he save money for college in this manner? What could be done to improve the return on the college fund while reducing taxes?

RECOMMENDED READINGS

Books

Investment Companies, New York: Wiesenberger Financial Services, Inc.
    This is the most complete annual reference on mutual funds. It provides the name,
    address, and performance record for every available fund. Public libraries general-
    ly have the most recent copy of the book.
Johnson's Investment Company Charts, Buffalo, N.Y.: Hugh A. Johnson Investment
    Company.
    This service provides performance charts for a large number of mutual funds and
    has a series of charts showing average performance for funds with different
    investment objectives. Public libraries often subscribe to the service.

Magazines

Forbes: (August 15 issue each year.)
    Forbes is a general-purpose investment magazine. The August 15 issue each year is
    devoted to rating the performance of most mutual funds. In addition to showing
    percentage returns for selected time periods, each fund is assigned a letter rating
    from A to F, based on its performance in both up and down markets. It is an
    excellent reference for quickly determining the better-performing funds.

Money:

"Major League Management for Minor League Investors," June 1973, pp. 64–66.
    The article discusses the pros and cons of investment management accounts with
    the trust departments of commercial banks.
"How the Fund Managers Let You Down," August 1975, pp. 27–29.
    The article discusses the recent performance of mutual funds relative to other
    investments and analyzes the reasons for mutual funds' poor showing. The article
    is worth reading before you decide whether or not to invest in funds.

Chapter 21

Retirement and Estate Planning

After completing this chapter you should be able to:

recognize the importance of early planning to achieve an adequate retirement income.

identify the major sources of retirement income for most people.

explain the various ways capital may be accumulated through the use of tax-sheltered investments.

estimate the amount of money which must be saved annually to provide a desired level of retirement income.

recall the principal provisions of a will and explain why a will is necessary for most people.

explain how estate tax computations are made.

illustrate several methods of legally reducing estate taxes.

recall the major features of the gift tax laws.

distinguish among the major types of trust agreements.

explain specific uses for the three principal types of trust agreements.

Picture this scene: A lawyer's office. Sitting before the lawyer's desk for the reading of a will is the bereaved family of the deceased, all potential heirs, all mourning but expecting something. The lawyer begins to read the will: "Being of sound mind, I spent every damn cent I had before I died."

This represents a highly practical way to dispose of one's assets—to use and enjoy to the fullest all our material things and our money, exhausting them at the same time we expire, leaving nothing behind. But it is not possible to do so. We must plan and invest during our early working years to have investments producing income regularly and indefinitely during our retirement years. When we no longer need the income, which of course is when we are dead, we should have prepared to leave to our heirs what remains of our investments and material things in an orderly and efficient manner.

While retirement planning and estate planning may take place at distinctly different times in a person's life, they are closely related because they both involve a person's accumulated capital. Both topics may seem remote for young people just starting their working lives. Yet, without planning for retirement, it is highly probable that you can look forward to grinding poverty in your old age. Estate planning at an early age is also important; you should at least have a valid will.

Whether you are considering retirement or estate planning, there are excellent ways to accumulate capital or transfer it to others. The potential savings and benefits from a little planning are great. Tax shelters (ways of legitimately avoiding or deferring income taxes) are available to people of modest wealth as well as to the very wealthy. Many tax shelters are available through trust agreements; others may be available simply because of your occupation. Many people suffer great losses in their retirement and estates because they do not take advantage of what is allowed under the laws affecting retirement and estates.

RETIREMENT PLANNING

The crux of retirement planning is making an early commitment to saving regularly. In Chapter 1 it was shown how savings grow at various interest rates. The more you save, the higher the rate of interest you earn, and the longer the money earns interest, the more you will have at the time you retire.

The major sources of retirement income for most people are one or more of the following: (1) social security benefits, (2) private pension plans, (3) payments from individual tax-sheltered annuities, (4) liquidation of investments, and (5) income from investments.

Social Security Benefits

Providing retirement income was the original purpose of social security. Social security was extended to also provide disability income and survivor's benefits, but the retirement portion is still the largest part of the program.

Benefits provided by social security have grown rapidly in the last decade, and the formula used to determine them guarantees that they will increase as prices rise. Social security constitutes a major portion of retirement income for many people. But the payments do not provide enough income for most people to maintain the standard of living they would like.

Eligibility   Eligibility for retirement benefits is determined by the number of quarters (three consecutive months) an individual has worked. A person receives credit for a quarter if he or she is paid $50 or more in a 3-month calendar period. If a person is self-employed, a full year's credit will be given if income for the period is above $400, even if the earnings occur in only a portion of the year. Exhibit 21–1 shows the number of periods required for full coverage.

Level of Benefits   The amount of benefits depends on the worker's average earnings subject to social security. Benefit levels for retired individuals are given in Exhibit 21–2. For example, if a woman retires at age 65, having had yearly average earnings subject to social security of $7,000, she will receive $335.50 per month. Should she retire at 62, the monthly benefit would drop to

Exhibit 21-1   Number of Years Needed for Full Social Security Coverage

Work credit for retirement benefits		Work credit for survivors checks		
If you reach 62 in	Years you need	Born after 1929, die at	Born before 1930, die before age 62	Years you need
1974	6*	28 or younger		1½
1975	6	30		2
1976	6¼	32		2½
1977	6½	34		3
1978	6¾	36		3½
1979	7	38		4
1981	7½	40		4½
1983	8	42		5
1987	9	44	1973	5½
1991 or later	10	45	1974	5¾
		46	1975	6
		48	1977	6½
		50	1979	7
		52	1981	7½
		54	1983	8
		56	1985	8½
		58	1987	9
		60	1989	9½
		62 or older	1991 or later	10

*For 1974 a woman needs only 5¾ years.
Source: U.S. Department of Health, Education, and Welfare.

Exhibit 21-2   Examples of Monthly Social Security Payments (effective June 1974)

Benefits can be paid to	$923 or less	$3,000	$3,500	$4,000	$5,000	$6,000	$7,000	$8,000	$9,000	$10,000
					Average yearly earnings since 1950					
You, the worker										
Retired at 65	93.80	194.10	210.40	228.50	264.90	299.40	335.50	372.20	393.50	412.40
Under 65 and disabled	93.80	194.10	210.40	228.50	264.90	299.40	335.50	372.20	393.50	412.40
Retired at 62	75.10	155.30	168.40	182.80	212.00	239.60	268.40	297.80	314.80	330.00
Your wife										
At 65	46.90	97.10	105.20	114.30	132.50	149.70	167.80	186.10	196.80	206.20
At 62, with no child	35.20	72.90	78.90	85.80	99.40	112.30	125.90	139.60	147.60	154.70
Under 65 and one child in her care	47.00	102.70	130.90	162.00	224.00	249.90	262.40	279.20	295.20	309.40
Your widow										
At 65 (if worker never received reduced retirement benefits)	93.80	194.10	210.40	228.50	264.90	299.40	335.50	372.20	393.50	412.40
At 60 (if sole survivor)	74.90	138.80	150.50	163.40	189.50	214.10	239.90	266.20	281.40	294.90
At 50 and disabled (if sole survivor)	56.80	97.10	105.30	114.30	132.60	149.80	167.80	186.20	196.80	206.30
Widowed mother and one child in her care	140.80	291.20	315.60	342.80	397.40	449.20	503.40	558.40	590.40	618.60
Maximum family payment	140.80	296.80	341.30	390.50	488.90	549.30	597.90	651.40	688.70	721.80

A word of explanation: Some people think that if they've always earned the maximum amount covered by social security they'll get the highest benefit shown on the chart. This isn't so. Although retirement benefits as high as $412.40 a month are shown, payments this high can't be paid to a worker retiring at 65 now. The maximum retirement benefit for a man who become 65 in June 1974 is $304.90 a month, based on average covered yearly earnings of $6,132.

Source: U.S. Department of Health, Education, and Welfare.

$268.40. It is important to recognize that most people will be ineligible for the maximum benefit since the greater part of their coverage will be at the lower income levels of earlier years.

Private Pension Plans

Many people working for large and small organizations are covered under their employer's group pension plan. Most of these plans provide excellent retirement benefits for people who have been covered for the full term of the plan. However, the problem with many pension plans is the vesting schedule which shortchanges people who must withdraw from a plan for one reason or another.

Vesting Vesting is the technical term which describes the conditions under which the money paid into a pension plan for your retirement income becomes irrevocably yours. With some pension plans you are vested immediately, which means that, beginning with the very first payment, the money is yours and set aside for your retirement. With other plans, you are not vested until you have participated in the plan for 10 years (sometimes longer). Thus, even though your employer has been making payments into the plan, you have no assurance of retirement income until you have participated in the plan for 10 years. If, for example, you change jobs before 10 years, you will lose the potential benefits from the employer's contributions. Any contributions you made to the plan would, of course, be returned to you.

When you are vested, all contributions, whether yours or your employer's, belong to you. You may not be able to use the money until normal retirement, but the money is yours and will be available when you retire. Obviously, the sooner you become vested, the better the plan is for you.

You should not accept a job solely because of the vesting provisions of the pension plan that comes with the job. Nevertheless, if you have two job offers that are equal, but one provides a better vested pension plan, that is the job you should accept. After accepting a position, it is important to understand the vesting schedule so that you will not leave an employer at a bad time. Thousands of men and women have taken new jobs only to discover that they left their last jobs a year or two too early to be fully vested under the plan of their old employers. The vested benefits they relinquished in many cases were worth $50,000 or more. That is, the value of the pensions they lost were worth $50,000 or more. A new job would have to be extremely attractive to be worth that kind of sacrifice.

Other Important Pension Features In addition to understanding the vesting schedule in your company's pension plan, you should investigate other, equally important provisions. Things you should be concerned with are: waiting periods, contributions, benefit levels, eligibility for participation, death benefits, early retirement provisions, and disability income provisions. Exhibit 21–3 is a series of questions which can be asked about any pension plan. After each of the questions, the characteristics of the best type of plan are outlined.

Exhibit 21-3   Questions and Answers for Evaluating a Corporate Pension Plan

1. Does eligibility for the plan start at the time of employment, or is there a waiting period?
    The best plans do not have a waiting period. Less satisfactory plans may stipulate age and
    years of service for eligibility.
2. Is the plan contributory, or is it fully paid by the employer?
    Noncontributory plans are the best. However, contributory plans may be satisfactory if the
    employee's share is low and the plan's provisions are adequate in all other categories.
3. Is the benefit reduced by any social security payments?
    Good plans do not make the benefit subject to reduction because of social security
    payments.
4. Are benefits adjusted for inflation after retirement?
    The good plans are starting to include automatic adjustment provisions.
5. How are the benefits calculated?
    Formula plans determine benefits based on average salary at retirement and on years of serv-
    ice. Example: The formula may be 1.3 percent of final three-year average monthly salary for
    each year of service. A salary of $24,000 with 30 years' service would give a pension of $780
    per month. In money-purchase plans the employer takes the amount in the pension account
    and purchases the largest possible annuity. With inflation, the formula plans are best.
6. Is early retirement available?
    Early retirement should be available at age 55 or 60 if the employee has sufficient number
    of years of service.
7. Does the plan have a death benefit if the employee dies before retirement? That is, will your
    beneficiaries receive anything from the plan if you die before retirement?
    Failure of the plan to include a death benefit is a severe weakness.
8. Are there a variety of settlement options?
    The good plans will permit any of the options generally available with life insurance policies
    or individual annuity contracts.
9. Does the plan provide disability income benefits?
    It should. Furthermore, the period of disability should count toward credited service in
    determining retirement benefits.

Tax-Sheltered Accounts

One of the most effective ways of saving for retirement is through the use of
tax-sheltered accounts. Certain groups of people are eligible to invest a portion
of their income without having to pay taxes on the amount being invested. The
tax is deferred until the person retires. A person in the 35 percent marginal tax
bracket who puts $2,000 into a tax-sheltered investment will save $700 in
income taxes (at least for the present time). Moreover, the income earned by
the account is also tax deferred. When the investor retires and depletes the
investments, taxes must be paid, although presumably at a lower marginal rate.

Who Is Eligible?   Only three groups of people are eligible for tax-
sheltered investments. They are (1) self-employed individuals, (2) individuals
employed by firms not having pension plans, and (3) educators and others
working for nonprofit organizations.

Self-employed   Under the most recent revisions of the tax code, self-
employed individuals may use up to 15 percent of their annual income, or a
maximum of $7,500 annually, to invest in a tax-deferred retirement account.
For example, a dentist earning $30,000 could put $4,500 into a savings account,

an annuity, or common stocks. His taxable income for the year would be reduced by $4,500 and his tax savings could be as much as $1,500, depending on his other deductions.

Retirement plans for self-employed people are often referred to as HR-10 plans, or Keogh bill plans. Their only drawback is the regulation governing benefit payments. An investor must begin taking benefit payments no later than age 70 1/2 and cannot begin taking benefits before age 59 1/2 unless the investor is disabled. These are really minor drawbacks to an extremely attractive way for self-employed people to save tax money.

Individuals Not Covered by Pension Plans So-called Individual Retirement Accounts (IRAs) may be set up by people working for firms which do not have an employee pension fund. The maximum a worker can put into the fund is 15 percent of income or $1,500, whichever is lower.

The IRAs are an excellent way to save for retirement. Families with both the husband and wife working, particularly where one is covered by a pension and the other is not, should seriously consider setting up an account. Often, couples in this situation will feel that since one of them has a pension, an IRA account is unnecessary. Yet, these are just the people who can easily afford to join an IRA and can best benefit from the tax savings.

> **Strategy: If you meet the qualifications of a self-employed person or a person working for a firm which does not maintain a pension for its employees, some form of HR-10 or IRA plan is a wise investment. In setting up such a plan, try to get the counsel of a qualified tax advisor. Be cautious about listening only to a life insurance agent, banker, or mutual fund representative. Although all these people are selling legitimate vehicles for tax-sheltered plans, they may be somewhat biased in their advice. A good rule of thumb is to evaluate the investment just as you would any other investment.**

Educators Teachers and other employees of nonprofit educational organizations may use a portion of their income to invest in tax-sheltered annuities. The maximum amount that may be invested is determined by a complex formula which takes into consideration the amount being contributed to a regular retirement program by the employer (most educators are covered by pension plans). For educators, the tax shelter is restricted to annuities; the broader range of investment alternatives available under the HR-10 or IRA plans is not allowed. Moreover, to receive the tax advantages of such a plan, the payments must be deducted from the employee's salary by the employer. With the HR-10 and IRA plans, the individual purchases the investment and simply notes it on her or his tax return.

What Investments Are Acceptable? For educators, the tax shelter is limited to annuities offered through state retirement funds, private insurance companies, and the Teachers and Insurance Annuity Association (TIAA). However, the limitation is not quite so restrictive as it first appears, since each of these organizations offers both fixed and variable annuity contracts. Fixed annuities are, in effect, like bonds or long-term savings accounts where the principal is quite certain and the terminal value will be increased by annual earnings from the investment. Variable annuities do not guarantee a specific benefit; money is invested in common stocks and the value of the annuity depends on how well the stocks perform. Most educators electing a tax-sheltered annuity split their investment evenly between fixed and variable annuities. They are thus guaranteed a certain monthly income from the fixed investments and they will benefit from any increase in stock prices, which of course may not happen.

Under the other two tax-sheltered plans, many kinds of investments are allowed. Money for either HR-10 or IRA plans can be invested in annuities, life insurance, common stocks, mutual funds, savings accounts, or bonds.

Liquidation of Investments

For most people, the dividends and interest from their investments do not provide sufficient retirement income. Nevertheless, they usually struggle along indefinitely on what they receive in dividends and interest, and they never think about the capital value represented by their investments. They do not realize that their investments can be liquidated (i.e., sold or redeemed) to provide money income. And it can be done carefully and methodically. It is possible to achieve a higher monthly income by gradually liquidating a small portion of the investments, that is, turning it into cash, plus the dividends and interest from the balance of the investments not liquidated. If planning is done perfectly, the cash value of the investments should be exhausted by the time the retired person dies. Obviously such a calculation is virtually impossible. Consequently, the investments must be liquidated rather conservatively.

Annuities   Purchasing an annuity is the best and most conservative way of liquidating the value of your investments to make sure that your income will continue for as long as you live. An annuity is a contract which guarantees that you will receive a set income every year for life. Through the process of risk sharing, much like that found in life insurance, people living too long continue to receive income at the expense of those who died too early. Annuities are really similar to the settlement options discussed in Chapter 14, Life Insurance. They are available with guranteed payments, refund features, or even joint life agreements.

There are two types of annuities: deferred annuities and single-payment annuities.

Deferred annuities are purchased through regular payments over a period of years. The annuity can begin to provide income at the end of the payments or be deferred until a specified later time. Deferred annuities are suitable for people who are about 10 or 15 years away from retirement and want to accumulate money during that time for retirement income.

Single-payment immediate annuities are obviously purchased with a single payment, and the income starts immediately upon purchase. Single-premium immediate annuities are suitable for people who have just retired with a sum of money which they want to make sure will provide income for as long as they live. Often, at the time people retire they sell their house and since the house is probably paid for, it represents a substantial amount available for the purchase of an annuity.

Deferred annuities not only guarantee income; they also provide certain tax advantages. For example, the interest earned by the annuity is not taxable during the deferral period. It is taxable when the investor begins to receive income payments from the annuity, and then only the portion of the payments representing earned interest is taxable. Currently, some annuities are being offered which are earning about 8 percent on their investments. An 8 percent effective after tax yield is quite good. A person with a 30 percent marginal tax rate would have to invest in something earning at least 11.4 percent interest; after paying taxes on that interest, it would be equivalent to the 8 percent interest on nontaxable annuities. Similarly, a person with a 50 percent marginal tax rate would need an investment earning 16 percent taxable interest to compete with the nontaxable 8 percent interest of the annuity. Those yields are difficult to obtain and to maintain over a period of years without incurring high risk.

Other Self-liquidating Investments   If your investments are large enough so that you can manage to live on the income from the interest (or dividends), you are quite fortunate. And so are your heirs. Because you will not have to liquidate your investments, your heirs (if you name them in your will) will inherit them. But most people do not have large enough investments to provide sufficient retirement income from the interest alone. These people can increase their retirement income by liquidating a part of their investments each year. How long an investment will last until it is entirely liquidated depends on three things: (1) the total amount of the investment, (2) the annual interest rate earned by the investment, and (3) the amount liquidated each year.

For example, see Exhibit 21-4. This exhibit shows how long an investment worth $50,000 will last at various interest rates and with various amounts, representing interest plus a liquidated portion of the investment, withdrawn as

Exhibit 21-4   Number of Years $50,000 Will Last with Different Withdrawal and Earnings Rates

Amount taken out yearly	Interest rate				
	5%	6%	7%	8%	9%
$ 4,000	20	24	30		
5,000	14	15	18	21	26
6,000	11	12	13	14	15
7,000	9	9.5	10	11	12
8,000	7	8	8.5	9	10.5
9,000	6.5	7	7.5	8	8
10,000	5.5	6	6.5	7	7

retirement income each year. If you want your money to last as long as possible, you should invest at the highest rate but at a safe risk level, and withdraw as little as necessary.

Let us take another view and assume you have $50,000 earning 7 percent annual interest, and you withdraw $5,000 annually in interest plus a liquidated portion of the investment. According to Exhibit 21–5, your money will last for 18 years.

> **Strategy: In no case should self-liquidating investments be used as the only source of income. Such a withdrawal plan may be beneficial, but only if there are other sources of income which will be available should the principal amount be exhausted. For people who must rely exclusively on liquidating their capital, the purchase of a single-premium immediate annuity is better than self-managed liquidation. The annuity guarantees income indefinitely; self-liquidation does not.**

Income from Investments

How much money should you have invested to provide the interest income you think you will need during retirement? The answer depends on several things: your basic living needs, your expected income from pensions and social security, and, of course, how much interest you can earn on your investments.

For example, Sam Brown and his wife Georgia are both sixty-seven years old. Sam is receiving a pension of $500 monthly, and social security adds another $350. Sam and Georgia have living expenses of $1,500 a month including taxes. The difference between their needs and their pension and social security income is $650 a month, or $7,800 a year. If the Browns had $111,428 invested at 7 percent interest, they would receive the needed $7,800 each year and would not have to use their capital. If they could earn 8 percent, they would need $97,500; and at 10 percent it would take only $78,000 to provide the additional income they need. Remember, however, higher returns mean higher risk. Expecting too high a return for income can be dangerous.

The following rules of thumb will be helpful for people trying to meet living expenses on invested capital. If your investments are so large that they are generating more income than you need, you can probably afford some degree of risk in your investments. If not, and total value of your investments will provide just enough interest and dividend income to meet your retirement

Exhibit 21-5   Example of $50,000 Earning 7 Percent and Providing $5,000 Annually

Period	Principal	Interest	Interest plus principal	Withdrawal	Remaining balance
Start of 1st year	$50,000	0	$50,000	0	$50,000
End of 1st year	50,000	$3,500	53,500	$5,000	48,500
End of 2d year	48,500	3,395	51,895	5,000	46,895
End of 3d year	46,895	3,283	50,178	5,000	45,178
↓	↓	↓	↓	↓	↓
End of 18th year	4,673	327	5,000	5,000	0

living expenses, you should invest very carefully; the bulk of your investments should be made up of intermediate-term Treasury notes, bank certificates of deposit, and high-grade corporate bonds. A small emergency reserve should be maintained in a passbook savings account which can be liquidated quickly and easily. Investments in common stocks should constitute no more than 50 percent of the portfolio. Moreover, the stocks should be limited to high-quality issues which have paid regular dividends for an extended period of time. You should not invest in speculative common stocks, very long term bonds, and aggressive mutual funds.

A reasonable portfolio for a retired couple with $120,000 to invest might consist of the following securities:

$30,000—five-year Treasury notes
$25,000—four-year certificates of deposit, bank or S&L
$ 5,000—passbook savings account, bank or S&L
$20,000—corporate bonds rated A or better, maturities of less than 20
        years
$40,000—common stocks-in-round lots of approximately 10 issues

This type of investment portfolio would give a high current return, little price risk, and a great deal of liquidity. The hedge against inflation is somewhat weak, but if inflation eventually erodes the purchasing power of the income from the portfolio, you could then begin to self-liquidate the portfolio, thus gaining much higher income.

How Much Retirement Income?

One thing is certain: It will take more income to maintain a satisfactory standard of living 40 years from now than it does today. But for people just starting their working lives, 40 years ahead represents the point at which they stop working. The average person can look forward to about 20 years of retirement after stopping work. Somebody aged 25 should be making 60-year projections to plan adequately for retirement. That seems like a formidable task. But it is just like planning for major expenditures. It is impossible to determine how to meet your goals unless you project the goals.

With continued inflation expected over the foreseeable future, long-range retirement planning is becoming ever more critical. Many people have retired early with seemingly adequate pensions, yet within a few years the increase in living costs reduces those pensions to little more than subsistence income levels. For example, a pension providing $1,000 a month today will have the purchasing power of $614.00 in 10 years if inflation persists at 5 percent, and after 20 years it will only be worth $377. Inflation at 7 percent reduces purchasing power of $1,000 to $508 in 10 years and $258 in 20 years.

Deciding on the amount of retirement income which you feel is adequate calls for a careful appraisal of all your living costs. Undoubtedly, after retiring, your income will be smaller, forcing a cutback in some areas of spending. One way to see where the spending can be reduced is to go back to the income statement developed in Chapter 3 and project what will be your income and spending in each of the categories when you retire. It is probably best to begin by estimating your expenses. This will give you an idea of the adjustments you may have to make in your expenses when you compare total expenses with a realistically achievable income level.

First estimate how much income, in today's dollars, you will need during retirement; then convert that amount to inflated dollars for when you retire. Next, calculate how much must be saved annually to provide that level of retirement income. There are a number of key assumptions which must be included in the calculations. These include:

1   Desired income level in today's dollars
2   Rate of inflation
3   Years to retirement
4   Years expected after retirement
5   Rate that can be earned on investments

The steps involved in this approach to retirement income planning are summarized in Exhibit 21–6.

An example will illustrate how much you should save to obtain the retirement income you need. Jason Smith, age twenty-five, estimates that he

Exhibit 21-6   Retirement Income Planning

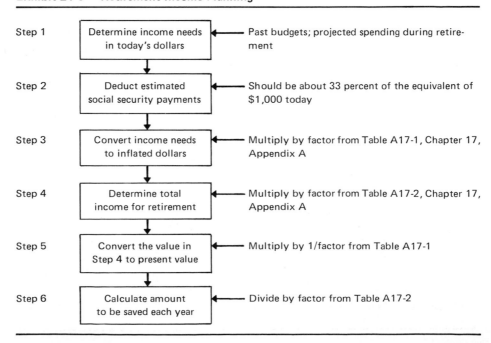

Step 1	Determine income needs in today's dollars	◄── Past budgets; projected spending during retirement
Step 2	Deduct estimated social security payments	◄── Should be about 33 percent of the equivalent of $1,000 today
Step 3	Convert income needs to inflated dollars	◄── Multiply by factor from Table A17-1, Chapter 17, Appendix A
Step 4	Determine total income for retirement	◄── Multiply by factor from Table A17-2, Chapter 17, Appendix A
Step 5	Convert the value in Step 4 to present value	◄── Multiply by 1/factor from Table A17-1
Step 6	Calculate amount to be saved each year	◄── Divide by factor from Table A17-2

will need today's equivalent of $1,000 a month when he retires in 40 years. At an annual inflation rate of 5 percent, he must have an income of $7,040 monthly 40 years from now to buy what $1,000 buys now. Assuming that social security will provide one-third of his monthly income, he must provide approximately $4,695 of the total. Annually, this is $56,348. His total retirement income needs will be $1,863,428, assuming a 20-year retirement with inflation continuing at a rate of 5 percent. The amount that he must have at the start of retirement to provide this total income is $702,385, assuming that he can earn 8 percent on his investments. Finally, if Jason is to have $702,385 in a retirement fund 40 years from now, he must save $2,711 a year, again assuming an interest rate of 8 percent. The details of Jason's retirement income computation are shown in Exhibit 21–7. This exhibit follows the format specified in Exhibit 21–6.

Are 40-Year Projections Worthwhile? This is a difficult question to answer. Forty years is certainly a long time to consider. But regular savings should be started early, even if formal retirement planning is not being done. By the time a person is forty years old, retirement planning becomes critical. If it is postponed much beyond that point, it will be almost impossible to accumulate the capital needed to provide an adequate retirement income. If you wait until fifty or fifty-five years of age to start saving for retirement, you

Exhibit 21-7   Calculation of Retirement Income Needs for Jason Smith

Assumptions

1. Income in today's dollars:		$1,000
2. Rate of inflation:		5 percent
3. Years to retirement:		40
4. Years expected after retirement:		20
5. Rate earned on investments:		8 percent

		Monthly	*Annually*
Step 1	Income (today's dollars)	$1,000	$12,000
Step 2	Less: one-third social security	333	3,996
	Net requirement	$ 667	$ 8,040
Step 3	Income in inflated dollars		
	($667 × 7.040)	$4,695	$56,348
	Factor: Table A17-1, 5 percent		
	40 years		
Step 4	Total income requirements		
	($56,348 × 33.07)	—	$1,863,428
	Factor: Table A17-2, 5 percent,		
	20 years		
Step 5	Present value of income		
	($1,863,428 × 1/2.653)	—	$702,385
	Factor: Table A17-1, 5 percent,		
	20 years		
Step 6	Amount to be saved monthly and		
	annually for 40 years		
	($703,071 ÷ 259.06)	$ 226	$2,711
	Factor: Table A17-2, 8 percent,		
	40 years		

may as well forget it. Unless you are able to save large amounts of money in a very short period of time—which most people cannot—reaching a reasonable retirement income goal is a virtual impossibility. For example, if Jason postpones saving for retirement until he is thirty-five, he must save $6,206 annually. If he does not start until forty-five, he will have to save $15,364 a year to reach his goal. Saving $2,700 a year is possible; saving $15,364 is unrealistic for most people.

Special Retirement Considerations

Retirement brings with it some special problems and some opportunities. Insurance can be troublesome for retired couples, particularly health and automobile insurance. Housing deserves special attention since it represents such a major expenditure and one where significant tax savings may be available for retired individuals. Also, a national organization of retired people is worth investigating. Membership in it may save you money through its special insurance packages, and it makes vacation tours available on a group basis at very competitive rates.

Insurance Health insurance can be a poor buy, because of policy restrictions, even for young, healthy people. Health insurance for retired couples is even more expensive and carries far more restrictions. The best advice is to continue the health insurance you had while working. Your insurance will probably be maximized, at the lowest possible cost, by extending or converting your group coverage. If you have to purchase an individual policy, try to get the best one available, using the guidelines we set out in Chapter 15.

Auto insurance may also be a problem. Policy cancellation is a distinct possibility facing anyone over sixty-five years old, and obtaining new insurance at that age can be difficult. Probably the best course of action is to have a policy that is noncancelable because of age. Many companies are now including statements to that effect in their contracts. When approaching retirement, think seriously about buying a noncancelable policy. It will be easier to purchase before you retire than after you turn sixty-five.

Housing   By the time you retire, you may own a house worth $40,000 or more, and you probably will have paid off the mortgage. The money invested in the house could be used to generate a substantial amount of income. Moreover, the house may be too large or too expensive for your needs, and a smaller home or apartment may be a better alternative.

If you decide to sell, try to postpone the sale until you are over sixty-five. The tax laws give a special break on capital gains to individuals over this age. By comparing the cost of keeping the house and living in it with costs of renting an apartment, selling the house, and investing the proceeds of the sale, you can evaluate which is the better alternative. For example, suppose you own a home, mortgage free, worth $40,000. Real estate taxes, heat, insurance, and upkeep cost you approximately $215 a month. Your alternative is an apartment which rents for $325, utilities are an extra $40 monthly, and insurance costs $5 a month. The question is, would you be better off selling the house, investing the proceeds, and renting the apartment? The economic aspects of the decision are summarized in Exhibit 21-8.

In comparing this calculation of ownership versus rental with the comparison given in Chapter 12, it should be apparent that circumstances play an important role in determining the relative attractiveness of ownership. Price appreciation has been excluded as a variable, because it is not important to retired people. Their objective is to minimize the cash outflow associated with shelter costs. In the long run, appreciation may still make ownership less expensive, but in the long run they will also be dead. Note also that Exhibit 21-8 excludes tax savings as an offsetting factor. The lower tax bracket of retirees and the smaller amount of tax-deductible expenses make this a

Exhibit 21-8   Comparison of Home Ownership with a Rental Alternative

	Ownership, $40,000 home, no mortgage	Renting an apartment, selling your $40,000 home, and investing the proceeds
Rent	—	$325
Heat and light	$ 72	40
Insurance	10	5
Upkeep	33	—
Taxes	100	—
Total expenses	$215	$370
Less: Interest on $40,000 at 7.5%	—	250
Net cost	$215	$120

reasonable assumption. On balance, it appears that with a large equity investment in a home (that means the house is all or mostly paid for), most retired people would be financially better off selling their home and renting living accomodations.

AARP   The American Association of Retired Persons may help fulfill some retirement needs. AARP sells supplemental health insurance to its members and makes automobile insurance available to members who have had their policies canceled because of age. It offers an extensive travel program and other activities designed to stimulate retired individuals. Information about AARP is available at the following address:

American Association of Retired Persons
1225 Connecticut Avenue, N.W.
Washington, D.C. 20036

ESTATE PLANNING

Estate planning is the process of choosing the best way to dispose of whatever a person owns. The disposition of an estate may take place prior to, at the death of, or many years after, the death of the person holding the assets. The tools of estate planning are wills, trusts, and predeath gifts. They are not and should not be exclusively the domain of the rich. Most people should have a will, and many could benefit from the use of trusts. Gifts can also be used advantageously by many people as a way of reducing tax liabilities.

Before you reject estate planning as unnecessary for the average person, consider Ichabod, a typical young college graduate. At age thirty, after being out of school for six or eight years, he will probably be married and have several children. He may feel broke all the time, but he probably has a fairly large net worth. If he is earning $16,000 a year working for a large company, he will most likely have twice his salary in group life insurance. The equity in his house may be $10,000. He undoubtedly owns at least one car worth several thousand dollars, and other personal property may total $5,000. A modest savings account and the balance in his checking account might total $2,500. Finally, additional life insurance of $25,000, often in the form of mortgage-redemption insurance, will give this young man an estate of over $65,000. A person like this should make use of at least one of the tools of estate planning—a will—and is also a prime candidate for some of the types of trust agreements we will discuss.

Wills

One thing is certain if you die without having made a will—you will never notice the unnecessary trouble and chaos you will have caused your family. All your worldly possessions, everything you own, which upon your death is called your estate, will be assigned to a court of law to decide who gets what. The process can be very complicated, time-consuming, costly (the expenses are paid out of your estate), and in the end, the heirs may not be the ones you may have preferred. In cases where the immediate survivors are minors, the court must appoint a guardian or trustee, whose fee comes out of the estate, and put the estate in trust until the minors become legal adults. All these problems can occur if there is no will, and most of them can be avoided or reduced if there is a will.

Writing a will is a relatively straightforward and inexpensive procedure. Most lawyers are happy to draft wills, and the fee for a standard one may run from $50 to $150. Despite the ease of making a will and its modest cost, most people who should have one do not.

Do Not Do It Yourself   Trying to avoid the legal fee by doing the will yourself can be a costly mistake. Even simple wills must comply with state laws regarding the details of execution, such as proper witnessing. The cost of having an attorney prepare the document is a small price to pay for the assurance that it satisfies all the legal requirements. If you write the will yourself, even if your intent is clear and reasonable, failure to properly execute it may cause your family a great deal of expense and legal complications. Why even take the chance when you can be sure everything is properly done by having a lawyer do it?

Intestate   A person who dies without an executed will is said to have died intestate. The distribution of an estate which is intestate is determined by state laws, not by the wishes of the deceased. Often the distribution will be in conflict with the interests of the deceased's survivors. Yet, without a will, there is nothing that can be done about it.

A typical state law may call for property to be distributed to both the surviving spouse and the children. The major problems occur when one or more of the children is a minor. In such cases, a trustee must be appointed to oversee the child's money. Usually, the trustee will have to post a bond and file annual reports with the court under whose jurisdiction the trust was set up. All this costs money which could easily be saved through the use of a will. Exhibit 21–9 gives typical intestate distribution provisions for married and unmarried individuals.

Exhibit 21-9   Distribution of Property Where No Will Exists

Status of deceased	Property to:
1. Married, one child	Spouse, 50 percent Child, 50 percent
2. Married, two or more children	Spouse, 33 percent Children, 67 percent
3. Married, no children, parent(s) surviving	Spouse, 75 percent Parent(s), 25 percent
4. Married, no children, parents deceased	Spouse, all
5. Unmarried, parent(s) surviving	Parent(s), all
6. Unmarried, no parents, brother(s) and/or sister(s) surviving	Brother(s) and/or sister(s) equally, all

Probate   When a person dies, his or her will is validated by a court hearing. The process is known as probating a will. All assets which pass to heirs through the will are thus subject to probate. Legal fees for probating a will are usually based on the value of the estate. Consequently, the greater the value of the property subject to probate, the greater the legal fee. Property can be distributed without probating if it is held in a trust or registered in certain forms of joint ownership. The details of these trusts and joint ownership will be discussed more fully in a later section.

Major Provisions of a Will   Wills may vary in length and the degree to which they specify the distribution of the individual's property. In general, however, standard wills have many or all of the following features:

1   An introductory statement: "I, John Doaks, of Oshkosh, Wisconsin, being of sound mind do hereby make this my last will and testament, etc."
2   A statement calling for the prompt payment of all debts and funeral expenses. This is to ensure that such expenses will be considered legitimate deductions from the estate.
3   Specific instructions on funeral arrangements. If you would like to be buried in a pink and purple casket, you may include the instruction in your will (the instructions should also be in the letter of last instructions, since the will may not be located before the funeral).
4   Appointment of a guardian for minor children. Failure to include this provision means that the guardian will have to be appointed by the court. Although the surviving parent will usually be appointed, the court may require a guardianship bond (a sum of money to ensure that the guardian fulfills his or her obligation) and an annual report by the guardian on the management of the minor's money.
5   Appointment of an executor. If you do not appoint an executor (person who administers the estate), the court will. As with the guardianship appointment, the court may require that the executor it appoints must post a bond. You may appoint, as executor, an individual, such as a relative or friend, or the trust department of a commercial bank. Be sure that the executor is capable of settling an estate. The legal aspects of estate settlement are sufficiently complicated to require a high level of competence in estate administration.
6   A statement calling for guardians and executors to serve without bond. This provision eliminates the expense of bonds for these functions. The savings can be substantial, about $1,000 to $1,500.
7   A statement detailing the distribution of property. Specific articles, such as jewelry or silver pieces, may be left to designated individuals. If a friend or relative is to be left a flat amount of money, this can also be specified in the will. The simplest and the most common disposition of property is to leave everything to the surviving spouse. This type of blanket provision eliminates the need for specific bequests (that is, specifying set amounts of money for individuals).

Updating Your Will   You are, of course, free to change your will at any time. You should definitely reevaluate your will when any of the following events happen:

TO MY BROTHER FELIX
I LEAVE MY RUBBER BAND COLLECTION,
MY PET SKUNK, AND TWO STICKS
OF JUICY FRUIT GUM...

1   Change in marital status. If you get married or divorced, or if your spouse dies, changes are undoubtedly necessary.

2   Birth of children. Failure to change a will after children are born could create problems.

3   Change in state residence. Differences in state laws may necessitate changes. This is particularly true if you move to or from a so-called community property state—that is, one which treats the total assets of a husband and wife as belonging equally to each.

4   Accumulation of capital. The will you made when you had a total estate of $10,000 may be inappropriate now that you are worth $500,000.

5   Loans to relatives. Money lent to a family member cannot be forgiven unless a specific provision to that effect is included in the will. Failure to make such stipulation will force the executor to collect the debt, even if your intent was to cancel the obligation when you die.

6   Change in beneficiaries. If you elect to change beneficiaries of your estate, the change must be done by writing a new will or updating the will with a codicil (the legal term for an addition to an existing will).

7   Death of a named guardian, trustee, or executor. Should any of these parties to a will die, a new will must be written to appoint a new individual to the job in question.

Letter of Last Instructions

In discussing financial records back in Chapter 3, it was stated that a letter of instructions should accompany a will. The letter simply provides information which is of assistance for the executor of the estate. Updating a letter to reflect changed circumstances does not require legal assistance. The letter should include the location and identifying numbers for:

  1 Bank accounts
  2 Life insurance policies
  3 Certificates of automobile ownership
  4 Deeds to real estate
  5 Prior income tax returns
  6 Canceled checks
  7 Stock brokerage accounts
  8 Mutual fund investments
  9 Other insurance policies
 10 Location and contents of safe-deposit box

By making this information available in one place, the process of estate administration can be greatly simplified.

Estate Taxes

Every estate with assets of more than $60,000 must file an estate tax form. Estate taxes are graduated similar to the federal income tax. Like the federal income tax, there are also legitimate ways to avoid much of the tax liability.

The basic estate tax rates are shown in Exhibit 21–10. A person having a taxable estate of $7,500 would pay a tax of $325. The total consists of $150 payable on the first $5,000 of taxable estate, and $175, a 7 percent tax on the amount in excess of $5,000 ($2,500).

Calculating the Taxable Estate   Estate taxes are levied on what is left of the estate after all debts have been paid and all allowable deductions and exemptions have been taken. All estates qualify for certain deductions and a $60,000 exemption.

Exhibit 21-10   Federal Estate Tax Rates

Amount of taxable estate (A)	Tax on amount in (A) (B)	Percentage rate on excess (C)
$ 0	$ 0	3
5,000	150	7
10,000	500	11
20,000	1,600	14
30,000	3,000	18
40,000	4,800	22
50,000	7,000	25
60,000	9,500	28
100,000	20,700	30
250,000	65,700	32
500,000	145,700	35
750,000	233,200	37
1,000,000	325,700	39
1,250,000	423,200	42
1,500,000	528,200	45
2,000,000	753,000	49
2,500,000	998,200	53
3,000,000	1,263,200	56
3,500,000	1,543,200	59
4,000,000	1,838,200	63
5,000,000	2,468,200	67
6,000,000	3,138,200	70
7,000,000	3,838,200	73
8,000,000	4,568,200	76
10,000,000	6,088,200	77

First, all legitimate debts incurred by the deceased, the expenses incurred in the settlement of the estate, and funeral expenses paid by the estate are deducted from the gross estate. What remains is called the adjusted gross estate.

Next, the adjusted gross estate is reduced by the allowable deductions. If the estate is left to a spouse, a marital deduction is allowed which is equal to half the adjusted gross estate. Also, qualifying charitable contributions are deducted from the adjusted gross estate. If the estate is left to a spouse, the order for calculating these deductions is: first the marital deduction, then the charitable deductions.

Finally, after these deductions, the estate is reduced by the $60,000 exemption. What is left is taxable and is called the net taxable estate.

To summarize, the formula for computing the taxable estate is:

Gross Estate
Less: Deductions for funeral expenses, debts, and estate administration expenses
Gives: The adjusted gross estate
Less: The marital deduction (one-half the adjusted gross estate)

Less: Charitable contributions
Less: The $60,000 exemption
Gives: Net taxable estate (calculate tax liability using federal estate tax rates)

An example should help clarify the calculation. Suppose Grandpa Smith died, leaving a gross estate of $280,000. Deductions for funeral expenses, estate settlement fees, and debts incurred by Grandpa were $12,000. Since he left his estate to his wife, it qualified for the 50 percent marital deduction. There were no charitable bequests. The calculation to figure Grandpa's estate tax is:

Gross estate		$280,000
Less: Deductions		12,000
Adjusted gross estate		268,000
Less: Marital deduction	134,000	
$60,000 exemption	60,000	194,000
Taxable estate		$74,000
Estate tax		$13,420

What Is Included in the Gross Estate?   Items which must be included are:

1   The value of all stocks, bonds, real estate, and other financial assets
2   Jointly owned property except the portion paid for by the surviving spouse (which usually refers to the home)
3   Any gifts made in contemplation of death
4   Life insurance proceeds payable to the estate or when the insured owned the policies
5   Personal property, such as furniture, jewelry, art, and coin collections

The value of the estate may be difficult to determine, particularly when it consists heavily of personal property which may be appraised quite differently by two individuals. When the internal revenue service is setting the value of an estate, you can be sure that it will be very generous in appraising such items. If you had a personal inventory, with supporting appraisals, included with your letter of instructions, the IRS would most likely accept those values.

Property Ownership   The way property is owned can have a significant impact on estate tax liability and the ease with which property is distributed to heirs. Property, of course, may be owned individually. In that event, it would be subject to estate taxes if the amount is large enough, and it would be subject to probate. Some of the forms of joint ownership can avoid the probate process. There are three types of joint ownership, which are discussed in the following paragraphs.

Tenants by the Entirety   This kind of joint ownership is restricted only to a husband and a wife and may be used only for real estate. The real estate property may not be sold or transferred without the agreement of both the husband and wife. Upon the death of one spouse, the entire real estate property will pass to the sole ownership of the surviving spouse, and the transfer of ownership is completely unaffected by the will of the deceased spouse. That means that the property does not have to pass through probate. However, the portion of the property owned by the deceased is subject to estate taxes, if the value is large enough.

Joint Tenancy This is a form of joint ownership, much like tenants by the entirety, except that the joint ownership is somewhat broader: (1) The partners do not have to be spouses (there can be more than two joint owners); (2) any one of the owners may dispose of his or her share of the property without permission (even against the wishes of the other owners); and (3) the property need not be real estate (the most common examples of property held in joint tenancy besides real estate are bank accounts, stock, and bonds). As with tenants by the entirety, the ownership of the property passes to the surviving owners upon the death of one of them, and the deceased owner's share of the property is not included among his or her possessions for distribution according to the will. The deceased's share of the property is subject to estate taxes.

Tenancy in Common Under this form of joint ownership, a deceased owner's share of the property cannot be excluded from his or her will. The owner's share must be probated and distributed in accordance with the provisions of the will. Except for this major difference, tenancy in common has the same features as enumerated for joint tenancy.

> **Strategy: The limitations of tenancy in common make it inappropriate for most people. There are very few circumstances where tenancy in common is preferable to other forms of ownership.**

It is extremely important with jointly owned property to have acceptable documentation of each owner's respective investments. The case of Nellie and Sam Farquard illustrates this point. Nellie had received an inheritance of $80,000 from her parents. She and Sam used the money to buy their dream-house. Sam died shortly thereafter. Nellie was unable to prove that the entire $80,000 was hers. In the absence of acceptable proof, the IRS included the value of the property in Sam's estate. Estate taxes were paid on money which legitimately belonged to Nellie and should not have been included in Sam's holdings.

Gifts Can Cut Estate Taxes Estate taxes can be reduced by giving your money away before you die. While taxes are levied on gifts above a certain amount, there is a substantial exclusion which, in effect, makes most gifts tax free. Everybody may give a total of $30,000 under the lifetime gift exclusion. Moreover, you may also give up to $3,000 annually to as many people as you wish and it will not be subject to gift taxes. For example, a grandparent could give $9,000 to each of five grandchildren in one year; $3,000 would come under the annual exclusion, and $6,000 would count toward the lifetime exclusion ($30,000 total for the five grandchildren). The grandparent could give $3,000 a year to each grandchild each year thereafter, without incurring a tax liability.

A couple would have double these exclusions. A husband and wife together could give up to $60,000 over their lifetime and an additional $6,000 annually to as many people as they wish.

Even if a person elects to exceed the gift tax exclusions, a tax saving can be realized since federal gift taxes are less than estate taxes. It is quite possible that the gift tax rate may be only one-half, or less, of the estate tax.

If the donor dies within three years of making a gift, the Internal Revenue Service considers the gift to have been made in contemplation of death. In such a case, the amount given will be considered a part of the estate and will be taxed at the estate tax rate.

Life insurance proceeds may be eliminated from an estate simply by transferring the ownership of the policies, usually to the beneficiary. For example, Marvin Wright, a successful M.D., has $150,000 in life insurance. If he retains ownership of the policies, at the time of death, the proceeds will be considered part of his estate. If he transfers the ownership of the policies to the beneficiaries, the amount will not be subject to estate taxes. Should the policies have a cash value at the time of transfer, there may be a gift tax liability based on that value. With term insurance, there would be no tax since the policies would not have a cash value.

The case of Grandpa Smith shows how gifts could have reduced his tax. If he had given Grandma $33,000 five years earlier and followed it with successive

gifts of $3,000 for the next two years, his gross estate would have been reduced by $39,000. The new calculation for his estate tax would be:

Gross estate		$241,000
Less: Deductions		12,000
Adjusted gross estate		229,000
Less: Marital deduction	114,500	
Exemption	60,000	174,500
Taxable estate		54,500
Estate tax		$8,175

The estate tax saving would have been $5,745. The saving was produced by giving money to the person who was going to get it eventually anyway.

Strategy: Individuals with estates in excess of $120,000 who plan to leave the estate to a spouse should consider gifts as a method of reducing estate taxes. People with estates above $60,000 who are leaving the money to someone other than a spouse may find gifts advantageous for reducing taxes.

The federal gift tax rates are shown in Exhibit 21–11. Only the rates through $1 million are shown although the graduated tax continues until a maximum marginal rate of 57.75 percent is reached at $10 million. We doubt that many of us will ever have to worry about gift taxes on such amounts.

Trusts

The creation of trusts to facilitate the transfer of property should not be the exclusive domain of the rich. Trusts can be used by people of fairly modest net worth for a variety of reasons. A trust could be used to realize a tax saving or to ensure that the property is distributed in the intended manner. In this section, a

Exhibit 21-11 Federal Gift Tax Rates

Amount of taxable gift (A)	Tax on the amount in (A) (B)	Percentage rate on excess (C)
$ 0	$ 0	2.25
5,000	112.50	5.25
10,000	375.00	8.25
20,000	1,200.00	10.50
30,000	2,250.00	13.50
40,000	3,600.00	16.50
50,000	5,250.00	18.75
60,000	7,125.00	21.00
100,000	15,525.00	22.50
250,000	49,275.00	24.00
500,000	109,275.00	26.25
750,000	174,900.00	27.75
1,000,000	244,275.00	29.25

few of the most common types of trust arrangements and their uses will be discussed. *Caution:* This is one area where a little knowledge can be a dangerous thing. Our intent is not to make you an expert, but to show that trusts can be a useful tool for many people. No trust agreement should ever be executed without the assistance of a lawyer, a banker, a certified public accountant, or perhaps all three.

Revocable and Irrevocable Trusts   Trusts may be described in terms of their permanency. Revocable trusts are those which may be terminated or altered by the person originally setting up the trust. The advantage is obvious: Should the person have a change of mind, the agreement may be altered. The disadvantage is the loss of tax advantages which are available to irrevocable trusts.

Living Trusts   One of the most widely used trust arrangements is a living trust. Almost invariably, such a trust is executed to avoid the probate costs associated with settling a will. Under the provisions of a living trust, a person turns his or her property over to a trust. The ownership of the property rests with the trust. At the time of the death of the testator (creator of the trust), the assets of the trust are distributed to the trust's beneficiaries, without the necessity of probate. Potential savings are substantial. Probate costs for an estate of $100,000 may run as high as $5,000; they can be completely avoided through the use of a living trust. The cost of settling up a living trust runs from $250 to $1,000.

Testamentary Trusts   A testamentary trust is used to pass property to heirs. Tax avoidance is a major reason for using such a trust. A standard type of testamentary trust calls for the property to be held in trust for income beneficiaries with the corpus, or assets of the trust, to be distributed to the next generation upon the death of the beneficiaries. The estate tax is paid at the time the trust is activated, that is, when the individual creating the trust dies. There is no estate tax levied on the trust when the final distribution of assets takes place. Thus, using a testamentary trust to convey property permits the avoidance of one generation of estate taxes since the assets of the trust will be distributed without taxes at the time the income beneficiaries die.

Short-Term Reversionary Trusts   Trusts can be used for special short-term purposes, with the assets of the trust reverting to the original owner after a specified period of time, usually 10 years. Again, tax savings are the principal reason for the use of this type of trust. They may be used to provide a college education for a child or support for dependent parents.

An example of an educational trust can illustrate its use. A father in the 40 percent marginal tax bracket who is supporting a child in college must earn $3,333 to provide $2,000 of support (taxes at 40 percent take $1,333 from total income). By setting up a short-term reversionary trust with the child as the income beneficiary, the income would be shifted from the father's high tax bracket to the daughter's low tax bracket. In fact, unless the daughter's annual income exceeds $1,700, there will be no tax liability. If you are anticipating your child's starting college in 10 years, you could set up a trust with enough capital to produce $1,000 a year in dividends and interest. Invested at 7 percent—which is readily available today—the trust would have over $14,000 available for college expenses. Meanwhile, you would have saved $400 a year in taxes (if you are in the 40 percent tax bracket), and at the end of 10 years, you would get the property back from the trust. The tax savings over the 10-year period should be enough to pay for at least one year of college.

There are a couple of dangers in the use of a short-term reversionary trust that you should be aware of. First, if the income from the trust pays more than 50 percent of the student's support for the year, you cannot take the student as a dependent. Second, there will probably be a gift tax payable at the time the trust is set up. However, the tax is only for the present value of the income generated by the trust. You can usually get around this by the lifetime and annual gift exclusion. Even if you cannot, the liability would be quite small for all but very large gifts. Finally, some state laws may consider college support to be a legal obligation of the parent. In such a case, the income would be considered taxable to the parent. However, this contingency can be avoided with proper legal advice.

SUMMARY

1 Retirement planning and estate planning are both necessary for people of even modest means.
2 Retirement planning consists of projecting a desired income level and managing pensions and income-producing assets to achieve the projected income.
3 The major sources of retirement income for most people are payments from:
   a Social security
   b Private pensions
   c Tax-sheltered annuities
   d Liquidation of investments
   e Income from investments
4 Having an executed will is far more important than most people realize. A person dying without a will is said to have died intestate. In such circumstances, state laws, not the wishes of the deceased, determine the distribution of the estate's assets.
5 Estate taxes are levied on estates with net assets in excess of $60,000. The marital deduction and special bequests can reduce the tax.
6 Gifts may be used to transfer property with little or no tax liability. The gift tax rate is less than the estate tax rate, and reducing the estate through gifts saves estate taxes at the highest marginal rate.
7 Gift tax laws provide a $30,000 lifetime exclusion per donor. In addition, everybody may give up to $3,000 annually to as many recipients as they wish without incurring a gift tax liability.
8 Trust agreements are a legal and binding method for conveying property in a desired manner. Trusts may be revocable, permitting the donor to alter the trust

and/or recover the property, or irrevocable where the donor gives up forever all control over the property.

9 Living trusts are used to distribute property without going through the probate process. Probate fees can run as high as 5 percent of an estate's assets. Therefore the savings from avoiding probate can be substantial.

10 Testamentary trusts are used to convey property to subsequent generations. At the time the trust is activated, on the death of the first generation, an estate tax is payable. When the trust assets are distributed to the third generation, upon the death of the income beneficiaries, there is no estate tax liability.

11 Short-term reversionary trusts, which produce a substantial tax saving by transferring income to lower-bracket taxpayers, can be used for educational purposes or to provide support for other dependents.

REVIEW YOUR UNDERSTANDING OF

Retirement planning
Private pension plans
    Vesting
    Contributory
    Noncontributory
Tax-sheltered investments
    HR-10
    IRA
Annuities
AARP
Estate planning
Wills
    Intestate
    Probate
    Executors

Bequests
Letter of instructions
Estate taxes
Gross estate
Marital deduction
    Exemption
    Taxable estate
Gift taxes
    Contemplation of death
Trust
    Revocable
    Irrevocable
    Living
    Testamentary
    Short-term revisionary trusts

DISCUSSION QUESTIONS

1 Assuming a 5 percent inflation rate, how much retirement income per month will be needed 20 years from now to equal $1,000 at today's prices? 30 years from now? 40 years from now? (*Hint:* Use the tables from Chapter 17, Appendix A.)

2 Who is eligible to take advantage of tax-sheltered investments? What are the limits on the annual contribution for each of these groups?

3 Explain how the tax advantages of tax-sheltered investments work.

4 Using Exhibit 21–4, calculate the number of years it would take to liquidate $100,000 that is earning interest at 7 percent, if one withdraws $14,000 a year.

5 What are the advantages of using annuities rather than self-liquidating investments to provide retirement income?

6 What investment strategy should a person with $100,000 follow in order to have the bulk of his or her retirement income provided by investments without using any of the principal?

7 Why should most people have a will?

8 What is the purpose of the letter of instructions which should accompany the will? What are the major items that should be included in that letter for most people?

9 What are the problems associated with dying intestate? Is there any way to avoid them without the use of a will?

10 Under what conditions should a will be updated? List at least three situations which should cause you to reassess the contents of your will and explain why the changes are necessary.

11 Calculate the estate tax liability on Grandpa Smith's estate, using the following information.

Gross estate	$350,000
Gifts in anticipation of death	60,000
Charitable bequests	20,000
Estate settlement expenses	18,000

Grandpa left the money to his wife, so the estate has the full marital deduction.

12 How much would the tax liability on Grandpa's estate (question 11) have been reduced if the gifts were not deemed to be in anticipation of death?

13 What is the major advantage associated with the use of a testamentary trust? A living trust?

14 What alternatives for providing income for others are available in addition to a short-term reversionary trust? What are the advantages of the reversionary trust over these alternatives?

CASE PROBLEM—RETIREMENT

Franklin C. Hogg is starting to worry about having enough income for retirement 15 years from now. He will receive social security benefits which he expects will contribute about 30 percent of the amount he needs for retirement income. A company pension plan, according to its present formula, will pay him $500 a month. Frank currently has $14,000 in a passbook savings account at his local commercial bank, with interest credited at 5 percent annually. After completing his budget, Frank feels that he will need $1,000 a month at today's prices to be able to live. Frank expects prices to increase 5 percent a year between now and the time he retires, and he believes that prices will continue to rise at that rate during the expected 20 years of his retirement. Frank expects that the money he saves between now and retirement will earn 7 percent a year and that it will continue to earn at that rate after he stops working.

To help Frank find out how much he must save to reach his retirement income goal, you must answer the following questions.

a How much income will Frank need at retirement to equal today's $1,000?

b How much must he provide over and above his social security and company pension?

c How much must he have at the start of retirement to provide that income?

d How much must he save each year to have that amount available at the start of retirement?

e Do you have any advice which could help Frank achieve his goal?

CASE PROBLEM—ESTATE PLANNING

Rocky Shore is a successful beachcomber with a well-situated practice. His income last year was $30,000, and he expects that people will continue losing rings and wallets at a rate that will permit him to earn at least that much every year. Rocky is married, has two children, owns a home worth $75,000, owns two cars, and has investments in the stock market worth $100,000. Rocky knows that as a sole proprietor, he must provide for his own retirement. He currently is trying to add to his stock holdings to reach that goal.

He also wants to build up a college fund for his two children. The oldest, Sandy, will be starting school in six years, while the younger daughter, Pebbly, will start in eight years. Currently, there is no money earmarked for their education.

Rocky's life insurance program consists of $200,000 of 5-year renewable term insurance. He is the owner of the policies, and his wife and children are the primary and secondary beneficiaries, respectively.

What can Rocky do to straighten out his financial mess? Specifically:

a   How can he more effectively save for retirement?

b   How can he help provide for Sandy's and Pebbly's college education without paying high taxes?

c   What steps can he take to eliminate probate costs should he die?

d   What simple transfer could he make to sharply reduce the size of his estate when he dies?

RECOMMENDED READINGS

Books

Collins, Thomas, *The Complete Guide to Retirement.* Englewood Cliffs, N.J.: Prentice-Hall, Inc., 1972.
> The book provides a well-presented discussion of most of the important issues to be considered in planning for retirement.

Magazines

Money:

"Retire in Haste, Repent at Leisure," November 1974, pp. 49–52.
> Inflation and its impact on early retirement decisions are evaluated here. The article concludes with a series of questions which should be answered by anyone considering early retirement.

"Trusts Are More than a Means to the End," August 1974, pp. 66–71.
> This article discusses the tax savings possible with testamentary trusts and gives details of the different ways to set up such a trust.

Government publications

U.S. Department of Health, Education, and Welfare, "Your Social Security."
> This booklet, available at all Social Security Administration offices, gives the details on eligibility requirements and benefit levels for social security.

Index